RETAIL
MANAGEMENT

Robert F. Lusch
University of Oklahoma

Patrick Dunne
Texas Tech University

With the Assistance of
Myron Gable
Shippensburg University

SF62AA
PUBLISHED BY
SOUTH-WESTERN PUBLISHING CO.
CINCINNATI, OH   WEST CHICAGO, IL   DALLAS, TX   LIVERMORE, CA

Library of Congress Cataloging in Publication Data

Lusch, Robert F.
  Retail management / Robert F. Lusch, Patrick Dunne, Myron Gable.
    p.   cm.
  Includes bibliographical references.
  ISBN 0-538-80294-4
  1. Retail trade—Management.   I. Dunne, Patrick M.   II. Gable,
Myron   III. Title.
  HF5429.L785 1990
  658.8′7—dc20

Copyright © 1990
by SOUTH-WESTERN PUBLISHING CO.
Cincinnati, Ohio

1 2 3 4 5 6 7 D 4 3 2 1 0 9

Printed in the United States of America

Cover Photo: Sears, Perisur Mall, Mexico City
Courtesy of Retail Planning Associates,
645 South Grant Avenue, Columbus, OH 43206

To our fathers
for their early instruction in retailing.

Robert F. Lusch
Patrick M. Dunne

Contents

Preface

This book on retail management was written because we believe that the current offering of retail textbooks can be improved. We believe that most retail texts are too descriptive and do not focus on explaining retail phenomena. Retailing is not a simple process; thus simple description will not suffice at creating the understanding necessary to prepare students for careers in retail management. The understanding we attempt to develop is based on the premise that the sophisticated retail manager must apply both creative and analytical problem-solving skills. In addition, we believe that a solid understanding of the financial and performance dimensions of retail organizations is critical to success.

Retailing is a complex subject and, we believe, one of the most fascinating areas of study in marketing. Retailing combines not only marketing principles and concepts, but also concepts and theories from accounting, finance, economics, and management. In brief, the effective retail manager must be able to integrate all business disciplines in order to operate a successful retail organization.

This book begins in Part I to acquaint the student of retailing with the field of retail management by presenting a discussion of retail planning and management. Emphasis is placed on the need for good strategic planning as well as good operations and administrative management. In Part II of the text we examine the environmental factors that have an influence on the strategic planning process. Special attention is given to marketing channels, retail customers, competition in retailing, and the legal environment of retailing. Part III is a look at location analysis. Treatment is given to the proper market area in which to locate and then to the selection of the best store site in that market area. The location decision is the most long-term of the retail decisions. Management of retail operations is discussed in Part IV. Special attention is given to merchandising, pricing, promotion, store design and atmosphere, and customer service. It is not until Part V that retail planning, administration, and control are discussed in detail. Clearly, strategic development should come early in the retail management process; nonetheless we cover it late in the book because we believe the student must first develop a good understanding of operations management and the retail environments. We conclude the book with a chapter on the future of retailing in 2001. This chapter should help to prepare the student for the rapidly changing decade of the 1990s.

We believe that the ability to understand sophisticated retail concepts and theories requires an exploration of these concepts and theories through case study. Consequently this book incorporates 31 case studies. These case studies cover many retail lines of trade including department stores, hardware stores, furniture stores, drugstores, apparel stores, and many others. By being able to apply retail concepts and theories in these cases and by exploring them in classroom discussion, the student will be better able to grasp the complexity of retailing.

This book is "student-friendly." It is written with the student always in mind. The writing style is lively and clear. The graphics, design, photos, and plentiful examples are intended to capture the interest of the student. Each chapter includes at least two retailing-in-action vignettes that illustrate how retail enterprises are applying retail concepts and theories. In a sense these are mini-case studies for the student and serve to enhance student understanding of complex material. The end-of-chapter discussion questions, chapter summaries, case studies, and glossary were all developed and prepared with the student in mind. Happy reading!

Part I Photo: West Edmonton Mall
Part III Photo: Lukens Steel Company

Acknowledgments

The completion of any text is never the work of only the author or authors. In our case many outstanding individuals played an important role in shaping the final product.

First and foremost, we want to express our deepest appreciation to Dr. Myron (Mike) Gable of Shippensburg University. A past president of the American Collegiate Retailing Association, Mike not only served as our consulting editor, but also took over the arduous task of case editor.

We were also fortunate in having the expertise of three outstanding reviewers for our final draft: Dr. Charles Ingene, University of Washington; Dr. Frederick Langrehr, University of Nebraska at Omaha; and Dr. Antigone Kotsiopulos, Colorado State. Through their contributions, *Retail Management* not only resembles the real world of retailing, but also is student-oriented.

We also would like to acknowledge and thank the following professors who have reviewed, criticized, and made suggestions on earlier drafts and outlines of this text:

Dale Achabal, University of Santa Clara
Edward Blair, University of Houston-University Park
Terri Coons, University of Southern California
Jack Gifford, Miami University
Donald Granbois, Indiana University
Shelley Harp, Texas Tech University
Bruce Kellam, Eastern Washington University
George Lucas, Memphis State University
Louise Luchsinger, Texas Tech University
Donald McBane, Texas Tech University
Lewis Neisner, SUNY College at Buffalo
Charles Patton, Pan American University
Michael Pearson, Bowling Green State University
Rodger Singley, Illinois State University
Shirley Stretch, California State University—Los Angeles

Scott Vitell, University of Mississippi
Terrell Williams, Utah State University
Julian Yudelson, Rochester Institute of Technology

Several retailers and other organizations have provided us with valuable information for this text. We are particularly indebted to the Distribution Research Program at the University of Oklahoma, especially Dr. Bert C. McCammon, Jr.; Julie Davis of Seville Industries; Roy Chapman of J.C. Penney Co.; Randall Gebhardt of Retail Planning Associates, Inc.; Melissa Stenicka, H.E.B. Grocery Company; Mark Blankenship of Meier and Frank Department Stores; James Penny of J.W. Robinson Department Stores, and the staff at the National Retail Merchants Association (NRMA).

Not to be overlooked is the contribution of our wives—Virginia Lusch and Judith Dunne–who have contributed in so many ways to the completion of this book, especially Judy for typing the entire manuscript. Their enthusiasm and support helped to make the long hours involved in writing this text a more pleasant experience.

We are also indebted to the following people at South-Western Publishing Co.: Linda Sullivan, our Acquisitions Editor, who gave us the early encouragement to do this text the way we wanted; Sue Ellen Brown, our Production Associate Editor, who saw to it that production problems were minimal; and Jim Sitlington, our Publisher, who facilitated our endeavor whenever possible.

Finally, while many others have also provided invaluable contributions to this text, we authors take sole responsibility for any errors that may appear in the book.

Robert F. Lusch
Norman, OK
Patrick M. Dunne
Lubbock, TX

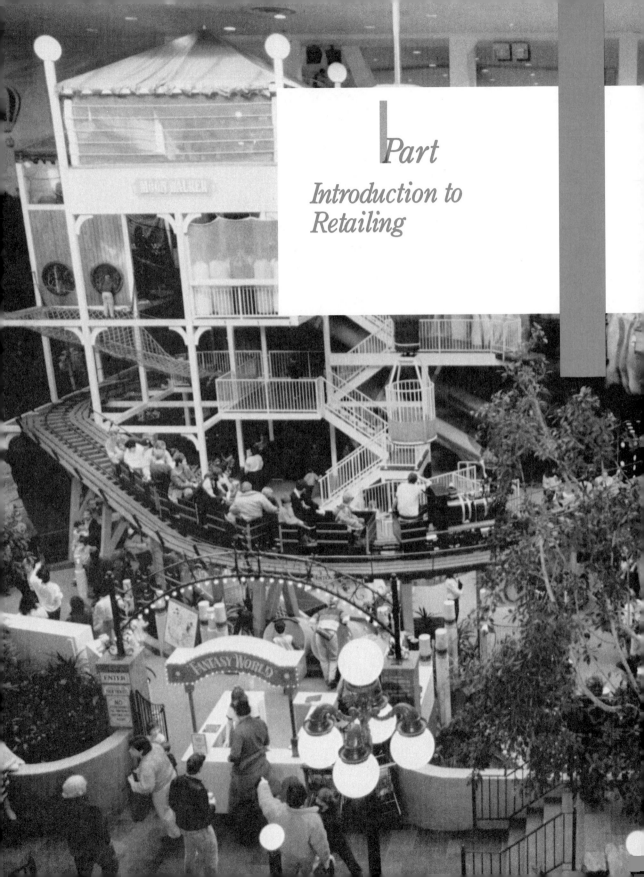

Part

Introduction to Retailing

1 Chapter

Perspectives on Retailing

The purpose of this chapter is to acquaint you with the nature and scope of retailing. It will look at retailing as a major economic force and as a significant area for career opportunities. Finally, it will introduce the approach to be used throughout the text to study and learn about the management of retail enterprises.

CHAPTER 1
Perspectives
on Retailing

Have you thought about the impact of retailing on a country's economic growth? On your way home from class today look around you. It is likely that you will see many fast food restaurants (such as Wendy's or Pizza Hut), convenience stores (such as 7-Eleven or Circle K), or a neighborhood shopping center with a grocery store (such as Food Giant or Safeway). You might even pass a regional shopping mall with several large department stores, hundreds of specialty stores, and approximately one million square feet of retail selling space.

Retailing is all around us and has contributed to the economic prosperity that we enjoy so much. Throughout history the nations that have enjoyed the greatest progress have been those with strong economic and retail sectors. Because strong retail performance is such an important factor in economic growth, this text will focus on how to manage and plan retail enterprises to achieve high levels of performance. To do this, we will be using a micro, rather than a macro, approach. We will concentrate on how individuals in retail enterprises manage and plan, rather than how the retail sector of the economy, in aggregate, should be structured, managed, or planned through government policies.[1]

Although progressive societies have always had strong retail sectors, the retail trades have not always been admired. Often, persons employed in retailing had low status. Consider the ranking of occupations that Aristotle developed:

> Now in the course of nature, the art of agriculture is prior, and next comes those arts which extract the products of the earth, mining and the like. Agriculture ranks first because of its justice: for it does not take anything away from men, either with their consent, as does retail trade and mercenary arts, or against their will, as do the warlike arts. Further agriculture is natural, for by nature all derive their sustenance from the earth.[2]

Thousands of years of commerce have now made retailers valued members of society. For example, when a McDonald's or a Wal-Mart decides to locate in a small town, there is a great deal of excitement in the community.

WHAT IS RETAILING?

Retailing is the final stage in the progression of merchandise from producer to consumer. Quite simply, any firm that sells merchandise to the final consumer is performing the retailing function. Regardless of whether a firm sells to the consumer in a store, through the mail, over the telephone, through a television shopping network, door to door, or through a vending machine, it is involved in retailing.

Although retailing is the final stage in the progression of merchandise from producer to consumer, it is not a static or homogeneous business function. Retailing is continuously changing in exciting ways. Consider,

Illus. 1.1
When a McDonald's or a Wal-Mart decides to locate in a small town, there is a great deal of excitement in the community. Photo courtesy of McDonald's Corporation.

for example, some of the major developments in retailing which have oc-curred over the past century: the development of department stores in the 1870s, of mail-order houses in the 1880s, of chain-stores in the early part of this century, of supermarkets in the 1930s, of discount stores in the 1940s, of shopping centers in the 1950s, of commodity-specialized mass merchandisers in the 1970s. In the 1980s there has been vast restruc-turing in the retail business: creative specialty chains like The Limited and the Foot Locker pioneered unusual merchandise and operational tech-niques; innovative department stores like Mervyn's and Main Street re-positioned themselves with new consumer-driven marketing strategies; and discounters like K mart, Wal-Mart, and 47th Street Photo helped make bargain-hunting respectable. Staid retailers were unable to adapt to the changing buying habits of the American consumer, like Gimbels.[3] These changes in retail operations were caused by environmental and competitive forces over which the retailer had little control, but was forced to respond to. Retailing is a profession of responding to change, and it will continue to be that way into the twenty-first century.

THE NATURE OF CHANGES IN RETAILING

What caused retailing to change so much in the recent past, and how will it change in the future? The answer to this question lies in the fact that retailers do not operate in a closed environment, but rather in a continu-ously changing environment. These changes will be discussed in greater detail in Chapters 3-6 and Chapter 18 will look at the future of retailing. For now we can point out the following changing environmental elements: the behavior of consumers, the behavior of competition, the behavior of channel members, the legal systems, the state of technology, and the socio-economic nature of society. Exhibit 1.1 depicts some elements that are external to retailing but that have a tremendous impact on retailing. For example, consider what the change in raising the legal drinking age from 18 to 21 did to campus pubs a decade ago.

As you see, retailing is basically a business of managing change. A retailer is a purchasing agent for an ever-changing consumer in an ever-changing world and the pace of these changes is accelerating. Demo-graphic changes such as the declining birth rate, the redistribution of in-come levels, and the increased participation of women in the work force have profound effects on our society. Technology is producing data faster than ever before. Entrepreneurs, not obliged to conform to old legal and social standards, are free to capitalize on emerging retail opportunities.

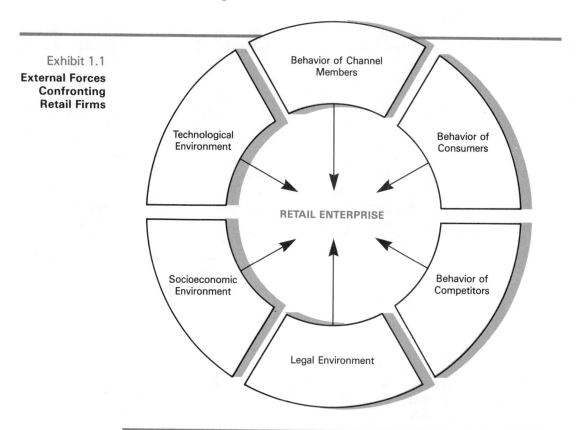

Exhibit 1.1
**External Forces
Confronting
Retail Firms**

Fashion trends that in the past would have lasted for years, now last only a few months. Recent industry studies have shown that the country already has more than sufficient retail space to meet the needs of the next half decade.

Thus, with market growth slowing, retailers will no longer be able to sustain long-term growth by adding new stores. Instead, growth must come at the expense of a competitor's market share. Today's retailer must be able to *analyze* these changes, *understand* these changes, *anticipate* other changes, and *adapt* to changes made by others. Successful retailers can look at the changing environment and see opportunities. The founder of McDonald's, Ray Kroc, saw the post-World War II baby-boom and the resulting demand for reasonably priced fast food as an opportunity. Unsuccessful retailers such as Revco, a large national drug store chain, fail because they do not foresee the actions that competitors might take. As the environment changes, retailers must change to survive and prosper. Success in retailing is dependent on being able to properly interpret what changes are occurring and building a strategy to respond to these changes. Therein lies the excitement and challenge of a career in retailing.

Illus. 1.2
**McDonald's
founder Ray
Kroc (*left*).
Source:
McDonald's
Corp.
A McDonald's
logo (*right*).**

THE MAGNITUDE OF RETAILING

The magnitude of retailing can, in part, be grasped by looking at some statistics from the *Census of Retail Trade*.[4] The U.S. Department of Commerce conducts a census of retailing every five years, in the years ending in 2 and 7, and releases the data about three years later. According to the Census Bureau, there were 1.9 million retail establishments in the United States in 1987. This figure is in disagreement with the 2.9 million total reached by both the Small Business Administration[5] and *Dun's Census of American Business*.[6] The difference is caused by different definitions of what constitutes a retail establishment: the Census Bureau does not count sole proprietorships. We will use Census Bureau data throughout the text unless otherwise noted. The Census Bureau also calculates that retail establishments in the United States had total sales of over $1,500,000,000,000. Based on Census Bureau data, there are 23 retail establishments for every thousand households. Census Bureau data also indicate that in 1987 retail establishments had average annual sales of over $750,000; but more than 50 percent of retail establishments had sales under $400,000.

EXEC 100: RETAILING'S TOP ACHIEVERS

In 1987, the largest retail chain in the United States in terms of total sales was Sears, with total sales of over $48 billion. K mart was second with sales of nearly $26 billion, followed by Safeway Stores ($18 billion),

Exhibit 1.2

Retailing Top 20 Performers (1987)

Chains	1987 Sales (millions)	1986 Sales (millions)	% Change	1987 Earnings (millions)	1986 Earnings (millions)	% Change	1987 Earnings as % of sales	1986 Earnings as % of sales	Return on equity	Return on assets	Existing units 1987	Units to be added 1988
1. Williams-Sonoma	$ 136.8	$ 100.4	36.0	$ 3.4	$ 1.2	183.0	3.0	1.0	17.0	16.0	86	14
2. Drug Emporium	322.2	241.0	34.0	4.5	1.5	141.0	1.0	0.7	18.0	9.0	137	N/A
3. Home Depot	1,453.7	1,011.5	44.0	54.1	23.9	127.0	4.0	4.0	22.0	10.0	75	21
4. Tiffany	230.5	182.5	26.0	16.2	7.4	118.0	7.0	4.0	14.0	12.0	10	1
5. Businessland	600.0	404.3	48.4	8.4	4.8	75.0	1.0	1.0	9.0	3.0	94	N/A
6. Circuit City	1,350.4	1,010.7	34.0	50.4	35.3	43.0	4.0	4.0	29.0	12.0	105	20
7. The Sharper Image	160.9	121.0	32.0	5.6	3.2	75.0	3.0	2.0	34.0	10.0	45	16
8. Costco	1,370.0	747.0	83.0	5.1	4.5	13.0	0.3	0.6	6.0	1.0	42	9
9. Big B	249.0	210.0	18.0	7.3	4.5	62.0	2.0	2.0	12.0	7.0	188	25
10. Wolohan Lumber	228.6	194.3	17.0	9.0	5.3	69.0	3.0	2.0	22.0	10.0	42	5
11. Wal-Mart	15,959.0	11,909.0	34.0	627.6	450.1	39.0	4.0	4.0	28.0	12.0	1,198	147
12. Agway[1]*	205.1	225.9	9.0	2.9	1.7	71.0	N/A	N/A	N/A	4.0	N/A	N/A
13. Gantos	133.0	98.4	35.0	6.2	4.5	37.7	5.0	5.0	22.0	9.0	84	23
14. Hechinger	725.1	588.4	23.0	41.9	28.2	49.0	6.0	5.0	16.0	7.0	79	7
15. Giant Food	2,721.3	2,528.5	7.0	75.6	46.5	63.0	3.0	2.0	23.0	9.0	144	4
16. Rite-Aid	2,486.3	1,756.7	42.0	144.5	78.0	85.0	6.0	4.0	28.0	12.0	2,233	50
17. Food Lion	2,900.0	2,400.0	21.0	85.8	61.8	39.0	3.0	3.0	21.0	11.0	475	100
18. Toys "R" Us	3,137.0	2,445.0	2.8	204.0	152.0	34.0	7.0	6.0	20.0	10.0	387	80
19. Dress Barn[2]	173.7	135.8	28.0	12.9	9.2	40.2	7.0	7.0	39.0	21.0	263	52
20. Pier 1 Imports	327.2	262.3	25.0	16.1	12.0	34.0	5.0	5.0	19.0	6.0	396	N/A

*Operating income
[1]Retail operations
[2]Figures for year ended July 30, 1987

SOURCE: Reprinted by permission from *Chain Store Age Executive* (August, 1988), p. 15. Copyright Lebhar-Friedman, Inc., 425 Park Avenue, New York, NY 10022.

Kroger ($18 billion), and Wal-Mart ($16 billion). Sears and K mart were also the leaders in total profits for 1987, followed by Wal-Mart, J. C. Penney, and McDonald's.[7] Based on these figures, the average Sears store had almost $34 million in annual sales, showing that a Sears store manager is managing a large and complex business. Edward Brennan, the chairman and CEO of Sears, had even bigger challenges directing the entire Sears complex, including catalog stores, real estate business, investment banking, foreign operations, television shopping, and mail order processing.

The summit of achievement in retailing today is reflected by *Chain Store Age's* annual summary of retailers' operating results: "The Exec 100: Retailing's Top Achievers." This ranking is based on percentage increases in sales, profit, and return on assets for the most recent fiscal year. The top five retailers for 1987 were Williams-Sonoma, a San Francisco-based mail-order and retail housewares operation, Drug Emporium, Home Depot, Tiffany, and Businessland. Each of these retailers had a well-defined retail concept, strong operating controls, and an ability to keep customers' needs clearly in focus. Exhibit 1.2 shows the results for the top 20 retail performers for 1987. The Exec 100 index is somewhat biased in favor of smaller firms because they have an easier time gaining large percentage increases. Yet eight retailers with sales in excess of $2 billion annually are included. Annual sales of the top five Exec 100 retailers show that newcomers always have the opportunity to succeed in retailing. One chain missing from the list in 1987 was The Limited, a specialty women's apparel chain, which dropped to number 61 after many years of outstanding percentage growths. The Limited's rather poor earnings growth of 3% was caused, in part, by a misreading of women's fashions resulting in high levels of markdowns.[8] The Limited is expected to be back on this list soon.

ENTRY BARRIERS

Together, the statistics on aggregate retailing activity in the United States and on the largest retail chains suggest that retailing is large and complex. In addition, retail management decision making is becoming increasingly sophisticated. Once it was considered an easy industry to enter, but now substantial barriers are rising, especially if one desires to locate in large regional malls or other prime locations. Competition is intense for high-traffic locations, and construction costs and lease payments have risen drastically over the last decade. Consider the data in Exhibit 1.3, which shows the capital expenditures required in 1987–88 to construct various types of new stores. The average supermarket constructed was 52,000 square feet, and construction costs were over $3.3 million. This did not include the cost of land, which was probably $500,000 to $1,000,000 or inventory to stock the store, which was probably another $750,000 to $900,000. Thus, to enter the supermarket busi-

Exhibit 1.3

Capital Expenditures for Constructing Outer Exterior Shells for New Store and Completing the Store (1988)

Line of Trade	Average Existing Store Size Two Years Prior	Average New Store Size (sq. ft.)	Capital Expenditures For Outer Shell Per New Store	Capital Expenditures for Interior and Exterior per New Store*
Supermarkets	48,800	52,000	$1,612,000	$3,304,600
Department Stores	148,300	111,085	4,243,447	8,911,239
Drugstores	14,300	20,600	597,400	1,224,670
Discount Department Stores	88,700	67,700	1,550,330	3,178,177
Home Improvement Center	28,300	31,800	887,680	1,755,360
Specialty Apparel Stores	21,200	21,548	571,022	1,216,277

*Includes fixtures, ceiling, interior signage, roofing, flooring, interior lighting, and HVAC system.
SOURCE: Reprinted by permission from *Chain Store Age Executive* (July, 1986 and 1988; August, 1988). Copyright Lebhar-Friedman, Inc., 425 Park Avenue, New York, NY 10022.

ness with a single new store in a good location with adequate inventory, approximately $5 million in investment capital would be required. Of course if the retailer decided to lease space rather than buy, the initial investment would be considerably less. The cost for a new specialty apparel store complete with fixtures would be $1.2 million without land or inventory. In light of this, the number of new retail enterprises that have been developed in the last two decades is truly amazing. Most of these new businesses have been new kinds of retailers; e.g., warehouse retailing, discount drugs, or home-delivery fast foods. This seems to be the driving force behind retailing today. *Retailing in Action 1-1* describes one of the new forms of retailing: warehouse clubs.

RETAILING IN ACTION   **1-1**

A Recent Successful Retail Innovation

Unlike many other new retail institutions, which start with a bang only to fade away, warehouse clubs, with a projected $18 billion in sales in 1989, are now the fourth largest form of mass merchandise distribution in the country, behind only supermarkets, discount stores, and department stores. Warehouse clubs have created a new, more cost-efficient form of distribution for small-business customers. Most small businesses have yet to realize the tremendous benefits of warehouse clubs and modify their shopping habits accordingly. But then, warehouse clubs, which had their beginnings with the Price Club in 1976, are still learning how to merchandise to the needs of small businesses as well as individual customers.

Warehouse clubs are one of the few wholesale or retail concepts developed over the last quarter century that have the potential to become a permanent part of the American retailing system.

Below are two tables that illustrate this growth. Table 1 shows the growth in number of units and Table 2 shows the growth in sales dollars.

Table 1

Wholesale Club Growth

	Number of Warehouses Based on Calendar Year			
	1986	1987	1988*	1989*
Price Company	25	34	42	50
Sam's Wholesale Club	49	84	101	120
Costco Wholesale Club	37	43	49	57
PACE Membership	25	32	39	45
BJ's Wholesale Club	4	19	22	25
Price Savers	15	12	16	24
Makro	9	4	6	9
The Wholesale Club	11	15	18	20
Warehouse Club	14	12	12	14
Buyer's Club	3	4	5	6
Club Wholesale	3	6	6	6
American Wholesale	1	4	2	2
Net Cost Club	1	1	1	2
Save Club	1	1	1	1
Super Savers	21	—	—	—
Saveco	2	2	—	—
Wholesale Plus	1	1	1	—
Buy It Wholesale	1	2	1	—
TOTAL:	223	276	320	381

Note: Super Savers was acquired by Wal-Mart in June, 1987. Wholesale Plus, Buy It Wholesale, and Saveco ceased operation in 1988.

Illus. 1.3
Sam's Wholesale Club.

Table 2
Wholesale Club Sales

	Sales ($ millions) Based on "Calendar Year"			
	1986	1987	1988*	1989*
Price Company	$2,806	$ 3,487	$ 4,280	$ 5,050
Sam's Wholesale Club	1,678	2,711	3,700	5,030
Costco Wholesale Club	843	1,548	2,140	2,710
PACE Membership	595	940	1,250	1,500
BJ's Wholesale Club	350	580	800	1,000
Price Savers	175	299	610	800
Makro	290	300	450	525
The Wholesale Club	158	272	380	475
Warehouse Club	185	231	270	285
Buyer's Club	65	80	80	100
Club Wholesale	50	66	70	76
American Wholesale	35	100	60	65
Net Cost Club	20	20	28	40
Save Club	2	2	2	2
Super Savers	350	150	—	—
Saveco	11	38	—	—
Wholesale Plus	30	30	—	—
Buy It Wholesale	25	10	—	—
TOTAL:	$7,668	$10,864	$14,120	$17,658

Note: Super Savers was acquired by Wal-Mart in June, 1987. Wholesale Plus, Buy It Wholesale, and Saveco ceased operation in 1988.

SOURCE: "Keeping Up With The Wholesale Club," *Discount Merchandiser Magazine* (November 1988), pp 30 + 32. Courtesy of *Discount Merchandiser Magazine*.

Look at the average size of store for the various retail categories in Exhibit 1.3. The biggest increases over the two years ending in 1988 were in the drug store business, a reflection of the rapid growth of deep discount drug stores like Phar-mor, Rite-Aid, and Osco. These stores also handle many nondrug items, such as auto parts, motor oil, food products, and even some clothing. This handling of many different unrelated items by a retailer is called **scrambled merchandising**. There was also a slight increase in supermarkets and home improvement centers, reflecting the fact that even operators not involved in the warehouse business *per se* are building larger stores to add more merchandise. Department stores and discount stores are starting to grow smaller as a result of increased competition from specialty stores and better use of space caused by high rents.

RETAILING FROM TWO PERSPECTIVES

All economic systems have both a supply and a demand component. The supply component consists of private and public enterprises producing and marketing goods and services to the demand side of the economy. The demand side consists of households and private and public enterprises that purchase goods and services. The interaction between supply (sellers) and demand (buyers) determines prices, competitive intensity, and profit levels. Students and retail managers alike need to study an economic sector like retailing from both the demand and supply perspectives to properly understand it. Retail executives cannot maximize store profits by focusing only on supply factors such as labor, merchandise, and store layout. They must also pay attention to demand factors such as household income, household transportation costs, households per square mile, and consumer lifestyles.

Imagine yourself as a retail entrepreneur who recently designed and built a 10,000-square-foot drugstore. You are working long hours and are doing an excellent job managing your employees and merchandise. You built your drugstore in a small town where land and building costs were relatively low but where there was already an abundance of drug retailers. The town is characterized by a stagnant economy: average household incomes have remained stable for several years and many younger households are moving away. Profits are not what you expected. Why? You did not properly balance supply and demand factors in your decision-making process.

The major problems in managing a retail enterprise are related to either the supply or demand side of retailing or both. Retailers must interrelate supply and demand factors effectively in order to produce a profit sufficient for survival and growth. Everything in retailing must be related to dollars and cents. It is this bottom-line objective that cannot be ignored—in the short, the intermediate, or the long run.

A RETAIL CAREER

In order to manage demand and supply factors to achieve profit sufficient for survival and growth, a retail store manager needs to be capable in:

Economics	yes _____	no _____
Accounting	yes _____	no _____
Financial Analysis	yes _____	no _____
Personnel	yes _____	no _____
Marketing	yes _____	no _____

The answer is yes to all of the above! In this section, we will demonstrate the validity of this statement. Few industries offer an environment as fast-paced and ever-changing as retailing, where results are readily seen on the bottom line. Retailing will train you to become an expert not in just one field, but in all business disciplines. It offers the economist's job of forecasting sales growth, the marketing manager's job of determining what styles will be in during the coming season, the personnel manager's job of developing work schedules and hiring the right people, the traffic manager's job of arranging deliveries, and the accountant's job of arriving at the bottom line. In summary, no other occupation offers the immediate opportunities that retailing does, yet many students do not consider a career in retailing.

COMMON BELIEFS

Students may have certain perceptions of retailing that tend to turn them away from pursuing it as a career. Sometimes this is good, since not all individuals are suited for retailing. However, it is unfortunate when inaccurate perceptions turn a student from a potentially rewarding retail career to another career that may only appear to be more promising. By examining some common beliefs, we will try to construct an accurate picture of retailing.

College Education.   Is college a prerequisite to a career in retailing? It depends. To be an assistant buyer or department manager, the answer is probably no. A college degree would be helpful but not required. However, for career advancement with a fast-track progressive retailer or a career in top management (store manager, vice president, chief executive officer), college training is generally a prerequisite. Many large retailers will not consider anyone without a college degree for their training programs. Some retail firms even recruit MBAs to fill entry-level management positions, and then advance them rapidly.

Salary.   Is retailing competitive in terms of compensation? A recent graduate with a bachelor's degree seeking an entry-level position can probably get a higher salary in other fields. In general, retailers offer 10 to 15 percent below what college graduates can earn from manufacturers, insurance companies, and many other campus recruiters. Starting salaries in executive training programs approximate $20,000–$24,000 a year. That is only the short-run perspective, however. In the long run, a retail manager or buyer is directly rewarded on performance. An entry-level retail manager or buyer who does exceptionally well can double or triple his or her income in three to five years and often be ahead of classmates who chose other career fields.

High-level retail managers receive salaries comparable to their counterparts in other industries. Consider, for example, the data in Exhibit 1.4, which shows the total annual compensation of a variety of chief executives in retailing, including Charles Lazarus, the chairman and founder of Toys 'R' Us, who became the highest paid U.S. executive ever with a 1987 salary of over $60 million. Shareholders who invested $100 in Toys 'R' Us in 1978 would have had a $4,000 profit by December 1987.[9] *Retailing in Action 1-2* presents a biographical sketch of another highly successful retailer, Sam Walton, the founder of Wal-Mart.

RETAILING IN ACTION

1-2

Sam Walton:
A Retail Success Story

Illus 1.4
Sam Walton, founder and Chairman of Wal-Mart Stores Inc. Source: Wal-Mart Stores Inc.

In July 1988, *Forbes* magazine listed Sam Moore Walton as the richest man in America, with a net worth of $6.5 billion. Walton, called a "merchant by instinct" by retail stock market analysts, started with J. C. Penney in Des Moines then opened his own Ben Franklin store in 1945 in Newport, Arkansas. He saw the potential of operating in small towns and with his brother James opened a discount store in Rogers, Arkansas, in 1962. Operating with the strategy of saturating small-town markets, watching costs, and generating employee enthusiasm, Walton's Wal-Mart Stores Inc. now operates over a thousand stores, mostly in small towns but expanding into metropolitan areas. At the time of Mr. Walton's retirement as chief executive officer in 1988, Wal-Mart had sales of $16 billion and earnings of $627.6 million.

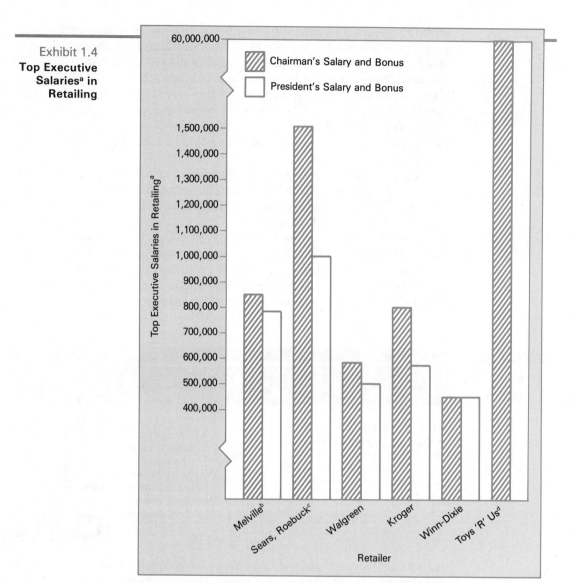

SOURCE: Based on data from *Business Week* (May 2, 1988), p. 75 and
(May 16, 1988), p. 42.

Career Progression.   Can you advance rapidly in retailing? The answer depends on both the retail organization and the individual. A person capable of handling more responsibility than he or she is given can move up quickly; even if that person works for a firm too small or growing too slowly to promote, he or she can easily advance by joining another retail organization.

There is no standard career progression, but a typical example may be useful. A college graduate starting a career with a department store chain might first work as a management trainee and then progress as shown in Exhibits 1.5 and 1.6. *Retailing in Action 1-3* is a description of a divisional merchandise manager's career that was published by the editors of *Chain Store Age.*

RETAILING IN ACTION	1-3

In Focus: Divisional Merchandise Manager

Three months after joining Jordan Marsh, a full-line department store chain that operates in New England, Dan England was supervising a staff of 32 people and was responsible for multimillion-dollar volume selling areas. Not bad for a young man just out of college without any prior business experience. As England recalls, it was "a sobering, and enthralling, experience."

That was ten years ago. Today, England, 31, is divisional merchandise manager, overseeing a group of buyers in home furnishings, including furniture, electronics, decorative accessories, and tabletops. His buyers buy for the entire chain, not just one store. And while working with his buyers, England is also charged with keeping up with consumer trends in his market, with financial planning, and with overall enhancement of his areas' sales and profits.

In many ways, England's current position represents the sum total of all he's done to date. Step-by-step up the career ladder, he's added skills and knowledge necessary for the next move up the career ladder.

After all, acquiring certain skills and knowledge was England's goal from the very start. He recalls: "Just before graduating (from the University of Pennsylvania), I did some soul-searching and came to the conclusion that I wanted to enter the business world. I concluded that a retail background would be very good training for someone who wanted a broad-based experience in general business practices."

After shopping for a retailer that met his criteria for personal and professional growth opportunities, England signed on with Jordan Marsh. Like other college recruits, England first had to successfully complete a 12-week training regimen. It was an experience that became the springboard for his professional growth: "The training immediately acquaints you with the basics of department store retailing," England says. "You get classroom training. You get hands-on experience. You're with a sales manager running a department and all that entails, which can be anything from supervising the activities of sales (personnel), to receiving merchandise, to arranging it on the floor, to rearranging the department to better maximize traffic." What's more, England also had a chance to observe buyers at work, getting a feel for new product planning, merchandise selection, and such subjects as advertising.

After training, England became sales manager in his own right. Assigned to home furnishings, he was suddenly supervising 32 people and responsible for building business in such areas as appliances and consumer electronics.

England stayed in that position about a year, then was promoted to assistant buyer, in the upholstered furniture division. It was a job that built logically on his previous activities, but opened up new areas of knowledge by being "a bit more focused, more analytical, more long-term planning oriented," England says. Next, England was named divisional sales manager, supervising a group of sales managers.

After a year as divisional sales manager, England became a buyer, in domestics. He says: "A good buyer will have several skills and also some character traits that are necessary for successful buying activities." These include analytical skills, "both quantitative and qualitative; a good sense of fashion," which England says, "applies to any number of merchandise areas besides apparel"; interpersonal skills; supervisory and administrative skills ("your office must be prepared to instantly capitalize on things as they occur because there are fast changes in retail buying"); as well as negotiation skills; merchandising skills; and marketing instincts (knowing how to advertise a product and what kinds of sales promotions work best in any given situation).

England worked as a buyer for two years, then was promoted to assistant store manager, supervising divisional sales managers. A year later, he was named divisional merchandise manager.

England's future career path could lead him to either a position as regional director of stores or general merchandise manager. But his prediction of 10 years ago—that retailing would give him a wide-ranging business background—came true long ago. "In retailing," he says, "You're involved in four or five different things. Each is a function of doing business, but not a specialty. In other words, I've learned some accounting, but I'm not an accountant. I've learned some of the principles of marketing, sales promotions and advertising, but I'm not in the world of advertising. I've learned a bit about finance and the like, but I'm not working in a bank. Retailing gives you a general flavor of many different ingredients of the general business communities, and I'm not so sure that a lot of industries can do that."

Source: *Careers in Retailing,* Published by Lebhar-Friedman, Inc., 425 Park Avenue, New York, NY 10022, pp. 24–25. Reprinted with permission. Copyright Lebhar-Friedman, Inc.

Exhibit 1.5
**JC Penney
Career
Progression
Chart**

Opportunities for Promotion

Today, the Manager of a large JCPenney store gains wide experience in store functions, including operations and personnel assignments, and often is a part of the staffs of our regional or district offices. Store Manager jobs are highly prized for their independence, responsibility, and level of compensation.

The key to advancement is job performance and, of course, the availability of positions. A career path in Store Management usually looks like this:

Management Responsibilities

The responsibilities that correspond with each successive management position represent their own unique challenges and opportunities:

Corporate Office
Regional Office
District Manager

Store Manager
— Accountable for all phases of retail store operation. Responsible for meeting store sales and profit objectives and developing future managers.

District Office Staff
— Coordinates activities for a group of stores in terms of Personnel, Operations, Presentation, and Publicity.

Business Planning Manager
— Coordinates one of the four business entities (Women's, Men's, Children's, and Home Furnishings) for a market.

General Merchandising / Personnel Manager / Operations Manager
— Second-level management positions in stores. Accountable for merchandising functions, personnel policy and procedures, and sales support and service areas.

Senior Merchandising Manager
— Same responsibilities as Merchandising Manager, but with a larger volume. Assistant Buyers are selected from this position.

Merchandising Manager
— Responsible for merchandise lines in one or more departments of a store. Manages a store-within-a-store: responsibilities include selection of merchandise, departmental sales and profits, and managing a floor sales team.

Management Trainee
— Participates in a 12-month in-store training program that emphasizes merchandising systems, personnel procedures, and operations.

SOURCE: Reprinted with permission of J.C. Penney.

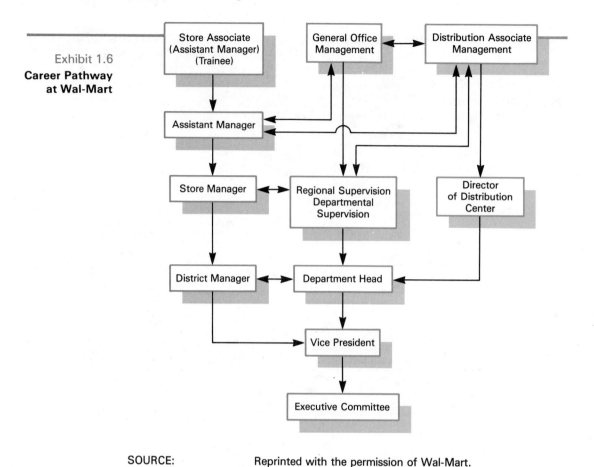

Exhibit 1.6
Career Pathway at Wal-Mart

SOURCE: Reprinted with the permission of Wal-Mart.

Geographic Mobility.   Will retailing allow you to live in the area of the country where you desire? Yes and no. Retailing exists in all geographic areas of the United States. In the largest 300 cites in the United States, there are sufficient employment and advancement opportunities in retailing. However, in order to progress rapidly, a person must often be willing and able to make several geographic moves, all of which may not be attractive. Rapidly growing chain stores almost always transfer individuals in order to open stores in new areas. These transfers are generally coupled with promotions and salary increases. A person may stay in one area if he or she wants to, but it may cost that person opportunities for advancement.

Women in Retailing.   In the past, retailing was viewed as a good career for women. But the role of women in retailing was most often restricted to the sales floor, the buying office, or middle management. Women typically found the door shut when it was time to move into the executive suite. But by the mid 1980s, statistics compiled by Gable, Gillespie and Topol showed that females constitute close to 44 percent of all department store executives, making it the profession where women have achieved the highest level of attainment.[10] However, most female executives are still only at the lower levels of corporate management.[11] In the past several years, breakthroughs into the retail presidential ranks have included:

Judith K. Hofer, president of May Company's Famous-Barr Co. division;

Pamela Grant, president of May Company's Goldwater's division;

Marilyn Lewis, chairman of Hamburger Hamlets;

Joanna Bradshaw, president of Workbench Inc., an independent chain of life-style furniture stores;

Judy Stewart, president of August Max, a specialty chain, a division of U.S. Shoe;

Eve Levinson, president of Contempo Casuals, a specialty retail division of Carter Hawley Hale;

Lana Jane Lewis-Brent, president of Sunshine-Jr. Foods Inc. of Florida;[12]

Mrs. M. Pollack, chair of Palais Royale;

Evelyn Goodman, president and GMM of Lipton's Fashion Wear, Ltd.

Societal Perspective.   Merchants have never been viewed with great favor. Now, however, merchants are respected and desirable members of their communities, their state, and their nation. Leading retail executives are well-rounded individuals with a high social consciousness. Many of them serve on the boards of nonprofit arts organizations, as regents or trustees of universities, on local chambers of commerce, on school boards, and in other service-related activities. Retailers serve society not only outside their retailing career, but also within it. Take a moment to envision a world without merchants or retailers. How could any advanced industrial society survive in their absence? It couldn't. It is not the profession that determines one's contribution to society but the soundness of one's ethical principles. You need to develop a firm set of ethical principles to guide you throughout your career.

PREREQUISITES FOR SUCCESS

What is required for success as a retail executive? Many people respond to this questions with the simple answer, "hard work." The work is hard, the hours almost always exceed forty per week, and a six-day week is not unusual for a retail executive. However, work is not the only prerequisite. Let us look at some other requirements for success in retailing.

Analytical Skills.   To be successful, the retail executive must be able to analyze facts and data in order to plan, manage, and control. Every day, the retail executive must solve problems. An understanding of the past and present performance of the store, its merchandise lines, and its departments is necessary. The analysis of the store's performance data forms the basis for future actions.

Creativity.   The ability to generate novel ideas and solutions is known as creativity. Retail executives cannot operate a store totally by a set of pre-programmed equations and formulas; they need to be idea people as well as analysts. Success in retailing is the result of sensitive, perceptive decisions and imaginative, innovative techniques. For example, a buyer must be able to detect environmental changes and relate these changes to new needs or products in the marketplace.

Decisiveness.   Decisiveness is the ability to render judgments, take action, and commit oneself to a course of action until desired results are achieved. A retail executive must be decisive. Sometimes better decisions could be made if more time were available, but variables such as fashion trends and consumer desires change quickly. In order to be successful, an executive must make decisions quickly, confidently, and correctly, even if complete information is not available.

Flexibility.   Flexibility is the ability to adjust to ever-changing situations. The retail executive must have the willingness and enthusiasm to do whatever is necessary to get the job done, even if it means changing plans. In retailing, surprises never cease. Because plans must be altered quickly to accommodate changes in trends, styles, and attitudes, successful retail executives must be flexible.

Initiative.   Retail executives must have the ability to originate action rather than wait to be told what to do. This ability is called initiative. To be a success, the retail executive must monitor sales volumes, profits, and inventory levels and seize opportunities for action.

Leadership.   Leadership is the ability to inspire others to trust and respect your judgment and to do what you ask. Retail executives must be managers. One person cannot do it all. In any large-scale retail enterprise, the executive must depend on others to get the work done.

Organization.   Organization is the ability to establish priorities and courses of action for yourself and others and the ability to plan and follow up to achieve results. Retail executives are often forced to coordinate many different factors, issues, functions, and projects at the same time.

To achieve goals, the successful retailer must set priorities and organize personnel and resources.

Risk Taking.   Retail executives must be willing to take risks based on thorough analysis and sound judgment; they must also be willing to accept responsibility for the results. Success in retailing often comes from taking calculated risks and having the confidence to try something new before someone else does.

Stress Tolerance.   As the other prerequisites to success in retailing suggest, retailing is fast-paced and demanding. Retail executives must be able to perform consistently under pressure and to thrive on constant change and challenge. They must be resilient.

These nine prerequisites to success in retailing are not intended to scare you off. You probably do not yet possess all nine. The important thing is that a person beginning a retail career should have the desire to acquire them. If you desire these abilities, this book will help you move toward a career in retailing.

TWO METHODS OF RETAIL MANAGEMENT

As we have seen, the first two prerequisites to success as a retail executive are analytical skills and creativity. These attributes also represent two common approaches to retail management.

ANALYTICAL METHOD

The analytical retail executive is a finder and investigator of facts: reducing, synthesizing, and dissecting facts in order to make decisions systematically. To make these decisions, the executive uses models and theories of retail phenomena that enable her or him to structure all dimensions of retailing.[13] An analytical perspective usually results in a standardized set of procedures, success formulas, and guidelines.

Consider, for example, the manager of a McDonald's restaurant, where everything is preprogrammed, including the menu, decor, location, hours of operation, cleanliness standards, customer service policies, and advertising. The store manager needs only to gather and analyze facts to determine whether the preestablished guidelines are being met and to take appropriate corrective actions if necessary.

CREATIVE METHOD

The creative retail executive is a producer of ideas. This executive tends to be a conceptualizer and is very imaginative. She or he uses insight and intuition more often than facts, and the result is usually a novel way to look at or solve a retail problem. It is possible to operate a retail establishment with creativity, but in the long run, using *only* creativity will be inadequate. Analytical decision making must be used to profitably respond to unforseen events in the environment.

An example is Kaleidoscope, Inc., a retail mail-order firm. Susan Edmondson invested $5,000 and began operating her business out of the carriage house in her backyard. Her buying technique was creative and nonanalytical. She bought what her insight and intuition suggested—jewelry, home furnishings, gourmet foods and cookware, children's toys, and some clothing. Basically, all were items that appealed to her. As a result, her target market was a reflection of Susan Edmondson, an affluent woman between thirty and fifty years old. In spite of these purely intuitive methods, Kaleidoscope prospered. In fact, within four years the firm's sales had reached $16 million. Unfortunately, the story doesn't end there. Susan and her husband had made no analytical assessment of the company's financial future and the capital requirements necessary to enlarge the business. Soon they found that order processing couldn't keep up with the incoming mail. Inadequate computers bled the firm of money. Lawsuits followed. Susan and her husband were divorced, which cut communication between the management team. Soon employees with no formal knowledge of business or finance were making spur-of-the-moment decisions without any regard for the future. Finally, five years after its founding, and only a few months after reporting a $16 million sales year, Kaleidoscope, Inc., filed for bankruptcy.[14]

A TWO-PRONGED APPROACH

As shown through the McDonald's and Kaleidoscope examples, retailing can be practiced by either of two extremes. The retailer who employs both approaches is most successful in the long run. It is obvious what went wrong at Kaleidoscope, but isn't McDonald's very successful using only the analytical method? No. The McDonald's store manager can operate quite successfully in a purely analytical mode. However, behind the manager is a corporation that is creative as well as analytical. Examples of the corporation's creative dimensions include the development of McDonald's characters (Ronald McDonald, Grimace, and Hamburglar) and selected menu items (McDLT, Egg McMuffin, and Big Mac). McDonald's strong analytical dimension is reflected in its standardized layouts, fixtures, equipment, and employee training. It is the combination of the creative with the analytical that has made McDonald's what it is today.

In all fields of retailing, the synthesis of creativity and analysis is necessary. Roger Dickinson, a former retail executive and now professor of marketing, has stated that "many successful merchandisers are fast duplicators rather than originators."[15] To decide who or what to duplicate requires not only creativity but an analysis of the strategies that retailers are pursuing. Dickinson further states that "creativity in retailing is for the sake of increasing the sales and profits of the firm."[16] If creativity is tied to sales and profits, analysis cannot be avoided.

Retailers in the 1990s and beyond cannot do without either creativity or analytical skills. In this book, we will attempt to develop your skills in both areas. At the outset, however, you should note that the analytical and creative approaches to retailing are not that different. Whether you use creativity or analytical skills, you will always be solving problems. The similarities between the creative and analytical methods of solving problems are presented in Exhibit 1.7.

A PROPOSED ORIENTATION

The approach to the study of retailing used in this book has four major orientations: (1) environmental, (2) management planning, (3) profit, and (4) decision making.

Retailers should have an environmental orientation, which will allow them to continuously adapt to external forces in the environment. Retailing is not static. With social, legal, technological, economic, and other external forces always in flux, the retailer finds it necessary to assess these changes in an analytical perspective and to respond with creative actions.

Retailers should have a planning orientation, which will help them to adapt systematically to a changing environment. Planning is deciding today what to do tomorrow. A retailer who wants to have a competitive edge must plan for the future. This text will place special emphasis on the development of creative retail strategies.

Retailers should have a profit orientation, since all retail decisions have an effect on the income statement, the balance sheet, or both. This text will therefore focus on management of the balance sheet and income statement. Analytical tools that show how to evaluate the profit impact of retail decisions will be discussed.

Retailers should have a decision-making orientation, which will allow them to focus on collecting and analyzing data for making intelligent retail decisions. A retail information system is needed to help retail executives program their operations for desired results.

THE BOOK OUTLINE

This book consists of 18 chapters and 30 retail case studies. The material in the text and the case studies are intended to reinforce each other. The cases bring the real world into your studies, and give you insight into the kind of situation you might face some years from now as a retail execu-

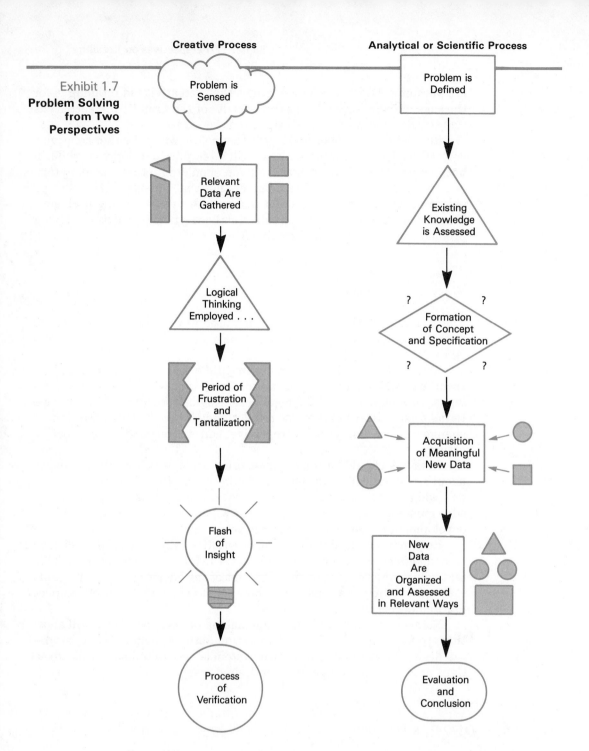

Creative Process

Analytical or Scientific Process

Exhibit 1.7
**Problem Solving
from Two
Perspectives**

Problem is
Sensed

Problem is
Defined

Relevant
Data Are
Gathered

Existing
Knowledge
is Assessed

Logical
Thinking
Employed . . .

? ?
Formation
of Concept
and Specification
? ?

Period of
Frustration
and
Tantalization

Acquisition
of Meaningful
New Data

Flash
of
Insight

New
Data
Are
Organized
and Assessed
in Relevant Ways

Process
of
Verification

Evaluation
and
Conclusion

SOURCES: Lewis E. Walkup, "Creativity in Science Through Visualiza-tion," *Journal of Creative Behavior,* 1 (Summer 1967), pp. 283-84; and Gerald Zaltman, Christian R. A. Pinson, and Reinhard Angelmar, *Mothatheory and Consumer Research* (New York: Holt, Rinehart and Winston, 1973), pp. 13-15.

tive. Through careful analysis of the cases and discussion with fellow students you will discover retailing concepts. The concepts will be vividly retained because of the concrete context in which they were learned. Furthermore, the cases require you to think of yourself as a retail decision maker who must work with less-than-perfect information.

INTRODUCTION TO RETAILING

This book is divided into six parts. The first part, *Introduction to Retailing*, has two chapters. You have already learned something about the nature and scope of retailing. In Chapter 2, "The Retail Planning and Management Process," you will be exposed to the basic concepts of strategy, administration, and operational planning and management in retailing.

THE RETAILING ENVIRONMENT

Part 2 of this book focuses on external factors the retailer faces in making everyday business decisions. The four chapters examine the factors shown in Exhibit 1.1 in greater detail.

Chapter 3 "Understanding Channel Behavior," will focus on the behavior of the various members of the channel of distribution and their effect on the retailer.

Chapter 4 "Understanding the Retail Customer," will look at the behavior of the retail consumer and the socioeconomic environment.

Chapter 5 "Competition in Retailing," will examine the behavior of competitors as well as the technological advances taking place in the market.

Chapter 6 "Understanding the Legal Environment," will analyze the effect of the legal constraints on today's retailer.

LOCATION ANALYSIS

It has been said that the three keys to success in retailing are location, location, and location. In Part 3, we discuss some of the elements considered in determining the feasibility of entering a given retail market, and how to select a site after the decision to enter the market has been made.

MANAGING RETAIL OPERATIONS

In Part 4, *Managing Retail Operations*, we discuss the merchandising operations of a retail firm. This part deals with the day-to-day tasks facing retailers, such as financial planning, buying, pricing, promotion, store design, and customer service.

Chapter 9   "Introduction to Financial Planning"
Chapter 10 "The Merchandise Buying and Handling Process"
Chapter 11 "Pricing Merchandise"
Chapter 12 "Retail Promotion"
Chapter 13 "Store Design and Atmosphere"
Chapter 14 "Servicing the Retail Customer"

RETAIL PLANNING, ADMINISTRATION AND CONTROL

In Part 5, we discuss retail planning and control. Our concern is how to maximize the efficiency of operations.

Chapter 15   "Retail Planning and Control," will present the overview of the entire section.
Chapter 16   "Management of Human Resources" will examine the role of human resources in a retail firm.
Chapter 17   "Retail Information Systems," will develop a framework for collecting and gathering information that you need for optimal planning, administration and control.

FUTURE OF RETAILING

Part 6 looks into the future of retailing. It discusses what environmental changes are anticipated over the next decade, and how those changes will affect the retailing sector.

SUMMARY

Retailing is the final stage in the progression of merchandise from the producer to the consumer. It involves effectively combining creative and analytical skills to make a profit in an ever-changing environment.

What possibilities does a retailing career offer to the student? In the long run, a retail career can offer salary comparable to other careers, opportunities for career advancement, and geographic mobility.

What are the prerequisites for success as a retailing executive? Besides hard work, the nine prerequisites for success are analytical skills, creativity, decisiveness, flexibility, initiative, leadership, organization, risk-taking, and stress tolerance. All are important, but it is most important for the retail executive to have an attitude of openness to new ideas and a willingness to learn.

From what perspective should retailing be studied? Since retailing represents an economic sector, it should be studied from both a supply and demand perspective. It is the interaction between supply (sellers) and demand (buyers) that establishes price levels, competitive intensity, and profit levels.

In this book, we utilize four orientations to the study and practice of retailing: an environmental orientation, a planning orientation, a profit orientation, and a decision-making orientation.

QUESTIONS FOR DISCUSSION

1. No specific mention was made of marketing in this first chapter. What do you see as the relationship between retail management and marketing management?
2. What concepts and techniques from economics and/or finance do you believe would be most helpful in retail decision making? Why?
3. A retail manager who is both creative and analytical will definitely succeed. Agree or disagree with this statement and defend your position.
4. Is managing a franchise of a large retail chain with 100 employees any different than managing your own store with only two employees? Why?
5. Regardless of what they sell, the major problems of many retail enterprises are identical. Agree or disagree with this statement and defend your position.
6. If you were on the board of directors of one of the largest retail chains in the United States and had to head a committee to select a new president for the retail chain, what criteria would you use to evaluate the potential candidates? Why?
7. Many of today's environmental trends will have an impact on retailing operations over the next decade. Discuss three such trends and their effects on retailing.
8. Ask some local retailers how they view the outlook for opportunities in retailing. Do they believe a college education is necessary for success in retailing?

SUGGESTED READINGS

Jakobson, Cathryn. "They Get It For You Wholesale." *The New York Times Magazine* (December 4, 1988): 24–25, 54–57.

Nowakhtar, Susan and Richard Widdows. "Research Note: The Structure of the General Merchandise Retailing Industry 1959–1983: An Empirical Analysis." *Journal of Retailing* (Winter 1987): 426–435.

Schwartz, Joe. "The Evolution of Retailing." *American Demographics* (December 1986): 30–37.

Swineyard, William R. "The Appeal of Retailing as a Career." *Journal of Retailing* (Winter 1981): 86–97.

ENDNOTES

1. Some examples of the macro approach to retailing are Elizabeth C. Hirschman, "A Descriptive Theory of Retail Market Structure," *Journal of Retailing* (Winter 1978): 29–48; Louis P. Bucklin, *Competition and Evolution in the Distributive Trades* (Englewood Cliffs, N.J.: Prentice-Hall, 1972); Margaret Hall, John Knapp, and Christopher Winsten, *Distribution in Great Britain and North America* (London: Oxford University Press, 1961).

2. E. E. Foster, translator, "The Works of Aristotle," *The Oeconomica*, Oxford 10 (1920): 1343a–43b.

3. For a further discussion of changes that have occurred in retailing, see William R. Davidson, Albert Bates, and Stephen Bass, "The Retail Life Cycle," *Harvard Business Review* (November–December 1976): 89–96; Delbert J. Duncan, "Responses of Selected Retail Institutions to Their Changing Environment," in Peter Bennett, ed., *Marketing and Economic Development* (Chicago: American Marketing Association, 1965): 483–602; William J. Regan, "The Stages of Retail Development," in Reavis Cox, Wroe Alderson, and Stanley Shapiro, eds., *Theory in Marketing* (Homewood, Il.: Richard D. Irwin, 1964): 139–53; Leonard L. Berry, "Retail Positioning Strategies for the 1980s," *Business Horizons* (November–December 1982): 45–50; Aimee Stern, "Retailers Restructure," *Dun's Business Month* (February 1986): 28–32.

4. U.S. Department of Commerce, Bureau of the Census, *1982 Census of Retail Trade* (Washington, D.C.: U.S. Government Printing Office, 1982).

5. *The State of Small Business: A Report of the President 1988* (Washington, D.C.: U.S. Government Printing Office, 1988), 237.

6. *Dun's Census of American Business 1988*: 18–119.

7. "The 50 Largest Retailing Companies," *Fortune* (June 6, 1988): D29.

8. "Exec 100: Retailing's Top Achievers," *Chain Store Age* (August, 1988): 14–20.

9. "The $60 Million Chairman," *Business Week* (May 16, 1988): 42.

10. Myron Gable, Karen R. Gillespie, and Martin Topol, "The Current Status of Women in Department Store Retailing: An Update," *Journal of Retailing* (Summer 1984): 92; Myron Gable and B.J. Read, "The Current Status of Women in Professional Selling," *Journal of Personal Selling and Sales Management* (May 1987): 33–39.

11. Pete Arlow and Myron Gable, "Size, Industry Segment, Financial Performance: Their Relationship to Women in Executive-Board Positions in Major Firms," *Managerial Frontiers: The Next Twenty-Five Years*, (proceedings of Eastern Academy of Management Meetings, 1987: 39–41.

12. "Equal Opportunity for Women Comes Slowly in the Executive Suite," *Chain Store Age Executive* (June 1980): 27–29. For a study of women in larger

firms see Kaylene C. Williams, James C. Feltet and Claire Madaire, "A Comparison of Women in Department and Specialty Store Management," *Journal of Retailing* (Winter 1983): 107–115; "Women At the Top: Lana Jane Lewis-Brent," *C Store Business* (May 1983): 43–45; "Top Women Execs," *USA Today*, 20 March 1986, 4B.

13. The analytical approach to retailing has been espoused for over fifty years. See Walter Hoving, "More Science in Merchandising," *Journal of Retailing*, (October 1929): 3–9 and Paul H. Nystrom, *The Economics of Retailing*, (New York: Ronald Press, 1915).

14. "A High Fashion Sales Whiz Who Was," *INC* (May 1979): 80–82.

15. Roger Dickinson, "Creativity in Retailing," *Journal of Retailing* (Winter 1969-1970): 4.

16. Dickinson, 4.

2 Chapter

The Retail Planning and Management Process

OVERVIEW

This chapter will explain the importance of planning in retail management. To facilitate this discussion we will introduce a retail planning and management model, which will serve as a frame of reference for the remainder of the text. This simple model will illustrate the importance of strategic planning, operations management, and administrative management. These three activities, if properly conducted, will result in high-performance financial results for the retail firm.

**CHAPTER 2
The Retail
Planning and
Management
Process**

In most endeavors, a well-defined plan of action means the difference between success and failure. For example, a traveler cannot go from Cincinnati to Kansas City without a plan of which highways to use. The quarterback and the coach develop a game plan of offensive plays before every game. Successful college students plan their assignments so that they are not forced into an "all nighter" the night before an assignment is due. Similarly, a clearly defined plan of action is an essential ingredient of retail management.

THE NEED FOR PLANNING

Planning is the anticipation and organization of what needs to be done to reach an objective. This sounds simple enough, but it is difficult to know in advance of an upcoming merchandising season what styles, quantities, and sizes customers will want, and how these wants are changing. Superior planning can offset some of the advantages the competition may have. People not familiar with retailing often wonder how retailers can anticipate what consumers are going to want next season. They may assume that retailers do it with some sort of magic. However, success for all retailers, large and small, is generally a matter of planning and its implementation. Many small specialty stores have taken significant market share away from larger department stores by studying environmental changes, anticipating future changes, and planning accordingly. **Strategic planning** is a type of planning that involves adapting the resources of the firm to the opportunities and constraints of an ever-changing environment. Through strategic planning, retailers achieve and maintain a balance between resources and opportunities. Let's take a closer look at the components of the strategic planning process.

COMPONENTS OF STRATEGIC PLANNING

Strategic planning consists of three components:

1. Development of a *statement of purpose or mission* for the firm
2. Definition of *specific goals and objectives* for the firm
3. Development of *basic strategies* that will enable the firm to reach its objectives and fulfill its mission.

STATEMENT OF MISSION

The beginning of the planning process is the formulation of a mission statement. The **mission statement** is a description of the fundamental nature, rationale, and direction of the firm. While these statements vary from firm to firm, they usually include three elements:

1. How the retailer uses or intends to use its resources
2. How it expects to relate to the ever-changing environment
3. The kinds of values it intends to offer in order to serve the needs and wants of the consumer.

Consider the mission statement for a chain of prerecorded music stores in the northeastern United States with over 100 outlets at the beginning of 1990.

"This chain is in business to provide prerecorded entertainment in all modes desired by consumers. Our target market consists of all viable segments of the population shopping in locations, primarily malls, where our stores are situated in the northeast and mideast regions of the United States. In addition to a broad assortment of merchandise, we strive to provide our customers with both value and personal service. In the long run, we will have the dominant market share in all the market segments we serve. We endeavor to increase our sales by one hundred percent in the next five years, primarily through improved market and merchandise development, and secondarily through market penetration."

Strategic Trust

"During the next five years we will double our sales through market development, merchandise development, and market penetration. We will open five to ten new stores a year, and over the next ten years remodel, where necessary, our existing stores in a contemporary fashion. We will improve our budget/cut-out merchandise to have them account for a greater percentage of total sales. Further, our video stock will also be increased with the goal of having video provide increased sales volume."[1]

In summary, the mission statement really answers the question of "What business are we in?"[2] This chain's mission statement says that they want to be, not a record store leader, but a "value oriented" retailer of all prerecorded entertainment.

Consider how this poor mission statement for the Avon Drive-In Theater can be improved by addressing the omissions in parentheses. "We are in the movie (not the entertainment) business and we shall only show PG13 movies (not what the customers want) at the lowest prices in our trading area (failure to recognize that their market might not be exclusively price sensitive)."

STATEMENT OF GOALS AND OBJECTIVES

The second step in the planning process is to define specific goals and objectives. These **goals and objectives** should be derived from, and give precision and direction to, the firm's mission statement. The objectives should identify the performance results that the retailer intends to bring about through the execution of its major strategies. The statement of goals and objectives serves two purposes. First, it provides specific direction and guidance to the firm in the formulation of its strategy. Second, it provides a standard against which the firm can measure and evaluate its performance results.

Let's look at the prerecorded music chain's goals and objectives for one fiscal year:

1. Open or acquire five to ten new stores.
2. Remodel six to eight stores.
3. Increase net profit for each six month period by one percent over last year's net profits by featuring and increasing the merchandise assortment of higher gross margin products such as accessories and budget/cut-out merchandise.
4. Increase video sales by 50 percent over last year.
5. Improve performance in classical music by increasing turnover by one percent over preceding year.
6. Improve the quality of promotion activities, including in-store appearances, publicity, contests, cross-promotions, school promotions, and in-store circulars.
7. Achieve awareness/recognition level by consumers in newer market areas (i.e., Washington/Baltimore) equal to that in New Jersey/Long Island areas.

8. Improve communication among top-level executives, especially those at similar management levels.
9. Restructure buying operation to better interact with other corporate activities (i.e., promotion).
10. Have advertising department *totally* within house.
11. Complete modernization of warehouse.
12. Maintain inventory levels at stores so as not to exceed budgeted inventory levels.

Notice how goal number 3 did not just say that the record chain wanted to increase profits, but stated a percentage (1%) by which it wanted to increase profits over each six month period. To be useful, a goal must not only state what the company wants to accomplish, but the amount that it wants to achieve and the time period involved.

Objectives and goals should be established for each department or performance area in the business. While these goals can be expressed in many different ways, usually a retailer will break them down into two dimensions: **market performance objectives**, which compare a firm's actions against its competitors, and **financial performance objectives**, which analyze a firm's ability to provide adequate profit to continue in business.

These two dimensions can be further subdivided. Market performance objectives can be expressed in terms of sales volume or as a market share percentage. Financial performance objectives include profitability and liquidity.

Profitability can be measured in a variety of ways but is generally expressed in terms of return on total assets or return on net worth (the amount of money invested by the owner). Many small- and medium-size retailers do not really manage profitability. They treat it as a residual of good market performance and good merchandising. These retailers overlook the fact that every decision they make has an impact on profitability. Because profitability is such an important measure of successful planning, it is one of the most vital aspects of a retailer's responsibilities.

Liquidity, the second financial performance objective, is a measure of how many of the firm's assets can readily be converted to cash. A variety of specific financial ratios for measuring liquidity will be discussed later in this chapter.

STRATEGIES

After stating the firm's mission and establishing some goals and objectives, a retailer must develop a *strategy*; that is, a course of action to accomplish the goals. The strategy is a plan that, when executed, will produce the desired levels of performance.

Notice the close relationship between a retailer's objectives and its strategies. Objectives indicate what the retailer wants to accomplish.

Strategies indicate how the retailer will attempt to accomplish those goals with the resources available.

Separate strategies must be developed for the market performance goals and the financial performance goals. Thus, a retailer should have a market strategy and a financial strategy.

A fully developed retail market strategy includes:

1. The specific target market that the retailer is seeking to serve.
2. The sales volume and market share sought.
3. The specific retail mix (location, price, promotion, display, customer service, merchandise assortment) that the retailer intends to use to appeal to this target market to gain this market share or sales volume.

A fully developed retail financial strategy shows:

1. The particular levels of financial performance that the retailer is seeking to achieve.
2. The specific mix of financial statement components such as cost of merchandise, human resources, types of assets, expenses, etc. needed to achieve a targeted financial performance level.

Exhibit 2.1 illustrates the strategy planning process. The following four case histories also depict the strategic planning process.

S. S. Kresge.   S. S. Kresge was a declining old-line variety store chain muddling through the post-World War II era. With astute planning, however, it became one of the fastest growing retailers in the period from 1960–1988.[3] Let us examine how this was accomplished.

In 1957, Harry B. Cunningham, a general vice president of the firm, was assigned to travel the country to study, first-hand, retail trends. Cunningham traveled for two years and finally confirmed that variety stores—like the earlier five-and-dime stores—had somehow drifted away from their original formula for success: low margins and high turnover. Instead of pricing merchandise to stimulate sales, they were pricing it on the basis of current costs. Variety stores were extremely vulnerable; supermarkets, discount houses, and other new mass merchandisers were beating them at their own game and many wanted to enter a new form of retailing.

In 1959, Cunningham was named president and chief executive officer and ordered another two-year study to focus exclusively on discounting. When the results were in, Cunningham gave discounting the final go-ahead. He was determined to avoid the merchandising mistakes of the other discounters flooding the market. The result was K mart, a conveniently located, one-stop shopping unit, where customers could buy quality merchandise at discount prices. In March, 1962, Kresge opened its first K mart in Garden City, Michigan and by the late 1960s, Kresge was the

Exhibit 2.1
**Retail Strategic
Planning
Process**

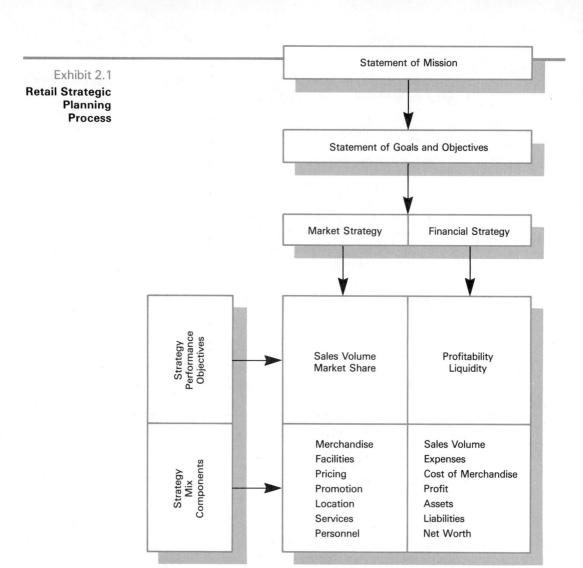

Statement of Mission

Statement of Goals and Objectives

Market Strategy	Financial Strategy

Strategy Performance Objectives	Sales Volume Market Share	Profitability Liquidity
Strategy Mix Components	Merchandise Facilities Pricing Promotion Location Services Personnel	Sales Volume Expenses Cost of Merchandise Profit Assets Liabilities Net Worth

SOURCE: Adapted from William R. Davidson, Daniel J. Sweeney, and Ronald W. Stampfl. Used with authors' permission.

Illus. 2.1
**A K mart store.
By 1987, K mart
was the second
largest retailer
in the United
States.**

unquestioned leader in the discount arena. In fact, by 1987 K mart had become the second largest retailer in the United States, with annual sales in excess of $24 billion.

Montgomery Ward. Our second example is of an inaccurate assessment of the environment coupled with a failure to recognize that the assessment was inaccurate, resulting in a very unsuccessful plan. In this situation the retailer continued to pursue a strategy designed for the wrong environment.

After World War II, Sewell Avery, chairman of the board at Montgomery Ward, believed that a depression was imminent.[4] Avery believed that after the war, the economy would not be able to maintain its growth because of the halt in war production and the large number of servicemen trying to find employment. At the time, Montgomery Ward had the managerial and financial resources to expand, but decided on a no-growth strategy based on Avery's prediction of a depression. Had a depression occurred, Avery would have been a hero; as it was, he was far from a hero.

Even after it was clear that no depression was on the horizon, Avery still insisted on a no-growth policy. At the same time, Sears was aggressively adding new stores and remodeling existing ones. As a result, sales at Sears accelerated from $1.9 billion in 1948 to $2.9 billion in 1954. In comparison, sales at Wards slipped from $1.1 billion in 1948 to $0.9 billion in the same period.

Retailing in Action 2-1 provides an analysis of how Montgomery Ward's more recent planning has fared.

RETAILING IN ACTION

2-1

Montgomery Ward Adapts to a Changing Consumer

The decade between 1975 and 1985 was a period of adjustment for retailers, as competitive pressures dramatically changed the market place. Shopping center selling space increased 80 percent during this period, while the population grew only by 12 percent. America's retailers became considerably more competitive and offered the customer far more spending options.

During this time period, the consumer started to support the specialty retailer to a much greater degree than national chain stores, discount stores, or department stores. Specialty stores enjoyed substantial growth, while market share and sales productivity of most other retailers diminished or at best kept pace with inflation.

In 1985, Montgomery Ward, seeking to take advantage of this trend, opened six prototype stores that combined specialty store retailing with value-driven merchandise assortments and aggressive promotional programming.

The largest prototype (100,000 + square feet of selling space) represented Ward's plans to abandon general merchandising and to imitate the success of such specialty retailers as Toys "R" Us and The Limited.

Specialty retailers are known for their depth in narrow categories of merchandise, such as fashionable women's clothes, toys, or automotive supplies. Ward officials wanted their stores to be seen as a collection of seven independent specialty shopsunder one roof: apparel, home electronics, appliances, auto care, home improvement and hardware, home furnishings, and sporting goods.

To promote the impression of wide selection in each of these areas, Ward moved much of its inventory out of the stockroom and on to the selling floor. To accommodate these extra goods, shelves ran farther up the walls and some racks were taller than presentation enhancements and other fixtures. The large prototype was built so that it could have as many as seven individual stores within the store, the medium prototype, five individual stores, and the small prototype, four individual stores.

After a year of testing, Ward's announced in 1986 that the remodeling program would continue but that two of the original seven specialty shops—home improvement and hardware and sporting goods—would be eliminated. The space used by these shops was to be devoted to the remaining shops.

Chain Store Age reported that perhaps no other retailer bases so many of its decisions on consumer research as Montgomery Ward. This might account for the firm's recent success.

In 1988, Ward's management conducted a $1.5 billion buy-out of the firm from Mobil, indicating the success of the remodeling program. Mobil's white elephant was now a successful and very profitable retailer.

Source: Information supplied in personal correspondence by J. A. Daynard, Senior Vice President, Montgomery Ward and "Market Research Put To Creative Use," *Chain Store Age* (May 1988): 23–26.

Price Club.   The last decade has seen a new retail concept emerge: the warehouse club, a cash-and-carry business which offers members brand name merchandise marked up as little as 11 percent. Many large retailers have now entered this business, but no one will deny that Sol Price and his Price Club were the pioneers in the development of this new retail concept. The Price Club has been successful both in terms of market performance and financial performance. By operating out of a 100,000 square-foot building in a low rent district, devoid of advertising, with a stark, industrial decor and maximum of 3,500 stockkeeping units (SKU) (an SKU is the lowest level of identification of merchandise. SKUs are usually defined by department, store, vendor, style, color, size, and location), Price has been able to operate at an 11 percent markup, while most traditional retailers operate at a gross margin two to three times as great. In addition to cutting expenses down to 7 percent of total sales, Price has been able to generate $1,000 of sales per square foot with an inventory turn of 16 to 18 times a year and a net profit to net worth ratio of 19.3 percent (also called return on net worth). By comparison, a traditional department store turns its inventory four-and-half times a year with sales of $100–$150 per square foot and a 15% net profit/net worth ratio.[5]

W. T. Grant.   Many different reasons have been given for the demise in 1976 of W. T. Grant, after 90 years as a merchandising giant. Reasons given include (1) increase in sales but decreased net profit due to lack of a strategic plan to accommodate sales increases, (2) inadequate controls over management, and (3) lack of internal communication.[6] However, closer analysis reveals another, overlooked reason. Many times a retailer will use someone else's money in normal operations. Earlier we spoke of two different financial profitability measures: return on assets and return on net worth. If a retailer does not borrow money from anybody and earns $50,000 on an investment of $450,000, the retailer's return on investment on total assets is 11.1 percent. If the retailer borrowed $200,000 in capital from a bank and/or from suppliers in the form of trade credit and invested $250,000 of its own, the retailer would still have $450,000 in total assets but its net worth would be $250,000, and its return on net worth would be 20 percent ($50,000 divided by $250,000).

The retailer's leverage ratio represents the dollars of total assets that can be acquired or supported for each dollar of net worth. It is calculated as total assets divided by net worth. This ratio measures the extent to which the retailer is utilizing debt; a normal ratio for retailers is between 2.0 and 2.5. In the year prior to filing for bankruptcy in 1976, W. T. Grant's leverage ratio was 9.5.[7] This means that for every $1 of net worth, W. T. Grant had total assets of $9.50. While a higher leverage ratio does increase the return on net worth, it also increases the retailer's risk, because as the proportion of debt increases the retailer is faced with ever-higher interest payments. This is where W. T. Grant became vulnerable. In addition, their financial planners did not forecast the economic downturn of the mid 1970s. Grant's financial strategy was not compatible with its marketing strategy of expansion and the changing environment. Other errors in Grant's strategic planning will be discussed in the W. T. Grant case on page C39.

What lessons can be learned from our four case histories? Did you see how Kresge's successfully reached out for a new target customer, the suburbanite of the 1960s? Did you see how Harry Cunningham developed a new retail mix for this consumer that was better than the offerings of the supermarkets, discounters, and other mass merchandisers, while Montgomery Ward continued with its traditional ways? Did you see how the Price Club developed a whole new financial strategy while W. T. Grant's lack of concern about the financial dimensions of retail operations contributed greatly to its demise?

THE RETAIL PLANNING AND MANAGEMENT MODEL

In Chapter 1 we mentioned that this book would have a management planning orientation, an environmental orientation, a profit orientation, and a decision-making orientation. These four orientations will be explained throughout this text with the aid of the retail planning and management model presented in Exhibit 2.2.[8]

The model suggests that a retailer must engage in three types of planning and management tasks: (1) strategic planning, (2) operations management, and (3) administrative management. Each task is undertaken to achieve high-performance results. For now, just think of high performance results as financial results substantially superior to the industry average. Later we will present a more precise definition.

STRATEGIC PLANNING

Strategic planning is concerned with how the retailer responds to the environment in an effort to establish a course of action to follow. This involves determining which marketing, financial, and locational strategy best reflects the line(s) of trade in which the retailer will operate, which market(s) will be pursued, and which retail mix to use.

The initial step is to define the firm's mission and establish goals and objectives. The next step is to develop a strong marketing plan or strategy in terms of both market and financial performance. We can best begin strategic planning by assessing the external environment. What we are looking for is an opportunity to fulfill the needs of a defined group of consumers (our target customers) in a method different from our competition; i.e., to seek a differential advantage over our competition.[9] Rarely will retailers discover a way to gain a differential advantage over their competitors merely by reviewing their own internal operations or focusing exclusively on the conventional industry structure. An effective retail strategy can result only from matching environmental forces with a retail marketing program that satisfies the customer better than any other retailer. The major environmental forces that should be assessed are profiled in Exhibit 2.2. Briefly they are:

1. **Channel Behavior.** The behavior of members of the retailer's marketing channel, the flow from manufacturer to consumer, can have a significant impact on the retailer's future. For example, are certain channel members, such as manufacturers or wholesalers, establishing their own retail outlets? Are wholesalers requiring larger minimum orders and offering less attractive credit terms? Behaviors such as these have implications for the retailer's strategy.

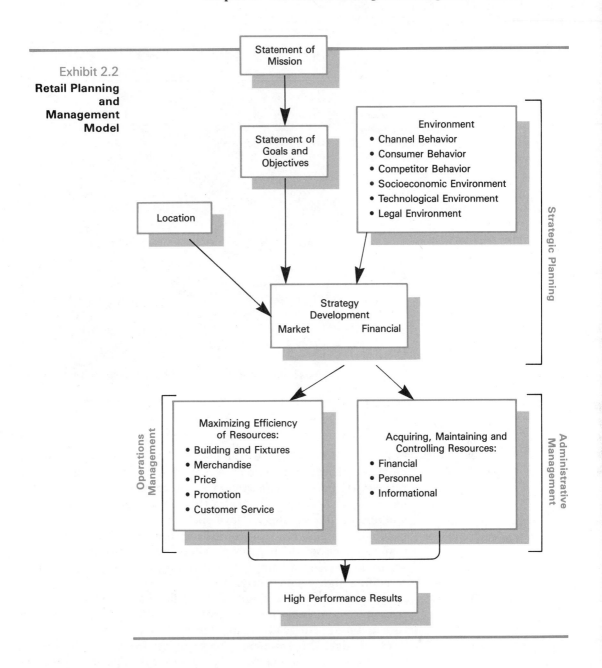

Exhibit 2.2
**Retail Planning
and
Management
Model**

Statement of Mission

Statement of Goals and Objectives

Environment
• Channel Behavior
• Consumer Behavior
• Competitor Behavior
• Socioeconomic Environment
• Technological Environment
• Legal Environment

Location

Strategy Development
Market   Financial

Strategic Planning

Maximizing Efficiency of Resources:
• Building and Fixtures
• Merchandise
• Price
• Promotion
• Customer Service

Acquiring, Maintaining and Controlling Resources:
• Financial
• Personnel
• Informational

Operations Management

Administrative Management

High Performance Results

Illus. 2.2
The retailer needs to understand consumer behavior in order to develop an effective retail strategy.

2. **Consumer Behavior.** The behavior of consumers will obviously have a significant impact on the retailer's future. Specifically, the retailer will need to understand the determinants of shopping behavior so that likely changes in that behavior can be identified and appropriate strategies developed.
3. **Competitor Behavior.** How competing retailers behave will have a major impact on which strategy will be most appropriate. Retailers must develop a competitive strategy that is not easily imitated in a highly competitive arena.
4. **Socioeconomic Environment.** The retailer must understand how economic and demographic variables will influence sales in the future and must adapt its strategy accordingly.
5. **Technological Environment.** The technical frontiers of the retail system offer new and potentially better ways of performing standard retail functions. The retailer must always be cognizant of opportunities for improving operating efficiency.
6. **Legal Environment.** The retailer should be familiar with local, state, and federal regulation of the retail system, as well as evolving legal patterns, in order to design retail strategies that are legally defensible.

Retailing in Action 2-2 illustrates what kinds of things can happen when retailers fail to understand their environment.

A single retailer cannot control these environmental forces, but the threats emanating from these forces can be translated into advantages by a successful retailer; e.g., the way Macy's changed from a store for the working classes of New York to a trendy boutique store catering to the upper middle class.

RETAILING
IN
ACTION

2-2

A Failure in Understanding the Market for Your Product

One of the hottest retailing ideas of the early 1980s was not even around to celebrate its fifth birthday in 1985. Wall Street originally praised the concept of Pizza Time Theatre Inc. Pizza Time planned to make unexceptional pizza irresistible by surrounding the eating area with electronic entertainment calculated to entice families into supermarket-size, windowless "entertainment centers." Financial experts felt the company's idea to combine dining and entertainment was ingenious and that future profits would be unlimited. At first, this appeared to be the case—revenues went from $36 million in 1981 to $99 million in 1982. However, the firm's estimate of $400 million in revenues by 1986 was halted by a filing of bankruptcy under Chapter 11 in 1984.

What could have caused such a rapid turnaround? Pizza Time's decline came as a result of a poorly thought-out marketing strategy. Primarily, it was a problem of target market selection. While the children loved the idea, the needs of their parents who were paying for the excursion were not met. Couples who worked all day did not relish the idea of child-infested video arcades. Also, management was the first to admit the quality of the pizza was not outstanding, at least not outstanding enough to justify the $22-24 the average family spent per visit. In addition, no liquor or beer was available for the adults; and they had to see the same show each visit, since the robots could not be easily reprogrammed.

A changing environment did not help the situation either. The video game craze became passe, and other fast food concepts, such as Mexican foods, started coming on strong. In short, Pizza Time's biggest mistake was a failure to realize that it had two markets: the kids and their parents. Each market required a different retail mix to be satisfied.

Source: Based on data from Gwen Kinkead, "High Profits from a Weird Pizza Combination," *Fortune* (July 26, 1982): 62-66; Scott Hume, "Why the Fun's All Gone for the Pizza-Video King," *Advertising Age* (March 26, 1984): 1 and 78; and Peggy Barnes, "Pizza Time Draws its Profits in Cheese," *Arizona Daily Star,* 12 April 1983, p. 1-D.

Another uncontrollable factor that will influence the retailer's ability to develop a strategic plan is location. Most retail managers have little control over location decisions. In most cases it is a decision which has already been made and the retailer must live with it. A newly appointed manager for a chain department store could change promotional policy, personnel, service levels, credit policies, or even prices but would probably be constrained by a long-term lease. Only the upper management of most chains are ever involved in location decisions. For the small retailer just starting out, or the retailer considering expansion into a new area, location is an important decision. Retailers should insist on an "out clause" in the lease if the location doesn't meet expectations. A full discussion of location and site decision-making will be covered in Chapters 7 and 8.

After reviewing its mission, objectives, environment, and location, the retailer should develop alternative uses of resources in order to obtain the highest performance level. After determining which strategy will yield the best results, the retailer is able to concentrate on operations and administrative management.

OPERATIONS MANAGEMENT

Operations management is concerned with maximizing the efficiency with which the retailer converts resources into sales and profits. When a retailer does a good job at operations management, that is, efficiently uses the resources available, then the retailer is said to be operations effective.

Most of the retailer's time and energy on a day-to-day basis is devoted to operations management. The retail planning and management model (Exhibit 2.2) shows that operations management involves managing the building and fixtures, merchandise, price, promotion, and customer service. All of these activities require daily attention. For example, the selling floor must be maintained, customers served, merchandise managed, advertisements run, and pricing decisions made every day. In other words, operations management is running the store.

A well-defined marketing strategy cannot ensure profitability for the retailer if operations are not maintained. This is precisely what retail analysts say happened to Kentucky Fried Chicken in the mid-1970s. Too much attention was paid to long-range strategic planning "and not enough time to running the store."[11] However, new management took over Kentucky Fried Chicken, and with emphasis on store operations, earnings tripled in just three years.[12]

In Part 4 of this text, *Managing Retail Operations*, we will focus on operations management, the real guts of retailing. In the first several years of your retail career, your concern will be almost exclusively with operations management. Strategic planning and administrative management will be handled by senior executives. If you enter retailing via a small- or medium-size firm, you will be making administrative, and even strategic, decisions sooner.

ADMINISTRATIVE MANAGEMENT

Administrative management involves the acquisition, maintenance, and control of resources necessary to carry out the retailer's strategy. It involves structuring and designing resources in order to maximize the retailer's performance potential. As shown in the retail planning and management model, the retailer is concerned with acquiring three categories of resources: financial, personnel, and informational.

Part 5 of this text is devoted to administrative management with a separate chapter on each type of resource. For now, just remember that a retailer can develop a good strategy with a good operations manager, but, if the proper financial, personnel, or informational resources are not acquired and used to implement that strategy, all is wasted.

HIGH PERFORMANCE RESULTS

The bottom portion of the retail planning and management model suggests that the cumulative effect of well designed and executed strategic, operations, and administrative plans will be high-performance results. Mistakes in any of these three areas will severely hamper the retailer's performance and prevent it from achieving high-performance status. Remember how Sears was forced in the late 1980s to reduce prices on its entire merchandise line, despite having higher operating costs than its competitors, and how Revco's mistaken sales projections resulted in the failure of its leveraged buyout.

THE HIGH-PERFORMANCE IMPERATIVE

The need for high-performance results is tied to the extremely competitive nature of retailing. Entry barriers are still relatively low in retailing, and new retail entrepreneurs are continually entering the marketplace. Because of this increased competition, margins and profit levels deteriorate. Retailers are forced to set high financial performance objectives so that if planned results are not achieved, at least there is a chance of achieving average operating results. The retailer that aims for only average results will often have to confront a sobering income statement and balance sheet.

PERFORMANCE MEASURES

What are the high-performance measures in retailing? As in any other business, the primary objective is to make a profit. After profitability, the next most important financial performance criteria in retailing is liquidity. Finally, today's retailer must be concerned with growth. Each of these objectives will be discussed briefly here and in more detail in Chapter 16.

PROFITABILITY

When retailers speak of "making a profit," the definition of profit is often unclear. The most common definition of **profit** is net profit after taxes—the bottom of the income statement. A common way to express profit is as a percentage of net sales. However, most retailers report profit as a percentage of investments.

Reporting profits as a percentage of investments is complicated by the fact that there are two different ways to define the term *investment*. Return on assets (ROA) reflects the return on all capital used in the business whether provided by owners or creditors. Return on investment (ROI), also referred to as return on net worth (RONW), reflects only the return on the amount that the owners have invested in the business. ROI or RONW can be expressed as profit divided by investment in business, or net worth.

Exhibit 2.3 gives the basic ROI model. Study it to understand the differences between ROA and RONW. Exhibit 2.4 defines the important terms in Exhibit 2.3.

By combining the information in the seven boxes on the extreme left of Exhibit 2.3, we can analyze the retailer's profit performance. (We will assume that the information contained in this model has been covered in previous course work. If it has not been covered, then Exhibit 2.4 provides the reader with a description of the terms involved in the basic ROI model.) This ROI model multiplies a retailer's profit margin by its rate of asset turnover to arrive at its return on assets. Thus, if a retailer has a profit margin of 4 percent and a rate of asset turnover of 3.0, it will have a return on assets of 12 percent (4% times 3.0 = 12%). The retailer's return on assets depicts the profit return achieved on all assets invested, regardless of whether the assets were financed by the firm's owners or creditors.

The return on asset figure is multiplied by the firm's financial leverage ratio to calculate return on net worth. In our example, if the firm had a financial leverage ratio of 2.0 (meaning its total assets were twice its net worth) and this was multiplied by the return on assets of 12 percent, the result would be a return on net worth of 24 percent (12% times 2.0 = 24%). The retailer's return on net worth depicts the profit the owners achieved on the dollars they had invested in the firm.

Some retailers only look at these seven elements of the basic ROI model when evaluating profitability. They call this combination of profit margin, asset turnover, and financial leverage the **strategic profit model (SPM)**. Exhibit 2.5 is a visualization of the SPM. A more detailed description of profit margin, asset turnover, and financial leverage follows.

Profit Margin.   The **profit margin** is the ratio of net profit (profit after taxes) to net sales. It shows how much profit a retailer makes on each dollar of sales after all expenses and taxes have been paid. For example, if a retailer is operating on a profit margin of 2 percent, it is making two

Exhibit 2.3

Basic Return on Investment Model

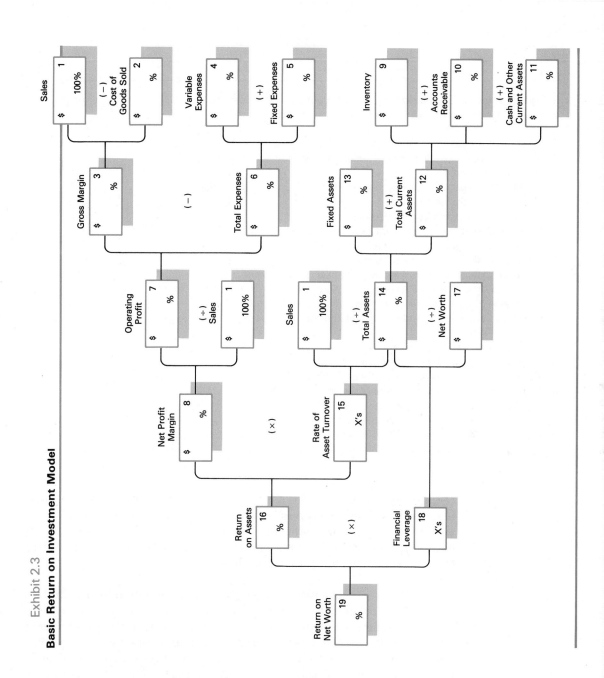

Exhibit 2.4

Definition of Terms in the Basic ROI Model

Item and Calculation	Source Statement
1. **Sales:** all revenues from exchange of merchandise and/or services	Income
2. **Cost of goods sold:** cost value of those sales which are made during a period.	Income
3. **Gross Margin:** subtract Cost of Goods Sold from Sales.	Income
4. **Variable Expenses:** all expenses which change with changes in sales volume; short run concept.	Income
5. **Fixed Expenses:** All expenses that stay the same over a wide range of sales volume and a long time period.	Income
6. **Total Expenses:** add Variable Expenses and Fixed Expenses.	Income
7. **Operating Profit:** subtract Total Expenses from Gross Margin.	Income
8. **Net Profit Margin:** operating profit divided by sales.	
9. **Inventory:** value of merchandise in stock	Balance
10. **Accounts Receivable:** money owed retailer by customers.	Balance
11. **Cash and other Current Assets:** cash and any asset other than Accounts Receivable or Inventory which can easily be converted into cash.	Balance
12. **Total Current Assets:** add Cash and Other Current Assets, Inventory, Accounts Receivable.	Balance
13. **Fixed Assets:** assets which are depreciated over time.	Balance
14. **Total Assets:** add Current Assets and Fixed Assets.	Balance
15. **Rate of Asset Turnover:** divide Sales by Total Assets.	
16. **Return on Assets:** multiply Rate of Asset Turnover times Net Profit Margin.	
17. **Net Worth:** subtract total Liabilities (debt) from Total Assets.	Balance
18. **Financial Leverage:** divide Total Assets by Net Worth.	Balance
19. **Return on Net Worth:** multiply Return on Assets by Financial Leverage.	

cents on each dollar of sales. In general, retailers operate on lower profit margins than manufacturers. The profit margin ratio is derived exclusively from income or operating statement data and does not include any data from the retailer's balance sheet. Thus, it does not show how effectively a retailer is using the capital at its disposal.

Asset Turnover.   The **rate of asset turnover** is computed by dividing the retailer's net sales by total assets. This ratio measures how productively the firm's assets are being utilized. In other words, it shows how many dollars of sales a retailer can generate on an annual basis with each dollar invested in assets. Thus, if a retailer has a rate of asset turnover of 3.0, it is generating three dollars in sales for each dollar in assets. The asset turnover ratio incorporates data from the income statement (sales) and the balance sheet (assets) and, as such, shows how well the retailer is utilizing its capital to generate sales. In general, retailers experience higher rates of asset turnover than manufacturers.

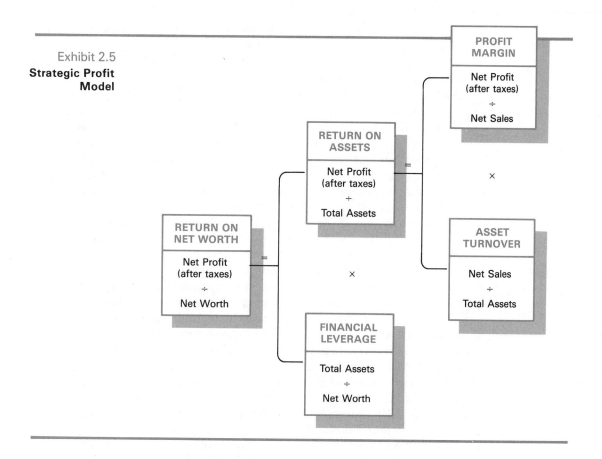

Exhibit 2.5
Strategic Profit Model

Department or specialty stores have higher gross margins and lower asset turnover rates than discounters, because discounters generally have few capital assets other than inventory. Thus, specialty stores and discounters compete very differently. Discounters expect to gain a higher turnover by reducing their margins, and specialty stores expect their higher margins to make up for their lower turnover rate.

Attempts to increase asset turnover by reducing stock levels can have serious consequences for a retailer. Lower stock levels may produce higher turnover rates, but they can also kill a business. Revco didn't replenish its shelves for the 1987 Christmas season, resulting in lost sales, lost customers, and ultimately in the firm's failure the following year.[13]

Financial Leverage. In our discussion of the demise of W. T. Grant, we mentioned leverage. The **financial leverage ratio** is found by dividing total assets by net worth. This ratio shows the extent to which a retailer is utilizing debt in its total capital structure. The low end of this ratio is 1.0 and represents a situation in which the retailer is using no debt in its capital structure. As the ratio increases the firm is using a heavier mix of debt versus equity. For example, when the ratio is 2.0, the firm has two dollars in assets for every dollar in net worth.

When the cost of borrowing is high and the economic outlook is uncertain, a high leverage ratio can be extremely dangerous, as was shown in the W. T. Grant example. Generally, retailers operate with a leverage ratio of 2.0 to 2.5. The dangers of a high leverage ratio in a poor economic environment can be illustrated by examining the plight of Revco Drugstores today. In 1987, Revco's management took the firm private with a leveraged buy-out. In doing this they increased their leverage ratio to over 5.0. In 1988 competition in the drugstore industry intensified, as more discount operations popped up and supermarkets expanded their pharmacy operations. Revco was forced to cut its prices to compete. This eroded profit margins and left Revco unable to pay its $150 million annual interest bill.[14] One study has found that one of the key factors in many retail bankruptcies is a high leverage ratio.[15]

Retail managers need the advice of financial experts inside and outside of the firm in the use of the SPM components, especially the leverage ratio. The proper programming of profit margin, asset turnover, and financial leverage allows retailers to achieve their target rate of return on assets and return on net worth. While each firm and each type of retailer requires a different combination of the three ratios, retailers can get some insight on the proper mix for them by examining past performance. Another approach would be to compare your plan and results with similar stores. Industry figures can be obtained from a variety of sources, including Dun & Bradstreet's, *Dun's Review, Robert Morris Associates' Annual Statement Studies*, trade association data, and academic studies. Exhibit 2.6 shows the profitability profile of leading retailers by category of business; Exhibit 2.7 gives some individual profiles of high performance retailers by various categories.

LIQUIDITY

Profitability reflects only part of the retailer's financial performance. An equally important dimension is liquidity. **Liquidity** represents the firm's ability to meet its current payment obligations. It has been said that financial analysts look at profitability, but credit analysts look at liquidity. Liquidity is crucial to the retailer for two reasons. If a retailer has too much liquidity, then working capital is not being fully utilized. If this is the case, attractive options for using this working capital are probably being ignored in order to minimize the risk of being insolvent. Not enough liquidity can mean that a retailer may not be able to take advantage of opportunities to purchase merchandise at attractive prices.

In general, then, liquidity is important to the retailer because it protects the company from economic downturns and potential insolvency and also provides the flexibility needed to capitalize on unexpected merchandising opportunities.

Exhibit 2.6

Financial Profile Of Leading Retailers

The Ratios Of High Performance Management	Department Stores	Discount Department Stores	Departmentalized Specialty Stores	Specialty Stores	Off-Price Merchandisers	Drug Stores	Diversified Retailers
Strategic Profit Model Ratios							
Net Profits/Net Sales (Percent)	2.9%	2.6%	4.2%	6.8%	4.7%	2.5%	3.4%
Net Sales/Total Assets (Times)	1.8×	2.5×	1.8×	1.9×	2.4×	2.7×	2.1×
Net Profits/Total Assets (Percent)	5.0%	6.5%	7.2%	12.9%	11.3%	6.7%	7.2%
Total Assets/Net Worth (Times)	2.3×	2.6×	2.2×	1.8×	2.0×	2.2×	2.0×
Net Profits/Net Worth (Percent)	11.7%	16.8%	15.6%	23.5%	22.5%	14.8%	14.6%

SOURCE: Bert C. McCammon, Jr., Deborah S. Coykendall and Mary Brett Whitfield, Distribution Research Program, College of Business Administration, The University of Oklahoma, 1988. Reprinted with permission.

Exhibit 2.7
Strategic And Financial Profile Of High Performance Retailers

Company (Sales In Thousands of Dollars)	Profitability Profile					Liquidity Ratios		
	Net Profits/ Net Sales (Percent)	Net Sales/ Total Assets (Times)	Net Profits/ Total Assets (Percent)	Total Assets/ Net Worth (Times)	Net Profits/ Net Worth (Percent)	Current Assets/ Current Liabilities (Times)	Current Assets (Minus Inventory)/ Current Liabilities (Times)	Cash/ Current Liabilities (Percent)
Close-Out Retailers								
Consolidated ($397,221)	4.9%	1.9×	9.5%	1.8×	17.0%	2.6×	.7×	9.3%
Pic 'N' Save ($303,324)	13.1	1.6	21.1	1.2	26.1	4.1	2.0	190.8
Price Value Specialty Retailers								
Arbor ($151,480)	3.5%	2.8×	9.7%	1.7×	16.4%	2.2×	1.0×	86.7%
Clothestime ($160,334)	7.4	3.0	22.1	1.6	34.3	2.1	.6	19.9
Dress Barn ($135,828)	6.7	3.0	20.1	1.7	36.0	1.9	1.0	87.8
Shoe City ($35,348)	4.9	3.1	14.9	1.5	21.7	5.4	1.4	91.5
Specialty Retailers								
Claire's ($87,205)	6.1%	2.2×	13.3%	1.7×	22.5%	.9×	.2×	9.7%
Merry-Go-Round ($207,483)	3.6	2.9	10.3	1.7	17.6	1.2	.3	14.8
Sound Warehouse ($131,183)	5.7	2.0	11.4	2.0	23.1	1.6	.2	16.7

Tandy ($3,035,969)	6.5	1.5	9.5	1.6	15.1	2.8	.9	53.4
The Gap ($848,009)	8.0	2.3	18.7	1.7	32.1	1.9	.7	53.4
Power Retailers								
Highland ($656,456)	3.1%	2.7X	8.2%	2.2X	17.7%	2.7X	.9X	70.5%
Circuit City ($1,010,692)	3.5	2.8	9.8	2.4	23.7	2.0	.5	34.4
Seaman Furniture ($168,696)	6.7	3.0	20.3	2.7	53.7	1.4	.9	53.0
Toys "R" Us ($2,444,903)	6.2	1.6	10.0	1.7	16.9	1.3	.3	16.9
Portfolio Retailers								
Cullum ($1,036,450)	1.8%	4.3X	7.5%	2.0X	15.2%	1.5X	.4X	12.5%
Melville ($5,262,364)	4.5	2.6	11.9	1.6	18.9	2.5	.8	61.1
The Limited ($3,142,696)	7.3	2.3	16.5	1.8	29.1	1.4	.3	1.0
Wal-Mart ($11,993,699)	3.8	3.0	11.1	2.4	26.6	1.8	.2	12.4
Woolworth ($6,531,000)	3.3	2.3	7.5	1.9	14.4	1.9	.4	27.1
Secondary Market Retailers								
Casey's General ($284,721)	2.2%	4.0X	8.7%	1.5X	13.1%	1.1X	.3X	6.1%
Family Dollar ($487,735)	6.3	2.2	14.0	1.5	21.6	2.2	.4	36.7
Weis Markets ($1,101,473)	5.9	2.3	13.8	1.2	16.0	5.7	4.5	429.2
Merchandising Intensification Retailers								
Mercantile ($2,028,202)	5.5%	1.6X	8.8%	1.6X	14.5%	4.7X	3.2X	49.7%
Walgreen ($3,660,563)	2.8	3.1	8.6	2.2	18.6	1.9	.4	25.2
Winn-Dixie ($8,225,244)	1.4	6.1	8.6	1.9	16.5	1.7	.6	36.2

SOURCE: Bert C. McCammon, Jr., Deborah S. Coykendall and Mary Brett Whitfield, Distribution Research Program, College of Business Administration, The University of Oklahoma, 1988. Reprinted with permission.

Financial analysts generally use three financial ratios to evaluate liquidity. The most popular is the **current ratio** which measures current assets to current liabilities. This ratio is the basic measurement of a retailer's solvency. Conventional wisdom suggests that retailers should maintain a current ratio of approximately 2.0.

A second ratio is called the **quick ratio** and is computed as current assets, less inventory, divided by current liabilities. The quick ratio is a more stringent measure of a firm's ability to repay its current debt. Conventional wisdom suggests that retailers should maintain a quick ratio of 1.0.

The third and final ratio, the **liquidity ratio**, is cash and its equivalent divided by current liabilities. It is sometimes referred to as the *acid-test ratio*. This ratio received considerable attention during the mid-1980s credit crunch. Analysts contend that a retailer's cash should equal 15 to 20 percent of current liabilities. The liquidity ratios for some high performance retailers by various categories are shown in Exhibit 2.7.

GROWTH

A high-performance retailer must have growth significantly greater than the industry average. To achieve a position apart from other retailers, a high-performance retailer must increase sales by at least 1.5 times the industry rate of growth. Thus, if the industry over the last year grew at 10 percent, a high-performance retailer would need to achieve a growth in sales of at least 15 percent. Sometimes retailers tend to seek growth opportunities outside their fields of expertise and meet failure as shown in Retailing in Action 2-3.

RETAILING IN ACTION | **2-3**

Good Strategy Is Also Doing the Things You Do Best

Many retailers are guilty of too much diversification. They stick their fingers into too many pies and forget their primary business, which is usually their strength. Such was the case with Walgreen Stores during the 1970s. The nation's oldest drugstore chain made ill-fated diversification moves into discount stores and restaurants in the United States and Mexico, neglecting their primary drugstore business. In doing so, Walgreen, traditionally the drugstore industry's profit leader, lost ground to more aggressive chains such as Jack Eckerd Corp., Revco, and Rite Aid Corp.

In the late 1970s and early 1980s a back-to-basics strategy returned Walgreen to second place in drugstore profits behind only Jack Eckerd. In five years the Illinois-based retailer sold off its discount department stores, severed its ties with independent druggists, shut down thirty in-store optical shops and a third of its 293 in-store lunch counters. During this period Walgreen concentrated on what it does best — the drugstore business. CEO Charles Walgreen III strengthened management by recruiting key managers from outside, increased store size by 30 percent, and increased the number of drugstores by 50 percent. Many of these new stores were located downtown in major metro areas. With Walgreen's medium-range pricing, the company can virtually blanket an entire metro area. This market clustering offers Walgreen three advantages over those chains with only a few retail outlets in the area: more extensive coverage with radio and television ads, cheaper per-store distribution, and more efficient use of regional supervision. As a result, Walgreen is the first or second leading drugstore chain in 27 of the 34 markets it serves.

The chain has resisted industry trends towards discount outlets, combination stores, and stores larger than 13,000 square feet. Walgreen wants "the consumer to get in the store in a hurry, get a good selection of merchandise, and get out in a hurry."

That's how Walgreen got to be number one in the first place, and how it plans to get there again.

Illus. 2.3
Walgreen is the first or second leading drugstore chain in 27 of the 34 market areas it serves.

Source: Based on data obtained in "The Walgreen formula: Digging In for New Growth in Drug Retailing," *Business Week* (March 1, 1982): 84–85 and Al Urbanski, "The Re-Greening of Walgreen," *Sales and Marketing Management* (July 4, 1984).

COMBINING MARKETING AND FINANCIAL PERFORMANCE

Earlier we spoke of the need to integrate marketing objectives with financial objectives to achieve a high-performance level of operations. A sample strategic profit model for two hypothetical retailers is presented in

Exhibit 2.8

Comparison of Off-Price and Full-Price Retailers' Performances

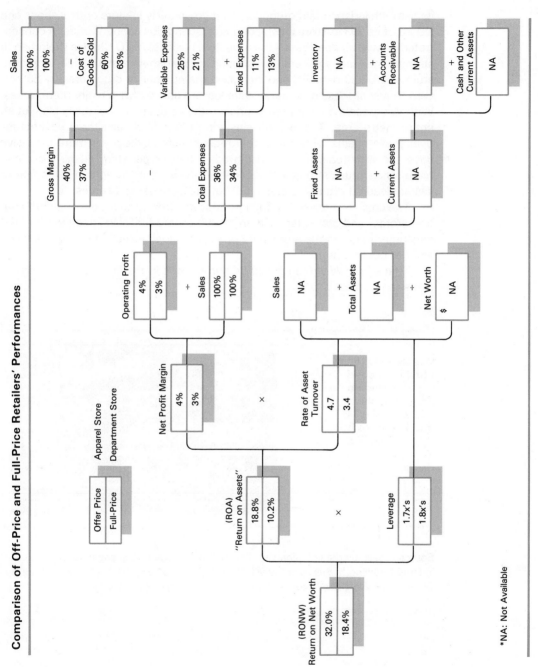

*NA: Not Available

Exhibit 2.8. One is an off-price retail apparel store and the other is a full price department store. **Off-price retailers** are usually retailers selling close-out brand name merchandise at independent locations. While off-price stores generally are able to sell their merchandise at 20 to 70 percent off retail, they maintain nearly the same markup as full price department stores. The price difference is partly attributable to the wholesale price paid for the merchandise. In addition, their out-of-the way locations enable off-price stores to have lower fixed expenses, and they are able to operate with a higher asset turnover (4 to 8 times a year compared to 3.0 to 5.0 times a year for a full-price department store). Both types of stores operate with leverage ratios near 2.0 and maintain similar gross margins. Yet lower fixed expenses and a higher turnover rate enable off-price firms to produce a better return on assets and net worth.

RETAIL PLANNING PERSONALITIES

You have seen the importance of planning in retail success. A retailer's **planning personality** may affect the way the firm views the future and the need to plan for it. There are four distinct planning personalities: (1) the near-sighted planner, (2) the extrapolator, (3) the goal setter, and (4) the cyberneticist.

A small retail operation may have only one person responsible for planning and thus one planning personality will project itself. A large retail chain, however, may have an entire staff of corporate planners. It is possible, therefore, that all four planning personalities would be projected in the planning process. This, however, is not likely because firms tend to hire planners that fit the personality mold already established. As we review these four planning personalities, try to identify the one that best describes your orientation toward the future.

THE NEAR-SIGHTED PLANNER

The **near-sighted planner** has little faith in planning. He or she believes that the future is terribly uncertain and that attempts to plan beyond the foreseeable future are futile. The concern is the immediate, the seeable. Planning is for next week's promotions or, at the extreme, for merchandise that needs to be purchased next season. In no way does this individual plan for two, five, or ten years in the future. The more distant events are, the more this planner discounts them in the present. The philosophy espoused is: "Why worry about the long run if we can't make it through the short run?"

Why does the near-sighted planner pay so little attention to the distant future? Frequently it is because previous attempts at gauging the market have failed. This individual may have misgauged when planning for next season, and feels strongly that assessing the retail environment five years hence is next to impossible. Or perhaps attempts to assess the retail environment over the long run have failed.

The near-sighted planner rationalizes that uncertainty rules out the value of planning. In reality, nothing could be further from the truth. If there were certainty, planning would not be needed. The more uncertainty, the greater the need for planning, not *vice versa*.

A retailer will not be able to achieve high-performance results over the long run if it continually neglects the future. The retailer must create its future.

THE EXTRAPOLATOR

The **extrapolator** is the manager who views the future as an extrapolation of the past. This retail planner feels that the systematic analysis of historical data will allow the retailer to plan successfully. From the 1940s to the 1960s, extrapolators were quite successful in planning. Retail sales and the economy in general were moving on a fairly predictable growth curve. But in the 1970s and 1980s, this approach to planning produced disquieting results. The basic historical relationships had changed: inflation rose and fell dramatically, consumer life-styles changed, energy prices exploded then fell just as rapidly, and peacetime federal budgets had record-setting deficits. Whenever basic historical relationships change, the extrapolation approach to planning meets with failure. Retail planners need to take historical patterns into account, but they should not become mere extrapolators of historical patterns and trends. Remember, yesterday does not necessarily predict how tomorrow will occur. This is why so many retailers had such bad results in the mid-1980s. For example, many large chains entered the Southwest market because they felt sure that OPEC was going to increase the price of oil to over $50 a barrel. When the price fell to below $10, they were not able to handle the present, much less the future. Given the ever-changing retail environment, it is imperative that a high-performance retailer not only look to the future but do it correctly.

THE GOAL SETTER

The **goal setter** is a visionary. This person establishes a goal in the distant future and devotes all her energy to achieving that goal. Often the goals set by the goal setters are unrealistic. Goal setters, in large part, ignore the reality of the past or present. Strengths and weaknesses do not matter to them as much as the desire to achieve the goal. Many notable historical figures were goal setters, such as Henry Ford, John D. Rockefeller, John F. Kennedy, and Lee Iacocca. Any of these individuals, if they had systematically analyzed the past and present, would not have tried to accomplish what they ended up accomplishing. But they did systematically ana-

Illus. 2.4
Henry Ford (*left*).
Source: Ford
Motor Company.
Lee Iacocca
(*right*). Source:
Wide World
Photos. These
two goal setters
systematically
analyzed the
future and
focused their
efforts totally on
their visionary
goals.

lyze the future and focus their efforts totally on their visionary goals.

Retailers that are pure goal setters tend to either be extremely successful or to fail. There is a tendency to recognize only the goal setters that succeed, but most goal setters fail. They often fail because they ignore the risks of what they are attempting to accomplish. The probability of success is so slim and that of failure so great that a strict goal-setting philosophy toward retail planning is not wise.

THE CYBERNETICIST

The type of planing orientation that is most appropriate for retailers is the cybernetics orientation. A **cyberneticist** is a systems thinker. This individual is oriented not only to all departments and functions within the firm but also to all external forces the retailer faces. Furthermore, this person can see the link between occurrences external to the firm and internal affairs.

In essence, the cyberneticist is a composite of the three preceding planning personalities. He recognizes the uncertainty of the future like the near-sighted planner, analyzes the historical path the retail enterprise has taken like the extrapolator, and sets goals for the future like the goal setter. In addition, the cyberneticist carefully analyzes the retailer's strengths and weaknesses and those of its competitors. In addition, he systematically assesses how the future might be different than the past. The cyberneticist combines all of this information to establish goals and develop plans for accomplishing them. His plans, if successfully carried through, can be expected to yield an attractive payoff on risks taken. The great majority of high-performance retailers adopt a cyberneticist planning orientation.

Don't feel that you must fit yourself into one of these four planning personalities. The categories are not rigid abstractions. Depending on the situation in which you find yourself, you might move from one personality type to another. Pure extrapolation may work for short-term labor scheduling, but the cyberneticist orientation might be more appropriate for planning long-term strategies. The key is to do the task of planning and be flexible.

SUMMARY

Planning and the financial performance of the retailer are intertwined. High-performance results do not just happen; they are engineered through careful strategic, operations, and administrative planning: deciding what needs to be done now and for the future and doing it. Not all retailers can achieve high-performance results, but the ones that do are those that do the best job of planning and managing. The components of strategic planning are: development of a statement of purpose or mission, definition of specific goals and objectives, and development of basic strategies that will enable the firm to reach its objectives and fulfill its mission.

In retailing, three types of planning are necessary. Strategic planning consists of matching the retailer's mission and goals with available opportunities. Administrative planning involves planning for the acquisition of resources that will be necessary to carry out the retailer's strategy successfully. Operations planning consists of planning the efficient use of available resources in order to manage the day-to-day operations of the firm successfully. When retailers succeed at these three types of planning, they achieve high-performance results.

High-performance retailers are distinguished by their profitability, liquidity, and growth. Profit is measured as a return on assets or net worth. Liquidity represents the firm's ability to meet its current obligations. Three liquidity ratios should be monitored by retailers: the current ratio, the quick ratio, and the acid-test ratio.

The most fundamental job of management in any retailing enterprise is strategic planning: the process of adapting the resources of the firm to the opportunities and constraints of an ever-changing environment. It's through strategic planning that retailers achieve and maintain the balance between resources and opportunities.

High performance retailers must also engage in operations management, which is concerned with maximizing the efficiency of the retailer's use of resources, and administrative management, which involves the acquisition, maintenance, and control of resources that are necessary to carry out the retailer's strategy.

Retailers tend to have one of four planning personalities. Nearsighted planners believe that the future is too uncertain to warrant planning; extrapolators believe the future can be planned by extrapolating from historical trends; goal setters focus exclusively on desired goals and ignore the reality of their strengths and weaknesses in the present. Cyberneticists are the systems thinkers, both internally and externally oriented. Cyberneticists consider past trends, present strengths and weaknesses, the uncertainty inherent in planning for the future, and desired goals. In short, they are a composite of the three preceding planning personalities.

QUESTIONS
FOR
DISCUSSION

1. Identify measures of financial performance, in addition to those mentioned in this chapter, that could be used to gauge a retailer's financial performance.
2. Return on assets is a better measure than return on net worth (or return on investment) for assessing a retailer's financial performance. Agree or disagree and explain why.
3. Rank the four planning personalities in terms of the most desirable to the least desirable. Would the type and size of retail firm affect your answer?
4. Given today's economic conditions, which retail firm would you most like to own and which one would you find least desirable? Explain your position.

Retailer	Asset Turnover	Profit Margin (Before Tax)	Financial Leverage
A	3.8x	7.0	2.4
B	5.0x	6.0	1.9
C	3.3x	6.3	3.2

5. Is planning in a high-inflation environment more or less difficult for a retailer than planning in a low-inflation environment? Why?
6. How do the retail firm's mission statement and goals and objectives statement relate to the retailer's development of competitive strategy?
7. How can financial ratio analysis be used in retailing?
8. Given the significant changes in retailing over the past decade, what do you see taking place over the next decade?
9. Which financial performance criteria is most important in retailing, profitability or liquidity? Defend your position.
10. Explain how the basic Strategic Profit Model can be used by retailers to evaluate different retail strategies.
11. Interview the manager of a local supermarket or apparel store to determine his or her philosophy on planning. Would you categorize the

manager as a near-sighted planner, extrapolator, goal setter, or cyber-neticist? Be sure to have a good idea of the questions you will ask during the interview before you make your visit.

12. Using the data below compute these financial ratios: current ratio, asset turnover, return on assets, profit margin, return on net worth, financial leverage, and acid-test ratio.

Annual Net Sales	$614,321
Total Assets	203,340
Net Profits (after taxes)	21,398
Net Worth	77,601
Cash	3,442
Current Liabilities	75,345
Current Assets	115,419

SUGGESTED READINGS

Bennett, Stephen. "Draw Your Own Debit Card, Pardner." *Progressive Grocer* (January 1988): 61–64.

Densmore, Max L. and Sylvia Kaufman. "How Leading Retailers Stay on Top." *Business* (April–June 1985): 28–35.

Kirby, Gail Hutchinson and Rachel Dardis. "A Pricing Study of Women's Apparel in Off-Price and Department Stores." *Journal of Retailing* (Fall 1986): 321–330.

"Information on Demographics and Psychographics Serves as Guidepost to Help Retailers Prepare for Turn of the Century." *Chain Store Age Executive* (May 1987): 19–25.

Scarborough, Norman M. and Thomas W Zimmerer. "Strategic Planning for the Small Business." *Business* (April–June 1987): 11–19.

"Thirty-One Major Trends Shaping the Future of American Business." *The Public Pulse* 2, no. 1 (1988): 1.

ENDNOTES

1. This mission statement was developed for a chain of prerecorded music stores by Myron Gable and is reprinted with permission.

2. Barton A. Weitz and Robin Wensley, *Strategic Marketing* (Boston: Kent Publishing, 1983), 5–7.

3. For a more detailed discussion of Kresge and K mart's early development, see "How Kresge Became the Top Discounter," *Business Week* (October 24, 1970): 62–63ff.; "Retailing: K is for Krunch," *Sales Management* (November 29, 1971): 3; "K mart: The Tail That Wags the Kresge Dog," *Merchandising Week* (July 9, 1973): 8ff.; and "What Woolworth Didn't Know Apparently Kresge Did," *Financial World* (May 22, 1974): 18–19. For a more recent discussion see "K mart: The No. 2 Retailer Starts to Make an Upscale Move—At Last," *Business*

Week (June 4, 1984): 50–51; "K mart's Antonini Moves Far Beyond Retail 'Junk' Image," *Advertising Age* (July 25, 1988): 1, 67; "Attention Non-K mart Shoppers: A Blue-Light Special Just for You," *Wall Street Journal* (October 6, 1987): 40.

   4. For an insightful discussion of Montgomery Ward during this time, see Robert F. Hartley, *Marketing Mistakes* (Columbus, Ohio: Grid, 1976), 7–17.

   5. Data presented here came from a paper presented by Bert C. McCammon, Jr. to J. C. Penney Executive University Program, Santa Clara University/ University of Florida, 1988 and "The Wholesale Club Industry," *Discount Merchandiser* (November, 1988): 38–39.

   6. "Investigating the Collapse of W. T. Grant," *Business Week* (July 19, 1976): 61.

   7. Albert D. Bates, "The Internalization of Retail Strategy," presented at Distribution Strategies for the 1980s, Norman, OK, January, 1979.

   8. This model is an adaptation and reflection of major concepts presented in H. Igor Ansoff, *Corporate Strategy* (New York: McGraw-Hill, 1965).

   9. For a more detailed description of the concept of differential advantage, consult Thomas A. Staudt, Donald A. Taylor, and Donald J. Bowersox, *A Managerial Introduction to Marketing*, 3d ed., (Englewood Cliffs, N. J.: Prentice-Hall, 1976), Chapter 2.

   10. "Foley's Digs In to Defend Its Turf," *HFD—Retailing Home Furnishings* (September 12, 1983): 8.

   11. "Kentucky Fried Chicken Bone in Heublein's Throat?" *Advertising Age* (March 7, 1977): 3, 56.

   12. "Chain's Fortunes Improved When It Rearticulated its Mission and Strategic Plan," *Marketing News* (July 9, 1982): 14.

   13. "The LBO Where Everything Went Wrong," *Business Week* (May 9, 1988): 47 and "Revco's Leveraged Buy-Out Comes Apart," *Wall Street Journal*, 14 June 1988, 6.

   14. "Revco's LBO Ends With A Whimper," *Business Week* (August 15, 1988): 46.

   15. Albert Bates, "The Internalization of Retail Strategy," paper presented at Distribution Strategies for the 1980s, Norman, Oklahoma, January, 1979.

II Part
The Retailing Environment

3 Chapter

Understanding Channel Behavior

This chapter addresses the retailer's need to analyze and understand the marketing channel to which it belongs. The chapter begins by discussing how all the activities in the marketing system must be performed by either the retailer or another channel member. Next we will review the various types of marketing channels and their benefits to the retailer. We conclude with some practical suggestions to improve channel relationships.

At the outset of this text, we stated that retailing is the final movement in the progression of merchandise from producer to consumer. Many other movements occur over time and geographical space, and all of them need to be executed properly for the retailer to achieve optimum performance. In this chapter we will discuss how these movements fit into the larger marketing system.

THE SYSTEM IS THE SOLUTION

Consider the following example. The final movement of a retail item occurs on November 17 at 10:47 a.m., when the customer of a specialty store in a suburban Chicago mall purchases a new coat for the winter season. At some prior time (probably six months to a year earlier) that coat was manufactured. Later, it was warehoused and placed on display in the manufacturer's showroom. Next, a quantity of these coats were purchased by the specialty retailer. Goods were shipped by the manufacturer to the retailer to be placed on display in the store in the Chicago mall. Manufacturing occurred in Taiwan, a Japanese freighter was used to transport the coats to the U. S., and the coats were warehoused in Los Angeles prior to being shipped to Chicago. Thus, before the final retail transaction could take place, many physical movements were needed, involving many firms other than the retailer. Retailers cannot properly perform their roles without these other firms. Retailers are part of a complex marketing system—an important component, but not the only one.

In order to understand the retailer's part in the marketing system, it should be viewed as a member of one, or even several, marketing channels. A **marketing channel** is a set of institutions that is necessary to move goods from point of production to point of consumption. As such, marketing channels consist of all the institutions and all the marketing activities in the marketing process. Each member of the marketing channel that collectively does the best job will achieve dramatically higher levels of performance. Entire marketing channels compete with each other; competition does not just take place at the level of the retailer. Firestone doesn't compete with Goodyear at just the local dealer level; rather, the marketing channel for Firestone tires competes with the marketing channel for Goodyear tires. Similarly, K mart doesn't compete with Target or Wal-Mart; rather the marketing channels that K mart utilizes are in competition with the marketing channels that Target and Wal-Mart have structured. We will discuss this competitive frame of reference in more detail in Chapter 5.

Why should the retailer view itself as part of a larger marketing system? Why can't it simply seek out the best assortment of goods for its customers, sell the goods, make a profit, go to the bank, and forget about the system? The answer is straightforward. The retailer could forget about the system and make a short run profit, but in the long run, the system will forget about the retailer. If that happens, profits sufficient for survival and growth will be difficult, if not impossible, to achieve. This doesn't mean that the system should, or can, never be changed. Sometimes an innovative retailer might see that the entire system needs changing as a result of other environmental changes and thus may in itself be a problem. Here an innovative channel member, like a retailer, might solve the problem by breaking out of the existing system and replacing it with a new system. For example, discounters established a new relationship with vendors by buying in large quantities, warehousing the merchandise, and shipping to their own stores as a means of obtaining lower prices. Understanding the system can help the retailer improve long-run, bottom-line performance.

THE MARKETING SYSTEM

The marketing system can be defined in a variety of ways. For instructional purposes, we will define the **marketing system** as that set of institutions performing marketing functions, the relationships among these institutions, and the functions that are necessary to create transactions with target populations. We will view the marketing system as largely synonymous with the marketing channel.

Exhibit 3.1 is a graphic representation of the marketing system. Study it closely. This exhibit portrays many of the links between institutions and functions that are necessary to bring about final exchange with some target populations. Note that the marketing system is affected by

Exhibit 3.1
The Marketing System

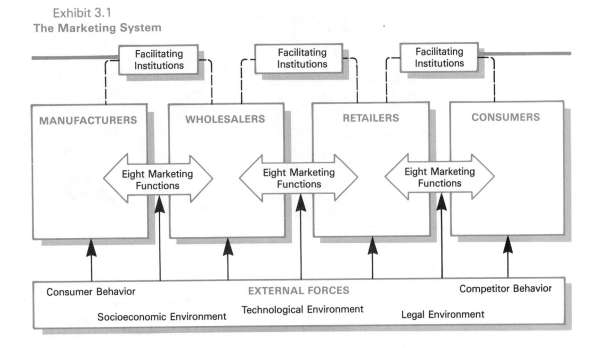

five external forces: consumer behavior, competitor behavior, the socioeconomic environment, the technological environment, and the legal environment. These external forces cannot be completely controlled by the retailer or any other institution in the marketing system, but need to be
taken into account when retailers make decisions. The retail management
and planning model (Exhibit 2.1) also dramatizes the importance of these
external forces in retail decision making.

THE MARKETING FUNCTIONS

What marketing functions need to be performed in the marketing system? Eight functions are necessary: buying, selling, storing, transporting, sorting, financing, information gathering, and risk taking.[1] Each will
be discussed briefly.

Buying.   Before a retailer can sell merchandise to the final consumer, the
retailer must purchase the merchandise from either the manufacturer or a
wholesaler who gets it from the manufacturer. The manufacturer of the
merchandise also needs to purchase many items (raw materials, subcomponents, supplies, etc.) before it can sell merchandise to the retailer or
wholesaler. Buying is as important to a retailer as selling.

Illus. 3.1
Manufacturers
of merchandise
must buy the
raw materials
needed to
produce it.
Source: Retail
Planning
Associates

Selling.   Selling is the function that most consumers associate with retailing, and it obviously is important. It involves all activities that are necessary and incidental to contacting customers and persuading them to purchase. Selling activities include advertising, personal selling, and sales promotions.

Storing.   Storage is necessary whenever there is a discrepancy between the time at which supplies are created and the time at which demand occurs.

For example, an apparel manufacturer may have a production run of one thousand blue dresses within two days, but since the demand for those dresses will not occur immediately, storage becomes necessary. Since the storage function involves expenses (rent for the warehouse, insurance, fixtures, wages, etc.), members of marketing systems often try to shift this function onto other members. For example, a manufacturer might offer the wholesaler or retailer a discount for accepting early delivery.

Transporting.   Transportation is necessary when the place of supply is removed from the place of demand. Production occurs in geographical pockets: apparel in the Northeast and Southeast, autos in the Midwest. But demand occurs throughout the United States, and as a result, merchandise needs to be transported. The only alternative would be to produce all products in all locations where people reside—which would obviously be extremely expensive. Imagine an auto plant and an apparel factory in every city and town in the United States. Transportation of merchandise from the store to the customer is also considered part of the transportation function.

Sorting.   Sorting needs to occur because both demands and supplies are heterogeneous.[2] Matching heterogeneous demands with heterogeneous supplies involves four sorting processes.

Accumulation means building up larger homogeneous supplies. For example, a number of small manufacturers or producers of a homogeneous product like corn might gather together so the larger quantity can be handled more economically.

Allocation is the breaking down of those homogeneous supplies into smaller lots. For example, a grain elevator that has accumulated large supplies of Grade 2 corn will sell it off in smaller quantities. Or a manufacturer of baseballs will divide its inventory into the smaller quantities needed by wholesalers and retailers.

Sorting out refers to the breaking down of heterogeneous supplies into more homogeneous groups. Here the baseballs might be further subdivided into big-league, high-school, and Little League categories.

Finally, **assorting** is the building up of assortments of products for use in association with each other. Consumers typically seek an assortment of goods, and retailers serve the consumer by building these assortments. In the above example, the retailer carrying the baseballs would also carry other baseball equipment such as gloves, bats, uniforms, and caps.

Financing.   If it is recognized that there are discrepancies between the time demand occurs and the time supplies are created, and also between points of production (supply) and points of consumption (demand), then it becomes clear that someone needs to finance these discrepancies. Ideally, the final consumer pays the retailer for the merchandise before the retailer must pay its supplier, but this generally doesn't happen. For example, most retailers have to pay for their Christmas merchandise long before Thanksgiving.

Information Gathering.   Sellers know what their supplies are and buyers know what their demands are, but without an exchange of information, the seller doesn't know what the buyer wants and the buyer doesn't know what the seller has. Information is essential to match suppliers properly with the demands of the retailer's market. It will not do any good to have suppliers producing tight jeans when the marketplace wants loose-fitting jeans.

Risk Taking.   It is obvious that demands cannot be forecast precisely. Products will be produced or purchased for resale and for which a demand might not materialize. In that case, the retailer can incur a loss. Consider, for example, the case of toy retailers. If they incorrectly assess the demand for certain toys at the Christmas toy shows in June and July, they may under- or over-stock certain toys. Either way, a loss will occur. No wonder retailers say, "risk taking's reward is profit." Remember how unexpectedly popular the "Cabbage Patch Kids" were a few years ago, only to be duds for retailers a few years later.

PERVASIVENESS OF THE FUNCTIONS

Whether the economic system is capitalistic, socialistic, or communistic, these eight marketing functions will exist. They cannot be eliminated. They can, however, be shifted or divided among the institutions and consumers in the marketing system.

All forms of retailing were created by rearranging the marketing functions among institutions and consumers. For example, department stores were created specifically to build a larger and better assortment of goods. They capitalized on the opportunity to perform more of the sorting process. No longer was it necessary to travel to one store for a shirt, another for slacks, and yet another for shoes; the necessary assortment was available in a single store. Supermarkets increased consumers' workload by shifting more of the information gathering, buying, and transporting functions to them. Before supermarkets, consumers could have the corner grocer select items and deliver them. But with the supermarket came self-service. Consumers had to locate the goods within the store, select them

Illus. 3.2
When customers perform channel functions, they can expect to pay lower prices.

from an array of products, and transport them home. For performing more of these marketing functions, the consumer was compensated with lower prices.

A marketing function does not have to be shifted in its entirety to another institution or to the consumer, but can be divided among several entities. For example, the manufacturer who does not want to perform the entire selling function could have the retailer perform part of the job through in-store promotions and local advertising. At the same time, the manufacturer could assume some of the task through national advertising.

No member of the marketing channel would want, or be able, to perform all eight marketing functions. For this reason, the retailer must view itself as being dependent on others in the marketing system.

MARKETING INSTITUTIONS

What institutions are involved in performing the eight marketing functions? There are many more than you might initially think. These institutions can be broken into two categories: **primary marketing institutions**, those which take title to the goods, and **facilitating institutions**, those which do not actually take title but facilitate the marketing process by specializing in the performance of certain functions. Exhibit 3.2 is a classification of the major institutions participating in the marketing system.

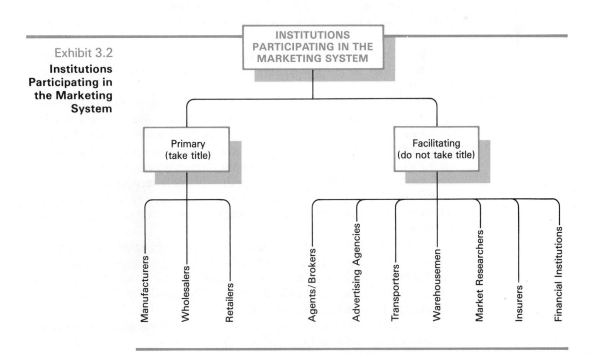

Exhibit 3.2

Institutions Participating in the Marketing System

Primary Marketing Institutions.   There are three types of primary marketing institutions: manufacturers, wholesalers, and retailers. Each takes legal title to the goods as they flow through the marketing channel.

Often, we don't think of manufacturers as marketing institutions, since they produce goods. But manufacturers cannot exist by only producing goods; they must also market the goods produced. They often need the assistance of other institutions in performing the eight marketing functions. There are over 360,000 manufacturers in the United States.

A second type of primary marketing institution is the wholesaler. Wholesalers buy and resell merchandise to retailers, other merchants, industrial institutions, and commercial users. There are nearly 438,000 wholesalers in the United States, each performing some of the eight marketing functions.

The third type of primary institution is the retailer. There are 1,406,846 retail stores and 1,711,834 service establishments in this country.[3] Retailers can perform portions of all eight marketing functions. Since the focus of this text is on retailing, let us examine how a typical retailer can contribute to the performance of these eight functions.

Buying is a side of retailing that the consumer rarely notices. When you walk into a department store, try to think about how much effort went into buying the assortment of merchandise you see. The merchandise comes from all over the world. Many top retail executives started their careers as assistant buyers, just as you might.

Selling is the function consumers identify most with retailing. Retailers need to sell, not just have merchandise available. To do this, they must advertise, use sales promotions, and frequently use personal selling, to ensure that merchandise is moved in adequate quantities.

The retail storage function comprises having the inventory and floor space necessary to make merchandise available at the time and place it is demanded.

Retailers also help perform the transportation function. Often retailers have to transport goods from the point of purchase (manufacturer or wholesaler) to the retail store. Other times, the retailer needs to deliver merchandise to the customer's residence. Retailers may need to be concerned with both inbound and outbound transportation. Thus, the location of retailers and their warehouses is extremely important.

Retailers do a considerable amount of sorting, especially assorting. Retailers build assortments of merchandise that match consumer demand patterns.

The retailer cannot operate on a profitable basis without information on consumer wants and needs, changing economic conditions, and competitive trends. A lack of such information will cause error in the retail planning and management process. The retailer needs timely and relevant information to make intelligent decisions.

The retailer cannot avoid risk taking. The consumer may reject the merchandise the retailer has selected. There may be a recession, or households may leave the retailer's trading area and new households may not move in. The merchandise may not arrive on time, it may arrived damaged, or it may not be what was ordered. The store may burn down, or customers may injure themselves in the store. The management of these risks is becoming an increasingly important function in retailing.[4] Risk can be decreased by retailers using insurance and/or securing "return privileges" in case the merchandise is a flop or the season is over before the merchandise arrives.

Finally, the retailer must perform part of the financing function. Retailers need to finance the preceding functions with either debt or equity capital.

Facilitating Institutions.   A variety of institutions facilitate the performance of the marketing functions. Most of these institutions specialize in one or two functions; none of them takes title to the goods. Institutions that facilitate buying and selling in the marketing system include:

1.   The **free-lance broker**, who has no permanent ties with any manufacturer and may negotiate sales for a large number of manufacturers over time. There is no limit on the territory in which sales may occur but the broker is strictly bound by the manufacturer regarding prices, terms, and conditions of sale. An example of a free-lance broker is someone who contracts with a manufacturer to sell the manfacturer's excess output. The broker is bound by the manufacturer's terms but may get the price changed by request. Once the products are sold, the free-lance broker is free to obtain the output of any other manufacturer and perform its duties again.

2.   The **manufacturer's agent** acts as the sales force for several manufacturers at the same time within a prescribed market area. The manufacturer's agent has a rather loose arrangement with the manufacturer that is seldom permanent beyond a year. This arrangement is usually renewed but can also be terminated on notice. The manufacturer's agent, like the free-lance broker, is strictly bound by the manufacturer for the prices, terms, and conditions of sale, but is additionally bound by territory. Manufacturer's agents usually have jurisdiction over only a part of the manufacturer's total output. Manufacturer's agents are extremely important in product lines like furniture, dry goods, apparel, and accessories.

3.   The **sales agent** has long-term arrangements with one or a very few manufacturers. This agent sells the entire output for the manufacturer and has no limitation on the territory, prices, terms, or conditions of sale. The sales agent also frequently finances the manufacturer. The sales agent is generally used in such product lines as home furnishings, textiles, and canned foods.

4. **Purchasing agents** specialize in seeking out sources of supply for some members of the channel. They operate on a contractual basis for a limited number of customers and receive a commission just as sales agents do. Purchasing agents, who are sometimes known as **resident buyers**, usually operate in the central market headquarters for a particular type of product. They are specialists on the availability of products; the reliability of suppliers; present and future market trends; and special deals, prices, shipping, and other considerations. Retailers make considerable use of two different types of resident buyers: store-owned and independent buyers. More details about these purchasing agents will be discussed in Chapter 10.

These facilitating agents and brokers are independent businessmen who receive a commission when they are able to bring buyer and seller together to negotiate a transaction. Seldom do agents or brokers take actual or physical possession of the merchandise. The purchasing agent aids in buying and the others assist in selling.

Advertising agencies also facilitate the selling process by designing effective advertisements and advising management on where and when to place these advertisements.

Institutions that facilitate the transportation function are motor, rail, and air carriers, and pipeline and shipping companies. These firms offer differing advantages in terms of delivery, service, and cost; generally, the quicker the delivery, the more costly it is. Transporters can have a significant effect on how efficiently goods move through the marketing system, and can be a major source of conflict when they fail to perform their jobs properly.

Imagine you are the lawn and garden department manager for a local discount store. You are waiting for a shipment of three hundred 50-pound bags of lawn food for a special national promotion. You placed your order in time and should have received the product two days ago. Upon calling the manufacturer, you discover that the product was sent out last week by truck for delivery to you two days ago. You try to trace the shipment through the trucking company, only to find that nobody seems to know where your shipment is or when it is expected to arrive. This type of incident is often a cause for considerable conflict between the retailer and transporter, the manufacturer and the transporter, the retailer and the manufacturer, and even the retailer and the customer—when the goods don't arrive on schedule after they have been advertised, customers become irritated with the retailer.

The major facilitating institution involved in storage is the public warehouse. A **public warehouse** will store goods for safekeeping in return for a fee. Fees are usually based on cubic feet used per month, but some warehouses charge daily fees. Frequently, retailers take advantage of special buys but have no space for the goods in their store or warehouse and find it necessary to use a public warehouse.

A variety of facilitating institutions assist in providing information in the marketing system. For example, the role of the mail and phone in transmitting information is pervasive. In addition, computers are playing an increasing role in information transmission. Retailers can now order many types of merchandise using an on-line computer. An order is keyed into a computer at the retail firm and is fed directly into the wholesaler's or manufacturer's computer. That computer will print out a purchase order and a warehouse routing slip to show what items are to be pulled from the warehouse and shipped to the retailer. Also assisting in the information function are market research firms, which provide problem-solving information in specialized areas.

There are also facilitating institutions that aid in financing, such as commercial banks, savings and loan associations, and stock exchanges. These institutions can provide, or help the retailer obtain, funds to finance marketing functions. Retailers frequently need short-term loans for working capital requirements (e.g., to handle increased inventory and accounts receivables) and long-term loans for continued growth and expansion (adding new stores or remodeling).

Finally, insurance firms facilitate by assuming some of the risks in the marketing system. Insurance firms can insure inventories, buildings, trucks, equipment and fixtures, and other assets for the retailer and other primary marketing institutions. They can also insure against employee and customer injuries.

After reviewing the various functions and institutions in the marketing system, we can now examine how the primary marketing institutions are arranged into a marketing channel.

CONVENTIONAL MARKETING CHANNELS

A large part of the marketing system consists of the marketing functions and the primary marketing institutions that perform them—but how are these functions and institutions arranged into a marketing channel? Bert McCammon has elaborated on two basic channel patterns: the conventional marketing channel and the vertical marketing system. Exhibit 3.3 provides an illustration of these major channel patterns.

A **conventional marketing channel** is one in which each member of the channel is loosely aligned with the others. Predictably, each member's orientation is toward the next institution in the channel. Thus, the manufacturer interacts with and focuses efforts on the wholesaler, the wholesaler focuses efforts on the retailer, and the retailer focuses efforts on the final consumer. In short, the marketing channel consists of a series of dyads in which the members recognize each other but not those outside.

The conventional marketing channel, although historically predomi-

Exhibit 3.3   **Marketing Channel Patterns**

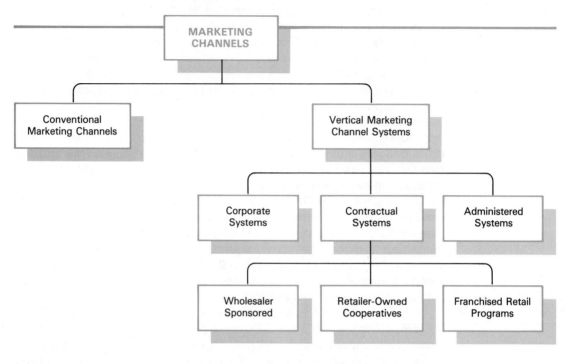

nant in the United States, is a sloppy and inefficient method of conducting business. It fosters intense negotiations in each dyad in the channel, and the channel members do not see the possibility of shifting or dividing the marketing functions among *all* channel participants. It is an unproductive mode for marketing goods, and has been on the decline in the United States since the early 1950s.

VERTICAL MARKETING SYSTEMS

Vertical marketing systems are rationalized, capital-intensive networks of several levels that are professionally managed and centrally programmed to realize technological, managerial, and promotional economies. There are three types of vertical marketing systems—corporate, contractual, and administered—each of which has grown explosively since the early 1950s.[5]

CORPORATE SYSTEMS

The **corporate vertical marketing system** typically consists of either a manufacturer who has integrated vertically to reach the consumer, or a retailer who has integrated vertically to create a self-supply network. The first type includes manufacturers such as Singer (sewing machines), Radio Shack (electronic products), Sherwin Williams (paint), Hart, Schaffner and Marx (men's apparel), Famolare (shoes), and Xerox (office equipment), which have created their own warehousing and retail outlets. The second type includes retailers such as Holiday Inns and Sears. For example, Holiday Inns has vertically integrated to control a carpet mill, furniture manufacturer, and numerous other suppliers needed to build and operate their motels. Sears obtains over 50 percent of its appliances from Whirlpool, over 50 percent of its apparel items from Kellwood, over 40 percent of its tires and tubes from Armstrong Rubber, and over 30 percent of its hand tools from EASCO—all organizations in which Sears has substantial equity.[6]

In corporate systems it is much easier to program the channel for productivity and profit goals, since a well-established authority structure already exists. Independent retailers that have aligned themselves in a conventional marketing channel are at a significant disadvantage when competing against a corporate vertical marketing system.

CONTRACTUAL SYSTEMS

Contractual vertical marketing systems include wholesaler-sponsored voluntary groups, retailer-owned cooperatives, and franchised retail programs. Each of these channel types allows for a more coordinated and system-wide perspective than conventional marketing channels; however, they are more difficult to manage than corporate vertical marketing systems because the authority and power structures are not as well defined. Channel members must give up some autonomy to gain system economies and greater market impact.

Wholesaler-Sponsored Voluntary Groups.   These groups are created when a wholesaler brings together a group of independently owned retailers (independent retailers is a term embracing anything from a single mom-and-pop store to a small local chain), grocers for example, and offers them a coordinated merchandising and buying program that will provide them with economies like those their chain-store rivals are able to obtain. In return, the independent grocers agree to concentrate their purchases with that wholesaler. It is a voluntary relationship; that is, there are no membership or franchise fees. The independent grocers may terminate the relationship whenever they desire, so it is to the wholesaler's advantage to build competitive merchandise assortments and offer other services that will keep the voluntary group satisfied.

It is common for the voluntary group wholesaler to offer the retailer the following services: store design and layout, store site and location analysis, inventory management systems, accounting and bookkeeping systems, insurance services, pension plans, trade area studies, advertising and promotion assistance, and employee training programs. The better the services and merchandising programs offered by the wholesaler, the more loyal the retailer. In such a situation, the wholesaler can become the channel leader and program the channel for high-performance results.

In the past, local food wholesalers used to get practically all of their business from independent grocers. Recently, however, as transportation costs have risen, major chains operating over a wide geographic area have started using local wholesalers, too. While welcoming this new business, wholesalers have tried to keep their independents happy by offering them even more services. Independent grocers still account for 40 percent of food wholesalers' business.[7]

Exhibit 3.4 profiles some of the retail support services a voluntary group wholesaler generally provides to its retailers. Examine the description of these services to get an understanding of how voluntary group wholesalers can assist independent retailers.

Exhibit 3.4

Support Services—A Voluntary Group Wholesaler Offers To Its Retailers

Support Service	Description
Financial counsel	Qualified personnel answer retailers' financial questions. Upon request, a retailer may receive advice on financing store expansion, cash-flow problems, loans, and other related financial concerns.
Engineering	The store engineering and development department offers retailers designs for new stores, additions, and remodelings. Expert advice on equipment and its procurement is offered. Market analysis services are provided, which prove invaluable to a retailer planning a new store or moving to a new location. Professional consumer research is offered to help retailers appraise customer acceptance. Energy saving advice is given directly, and tips are published in a weekly merchandiser.
Computer service	Wholesalers' data processing facilities provide case labels as a pricing aid to retailers; electronic ordering for speed, accuracy, and backroom space saving; commodity purchase analysis reports on a scheduled basis; and many other benefits.
Advertising	The emphasis of the advertising program is built around private brands, and by continuous use of banners and themes gives the impression of a large chain-like advertising campaign rather than a small one-store effort. In addition to placing newspaper, handbills, radio, and TV ads, the department lends assistance in planning special sales, promotions, anniversary sales, and grand openings.
Retail accounting	The accounting department handles bookkeeping, tax preparation, bill-out service, computerized payrolls, and many other accounting-oriented functions. Assistance is communicated by standardized forms, computer printouts, telephone calls, and visits by wholesaler's accountants for special problems.
Retail training	The training department provides retailers with a comprehensive training program for management and employees which includes all facets of merchandising, marketing, in-store security, and other appropriate functions.
Printing	The printing department continually provides printed material including letterheads, cash register refund forms, bag stuffers, envelopes, store directories, etc.

Wholesaler-sponsored voluntary groups have been a major force in marketing channels since the mid 1960s. They are now prevalent in many lines of trade. Independent Grocers' Alliance (IGA), Ace Hardware, Western Auto, Ben Franklin, and Economost are all examples of wholesaler-sponsored voluntary groups.

Retailer-Owned Cooperatives.   Another common type of contractual vertical marketing system is retailer-owned cooperatives. These systems are organized and owned by retailers and are most common in the grocery field (for example, Associated Grocers and Certified Grocers). They offer scale economies and service to member retailers, allowing their members to compete with larger chain-buying organizations.

Wholesaler-sponsored voluntary groups and retailer-owned cooperatives have very different leadership patterns, and these differences impact on their competitive intensity. Generally, wholesaler-sponsored voluntary groups are more effective competitors, but both types of groups have advantages and disadvantages. For example, a wholesaler can provide more leadership to its voluntary group because it represents the locus of power within the system. In retail-owned cooperatives, power is diffused throughout the retail membership, making it difficult to define roles and allocate resources. On the other hand, members of wholesaler-sponsored voluntary groups have relinquished some of their autonomy by making themselves highly dependent on specific wholesalers for expertise. In retailer-owned cooperatives, members retain more autonomy and thus tend to depend much less on the supply unit for assistance and direction.[8]

Franchise.   The third type of contractual vertical marketing system is the franchise.[9] The term originally came from the French word meaning *to be free from servitude*. Today, franchising gives individuals the opportu-

Illus. 3.3
IGA is a wholesaler-sponsored voluntary group, a major force in marketing channels since the mid 1960s.

nity to own their own business, even if they are inexperienced and lacking adequate capital. During recent years, franchising has been expanding rapidly and entering new areas of application. This growth is the result of individuals trying to overcome two of the most common causes of retail failure: lack of management know-how and inadequate financial resources. Statistical evidence of such expansion is contained in the study entitled *Franchising in the Economy*, published annually by the United States Department of Commerce, International Trade Administration. The latest study, shown in Exhibit 3.5, revealed that franchised businesses accounted for $640 billion in sales in 1988. Franchise sales in goods and services, excluding supplier-dealer businesses such as automobile dealers and gasoline service stations, were $212.2 billion in 1988—up almost 280 percent over the last ten years. Retail franchising in 1988 was equal to 33 percent of total United States retail sales.

Exhibit 3.5

Franchise Sales Volume and Changes in Sales Volume: 1978–1988

		1978 Sales (in millions)	1988* Sales (in millions)	Percent Change
Product and Tradename Franchises	Automobile and truck dealers	$147,274	$335,445	128%
	Gasoline service stations	59,663	91,894	54
	Soft-drink bottlers	10,960	22,134	102
Business Format Franchises	Automotive parts and service	6,803	13,740	102
	Business aids and services	5,046	16,841	234
	Construction, home improvements, maintenance, and cleaning services	1,269	6,246	392
	Convenience stores	5,013	13,562	171
	Educational products and services	284	1,181	316
	Restaurants (all types)	21,101	63,231	200
	Hotels, motels, and campgrounds	5,764	19,700	242
	Laundry and drycleaning services	245	406	66
	Recreation, entertainment, and travel	291	4,990	176
	Rental services (auto-truck)	2,526	6,978	258
	Rental services (equipment)	236	767	225
	Retailing (nonfood)	9,335	28,469	205
	Retailing (food other than convenience stores)	6,120	12,088	98
	Miscellaneous	284	1,934	581
	Total—all franchising	$282,214	$639,606	127%

*estimated by respondents
SOURCE: U.S. Department of Commerce, *Franchising in the Economy: 1986-1988* (Washington, D.C.: U.S. Government Printing Office, February 1988).

Franchising is a form of licensing by which the owner of a product, service, or method (the franchisor) obtains distribution through affiliated dealers (franchisees). The holder of the franchise right is often given exclusive access to a defined geographical area. The product, method, or service being marketed is identified by a brand name, and the franchisor maintains control over the marketing methods employed.

In many cases the franchise operation resembles a large chain with trademarks, uniform symbols, equipment, storefronts, and standardized services, products, and practices as outlined in the franchise agreement.

The International Franchise Association defines franchising as "a continuing relationship in which the franchisor provides a licensee privilege to do business, plus assistance in organizing, training, merchandising, and management in return for a consideration from the franchisee."

Franchising has also been described as a convenient and economic means of fulfilling the desire for independence with a minimum of risk and investment and maximum opportunities for success, through the utilization of a proven product or service and marketing method. However, the owner of a franchise gives up some freedom in business decisions that the owner of a nonfranchised business would have. Retailing in Action 3-1 provides a discussion of the factors to be considered in the selection of a franchise.

RETAILING
IN
ACTION

3-1

So You Want to Own a Franchise?

They are everywhere across the United States, from McDonald's with 1,800 franchisees, to the three Al's Bar BQ franchisees in Illinois. Franchises are taking over a large part of retail trade and you want to become a part of the action. But where do you start?

With more than 2,300 franchises to choose from, finding the one best for you can be almost as difficult as starting your own business. And while it's true that McDonald's franchises have proven themselves more golden than their arches, most franchises aren't that profitable. Besides, franchising isn't for everybody. The franchisee agrees to do practically all the work, in exchange for only part of the profit. Also, most franchisors provide little leeway in their rules on how to produce and market the product. Still, the franchisor does provide the expertise that you may feel is needed.

The first step you must take on the road to being a franchisee—and this is often the most difficult one—is to take a hard look at yourself. Are you ready to make the personal sacrifices—long hours, hard work, and financial uncertainty—that a franchise requires? Do you enjoy working with others? Are you a good leader? Are you an organized person? Or do you just want the gold at the end of the rainbow?

The second decision you'll have to make is what kind of franchise to buy and where. The place to find this information is the *Franchise Opportunities Handbook,* published by the Commerce Department, which lists most of the major franchisors.

Once you have found your target, don't just rely on your regular lawyer to help with the paperwork that awaits you. You'll need an experienced franchise attorney to sift through the documents and negotiate your contract.

A franchise isn't quite like running your own company. You'll have to follow the franchisor's instructions almost to the letter or you could risk losing your investment.

Perhaps most importantly, you and your attorney should take a hard look at what the franchisor has to offer. The fee should entitle you to more than the franchisor's name and trademark. A reputable franchisor will offer you a lot more: location analysis, help in constructing the facilities (if they don't lease them to you), extensive and ongoing training for both you and your staff, a discount on supplies if the franchisor insists upon being your supplier, national advertising (usually for an additional fee), and merchandising strategy.

How a franchisor operates is also crucial. Experts say a good franchisor will always own some of its own units. There are other tests: Does the company make most of its money selling franchises rather than a product or service? If so, beware: That franchisor has no inherent stake in your continued success. But don't be put off by franchisors who demand hefty royalty fees and monthly advertising and promotion contributions. Most do—and even though that means you'll have to surrender a portion of your gross each month, the franchisor will have a real interest in your success. If the franchisor wants you to purchase your products from central suppliers, determine whether these products are truly distinctive or whether you're being forced to pay a premium for goods you could buy cheaper elsewhere.

What happens if you want out? Almost all franchisors reserve the right to approve your buyer should you want to sell. Some of the better ones will buy your franchise back if you can't make a go of it. But most smaller franchisors can't afford to do that.

Before you sign on the dotted line, talk to some franchisees who have been in the business for a while. Ask the company for a list of all its franchisees. And don't just talk to the people the franchisor suggests. How many franchises have been terminated? If any of the franchisees are selling their franchises, find out why. And get a list of all pending lawsuits against the franchisor. You should also check with the Federal Trade Commission and the Attorney General in the states the franchisor operates in to see whether the company is registered and if any complaints have been lodged against it.

Source: U.S. Department of Commerce, *Franchise Opportunities Handbook* (Washington: U.S. Government Printing Office, 1988); James Areddy, "The Buyer's Guide," *Wall Street Journal,* 10 June 1988, pp. 32R-33R and Thomas Petzinger, Jr., "So You Want to Get Rich?" *Wall Street Journal,* 15 May 15 1987, p. 15D.

In a way, franchisees are not their own bosses. In order to maintain uniformity of service and to insure that the operations of each outlet will reflect favorably on the organization as a whole, the franchisor usually exercises some degree of control over the operations of franchisees, requiring them to meet stipulated standards of quality. The extent of such control varies. In some cases, franchisees are required to conduct every step of their operation in strict conformity with a manual furnished by the franchisor—and this may be desirable. In return for this surrender of freedom, the individual franchisee can share in the goodwill built up by all other outlets that bear the same name.

Since the last years of the 1980s, a change has been evolving in franchising. Mom-and-pop franchisees were replaced by a new breed of franchise owners. For years, most franchisors sought to sell their operations almost exclusively to would-be entrepreneurs with little or no business experience. Now the profile of the typical franchise owner is changing. A growing number of cash-rich investors and companies are sinking money into franchises, or buying rights to an entire state or foreign country. Business executives who lost their jobs in the mergers of the late 1980s are turning to franchise ownership. Independent store owners are converting to franchises to gain advertising clout. And franchisees experienced in one field are snapping up franchises in other fields. While the mom-and-pops are still important to the growth of the franchise operation, there has been a marked shift recently toward more sophisticated buyers with proven business skills and deep pockets. A survey of franchisors revealed that the most common reason for franchise failure was that the buyer had little or no previous business experience. On the other hand, most successful franchisees had previously owned businesses or franchises.[10]

Franchisors participate in many aspects of the marketing channel. The franchisor could be a manufacturer, such as Chevrolet or Midas Mufflers; a service specialist, such as Kelly Girl, Century 21 Real Estate, or Manpower; or a retailer, such as McDonald's, Kentucky Fried Chicken, 7-Eleven, or Dunkin Donuts. Franchisors depend upon the successful operation of franchise outlets for continued growth and need individuals who are willing to learn the business and who have the energy for a considerable amount of effort. The franchisor can supply the other essentials for successful operation of the outlet. Among the services franchisors may provide to franchise operators are: (1) reduced uncertainty, since the approach to doing business has been proven successful by the franchisor; (2) location analysis and counsel; (3) store design and equipment purchasing; (4) initial employee and management training and continuing management counseling; (5) advertising and merchandising counsel and assistance; (6) standardized procedures and operations; (7) centralized purchasing with consequent savings; (8) financial assistance in the establishment of the business; and (9) store development aid, including lease negotiation.

To the franchisor, franchising offers these advantages:

1. Capital advantages will be gained since franchisees are typically charged a franchise fee. The franchisor can use these fees as a major source of working capital, allowing the franchise to grow at a rapid pace without diluting its equity in the business.
2. Reduction in fixed overhead expenses will accrue to the franchisor, since the high cost of maintaining company-owned outlets will be eliminated.
3. More motivated managers will be obtained because the franchisees, as independent businessmen, will be more committed to developing markets than salaried employees would be.[11]

Although franchises offer significant advantages to both franchisor and franchisee, conflict is common. Franchisor-franchisee conflict frequently occurs over the following issues:

1. How should the direct channel profits be divided? The establishment of fees and margins, specification of investment requirements, and location of expense-incurring activities are involved.
2. When should franchisee investment in new or upgraded facilities be required, and who should participate in this decision?
3. How far should the franchisor go in saturating a single market area with franchise outlets?[12]
4. What amount of capital reserves and expertise are needed by the franchisee?[13]

The most important determinant in avoiding conflict in a franchise system is the contract. The contract should not be one-sided in favor of the franchisor. Several principles to guide franchise contract development have been suggested:

1. The contract should be frank, completely disclosing the relationship between franchisor and franchisee. The objective is to make explicit all mutual rights and obligations with performance standards to ensure that neither party may reasonably claim that it was deceived by the other.
2. The provisions should be fair so that neither party may claim unreasonable dominance by the other.
3. The contract should be tailored to the specific situation, recognizing the uniqueness of individual franchise systems and the difficulty of designing a generalized franchise contract.
4. Contract provisions should be enforceable so that no party can use economic strength for cavalier violation of agreed-on covenants.[14]

Ambiguity, a major source of conflict, can be removed by:

1. Specifying the unique roles of the contracting parties.

2. Making operating procedures as specific as possible within the confines of antitrust regulations and local market differences.
3. Specifying in substantial detail the performance obligations of both parties.
4. Specifying how performance standards will be established and revised.
5. Specifying criteria for new outlet penetration of given markets.
6. Specifying reasonable causes leading to termination.[15]

The franchise contract gives the franchisor legitimate power to control the marketing channel. In addition, the franchisor obtains power by providing the franchisee with services and assistances that increase franchisee dependence, and thus franchisor power.[16] These assistances are provided when the franchisor helps the franchisee establish business and include: market survey and site selection, facility design and layout, lease negotiation advice, financing advice, operating manuals, and management and employee training programs. After the franchisee is established, ongoing assistance is provided by the franchisor to help ensure that the franchisee continues to do a good job. This ongoing assistance typically includes: field supervision, merchandising and promotional materials, management and employee training, quality inspection, national advertising, centralized purchasing, market data and guidance, auditing and recordkeeping, management reports, and group insurance plans. Many legal problems arise in controlling a franchise system. These legal problems are discussed in considerable detail in Chapter 6.

ADMINISTERED SYSTEMS

The final type of vertical marketing system is the administered system. **Administered vertical marketing systems** are similar to conventional marketing channels, but one of the channel members takes the initiative to lead the channel by applying the principles of effective interorganizational management. Administered systems, although not new in concept, have grown substantially since the 1960s.

Frequently, administered systems are initiated by manufacturers. As McCammon has observed,

> Manufacturing organizations . . . have historically relied on administrative expertise to coordinate reseller marketing efforts. Suppliers with dominant brands have predictably experienced the least difficulty in securing strong trade support, but many manufacturers with "fringe" items have been able to elicit reseller cooperation through the use of liberal distribution policies that take the form of attractive discounts (or discount substitutes), financial assistance, and various types of concessions that protect resellers from one or more of the risks of doing business.[17]

Exhibit 3.6

Common Concessions Manufacturers Offer to Gain Retailer Support

Price Concessions

Discount Structure	*Discount Substitutes*
Trade (functional) discounts	Display materials
Quantity discounts	Premarked merchandise
Cash discounts	Inventory control programs
Anticipation allowances	Catalogs and sales promotion literature
Free goods	Training programs
Prepaid freight	Shelf-stocking programs
New product, display, and advertising allowances (without performance requirements)	Advertising matrices
	Management consulting services
	Merchandising programs
Seasonal discounts	Sales "spiffs"
Mixed carload privilege	Technical assistance
Drop shipping privilege	Payment of sales personnel and demonstrator salaries
Trade deals	Promotional and advertising allowances (with performance requirements)

Financial Assistance

Conventional Lending Arrangements	*Extended Dating*
Term loans	E.O.M. (end of month) dating
Inventory floor plans	Seasonal dating
Notes payable financing	R.O.G. (receipt of goods) dating
Accounts payable financing	"Extra" dating
Installment financing of fixtures and equipment	Post dating
Lease and note guarantee programs	
Accounts receivable financing	

Protective Provisions

Price Protection	*Inventory Protection (cont.)*
Premarked merchandise	Reorder guarantees
"Franchise" pricing	Guaranteed support of sales events
Agency agreements	Maintenance of "spot" stocks and fast delivery
Inventory Protection	*Territorial Protection*
Consignment selling	Selective distribution
Memorandum selling	Exclusive distribution
Liberal returns allowances	
Rebate programs	

SOURCE: Bert C. McCammon, Jr., "Perspectives for Distribution Programming," in Louis P. Bucklin, ed., *Vertical Marketing Systems* (Glenview, Ill.: Scott, Foresman and Company, 1970), 36–37. Reprinted with permission of the author.

Exhibit 3.7
Plans and Activities Covered in Programmed Merchandising Agreements

Merchandising Goals

1. Planned sales
2. Planned initial markup percentage
3. Planned reductions, including planned markdowns, shortages, and discounts
4. Planned gross margin
5. Planned expense ratio (optional)
6. Planned profit margin (optional)

Inventory Plan

1. Planned rate of inventory turnover
2. Planned merchandise assortments, including basic or model stock plans
3. Formalized "never out" lists
4. Desired mix of promotional versus regular merchandise

Merchandise Presentation Plan

1. Recommended store fixtures
2. Space allocation plan
3. Visual merchandising plan
4. Needed promotional materials, including point-of-purchase displays, consumer literature, and price signs

Personal Selling Plan

1. Recommended sales presentations
2. Sales training plan
3. Special incentive arrangements, including "spiffs," salesmen's contests, and related activities

Advertising and Sales Promotion Plan

1. Advertising and sales promotion budget
2. Media schedule
3. Copy themes for major campaigns and promotions
4. Special sales events

Responsibilities and Due Dates

1. Supplier's responsibilities in connection with the plan
2. Retailer's responsibilities in connection with the plan

SOURCE: Bert C. McCammon, Jr., "Perspectives for Distribution Programming," in Louis P. Bucklin, ed., *Vertical Marketing Systems* (Glenview, Ill.: Scott, Foresman and Company, 1970), 48–49. Reprinted with permission of the author.

Exhibit 3.6 provides a list of some common concessions that manufacturers might use to get retailers to support their marketing programs. These terms will be discussed in detail in Part 4.

Manufacturers can also develop an administered system through *programmed merchandise agreements*. McCammon defined these agreements as "a joint venture in which a specific retail account and a supplier develop a comprehensive merchandising plan to market the supplier's product line. These plans normally cover a six-month period but some use a longer duration."[18] Exhibit 3.7 profiles the activities covered in programmed merchandising agreements. Manufacturers that have used programmed merchandising agreements include General Electric (on major and traffic appliances), Baumritter (on its Ethan Allen furniture line in nonfranchised outlets), Sealy (on its Posturepedic line of mattresses), Villager (on its dresses and sportswear lines), Scott (on its lawn care products), Norwalk (on its upholstered furniture), Keepsake (on diamonds), and Stanley (on hand tools).

Retailers that use this type of an agreement include Sears, Kroger, and Wal-Mart. Sears, for example, administers its relationships with almost all of its suppliers. In fact, very few suppliers would have the power to administer to Sears. For example, in white goods (appliances such as washing machines, dishwashers, refrigerators, etc.) Sears accounts for over 25 percent of all United States sales. It is not surprising that Sears dominates its relationship with the manufacturers of these products.

MANAGING RETAILER/SUPPLIER RELATIONS

Retailers who are not part of a contractual system or corporate channel will probably participate in several marketing channels, since they will need to acquire merchandise from many suppliers. These marketing channels will either be conventional or administered. If retailers desire to improve their performance in these channels, they must understand the principles of interorganizational management.

Interorganizational management is the management of relationships between organizational entities. In a marketing channel, it involves one member, such as a retailer, managing its relations with other organizations in the channel, such as wholesalers and manufacturers. The retailer operating in a conventional marketing channel could apply the concepts of interorganizational management to move the channel toward becoming an administered channel. Alternatively, if the retailer participates in an administered channel, an understanding of interorganizational management will help the retailer appreciate the need for one channel member to lead and organize the channel and for all channel members to work in unison.

What are the basic concepts of interorganizational management that a retail executive needs to understand? They are dependency, power, and conflict.

DEPENDENCY

As we mentioned earlier in this chapter, all marketing systems need to perform eight marketing functions. These functions are performed by a multitude of institutions in the marketing channel. None of the respective institutions can isolate itself; each depends on others to do an effective job.

Retailer A is dependent on Suppliers X, Y, and Z to get goods delivered on time and in the right quantities. Conversely, Suppliers X, Y, and Z depend on Retailer A to put a strong selling effort behind the goods, displaying the merchandise and helping to finance consumer purchases. If Retailer A does a poor job, each supplier can be adversely affected; if even one supplier does a poor job, Retailer A can be adversely affected. In all channel alignments, each party depends on the others to do a good job.

When each party is dependent on the others, we say that they are interdependent. Interdependency is the root of conflict in marketing channels.[19] When conflict arises, someone needs to exercise power. However, before we explore the concepts of power and conflict, let us examine the concept of dependency in more detail.

Generally, the retailer's dependency on the supplier is (1) directly proportional to the retailer's motivational investment in goals that the supplier can mediate and (2) inversely proportional to the retailer's alternatives for achieving its goals outside of its relationship with the supplier.[20] This relationship can be better understood through a hypothetical example. Assume that the management of Lifestyles, a catalog showroom, is highly committed to achieving a 20 percent return on investment. Lifestyles purchases the majority of its merchandise from a single supplier, who provides a merchandise line that yields a very attractive profit margin. It is clear that this attractive margin will significantly help Lifestyles attain its goal. Further assume that Lifestyles is not able to locate any other suppliers that can supply merchandise lines with such attractive profit margins. Obviously, then, the retailer is very dependent on the supplier. To see if you comprehend the concept of dependency, create a situation in which the retailer would not be very dependent on the supplier.

POWER

We can use the concept of dependency to explain power; but first we must define power. The **power** of the supplier over the retailer is the ability of the supplier to affect the decision variables of the retailer.[21] The more dependent the retailer is on the supplier, the more power the supplier has over the retailer. For example, a powerful beverage distributor could get a dependent convenience store to give its products prime shelf space and special promotional emphasis. It is a fact of life in marketing channels that the more a retailer allows itself to become dependent on a supplier, the more the supplier will be able to influence the retailer's actions.[22]

A second explanation of power is that the more sources of power that A has over B, the more power A has over B.[23] In this framework, A (the power holder) could be either the supplier or the retailer. There are five sources of power:

1. **Reward power** is based on the ability of A to mediate rewards for B.
2. **Expertise power** is based on B's perception that A has some special knowledge.
3. **Referent power** is based on the identification of B with A. B wants to be associated or identified with A.
4. **Coercive power** is based on B's belief that A has the capacity to punish or harm B if he doesn't conform to A's desire.
5. **Legitimate power** is based on A's right to influence B, or B's belief that he should accept A's influence. The appearance of legitimate power is most obvious in contractual marketing systems.

The retailer can use the concepts of dependency and power to develop strategies to equalize its power with the supplier or even to become more powerful than the supplier. Here are some realistic examples of what the retailer might do in this regard:

1. The retailer could develop expert power by obtaining information on consumers' needs and providing this information to suppliers.
2. The retailer could maintain multiple sources of supply in order to avoid the coercive power of any single supplier.
3. The retailer could use scarce shelf space to reward key suppliers (this is especially true today in supermarkets).
4. The retailer could establish referent power by building a strong consumer franchise so that the consumer becomes more loyal to its store than to a supplier's brand.
5. The retailer could develop a strong store brand program to avoid the coercive power of national producers.
6. The retailer could band together with other retailers in order to purchase in larger quantities and employ reward power with suppliers.

This is not an exhaustive list. Take a moment to see if you can add three more examples.

CONFLICT

Conflict between retailers and suppliers is inevitable since retailers and suppliers are interdependent.[24] Interdependency has been identified as the root of all conflict in marketing channels; however, there is more to understanding conflict than its direct tie to interdependency. Exhibit 3.8 provides a model of the conflict process to serve as a frame of reference for the following discussion.

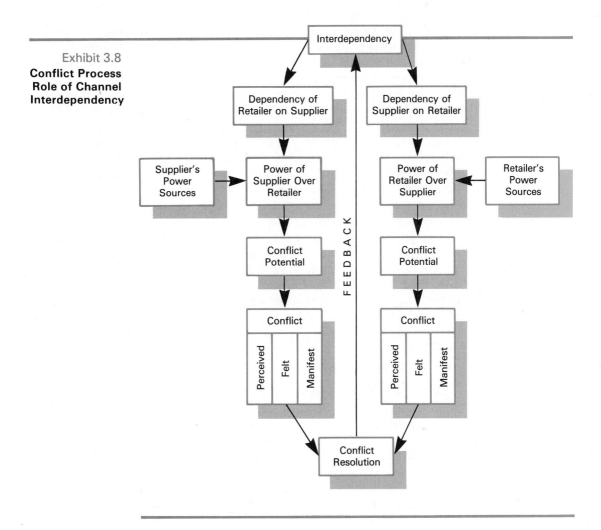

Exhibit 3.8
Conflict Process Role of Channel Interdependency

Interdependency and Conflict Potential.   As Exhibit 3.8 shows, conflict involves several stages.[25] First, interdependency needs to exist among the retailer and supplier. Dependence on another channel member to achieve your goals results in the other member having power over you. This power can be from any of the five different sources. The fact that one channel member is dependent on another member causes the potential for conflict to enter the channel. However, more than just a potential for conflict needs to exist for a retailer and supplier to engage in conflict. Latent sources of conflict are also necessary.

Latent Conflict is an underlying situation that, if left unattended, could eventually result in conflicting behavior. In the retailer-supplier dyad, there are three major sources of latent conflict: perceptual incongruity, goal incompatibility, and domain dissensus.

Perceptual incongruity occurs when the retailer and supplier have different perceptions of reality.[26] A retailer may perceive that the economy is entering a recession and therefore want to cut inventory investments, while the supplier may perceive that the economy will remain strong and therefore feel that inventory investments should be maintained or possibly increased. Perceptual incongruity is a major source of conflict in the marketing channel. For example, consider the following areas which the retailer and supplier might perceive differently: the quality of the supplier's merchandise, the potential demand for the supplier's merchandise, the consumer appeal of the supplier's advertising, and the best shelf position for the supplier's merchandise.

A second source of latent conflict is **goal incompatibility**, a situation in which the goals of the supplier or retailer if pursued would hamper the goal attainment of the other.[27] For instance, consider an apparel supplier with a sportswear line that it wants the consumer to perceive as having a status image. A high retail price would be consistent with this goal. However, the retailer might believe that its return-on-investment goals could be better achieved if the sportswear were heavily discounted and a higher volume could be sold. Clearly, the retailer's profit goals are not compatible with the supplier's image goals.

Three other examples of where the retailer's goals are incompatible with the supplier's goals are:

1. The manufacturer entering the retail business by opening an outlet store in competition with an established retailer carrying the product line.
2. The retailer seeking to gain an exclusive territory agreement, when the supplier wants to have as many retailers as possible carrying the line. In Chapter 6 we will discuss the legal issues involved with these agreements.
3. The manufacturer selling excess production to off-price or discount stores, placing the established retailer, who feels that he or she helped to develop the demand for the product, in price competition. Often this will result in the original retailer replacing the national brand with a private label.

The problem is not necessarily one of profit goals vs. image goals. Even if the retailer and supplier both have a return-on-investment (ROI) goal, they can still be incompatible, because what is good for the retailer's ROI may not be good for the supplier's ROI. Consider the price element in the transaction between the supplier and retailer. If the supplier obtains a higher price, his ROI will be higher but the ROI of the retailer will be lower. Similarly, other key elements in the transaction between the retailer and supplier—such as advertising allowances, cash discounts, order quantity, and freight charges—can result in conflict.

Because suppliers have different goals than the retailers they serve, they often engage in behavior that is in conflict with the retailer. For instance, when retailers place orders with suppliers they often give a cancellation date. This date tells the supplier that if the merchandise can't be shipped by that date then the order should be cancelled. But many suppliers ignore the cancellation dates and ship the merchandise late. What can a gift shop do with a shipment of Valentine cards that arrive on February 15? Another common practice is the substitution of merchandise when the supplier is out of the ordered items. The supplier may substitute colors and styles that the retailer does not want. A fabric store in a college town may place an order for midnight blue and gold, the team colors, for the homecoming celebration. In the past, there has been a sellout of all material in these colors, and this year the celebration is expected to be even bigger. Imagine the retailer's dismay when unpacking the order to find that the supplier has substituted royal blue for the darker shade. Finally, retailers will often receive invoices requesting immediate payment before they receive the merchandise.

Another example of goal incompatibility is when an individual franchisor of a fast food chain is concerned only with selecting the profit-maximizing location for one outlet in a geographic area, while the franchisor is concerned with maximizing its profits from a set of outlets.

A third source of latent conflict is **domain dissensus**.[28] Domain refers to the decision variables that each member of the marketing channel feels it should be able to control. When the members of the marketing channel agree on who should make which decisions, **domain consensus** exists. Where there is disagreement on who should make decisions, domain dissensus exists.

Consider the case of an automobile manufacturer and an automobile dealer. The dealer believes it should be able to make decisions regarding employees, local advertising, retail pricing, hours of operation, and remodeling and expansion. However, the manufacturer believes that it should be consulted on hours of operation and remodeling and expansion. As a consequence, there exists some domain dissensus in the auto manufacturer-auto dealer dyad.

Perceived Conflict.   **Perceived conflict** is a cognitive stage. It represents the point at which either the supplier or retailer becomes aware of one or more of the preceding sources of latent conflict. For instance, in our example of the apparel supplier that was pursuing a high-priced, quality image for its sportswear line and the retailer that was heavily discounting the brand to achieve a higher return-on-investment goal, perceived conflict would not occur until the supplier became aware of the retailer's pricing strategy. Note that none of the three sources of latent conflict are necessarily ever perceived. If they are not perceived, conflict will not progress beyond the latent stage. Retailing in Actions 3-2 and 3-3 describe two major sources of conflict involving the retailer and manufacturer.

RETAILING
IN
ACTION

3-2

A Source of Conflict: Off-Price Retailers

The last decade has been an extremely nervous time for most of the nation's clothing manufacturers. Beset with declining economic conditions and sudden changes in market demand, manufacturers began to more fully utilize an old marketing channel member: the off-price retailer.

Off-price retailing actually began in 1920, when Loehmann's set up a cut-rate back-door outlet in Brooklyn for "better" women's wear that had been traditionally sold only through dignified stores like Saks Fifth Avenue, Best's, and Lord & Taylor. Upset retailers put pressure on the manufacturers, who in turn persuaded Loehmann's to cut all the labels from the garments or to replace labels with different brand names so customers could not compare prices between the stores. This practice persists today in some off-price outlets, although astute shoppers have long since learned to identify manufacturers by other means.

Off-price retailers make their money because of miscalculations on the manufacturer's part. For example, a women's apparel manufacturer must decide which fabrics to use and what quantities to order from the mill a full 18 months before the final product appears in the store. If the manufacturer does not sell what it expected to, it must find some way to unload the excess production. The off-pricer is therefore able to pick up this excess production at a fraction of the cost a regular or traditional retailer must pay. For example, a traditional retailer might pay $100 for a suit and price it at $200. The off-pricer would only pay $60 for the same suit and mark it at $99.

The impact of off-pricers on retailing has been tremendous. Traditional retailers are now emphasizing value for the customer and questioning the use of national brands vs. in-house private brands. After all, why should retailers develop a manufacturer's brand into a hot item, only to be later undersold by off-pricers? That can't happen with a private label. Manufacturers are worried about possible retailer reactions. After all, they need an outlet for excess production.

The next few years will be an exciting time as we watch how manufacturers and retailers react to this new force in the retail channel.

Felt Conflict. **Felt conflict** consists of stress, tension, or hostility resulting from perceiving a conflict. It is the affective dimension of conflict. Not all suppliers and retailers that perceive conflict will experience felt conflict; some may have a high tolerance for perceived conflicts. They may realize that there is a basic source of conflict but feel that it isn't worth

RETAILING
IN
ACTION

3-3

Conflict Between Manufacturers and Retailers

Grocery manufacturers often offer trade promotions, or cooperative merchandise allowances (such as free goods and percentage off), to retailers. The intent is that these trade promotions will encourage the retailer to promote the items, building traffic and increasing sales for both parties.

In the past, manufacturers and retailers frequently came into conflict over the form and amount of trade promotions. Retailers viewed promotional efforts initiated by manufacturers as encouraging profitless brand-switching rather than increasing sales and profits. Manufacturers, on the other hand, complained that retailer-initiated promotions sometimes damage brand names which have been carefully and expensively nurtured over years or that retailers wanted the manufacturer to sponsor an event or sale that would benefit only the retailer. Worse yet, manufacturers complained that retailers frequently took advantage of them by absorbing trade promotions without passing their benefits along to consumers, sending the savings to the retailer's bottom line.

In the late 1980s, the promotional allowances accompanying new products took a new twist. The retailers began demanding slotting allowances, or fees when accepting new products. The retailers saw these allowances as means to defray the cost of adding a new product to their computer, finding space in the warehouse, redesigning store shelves and notifying individual stores about this latest new product. The manufacturers saw it as blackmail.

Retailers, thanks to the scanner, no longer were held captive to manufacturers' market share data or dazzled by claims of future sales and began to exercise their new power. Supermarket managers weren't concerned about brand loyalty either and didn't buy the manufacturers' argument that the slotting allowances must come from trade promotions, resulting in lower projected sales for both the retailer and manufacturer.

The power base between supermarkets and manufacturers shifted in the late 1980s. How it will be resolved is anybody's guess.

getting upset about. Or, they may simply be too busy with other matters to waste time worrying and getting frustrated over the source of conflict.

Manifest Conflict.   **Manifest conflict** is the behavioral or action stage of conflict. This stage is often characterized by verbal or written threats or other actions by the supplier or retailer to block the other from what she is doing. Manifest conflict will not always follow felt conflict for a variety of reasons. Possibly the supplier or retailer experiences felt conflict but determines that there is little to gain by engaging in manifest conflict. Or the retailer may experience felt conflict but also realize that the supplier has considerably more power, rendering any engagement in manifest conflict futile.

Conflict Resolution.   Not all conflict in the channel is bad. Sometimes the appearance of conflict may stimulate members to improve channel efficiency. For example, a wholesaler might at first become angry toward a retailer, with whom it has had a long and satisfying relationship, when the retailer seeks to buy certain items directly from the manufacturer. This initial anger might develop into a manifest conflict situation that would destroy the relationship or it might cause both members to put forth a better effort in the future. In this case, channel efficiency would be improved. In most instances, though, conflict reduces channel efficiency and must go through a resolution process.[29] Manifest conflict threatens the most potential harm to the retailer-supplier dyad and thus needs to be resolved as soon as possible.

There are two major conflict resolution mechanisms—**withdrawal** and **procedural resolution**.[30] In a retailer-supplier conflict, withdrawal should be viewed as a last resort. However, if the retailer and supplier fail, through all reasonable means, to resolve their conflict, then their relationship may be dissolved. In that case, each will need to seek a new channel partner.

Procedural resolution is more common than withdrawal. If the retailer and supplier are each dependent on the other and interested in a continuing relationship, most conflicts can be resolved. There are three means of procedural resolution: reconciliation, compromise, and award.

Reconciliation is a situation in which "the value systems of . . . the parties so change that they now have common preferences in the joint field: they both want the same state of affairs or position in the joint field and so conflict is eliminated."[31] For example, in the situation discussed earlier, the retailer perceived that a recession was on the horizon and the supplier perceived continued prosperity. As a result, the retailer desired to reduce inventories and the supplier wanted to maintain or even increase inventory. Ultimately, the supplier and retailer got into a heated argument. Finally, the supplier was able to present evidence that caused the retailer to revise his perceptions and come to hold the same view as the supplier. In another situation, retailers who doubt the saleability of a new product might secure a "return clause" in order to minimize losses if the item doesn't sell.

A second form of procedural resolution is **compromise. Compromise** is the result of a situation "in which the value systems are not identical and the parties have different optimum positions in the joint field; however, each party is willing to settle for something less than his ideal position rather than continue the conflict."[32] To continue the preceding example, the supplier and retailer, after heated debate, may decide to compromise on their original positions. The retailer may decide not to cut inventory as much as he had initially planned if the supplier will finance more of the retailer's inventory investment by providing 45-day instead of 30-day payment terms. In a conflict resolved by compromise, each party relinquishes part of its initial position. In marketing channels, compromise is the most common form of conflict resolution.

Award is a settlement that is reached "because both parties have agreed to accept the verdict of an outside person or agency rather than continue the conflict."[33] An award is typically the result of a legal trial or arbitration. The courts have settled many conflicts in marketing channels, specifically between retailers and suppliers.

In addition, state and federal legislatures have passed legislation to equalize the balance of power between retailers and their suppliers and thus reduce or resolve conflict. For example, when automobile dealers and manufacturers clashed over distribution and marketing policies, state and federal legislation was passed in an attempt to equalize the balance of power between them.[34] Similar legislation resulted in regulating franchisors in the 1970s.[35]

When **arbitration** is used to resolve a conflict, parties voluntarily submit their dispute to a third party whose decision will be considered final and binding.[36] Many franchise channels and administered vertical marketing systems have established formal arbitration boards.[37] These boards consist of industry representatives and are chaired by an independent arbitrator, perhaps a retired judge. This approach "provides for a third party to enter and resolve a dispute before it becomes too difficult to settle in a reasonably friendly fashion."[38] Using arbitration to resolve channel conflicts offers five advantages:

1. Arbitration is fast. The parties to a dispute can be quickly informed that a quarrel exists and told the time of a hearing; the

Illus. 3.4
Arbitration is the voluntary submission of dispute to a third party whose decision will be considered final and binding.

evidence can then be heard by a panel and the decision rendered within a few weeks.

2. Arbitration preserves secrecy. Outside parties can be banned from the hearings. Decisions that are not matters of public record can be kept secret.

3. Arbitration is less expensive than litigation, reducing the cost of a tolerable decision.

4. Arbitration confronts problems in their incipient stage, when they are easier to solve. The attitude is, "We have a potential problem here; let's solve it before positions and options get too fixed."

5. Arbitration often takes place before industry experts. The arbitrator panel is composed of those who know an industry and its practices. Some argue that this produces a fairer decision than the courts.[39]

Feedback.   If you refer to Exhibit 3.8, you will notice that conflict doesn't end with resolution. After the conflict is resolved, there will be feedback. In other words, the outcome of the conflict will affect the future balance of dependency between the channel members. It will also result in a change in the power each member has over the other. How satisfactory the resolution was to the parties and what they learned about each other during the entire conflict process will influence their future behavior toward each other. Also, a retailer's conflict with one supplier may provide useful information on how to handle similar conflicts with other suppliers.[40]

SUMMARY

The system must be viewed as the solution. If the retailer ignores the marketing system in order to maximize short-run profits, then in the long run, the system will forget about the retailer. And if the system forgets the retailer, then profits sufficient for survival and growth will vanish.

In learning to work within the marketing system, the retailer needs to recognize the eight marketing functions necessary in all marketing systems: buying, selling, storing, transporting, sorting, financing, information gathering, and risk taking. The retailer can seldom perform all of these functions and therefore must rely on other primary and facilitating institutions in the marketing system. Although the marketing functions are pervasive, they can be shifted or divided among the institutions in the marketing system.

The institutions in the marketing system can be arranged into two primary marketing channel patterns—conventional and vertical. A conventional marketing channel is one in which each member of the channel is loosely aligned with the others, each member recognizing those it directly interacts with but ignoring all others. Conventional marketing channels are on the decline in the United States and vertical marketing systems are becoming dominant. In the vertical marketing system, all parties to the channel recognize each other and one party programs the channel to achieve technological, managerial, and promotional economies. Three types of vertical marketing systems are corporate, contractual, and administered.

The retailer, in order to operate efficiently and effectively in any marketing channel, needs to understand the basics of interorganizational behavior. Key concepts that need to be understood are dependency, power, and conflict. By understanding these concepts, the retailer can learn to interact productively with other marketing channel members.

QUESTIONS FOR DISCUSSION

1. In this chapter we stated that K mart's marketing channels are in competition with Target and Wal-Mart. Would this be the case if both K mart and Target buy from some of the same suppliers? For example, assume both buy calculators from Texas Instruments.
2. Facilitating marketing institutions are powerless in the marketing channel. Agree or disagree and explain your reasoning.
3. How might a small local chain of five grocery stores increase its power in the marketing channel?
4. Can a retailer lead the marketing channel?
5. During economic recession, conflict in the marketing channel is likely to increase. Agree or disagree and explain why.
6. Using the strategic profit model (Exhibit 2-5) as a frame of reference, show how certain components of the model help explain conflict between retailers and their suppliers.
7. What are the marketing functions performed in a marketing channel?
8. Define and give an example of the three sources of latent conflict.
9. How do wholesaler-sponsored voluntary groups benefit independent retailers?
10. What are advantages of the franchise form of distribution/marketing to the franchisor and franchisee?
11. What are the advantages of using arbitration to resolve conflict in the marketing channel?
12. What are some of the factors that complicate the study of marketing channels?
13. What is a vertical marketing system?
14. What is the primary difference between a conventional marketing channel and a vertical marketing system?

15. How does sorting overcome the problems inherent in heterogenous supply and demand?
16. Why would a manufacturer elect to use multiple channels of distribution for the same product?
17. Describe the complex relationship between power and conflict.
18. Define the five sources of power that can be used in a marketing channel.

SUGGESTED READINGS

Frazier, Gary L. "Interorganizational Exchange Behavior in Marketing Channels: A Broadened Perspective." *Journal of Marketing* (Fall 1983): 68–78.

Frazier, Gary L. "On the Measurement of Interfirm Power in Channels of Distribution," *Journal of Marketing Research* (May 1983): 158–166.

Frazier, Gary L., and John O. Summers. "Interfirm Influence Strategies and Their Application Within Distribution Channels," *Journal of Marketing* (Summer 1984): 43–55.

Gaski, John. "The Theory of Power and Conflict in Channels of Distribution," *Journal of Marketing* (Summer 1984): 9–29.

Hunt, Shelby D., Nina M. Ray, and Van R. Wood. "Behavioral Dimensions of Channels of Distribution: Review and Synthesis," *Journal of the Academy of Marketing Science* (Summer 1985): 1–24.

Jackson, Donald M., Robert F. Krampf, and Leonard J. Konopa. "Factors that Influence the Length of Industrial Channels," *Industrial Marketing Management* (October 1982): 263–268.

Sibley, Stanley D., and Donald A. Michie. "An Exploratory Investigation of Cooperation in a Franchise Channel," *Journal of Retailing* (Winter 1982): 23–45.

Zeller, Richard E., Dale D. Achabal, and Lawrence A. Brown, "Market Penetration and Locational Conflict in Franchise Systems," *Decision Sciences* (January 1980): 58–80.

ENDNOTES

1. For a more detailed discussion of marketing functions consult Franklin W. Ryan, "Functional Elements of Market Distribution," *Harvard Business Review* (January 1935): 205–21; and Edmund D. McGary, "Some Functions of Marketing Reconsidered," in Reavis Cox and Wroe Alderson, eds., *Theory in Marketing* (Homewood, IL: Richard D. Irwin, 1950), 263–79.

2. Alderson was one of the first to discuss the sorting function in detail. See Wroe Alderson, *Marketing Behavior and Executive Action* (Homewood, IL: Richard D. Irwin, 1957). Some current authors use the term *standardization and grading* instead of sorting. For example, see E. Jerome McCarthy and William D. Perreault, *Basic Marketing*, 9th ed. (Homewood, IL: Richard D. Irwin, 1987), 18 and William F. Schoell and Joseph P. Guiltinan, *Marketing*, 3d ed. (Boston: Allyn & Bacon, 1988): 9.

3. *County Business Patterns: 1986* (Issued November, 1988), Table 1A.

4. For a more detailed discussion see "The Perils and Premiums of Retailing," *Chain Store Age Executive* (July 1980): 34–51 and "The Man Who Makes Millions on Mistakes," *Fortune* (September 6, 1982): 106–116.

5. Bert C. McCammon, Jr., Alton F. Doody, and William R. Davidson, "Emerging Patterns of Distribution" (paper presented at the annual meeting of the National Association of Wholesalers, Las Vegas, 15 January 1969). Reprinted in Bruce J. Walker and Joel B. Haynes, eds., *Marketing Channels and Institutions: Selected Readings*, 2d. ed. (Columbus, Ohio: Grid, 1978), 195.

6. "The Leaning Towers of Sears," *Fortune* (July 2, 1979): 78–85.

7. "Wall Street Warms to Supermarkets," *Fortune* (November 29, 1982): 146.

8. Louis W. Stern and Adel I. El-Ansary, *Marketing Channels*, 3d. ed. (Englewood Cliffs, NJ: Prentice Hall, 1988), 331.

9. This section is based on information obtained from U.S. Department of Commerce, *Franchise Opportunities Handbook* (Washington D.C.: U.S. Government Printing Office, 1988), xxix.

10. "New Owners of Franchises Belie Mom-and-Pop Image," *Wall Street Journal*, 29 August 1988, p. 13.

11. Bert Rosenbloom, *Marketing Channels*, 3d. ed. (Hinsdale, IL: Dryden Press, 1983), 374–376.

12. Ronald Stephenson and Robert G. House, "A Perspective on Franchising," *Business Horizons* (August 1971): 35–42.

13. R. Richard Bruno, "Capital Reserves and Expertise are Mandatory Before Taking Plunge Into Business Franchising," *Marketing News* (February 17, 1984): 3.

14. Better Business Bureau, *Facts on Selecting a Franchise*, 1975 and International Franchise Association, *Answers to the Twenty-One Most Commonly Asked Questions About Franchising*, 5.

15. Stephenson and House, "Perspective on Franchising,": 38.

16. Shelby D. Hunt and John R. Nevin, "Power in a Channel of Distribution: Sources and Consequences," *Journal of Marketing Research* (May 1974): 186–93.

17. Bert C. McCammon, Jr., "Perspectives for Distribution Programming," in Louis P. Bucklin, ed., *Vertical Marketing Systems*, (Glenview, IL: Scott Foresman, 1970), 45. Reprinted with permission of the author.

18. McCammon, p. 48.

19. Louis W. Stern and Ronald H. Gorman, "Conflict in Distribution Channels: An Exploration," in Louis W. Stern, ed., *Distribution Channels: Behavioral Dimensions* (Boston: Houghton Mifflin, 1969), 156.

20. Richard M. Emerson, "Power-Dependence Relations," *American Sociological Review* (February 1962): 31–41.

21. James R. Brown, Robert F. Lusch, and Darrel D. Muehling, "Conflict and Power-Dependence Relations in Retailer-Supplier Channels," *Journal of Marketing* (Winter 1983): 54.

22. For a more detailed discussion of the power-dependence relationship see Steven J. Skinner and Joseph P. Guiltinan, "Perceptions of Channel Control," *Journal of Retailing* (Winter, 1985): 65–88.

23. J. R. P. French and Bertram Raven, "The Bases of Social Power," in Darwin Cartwright and Alvin Zoner, eds., *Group Dynamics: Research and Theory* (New York: Harper and Row, 1968).

24. For an investigation of conflict across channels rather than within a par-

ticular channel see John Robbins, Thomas Speh, and Morris Mayer, "Retailers' Perceptions of Channel Conflict Issues," *Journal of Retailing* (Winter 1982): 46–67.

25. This process model of conflict relies heavily on Louis R. Pondy, "Organizational Conflict Concepts and Models," *Administrative Science Quarterly*, (September 1967): 328–41.

26. Perceptual incongruity is identified as a source of conflict in Morton Deutsch, *The Resolution of Conflict* (New Haven: Yale University Press, 1973): 16; Joseph A. Litterer, "Conflict in Organizations: A Re-Examination," *Academy of Management Journal* (September 1960): 183; and Louis W. Stern and James L. Heskett, "Conflict Management in Interorganizational Relations: A Conceptual Framework," in Louis W. Stern, ed., *Distribution Channels: Behavioral Dimensions* (Boston: Houghton Mifflin, 1969): 294.

27. Goal incompatibility is identified as a source of conflict in Stuart M. Schmidt and Thomas A. Kochon, "Conflict: Toward Conceptual Clarity," *Administrative Science Quarterly* (September 1972): 359–70; Bertram H. Raven and H. T. Eachus, "Cooperation and Competition in Means-Interdependent Triads," *Journal of Abnormal and Social Psychology* (1963): 307–316; and Stern and Heskett, "Conflict Management in Interorganization Relations," 294.

28. Domain dissensus is identified as a source of conflict in Louis W. Stern and Ronald H. Gorman, "Conflict in Distribution Channels: An Exploration," in Louis W. Stern, ed., *Distribution Channels*, 156–75. The reader also might want to see Patrick L. Schul, William Pride, and Taylor E. Little, "The Impact of Channel Leadership Behavior on Intrachannel Conflict," *Journal of Marketing* (Summer 1983): 21–34.

29. Bert Rosenbloom, "Conflict and Channel Efficiency: Some Conceptual Models for the Decision Maker," *Journal of Marketing* (July 1973).

30. Kenneth E. Boulding, *Conflict and Defense* (New York: Harper and Brothers, 1962).

31. Boulding, 310.

32. Boulding, 310.

33. Boulding, 310.

34. Stuart Macaulay, *Law and the Balance of Power* (New York: Russell Sage Foundation, 1966).

35. Shelby D. Hunt and John R. Nevin, "Tying Agreements in Franchising," *Journal of Marketing* (July 1975): 24–25; Shelby D. Hunt and John R. Nevin, "Full Disclosure Laws in Franchising," *Journal of Marketing* (April 1976): 53–62; and James T. Haverson, "What's in Store at the Federal Trade Commission," *Franchising and Antitrust* (Washington, D.C.: International Franchise Association, 1975), 20–29.

36. Stern and El-Ansary, *Marketing Channels*, 296.

37. Robert F. Weigand and Hilda C. Wasson, "Arbitration in the Marketing Channel," *Business Horizons* (October 1974): 39–47.

38. Weigand and Wasson, "Arbitration," 39.

39. Weigand and Wasson, 39.

40. For a discussion of how members' satisfaction is related to the channel's climate see Patrick L. Schul, Taylor E. Little, Jr., and William M. Pride, "Channel Climate: Its Impact on Channel Satisfaction," *Journal of Retailing* (Summer 1985): 9–38.

4 Chapter

Understanding the Retail Customer

OVERVIEW

The purpose of this chapter is to examine the effects of the socioeconomic environment and the buying behavior of the individual consumer on the retailing sector of the economy. The chapter discusses the effects of recent demographic, economic, and psychographic changes on retail behavior and focuses on the individual retail purchasing decision process. A retail patronage model is developed to explain how consumers make retail patronage decisions.

CHAPTER 4
Understanding
the Retail
Customer

2. Never Marrieds
3. Divorce
4. Unrelated Two-Person Households

D. Economic Trends
1. Income Growth
2. Current Buying Patterns
3. Personal Savings
4. Employed Women
5. Affluent Superclass

II. Economic Factors
A. Gross National Product
B. Interest Rates
C. Economic Turbulence
D. National Debt
E. Unemployment

III. Psychographic Trends
A. Turning from Casualness Back to Neatness
B. Male/Female Role Flexibility
C. Deterioration of Institutional Confidence
D. Management of Time vs. Money
E. A Movement Toward Inner-Directedness

IV. A Retail Patronage Model

V. Problem Recognition
A. Arousing Problem Recognition
B. Ideal State
C. Actual State
D. Retailer-Induced Problem Recognition
E. Types of Problem Recognition

VI. Store Choice
A. Shopping Alternatives
B. Four Situations
C. Information Search
D. Shopping Orientations
E. Evaluative Criteria
F. Attitude Formation
G. An Example
H. Situational Factors
I. Retailer Implications

VII. The Store Visit Process
A. Evaluative Criteria
B. In-Store Effects
1. Point of Purchase Advertising (POP)
2. Store Personnel
3. Atmospherics
4. Merchandise Inspection
D. Closure
E. Outcome

In Chapter 3, the role of retailing in the marketing system was discussed with special emphasis on the role of the retailer in the marketing channel. In this chapter, we will show that the retailer's performance within the marketing channel is heavily influenced by the socioeconomic environment and the behavior of consumers. (See the retail planning and management model in Chapter 2.) The chapter begins with a discussion of the demographic, economic, and psychographic factors influencing consumer behavior. Then we present a model of retail patronage to describe the various factors in a retail purchase decision. Finally, we will look at how this patronage model can be adapted for nonstore purchasing behavior.

DEMOGRAPHIC TRENDS

The four components of demographic trends are population trends, geographic shifts, social trends, and economic trends.

POPULATION TRENDS

Population Growth.   Retailers have long viewed an expanding population base as synonymous with growth in retail markets. Unfortunately, this natural growth in markets has been declining during the past three decades as families have fewer children. Exhibit 4.1 shows the birth rate per thousand from 1960 to 1986. Experts disagree as to the trend of this birth rate over the next century.[1] The current projections range from a fertility rate (lifetime births per woman) of 2.3 to 1.6, with a median of 2.0. From an historical viewpoint, the United States fertility rate has never been as low as its current level. Between 1924 and 1933, the fertility rate declined from 3.1 to 2.2, where it remained throughout the 1930s. During the 1940s and 1950s, the baby boom era, it increased to 3.6. Throughout the 1960s and 1970s, the fertility rate declined steadily to a low of 1.7 in 1976. Since then it has remained around 1.8. The Census Bureau estimates that it will increase to an average of 1.9 over the next four decades. By comparison, the rate for Western Europe ranged from a high of 3.2 in Ireland to a low of 1.4 in West Germany and Denmark, with only four other countries having a rate higher than the United States.[2]

Two other important influences on population growth are life expectancy and net immigration totals. When people live longer, the population base gets larger, and Americans have been living longer. In 1970 the average life expectancies for a male and female at birth were 67.1 and 74.9

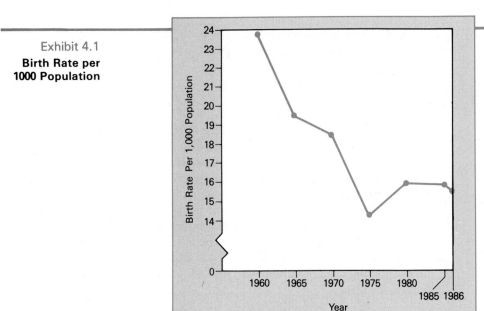

Exhibit 4.1

**Birth Rate per
1000 Population**

SOURCE: U.S. Bureau of the Census, *Statistical Abstract of the United States* (Washington, D.C.: U.S. Government Printing Office, 1988), Table #81.

years respectively. By 2000 these figures are projected to increase to 73.9 and 80.8 years. Since immigration laws are under the control of Congress, they are difficult to project. Estimates on future net immigration range from 250,000 to 750,000 annually, with a median projection of 500,000 annually.[3]

Exhibit 4.2 shows the expected population for the United States in future years assuming projected changes in life expectancy and net immigrations. Each column reflects a different fertility rate.

It is interesting to look further down the road, to just past the year 2020. If the median fertility, immigration, and death rate projections are correct, the United States could begin to experience zero or negative population growth. A decline in population will mean decreased demand for goods and services domestically. The key to retail success is shifting from new store openings and expansion to strategies built upon market-share dominance and margin management.

Retail analysts must pay close attention to fertility rates, life expectancy levels, and net immigration totals in their long-range forecasting of market potential. This is especially true of retailers catering specifically to young children or the elderly.

Age Distribution.   Various segments of the retail industry tend to serve different age groups in society. For example, adults over 55 purchase four

Exhibit 4.2

**Total Population
Projections,
1990–2060
(Thousands)**

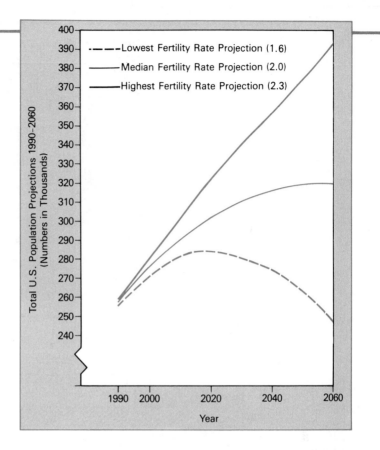

SOURCE: *Social Security Area Population Projections: 1987*
(Washington : U.S. Department of Health and Human Services, August 1987),
Table 20.

times as much as other consumers at drug stores. Furniture, appliance, and home-center retailers obtain most of their patrons from the 25–45 age segment. Record retailers appeal mostly to the 12–25 year-old market, while children's apparel retailers are aimed at the pre-teenage market.

The retailer must examine not only total population figures but age distribution. Exhibit 4.3 gives the Census Bureau's age distribution projections through 2020 using median fertility, death, and immigration rates. We see that the age groups that are projected to experience the largest percentage gains are those over 65, while teenagers and younger children are projected to remain relatively stable. Retailers catering to this over-65 segment have the potential for significant growth during the 1990s and the twenty-first century, while those serving the children's market will probably experience an unfavorable environment, unless they are able to adjust their product offerings to cater to all age groups, as Toys 'R' Us has done. Retailing in Action 4-1 provides a glimpse of how

Illus. 4.1
**An example of
age distribution.
Record retailers
appeal mostly
to the 12-to-25-
year-old market.**

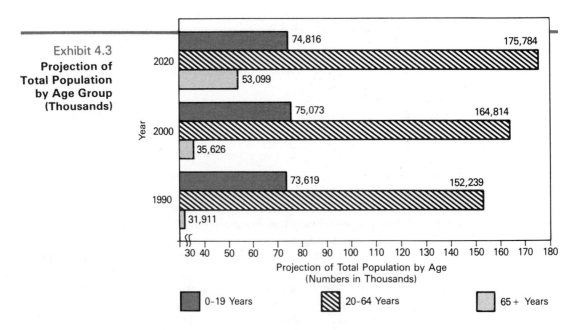

Exhibit 4.3
**Projection of
Total Population
by Age Group
(Thousands)**

Year

2020   0-19: 74,816   20-64: 175,784   65+: 53,099

2000   0-19: 75,073   20-64: 164,814   65+: 35,626

1990   0-19: 73,619   20-64: 152,239   65+: 31,911

Projection of Total Population by Age
(Numbers in Thousands)

0-19 Years   20-64 Years   65 + Years

SOURCE: *Social Security Area Population Projections: 1987*
(Washington: U.S. Department of Health and Human Services, August 1987),
Table 20.

RETAILING
IN
ACTION

4-1

How Retailers Can Make Shopping Easier for the Elderly

Several studies have been conducted to help retailers better meet the needs of older consumers. Generally these recommendations fall into three broad classifications:

• Make them feel important
• Make shopping more interesting for them
• Help them obtain a good value for their money

Specific recommendations include the following:

1. Offer senior citizens special attention with promotions like "Senior Discount Days."
2. Have special "Savings for Seniors" sales that go beyond senior citizen discount days and feature products for older people. However, do not make it appear that these specials are necessary because of the financial limitations of seniors.
3. Have someone available to help older shoppers find items in the store. Seniors prefer to have special products such as low- or no-salt, sugar, and caffeine items grouped together and not stocked with regular products.
4. Train all employees to understand older citizens better, including their need for clear explanations and reassurance. Train clerks to speak clearly and not mumble.
5. Employ an older person on every shift to help other older people.
6. Pay special attention to rest areas and restroom needs when developing your floor plan. Older customers require a place to sit and rest when shopping.
7. Provide older people with the facilities to be able to order merchandise by telephone or mail.
8. Use large print when putting signs in the store. Use bright lights to enable the elderly to see clearly.
9. Do not constantly move products to new locations; this causes more confusion for the elderly.

Source: Based on James R. Lumpkin, Barnett A. Greenberg, and Jac L. Goldstucker, "Marketplace Needs of the Elderly: Determinant Attributes and Store Choice," *Journal of Retailing* (Summer 1985): 75–105; "Aging Americans Give Marketing Advice," *Chain Store Age Executive* (August, 1988): 80; and Myron Gable, Lynn Harris, Susan Stone Sipkoff, and Martin Topol, "Shelf Space Strategy For No- Or Low- Salt and Sugar Products," Presentation for ACRA Meeting, Atlanta, GA, April, 1986.

retailers catering to the elderly are responding to the special shopping needs of this market.

In 1984 Americans over 65 outnumbered teenagers for the first time in history. This "graying of America" will have enormous consequences for business in general, not just retailing. Besides the increase in health-care services, restaurants (where the over-60 category accounts for more than 30 percent of the breakfast and dinner trade) will have to consider such items as the design of their tables and seats; financial service firms will have to reconsider their product offerings to this fixed-income category of consumers; and retailers in general will have to rethink the way they portray and target senior citizens in their advertising. The elderly have been shown to resist change in general and technological change in particular. It is extremely important for the retailer to consider the effects of any technological adoption upon this target market, since senior citizens have been found to reject some retailing innovations (automatic teller machines) while readily adopting others (grocery scanners).[4]

Another fact for the retailer to note is that nearly 30 percent of those in the 50 to 70 age group have no mortgage payments. They are an ideal market for travel and other fun retailing experiences.

Over the next decade the baby boomers are going to move from one age group to another. During the 1990s, they will advance to the 40- to 50-year-old group. Retailers should be aware that consumers over 40 tend to focus on their families and finances more than other age groups, creating high sales potentials for firms serving these needs. This age group also consumes more reading material than any other group. Bookstores should do well this decade.

In 1986, the United States was fourth in percentage of population over 65, with 12.1 percent. First was Sweden at 17.9 percent, followed by Britain with 15.1 percent, and France with 13.1 percent. Japan was fifth with 10.9 percent.[5]

GEOGRAPHIC SHIFTS

Shifting Population Centers.   Retailers should be concerned not only with numbers of people and their ages but also where they reside. Consumers, as we will point out in Chapter 7, will not travel great distances to make retail purchases. Consumers want convenience and will, therefore, patronize local retail outlets, even though the local outlet may be part of a national chain. Because the United States population for the past 200 years has been moving west and south, growth opportunities in retailing should be greatest in these areas.

Exhibit 4.4 shows the changing population center of the United States population. In 1790, the year the first census was taken, the population center of the nation was 23 miles east of Baltimore, Maryland. By 1900, it had moved to 6 miles southeast of Columbus, Indiana. In 1980, it was one-quarter mile west of DeSoto, Missouri, 40 miles southwest of St. Louis.

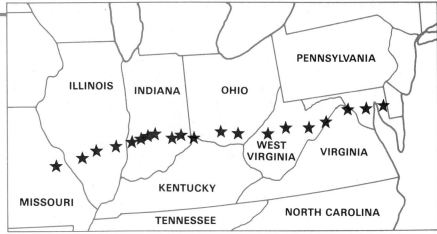

SOURCE: U.S. Bureau of the Census, *Statistical Abstract of the United States* (Washington, D.C.: U.S. Government Printing Office, 1988), p. 9.

In Exhibit 4.5, we see how the four geographic areas of the country grew, in percentage of total United States population, between 1960 and 1986, and projected shifts to the year 2000. These figures show that between 1960 and 1986, the South and West grew and the other two regions declined in population percentages. Demographers contend that this trend will continue throughout this century. This geographic shift meant midwestern retailers experienced slower growth and national retailers began adding distribution centers in the South and West.[6]

Urban Centers.   Most of the population of this country resides in metropolitan areas with populations greater than 50,000, which the Census Bureau calls **metropolitan statistical areas (MSAs).** The proportion of the population residing in these cities has increased dramatically, from 56.1 percent in 1950 to 76.6 percent in 1986.[7]

This migration to MSAs is not toward the central city but toward its suburbs. Several reasons have been advanced to explain this population shift. First, the baby boomers demonstrate a desire to move out of inner-cities and apartments to raise their children in an environment of backyards, good schools, and safe streets. Second, the economy of the 1980s was good, enabling the financing of this move. Third, society moved from a manufacturing-based economy, which attracted people to the central cities, to a white-collar service- and information-based economy located in the suburbs. This new economy is not dependent on the inner-city infrastructure of railroad tracks and utilities. Finally, the suburbs have become more than bedroom communities—they are now independent, self-supporting trade areas with their own jobs, retail districts, schools, entertainment, and employment bases.[8] While this has resulted in a de-

Exhibit 4.5
Percent of United States Resident Population by Region

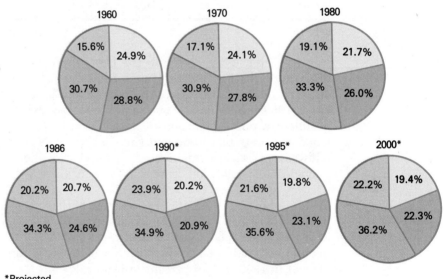

Percent of U.S. Resident Population by Region

1960

15.6% 24.9%
30.7% 28.8%

1970

17.1% 24.1%
30.9% 27.8%

1980

19.1% 21.7%
33.3% 26.0%

1986

20.2% 20.7%
34.3% 24.6%

1990*

23.9% 20.2%
34.9% 20.9%

1995*

21.6% 19.8%
35.6% 23.1%

2000*

22.2% 19.4%
36.2% 22.3%

*Projected

SOURCE: U.S. Bureau of the Census, *Statistical Abstract of the United States* (Washington, D.C.: U.S. Government Printing Office, 1988), Table 23.

cline in downtown retail sales, sales increases in large regional malls have more than made up for any decline. Retail analysts have cited this as a major factor to the merger mania in the supermarket industry during the late 1980s. Suburban location attracted American Stores to acquire Lucky Stores and A & P to acquire Shopwell, Food Emporium, and Wald-baum's Supermarkets.[9]

However, there are opportunities in the smaller markets. During the past decade, retailers have witnessed a rapid growth in secondary markets, those with a population of less than 50,000. Historically, most chain retailers have ignored these markets. But as MSAs began to stabilize and secondary markets continued to grow, retailers began to notice the success of retailers such as Ames Department Stores, Wal-Mart, and Family Dollar Stores in secondary markets.

Mobility.   In many countries, people are born, raised, marry, are widowed, and die in the same city or immediate geographic area. While this used to be true in the United States, it certainly is not true of contemporary America. Today's population is extremely mobile. For example, between 1985 and 1986, 3 percent of the United States population moved to another state, 3.7 percent moved to a different county in the same state, and 11.3 percent moved to a new house in the same county.[10] At this rate, the total population would relocate on average every decade.

This is important to retailers because they tend to serve local markets and cater to well-defined demographic groups. A retailer may find that its target market no longer resides in its trading area. Retailers in areas undergoing population growth want to be prepared to serve new consumers. After a move, consumers must locate new sources for food, clothing, household goods, and recreation. This presents an advantage for chain operations, in that a consumer moving from Des Moines to New Orleans knows what to expect at a Limited, Gap, Wal-Mart, K mart, or Pizza Hut.

SOCIAL TRENDS

Education.   The education level of the average American is increasing. In 1986, the median years of school completed was 12.6 for all individuals over the age of 25, compared with 10.6 years in 1960.[11] There is a close correlation between formal education and consumer expectations. Since education levels for the population are expected to continue to rise, retailers can expect consumers to become increasingly sophisticated and discriminating.

Never Marrieds.   A relatively new social phenomenon has occurred during the past quarter century. In 1970, only 9.4 percent of the United States male population between the ages of 30 and 34 had never married, and only 6.2 percent of the female population had never married. By 1986, these percentages had increased to 22.2 and 14.2 percent, respectively, and no change in these percentages is projected.[12] Married couples are one of the slowest growing household types. This trend presents many opportunities for the retailer, because the need for a large number of smaller houses complete with home furnishings will occur.

Exhibit 4.6

Marriage and Divorce Rates per 1000 Population

SOURCE: U.S. Bureau of the Census, *Statistical Abstract of the United States* (Washington, D.C.: U.S. Government Printing Office, 1988), Table 126.

Divorce. There has been a rapid increase in the divorce rate in the United States over the last several decades. Exhibit 4.6 shows the marriage and divorce rate per thousand since 1960. During this period, the divorce rate increased by 227 percent. Divorces are not happy events, but when a divorce occurs many retail purchases occur: a second household is formed almost immediately. These new households need furniture and kitchen appliances, televisions, stereos, and even linens. As a result of the increasing number of single and divorced people, the number of individuals living alone has increased from 10 million in 1970 to 21 million in 1986.[13]

Unrelated Two-Person Households. The number of primary individuals in the United States is expected to nearly double between 1970 and 1990. A **primary individual** is a household head living alone or with nonrelatives. Between 1980 and 1987, the number of unmarried couples ("mingles") increased by 18 percent.[14] This trend is significant to retailers because it represents a new kind of purchasing unit that is hard to understand by conventional household or family norms. The retailer, as well as the social scientist, has little understanding of how joint decision making occurs or does not occur in such households.

Today, the combination of mingles, singles, and "dinks" (Dual Income, No Kids households) accounts for more than 50 percent of all United States households. This market is not concerned about back-to-school sales or other traditional, family-oriented retail activities. This market is interested in CD players, high fashion, and gourmet foods.

ECONOMIC TRENDS

Income Growth.   People or households must have purchasing power to represent a market. Unfortunately, the trend in **real income growth**, income minus the effect of inflation, is not encouraging. Median household income in constant dollars declined every year between 1978 and 1982, and after some growth between 1983 and 1986, it was still 1 percent less than it was in 1978.[15] This decline in household income contributed to the success of discounters and manufacturers' outlets during the early 1980s.

Current Buying Patterns.   Each month the Bureau of Labor Statistics announces the Consumer Price Index (CPI) for the previous month. The CPI measures price changes in a fixed market basket. That is, it compares the current cost of purchasing a fixed set of goods and services with the cost of the same set last month, last year, etc. Keeping the market basket constant enables the CPI to measure price changes exclusive of purchasing pattern changes.

In 1987, the bureau revised its market basket to reflect consumers' current spending habits. Exhibit 4.7 compares the distribution of expenditures for urban wage earners for 1987 with the CPI developed in 1977. The shifts between product categories are relatively small when measured monthly or yearly. However, Exhibit 4.7 shows that over a longer period, these small shifts can develop into a pattern. Consider the percentage drops in food and housing categories. Rising income levels explain part of this shift. As discretionary income increases, consumers spend some of it on fancier food and better housing, but they spend a larger percentage of this increased income on apparel and medical care.

Another reason consumers might change the way they allocate their dollars is that price changes vary for different products. Consumers tend to cut back on buying items whose prices rise particularly fast. Even so, if the price increase is steep and consumers need the product, the product may command a larger share of the consumer's total expenditures. Such is the case with medical care today. Retail executives should be constantly aware of shifts in demand in order to identify changing consumer tastes.

Personal Savings.   A major criticism of this nation's economic system is that it does not reward personal savings. Changes in tax laws during the 1980s sought to rectify this. Increased savings would be used to finance capital growth in the economy. The average American consumer has been spending more and saving less in recent years. Americans spent 95.8 percent and saved only 4.2 percent of their personal disposable income in

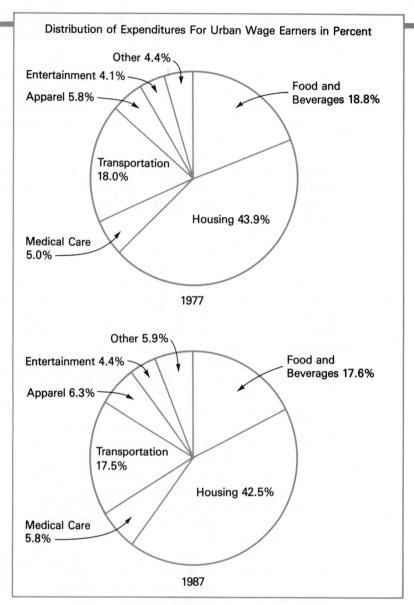

Exhibit 4.7
Distribution of Expenditures for Urban Wage Earners, Percentages

Distribution of Expenditures For Urban Wage Earners in Percent

Other 4.4%
Entertainment 4.1%
Apparel 5.8%
Food and Beverages 18.8%
Transportation 18.0%
Housing 43.9%
Medical Care 5.0%
1977

Other 5.9%
Entertainment 4.4%
Apparel 6.3%
Food and Beverages 17.6%
Transportation 17.5%
Housing 42.5%
Medical Care 5.8%
1987

SOURCES: *CPI Detailed Report,* (Washington: Bureau of Labor Statistics, June 1988) and *BLS Handbook of Methods, Vol. II, The CPI* (Washington: Bureau of Labor Statistics, April 1984).

1986, up from 92.2 percent in 1973.[16] Retailers enjoyed continued sales growth during this period, because even though median household income remained stable, spending percentages increased.

Employed Women.   Over the past 25 years, women have become a dominant factor in the labor force. In 1960, 37.7 percent of all women over 16 were in the labor force; by 1986, participation had increased to 55.3 percent.[17]

This trend is true of all age groups, even women 25 to 34, who would be expected to be raising families. In 1986, 71.6 percent of all women aged 25 to 34 were in the labor force, compared to only 36 percent in 1960. The percentage of married women with preschoolers in the labor force has increased from 45.3 to 56.9 percent between 1980 and 1987.[18]

This significant increase in the number of working wives has protected many households from inflation and recession. In 1987, the median earnings of married couples were $24,556 if the wife didn't work, but $36,431 if both spouses worked full time.[19]

The increase in the number of working women has many retail implications. Consider the following assumptions about working wives:

1.   Working wives are often unable to shop during regular retailing hours. Thus they might prefer sales and special events held in the evening.
2.   Working women place a premium on youthful appearance and maintenance of self.[20]
3.   Working wives might find that price is sometimes less important than convenience, availability, service, and time savings.

These assumptions might lead you to conclude that working women are more likely to be in-home shoppers. One study found this to be true for part-time working mothers of preschoolers, but not full-time working mothers of preschoolers.[21] Retailers should use strategies like direct mail, different store hours, and even baby-sitting services for their working female customers.

Affluent Superclass.   Recent trends toward being unmarried, getting married later, and having two spouses working have resulted in the growth of a new retail market, the **affluent superclass**—households with incomes of more than $50,000 annually. While they number only 5.4 percent of all United States households, they produce 17.2 percent of the nation's income. They are highly concentrated in the nation's largest cities, enabling retailers to reach this high income segment with a concentrated effort and a limited number of outlets.

ECONOMIC FACTORS

The previous discussion focused on how economic trends have influenced consumer behavior. It is also important to understand the broader economic environment which influences retail enterprises.

The economic environment in which retailers operate is complex. Few business people or government officials really understand the economic forces shaping society. Consider all the conflicting economic predictions you have heard during the past month. Our brief overview will not pretend to explain the complexities of this environment; rather, it will focus on five important factors that the retail executive should regularly monitor. They are: gross national product, interest rates, economic turbulence, national debt, and unemployment.

GROSS NATIONAL PRODUCT

The most important long range economic indicator for the economy is **gross national product** (GNP). **Gross national product** is the total value of all the goods and services produced in the United States during one year. Retailers want GNP to grow at a moderate and steady rate. Too-rapid growth in GNP will produce inflation (a decline in buying power due to prices rising faster than income), and too-slow growth or no growth will result in recession. GNP figures are very useful for projecting future national disposable income levels, which in turn can be used to project future sales figures. An ideal growth rate is between 3 and 5 percent annually. Between 1960 and 1988, the country's real GNP (real GNP discounts the effects of inflation) has grown at an annual rate of 3.6 percent. This growth rate was translated into a growth in retail sales.

INTEREST RATES

An **interest rate** is the price paid for the use of money. Consumers and retailers alike use other people's money to purchase merchandise. Consumers use credit cards or installment plans to purchase a large number of goods—especially durables such as household appliances, furniture, and automobiles. Retailers use bank credit to help finance their heavy investment in inventory. For example, the typical new car dealer with a modest inventory of 200 cars has to finance between $1 and $2 million in inventory investment. At an interest rate of 10 percent, the daily interest expense to carry this inventory would be over $500.

Because the interest rate is the price of money, and because the consumer needs this money to buy merchandise, the effective price of merchandise rises each time the interest rate rises. We know from basic economics that as the price of merchandise rises, the quantity demanded declines. Consider for example, a young couple considering purchasing three rooms of furniture at a cash price of $4,000. If the total purchase price is financed at 12 percent over 30 months, the monthly payments would be $155, which would work out to a deferred payment price of $4,670 ($155 times 30). If the interest rate is 18 percent, the monthly payments would be $165.96, which would equal a deferred price of $4,978.80 ($165.96 times 30). Thus, because the price of money (the interest rate) went up, the price of the furniture increased. Each time the interest rate rises, potential customers are eliminated from the market because they cannot afford the purchase. Just as rising rates slash the size of the market, declining rates expand it.

Retailers, likewise, must purchase merchandise on credit. Retailers typically buy merchandise with the idea of using the proceeds from the sale to pay for the purchase and store overhead expenses, and to make a profit. They need to be cognizant of interest rate fluctuations.

ECONOMIC TURBULENCE

The United States economy is beginning to be characterized by frequent swings in the business cycle. Economic turbulence has become one of the realities of retail planning. Today's consumers are confused—they don't know whether they should purchase an item today because its price might increase, or postpone the purchase in hopes of a price decrease. Because the economy is so volatile, consumers have become more pessimistic and conservative in their purchasing activities.

This makes the retailer's job more difficult. Does the retailer increase inventory in hopes of a good season or keep inventory stable? Since it takes time to order and receive merchandise (usually several weeks to months), the retailer can easily over- or under-commit inventory stock. For example, the city's economy may be booming in mid-July when a department store buyer orders for the Christmas season. However, what would happen if the city's leading manufacturer were to cut production by 50 percent and lay off 60 percent of the work force on October 19? This happened in Lubbock, Texas, when Texas Instruments laid off more than 2,000 employees and retailers were forced to cope with this economic bombshell in the middle of their Christmas season. The Christmas season normally accounts for 30 to 40 percent of annual department store sales.

NATIONAL DEBT

The national debt is a composite of the nation's annual budget deficit (when the government spends more than it receives) and negative balance of trade (when imports exceed exports). As the debt level increases, the Federal Reserve is forced to raise interest rates to fund this debt. As interest rates rise, the cost of money for retailers increases. Consumers, fearful of even higher rates, generally reduce their spending, thus reducing retail sales. This increase in interest rates especially affects retailers selling higher-priced durable goods, which are typically bought on credit.

UNEMPLOYMENT

In the past, unemployment data was rather simple to analyze. Retailers wanted to see unemployment rates decrease, because that meant more people had jobs, and these jobs produced income, and this income led to increased retail sales. When unemployment increases, consumer demand decreases.

When unemployment falls below 6 percent, many experts feel that the economy is nearing full employment. At full employment, a shortage in the supply of laborers forces wages up. Many fast food retailers in regions of the country with low unemployment recently began to experience this upward pressure, resulting in starting salaries for counter clerks of over $7 an hour. A similar employee in other geographic locations made only $4 an hour. The unemployment rate in the Northeast was only 3.9 percent at the end of 1987, while rates in the rest of the country ranged between 5.7 percent and 6.5 percent.

The unemployment issue is complicated by the fact that as unemployment falls and wages increase, the Federal Reserve may raise interest rates in an attempt to halt inflation.

PSYCHOGRAPHIC TRENDS

Changing demographic and economic factors are not sufficient to explain changing consumption patterns in the United States; an understanding of psychographics is also fundamental. **Psychographics**[22] is the examination of the activities, interests, and opinions of a meaningful segment of the population. Psychographics is commonly referred to as life-style analysis by retailers. Life-style can be defined as "the patterns in which people live and spend time and money."[23]

A discussion of psychographics can be phrased in terms of general or specific trends. One could profile the activities, interests, and opinions of the general populace about life in general, or, alternatively, one could profile the activities, interests, and opinions of a specific populace about a specific aspect of life. An example of the latter would be McDonald's using life-style positioning to achieve its market dominance.[24] McDonald's achieved this dominance by selling only one specialty product—hamburgers—when other fast food restaurants offered complete menus. Its menu appealed to young couples with children, who wanted to avoid long waits and the resulting opportunities to spill drinks, make messes, etc. Wendy's, on the other hand, sought to appeal to people without children. Wendy's avoided the McDonald's crowd—those with young children—by decorating with carpet and Tiffany lamps and by not providing a playground area. Additionally, Wendy's appealed to busy life-styles by having the first drive-through window and extensive buffet bars including salads and Italian and Mexican foods.

Several of the major changes in life-styles that have or will impact retailing in the remaining years of this century are outlined in the sections that follow.

TURNING FROM CASUALNESS BACK TO NEATNESS

During the Vietnam War era of the 1960s, people adopted an air of casualness. Students began to wear jeans to social functions, cars were replaced by pickup trucks, and neckties were replaced by open collars. The late 1980s saw a revival of neatness, as people began to dress up again and behave in a more formal manner. Some claim that this life-style is merely the result of the protestors of the 1960s and 70s reaching middle age. Apparel stores will have to reevaluate their merchandise mixes if this trend continues.

MALE/FEMALE ROLE FLEXIBILITY

The distinction between male and female roles in society is becoming blurred. Women are entering traditionally male jobs: bus drivers, telephone repair persons, police officers, and business executives. Some males are taking traditionally female jobs. The number of male nurses, telephone operators, and airline attendants are increasing dramatically. More men are deciding to stay home to take care of households as their wives become major breadwinners. With more men at home, supermarkets will have to direct promotions toward their needs.

DETERIORATION OF INSTITUTIONAL CONFIDENCE

Recently the American public has shown an increasing distrust of government and other institutions. Much of this distrust became overt after religious scandals and Irangate. Skepticism regarding business, religious, and educational institutions may be based on feelings that these institutions are more interested in satisfying their own goals than the public's wants and needs. Many old established retailers (e.g., Neiman-Marcus,

Illus. 4.2
Due to time-poverty, home television shopping and mail order sales are increasing.

Bloomingdale's, Carter Hawley Hale) no longer enjoy the customer loyalty they once had.

MANAGEMENT OF TIME VS. MONEY

Many households, especially multiple-income households, are becoming more concerned with the management of time versus money. Money management obviously cannot be ignored, but households frequently realize that it is time, not money, that determines whether they can participate in an activity. Many American households are experiencing a new phenomenon—"time poverty." Consumers who fit this description want to reduce the amount of time spent in retail stores. They don't want to wander around in search of a particular product. They have too many other things to do. In view of this, it is not surprising to find estimates that home television shopping will ring up sales of over $5 billion in 1992. Mail order sales are expected to exceed $70 billion.[25]

A MOVEMENT TOWARD INNER-DIRECTEDNESS

In what is considered the most advanced study of this nation's future lifestyle patterns, SRI developed its **Values and Lifestyle (VALS)** program. VALS is a systematic classification of American adults. It consists of four comprehensive groups, divided into nine life-styles, each defined by distinct values, drives, beliefs, needs, dreams, and points of view. The four comprehensive groups are need-driven (those people farthest removed from the cultural mainstream and living in extreme poverty); outer-directed (those people who represent the mainstream of society, buy with an eye towards appearance and gear their life to visible, tangible, materialistic goals); inner-directed (those self-reliant consumers who are indifferent to social status and money and seek only inner satisfaction); and outer- and inner-directed (those people who combine the qualities of the inner- and outer-directed groups).

The VALS typology represents a general view of life-style patterns. It is a basis for segmenting the entire consumer market. SRI forecasts that the number of people who are inner-directed will increase dramatically during the rest of this century. The inner-directed category will total 33 percent of total population by1995, as opposed to 20 percent in 1980. The outer-directed category will decline from 67 to 52 percent.[26] For the retailer this means that the mass market will be replaced by a number of new highly segmented inner-directed markets, each having individual tastes and not satisfied with emulating others. This life-style data indicates that there is more to consumer research than just demographic data. The retailer of the twenty-first century will need to know the consumer's life-style orientation. For an example of how a group of department stores used the VALS program to study their consumer, see Retailing in Action 4-2.

RETAILING IN ACTION 4-2

Los Angeles Newspaper Instrumental in Organizing Consumer Study

Five Los Angeles area department stores cooperated with the marketing research staff of the *Los Angeles Times* to use SRI International's VALS (Values and Lifestyles) program to learn more about their customers. A representative sample of 7,000 female customers was questioned about demographic characteristics, shopping patterns and preferences, values, attitudes, life-styles, and media utilization.

John Mount, director of marketing research for the *Times,* stated that "this was the first time department stores cooperated with the newspaper in such a major research undertaking". It also represented the first time that the VALS program, which was developed by Arnold Mitchell in the late 1970s, was used in a total retail setting.

The *Times* found the median household income of respondents was $27,165, the median age was 40, 62 percent of the respondents were married, 65 percent of this group had children, and 30 percent had professional jobs.

The study revealed that 67 percent of "very frequent" LA shoppers fell into the outer-directed category (the SRI national study found this percentage to be 69 percent), 32 percent were inner-directed (compared to the national average of twenty percent), and only 1 percent was needs-driven (11 percent in the national study). The large difference in the needs-driven group could be accounted for by the fact that metropolitan growth markets tend to be upscale.

An interesting sidelight to the study was the fact that outer directed frequent department store shoppers also tended to make frequent use of discount stores and direct mailers, while the inner-directed group also shopped specialty stores and off-price retailers.

As a result of this study, Mount added, the five retailers (The Broadway, Bullock's, May Company, J.C. Penney, and Robinson's) adjusted their inventories, redesigned their decor, alerted their sales staff to the types of consumers the store was attracting, and redeveloped their advertising strategy.

Source: Based on data supplied by John Mount, Marketing Research Department, *Los Angeles Times*. Reprinted with the permission of the *Los Angeles Times*.

A RETAIL PATRONAGE MODEL

Now that we have reviewed the demographic, economic, and life-style factors affecting the retail consumer's behavior, let's explore the consumer's behavior when undertaking a retail purchase. Before presenting the retail patronage model, we should recognize several important points. First, any model, by its very nature, is an abstraction (that is, the model is not the real thing; it is only a representation of reality). However, it should be relatively representative of reality. Second, this model is not proposed as a framework for serious empirical testing. Rather, it is intended to assist in a clearer understanding of the major factors involved in a retail purchase decision from the viewpoint of the consumer. Finally, the model presented depicts patronage behavior involving only in-store purchases, thus excluding nonstore retailing. The nonstore retail transaction will be discussed after the model is fully explained.

Now examine the patronage model in Exhibit 4.8. It is a process model, moving from left to right. The process begins when the consumer recognizes a need to shop: to buy, to obtain information, to socialize, or for other personal reasons. The consumer then evaluates shopping alternatives and selects a store or stores to visit. Each store as it is visited is continuously evaluated so the consumer can decide whether to stay in the store and shop or leave. The consumer will reach closure if the offerings in the store are favorably evaluated. Finally, we move to the outcome stage, in which the consumer either purchases, postpones purchase and does ad-

Exhibit 4.8   **A Retail Patronage Model**

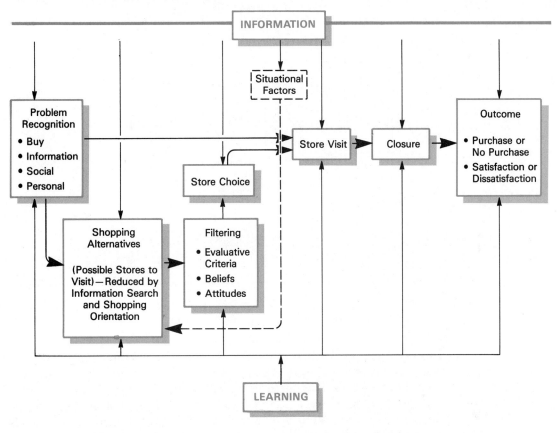

ditional searching, or decides not to buy. Consumers are continuously storing information for future use in shopping situations and, therefore, the model has a feedback loop. In addition, each stage of the model is affected by the information sources that continually bombard the consumer.

PROBLEM RECOGNITION

The first step in the retail patronage model is problem recognition. **Problem recognition** occurs when the consumer's ideal state of affairs departs sufficiently from the actual state of affairs to place the consumer in a state of unrest. In short, problem recognition occurs when consumers are disturbed enough by the difference between their actual and ideal state that they begin thinking of ways to resolve the difference. Exhibit 4.9 is a detailed illustration of the problem recognition stage.

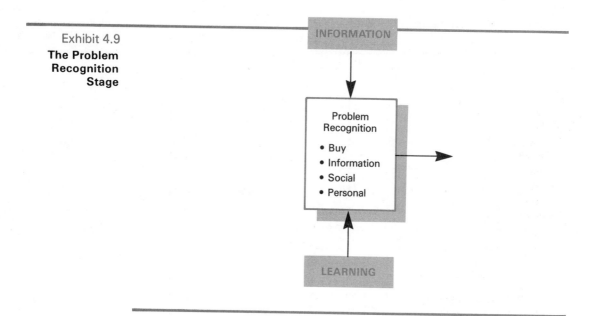

Exhibit 4.9
The Problem Recognition Stage

AROUSING PROBLEM RECOGNITION

Problem recognition can be aroused by either information sources or learning processes. Information sources may alert or remind the consumer of a discrepancy between the actual and ideal state. For example, the consumer may see an advertisement for a sleeper sofa on sale at a local department store. While seeing the advertisement, the consumer recalls that relatives will be visiting in the near future to spend a week. Almost instantly this person recognizes the problem of not having a place for the relatives to sleep.

Problem recognition may also be the direct outgrowth of learning processes. For example, the consumer may learn through experience that approximately every other day the household runs out of milk and bread. Thus, every other day (even without checking) the consumer recognizes the need to replenish these staples.

The last time you went shopping, how did you recognize the need to shop? Did an information source cause you to recognize the problem or did the problem recognition result from a psychological process such as learning?

IDEAL STATE

The **ideal state** is consumer or household specific. What may be the ideal for one consumer is not the ideal for another. The retailer must not use its ideal to gauge the consumer's ideal. For example, a TV retailer may believe that the ideal is a TV in each room of the house and that any house with fewer televisions has a problem the retailer can solve. This is clearly not realistic. The ideal is determined by a host of factors such as income, social class, reference group, age, educational level, and occupation, most of which the retailer has little or no control over.

ACTUAL STATE

The retailer cannot measure the consumer's actual state by casual observation. The consumer's **actual state** depends on how the consumer perceives it. An outsider may look at a family of eight in a small house and conclude that the actual state is undesirable. The household itself, however, may perceive the actual state quite differently. Retailers generally have little control over a household's actual state.

RETAILER-INDUCED PROBLEM RECOGNITION

Should the retailer try to stimulate problem recognition? To do so, the retailer would have to alter the consumer's actual or ideal state. However, as we have previously indicated, the retailer has little control over these states. Therefore, the retailer would, in most part, be wasting dollars by attempting to induce problem recognition.

The consumer is bombarded by thousands of messages daily and screens out most of them. The stimuli (information) that will be perceived are those which relate to problems he or she has already recognized. Consequently, retailers can better spend their dollars by focusing efforts on consumers who have already recognized the need to shop.

TYPES OF PROBLEM RECOGNITION

Up to this point, we have assumed that consumers shop because they recognize the need to buy a particular item. However, shopping behavior may be triggered by the recognition of needs other than buying. As shown in Exhibit 4.9, shopping behavior can be the outgrowth of four types of problem recognition: (1) recognition of the need to buy; (2) recognition of the need to gather information; (3) recognition of the need to socialize; and (4) recognition of other personal needs.

The first two needs are quite obvious and are the ones that most frequently come to mind when one thinks of shopping. That is, consumers frequently shop simply to buy the things for which they recognize a need. They may also shop to gather information. They may want information on which product is superior, or which retailer has the best price.

The second pair of needs, social and personal, have been elaborated upon by Edward Tauber.[27] These motives are only tangentially related to purchasing behavior. Rather, they use the shopping experience to satisfy other needs that have been recognized by the consumer.

According to Tauber, **social motives for shopping** include the following:[28]

1. Social experiences outside the home. The marketplace has traditionally been a center of social activity ... many parts of the United States still have market days, county fairs, and town squares that offer a time and place for social interaction. Contemporary equivalents exist in sidewalk sales, auctions, and swap meets. . . .

2. Communication with others having a similar interest. Many hobbies center around products or services, such as boating, collecting stamps, car customizing, and home decorating. Stores that offer hobby-related goods serve as a place for people with similar interests to interact. People like to talk with others about their interests, and sales personnel are frequently sought to provide special information concerning the activity.

3. Peer group attraction. The patronage of a store sometimes reflects a desire to be with one's peer group or a reference group to which one aspires. For instance, record stores are common hangouts for teenagers. This shopping attraction is not necessarily related to the motive of common interest since the gathering spot tends to change over time; in many cases the shopper may have limited interest in the product category and little intention to make a purchase. . . . Peer group success may, however, present a retailer with problems. Consider the situation where a middle-aged customer avoids a record store filled with teenagers.

4. Status and authority. Many shopping experiences provide the opportunity for an individual to command attention and respect. In few other activities can a person expect to be waited on without having to pay for this service. A person can attain a feeling of status and power in this limited master-servant relationship. . . .

5. Pleasure of bargaining. For many shoppers, bargaining is a degrading activity; haggling implies that one is cheap. Others, however, appear to enjoy the process, believing that with bargaining, goods can be reduced to a more reasonable price. . . . An individual prides himself in his ability to make wise purchases or obtain bargains.

Some of these social motives can be combined with buying and information motives. Shopping does not necessarily arise from any single motive.

Retailing in Action 4-3 identifies and describes a set of personal motives for shopping.

**RETAILING
IN
ACTION**

4-3

Personal Motives for Shopping

Edward Tauber has identified and described a set of six personal motives for shopping. These include:

1. Role playing. Many activities are learned behaviors, traditionally expected or accepted as part of a certain position or role in society—mother, house-wife, husband or student. . . .
2. Diversion. Shopping can offer an opportunity for diversion from the routine of daily life and thus represents a form of recreation. . . .
3. Self-gratification. Different emotional states or moods may be relevant for explaining why (and when) someone goes shopping. For example, a person may go to a store in search of diversion when he is bored or go in search of social contact when he feels lonely. Likewise, he may go to a store to buy "something nice" for himself when he is depressed. . . .
4. Learning about new trends. Products are intimately entwined in one's daily activities and often serve as symbols reflecting attitudes and life-styles. An individual learns about trends and movements and the symbols that support them when he visits a store. . . .
5. Physical activity. An urban environment characterized by mass transportation and freeway driving provides little opportunity for individuals to exercise at a leisurely pace. Shopping can provide people with a considerable amount of exercise. . . .
6. Sensory stimulation. Retail institutions provide many potential sensory benefits for shoppers. Customers browse through a store looking at the merchandise and at each other; they enjoy handling the merchandise and are either trying it on or trying it out. Sound can also be important, since a "noisy" environment creates a different image than one which is characterized by silence or soft background music. Even scent may be relevant; for instance, stores may possess a distinctive odor of perfume or of prepared food. . . .

Source: Reprinted with permission from Edward M. Tauber, "Marketing Notes and Communications—Why Do People Shop?" *Journal of Marketing* 36 (October 1972): 47–48, published by the American Marketing Association.

STORE CHOICE

Once consumers have established a need to shop, they proceed to an evaluation of the shopping alternatives, which will yield a set of store choices. These store choices will strongly influence the actual store visit. The store choice process portion of the model is presented in Exhibit 4.10.

SHOPPING ALTERNATIVES

After recognizing the need to shop, the consumer may consider shopping alternatives before deciding which store to visit. We are careful to state that the consumer *may* consider alternatives, because it is possible that the store choice will be based on habitual behavior. This is one reason that in Exhibit 4.10, learning processes are shown as influencing shopping alternatives. For example, if the consumer has learned from prior experience that when the household depletes its supply of milk, soda pop, bread, or other convenience goods, the best way to acquire these goods is to go to the local Circle K, 7-Eleven, Stop and Go, or another convenience food-store, then no shopping alternatives are considered. The consumer driven by habit patronizes the store that was traditionally patronized.

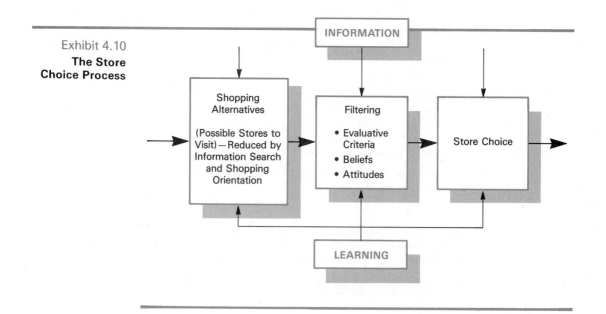

Exhibit 4.10
The Store Choice Process

FOUR SITUATIONS

If we assume that the consumer is shopping primarily to buy or obtain information, rather than to socialize or satisfy other personal needs, we can identify four basic situations that might confront the consumer at the shopping alternative stage of the model.

1. The consumer knows the exact product wanted and at which store to purchase the item. Using past experience, the consumer may have arrived at an adequate solution for many shopping problems. Items of relatively low value that are frequently purchased tend to belong in this category (toothpaste, milk, bread, soda pop). However, goods of higher value can also fall in this category. Some people, when they recognize a need to buy a new car, are both brand and store loyal. When confronted with a need to buy a new car, they may go directly to the local Lincoln-Mercury dealer and purchase a new Lincoln, because they have learned that this is an acceptable and satisfying method of problem solving.

2. The consumer recognizes a shopping problem and, from prior learning, knows which store to visit but does not know the specific product or brand that is desired. This situation may occur more often than you might expect. For example, a household has recognized the need to purchase a used automobile for their teenage daughter. They have come to trust a local used car dealer and decide to not consider any other dealers. However, they have not decided on the exact make of car to purchase and plan to follow the dealer's advice, since he has always treated them fairly.

3. The consumer may not have a store choice in mind but may have decided on the product and brand to purchase. Since the product and brand have been determined, the customer has restricted the evaluative process to those stores that carry the item. The consumer, however, may not have knowledge of all of the stores that carry the item and thus some searching may be required. For example, a household decides to purchase a new television set. Their old set was an RCA and it operated perfectly for 12 years. They have noticed several ads on TV for RCA sets, and they decide to buy a new RCA color, 25-inch console. The dealer they bought their old set from 12 years ago is no longer in business. Therefore, they start to watch the newspaper for appliance, furniture, and department stores that advertise RCA sets.

4. The consumer recognizes a shopping problem but has not decided on either the store or the product and brand. This situation requires the largest amount of information search and decision making. For example, one spouse has just received a promotion and a 25 percent salary increase. The couple, over the last year, has put

off purchasing several major durable goods that needed replacing—a car, living room furniture, and a washer and dryer. Even with the 25 percent raise, they cannot afford all of these items. More importantly, since they are young, they have little prior information and experience regarding various retailers in the city. Therefore, this couple must engage in extensive search for both products and retail outlets.

INFORMATION SEARCH

Shopping alternatives are influenced by learning processes and information sources. This basic relationship is illustrated in the store choice process model in Exhibit 4.10. The consumer can search for information either internally or externally. **Internal search** is the mental recall or review of what the consumer has learned from prior shopping behavior or prior processing of information (e.g., friends' comments about stores or advertisements for selected retailers). **External search** is the seeking of information from any source outside the individual. External search could include going to the yellow pages, calling a friend for advice, or looking through the morning newspaper for store advertisements.

The retailer can influence the shopping alternatives in the consumer's choice set several ways. Through past actions and interactions with the consumer, the retailer will in part influence what the consumer has learned. If the retailer has satisfied the consumer in the past, the consumer will remember; if the retailer dissatisfied the consumer in the past, the consumer will remember. For example, if the retailer has a high level of advertising, the consumer is more likely to recall the retailer in internal search activity. Likewise, the retailer can affect the set of shopping alternatives considered by manipulating retailer-controlled information sources. This involves the careful design of the retailer's current promotion activities. There are other ways that prior retailer actions influence the consumer's internal search. Try to think of some examples on your own.

SHOPPING ORIENTATIONS

Once the consumer has decided on a set of shopping alternatives, the next step is to evaluate each store in the set to decide which to visit first. Consumers possess different shopping orientations; and these orientations have a profound effect on the evaluative process.[29]

Gregory Stone identified **four major shopping orientations:** (1) economic, (2) personalizing, (3) ethical, and (4) apathetic. Quoting directly from Stone's research, each type can be profiled.[30]

1. *The economic consumer.* Here was the closest approximation to the "economic man" of the classical economist. This type of shopper expressed a sense of responsibility for her household purchasing duties: she was extremely sensitive to price, quality, and assortment of merchandise, all of which entered into the calculus of her behavior in the market. She was interested in shopping. Clerical personnel and the store were, for her, merely the instruments of her purchase of goods. Thus, efficiency or inefficiency of sales personnel, as well as the relative commensurateness of prices, quality, or the selection of merchandise, were decisive in leaving her with a pleasant or unpleasant impression of the store. The quality she demanded of a "good" clerk was efficiency.

2. *The personalized consumer.* This type of consumer shopped "where they know my name." It was important that she shop at "her" store rather than "public" stores. Strong personal attachments were formed with store personnel, and this personal relationship, often approaching intimacy, was crucial to her patronage of a store. She was highly sensitized to her experiences in the market; obviously they were an important part of her life. It followed that she was responsive to both pleasant and unpleasant experiences in the store. Her conception of a "good" clerk was one who treated her in a personal, relatively intimate manner. For an example of the importance of this shopping orientation see Retailing in Action 4-4.

3. *The ethical consumer.* This type of shopper shopped where she "ought to." She was willing to sacrifice lower prices or a wider selection of goods "to help the little guy out" or because "the chain store has no heart or soul." Consequently, strong attachments were sometimes formed with personnel and store owners or with "stores" in the abstract. These mediated the impressions she had of stores, left pleasant impressions in her memory, and forced unpleasant impressions out. Since store personnel did not enter in primarily as instrumentalities but rather with reference to other, more ultimate ends, she had no clear conception of a "good" clerk.

4. *The apathetic consumer.* This type of consumer shopped because she "had" to. Shopping for her was an onerous task. She shopped "to get it over with." Ideally, the criterion of convenient location was crucial to her selection of a store, as opposed to price, quality of goods, relationships with store personnel, or others. She was not interested in shopping and minimized her expenditure of effort in purchasing goods. Experiences in stores were not sufficiently important to leave any lasting impression on her. She knew few of the personnel and had no notion of a "good" clerk.

RETAILING
IN
ACTION

4-4

Failure to Understand Your Market Means "Failure"

In early 1987, J. Bildner & Sons was on its way to becoming a yuppie dynasty, with 19 upscale groceries in five cities and plans for 30 more. Eighteen months later, the company filed for protection under Chapter 11 of the Federal Bankruptcy Code.

What was the cause of this? Was Bildner a victim of overly ambitious expansion and an ill-conceived plan to sell groceries in department stores? Or was the failure caused by a downturn in the economy that should have been spotted by management? Let's go back to the beginning.

Bildner, founded in 1983, quickly achieved an important niche in the upscale areas of Boston and in smaller, upscale towns by following its mission statement: offer the full service of a grocery chain with the personalized service of a neighborhood deli or caterer, with special services such as delivery of Sunday brunch.

Three years later Bildner was in the middle of a major expansion into new markets. Bildner left its home base of Boston for expansion into New York, where its decision to build free-standing stores turned out to be too pricy and incurred long delays in construction, and into Chicago and Atlanta where it had agreements to operate the food section of leading department stores, imitating Harrod's food halls in London. Actual sales never reached expectations despite the lack of any major delays in start-up. These failed expansions resulted in a quick pullback and $4 million in costs related to cancelling leases.

In looking back, Bildner, which *Newsweek* once called "a yuppie's dream," felt it failed because its expansion plans were too ambitious, construction costs and delays exceeded budget, and the economy went sour. However, the problem was more simple. Bildner was not prepared for the loyalty that the citizens of these other cities had for their own well-entrenched institutions, such as upscale groceries Balducci's and Zabar. The attachments of these "personalized customers" to existing stores was too much for Bildner to overcome.

Source: Based on Stephen Dowdell, "Bildner's Experiment," *Supermarket News* (October 12, 1987): 8; William M. Bulkeley, "J. Bildner Files For Protection Under Chapter 11," *Wall Street Journal* (13 July 1988): 27; Alan Radding, "Bildner's backfire," *Advertising Age* (July 25, 1988): 425; and Buck Brown, "James Bildner's Spectacular Rise and Fall," *Wall Street Journal* (24 October 1988): B1.

EVALUATIVE CRITERIA

Shopping alternatives are assessed by the consumer on a set of evaluative criteria. **Evaluative criteria** are typically expressed in the form of the attributes or specifications used to compare various alternatives. The evaluative criteria we are concerned with here are **store attributes.**

Three things should be recognized about evaluative criteria. First, the attributes of a store are both objective and subjective. Take, for example, the physical attributes of a store. The size of the store can be objectively measured, but the effect of the store layout (also a physical attribute) on how comfortable the consumer feels while shopping in the store rests solely in the mind of the consumer and thus is subjective. Second, the number of evaluative criteria that most individuals can mentally handle when evaluating alternatives is between six and nine.[31] Third, an individual's evaluative criteria are shaped by shopping orientations and learning processes.

Several studies have been conducted on the attributes that consumers use to evaluate stores.[32] Eight of the most frequently used attributes are:

1. Price
2. Merchandise (including quality, style and fashion, assortment, national versus private labels)
3. Physical characteristics (including decor, layout, and floor space)
4. Sales promotions
5. Advertising
6. Convenience (including hours, location, ease of finding items, and parking)
7. Services (including credit, delivery, returns, and guarantees)
8. Store personnel (including helpfulness, friendliness, and courtesy)

This list of attributes is not exhaustive, and not all components of all attributes apply to all store types.[33] For example, when evaluating grocery stores, the style or fashion of merchandise is not relevant. In a cross-cultural study, Arnold, Oum, and Tigert found locational convenience and lower prices were clearly the most important attributes in choosing a retail grocer. They also found insignificant seasonal changes of these attributes in a single market, but significant changes in a single market over a seven year period, between markets and across cultures.[34]

ATTITUDE FORMATION

Exhibit 4.10 shows that the process of developing store choices is heavily influenced by the attitude formation process.

An attitude is a mental and neural state of readiness to respond, which is organized through experience and exerts a directive or dynamic influence on behavior.[35] Attitudes have traditionally been viewed as being

Illus. 4.3
Locational convenience and lower prices are the most important attributes in choosing a retail grocer.

comprised of three dimensions: cognitive, affective, and behavioral. The **cognitive dimension** refers to the understanding or perception of an attitude object. The **affective dimension** concerns the feelings of like or dislike towards an object. The **behavioral dimension** refers to the action tendencies toward the attitude object. In terms of store-related behavior, we can speak of a person's understanding or perception of a store, a person's like or dislike of a store, and a person's tendency to shop at a store. Communication theory suggests that people move through these same cognitive, affective, and behavioral stages in the purchase process.[36] However, there is disagreement regarding the order in which the stages occur.[37]

The basis of contemporary attitude models is as follows:

$BI \simeq A = f(E, B)$, where:
BI = behavioral intention toward an object
A = attitude toward an object
E = importance of evaluative criteria on which an object is evaluated
B = belief about the object based on various attributes or evaluative criteria

Think of the object as the store. Behavioral intentions are separate from attitude, and a favorable attitude does not necessarily lead to behavior, only to a behavioral intention. Precise definitions of the major items in the attitude model follow:

1. **Evaluative criteria:** Desired outcomes from choice or use of alternatives; expressed in the form of the attributes or specifications used to compare various alternatives.
2. **Beliefs:** Information that links a given alternative to a specified evaluative criterion, specifying the extent to which the alternative possesses the desired attribute.
3. **Attitude:** A learned predisposition to respond consistently in a favorable manner with respect to a given alternative (referred to earlier as the affective dimension).
4. **Behavioral Intention:** The subjective probability that beliefs and attitudes will be acted on.[38]

In Exhibit 4.10, the four components (evaluative criteria, beliefs, attitude, and store choice) lead up to the actual store visit. Fishbein and Rosenberg have both developed models for relating some or all of these components.[39] Market researchers have developed their own attitude models, frequently referred to as multi-attribute models. A useful multi-attribute model is the one developed by Talarzyk and Moinpour.[40] We will formulate their model in terms of an attitude toward a retail outlet.

$$A_b = \sum_{i=1}^{n} W_i B_{ib}$$

where:

A_b = attitude toward retail outlet b
W_i = weight or importance of store attribute i
B_{ib} = evaluative aspect or belief with respect to utility of alternative outlet b to satisfy attribute i
$\sum_{i=1}^{n}$ = number of attributes important in selection of a retail outlet.

This is a **compensatory model** because the strength in one attribute can offset a weakness in another.[41]

AN EXAMPLE

A consumer is evaluating three retail outlets to decide which one to visit. This consumer believes that for the type of shopping being undertaken, six evaluative criteria (store attributes) are relevant: (1) competitive prices, (2) convenient location, (3) helpful store personnel, (4) wide merchandise assortments, (5) attractive store decor, and (6) informative advertising. The weights (W_i) the consumer attaches to each of these attributes, on a scale of one to five, are presented in Exhibit 4.11. This consumer has evaluated three retail outlets and has formed beliefs about how each store performs on each of the respective attributes. The rating each store

Exhibit 4.11

A Consumer's Multi-attribute Evaluation of Three Retail Outlets

Attribute	Importance (W_i)[a]	Rating (B_{ib})[b]		
		Outlet A	Outlet B	Outlet C
Competitive prices	4	2	3	5
Convenient location	3	5	4	2
Helpful store personnel	4	3	3	4
Wide merchandise assortment	5	2	4	5
Attractive store decor	2	1	2	4
Informative advertising	2	4	3	4

[a]Scale values: (1) very low importance, (2) low importance, (3) average importance, (4) high importance, (5) very high importance

[b]Scale values: (1) strongly disagree, (2) disagree, (3) neutral, (4) agree, (5) strongly agree

received on each attribute by this consumer is also provided in Exhibit 4.11.

Using the formal multi-attribute model that we presented and the data presented in Exhibit 4.11, we can compute the attitude score (A_b) for this particular consumer for each of the three retail outlets. The appropriate computations are as follows:

Outlet A = $(4 \times 2) + (3 \times 5) + (4 \times 3) + (5 \times 2) + (2 \times 1) + (2 \times 4) = 55$
Outlet B = $(4 \times 3) + (3 \times 4) + (4 \times 3) + (5 \times 4) + (2 \times 2) + (2 \times 3) = 66$
Outlet C = $(4 \times 5) + (3 \times 2) + (4 \times 4) + (5 \times 5) + (2 \times 4) + (2 \times 4) = 83$

These computations lead us to expect that the consumer will most likely patronize retail Outlet C. The highest attitude score for Outlet C suggests that this outlet performs best (in the mind of the consumer) on the attributes the consumer believes to be of highest importance. A careful examination of the data in Exhibit 4.11 will validate this suggestion.

SITUATIONAL FACTORS

There is not always a perfect correlation between store choice, which results from attitude formation, and store patronage. Situational factors, such as hearing an ad for a competitor's store while traveling to the intended retailer, will inevitably intervene between the time intentions are formed and shopping in the store begins. Situational factors are of three broad types: economic, social, and informational.

The consumer's economic status may change, which could trigger a change in problem recognition or evaluative criteria. Assume, for example, that the consumer is laid off. What was previously a problem (need to buy a new stereo) may no longer be perceived as a problem, or price may become a much more important criterion.

The consumer may also experience a change in the social environment. Most important in this regard is a change in reference-group orientation. Reference groups are of three major types: membership, aspirational, and dissociative. A **membership group** is one in which a person is a recognized member. An **aspirational group** is one to which a person does not currently belong but to which one aspires to be a member. **Dissociative groups** are those with which the individual does not want to be identified.

Reference groups provide a frame of reference for how individuals behave. Let us illustrate the concept in terms of our store patronage model. A college freshman, arriving on campus, decides that she needs to buy some new clothes. Her parents gave her a Penney's charge card to use while she is away at college. She intends to take the bus to the Penney's store downtown. That evening she goes to her first sorority rush. The next morning she runs across a few of the sorority girls she met the evening before and they are excited about the prospect of her becoming a sorority sister. They invite her to spend the afternoon with them shopping at a few campus dress and sportswear shops. Since she needs some new clothes, she decides to purchase them that afternoon at one of the campus shops that the girls think is a fabulous place to shop.

A final situational factor may be the receipt of new information. The new information could change the degree to which a problem is recognized, or one's attitude toward various stores. For example, the consumer is driving to the hardware store and hears an advertisement over the radio that Sears is having a sale on all carpentry tools and home decorating items. The consumer drives past the hardware store and travels the additional four miles to Sears. Another example: The consumer decides to buy a new stereo and has decided to spend Saturday afternoon visiting several local stereo dealers. On Friday afternoon, while sitting in the doctor's office, the consumer reads an article in *Popular Science* that states that within the next year there will be major improvements in stereo technology. The consumer decides to put off buying the stereo and keep the money in the bank.

RETAILER IMPLICATIONS

The store choice section (Exhibit 4.10) of the retail patronage model (Exhibit 4.8) has several managerial implications.

The attitude scores that were developed from the multi-attribute attitude model can be used to predict retail sales or market share. To do this, the retailer needs to develop an ongoing research program to gather data on consumer attitudes toward its store and competing stores.

The retail analyst who conducts a continuing attitude survey will want to examine at least two phenomena. First, the analyst will want to examine how the importance that consumers attach to various store attributes changes over time. This will reveal whether consumers are seeking different benefits over time or the benefits sought are longitudinally stable.[42] Next, the analyst will want to examine consumer beliefs regarding how each retailer performs on each of the attributes over time.

To illustrate this point, consider the data presented in Exhibit 4.12. These data show the attitude toward two retail outlets over three years, in terms of components of the multi-attribute attitude model. Consumers are increasingly seeking retail outlets that have more competitive prices and more convenient locations. The importance of helpful store personnel, wide merchandise assortments, attractive store decor, and informative advertising have remained relatively constant over the three-year period. However, we see that consumers believe that Retailer A's prices have become less competitive and that store personnel are not as helpful as previously. On the favorable side, consumers perceive an increase in the informativeness of Retailer A's advertising. Turning to Retailer B, we see that consumers believe that its prices have become more competitive and its personnel more helpful. On all other store attributes, the consumer perceives Retailer B as doing as well or slightly better than three years ago. In the eyes of the consumer, then, Retailer B is doing a better job in increasing its performance than Retailer A.

If one were to compute the composite attitude score for Retailer A and Retailer B over the three-year period (using the equation on page 141), it would be seen that consumers overall still have a more favorable attitude toward Retailer A. However, this situation is quickly changing. Ex-

Exhibit 4.12

Multi-attribute Ratings of Two Retail Outlets Over Three Years

Attribute	Importance (W_i)[a]			Retailer A Rating (B_{ib})[b]			Retailer B Rating (B_{ib})[b]		
	1988	1989	1990	1988	1989	1990	1988	1989	1990
Competitive prices	3.9	4.0	4.3	2.2	2.2	2.0	3.4	3.6	3.9
Convenient location	3.1	3.4	3.6	3.2	3.2	3.1	3.6	3.6	3.7
Helpful store personnel	4.0	4.0	4.0	4.2	4.2	4.0	2.9	3.0	3.3
Wide merchandise assortment	2.7	2.7	2.8	3.9	3.8	4.0	3.1	3.1	3.2
Attractive store decor	3.4	3.3	3.4	4.4	4.5	4.5	1.9	1.9	2.0
Informative advertising	3.7	3.6	3.8	2.7	2.9	3.1	2.4	2.4	2.5

[a]Scale values: (1) very low importance, (2) low importance, (3) average importance, (4) high importance, (5) very high importance
[b]Scale values: (1) strongly disagree, (2) disagree, (3) neutral, (4) agree, (5) strongly agree

hibit 4.13 dramatically reveals that Retailer A is quickly losing its favorable position. Since a change in attitude is a lead indicator of a change in sales or market share, we would predict that the market share of Retailer B will increase in the forthcoming year unless Retailer A is effective in reversing its decline in relative performance.

Another use of attitude data is fine-tuning retail strategy. It is clear that Retailer A needs to do something—but what? The retailer should do something that is important to the consumer and that will give it a unique competitive advantage. Retailer B stands out in terms of having competitive prices, and consumers are increasingly placing heavier emphasis on prices in their attitude formation. If Retailer A decided to offer more competitive prices, that would not create a differential competitive advantage. Retailer A would be better off trying to develop a stronger nonprice strategy, perhaps on the store personnel or advertising attributes. Take a moment to see if you could develop a nonprice strategy for Retailer A.

Finally, the retail analyst can use the multi-attribute data to perform segmentation. **Segmentation** is a procedure for breaking a heterogeneous market into more homogeneous groups. It will be discussed in more depth in Chapter 15. For now, all you need to recognize is that not all shoppers look for the same benefits from stores. Some consumers attach a very high weight to competitive prices, whereas other consumers attach low weight to competitive prices. In this regard, Exhibit 4.14 continues our

Exhibit 4.13

Ratio of Two Retailers' Composite Scores over Three Years

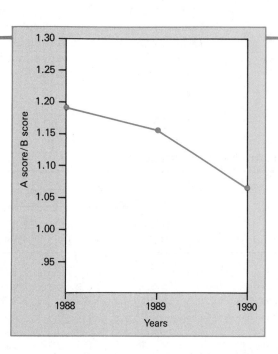

hypothetical example. Here Retailers A and B can see that there are five unique segments in terms of benefits being sought. This is not meant to imply that a consumer will be in the same profile segment for all products; rather, the consumer of the 1990s will probably be a situational shopper, switching from segment to segment depending on product and situation. In any case, the segments have the following profiles:

1. **Economic segment.** This segment represents 34 percent of the market and attaches highest importance to competitive prices, helpful store personnel, and informative advertising. These benefits help this shopper to make economically good purchase decisions.
2. **Elegant segment.** This segment represents 16 percent of the market and attaches highest importance to attractive store decor and helpful store personnel. These benefits help make this shopper feel elegant and important while shopping.
3. **Convenience segment.** Representing a substantial 26 percent of the market, this segment is more interested in convenient location and informative advertising. Both of these attributes help this consumer do his or her shopping chores quickly.
4. **Naive segment.** This segment comprises 14 percent of the market. This segment is "naive" because they expect everything from a store. They want competitive prices, convenient location, helpful personnel, relatively wide assortments, attractive store decor, and informative advertising. Thus, they are always complaining about stores, because no store performs well on all attributes.
5. **Other segment.** Representing 10 percent of the market, this segment includes people that cannot be categorized in any of the preceding segments. It is difficult to determine what motivates this segment.

Exhibit 4.14

Ratings of Store Attributes by Shopper Segments

	Ratings by Segment					
Attribute	Economic (34%)	Elegant (16%)	Convenience (26%)	Naive (14%)	Other (10%)	Total (100%)
Competitive prices	4.9	3.7	3.5	4.7	4.4	4.3
Convenient location	3.7	2.9	4.5	4.0	2.3	3.6
Helpful store personnel	4.1	4.7	3.5	4.2	3.3	4.0
Wide merchandise assortments	3.0	2.3	3.2	3.0	2.0	2.8
Attractive store decor	2.9	4.3	3.3	3.9	3.2	3.4
Informative advertising	4.1	3.1	3.8	4.0	3.7	3.8

With this additional information, which was derived from the multi-attribute data, Retailer A could fine-tune its retail strategy. In short, it could decide which segments(s) of the market it should attempt to attract. Where do you believe Retailer A should place its emphasis? What additional information might it need to make this decision?

THE STORE VISIT PROCESS

We are at the point in the store patronage model where the consumer has arrived at the store. The consumer has progressed through problem recognition, evaluation of shopping alternatives, shopping intentions, and is now at the store. Remember, however, that the store that consumers may find themselves in may not be the one that they intended to visit because of the possible intervention of situation factors. In Exhibit 4.15 we provide the store visit process model, which is a component of the store patronage model presented in Exhibit 4.8.

EVALUATIVE CRITERIA

The evaluative criteria mentioned in the store choice model are still covertly operating after shoppers enter a store. Specifically, consumers who enter a store and immediately realize it is not the type of store they expected, may directly turn around and leave the store. For example, the consumer may have expected the store to have friendly and helpful em-

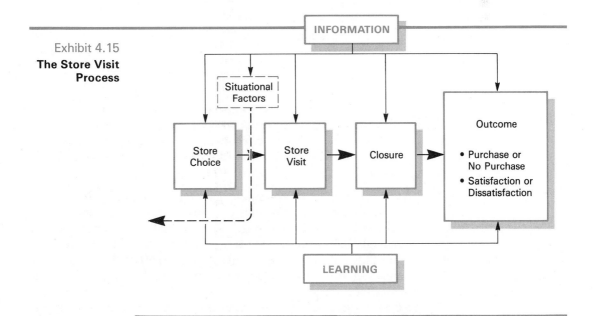

Exhibit 4.15
The Store Visit Process

ployees but on entering cannot find any sales assistance. What the consumers believe about the store must be reinforced during the visit or else they will change that attitude or behavior.

IN-STORE EFFECTS

Every consumer who enters the store is a better prospect than the consumer who does not enter. However, prospects are converted to consumers through in-store effects. In-store effects are of four major types.

Point of Purchase Advertising (POP). Any communication vehicle within the store is called point-of-purchase advertising, including signs, banners, special merchandise displays, counter signs, price cards, window signs, posters, elevator cards, flags, and similar devices that inform the consumer about the product or store offering. These promotion vehicles provide consumers with information that can be used in deciding whether the product fits their needs. POP ads can alert consumers about products they had not thought about purchasing on entering the store. Since many purchases are unplanned, point-of-purchase advertising can trigger a need in the consumer's mind.

Store Personnel. Personnel, especially sales personnel, are the second major in-store influence. Sales personnel can assist the consumer in finding merchandise and can answer questions about various products. Increasingly, retailers in the United States have become self-service; therefore, the role of sales personnel has declined. This trend, however, is not pervasive. For example, jewelry stores and automobile dealers still rely heavily on sales personnel to influence the in-store customer.

Atmospherics. Atmospherics is the conscious designing of space and its various dimensions to evoke certain effects in buyers. It concerns how consumers perceive the in-store environment and whether they are comfortable in it. Philip Kotler identifies four situations in which atmosphere will be an especially important in-store influence:[43]

1. "Atmospherics is a relevant marketing technique, primarily in situations where the product is purchased or consumed and where the seller has design options." For example, atmospherics are more likely to be important to a restaurant with table service than to one that only has a carry-out service. Also, manufacturers of consumer goods are less likely to be able to use atmospherics than are retailers.
2. "Atmospherics becomes an important marketing tool as the number of competitive outlets increases." Atmospherics is another

means by which one business can be differentiated from another. This kind of competitive action is more difficult for competitors to counter than price changes or assortment.

3. "Atmospherics is a more relevant marketing tool in industries where product and/or price differences are small." Savings and loan associations often seek differentiation through the use of atmospherics because regulatory requirements necessitate considerable similarity among them. Their efforts typically take shape through the skillful use of interior decor and related promotional strategy.

4. "Atmospherics is a more relevant marketing tool when product entries are aimed at distinct social classes or life-style buyer groups." The May Company basement, with its unique merchandising strategy, is likely to appeal to the working class. Its atmosphere must be consistent with bargain-basement retailing. This environment is in considerable contrast to other departments in the very same store that cater to an upper-middle class clientele.

Merchandise Inspection.   The final in-store influence is merchandise inspection. The consumer inspecting merchandise will be either favorably or unfavorably impressed. Much of this the retailer will have relatively little influence over—the package, label, information on label, etc. However, the retailer can control the extent to which the consumer is allowed to handle the merchandise. Although it is necessary to keep some items, like diamonds, under lock and key, extensive security measures discourage customers. Furniture stores with signs reading "do not sit on the furniture" or glassware shops that warn you not to touch discourage customers, and

Illus. 4.4
The ability to inspect merchandise is a very important in-store influencer.

these measures can cost more in lost sales than they save the retailer in merchandise. An appliance store needs floor samples that customers can see at work; not everything can be on a shelf in a box. The ability to inspect merchandise is a very important in-store influence. Recognizing this, Target Stores has a display model for each item in their housewares department.

CLOSURE

During the store visit the consumer should be brought to closure. **Closure** is the point where the evidence conclusively suggests that the product or service being offered should be bought. Closure needs to be differentiated from outcome: closure is deciding to buy; the actual buying (which sometimes may not follow closure) is outcome. Instrumental in obtaining closure is positive reinforcement from each of the in-store influences we have delineated.

Closure should not be forced on the consumer. If the retailer is concerned about long-run goodwill, the customer should not be pressured or persuaded to purchase a product or service that is not in his or her best interest. This is simply good retail ethics, on which high performance retailing must rest.

One of the most frequent causes of not obtaining closure is that the retailer is out of stock on the item the consumer is seeking to purchase.[44] However, even if the item is out of stock, closure may still occur, and the effect on the retailer may still be favorable.

There can be three possible effects of being out of a stock: favorable, unfavorable, or questionable.

Possible favorable effects are brand switching, switching attributes within brands, and product-class substitution. Assume a consumer goes to a store to buy two six-packs of Pepsi in twelve-ounce cans, and finds that this item is not in stock. The consumer could switch to another brand, perhaps Coke or R.C. Or, she could switch attributes; for example, she could buy twelve-ounce bottles rather than cans. Or, she could switch to another product class and decide to buy ice tea mix. In the short run, all of these effects are good for the retailer, because the consumer does reach closure in the store. However, if the retailer repeatedly is out of stock on items, the consumer will begin to patronize that store less often.

Item stockout could be unfavorable to the retailer in the short run. This could happen for two reasons. The consumer may, on finding the item out of stock, simply decide to shop at another store. Or, the consumer may terminate shopping altogether. The consumer may become frustrated and decide that it is no longer worth the time and effort to search for the item.

The effect on the retailer could be questionable if we know only in the long run whether the consequence was favorable or unfavorable. An example of a questionable effect is when consumers take a raincheck and postpone shopping. If consumers finally use the raincheck to purchase the item, or if they come back to the store at some later date, the consequence was favorable to the retailer. However, if the raincheck is not used, or customers resume shopping at a different store, the consequence is definitely unfavorable.

OUTCOME

The final step in the store-patronage process is called outcome. There are two basic outcomes: a purchase occurs or a purchase does not occur. Let us examine the latter category first.

If the consumer decided not to purchase, the consumer was disappointed with the retail outlet, the merchandise available at the outlet, or both. Many of you have experienced the situation of going to purchase something and being treated so poorly that you left the store in disgust. Other times, you may be treated well but simply not be satisfied with the merchandise that is available. For example, it may not look as good as it did on the television advertisement. There are also circumstances where the consumer is upset with both the retailer and the merchandise available. For example, the merchandise isn't what you want but the retail salesperson continues to pressure you to purchase the item. You leave in disgust and are not likely to forget this distasteful experience.

Consumers base future behavior on whether their shopping trips have been rewarding or punishing. If the visit to the retail outlet was rewarding, future visits will be more probable. The retailer needs to recognize that many consumers are very vocal about their pleasures and displeasures with retailers. Consumers who might not tell anyone about a pleasant shopping experience will not hesitate to tell their friends, acquaintances, and even strangers about unhappy experiences, thus creating unfavorable word-of-mouth advertising.

The logical alternative to the nonpurchase outcome is to enter into, and complete, a transaction with the retailer. It is hard for consumers to know, before making a purchase, whether they will be totally satisfied with that purchase after the transaction has taken place. The four possible states of post-purchase satisfaction are presented in Exhibit 4.16.

One possible state is that the patrons are satisfied with the product purchased and the retail outlet. This state is quite good for the retailer and the manufacturer of the product, since consumers' behaviors are strongly reinforced and future loyalty to the brand and retailer will be enhanced. But all of the other states involve some degree of dissonance in regard to the product, retail outlet, or both. **Dissonance** is post-choice doubt motivated by awareness that unchosen alternatives also have desirable attributes.[45]

A consumer who has just purchased a new Ford may be very satisfied with its performance, handling characteristics, and gasoline consumption. But after owning the car for a week, the consumer sees the same

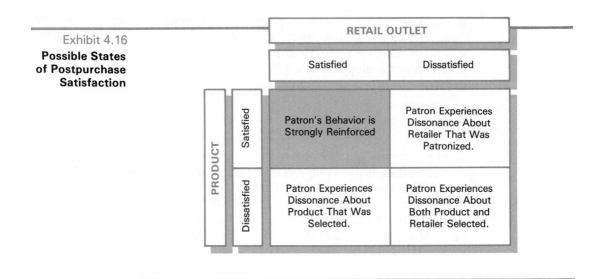

Exhibit 4.16
**Possible States
of Postpurchase
Satisfaction**

automobile advertised by another local dealer for $300 less. The consumer experiences dissonance because of not having shopped both Ford dealers.

How do consumers handle dissonance? There are two basic ways: the consumer can reassess the attractiveness of unchosen alternatives, or search for information to validate the choice made. For example, the consumer who bought the Ford may ask friends about the reputation of the dealer offering the lower price. The consumer may hear that this dealer offers very poor service and does not stand behind the factory warranty. The buyer rationalizes that the extra $300 was probably worth it in the long run since the patronized dealer is reputed to offer excellent service.

Or there may be a situation where the consumer is satisfied with the Ford dealer but is dissatisfied with the car itself. Shortly after the customer took delivery, the car developed a leak in the transmission. The dealer was very cooperative and immediately repaired the leaky transmission. One hundred miles later a rattle developed in the dashboard. Again the dealer was cooperative and found the source of the problem. The consumer, at this point, is experiencing a high level of dissonance regarding the purchase of the Ford, although very satisfied with the dealer's service and attitude.

A third situation could occur. Perhaps this customer discovers that the automobile could have been purchased at a lower price from another dealer that has a better reputation for service and fair treatment of the customer than the dealer who was patronized.

This discussion on post-purchase satisfaction demonstrates that the retailer's job is not finished just because a transaction has been completed. The consumer will naturally engage in post-purchase evaluation. If the result is satisfaction with the retailer, the retailer will occupy a favorable position in the consumer's mind. If the result is dissonance about the retailer and the dissonance cannot be adequately resolved, the retailer will occupy an unfavorable position in the consumer's mind. Since the consumer may attempt to reduce dissonance by gathering additional information, the retailer might find it useful to direct some of its promotional activity at those who already have purchased, attempting to assure them that they patronized the right retailer. This is especially true for retailers who sell major durable goods. For example, dissonance can be reduced substantially by the mere receipt of a letter from the salesperson who sold you your car urging you to not hesitate to stop by or call if you experience any problems or have any questions on how to care for your new car.

THE NONSTORE RETAIL PATRON

The preceding discussion of the retail patronage model focused exclusively on store retailers. However, the model is equally applicable to nonstore retail situations. Let us briefly examine several aspects of the model for nonstore retailers.

PROBLEM RECOGNITION

Nonstore retailers can play an important role in arousing problem recognition. For instance, the direct mail, door-to-door sales, television shopping networks, or party retailers get better exposure in the home than store retailers and, therefore, may have a better chance of creating problem recognition.

Nonstore retailers can also be an important source of information in the buying process. For example, consumers may consult catalogs to learn about price ranges and competitive offerings. Consumers can use personal computers to scan the offerings of national manufacturers through the use of services such as Comp-U-Shop.

SHOPPING ALTERNATIVES

When consumers evaluate shopping alternatives they may be favorably predisposed toward certain nonstore retailers because of their performance on certain attributes. For example, many nonstore retailers offer competitive prices, wide merchandise assortments, and the convenience of in-home shopping.

Also, the nonstore patron may have different shopping orientations than the patron of a store. The nonstore patron may view shopping as an onerous task to be done as quickly as possible. Thus, the consumer may prefer the nonstore alternative.

Finally, the consumer may be favorably predisposed toward a nonstore retailer because it offers well-known products.

STORE VISIT

The nonstore patron may not be able to visit stores or have no desire to visit stores. Possibly the patron is quite content with purchasing convenience goods, such as a cola and candy bar from a vending machine at school or by being able to purchase a specialty product, such as a Sears Craftsmen tool, from the QVC television shopping network. In these cases, the shopper has no need or desire to visit a retail store.

COMMENT

The retail patronage model is general enough to explain both store and nonstore patronage behavior. Take a moment to place yourself in a nonstore retailing situation and anticipate your behavior in terms of the retail patronage model.

SUMMARY

This chapter has concentrated on the major socioeconomic changes affecting consumer demand and on developing a model to explain and describe the behavior of consumers during a retail purchase decision. Rapid changes in the socioeconomic environment necessitate good management in the retail industry. Retailers need managers who can provide leadership—meeting the challenges of, and profiting from, the opportunities these changes present.

Chapter 4 began with a discussion of major demographic trends, including population growth, age distribution, geographic shifts, urban centers, mobility, education, never marrieds, divorce, unrelated two-person households, income growth, current buying patterns, level of personal savings, employment of women, and the affluent superclass. Next we examined the five economic factors that significantly influence both the retailer and the consumer: gross national product, interest rates, economic turbulence, national debt, and unemployment.

We concluded our examination of the socioeconomic environment with a look at life-style trends, including higher inflation, unemployment, a turning away from casualness, male/female role flexibility, a deterioration of institutional confidence, the management of time vs. money, and the movement toward inner-directedness.

Next, we presented a model to explain and describe the behavior of retail patrons. This systematic process model moved the consumer through problem recognition, to evaluating shopping alternatives, to the development of store choice intentions. Intentions, in turn, lead to a store visit. Situational factors which may prevent the consumer from behaving according to initial intentions were discussed. The consumer's continued evaluation process inside the store was also considered. We also looked at closure, resulting in either purchase or nonpurchase, and at purchase resulting in satisfaction or dissatisfaction toward the store, the product, or both. We concluded discussion of the model with an examination of ways to overcome dissonance resulting from the purchase.

Finally, we examined the adoption of our model for use in explaining and describing nonstore purchase decisions.

QUESTIONS
FOR
DISCUSSION

1. What demographic and economic trends occurring in the United States support the prediction that by 1992, $5 billion of retail sales will be made through television shopping networks?
2. Why is it more difficult for retailers to manage their enterprises in a roller-coaster economy?
3. In the chapter is an example of how two retailers selling the same product line sought to appeal to different life-style markets. Can you think of another example of life-style strategy?
4. How does a demographic trend, such as the increasing number of working wives, affect retailing?
5. What strategies should retailers develop in the face of slower population growth?
6. Develop a list of things an apparel retailer could do to increase the probability that, once consumers entered the store, they would not leave without making a purchase.
7. Discuss the interrelationships between demographic and psychographic trends. This may best be handled by using examples. Should retailers be more concerned with gathering data on demographic or psychographic trends?
8. Develop a scenario for retailing in 2000, assuming that real incomes between 1990 and 2000 do not rise and population growth is stagnant.
9. Obtain the most recent edition of the *Statistical Abstract of the United States*. Obtain current data for all the demographic and economic variables discussed in this chapter. Do you see any other data in the *Statistical Abstract* that may be useful to retailers?
10. Compare your life-style with that of your parents. How does the difference influence the stores you shop?
11. What are evaluative criteria? What criteria did you use when you purchased your last shirt?
12. Do consumers shop in a rational manner?
13. How much control does the retailer have over patronage behavior?

14. Discuss the concept of post-purchase dissonance. How can the retailer overcome it?
15. Using some recent research, a supermarket retailer has found that consumers evaluate supermarkets on five dimensions: (1) convenient location, (2)competitive prices, (3) attractive and clean store decor, (4) speed of check-out lines, and (5) wide merchandise assortment. This retailer also had research conducted on the components of the consumer's multi-attribute model. Interpret the following:

Attribute	Importance Weight[a]	Supermarket Rating[b]	Competition Rating[b]
Convenient location	8.3	9.1	7.8
Competitive prices	8.9	6.3	9.1
Attractive and clean store decor	6.2	7.1	6.8
Quick checkout lines	6.4	8.4	8.3
Wide merchandise assortment	5.9	6.3	8.1

[a]Values range from 1 to 10 with 1 denoting low importance and 10 denoting high importance.

[b]Values range from 1 to 10 with 1 representing strongly disagree and 10 representing strongly agree.

SUGGESTED READINGS

Bateson, J. E. G. "Self-Service Consumer: An Exploratory Study," *Journal of Retailing* (Fall 1985): 49–76.

Bearden, William O., Donald R. Lichtenstein, and Jesse E. Teel. "Comparison Price, Coupon, and Brand Effects on Consumer Reactions to Retail Newspaper Advertisements," *Journal of Retailing* (Summer 1984): 11–34.

Bernhardt, Kenneth L. "Consumer Problems and Complaint Actions of Older Americans: A National View," *Journal of Retailing* (Fall 1981): 107–123.

Bruner II, Gordon C. "Problem Recognition Styles and Search Patterns: An Empirical Investigation," *Journal of Retailing* (Fall 1986): 281–297.

Black, William C. "Choice-Set Definition in Patronage Modeling," *Journal of Retailing* (Summer 1984): 63–85.

Cobb, Cathy J. and Wayne D. Hoyer. "Planned Versus Impulse Purchase Behavior," *Journal of Retailing* (Winter 1986): 384–409.

Hyman, Michael R. "Long-Distance Geographic Mobility and Retailing Attitudes and Behaviors: An Update," *Journal of Retailing* (Summer 1987): 187–204.

Lumpkin, James R., Barnett A. Greenberg, and Jac L. Goldstucker. "Marketplace Needs of the Elderly: Determinant Attributes and Store Choice," *Journal of Marketing* (Summer 1985): 75–105.

ENDNOTES

1. "Another Baby Boom Seems Near, But Experts Disagree on Its Size," *Wall Street Journal*, 4 March 1982, p. 27 and "Birth Dearth: Some Thinkers Expect Population to Drop and Trouble to Result," *Wall Street Journal*, 18 June 1987, pp. 1, 20.

2. U.S. Department of Health and Human Services, *Social Security Area Population Projects: 1988* (Washington D.C.: U.S. Government Printing Office, June 1988), 5.

3. *Social Security Projections*, p. 18.

4. Valarie A. Zeithaml and Mary C. Gilly, "Characteristics Affecting the Acceptance of Retailing Technologies: A Comparison of Elderly and Nonelderly Consumers," *Journal of Retailing*, (Spring 1987): 49–68.

5. "Those 65 and Older," *Parade Magazine* (February 14, 1988): 10.

6. "New Sunbelt Migration Patterns," *American Demographics* (January 1987): 38–41.

7. U.S. Department of Commerce, *Statistical Abstract of the United States: 1988* (Washington D.C.: U.S. Government Printing Office, 1988), Table 33.

8. Joe Schwartz, "On the Road Again," *American Demographics*, (April 1987), pp. 38–42.

9. "Company Delivers Goods to Busy Grocery Shoppers," *Lubbock Avalanche-Journal*, 4 September 1988, p. 4-F.

10. Statistical Abstract, 1988, Table 24.

11. Statistical Abstract, 1988, Table 201.

12. Statistical Abstract, 1988, Table 49.

13. Statistical Abstract, 1988, Table 59.

14. Statistical Abstract, 1988, Table 56.

15. Statistical Abstract, 1988, Table 700.

16. "Baby Boomers Find It Hard to Save Money." *Wall Street Journal* (February 13, 1989): A1.

17. Statistical Abstract, 1988, Table 607.

18. Statistical Abstract, 1988, Table 625.

19. Statistical Abstract, 1988, Table 704.

20. William Lazer and John E. Smallwood, "The Changing Demographics of Women," *Journal of Marketing* (July 1977): 21–22.

21. Jean C. Darian, "In-Home Shopping: Are There Consumer Segments?," *Journal of Retailing* (Summer 1987): 163–186.

22. For a detailed discussion of the general use of psychographics in business, the reader is referred to Peter W. Bernstein, "Psychographics Still an Issue on Madison Avenue, *Fortune* (January 16, 1978): 78–84.

23. James F. Engel and Roger D. Blackwell, *Consumer Behavior*, 4th ed. (Chicago: The Dryden Press, 1982), 188.

24. This example is adapted from Roger D. Blackwell and W. Wayne Talarzyk, "Life-Style Retailing: Competitive Strategies for the 1980s," *Journal of Retailing* (Winter 1983): 10–11.

25. "Electronic Sales," *Chain Store Age-Executive* (August 1988): 15.

26. Arnold Mitchell, *The Nine American Lifestyles* (New York: MacMillan Publishing Co., 1983), 232.

27. Edward M. Tauber, "Marketing Notes and Communications—Why Do People Shop?" *Journal of Marketing* (October 1972): 47–48.

28. Reprinted with permission from Edward M. Tauber, "Marketing Notes and Communications—Why Do People Shop?" *Journal of Marketing* (October 1972): 47–48.

29. For an empirical study which demonstrates that consumers with different shopping orientations exhibit different preferences for sources of information, see George P. Moschis, "Shopping Orientations and Consumer Uses of Information," *Journal of Retailing* (Summer 1976): 61–70, 93.

30. Reprinted from Gregory P. Stone, "City Shoppers and Urban Identification: Observations on the Social Psychology of City Life," *American Journal of Sociology* (1954): 36–45, with permission of the University of Chicago Press.

31. Engel and Blackwell *Consumer Behavior*, p. 418 suggest six or fewer criteria are used. However, Fishbein suggests that as many as nine are used. Martin Fishbein, "Attitude, Attitude Change and Behavior: A Theoretical Overview," in Philip Levine (ed.), *Attitude Research Bridges the Atlantic* (Chicago: American Marketing Association, 1975), 3–16.

32. Many of these studies fall under the guise of store image studies. A review of more than 20 of these studies is provided in Douglas J. Lincoln and A. Coskun Samli, "Definitions, Dimensions, and Measurement of Store Image: A Literature Summary and Synthesis," in Robert S. Franz et al. (ed.) *Proceedings, Southern Marketing Association*, (Southern Marketing Association, 1979), 430–433.

33. For an approach to designing and analyzing complex multi-attribute consumer judgment and decision making in supermarket choices see Jordan J. Louviere and Gary J. Gaeth, "Decomposing the Determinants of Retail Facility Choice Using the Method of Hierarchical Information Integration: A Supermarket Illustration," *Journal of Retailing* (Spring 1987): 25–48.

34. Stephen J. Arnold, Tac H. Oum, and Douglas J. Tigert, "Determination Attributes in Retail Patronage: Seasonal, Temporal, Regional, and International Comparisons," *Journal of Marketing Research* (May 1983): 149–157.

35. G. Allport, "Attitudes," in C. Murchison, (ed.), *Handbook of Social Psychology* (Worcester, MA: Clark University Press, 1935), 798–884.

36. Philip Kotler, *Marketing Management: Analysis, Planning and Control*, 4th ed. (Englewood Cliffs, N.J.: Prentice-Hall, 1980), 474–475.

37. Michael L. Ray, *Marketing Communication and the Hierarchy-of-Effects* (Cambridge, MA: Marketing Science Institute, 1973).

38. Engel and Blackwell, *Consumer Behavior*, 445.

39. Martin Fishbein, "The Relationship Between Beliefs, Attitudes and Behavior," in Shel Feldman (ed.) *Cognitive Consistency* (New York: Academic Press, 1966), pp. 199–223; Milton J. Rosenberg, "Cognitive Structure and Attitudinal Effect," *Journal of Abnormal and Social Psychology* (1956): 367–72.

40. W. W. Talarzyk and Reza Moinpour, "Comparison of an Attitude Model and Coombsion Unfolding Analysis for the Prediction of Individual Brand Preference" (paper presented at the Workshop on Attitude Research and Consumer Behavior, University of Illinois, 1970).

41. A **noncompensatory model** is one in which a weakness on a given attribute cannot be offset by strength on another—if an attribute is rated too weak, the retailer outlet is eliminated from the choice set. Compensation models have received more attention in the literature and thus we will limit discussion to them.

42. Arnold, Oum and Tigert, "Determinant Attributes . . ." 154–156.

43. Philip Kotler, "Atmospherics as a Marketing Tool," *Journal of Retailing* (Winter 1973–74): 52–53. Reprinted with permission.

44. A model of consumer stock-out behavior can be found in Philip B. Schary and Martin Christopher, "The Anatomy of a Stock-Out," *Journal of Retailing* (Summer 1979): 59–70.

45. Engel and Blackwell, *Consumer Behavior*, p. 505.

5 Chapter

Competition in Retailing

The behavior of competitors is an important component of the retail planning and management model. Effective planning and management in a retail enterprise cannot be accomplished without the proper analysis of competitors. In this chapter, we will review five ways of categorizing retailers and develop a model of retail competition. We will then discuss the evolution of retail competition and look at the upcoming retail revolution—nonstore retailing. Finally, we will show that retail technology, both in new forms of retailing and in innovative equipment and fixtures, is continually changing competitive practices in retailing.

CHAPTER 5
Competition
in Retailing

So far in Part 2, we have discussed how retailing fits into the marketing channel and have looked at the consumer's behavior in the retail marketplace. We will now discuss how the retailer can become an effective competitor. A high-performance retailer must always be on the offensive and set the trend for others to follow. A retailer will have a substandard performance if it is forced to compromise or follow the path of others.

No retailer can design a strategy that will totally insulate it from the competitive actions of others. Merchandising innovations can easily be copied and cannot be patented. Furthermore, the relatively low entry barriers in retailing mean that the successful retailer can count on being copied by others when it unveils a profitable strategy. The rapid growth of fast-food restaurants, television shopping networks, discount department stores, and one-hour photo shops attest to that.

If you plan to become a retail executive, you must develop the talent for designing and implementing innovative competitive strategies. Furthermore, you need to recognize that in retailing, competition is a fact of life.

CATEGORIZING RETAILERS

Categorizing retailers can help you understand competition in retailing. There is no single, accepted method of classifying retail competitors, although many classification schemes have been proposed. The five most popular schemes are described in Exhibit 5.1.

CENSUS BUREAU

The United States Bureau of the Census, for purposes of conducting the census of retail trade, classifies all retailers using two-digit standard industrial classification (SIC) codes, shown below.

1. Building materials, hardware, garden supply, and mobile home dealers (SIC 52)
2. General merchandise group stores (SIC 53)
3. Food stores (SIC 54)
4. Automotive dealers and gasoline service stations (SIC 55)
5. Apparel and accessory stores (SIC 56)

Exhibit 5.1

Categorizing Retailers

Census Bureau	Number of Outlets	Margin/ Turnover	Location	Size
2-digit SIC code	Single unit	Low margin/ low turns	Traditional	By sales volume
3-digit SIC code	2–10 units		Central Business	
4-digit SIC code	11 + units	Low margin/ high turns	Districts	By number of employees
		High margin/ low turns	Shopping Centers	
			Free-standing	
		High margin/ high turns	Non-traditional	

6. Furniture, home furnishings, and equipment stores (SIC 57)
7. Eating and drinking places (SIC 58)
8. Miscellaneous retail stores (SIC 59)

Generally, these two-digit SIC codes are too broad to be of much use to the retail analyst.

The three-digit SIC codes provide much more information on the structure of retail competition. Exhibit 5.2 is a partial listing of the statistics on these codes. The average department store (SIC 531) has a sales volume of $5,698,576; the typical variety store (SIC 533) had annual sales of $550,496; and the average eating place (SIC 5812) had sales of $418,358.

In almost all instances, the SIC code reflects the type of merchandise the retailer sells. The major portion of a retailer's competition comes from other retailers in its SIC category. General merchandise stores (SIC 53) are the exception to this rule, especially department stores (SIC 531). General merchandise stores, due to the breadth of merchandise carried, compete with retailers in most other SIC categories. Likewise, most retailers must compete to a considerable extent with general merchandise stores, because those larger stores probably handle many of the same types of merchandise that smaller, more limited retailers sell. Of course, in a very broad sense, all retailers compete with each other since they are all vying for the same limited consumer dollars.

Exhibit 5.2

Scope of Retail Trade by Type of Store (1987)

SIC Code	Line of Trade	Number of Establishments	Sales (millions)	Sales per Establishment
553	Auto/home supply stores	111,747	$ 27,012	$ 241,725
562	Women's Ready-to-	42,495	31,171	733,522
563	wear, accessories,			
568	furs			
591	Drug and proprietary	52,463	56,000	1,067,419
	stores			
541	Grocery stores	174,073	296,105	1,701,039
531	Department stores	26,617	151,679	5,698,576
533	Variety stores	15,328	8,438	550,496
5812	Eating places	323,008	135,133	418,358

SOURCES: Establishment data from *Dun's Census of American Business 1988,* pp. 18–119; Sales data from the *Revised Monthly Retail Sales and Inventory, January 1978 through December 1987.*

NUMBER OF OUTLETS

Another method of classifying retailers is by the number of outlets each operates. Generally, retailers with several units are a stronger competitive threat because they can spread many fixed costs, such as advertising and top management salaries, over a larger volume of sales and can achieve economies in purchasing. However, single-unit retailers do have advantages. They are generally owner- and family-operated and tend to have harder working, more motivated employees. Also, they can focus all their efforts on one trade area and tailor their merchandise to that area.

Any retail organization that operates more than one unit is technically a chain, but this is really not a very practical definition. The Census Bureau breaks down chain stores into two size categories: two to ten stores and eleven or more.

Exhibit 5.3

The Importance of Large Chain Operations (11 or more units)

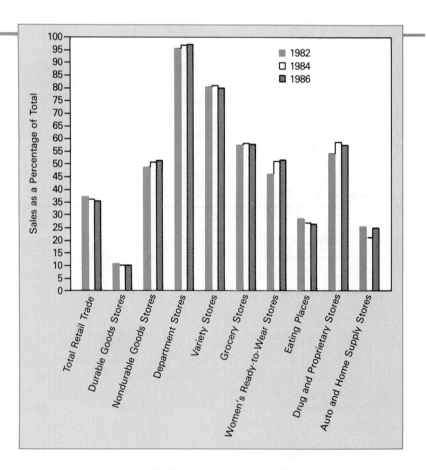

SOURCE: *Statistical Abstract of the U.S. 1988,* Table 1306.

Exhibit 5.3 shows sales by chain stores (eleven or more units) as a percentage of total United States sales for ten different merchandise lines. The statistics in this table reveal that chain-store retailing is significant and that nearly 36 percent of all retail sales are accounted for by large chain stores (including 97 percent of all department store sales and 58 percent of all grocery store sales). Though large chain operations account for over 50 percent of nondurable goods store sales, they only account for one in ten durable goods sales.

Not all chain operations enjoy the same advantages. Small chains are local in nature and may enjoy some economies in buying and in having the merchandise tailored to their market needs. Large chains are generally regional or national and can take full advantage of the economies of scale that centralized buying and a standard stock list can achieve. Other national chains, recognizing the variations of regional tastes, give each store the necessary flexibility to adjust merchandise to local demands. This flexibility, which is used by national retailers such as J. C. Penney, is called the optional stock list approach. Both merchandising methods provide scale advantages in other retailing activities; for example, promotion savings when more than one store operates in an area. Finally, chain stores have long been aware of the benefits of vertically integrating their channels of distribution, as discussed in Chapter 3.

In recent years, chains have relied on their high level of consumer recognition to engage in private labeling (using their own brand name) as part of their overall strategy. In some cases, the private brands of national chains have become preferred national brands; e.g., Sears Craftsman.

MARGINS VS. TURNOVER

Retailers can be classified according to their average gross margin percentage and rate of inventory turnover. The gross margin percentage shows how much gross profit (sales less cost of goods sold) the retailer makes as a percentage of sales. A 40 percent gross margin indicates that on each dollar of sales, the retailer generates 40 cents in gross profit dollars. Inventory turnover refers to the number of times per year, on average, that a retailer sells its inventory. Thus, an inventory turnover of 12 indicates that, on average, the retailer turns its inventory 12 times each year or once a month. An average inventory of $40,000 (retail) and annual sales of $240,000 mean the retailer turns over its inventory 6 times a year ($240,000 ÷ $40,000).

High-performance retailers have long recognized the relationship between gross margin, turnover, and gross profit. Gross profit (the amount of money a firm has left after paying for the merchandise) is gross margin per unit times units sold. As shown in Exhibit 5.4, retailers can be classified into four basic types using the concepts of margin and turnover.

Typically, a *low-margin/low-turnover* retailer will not be able to gener-

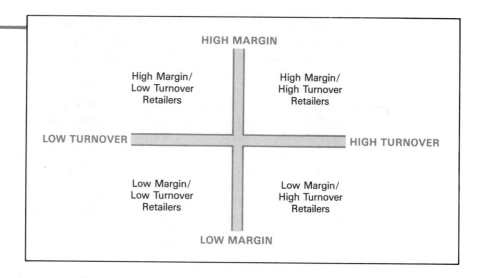

HIGH MARGIN

High Margin/
Low Turnover
Retailers

High Margin/
High Turnover
Retailers

LOW TURNOVER

HIGH TURNOVER

Low Margin/
Low Turnover
Retailers

Low Margin/
High Turnover
Retailers

LOW MARGIN

ate sufficient profits to remain competitive and survive. There are few good examples of this type of retailer. On the other hand, *low-margin/high turnover* retailers are common in the United States. Examples are discount department stores such as K mart and Target and full-line supermarkets such as Safeway, Kroger, or Food Giant. *High-margin/low-turnover* retailers are also common in the United States. Furniture stores, TV and appliance stores, jewelry stores, and hardware stores are examples of high-margin/low-turnover operations. Finally, some retailers find it possible to operate on both *high margins and high turnover.* As you might expect, this strategy can be very profitable. Convenience food stores such as 7-Eleven, Circle K, Stop N Go, or Quick Mart use this strategy.

Other types of retailers can also achieve high margin and high turnover status. An excellent example of this was when Dillard's Department

Illus. 5.1
Stop N Go is an example of a high-margin/high turnover retailer.

Stores acquired St. Louis-based Stix, Baer, & Fuller from Associated Dry Goods. Dillard's added more costly name-brand merchandise to appeal to affluent shoppers, doubled advertising, increased the sales force by 50 percent and installed a computer system to better manage inventory levels. The results were a high-performance gross margin and an improvement in turnover.

The low-margin/low-turnover retailer is the least able of the four to withstand a competitive attack because this retailer is barely profitable, and when competitive intensity increases, profits are driven even lower. On the other hand, the high-margin/high-turnover retailer is in an excellent position to withstand and counter competitive threats because profit margins enable it to finance competitive wars.

LOCATION

Retailers have long been classified according to their location within a metropolitan area, be it the central business district, a shopping center, or as a free-standing unit. These traditional locations will be discussed in greater detail in Chapter 8. However, the 1980s have witnessed a major change in retail locations. Retailers in this decade have become aware that opportunities to improve financial performances can be achieved by either improving the productivity of existing traditional stores or operating in nontraditional retail areas. The retail market growth of the past decade has slowed considerably in recent years. Retailers realize that most metropolitan areas have all the stores they can support. Therefore, rather than expand into unprofitable territories, retailers are renovating existing stores. Even when a retailer finds an ideal location for expansion, competitors are sure to follow. One retailer spent two years studying market conditions before deciding to open the first frozen yogurt store in Albuquerque, New Mexico. Within a year, four other yogurt stores were competing for his business on the northeast edge of town.

Other retailers are reaching out for nontraditional or alternative retail locations. Baskin-Robbins has ice cream shops on board U.S. Navy ships. Burger King is now on military bases as well as in Woolworth stores and Greyhound terminals, and even has twenty roving buses in Miami. McDonald's is in military bases, hospitals, museums, and schools.

SIZE

Many retail trade associations classify retailers by sales volume or number of employees. The reason for classifying by size is that the operating performance of retailers tends to vary according to size. For example, The American Floorcovering Association reports operating performance data by five sales volume categories (under $499,000; $500,000 to $999,999; $1 million to $1.9 million; $2 million to $4.9 million; and $5 million or more).

The National Retail Hardware Association classifies lumber and building materials stores into three categories by annual sales (under $500,000, $500,000 to $1 million, and over $1 million). The National Retail Merchants Association categorizes department stores into seven volume groups ($1-2 million; $2-5 million; $5-10 million; $10-20 million; $20-50 million; $50-100 million; and over $100 million). Other retail trade associations provide similar breakdowns. Generally, retailers should compare their results only against competitors of a similar size.

A MODEL OF RETAIL COMPETITION

Competition in retailing, as in any other industry, involves the interplay of supply and demand. One cannot appreciate the nature and scope of competition in retailing by studying only the supply factors, that is, the type and number of retailers that exist. One must also examine consumer demand factors. Let's examine a formal framework for describing and explaining competition in retailing.[1]

THE COMPETITIVE MARKETPLACE

When retailers compete for customers, they generally compete on a local level unless they are nonstore mail-order retailers. Retailers may compete nationally for financial capital, top executives, and college graduates, but for customers they compete locally. Why? Because households will not typically travel beyond local markets to purchase the goods they desire. When they do travel beyond local markets, it is usually because their city or town is too small to support retailers with the selection of merchandise they desire. But most cities of over 50,000 can provide the consumer with sufficient selection in almost all lines of merchandise. And in cities of less than 50,000, the household may need to travel to another town or city only for large purchases such as a new automobile, television, or furniture.

MARKET STRUCTURE

In terms of the four market structures economists use to describe competition (pure competition, monopolistic competition, oligopolistic competition, and pure monopoly*), retailing can be characterized as monopolistic

*Pure competition is a type of competitive market structure where there are no barriers to competition and where price cannot be controlled by individual buyers or sellers; monopolistic competition is a type of competitive market structure where there is a large number of sellers and where some product differentiation exists; oligopolistic competition is a type of competitive market structure where the industry is controlled by a few large producers; pure monopoly is a competitive market structure where there is only one producer.

or sometimes oligopolistic competition. As you may recall from microeconomics, the distinction between monopolistic competition and oligopoly lies in the number of sellers. An oligopoly means there are few sellers, so any action by one is noticed and reacted to by the others. Conventional economic thought suggests that for this to occur, the top four firms have to account for over 60 percent of the market. For retailing in the United States this does not occur on a national level and seldom occurs on a local level. Exhibit 5.5 shows that the market share of the four largest national food store chains is less than 20 percent and that of the four largest department store chains is less than 40 percent.

Obviously, retailing is much more concentrated within local markets than the preceding national statistics suggest. But seldom do the four

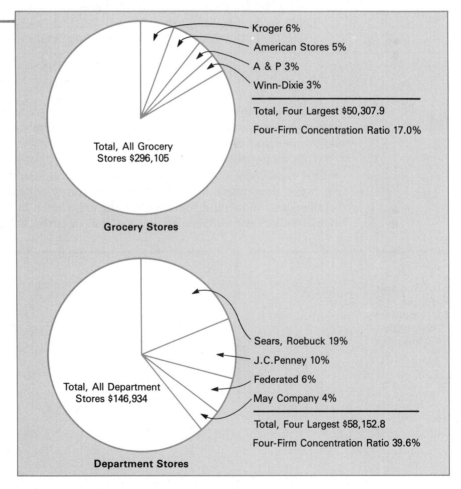

Exhibit 5.5
Total Sales of the Four Largest Firms in Two Retail Lines (Sales in Millions)

Kroger 6%
American Stores 5%
A & P 3%
Winn-Dixie 3%

Total, Four Largest $50,307.9
Four-Firm Concentration Ratio 17.0%

Total, All Grocery Stores $296,105

Grocery Stores

Sears, Roebuck 19%
J.C.Penney 10%
Federated 6%
May Company 4%

Total, Four Largest $58,152.8
Four-Firm Concentration Ratio 39.6%

Total, All Department Stores $146,934

Department Stores

SOURCE: *Chain Store Age Executive* (August 1988), pp. 17 & 18; *Revised Monthly Retail Sales and Inventories, January 1978 through December 1987,* Table 1.

leading retail firms in any trading area in the United States account for more than 60 percent of the market.

Leonard Weiss notes that even where retailing becomes concentrated at the local level, there are several checks on the retailers' power:

"The country is full of automobiles, so most customers have large numbers of alternatives. Moreover, many modern retailers are becoming less specialized. The supermarket that sells nylons and the drugstore where you cannot find the drug counter are famous. Any seller who tries to maintain high prices is apt to find the grocers or the gas stations or someone equally far removed trying to take over his profitable lines. At any rate, there seems to be a continuous supply of new shopkeepers, ready to appear whenever prospects are good, and often even when they are not. It takes a good deal more to break into such fields as food retailing than it once did, but the cost of entry is still much lower than in most concentrated segments of manufacturing."[2]

THE DEMAND SIDE OF RETAILING

Most retailers face monopolistic competition and we assume that market structure in our model, but our model would generally apply in oligopolistic competition as well.

In a monopolistically competitive market, the retailer is confronted with a negatively sloping demand curve. That is, as price is lowered the consumer demands a higher quantity. You may conclude that a typical retailer faces a demand function like the one shown in Exhibit 5.6. However, retailers are not confronted by such a curve because they face a

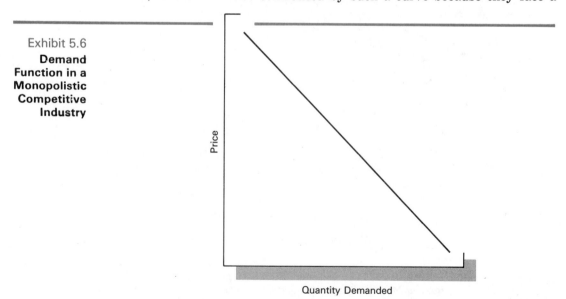

Exhibit 5.6
Demand Function in a Monopolistic Competitive Industry

Price

Quantity Demanded

three-dimensional demand function. The three dimensions are (1) quantity demanded per household, (2) price at the retail store, and (3) distance from the household's place of residence or work to the store. Quantity demanded by a household is inversely related to prices charged and distance to the store.

Higher prices result in less quantity demanded, because households have limited incomes and many alternatives for allocating their dollars. If a retailer raises prices and all else remains unchanged, then households will try to shift some of their purchasing power to other retailers. If other retailers also raise their prices this may not be the net effect. Also, if consumer incomes are also rising, this may not be the net effect. But in these examples all else does not remain unchanged.

The farther the consumer lives from the retailer, the more quantity demanded will drop. This happens because it costs the consumer dollars and time to travel to a store. The greater these costs are, the less the consumer will purchase from distant retailers. In the model to be developed, these costs will be comprised of three components: (1) the *actual dollar costs* of transporting oneself to the store and back; (2) the time involved, which is related to *opportunity costs* (that is, what else could you be doing with your time and what value do you attach to those alternative activities?); and (3) the *psychic costs* of traveling to the store and back (that is, if traffic arteries or public transportation are very congested, then you may get frustrated and upset). Exhibit 5.7 is a graphical representation of a three-dimensional demand function confronting the typical retailer.[3] Spend a few moments studying this model.

From the three-dimensional demand model we can derive several key concepts that you, as a retail manager, will need to understand.

1. There is a *maximum demand price* that the retailer can obtain for the goods or services it offers the consumer. Refer to Exhibit 5.7 to find this maximum demand price. Notice that the maximum demand price occurs only when the consumer's residence coincides with that of the store (an obviously unlikely occurrence) and when the retailer is willing to sell only a very small quantity of goods or services. Obviously, if the retailer desires to sell in large quantities to households located at increasing distances from the retailer's place of business, it must set its price below the maximum price it could theoretically establish.

2. There is a *maximum quantity* a consumer will demand from the retailer. This maximum quantity is obtained when the consumer lives very close to the store and the retailer's price on the good or service approaches zero. Find the maximum demand quantity on the three-dimensional demand model in Exhibit 5.7. Predictably, the retailer cannot operate profitably by selling at the maximum quantity price, since the revenues generated would not cover the retailer's expenses.

3. There is a *maximum distance* the consumer will travel to shop at a retail store. This distance is obtained by allowing price and quan-

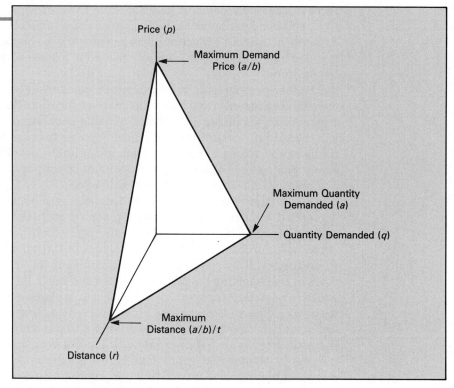

Exhibit 5.7

**The Three-
Dimensional
Demand Model**

In functional form the three-dimensional demand model can be stated as follows:

$$q = a - bp - btr$$

where: q = quantity demanded

p = price per unit

t = round trip transportation costs per mile, which includes actual transport costs and time and psychic costs

r = the radius or distance from the consumer's home or work to the store

a, b = parameters that describe shape of the demand function

Illustrating the three-dimensional demand model with a specific example:

$$q = 10 - 2p - 2(.25)r$$

Then we can determine: (1) the maximum demand price, by setting q and r equal to zero

$$0 = 10 - 2p - 2(.25)0$$

$$2p = 10$$

$$p = 5,$$

note that this is equivalent to (a/b), or $(10/2) = 5$; (2) the maximum distance by setting p or q equal to zero,

$$0 = 10 - 2(0) - 2(.25)r$$

$$0 = 10 - 2(.25)r$$

$$r = 20,$$

note that this is $(a/b)/t$, or $(10/2)/(.25) = 20$; and (3) the maximum quantity demanded, by setting p and r equal to zero,

$$q = 10 - 2(0) - 2(.25)0$$

$$q = 10$$

note that this is a, or 10 in the model.

tity to approach zero. Refer to Exhibit 5.7 to locate this point. The retailer will not typically attract customers from the maximum distance, since to do so would necessitate having to give merchandise or services away.

These three concepts suggest that retailers cannot be profitable by setting prices at the highest possible levels, trying to sell the largest quantity of goods or services possible, or trying to attract households from the greatest distance possible. Retailers will find it necessary to set prices somewhere below the maximum possible price but above zero. But where should they set prices? It seems reasonable retailers would want to set prices to maximize profits. To do so, they need knowledge of their costs, and that involves an examination of supply factors.

THE SUPPLY SIDE OF RETAILING

Retailers cannot operate without incurring costs, which can be classified as fixed or variable. These costs are portrayed graphically in Exhibit 5.8. **Fixed costs** are those the retailer incurs regardless of the quantity of goods or services sold. These costs are, in most part, related to the size of the store and the costs of maintaining and financing it, regardless of whether the store is open or closed. Examples of fixed costs in retailing include insurance, taxes, rent or lease payments, and security guards. **Variable costs** are those that increase proportionately with sales volume. The two largest variable costs in retailing are the cost of the goods or services sold and salaries and wages.

Not all costs can be categorized strictly into fixed or variable costs. **Semifixed costs** are constant over a range of sales volume, but past a crucial point they increase and then again remain constant at another,

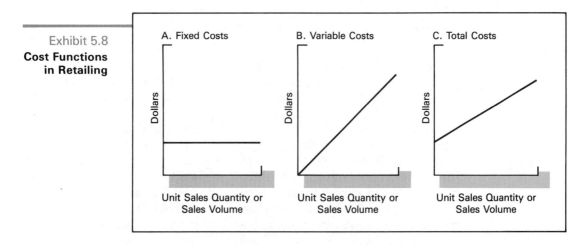

Exhibit 5.8
Cost Functions in Retailing

A. Fixed Costs

Dollars

Unit Sales Quantity or Sales Volume

B. Variable Costs

Dollars

Unit Sales Quantity or Sales Volume

C. Total Costs

Dollars

Unit Sales Quantity or Sales Volume

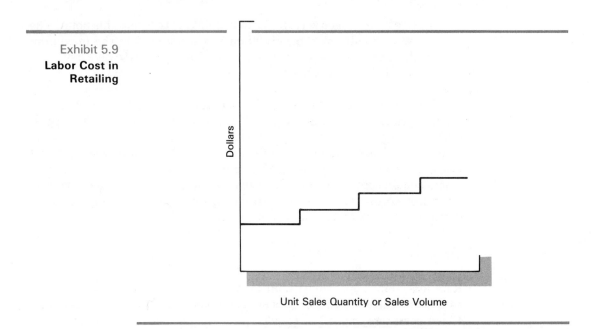

Exhibit 5.9
**Labor Cost in
Retailing**

Dollars

Unit Sales Quantity or Sales Volume

higher, sales volume range. For example, labor may be viewed as semi-fixed (see Exhibit 5.9). Before the doors of the store can be opened each day, a staff of employees must be on hand, but when store traffic volume rises past a crucial point, more employees would need to be added, since the existing staff would be inadequate.

Regardless of the exact form of the retailer's cost functions, the retailer must examine the supply side of retailing in order to set a profit maximizing price. The principles of microeconomic price theory cannot be ignored.

THE PROFIT-MAXIMIZING PRICE

Assume that a retailer has established the price level at which to sell its goods or services. Having established a price and knowing its costs, the retailer could construct a break-even (that quantity at which a retailer's total revenue equals total cost) chart as shown in Exhibit 5.10. The cost function is borrowed directly from Exhibit 5.8c and the total revenue function is obtained by multiplying the price the retailer has established by quantity Q. Note that Q is the total quantity the retailer sells and not the quantity any individual household demands (q) as portrayed in Exhibit 5.7. Let us examine how one might go about obtaining Q.

The retailer will sell to more than one household. Q is simply the summation of the individual household demand curves (q) shown in the three-dimensional demand model in Exhibit 5.8. As the retailer sets a lower price it will be able to attract customers from a greater distance. And the

Exhibit 5.10

A Retailer's Break-Even Chart

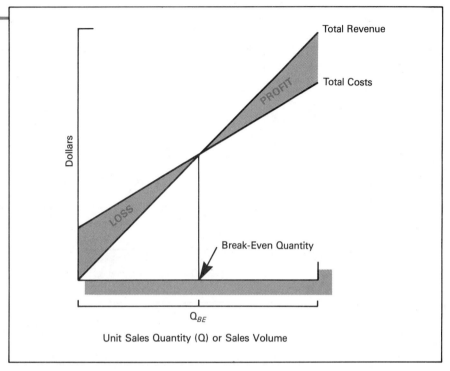

greater the density of households (households per square mile), the more households the retailer can attract to its store.

With an established price, the greatest distance a household will travel to a particular retail outlet can be defined as $((a/b) - (p))/t$, where a/b is the maximum demand price, p is the price the retailer has established, and t is the transport cost (round trip cost per mile). Let us construct a numerical example of the greatest distance a household would travel to purchase a particular item at a particular retail outlet.

Assume that the retailer has established a price (p) of $5 per unit and that the maximum price (a/b) the household would pay is $10 per unit. Further assume that the round-trip transportation cost per mile (t) is $.50. From this information and our formula for the maximum distance $((a/b) - (p))/t$, we can easily compute the maximum distance a household would travel as $(10-5)/.50$ or 10 miles. Households would simply not travel more than ten miles, because to do so they would spend more for the merchandise and the cost of transportation than the goods are worth to them. If a household traveled 20 miles to purchase the item, it would have spent $10 for transportation and $5 for the item—a total of $15. The maximum demand price the household was willing to pay was only $10.

The total quantity that a retailer sells is simply the sum of what all households purchase from the retailer. With an established price, the

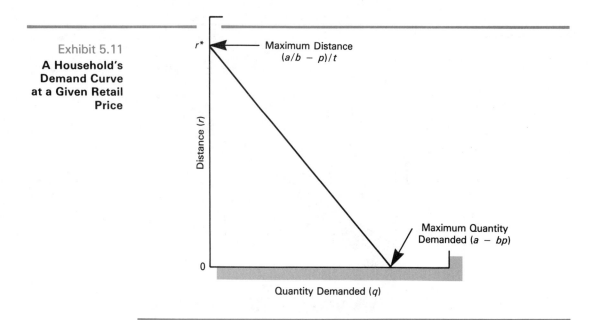

Exhibit 5.11

**A Household's
Demand Curve
at a Given Retail
Price**

quantity demanded by an individual household will vary inversely with
the distance from the retail outlet. In Exhibit 5.7, we portray the household's demand function given an established price. The maximum quantity demand is $((a) - (bp))$. Exhibit 5.11 verifies that as households are
closer to the retailer's place of business (i.e., as r^* approaches zero in Exhibit 5.11), they will purchase a larger quantity from that retailer.

If we now sum up the demand functions for all households located at a
distance of up to (r^*) from the store, we will obtain Q, the total unit volume the retailer will sell. We can now compare Q to the retailer's
breakeven quantity (Q_{BE}) in Exhibit 5.10. If Q exceeds Q_{BE} the price the
retailer established was profitable; but if Q fell short of Q_{BE}, the established price was unprofitable.

In theory, it is possible for a retailer to establish a profit-maximizing
price if the retailer has knowledge of its cost functions and the demand
functions of households in its trading area. The procedure would be similar to the procedure used in microeconomics when a manufacturer equates
marginal cost (the additional cost that results from the sale of one more
unit) with marginal revenue (the additional revenue that results from the
sale of one more unit). When the profit maximizing price is established,
retailers will attract customers from a well-defined distance, obtained by
inserting the profit-maximizing price into the formula $(a/b - p)/t$. To attract customers from a greater distance by cutting price would be unprofitable, since the marginal cost of doing so would exceed the marginal revenue generated.

NONPRICE DECISIONS

The retailer has more tools than just price to influence the quantity it will sell and profit level. Some important nonprice variables are merchandise mix, advertising, special promotions, personal selling, and store atmosphere. These and all other nonprice variables are directed at enlarging the demand that the retailer faces. Exhibit 5.12 shows the intended effect of nonprice variables in retailing. Notice that after successful implementation of a nonprice strategy, the maximum demand price consumers will pay, the maximum quantity they will demand, and the maximum distance they will travel to shop at the retailer's store all increase. How could this favorable shift in demand have occurred? Here are some possible explanations:

1. The retailer could have altered its merchandise mix in the direction of higher quality shopping goods vs. convenience goods. This would increase maximum demand price and the distance consumers would travel to shop for these goods, thereby enlarging the retailer's trade area.

Exhibit 5.12

The Impact of Nonprice Strategies

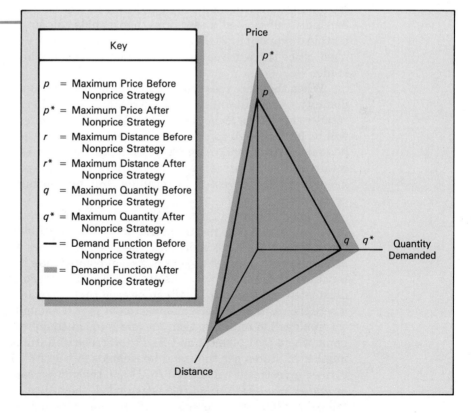

2. The retailer could have provided customers with free "park and shop" or "ride and shop" coupons, which would effectively lower transportation costs for customers. The lower transportation costs would increase the maximum distance the customer would be willing to travel, thereby increasing the retailer's trade area.
3. The retailer could have engaged in an extensive advertising campaign directed at persuading consumers to purchase more of the goods it sells. The net effect could have been an increase in the maximum quantity demanded.

All retail decision variables, whether price or nonprice, are directed at influencing demand. Of course, the profitability of the decisions depends on the marginal cost of the action vs. the marginal revenue it generates.

COMPETITIVE ACTIONS

In the retail competition model, we saw that retailers attract customers from a limited geographic area and that as prices are lowered, this area expands. But even at a zero price, households can only afford to travel a certain distance to get the goods and services retailers offer. Therefore, in most cities there are several, if not many, retailers in each line of retail trade.

When there are too many retail establishments competing in a particular city, the profitability of all the retailers will suffer. Eventually, some retailers may even leave the market. If there are too few retailers, profits will be high enough to attract new competitors, or existing retailers will be enticed to expand. A market is in equilibrium in terms of number of retail establishments if the return on investment is high enough to justify keeping capital invested in retailing, but not so high to invite more competition.

A good measure of competitive activity in a market is the number of retail establishments per thousand households ($N/1,000H$). If the stores are of the same approximate size, then as the number of stores per thousand households increases, the degree of competition intensifies. This intensified competition will tend to decrease the return on investment as illustrated in Exhibit 5.13. It can be seen that if $N/1,000H$ is at the level where the resulting return on investment is just enough to keep the capital employed in retailing, then the market is in equilibrium. This is at the point where $(N/1,000H)*$ and $ROI*$ intersect in Exhibit 5.13. When the number of stores per thousand households is below $(N/1,000H)*$, the return on investment will exceed $ROI*$ and the market can be characterized as *understored*. If $(N/1,000H)*$ is exceeded, the return on investment will fall below $ROI*$ and the market will be characterized as *overstored*.

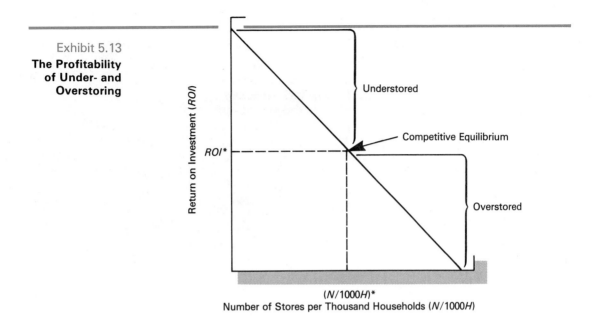

Exhibit 5.13

The Profitability of Under- and Overstoring

Note: *ROI** is the return on investment that will just be enough to keep the capital employed in retailing (the equilibrium *ROI*).

Competition is most intense in overstored markets, since many retailers are achieving an inadequate return on investment. These retailers face a major performance imperative and will implement both price and non-price actions in an all-out attempt to increase sales and profit levels. Since retailers operate in a relatively closed geographic market, with a fixed number of households and a limited number of dollars to compete for, any action by one retailer to increase its sales or profit level will warrant an action from competitors.

The easiest and quickest actions to copy are those which are price based. If a retailer cuts price, many competitors will respond with a similar price cut. Exhibit 5.14 gives an actual industry example of the profit effect of price competition. While this example is from the 1970s, it is very relevant today. A&P, the second largest food retailer in the United States at that time, engaged in a price-cutting strategy called WEO. WEO stood for *where economy originates* and was an attempt by A&P to recover market share it had been losing to other large chains over a ten-year period. As shown in Exhibit 5.14, the profit effect of this strategy for both A&P and its competitors was disastrous.

Illus. 5.2
Store closings can result from overstocked stores.

TYPES OF COMPETITION

INTRATYPE AND INTERTYPE COMPETITION

It is possible to merge the preceding discussion of competition in retailing with the classification schemes used by the Department of Commerce in conducting the Census of Retail Trade. **Intratype competition** occurs when any two or more retailers of the same type as defined in the Census of Retail Trade compete with each other for the same households. This is the most common type of retail competition. Firestone competes with Goodyear and Sears competes with Penney's. Historically, most competition in retailing has been of this form.

Recently many retailers have been moving toward **scrambled merchandising**, carrying any merchandise line which can be sold profitably. Thirty percent of sales at supermarkets are for nonfood items. 7-Eleven has emerged as one of the most powerful gasoline retailers in the country. Every time different types of retail outlets sell the same lines of merchandise and compete for the same limited consumer dollars, **intertype competition** occurs. Retailing in Action 5-1 illustrates how service stations and auto parts stores are now facing strong competition from other retailers.

As more types of retail firms handle a particular merchandise line, the gross margin on those items should decline. This has happened in the general merchandise category (nonfood items such as automotive, baby care, greeting cards, housewares, photo, and toys) of supermarket sales. Over a recent three-year period, the gross profit (sometimes referred to as the gross margin) percentage for this category declined from 37.0 percent to 35.5 percent.[4]

Exhibit 5.14
The Economics of Price Competition

	Profits as a Percentage of Net Sales			
Retailer	1970	1971	1972	1973
Chains with little A&P competition	1.4%	1.5%	1.5%	1.4%
Chains competitive with A&P	.9	.8	.2	.4
A&P	.9	.3	(.8)	.2
	Profits as a Percentage of Net Worth			
Retailer	1970	1971	1972	1973
Chains with little A&P competition	13.9%	14.8%	14.9%	14.3%
Chains competitive with A&P	9.9	8.7	2.3	4.8
A&P	7.4	2.2	(8.6)	2.0

SOURCE: Bert C. McCammon, Jr., Robert F. Lusch, and Bradley T. Farnsworth, "Contemporary Markets and the Corporate Imperative: A Strategic Analysis for Senior Retailing Executives," presented at Seminar for Top Management in Retailing, Graduate School of Business Administration, Harvard University (June 1976), p. 9. Reprinted with permission of the authors.

DIVERTIVE COMPETITION

Another concept that helps to explain the nature of competition in retailing is **divertive competition**.[5] This occurs when retailers intercept or divert customers from competing retailers. For example, a consumer on the way to the supermarket for bread and milk and also low on gas might buy all three at 7-Eleven and forget about going to the supermarket. Southland Corporation, the parent company of 7-Eleven, is one of the largest gasoline retailers in the country. To comprehend the significance of divertive competition, which can be either intertype or intratype competition, one needs to recognize that most retailers operate very close to their break-even point. For instance, supermarkets, with their extremely low gross margins, tend to have a break-even point of 94 to 96 percent of current sales. Even general merchandise retailers, with relatively large gross margins, face a break-even point of 85 to 92 percent of their current sales. A modest drop in sales volume could put these retailers in the red. The precise drop in sales volume needed to fall below break-even would depend on such factors as the retailer's cost structure, gross margin, current profit level, and a host of other factors.

RETAILING
IN
ACTION

5-1

Intertype Competition in Automotive Accessories

Traditionally, the place to purchase automotive accessories was at your local service station, auto dealer, or auto parts store. Today this is no longer the case, as more and more retailers, especially discount stores, supermarkets, and drug stores, are vying for the consumer's automotive dollars and as consumers are becoming more do-it-yourself oriented.

The typical comments by the managers of some of these retailers may help to substantiate this observation:

"In turns and ROI, the car care does as well or better than photos, videotapes, or housewares and doesn't need as much shelf space."

"I think we have enough space for HBA (Health and Beauty Aids) and school supplies. Car care sells and serves the consumers and their older cars. I don't need a calculator to see it."

"Automotive gives us variety; heck, I even see women buying it."

"Housewares is a one-time buy. Auto has a lot of consumption."

"I prefer to have more nonfoods departments with the best sellers than fewer sections with a complete line."

"Auto makes money because it's properly merchandised and helps us fulfill our role as a one-stop shopping location."

"The category always seems to have a promotion going on given the motor oils, cleaners, WD-40, and anti-freeze."

Based on "Automotive Takes The Long Road Back," *Progressive Grocer* (August 1987): 26–27 and "GM Scores Good Gains As Recession Recedes," *Progressive Grocer* (July 1984): 183–184.

Retailers are susceptible to any downturn in sales. New retail entrants in a community do not have to get all the business to hurt existing firms. On the contrary, all they have to do is divert or siphon off the 'plus' sales that existing firms need to operate profitably. For example, the late 1980s saw the advent of "category killers," a type of store that caused a stir in the retail industry. The category killer got its name from its marketing strategy: carry such a large amount of merchandise in a single category at such good prices that the competition is destroyed. Although the first category killer, Toys 'R' Us, began in the 1950s, the new breed, Phar-Mor, T.J. Maxx, Sportsmart, and Ikea, have only begun to make their presence known as they divert business from traditional outlets.

COMPETITION FOR MARKET SHARE

Historically, retailers in the United States have been confronted with an ever-expanding market. The population was growing, real per capita incomes were climbing, and the suburbs awaited new retail stores. The 1980s, however, were characterized by flat, or at best moderate, growth curves. Faced with a constant market, retailers began to realize that growth could only be achieved by aggressive expansion of market share.

DEVELOPING A PROTECTED NICHE

As competition intensifies in retailing, the retail manager will find it harder to be protected from competitive threats on the basis of the merchandise offered. Why? Because all retailers have access to the same merchandise. Therefore, retailers in the future will find it more rewarding to develop a protected niche in the marketplace. Careful store positioning can be used to accomplish this. In **store positioning**, one identifies a well-defined market segment using demographic or life-style variables and appeals to this segment with a clearly differentiated approach. A notable example of positioning is The Limited, which appeals to career-oriented women, 18 to 39 years of age, who are fashion conscious and upwardly mobile. The Limited's entire retail strategy—including store decor, merchandise, employees, background music, and prices—is geared to this segment. Targeting customers by age and income enables specialty stores like The Limited to respond quickly to changing trends. Most retail analysts contend that positioning will be even more important in the 1990s than it was in the 1980s. Even K mart is gearing up to reposition itself for the 1990s with an upmarket image, leaving its "blue light special" image behind.

EVOLUTION OF RETAIL COMPETITION

There are several theories to explain and describe the evolution of competition in retailing. We will review five of them briefly.

THE WHEEL OF RETAILING

Professor Malcolm P. McNair developed the wheel of retailing hypothesis to describe patterns of competitive development in retailing.[6] McNair contends that new types of retailers enter the market as low-status, low margin, low-price operators. This modest strategy allows these retailers to compete effectively and take market share away from the more traditional retailers. However, as they meet with success, these new retailers gradually acquire more sophisticated and elaborate facilities. This creates both a higher investment and a subsequent rise in operating costs. Predictably, these retailers must raise prices and margins, thus becoming vulnerable to new types of low-margin retail competitors who progress through the same pattern. This appears to be the case today in the fast food hamburger business. Burger King, Wendy's, and McDonald's have all upgraded their restaurants, promotions, and food selections leaving the door open for a number of very small regional chains. These chains have developed a back-to-basics approach, selling burger-only menus from buildings limited to drive-thru and walk-up service. Their competitive advantage is size, speed, location, and price (40 percent less than big-name competitors). Their strategy is to eliminate the frills, undercut the giants, and grow quickly.

Not all retailing scholars agree with the wheel of retailing theory. Hollander notes that, in both the United States and foreign retail environments, there are nonconforming examples. In reference to retailing in the United States he states, "The department-store branch movement and the concomitant rise of planned shopping centers also has progressed directly contrary to the wheel pattern. The early department-store branches consisted of a few stores in exclusive suburbs and some equally high-fashion college and resort shops."[7]

Furthermore, Hollander states in regard to retailing in underdeveloped countries that "the relatively small middle- and upper-income groups have formed the major markets for 'modern' types of retailing. Supermarkets and other modern stores have been introduced in those countries largely at the top of the social and price scales, contrary to the wheel pattern."[8] Tinsley, Brooks, and d'Amico have also taken issue with the wheel model, contending that changes in the retail environment increase the likelihood that retailers will seek to remain where they are, rather than move up the wheel.[9]

THE RETAIL ACCORDION

Several other theorists have noted that retail institutions evolve from outlets that offer wide assortments to specialized stores that offer narrow assortments, and then return to the wide assortment stores to continue through the pattern once more. This contraction and expansion suggests the term *accordion*.[10] In his history of Macy's, Ralph Hower writes:

"Throughout the history of retail trade (as, indeed, in all business evolution) there appears to be an alternating movement in the dominant method of conducting operations. One swing is toward the specialization of the function performed on the merchandise handled by the individual firm. The other is away from such specialization toward the integration of related activities under one management or the diversification of products handled by a single firm."[11]

Retail historians have observed that, in the United States, retail trade was dominated by the general store until 1860. The general store carried a broad assortment of merchandise ranging from farm implements to textiles to food. After 1860, due to the growth of cities and roads, retail trade became more specialized and was concentrated in the central business districts of cities. Here department and specialty stores were the dominant competitive force. Both carried more specialized assortments than the general store. In the 1950s retailing began to move again to wider merchandise lines. Typical was the grocery store, which added produce and dairy products, nonfood items such as kitchen utensils, health and beauty aids, and small household appliances. By the mid 1980s, specialization in merchandise lines once again became a dominant competitive strategy. Witness the recent success of such companies as Athlete's Foot, The Limited, Hickory Farms, Charming Shoppes, Benetton, Casual Corner, Pants West, Toys "R" Us, and Walden Books.

NATURAL SELECTION

The theory of natural selection in retailing is a direct adaptation of Darwin's theory of natural selection, which has been captured in the phrase, "survival of the fittest." Basically, Darwin's theory states that the species that most effectively adapts to its environment is most likely to survive and perpetuate its kind. Thus, management is continually monitoring environmental changes that can affect retail survival. While all retailing institutions have felt the effects of these environmental changes, department stores have had the most trouble adapting to change. For example, after World War II the conventional downtown department store dragged its feet, while growth in the suburbs was explosive. Delbert Duncan has observed:

> "Those firms whose management did recognize the challenge of the changing social and economic forces, however, and established branches of various sizes and types to serve these new markets, made the necessary shift in organization structure to accommodate multiunit operation, and adopted other innovations, have been richly rewarded. Moreover, in doing so, they helped to pioneer the development of the regional shopping center, one of the most important developments of the past two decades. Yet the measures adopted by the traditional department stores to meet the changing social and economic scene brought them face to face with problems not wholly anticipated. Moving from their long-established fortresses in downtown areas, they became vulnerable to the sharply increasing competition of other retailers quick to make innovations in policies and practices."[12]

Throughout the past two decades, consumer markets became more segmented. Department stores were slow to respond in a positive fashion. Consequently, many specialty stores experienced rapid growth because they were able and willing to design their total store offering to appeal to a select demographic or life-style group. For example, The Limited Inc. has tailored stores to many different women's markets with its Limited, Limited Express, Victoria's Secret, Lerner, Lane Bryant, Lerner Woman, and Henri Bendel retail outlets. It was not until the late 1980s that department stores began to recognize the magnitude of this challenge. Many responded by tailoring more than 20 departments within their stores to distinct groups, becoming, in effect, a group of specialty stores under one roof.

THE DIALECTIC PROCESS

A dialectic process of retailing, sometimes called the melting pot theory, was first proposed by Gist[13] and later validated by Maronick and Walker.[14] The dialectic process theory of retailing is based on Hegel's dialectic. According to Hegel, "Any idea, by the very nature of things, begets a negation of itself; the combination of the original idea, called the 'thesis' with its negation called the 'antithesis,' results in a 'synthesis'— which in turn, serves as the thesis when the process begins all over."[15]

A concise application of Hegel's dialectic to competitive behavior in retailing has been made by Thomas Maronick and Bruce Walker.

"In terms of retail institutions, the dialectic model implies that retailers mutually adapt in the face of competition from 'opposites.' Thus, when challenged by a competitor with a differential advantage, an es-

Illus. 5.3
**Many specialty stores have experienced rapid growth because of their appeal to a select demographic or life-style group.
Source: Retail Planning Associates**

tablished institution will adopt strategies and tactics in the direction of that advantage, thereby negating some of the innovator's attraction. The innovator, meanwhile, does not remain unchanged. Rather, as McNair noted, the innovator over time tends to upgrade or otherwise modify products and facilities. In doing so, he moves toward the 'negated' institution. As a result of these mutual adaptations, the two retailers gradually move together in terms of offerings, facilities, supplementary services, and prices. They thus become indistinguishable or at least quite similar and constitute a new retail institution, termed the synthesis. This new institution is then vulnerable to 'negation' by new competitors as the dialectic process begins anew."[16]

To illustrate the dialectic process in retailing, let us examine the evolution of competition in general merchandise retailing. First were department stores, with high margins, low turnover, high prices, full service, downtown locations, and plush facilities. These department stores were the thesis. The antithesis was the discount store, the post-World War II innovation which was able to offer lower prices due to lower margins, higher turnover, self-service operations, low-rent locations, and spartan facilities. The synthesis was the discount department store such as K mart and Target.

THE RETAIL LIFE CYCLE

The final framework we will examine for the evolution of retail competition is the retail life cycle. Davidson, *et al.*, argue that "retailing institutions, like the products they distribute, pass through an identifiable cycle."[17] This cycle can be partitioned into four distinct stages: (1) innovation, (2) accelerated development, (3) maturity, and (4) decline. Each stage will be briefly discussed.

Innovation.   The cycle begins with an aggressive, bold entrepreneur who is willing and able to develop an approach to retailing that departs sharply from conventional approaches. Many times the approach is oriented to cost reduction and passing the resulting savings on to the customer. For example, the supermarket in the early 1930s was able to operate on a gross margin of 12 percent, whereas conventional food outlets required 20 percent. Other times the innovation centers on a distinctive product assortment, shopping ease, locational convenience, advertising, or promotion. For example, self-service gasoline stations offered more convenient locations and lower prices than conventional service stations.

If the new advantage being offered is significant enough in the minds of consumers, sales will grow in the innovative stage. Profits, however, will not be attractive in the innovation stage and may be nonexistent. In any new business there are operating problems that need to be solved.

High start-up costs and the absence of scale economies due to relatively low sales put a damper on profits. But at the end of the innovation stage, sales begin to grow more rapidly and operating problems are overcome, stimulating profit levels.

Accelerated Development.   During development, sales and profit growth are explosive. Many new entrants arrive to share in the success of this new form of retailing. The market share of the innovators increases at the expense of conventional outlets. Firms that were astute enough to take part in the innovation stage expand their number of outlets by entering new geographic markets:

> "However, toward the end of the period these favorable factors tend to be counter-balanced by cost pressures that arise from the need for a larger staff, more complex internal systems, increased management controls, and other requirements of operating large, multi-unit organizations. Consequently, near the end of the accelerated development period both market share and profitability tend to approach their maximum level."[18]

Maturity.   In maturity, market share stabilizes and severe profit declines are experienced for several reasons. First, managers have become accustomed to managing a high-growth firm that was simple and small, but now must manage a large, complex firm in a stable market. Second, the industry has typically overexpanded. Selecting markets and building new stores takes a long planning horizon (12 to 36 months). It is inevitable that many stores planned in the accelerated development stage will open in the maturity state. Third, competitive assaults will be made on these firms by new forms of retailing (a bold entrepreneur starting a new retail life cycle).

One retail executive in a mature industry, the cafeteria business, reasoned that an aggressive building campaign would not be productive. However, Furr's/Bishop's Cafeterias, the nation's largest cafeteria chain, expanded by growing through acquisition of other smaller cafeteria chains, eliminating duplicate expenses and increasing its buying power and marketing muscle.[19]

Decline.   Although decline is inevitable, retail managers try to postpone it by serious attempts to reposition, modify, or adapt the firm. These attempts can postpone the decline stage, but a return to earlier, attractive levels of operating performance is not likely. Sooner or later decline will occur, and "the consequences are traumatic. Major losses of market share occur, profits are marginal at best, and a fatal inability to compete in the market becomes apparent to investors and competitors."[20]

A more complete profile of management activities throughout the retail life cycle is presented in Exhibit 5.15. Try to identify the exhibit's bottom-line implications for retail managers. There are three primary implications:

1. Retailers should remain flexible so that they are able to adapt their strategies to various stages in the life cycle.
2. Since profits vary by stage in the retail life cycle, retail managers need to carefully analyze the risks and profits of entering the market or expanding their outlets at various stages in the life cycle.
3. Retailers need to extend the maturity stage. Since retailers have substantial investments in a particular form of retailing by the time of the maturity stage, they should try to work that investment as long as possible.

These three points are reinforced by the fact that the retail life cycle is growing shorter. The downtown department store took 80 years to reach maturity, the variety store 45 years, the supermarket 35 years, the discount department store 20 years, and the home improvement center a short 15 years. Retail managers must recognize that high-performance results can be achieved only over the long run, by programming the firm to enter new lines of retail trade at appropriate points in time.

COMPETITION FROM NONSTORE RETAILERS

Several industry analysts contend that nonstore retailing sometimes called direct retailing, or direct marketing, will be the next revolution in retailing. The mechanics for such a revolution are already in place, as a variety of established selling techniques permit consumers to purchase goods and services without having to leave home. With accelerated communications technology and changing consumer life-styles, the growth potential for nonstore retailing is explosive. Traditional retailers need to continuously monitor developments in nonstore retailing.

NATURE AND SCOPE

The Census of Retailing classifies nonstore retailers into three major types:

1. **Mail-order houses**: establishments primarily engaged in the retail sale of products by catalog and mail order. Included are book and record clubs, jewelry firms, novelty merchandise firms, specialty merchandisers (such as sporting goods retailers), and the catalog divisions of large general merchandisers (such as Sears). Not included, however, are seasonal and special promotional catalog houses, which do three-fourths of their annual volume during the Christmas season. The number of catalogs distributed industry-wide increased to 11.8 billion in 1986 from 5.3 billion in 1981.[21]

Exhibit 5.15
The Retail Life Cycle

	Area or Subject of Concern	Stage of Life Cycle			
		Innovation	Accelerated Development	Maturity	Decline
Market characteristics	Number of competitors	Very few	Moderate	Many direct competitors, moderate indirect competition	Moderate direct competition, many indirect competitors
	Rate of sales growth	Very rapid	Rapid	Moderate to slow	Slow or negative
	Level of profitability	Low to moderate	High	Moderate	Very low
	Duration of new innovations	3 to 5 years	5 to 6 years	Indefinite	Indefinite
Appropriate retailer actions	Investment, growth, risk decisions	Investment minimization, high risks accepted	High levels of investment to sustain growth	Tightly controlled growth in untapped markets	Minimal capital expenditures and only when essential
	Central management concerns	Concept refinement through adjustment and experimentation	Establishing a preemptive market position	• Excess capacity and "overstoring" • Prolonging maturity and reversing the retail concept	Engaging in a "run-out" strategy

	Minimal	Moderate	Extensive	Moderate
Use of management control techniques	Minimal	Moderate	Extensive	Moderate
Most successful management style	Entrepreneurial	Centralized	"Professional"	Caretaker
Appropriate supplier actions — Channel strategy	Develop a preemptive market position	Hold market position	Maintain profitable sales	Avoid excessive costs?
Channel problems	Possible antagonism of other accounts	Possible antagonism of other accounts	Dealing with more scientific retailers	Servicing accounts at a profit
Channel research	Identification of key innovations	Identification of other retailers adopting the innovation	Initial screening of new innovation opportunities	Active search for new innovation opportunities
Trade incentives	Direct financial support	Price concessions	New price incentives	None

SOURCE: Reprinted by permission of the *Harvard Business Review.* Exhibit from "The Retail Life Cycle," by William R. Davidson, Albert D. Bates, and Stephen J. Bass 54 (November–December 1976), p. 92. Copyrighted © 1976 by the President and Fellows of Harvard College; all rights reserved.

2. **Automatic merchandising machine operators:** establishments primarily engaged in the retail sale of products by means of automatic merchandising units, also referred to as vending machines. This industry does not include coin-operated service machines, such as music machines, amusement and game machines, lockers, or scales. Retailing in Action 5-2 provides an insight into the early development of vending machines.

3. **Direct selling establishments:** primarily engaged in the retail sale of merchandise by telephone or house-to-house canvass. Included are individuals who are not employees of the organization they represent and employees of retail sales offices who sell merchan-

RETAILING IN ACTION   5-2

The Early History of Vending Machines

Today it is not uncommon for the average American to use a vending machine for soft-drinks, cigarettes, film, candy, soups, sandwiches, even toothbrushes. In fact, Americans spend nearly $20 billion every year in vending machines. Soft drinks are first in total sales with a 42 percent share, followed by cigarettes and packaged snacks. Yet, have you ever wondered about the origins of this nonstore retail outlet?

The first known American vending machine was a small, cast-iron machine which sold packaged pipe tobacco. It was invented some twenty years prior to the Civil War. However, it was not the world's first vending machine. During the eleventh century, Chinese merchants sold pencils through coin-operated machines. Archaeologists also found a coin-operated device in an ancient Egyptian temple. No one is sure who really did invent this modern-day miracle.

The use of the vending machine as we know it today started with the Industrial Revolution. With the increase in economic prosperity, various inventors sought to develop a machine to separate the newly prosperous businessman from his loose change. Between 1895 and 1915 more than 10,000 patents were issued for vending machines. Today's vending machines are undergoing major changes. No longer content to merely dispense the product and make change, machines now dispense coupons, make use of video sales presentations, give you the opportunity to play a game of skill before dispensing the product, talk to you, and even phone the plant to report an out-of-stock item.

Source: Based on data from Jeanne Lukasick, "Heavy Metal for Mass Appeal," *Beverage World* (January 1987): 28 and John Grossman, "Exploring the Slot Market," *American Way* (November 1983): 173–178.

Illus. 5.4
Avon is an example of a nonstore retailer.

dise door-to-door. Examples include house-to-house selling of magazines, jewelry and cosmetics such as Avon, as well as housewares; home delivery of milk and bakery goods; ice cream wagons; and party-plan merchandising (e.g., Stanley and Tupperware).

Davidson and Rogers note that the preceding classification, which was developed by the Department of Commerce prior to 1930, is quite archaic.[22] Nevertheless, the Census Bureau persists in its use. Davidson and Rogers elaborate on the restrictive nature of this classification.[23]

Mail order.   This was a term appropriate to the early days of Sears and Ward's, before they had retail stores. The terminology has persisted in spite of developments like consumers picking up catalogs at stores instead of receiving them by mail; orders being taken at catalog stores, catalog order desks within stores, or by 800 phone numbers, rather than being sent in by mail; and delivery by customer pickup or United Parcel Service rather than by mail.

Vending.   While commonly considered as nonstore, many vending machines are in stores, employee lunch rooms, or restbreak areas.

Direct selling.   This method is commonly referred to as house-to-house or door-to-door selling. There was a time when vacuum cleaner or hosiery salespeople actually went from door-to-door. While the vocabulary persists, the typical nonstore agent of a direct selling company does not walk the street but sells to selective prospects on a part-time basis (friends; fellow office workers, club members, and churchgoers; bowling league acquaintances, etc.)

Exhibit 5.16 highlights the inadequacy of the official census data on nonstore retailing. The shaded areas roughly show what the Census Bureau considers nonstore retailing.

Exhibit 5.16
Illustrative Types of Nonstore Retailing

Method of Operation	Nonstore Retailing Specialists	Nonstore Retailing as a Supplement to Conventional Retail Store or Wholesale Establishment Operations	Nonstore Retailing by Others
Catalog: general merchandise	Catalog divisions of Sears, Penney's, Wards, etc.	Seasonal and special promotional catalogs of conventional department stores such as Marshall Field, Lazarus, Higbee's, Bloomingdale's, Jordan Marsh, etc.	Catalogs of trading stamp companies, (S&H), premium companies in connection with sales incentive companies, etc.
Catalog: specialty	Catalog divisions of Lane Bryant, L. L. Bean, The Horchow Collection, J. C. Whitney, Figi's, The Talbots, etc.	Seasonal and special catalogs of specialty retailers such as Gump's, Bonwit Teller, Gattle's, Eddie Bauer, Sheplers, and resurrection of Abercrombie and Fitch by Oshman Sporting Goods.	Seasonal catalogs distributed to credit card customers by petroleum companies. In-flight shopping catalogs of major airline companies.
Direct advertising for telephone or mail orders and other forms of nonstore acquisition	Direct-mail solicitation by manufacturers or distributors such as New Process, Fingerhut, Bee Line, etc. Direct-response ads by nonstore specialists in magazines, newspapers, e.g., Walter Drake, club plans (books, records, cosmetics).	Department store and specialty store advertisements for mail or telephone order response in newspapers and magazines, by direct mail including bill stuffers, and by means of broadcast media.	Merchandise offers by magazines such as Apartment Life, Vogue, Playboy. Bank and Savings and Loan premium offers for new accounts. Merchandise promotional premiums to be redeemed by mail or newspaper coupons. Special item promotions by petroleum companies.

Exhibit 5.16   **Continued**

Method of Operation	Nonstore Retailing Specialists	Nonstore Retailing as a Supplement to Conventional Retail Store or Wholesale Establishment Operations	Nonstore Retailing by Others
At-home personal selling	Residential door-to-door selling (Avon, Electrolux, Fuller Brush, etc.) Party plan selling (Stanley, Tupperware). "Pyramid" selling plans (Amway).	Outside salesmen of conventional retailers for products such as appliances, carpeting, draperies, home improvements, lawn services, etc.	At-home selling by publishers of encyclopedias and other book sets.
Electronic retailing	Merchandisers of gadgets, records, tapes, etc., not available in stores.	Use of interactive cable TV as means of ordering merchandise (e.g., Qube Division of Warner Communications).	
Vending machines	Vending machine operating companies.	Vending machines as supplemental distribution by tobacco, candy, and novelty wholesalers.	Vending machines as supplemental distribution by bottlers of beverages, food processors or caterers.
Institutionalized or contract marketing of products formerly purchased as merchandise items in stores	Service retailing specialists who offer a complete system solution (Chemlawn, Barefoot Grass, Stanley Steamer, Carpet Cleaners).	Contract lawn or other home maintenance services offered by advertising or outside salesmen of store retailers, usually local.	Real estate developers offering residential units complete with appliances, carpeting, draperies, etc. Dispensing of pharmaceutical products in hospitals, nursing homes, and health maintenance organizations.
Borderline nonstore retailing situations	Duty-free shops at airports; concession stands at amusement parks and resorts; roadside stands of agricultural producers; auctions; merchandise sold at nonstore locations such as bowling alleys, golf clubs, tennis clubs, etc.; personal care products sold at barber shops and beauty salons, photo-finisher drive-through kiosks on the parking lots of retail premises; garage or yard sales of previously owned merchandise by relocating families, some handled by reselling experts; and catalog sales at wholesale prices to manufacturing plant employees through use of vendor catalogs.		

SOURCE: William R. Davidson and Alice Rogers, "Non-Store Retailing: Its Importance to and Impact on Merchandise Suppliers and Competitive Channels," *The Growth of Non-Store Retailing: Implications For Retailers, Manufacturers, and Public Policy Makers* (New York: Institute of Retail Management, New York University, 1979), p. 24. Reprinted by permission.

NONSTORE GROWTH

Chain Store Age has predicted that, as a result of several key forces at work today, over $100 billion of all retail sales will be nonstore by 1992, with electronic shopping accounting for the majority of these sales.[24] Some of these forces are:

- Consumers' need to save time.
- The erosion of fun in the shopping experience.
- The lack of qualified sales help in stores to provide information.
- The explosive increase in use of the telephone, the computer, and telecommunications.
- Consumer desire to eliminate the middleman's profit.[25]

Not everyone is convinced that nonstore retailing's prospects for growth are unlimited. Critics contend that the consumers' loss of discretionary income, the lack of personal touch in nonstore shopping, the limited number of products that are appropriate for nonstore use, failure by manufacturers to take control of this channel of distribution, and the reactions of store retailers threatened by this channel will limit nonstore growth. These critics believe that the nonstore revolution *will* take place but, because of the factors cited above, it will be slower than expected. In either case, high-performance retail managers must continue to monitor environmental changes, especially the technological changes which enable all the other environmental forces to change. Already, many traditional retailers have entered nonstore retailing, like Sears with its cable television shopping service.

TECHNOLOGICAL ENVIRONMENT

Technology is the application of science to develop new methods or ways of doing things. In retailing, technology occurs in two broad areas: new forms of retailing and new equipment or fixtures used in retailing.

NEW FORMS OF RETAILING

Retailing is continually evolving. New forms of retailing are born and old forms die out. Innovation in retailing is the result of a constant pressure to improve efficiency and effectiveness and to serve the consumer better. This pressure to better serve the consumer has also resulted in a shortened retail life cycle. The retail innovation process can be seen through two examples.

Grocery Retailing.   The food industry has witnessed three forms of innovation in grocery retailing: (1) warehouse stores; (2) limited item stores; and (3) hypermarkets. The **warehouse store** is a no-frills, low-service, high-tonnage approach to grocery retailing. Warehouse stores, such as the Price Club and Sam's, operate on a gross margin of 11 to 12 percent versus 20 to 24 percent for conventional supermarkets, and therefore offer significant price savings and good assortments. The **limited item store** was introduced by the Albrecht Company of West Germany. These stores are similar to warehouse stores, but they carry fewer than 1,000 grocery items. Limited item stores offer the consumer lower prices, but the customer must be willing to give up product assortment for this price saving.

Hypermarkets are like warehouse stores, but they also offer a wide variety of hard and soft goods. These cavernous (224,000 sq. ft.), one-stop supermarket and discount department stores, so popular in Europe, haven't enjoyed the same success in the United States. American consumers, who can choose from a much broader array of stores than Europeans, aren't that impressed with stores carrying over 70,000 products ranging from televisions to grapefruit to lawn rakes. These stores do, however, offer the customer one-stop shopping and lower cost in terms of time and miles traveled. They do not sacrifice service and variety as do the limited item stores and warehouse stores.[26]

It is difficult to predict which of these three innovations in grocery retailing, if any, will overtake the conventional supermarket. In the end, the consumer will be the judge. In terms of new forms and types of retail trade as well as technology, the consumer determines what is acceptable.

Electronic Shopping.   With increasing sophistication in computer and telecommunication technology, new forms of retailing are emerging. They revolve around a computer used to facilitate transactions between the consumer and the retailer.

Many national retailers are introducing interactive systems.[27] These kiosks aid the retailer in providing merchandising and sales information to customers, offer sales support in the retail setting, and facilitate sales promotions. According to research done by ByVideo, over 50 percent of all consumers leave stores empty-handed. The interactive kiosks are able to aid the retailer in providing the right merchandise to the right customer at the right time. Using touch-screen technology, customers can view directory and sales information, obtain coupons, and even view commercials.

Among the retailers using kiosks today are F. W. Woolworth, Herman's World of Sporting Goods, Sears, Roebuck & Co., Lucky Stores, Florsheim Shoes, and Kroger. The only retail category not having success with interactive kiosks is the home center retailers. The idea of using technology to improve customer service and eliminate the need for some sales help doesn't seem to work with the DIY (Do-It-Yourself) market, although no one has figured out why.[28]

One of the most elaborate of the current electronic in-store systems enables college students to order their class rings through kiosks. The

Illus. 5.5
Kiosks aid the retailer in providing merchandising and sales information to customers, offer sales support in the retail setting, and facilitate sales promotions. Source: Retail Planning Associates

video disks, owned by Balfour Inc., show students 10 to 15 versions of the official school ring, then tens of thousands of combinations of the basic options. It's always accurate, with up-to-date prices and availability.

Florsheim Shoe Co., one of the earliest kiosk users, introduced interactive video terminals in 1986 that allowed consumers to buy shoes by video. The terminals, manufactured by ByVideo, enabled the shoe retailers to increase sales without incurring any additional inventory cost. The terminal was an in-store device designed to supplement salespeople and eliminate walk-out customers. It was also an excellent tool to sell the low-demand, high-margin, odd sizes and styles not likely to be stocked by the retailer. Research has shown that as many as 54 percent of all men require some degree of specialized shoe fitting, making them ideal candidates for the infrared, touch-screen terminal catalogue—which features color video, photographs, and a twin-stereo soundtrack.

Industry sources estimate that by 1990, 30,000 transactional terminals and 70,000 informational terminals will be in use across the United States.[29]

Another innovative form of electronic shopping is the use of videocassette catalogs. First introduced when Marshall Field's sent 7,500 prime customer-prospects a tape describing their San Antonio store's amenities and products,[30] videologs have gained momentum among retailers trying to capitalize on two popular consumer pastimes: home shopping and video watching. Sears used an 18-minute tape to showcase electronic toys for Christmas in 1987 and Neiman-Marcus used a tape to show 15 expensive one-of-a-kind items in 1988.

However, the most significant advance in electronic shopping today is television shopping shows. Not only will consumers of the 1990s be able to make purchases from regular television shopping networks like Home Shopping Network and QVC, but they will also be able to use Telaction, an interactive television shopping channel. Telaction, which debuted in February 1988, works by having shoppers tune in to their interactive cable channel and dial a local phone number. While viewing still-frame video presentations from retailers offering merchandise (the original list included J. C. Penney, Marshall Field's, Dayton Hudson, Neiman Marcus, Sears, and Foot Locker), shoppers use the keypad of their phones to guide the system through a personalized shopping tour.

Unlike the other cable shopping networks, Telaction doesn't routinely offer discounted merchandise. Instead, it is more like catalog shopping. Customers pick what merchandise they want to see, rather than waiting passively for it to appear on their television sets.[31] It is predicted that Telaction will have $2 billion in sales by 1992.

EQUIPMENT AND FIXTURE INNOVATIONS

Innovations in retail equipment and fixtures are continually altering the nature and practice of retailing. Our discussion will not be exhaustive, but it will reflect a sampling of the innovations in equipment and fixtures.

Cash Handling Systems.   Retailers that handle large amounts of cash, such as gasoline stations and convenience stores, are very susceptible to robbery. These retailers are beginning to install cash-control systems, machines that allow employees to deposit excess cash. If the cash is needed for an especially large transaction, it can be retrieved after a preprogrammed delay. The time delay is long enough (two to ten minutes) that would-be robbers are not willing to risk waiting for the extra cash.

Telecommunications.   Retail executives can spend a considerable amount of time in travel: going to market, visiting branch stores and

Illus. 5.6
CheckRobot's automated checkout machines allow shoppers to check out merchandise themselves before paying a centrally located cashier. Source: CheckRobot Inc.

warehouses, etc. Much of this travel can be reduced through the sophisticated telecommunication systems available today. The Goudchaux/Maison Blanche chain in Louisiana has installed a telecommunications network designed to improve customer service, provide quick access to executives even at home, and expedite credit validation.[32] Technological advances in this area have improved management efficiency more than enough to offset any increases in the cost of phone rates.[33]

Scanning.   One of the most significant technological developments in retailing was the development and implementation of the Universal Product Code (UPC). The UPC consists of 12 vertical bars that are placed on the package of all grocery products. These 12 bars uniquely identify each product. Optical scanning machines at the checkout counter can be passed over the bars to compute the customer's bill automatically. Scanners have been a major profit producer for retail grocery stores by increasing worker productivity, reducing labor costs, and providing better and more timely information. The retailer can now quickly obtain item-movement data for any period of time it desires (weekly, daily, hourly, and so on). This data can be used to control inventory, to determine the response to advertised specials, to assess the change in demand due to a price change, and to determine the sales effect of altering shelf space. In short, this data allows the grocery retailer to manage the store more analytically. This data base helped retailers become the power brokers of their channel, as they no longer depend on the manufacturer for this information. In fact, many manufacturers now rely on retailers for information.

TRENDS IN INTERNATIONAL RETAILING

Retailing in other countries exhibits even greater diversity in its structure than it does in the United States. In some countries, such as Italy, retailing is composed largely of specialty houses carrying narrow lines. Finnish retailers generally carry a more general line of merchandise. The size of the average retailer is also diverse, from Harrod's in London and Mitsukoshi Ltd. in Japan, which serve over ten thousand customers a day to the small one-or two-person stalls in underdeveloped African and Latin American nations.

The rate of change in retailing appears to be directly related to the stage and speed of economic development in the countries concerned, but even the least developed countries are experiencing dramatic changes. Self-service, a retailing innovation developed in California in 1912, has grown at an overwhelming pace throughout the world. Supermarkets, a development of the United States depression, are now standard in both developed and undeveloped nations, although over 80 percent of European food sales are still in the hands of small retailers. Discount houses, a product of the post-World War II era, have gained market share in coun-

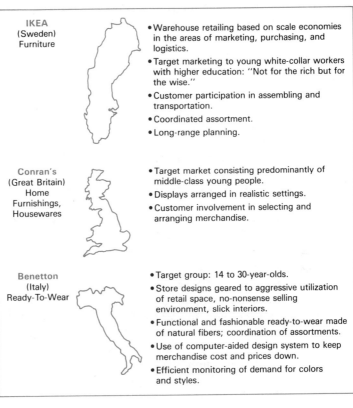

Exhibit 5.17
**Retailing
Concepts of
Three European
Specialty Stores**

IKEA
(Sweden)
Furniture

- Warehouse retailing based on scale economies in the areas of marketing, purchasing, and logistics.
- Target marketing to young white-collar workers with higher education: "Not for the rich but for the wise."
- Customer participation in assembling and transportation.
- Coordinated assortment.
- Long-range planning.

Conran's
(Great Britain)
Home
Furnishings,
Housewares

- Target market consisting predominantly of middle-class young people.
- Displays arranged in realistic settings.
- Customer involvement in selecting and arranging merchandise.

Benetton
(Italy)
Ready-To-Wear

- Target group: 14 to 30-year-olds.
- Store designs geared to aggressive utilization of retail space, no-nonsense selling environment, slick interiors.
- Functional and fashionable ready-to-wear made of natural fibers; coordination of assortments.
- Use of computer-aided design system to keep merchandise cost and prices down.
- Efficient monitoring of demand for colors and styles.

SOURCE: Madhau Kacker, "International Flow of Retailing Know-How: Bridging the Technology Gap in Distribution in *Journal of Retailing* (Spring 1988), pp. 41–67.

tries where such activity is legal. Electronic retailing spread to other countries from United States merchants. In 1983, 7-Eleven became the first chain in Japan to introduce computerized check-out systems.

However, as Kacker[34] has pointed out, new retail formats have emerged in countries other than the United States. This development can be attributed to a variety of factors in the economic and social environments: a wide-spread concern for health, a steady increase in the number of working women and two-income families, long, persistent energy shortages and the consequent upsurge in price levels, consumerism, and so forth. These factors, and their effects on consumer life-styles, encouraged high-performance retailers around the world to seek new market segments, make adjustments in the retail mix, alter location patterns, and adopt new multisegment strategies. In the process, many new retail concepts and formats have emerged and spread, not only from firm to firm but from country to country. Exhibit 5.17 presents unique retailing concepts applied by three European specialty chains operating in the United States.

SUMMARY

Retailers can be classified in a variety of ways. Five of the more popular schemes are by SIC code, number of outlets, margins vs. turnover, location, and size. None of these classifications, however, sheds adequate light on competition in retailing.

A model of retail competition was developed to aid in illustrating certain principles of retail competition. This model suggested that retail competition is typically local; the retail industry is monopolistically competitive or oligopolistic; the demand side of retailing must consider the distance of the consumer from the store; both supply and demand factors must be examined in developing price and nonprice strategies; and an action by a retailer to increase its trade area is likely to elicit a response from competitors.

The economics of intratype and intertype competition, divertive competition, and the struggle for market share in retailing can affect retail profits. Therefore, retailers need to develop a protected market niche. One increasingly popular way to do this is by a store positioning strategy.

Retail competition is both revolutionary and evolutionary. Five theories of viewing changing competitive patterns in retailing were reviewed. The wheel of retailing proposes that new types of retailers enter the market as low-status, low-margin, low-price operators. As they succeed, they become more complex, increasing their margins and prices and becoming vulnerable to new types of low-margin competitors, who, in turn, follow the same pattern. The retail accordion theory suggests that retail institutions evolve from outlets offering wide assortments to specialized narrow assortment stores and then return to wide assortments to repeat the pattern. The theory of natural selection argues that those retail institutions that most readily adapt to a changing environment will prosper and others will not. The dialectic process of retailing suggests that each new form of retailing (called the thesis) begets a negation of itself (called the antithesis), which results in a blending of the two called a synthesis. The synthesis ultimately becomes the thesis and the process begins again. Finally, the retail life cycle theory argues that retail institutions, like the products they distribute, pass through identifiable cycles during which the basics of strategy and competition change.

We followed with a discussion of nonstore retailing, since industry analysts contend that this form of retailing will be a major competitive force in the future. Types of nonstore retailing were discussed.

Technology was defined as the application of science to develop new methods or ways of doing things. In retailing, technology occurs in two broad areas: new methods of retailing and new equipment or fixtures used in retailing. Innovation in retailing is the result of constant pressure to improve efficiency and effectiveness and a continual effort to better serve the consumer. We used two examples: the continuing evolution in grocery store retailing and the emergence of electronic shopping. We also looked at recent innovations in fixtures and equipment and their impact on retailing.

We concluded our discussion of retail competition by looking at how retailing concepts and formats differ between countries as a result of differences in their economic and social environments.

QUESTIONS FOR DISCUSSION

1. Describe the wheel of retailing theory of retail competition. What is the theory's major strength and weakness?
2. Describe the retail accordion theory of competition. What is this theory's major strength and weakness?
3. What is the dialectic process of competition? How can it be used to describe the evolution in gasoline retailing?
4. What trends do you see taking place in retail competition over the next decade?
5. In terms of retail life cycle, what is likely to happen to the innovative retail firms of today?
6. What precautions should be taken when using Census Bureau data to categorize retail competition?
7. What is meant by classifying stores on the basis of margins and turnover ratios? Give an example of each category.
8. Which of the following retailers would you expect to face the strongest competition: gas station, flower shop, women's apparel store, pet shop, discount department store? Why?
9. Why are furniture stores able to attract customers from a greater distance than food stores?
10. Explain in your own words why retailers face a three-dimensional demand function. Do all retailers face a three-dimensional demand model?
11. Develop a list of expenses or costs for a department store and categorize them as fixed, variable, or semifixed.
12. Assume that you are in the market for a new Nissan. The local Nissan dealer will sell you the model you want for $11,875. However, you notice an advertisement by a Nissan dealer located in a city 180 miles away. The ad prices the car you want at $11,595. Should you travel to the distant city to purchase the Nissan?
13. Review the last twelve to eighteen issues of *Chain Store Age Executive* and identify recent innovations in retail equipment, fixtures, and buildings.

SUGGESTED READINGS

Feinberg, Sam. "A Study of Off-Price Retailing," *Home Furnishings Daily* (April 23, 1984): 161–184. This is a reprint of 11 columns Feinberg published in *Women's Wear Daily* on off-price retailing.

Popovich, Elizabeth. "Editor's Note: Can Direct Marketing Replace Stores?" *Product Marketing* (May 1984): 3.

Schlosberg, Jeremy. "The Demographics Of Convenience," *American Demographics* (October 1986): 36–42.

Sterlieb, George and James W. Hughes. "The Demise Of The Department Store," *American Demographics* (August 1987): 31–33, 59.

ENDNOTES

1. The framework is developed in elaborate detail by Charles A. Ingene and Robert F. Lusch, "A Model of Retail Structure, in Jagdish Sheth, ed., *Research in Marketing*, 101–64 and Jagdish Sheth, "An Integrative Theory of Patronage Preference and Behavior," in William Darden and Robert Lusch, *Patronage Behavior and Retail Management* (New York: North-Holland, 1983), 9–28.

2. Leonard W. Weiss, *Case Studies in American Industry* (New York: Wiley, 1971), 222–23.

3. In the simple model to be developed we assume the retailer sells a single item. This need not be the case for the validity of the model to hold up; it is done only to reduce the amount of mathematics in our discussions.

4. "General Merchandise Survey," *Progressive Grocer* (July 1984): 183 and (August 1987): 26.

5. The concept of divertive competition is discussed in Bert C. McCammon, Jack J. Kasulis, and Jack A. Lesser, "The New Parameters of Retail Competition: The Intensified Struggle for Market Share," in Ronald W. Stampfl and Elizabeth Hirschman (eds.), *Competitive Structure in Retail Markets: The Department Store Perspective* (Chicago: AMA, 1980), 108–118.

6. Malcolm P. McNair, "Significant Trends and Developments in the Postwar Period," in A. B. Smith, ed., *Competitive Distribution in a Free High-Level Economy and Its Implications for the University* (Pittsburgh: University of Pittsburgh Press, 1958).

7. Stanley C. Hollander, "The Wheel of Retailing," *Journal of Marketing* (July 1960): 41.

8. Hollander, "Wheel of Retailing," 40.

9. Dillard B. Tinsley, John R. Brooks, Jr., and Michael d'Amico, "Will the Wheel of Retailing Stop Turning?" *Akron Business and Economic Review* (Summer 1978): 26–29.

10. Stanley C. Hollander, "Notes on the Retail Accordion," *Journal of Retailing* (Summer 1966): 29–40, 54.

11. Ralph Hower, *History of Macy's of New York 1858–1919* (Cambridge: Harvard University Press, 1943), 73.

12. Reprinted from Delbert J. Duncan, "Responses of Selected Retail Institutions to Their Changing Environment," in Peter D. Bennett, *Marketing and Economic Development* (Chicago: American Marketing Association, 1965), 593.

13. Ronald R. Gist, *Retailing: Concepts and Decisions* (New York: John Wiley & Sons, 1968), 106–109.

14. Thomas J. Maronick and Bruce J. Walker, "The Dialectic Evolution of Retailing," in Barnett Greenberg, ed., *Proceedings: Southern Marketing Association* (Atlanta: Georgia State University, 1975), 147–151.

15. Thomas P. Neill, *Makers of the Modern Mind* (Milwaukee: Bruce Publishing Company, 1985), 298.

16. Maronick and Walker, "Dialectic Evolution," 147.

17. Reprinted by permission of the *Harvard Business Review*. From "The Retail Life Cycle," by William R. Davidson, Albert D. Bates, and Stephen J. Bass, (November–December 1976), p. 89. Copyright 1976 by President and Fellows of Harvard College: all rights reserved.

18. Davidson, Bates, and Bass, "Retail Life Cycle," 92. Reprinted by permission of the *Harvard Business Review*.

19. "Cafeteria Magnate Aims for Head of Line," *Wall Street Journal*, 18 August 1988, p. 18.

20. Davidson, Bates, and Bass, "Retail Life Cycle, 93.

21. "Last Chapter for Big Catalog?," *Advertising Age*, (July 18, 1988), p. 26.

22. William R. Davidson and Alice Rogers, "Non-Store Retailing: Its Importance to and Impact on Merchandise Suppliers and Competitive Channels" in Marcia Bielfield and Linda Nagel, eds., *The Growth of Non-Store Retailing: Implications for Retailers, Manufacturers, and Public Policy Makers* (New York: Institute of Retail Management, New York University, 1978), 22–29.

23. Davidson and Rogers, "Non-Store Retailing," 23.

24. "Electronic Shopping," *Chain Store Age Executive* (July 1988): 15.

25. "Will Food Retailing's Future Be Out-of-Store?" *Progressive Grocer* (December 1983): 23.

26. "The Return of the Amazing Colossal Store," *Business Week* (August 22, 1988): 59–61.

27. This section is based largely on material provided by ByVideo Inc.

28. "Some Home Centers Opt for DIY Videos," *Chain Store Age Executive* (September 1988): 61–52.

29. "Retailers Offering Electronic Shopping to Help Curb Consumers' Frustrations," *Lubbock Avalanche-Journal*, 18 July 1987, p. 8A.

30. "Marshall Field's Goes to the Videotapes," *Sales & Marketing Management* (December 1986): 60–61.

31. "Telaction: Is It Ready For Prime Time?," *Chain Store Age Executive* (July 1988): 16–19.

32. "Goudchaux Improves Service with Digital Network," *Chain Store Age Executive* (June 1984): 35–41.

33. "Phone Rates Squeeze Chains," *Chain Store Age Executive* (June 1984): 41–44.

34. Madhau Kacker, "International Flow of Retailing Know-How: Bridging the Technology Gap in Distribution," *Journal of Retailing* (Spring 1988): 41–67.

6 Chapter

Understanding the Legal Environment

OVERVIEW

In this chapter, we will discuss the legal constraints on retail decision making. The discussion revolves around the legal aspects of decisions about pricing, promotion, credit, franchises, products or merchandise, marketing channels, and mergers and acquisitions. Since decision making is discussed in detail in later chapters, you might find it useful to refer to this chapter again.

**CHAPTER 6
Understanding
the Legal
Environment**

We have seen that the retailer is constrained by several uncontrollable external forces. We will now explore another force that has a tremendous impact on retail decisions—the legal environment. Consider the impact of recent laws raising the legal drinking age to 21, or of a Washington state law which allows retailers to conduct only one yearly promotional game of chance. What about state "blue laws" that affect the retailer's ability to operate seven days a week? What about the cities that regulate garage sales? What about state regulations restricting the use of product samples? All these laws influence the ability of retailers to serve the needs of their target market.

To avoid costly legal blunders, the retail decision maker needs to understand its legal constraints. Knowledge of the legal environment can aid the retail executive in profitably managing the retail firm.

Retailers cannot make decisions without regard for the laws that regulate business trade. Federal, state and local laws limit the retailer's flexibility and freedom in making business-related decisions. Since local and state laws are quite varied, the emphasis of this chapter will be on federal legislation and its impact on retailers' actions. We will comment on some state and local laws, but will, in most part, leave it up to you and your class discussions to investigate the impact of state and local laws on retail activities in your state and community.

In the early 1980s, the cries for decreased governmental regulation of business became louder. Federal spending cutbacks also limited the activities of key regulatory agencies, like the FTC. Will the movement toward deregulation gain momentum? What direction will it take? We don't know yet.

The dynamic nature of retailing requires that it, like other economic sectors, be monitored. Most large retailers maintain legal departments and lobbyists to keep abreast of, interpret, and even influence government regulations. Such activities are usually beyond the resources of small businesses, but the government and the press do a reasonably good job of keeping businesses informed of pending and new legislation.

PRICING CONSTRAINTS

The price decision is the one that most frequently confronts retailers. Retailers continually have to establish prices for the many items they carry. In doing this, they have considerable, but not total, flexibility. The major constraining factors are summarized in Exhibit 6.1.

HORIZONTAL PRICE FIXING

When a group of competing retailers establish a fixed price at which to sell their merchandise, they are engaged in **horizontal price fixing**. For example, all retail grocers in a particular trade area may agree to sell eggs at 94 cents per dozen. Two supermarket chains were recently fined $2 million for price fixing,[1] while four other supermarkets were fined $830,000 after pleading no-contest to similar charges.[2] Another major supermarket pleaded no-contest to the price fixing charge of banding with competitors to eliminate double couponing.[3] Regardless of its actual or potential impact on competition or the consumer, this price fixing violates Section 1 of the Sherman Antitrust Act (1890), which states, "Every contract, combination in the form of trust or otherwise, or conspiracy, in restraint of trade or commerce among the several states, or with foreign nations is declared to be illegal."[4]

Since passage of the Sherman Act, the courts have viewed horizontal price fixing as a restraint of trade. Occasionally, retailers have argued that the Sherman Act does not apply to them, since they operate locally, not "among the several states"—the definition of **interstate commerce**. However, because the merchandise retailer's purchase typically originates in another state, the courts view retailers as involved in interstate commerce even if all of their customers are local. Also, most states have laws similar to the Sherman Act, prohibiting such restraints of trade as horizontal price fixing on a strictly local level.

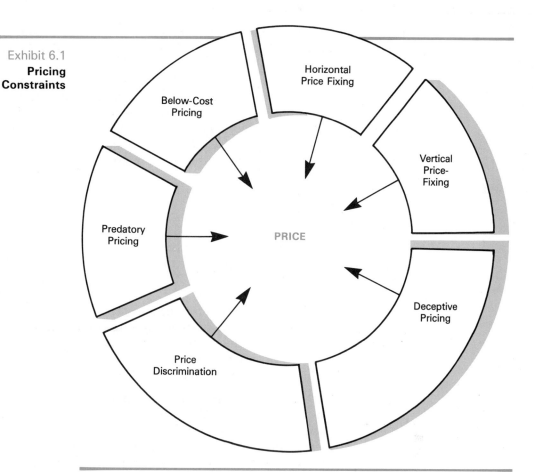

Exhibit 6.1
Pricing Constraints

Horizontal Price Fixing

Below-Cost Pricing

Vertical Price-Fixing

Predatory Pricing

PRICE

Deceptive Pricing

Price Discrimination

VERTICAL PRICE FIXING

When a retailer collaborates with its supplier to resell an item at an agreed-on price, **vertical price fixing** has occurred. This is also referred to as **resale price maintenance**, or fair trade. These agreements are illegal and are viewed as a violation of Section 1 of the Sherman Act.[5] Resale price maintenance does not mean that manufacturers cannot suggest to retailers a price at which they would like to see an item sold. But they cannot establish with the retailers a price for resale, nor can they legally threaten retailers with supply cutoffs if they do not sell at the recommended price.

Resale price maintenance agreements, or fair trade laws, were established during the depression as a means for small retailers to combat the price advantages of chain stores. They were banned by President Ford, with the consent of Congress, in 1976. Now some manufacturers and retailers are urging that fair trade laws be enacted again as a means to combat the inroads of the discounters. In May 1988, the use of price maintenance was again made quasi-legal when the Supreme Court ruled that a manufacturer's decision to cut off a retailer who is discounting prices isn't illegal, unless it involves an effort to fix retail prices. Since it would be difficult to prove that price fixing was the sole intent of such an action, some experts think that the ruling will lead to higher prices.[6] It appears that this matter will only be settled by legislative action, as discounters and their customers seek Congressional aid in preventing a return to fair trade.

PRICE DISCRIMINATION

When two retailers buy identical merchandise from the same supplier but pay different prices, that is **price discrimination**. Not all forms of price discrimination are illegal.

Legal Definitions of Price Discrimination.   Federal legislation addressed the legality of price discrimination in Section 2 of the Clayton Act, which made certain forms of price discrimination illegal.[7] Section 2 was amended and strengthened with passage of the Robinson-Patman Act in 1936.[8] This act had two primary objectives:

1. To prevent suppliers from gaining unfair advantage over their competitors by discriminating among buyers either in price or in providing allowances or services.[9]
2. To prevent buyers from using their economic power to get discriminatory prices from suppliers so as to gain an advantage over their own competitors.

The Robinson-Patman Act, like fair trade laws, grew out of the struggle of small independent retailers to compete with chain-store retailers during the 1930s. During this time many small grocers, druggists, and other retailers were quite vocal in complaining to their senators and congressmen about how suppliers frequently discriminated in price among different customers. It was quite disheartening to these small retailers that suppliers would often charge chain stores even less than they did the wholesalers that sold to the small, independent retailer. Times have changed, however, and the small, mom-and-pop grocer or druggist is now almost nonexistent. In its place are a large number of well-organized chain-store organizations that aggressively compete for market share and large groups of independent retailers who have banded together in cooperatives to be able to have the purchasing economies of the large chain-store organizations. Some scholars have thus argued that the Robinson-Patman Act should be repealed,[10] and FTC enforcement of the act is at a minimum.

For the retail manager, Section 2 of the Robinson-Patman Act (actually Section 2 of the amended Clayton Act) is the most important. Section 2(a) of the statute provides:

> That it shall be unlawful for any person engaged in commerce . . . to discriminate in price between different purchasers of commodities of like grade and quality . . . where the effect of such discrimination may be substantially to lessen competition or tend to create a monopoly in any line of commerce, or to injure, destroy, or prevent competition with any person who either grants or knowingly receives the benefit of such discrimination, or with customers of either of them. . . .

The retailer should recognize three things regarding this section of the act. First, the transaction must occur in interstate commerce, which the courts see as being almost universal, since customers can come from anywhere. Second, the actual competition does not have to be lessened; only a potential lessening of competition must exist. Third, the retailer who knowingly receives the benefit of discrimination is just as culpable as the supplier granting the discrimination. Thus, retailers should not coerce their suppliers into giving them discriminatory discounts that would put them at an advantage over their competitors. However, this does not mean that buyers can't negotiate the best deal possible; in most instances, buyers don't know what the best possible deal available is.

Considerable attention has been given to the phrase "commodities of like grade and quality." What does this phrase mean? Commodities are goods and not services. This implies that discriminatory pricing practices in the sale of services, like advertising space or the leasing of real estate, are not prohibited by the act. For example, shopping center developers frequently charge varying rates for equal square footage depending on the tenant and the type of merchandise sold. In a case brought by Plum Tree, Inc. (a franchisor of a nationwide chain of retail shops), against the N. K. Winston Corporation (a shopping center developer), Plum Tree charged the developer with price discrimination under the Robinson-Patman Act for charging different rents for equal space. "Plum Tree contended that the commodities under the act are equivalent to leaseholds in shopping centers and that a landlord must charge equal rent for equal space. The court held that a lease for real property is not "selling goods, wares, or merchandise".[11]

"Like grade and quality" has been interpreted by the courts to mean of identical physical and chemical properties. This implies that different prices cannot be justified merely because the labels on the product are different. Therefore, private labeling of merchandise does not make it different from identical goods carrying the seller's brand. However, if the seller can establish that an actual physical difference in grade and quality exists, then a price differential can be justified.

Retailer's Defenses of Price Discrimination.   The illegality of price discrimination is not clear cut. A variety of defenses are available to buyers and sellers charged with price discrimination. The principal defenses are:

1. A **cost justification** defense, which attempts to show that a differential can be accounted for on the basis of differences in cost to the seller in manufacture, sale, or delivery arising from differences in method or quantities involved.
2. A **changing market conditions** defense, which attempts to justify the price differential on the basis of danger of imminent deterioration of perishable goods or on the obsolescence of seasonal goods.
3. An argument based on **meeting competition** in good faith. The seller attempts to show that its lower price to a purchaser was made in good faith to meet an equally low price of a competitor provided that this matched price actually existed and was lawful in itself.

Thus, the retailer that knowingly receives a discriminatory price from a seller needs to be relatively certain that the seller is granting a defensible price break based on one of the three preceding criteria.

The cost justification defense is extremely difficult to use because the courts have never defined exactly how costs should be computed. The two most common defenses are changing market conditions and meeting competition in good faith. Recently, however, the courts ruled against Folger Coffee's good faith defense. The courts found that since Folger allowed retailers partial price reductions for coffee held by retailers in inventory and extended its discounts beyond the time period that its competitors provided discounted prices, it had negated its good faith argument.[12]

The Supreme Court has recently expanded the protection afforded sellers in charging different prices to retailers under the meeting competition defense. The case involved a manufacturer, Falls City Brewery, selling beer to wholesalers in Indiana and its neighboring state, Kentucky. Indiana law bans Indiana wholesalers from both buying or selling beer to out-of-state businesses and requires brewers to charge the same price throughout the state. Therefore, Falls City was entitled to sell beer at a lower price to Kentucky wholesalers, in order to meet competition, than it was charging Evansville, Indiana (a city on the Ohio River across from Kentucky) wholesalers.[13] This action hurt Indiana wholesalers and retailers as many Indiana consumers were able to cross the river and purchase Falls City at a lower price.

Discrimination in Services.   Sellers are not only prohibited from discrimination in price; they are also banned from providing different services and payments to different retailers. These services and payments frequently include advertising allowances, displays and banners to promote the goods, in-store demonstrations, and the distribution of samples or premiums. Sections 2(d) and 2(e) of the Robinson-Patman Act deal specifically with these practices and state that such services and payments or consideration must be made available on **proportionately equal terms** to all **competing customers**. Retailers have brought many more enforcement actions under these two sections than under Section 2(a).

Two questions arise in interpreting these sections: (1) Who are competing customers? and (2) What is proportionately equal? Let us illustrate some of the technical difficulties in answering these questions.

A manufacturer of household cleaning detergents is providing a large supermarket chain with an advertising allowance of 50 cents per case purchased. The supermarket chain buys directly from the manufacturer. A small grocer who operates a single store in the ghetto of a large city also sells detergent produced by this manufacturer, but is offered no allowance. This small grocer purchases all its merchandise through a local wholesaler and is six miles from the nearest store operated by the large supermarket chain. In reviewing this situation, the courts are most likely to be concerned with whether the small grocer and chain-store supermarket are competing customers.

It could be argued that the small grocer and chain grocer are not both customers of the detergent manufacturer, since the small grocer is, strictly speaking, a customer of a wholesaler. Courts have generally not accepted this argument. Competing customers has been held to include those buying for resale from a seller's customer, such as a wholesaler.[14] Another argument that might be presented is that the small grocer and chain grocer do not compete for the same customers. Expert witnesses may testify that consumers typically do not travel more than two to four miles to purchase groceries—especially in an urban environment. Since the two stores are separated by six miles they could hardly be viewed as competitors. This argument, if carefully constructed and supported by empirical evidence and expert testimony, might be considered plausible by the courts.

Let us now try to illustrate some of the ambiguity of the concept of proportionately equal terms. Assume that a cosmetics manufacturer offers a department store in Chicago a cosmetics demonstrator for one eight-hour day per month. A small drugstore in Chicago also handles this line of cosmetics but sells only one-eighth as much as the department store. The manufacturer believes that it would be impractical to furnish the drugstore a cosmetics demonstrator for one hour per month (a proportionately equal allowance). The drugstore retailer would also probably feel that this would be impractical. However, this does not relieve the manufacturer of its duty to the drugstore retailer for offering proportionate promotional service. The service need not be the same. A substitute could be offering a demonstration kit to the drugstore retailer, as long as both agreed this was adequate.

The same problem arises quite frequently in regard to advertising allowances offered retailers. A large appliance manufacturer may offer retailers an advertising allowance to be applied against any TV advertising they engage in. This is unfair to the very small appliance retailer, because

Illus. 6.1
Manufacturers must offer competing smaller retailers proportionate promotional services.

it cannot afford to advertise on TV even if the manufacturer picks up part of the cost. The small retailer has the right to some alternative promotional allowance (perhaps an allowance to be applied to advertising in the newspaper or to be used for window displays or banners). In a similar case, the FTC found that General Motors was unfair to smaller car rental companies when it supplied millions of advertising dollars to National Car Rental and Avis Rent-A-Car, but little or no money to smaller firms. The judge ruled that GM must advertise the availability of any future ad-support programs in specified publications and offer ad dollars to all interested rental and leasing firms on equal terms.[15]

Synthetic Brokerages.   Another aspect of the Robinson-Patman Act with which the retailer needs to be acquainted is Section 2(c). This important section prohibits the development of synthetic brokerages or any type of dummy brokerage payment. Any commission or allowance to a person directly or indirectly controlled by the buyer is prohibited. For example, a retailer who is buying through a broker may create a synthetic brokerage company through which to place its orders. The manufacturer would be instructed by the synthetic broker to ship the goods directly to the retailer and bill the retailer directly. The manufacturer would then remit to the broker a commission that would, in reality, end up in the hands of the retailer. Thus, the effective price that the retailer is paying for the goods is lower than the price competing retailers who transact their business through legitimate brokers are paying. Arrangements involving synthetic brokers are a form of price discrimination and have been treated as violations of the Robinson-Patman Act.

In summary, the Robinson Patman Act makes it illegal to discriminate in price of a product in interstate commerce (to sell goods of like grade and quality but not services to two nonretail buyers at different prices) if it lessens, injures, destroys or prevents competition or creates a monopoly (only the potential of a lessening, not an actual lessening, at any level in the channel is needed). The three defenses for charging different prices are: 1) the seller can show that a cost saving was realized from selling to a particular customer (often difficult to define), 2) the price differential was caused by normal market/price fluctuations (an important defense), and 3) the seller simply matched the equally low price of a competitor (retailers can be found guilty if they provide false information to the vendor).

DECEPTIVE PRICING

Retailers should avoid using a misleading price to lure customers into the store. Advertising goods at a price below what the retailer is actually willing to take or advertising an item at an artificially low price and then adding hidden charges are deceptive pricing practices, which are unfair methods of competition. The Wheeler-Lea Amendment (1938) of the Federal Trade Commission Act (1914) made illegal all "unfair or deceptive acts in commerce." Not only is the retailer's customer being unfairly treated when the retailer uses deceptive pricing, but the retailer's competitors are being potentially harmed because some of their customers may be deceitfully diverted.

In 1988, Sears was charged by the New York City Department of Consumer Affairs on several counts of deceptive pricing. One disputed practice involved the promotion of a discounted price, say 30 percent off, without explaining whether the markdown is based on the regular selling price of the merchandise or an inflated pre-sale price.

Another charge was that between September 1987 and January 1988, Sears advertised carpet cleaning services in the city for $34.98, urging readers to call by a certain date. For five months, the price remained the same, but the deadline to call kept changing, a tactic the Department of Consumer Affairs claimed was deceptive. In May, Sears increased the advertised price of the carpet cleaning service to $39.99, making the earlier claim legitimate.[16]

Washington and Minnesota have fined several major retailers for selling "sale items" that have never been on sale. Another form of deceptive pricing is using the term "lowest price guaranteed" when what is really meant is "we will match any price."[17] No wonder the consumer finds the pricing policies of many retailers deceptive, especially when experts report that as much as 85 percent of some general merchandise lines are sold "on sale" or that one jewelry chain has never sold a single item at regular price. These practices are causing retailers to lose credibility with their customers who no longer know the true price of any product.

PREDATORY PRICING

If a retail chain charges different prices in different geographical areas in order to eliminate competition in selected areas, it is in violation of Section 3 of the Robinson-Patman Act. This section forbids the sale of goods at lower prices in one area for the purpose of destroying competition or eliminating a competitor, or sales of goods at unreasonably low prices for such purpose. Deluxe Store, Handy Andy, and a local retail grocer's association have filed and won suits alleging that H. E. Butt Grocery Company engaged in predatory pricing in the San Antonio market.[18] A similar charge was filed against Kroger Company in its hometown of Cincinnati by sixteen members of the Independent Grocers Alliance (IGA) Distributing Company. The courts ruled in favor of Kroger, because IGA, while it proved that such action would result in irreparable injury to IGA, failed to prove that Kroger was operating below cost—a test for predatory pricing.[19]

BELOW-COST PRICING

In 1984, twenty-two states had sales-below-cost legislation governing the retail distribution of merchandise.[20] The specific content of these laws varies, but usually they prohibit the retailer from selling merchandise below cost plus some fixed percentage markup (6 percent is typical). These state laws are generally unclear as to whether the retailer can give merchandise away or offer prizes or premiums without increasing an item's price as a form of price reduction.

State laws have been generally ineffective in preventing sales below cost. First of all, they usually require that a competitor lodge a complaint or initiate a legal action against the retailer. Most retailers will not do this because they, too, may sometimes sell below cost. A second problem has been that most statutes do not clearly define cost. Is a retailer's cost the cash price paid, the invoice price before a cash discount, the delivered price, the average price paid over a year minus any end-of-year rebates, the price less any advertising or promotional allowance, or something else? Because of the technicalities in defining cost, litigation is time-consuming and expensive. In 1987, five small-town Oklahoma druggists sued Wal-Mart. These pharmacies charged Wal-Mart with violating an obscure 1941 state law requiring retailers to sell their goods above cost. Wal-Mart, with 77 stores in Oklahoma and 9,500 employees, is taking its case to the people in hopes that the law will be repealed.[21]

PROMOTION CONSTRAINTS

The ability of the retailer to make any promotion decision is constrained by two major pieces of federal legislation, the FTC Act (1914), especially section 5, and the Wheeler-Lea Amendment (1938) of the FTC Act. The retailer should be familiar with four promotional areas that are potentially under the domain of the FTC Act and the Wheeler-Lea Amendment. These areas are deceitful diversion of patronage, deceptive advertising, bait-and-switch tactics, and substantiation and retraction of advertising. Exhibit 6.2 depicts these four areas of constraint.

DECEITFUL DIVERSION OF PATRONAGE

If competitors publish or verbalize falsehoods about a retailer in an attempt to divert patrons from the retailer, they are engaging in an unfair trade practice. The retailer would be afforded protection under the FTC

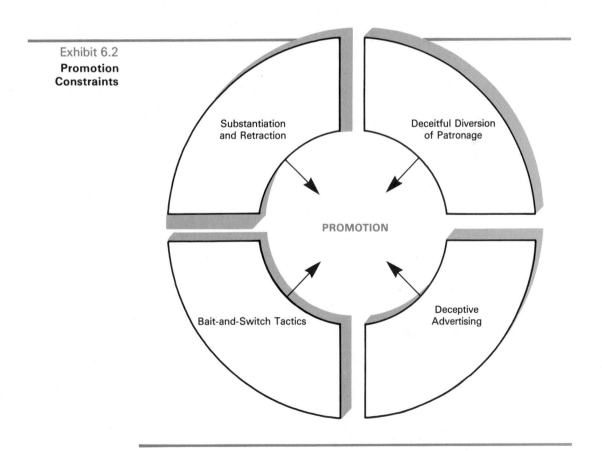

Exhibit 6.2
**Promotion
Constraints**

Substantiation and Retraction

Deceitful Diversion of Patronage

PROMOTION

Bait-and-Switch Tactics

Deceptive Advertising

Act but also could receive protection by showing that the defamatory statements were libel or slander. In either case, the retailer would have to demonstrate that actual damage had occurred. For example, assume that the salespeople of Retailer A try to convince consumers coming into their store that Retailer B is a good-for-nothing crook who is out to cheat the public. If Retailer B could prove in a court of law that the defamatory statements were falsehoods and that it lost market share or patrons as a result of these statements, then Retailer B would be entitled to damages. The loss of patrons is very difficult to demonstrate, and therefore cases involving the deceitful diversion of patronage are not common. Occasionally, however, such a case will surface, and therefore it is important that a retailer understand that it is not free to say whatever it pleases about a competitor. It is even more important that the retailer's sales force recognize this.

A form of deceitful diversion of patronage that occasionally occurs in retailing is palming off. **Palming off** occurs when a retailer represents merchandise as being made by a firm other than the true manufacturer. For example, consider an exclusive women's apparel retailer who purchases a group of nicely styled dresses at a bargain price and replaces their labels with those of a top designer. This is deception as to source of origin, and litigation could be brought under the FTC Act and the Wheeler-Lea Amendment. In addition, if the designer's label is a registered trademark, protection would be afforded under the major piece of federal trademark legislation—the Lanham Act (1946).

In a special report, the U.S. International Trade Council stated that United States industries are losing $20 billion a year as a result of foreign counterfeiting of trademarked United States products.[22] One of the more successful exhibits at the World Fair in New Orleans was a show of fake merchandise sponsored by the Customs Office. This exhibit displayed hundreds of different products—all fakes—copied overseas and shipped to the United States for retail sale. Examples included Rolex watches, Izod shirts, sunglasses, audiocassettes, and even Vicks Vapo-Rub.[23]

DECEPTIVE ADVERTISING

False or misleading advertising claims are illegal. It is often quite difficult to distinguish between what is false or misleading and what is simply puffery, which is not illegal. Saying, "this is an excellent buy, and you can't afford to pass it up," is probably puffery, even though the product may not be an excellent buy by all standards, and you may be able to afford to pass it up! It is important for retailers to recognize that the FTC is not concerned with the intent of the advertiser but with whether the consumer was misled by the advertising. Recently, the FTC has adopted a policy statement requiring proof that a consumer has been harmed as a result of a misrepresentation, omission, or a practice that is likely to mislead the consumer acting reasonably in the circumstances before an advertiser can be charged with deceptive advertising practices.[24] There is disagreement over whether requiring this proof constitutes a change in, FTC policy toward deception.[25] For example, an ad for "Danish pastry" would not be considered deceptive because "a few misguided souls believe . . . that all 'Danish pastry' is made in Denmark"[26] because a reasonable consumer would know what Danish pastry was.

The retailer should be concerned not only with its own advertising but also with that of manufacturers whose products it sells. If the manufacturer makes misleading statements, then the consumer will not only develop negative attitudes toward the manufacturer, but also toward retailers who carry that manufacturer's products. There is also a legal problem because retailers are liable for deceptive co-op ads (which they and the supplier paid for jointly). In a Supreme Court decision, Pay 'n' Save, a West Coast drug chain, was found liable for false and misleading advertisements of X-11 diet pills. The ads were prepared by an advertising agency for Porter & Dietsch, the manufacturer of X-11. The Supreme Court ruled that Pay 'n' Save's lack of knowledge of the false and misleading advertising claims was not a sufficient defense.[27]

BAIT-AND-SWITCH TACTICS

Another form of deceptive promotion is **bait-and-switch advertising**, advertising merchandise at unusually attractive prices and then, once the consumer is baited to come into the store, trying to persuade the customer that the low-priced model is not a good buy because of its poor quality or durability. Sears agreed with an FTC order prohibiting the use of bait-and-switch ads for 24 products, including vacuums and sewing machines.[28] Most states have similar laws. For example, New Jersey officials used state, rather than federal laws, in citing tactics used by auto dealers that promised cars that they knew they could not deliver.[29] Although not many retailers have used bait-and-swith tactics, consumer advocates are eager to lump all retailers into this unethical category. As a result, the FTC trade regulations have some very stiff penalties for retailers who constantly run out of advertised items. In 1988, the FTC amended these regulations by permitting food stores to issue rain checks or substitute items of comparable value when they run out of advertised specials. This benefited consumers because it eliminated the need for retailers to carry an excess inventory of all advertised items.[30] While retailers may legally use rainchecks, repeated use can negatively affect store image and result in lost customers.

SUBSTANTIATION AND RETRACTION

The FTC can request that the retailer substantiate its advertising claims about the safety, quality, or performance of its products.[31] The FTC issued a complaint against Sears and its advertising agency for making deceptive and unsubstantiated claims for the cleaning performance of its Lady Kenmore dishwashers. Statements challenged in the ads were "The do-it-yourself dishwasher. No scraping. No prerinsing. . . ." According to the FTC, the firm had no reasonable basis for these claims. Demonstrations did not prove the alleged cleaning ability, and the claims were inconsistent with the owner's manual, which instructs consumers to presoak and firmly scour cooked or baked-on foods.[32]

In 1987, the FTC charged Walgreen with making unsubstantiated claims for Advil pain reliever. Walgreen advertised Advil as a "prescription pain reliever. . ." and "anti-inflammatory . . . a source of comfort for people who experience arthritis pain." The FTC argued that Walgreen did not have a reasonable basis for its claims and Advil cannot be substituted for prescription forms of ibuprofen, the product's active ingredient. The Commission challenged only Walgreen's claims and not those of Advil's manufacturer, American Home Products.[33]

If the FTC finds that a retailer has made false or deceptive statements in advertising, it may require that a new advertisement be made in which the former statements are contradicted and the truth stated. This is called **retractive advertising**. In 1979, the FTC issued a complaint requiring Montgomery Ward to run retractive advertising. According to the complaint, Ward gave consumers false and confusing information that may have led them to install wood stoves at unsafe distances from combustible walls. The order required that Ward place full-page notices in its October 1979 house-clearance catalog and its Spring and Summer 1980 general catalog, offering to relocate wood-burning heaters to recommended distances from combustible walls.[34]

A new wrinkle on corrective advertising suits has been proposed by Borden, Inc.[35] The proposal is that the offending advertiser should put up the cash and let the victimized firm create the corrective campaign. Thus, if Retailer A's ads have wronged Retailer B, Retailer B and any other retailer affected by the original ads could create their own corrective ads with A's money.

PRODUCT CONSTRAINTS

A retailer's major activity is selling merchandise. Three areas of the law have a major effect on the products a retailer handles: patents, trademarks, and product safety. They are highlighted in Exhibit 6.3.

PATENTS

In mass retailing, the direct copying of popular product brands or lines is common. Retailers such as K mart, Ward's, and Sears often copy an item that has been a commercial success. Their goal is to produce the item at a lower cost so that they can offer it to the mass market at an attractive price.

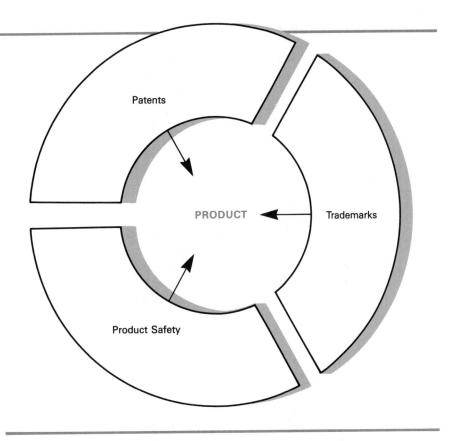

Exhibit 6.3
Product Constraints

Patents

PRODUCT

Trademarks

Product Safety

Acceptance of competition is so widespread in the United States that this practice is condoned unless a patent right is infringed on. A **patent** gives a 17-year legal monopoly for the marketing of a product or process to the patent holder. A person or company applying for a patent will usually receive it as long as application forms are completed properly. However, patent rights can be challenged in court on the basis that the patent was a product or process that didn't serve to advance the general well-being or welfare of society.[36]

An illuminating case in this realm is *Sears, Roebuck & Company vs. Stiffel Co.*[37] Stiffel developed a pole lamp that proved to be a commercial success. Sears then brought out a substantially identical lamp at a much lower price and Stiffel sued for unfair competition, claiming that Sears had caused confusion as to the source of the lamps. The initial judgment was in favor of Stiffel, but Sears appealed and the United States Supreme Court reversed the decision. The Supreme Court stressed that a patent could not be given to an article that did not advance the welfare of society. They argued that the pole lamp sold by Stiffel was not entitled to a patent based either on design or mechanical features. Therefore, the pole lamp was in the public domain and Sears had every right to design and sell almost identical lamps. The fact that Stiffel originated the pole lamp and made it popular was irrelevant.

Another interesting example of how retailers adjust to changing environmental conditions is probably being played out as you read this. In late 1985 and 1986, five of the most profitable prescription drugs—including the number one drug, Valium—had patent protection expire. How doctors, patients, and pharmacies will react to the onslaught of generic replacements is being determined daily.

TRADEMARKS

Retailers can often copy the product of manufacturers, but they cannot copy or use the manufacturer's trademark. A **mark** is any word, symbol, design, or combination of these used to identify a product or service. If the mark identifies a product, such as McDonald's Big Mac sandwich, it is called a **trademark**. When it identifies a service, such as the golden arches at McDonald's, it is called a **servicemark**. These marks, when registered with the appropriate federal agency, are protected from use by others according to the Lanham Act.[38] Therefore, the retailer cannot copy the mark of another, and its own mark cannot be copied if it is properly registered. If a person or firm has the right to use a mark, it may bring suit against a competitor duplicating or imitating the mark. The fundamental question in such litigation is whether the public is likely to be confused by the imitator's use of the mark and believe it identifies the person or firm being imitated. When there is sufficient danger of confusion, the court will prevent the imitator from using the particular mark.

Trademark rights can be lost if the mark loses its exclusive character by falling into the domain of the English language and becoming a generic label. For example, the terms aspirin, nylon, cellophane, thermos, and shredded wheat were once enforceable marks. But because they fell into the general language to describe a product class, the right to exclusive use was lost. Legal battles are generally waged before a mark falls into the public domain. It is probably not advisable for a retailer to try to be the first one to use a mark that it believes has fallen into the public domain. The free use of the mark should first be tested in a court of law.[39] This is why retailers such as McDonald's are vigilant in making sure that no one violates their trademark or that it becomes part of the public domain. For example, McDonald's not only wants to protect such registered trademarks as *McDLT* and *Quarter Pounder* which describe specific McDonald's sandwiches, they also want to protect the *Mc* prefix. In 1988, they filed suit against a motel chain called *McSleep* for infringing on their trademark.

PRODUCT SAFETY

Retailers are in a precarious position when it comes to product safety. Most retailers do not produce the goods they offer for sale but purchase them from wholesalers or manufacturers. Thus, they have little say about product quality or safety. (You might therefore believe that retailers are not responsible for the safety of products they sell; this is definitely not the case.) Yet according to Section 15 of the Consumer Product Safety Act (1972), the retailer has specific responsibilities to monitor the safety of consumer products.[40] Specifically, retailers (as well as manufacturers, other middlemen, and importers) are required to report to the Consumer Product Safety Commission any possible "substantial product hazard." Furthermore, Section 15 includes in the description of substantial hazards any failure to comply with an existing safety standard. Thus, a retailer may unknowingly violate the law by reselling products which do not conform to existing safety standards. Retailers may further violate the law by failing to repurchase from customers nonconforming products which were sold after the effective date of a standard.[41]

In one Consumer Product Safety Commission complaint, Sears was required to recall 70,000 allegedly hazardous household fans. Sears had to run national ads in hopes of coaxing consumers to return the fans.[42] More than 200 food products are recalled by manufacturers each year for reasons such as misbranding, product deterioration, or criminal adulteration. Moreover, retailers can become codefendants in tampering lawsuits if they allowed the tamperer access to the goods.[43] Many retailers have resorted to using disclaimers similar to the one in Retailing in Action 6-1 as a means of reducing their liability.

Retailers are also responsible for product safety and performance under conventional warranty doctrines. Under the current warranty law, the fact that the ultimate consumer may bring suit against the manufacturer or processor in no way relieves the retailer from its responsibility for the fitness and merchantability of the goods. In many states buyers have been permitted to name both the retailer and the manufacturer or processor in the same suit.

Retailers can offer express or implied warranties. **Express warranties** are the result of negotiation between the retailer and the customer. They may be either written into the contract or verbalized. They can cover all characteristics or attributes of the merchandise or only one attribute. An express warranty can be created without the use of the words *warranty* or *guarantee*. For example, a car salesperson might tell a buyer, "Everybody we've sold this type of car to has gone at least 60,000 miles with no problems whatsoever, and I see no reason why you can't expect the same. I wouldn't be surprised if you go 100,000 miles without any mechanical problems." This statement could create an express warranty. The court would be concerned with whether this was puffery or a statement of fact or opinion by the salesperson.

Implied warranties are not expressly made by the retailer but are based on custom, norms, or reasonable expectations. There are two types of implied warranties: an implied warranty of merchantability, and an implied warranty of fitness for a particular purpose.

An **implied warranty of merchantability** is made by every retailer selling goods. By offering the goods for sale, the retailer implies that they are fit for the ordinary purpose for which such goods are typically used. The notion of implied warranty applies to both new and used merchandise. For example, imagine that a sporting goods retailer located close to a major lake sells used inner tubes for swimming and a customer purchases one. The tube bursts while the person is floating on it and the person drowns. This retailer may be held liable. Because of the potential legal liability that accompanies an implied warranty, many retailers will expressly disclaim at the time of sale any or all implied warranties. This is not always legally possible; some retailers are unable to avoid implied warranties of merchantability.

The **implied warranty of fitness for a particular purpose** arises when the customer relies on the retailer to assist or make the selection of goods to serve a particular purpose. Consider a customer who is about to make a

**RETAILING
IN
ACTION**

6-1

Sample Disclaimer

The following is an example of a disclaimer that attempts to limit a seller's exposure when offering goods and services in the marketplace:

Seller warrants that the goods supplied hereunder will conform to the description stated herein; that it will convey good title thereto, free of all liens of any kind whatever unknown to the buyer; and that such goods will be of merchantable quality. This is seller's sole warranty with respect to the goods. SELLER MAKES NO OTHER WARRANTY OF ANY KIND WHATEVER, EXPRESS OR IMPLIED: AND ALL IMPLIED WARRANTIES OF MERCHANTABILITY AND FITNESS FOR A PARTICULAR PURPOSE THAT EXCEED THE AFORESTATED OBLIGATION ARE HEREBY DISCLAIMED AND EXCLUDED FROM THIS AGREEMENT.

Source: Steven Mitchell Sack, "Some Words on Warranties . . . ," *Sales & Marketing Management* (December, 1986): 52-54.

cross-country moving trip towing a two-wheel trailer behind her automobile. She needs a pair of tires for the rear of the automobile, and goes to a
local tire retailer. She asks the salesperson for a pair of tires that will allow
her to tow the loaded trailer safely. The customer is ignorant in this regard and is relying on the expertise of the retailer. If the retailer sells the
customer a pair of tires not suited for the job, the retailer is liable for
breach of an implied warranty of fitness for a particular purpose. This is
true even if the retailer did not have in stock a pair of tires to safely perform the job but instead sold the customer the best tire in stock to do the
job. Retailing in Action 6-2 provides a concise statement of what a salesperson should or should not state when making a sale.

Consumer product warranties have frequently been confusing, misleading, and frustrating to consumers. As a consequence, the Magnuson-
Moss Warranty Act[44] was passed. While nothing in federal law requires a
retailer to warrant a product under this act, anyone who sells a product
costing the consumer more than $15 and gives a written warranty (while
only written warranties are covered by federal laws, all types of warranties are subject to state laws) is required to provide the consumer with the
following information:

1.   The **identity** of the persons to whom the warranty is extended:
     whether the written warranty can be enforced only by the original
     consumer purchaser or covers every owner of the item during the
     term of the warranty.

**RETAILING
IN
ACTION**

6-2

No Bigmouths, Please

When salespeople make a warranty in the course of a sales call, they should be
certain that it:
- is concise and understandable;
- avoids extravagant or deceptive terms;
- states specifically what is promised and, in some cases, what is not;
- promises only what the company intends to perform;
- sets time or use limits, where applicable;
- limits the company's liability.

Source: Steven Mitchell Sack, "Some Words on Warranties . . .," *Sales & Marketing
Management* (December, 1986): 52-54.

2. A clear **description** of the products, parts, characteristics, compo-
    nents, and properties covered by the warranty; those items ex-
    cluded from the warranty must be described.
3. A **statement** of what the warrantor will do in the event of a defect,
    malfunction, or failure to conform with the written warranty, in-
    cluding which items or services the warrantor will pay for, and
    which items or services he or she will not pay for.
4. The point in **time** when the warranty begins (if it begins on a date
    other than the purchase date) and its duration.
5. A step-by-step **explanation** of the steps the consumer should fol-
    low to obtain performance of the warranty obligation and infor-
    mation regarding any informal dispute-settling mechanisms that
    are available.
6. Any **limitations** on the duration of implied warranties or any ex-
    clusions or limitations on relief, such as incidental or consequen-
    tial damages; together with a statement that under some state
    laws the exclusions or limitations may not be allowed.
7. A statement that the warranty gives the consumer certain addi-
    tional **legal rights** under state law, which may vary from state to
    state.

It is the retailer's responsibility to provide the prospective buyer with
the written terms of the warranty for review prior to the actual sale. The
retailer has two options: clearly and conspicuously displaying the text of
the written warranty near the product; or making warranties available for
examination by consumers upon request and posting signs advising consumers of the pre-sale availability of warranties.[45]
The FTC polices retailers' adherence to the Magnuson-Moss Warranty Act. For example, in 1979 the FTC took action against Korvette's
department store chain for not properly making warranties available to
consumers prior to the actual sales. Korvette's agreed to conduct a special
training program to instruct its sales personnel about the availability
and location of warranty information.[46] A nationwide investigation of
warranty practices began in early 1980, shortly after the FTC sent warn-
ings to 17 major chains, such as Sears, K mart, Montgomery Ward,
Woolworth, and Korvette's, pointing out that failure to disclose warranty
terms could subject the firms to fines of up to $10,000 for each
violation.[47]

CHANNEL CONSTRAINTS

Retailers are restricted in the relationships and agreements they may develop with channel partners. These restrictions can be conveniently categorized into six areas as shown in Exhibit 6.4.

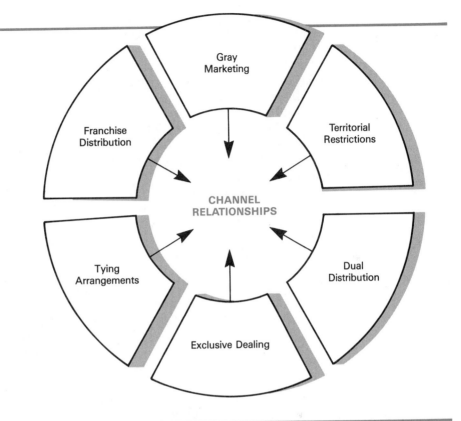

Exhibit 6.4
**Channel
Constraints**

TERRITORIAL RESTRICTIONS

Territorial restrictions are attempts by a supplier, usually a manufacturer, to limit the geographical area in which a retailer may resell its merchandise. The courts have viewed territorial restrictions as potential contracts in restraint of trade and thus in violation of the Sherman Antitrust Act. Even though the retailer and manufacturer may both favor territorial restrictions because of the lessening of intrabrand competition, the courts frown on such arrangements.[48]

The courts' views on territorial restrictions have changed several times since the early 1960s, making it difficult for retailers and suppliers to know what is legal and what is not. Let us review the changing view of the courts beginning with the White Motor case.[49] White Motor Company had insisted that its dealers confine their sales to well-defined territories. The legality of this agreement was challenged, and in 1963 the Supreme Court admitted that it did not know "enough of the economic and business stuff out of which the arrangements emerge to be certain" about the appropriate decision.[50] As a result, the Supreme Court decided to send the case to a lower court to assess the competitive consequences of the territorial restrictions. Thus, the Supreme Court was implying by its behavior that territorial restrictions were not a violation of the Sherman Act. Before the lower court could make a decision, White Motor consented to stop the contested practice, and the precedent was set that territorial restrictions would be assessed on their individual merits in regard to their effect or potential effect on competition.

Four years later, in 1967, the Supreme Court decided the Schwinn case, which dealt with territorial restrictions Schwinn had placed on its distributors and franchised retailers.[51] The court stated that suppliers could *not* prevent middlemen who held clear title to goods from selling to anyone of their choosing. Once title passed, the destination of goods could not be controlled. Not only Schwinn, but most other manufacturers were shocked by this ruling. In essence, the court was stating that territorial restrictions on retailers selling goods they have clear title to were a per se violation of the Sherman Act.

A decade later retail executives were again surprised. In 1977, in the GTE Sylvania case, the Supreme Court overruled the precedent of the Schwinn decision, claiming it had acted too hastily.[52] Continental TV, a retailer franchised by Sylvania, began to sell outside its defined territory. As a result, Sylvania refused to continue selling them merchandise. Continental sued Sylvania for treble damages. Sylvania successfully argued that the promise of territorial protection for its dealers strengthened competition, since it made the survival of their marketing system more likely. The Supreme Court accepted this argument and further proclaimed that territorial restriction should be decided on a case-by-case basis, thus reverting to the rule of reason established in the White Motor case.[53]

Recently, the courts upheld the right of Adolph Coors to terminate a wholesaler for violating the territorial restrictions of his agreement.[54] The Court, in reinforcing the Sylvania ruling, reasoned that a manufacturer has the right to set standards for quality control and to enforce those standards. In this case, it was concluded that the anticompetitive effect of reducing intrabrand competition was outweighed by an increase in interbrand competition as a result of the quality control standards achieved by territorial restrictions. Congress has, however, exempted soft drink bottlers from this legislation.[55]

The Justice Department, in 1985, issued 46 pages of guidelines supporting the legality of most vertical territorial restraints.[56] The guidelines, for example, contend that a vertical arrangement shouldn't be challenged if the manufacturer using it controls less than 10 percent of the market for the product it covers. The department also won't try to overturn vertical arrangements covering fewer than 60 percent of dealers or distributors in a specific geographic area.

It is important to note that while vertical territorial restrictions may be valid under the rule of reason, the rule applied to territorial restrictions arrived at by agreement between competitors is different. In such cases, the parties will have contracted, combined, or conspired in restraint of trade, a violation of Section 1 of the Sherman Act. Known as horizontal market allocation, such conduct is a violation.[57]

DUAL DISTRIBUTION

A manufacturer who sells to independent retailers and also through its own retail outlets is engaged in **dual distribution.** Thus, the manufacturer manages a corporately owned vertical marketing system that competes with independent retailers, which it also supplies through a conventional, administered, or contractual marketing channel. Retailers tend to get upset about dual distribution when the two channels compete at the retail level in the same trade area. For example, occasionally an auto manufacturer will open a dealership close to an independent dealer it sells to. Likewise, Ralph Lauren has over 25 wholly-owned retail outlets, and in addition uses major independent retailers as outlets. This can have a severe effect on manufacturer-retailer relationships. Independent retailers argue that dual distribution is an unfair method of competition and thus in violation of the Sherman Act. Dual distribution also takes place when manufacturers sell similar products under different brandnames for distribution through different channels. This kind of dual distribution is common in retailing with the use of private labels.

The courts have not viewed dual distribution arrangements as violations. In fact, they have reasoned that dual distribution can actually foster competition rather than reduce it. For example, the manufacturer may not be able to find a retailer to represent it in all trade areas or the manufacturer may find it necessary to operate its own retail outlet to establish market share and remain competitive with other manufacturers. The courts have applied rule-of-reason criteria. An independent retailer suing a manufacturer for dual distribution has to convince the court that it was competed against unfairly and competition was damaged. The retailer's best strategy would be to show that the manufacturer-controlled outlets were favored or subsidized (for instance, with excess advertising allowance or lower prices) to an extent that was detrimental to the independent retailer.

GRAY MARKETING

A new channel of distribution was given legal status in 1988, when the Supreme Court legitimized the so-called "gray market" that discounters exploit to give customers bargain-priced goods. In this channel, so-called gray marketers (unauthorized retail outlets), such as K mart or 47th

Street Photo Inc., buy goods (cameras, perfume, computers, etc.) either overseas or from authorized United States dealers (corporations, universities, and other large purchasers), who get the goods at quantity discounts of 30 to 40 percent. The large buyers can resell these products profitably for less than what a small retailer would normally pay for them. In many cases, they can make money simply by ordering huge quantities to earn big discounts and then selling the excess at cost. With regard to imported goods, the gray marketers usually rely on arbitrage. Here, when a strong dollar weakens the German mark against the Japanese yen, importers sometimes can acquire Japanese cameras from Germany at a much lower dollar cost than they could using the "authorized channel" from Japan.[58]

The troublesome thing about these practices is that the "unauthorized" retailers do not provide service and information. In addition, these "unauthorized" retailers may make unauthorized alterations in the product, or the product may have been produced to another country's specifications. Most importantly, these retailers undermine the efforts of the authorized retailers by getting a free ride on the authorized dealers' efforts to cultivate and educate potential customers. No wonder some retailers were confused when only a month after ruling manufacturers don't necessarily violate antitrust laws if they cut off discounters after getting complaints from full-price retailers, the Supreme Court legitimized "gray marketing." The ruling allows gray market imports to be blocked only in about 10 percent of situations.[59]

EXCLUSIVE DEALING

Retailers and their suppliers occasionally enter into exclusive dealing arrangements. In a **one-way exclusive dealing** arrangement, the supplier agrees to give the retailer the exclusive right to merchandise the suppliers' product in a particular trade area. The retailer, however, does not agree to do anything for the supplier; hence the term *one-way*. A weak manufacturer will often have to offer one-way exclusive dealing arrangements to get shelf space at the retail level. Truly one-way arrangements are legal.

A **two-way exclusive dealing** agreement occurs when the supplier offers the retailer the exclusive distribution of a merchandise line or product if in return the retailer will agree to do something for the manufacturer, such as, agree to not handle competing brands. Two-way agreements violate Section 3 of the Clayton Act (1914) if their effect may be to substantially lessen competition or to tend to create a monopoly. Specifically, the courts have been concerned with three potential negative consequences of two-way exclusive dealing agreements. First, strong manufacturers may attract strong retailers and the strength of the two reinforcing each other could lessen competition from smaller manufacturers and retailers. Second, since there are many more national manufacturers than there are retailers in any given smaller city, there would not be enough retail outlets for all manufacturers to be represented. Third, price competition at the retail level would be less, because intrabrand rivalry would be absent or severely restricted. The legality of two-way exclusive dealing agreements is determined case by case on a rule-of-reason basis, usually by considering the three preceding points.

TYING AGREEMENTS

When a seller with a strong product or service forces a retailer to buy a weak product or service as a condition for buying the strong one, a **tying agreement** exists. For example, a large national manufacturer with several very highly demanded lines of merchandise may force the retailer to handle its entire merchandise assortment as a condition for being able to handle the most popular merchandise lines. This is called a full-line policy. Alternatively, a strong manufacturer may be introducing a new product and, in order to get shelf space or display space at the retail level, it may require retailers to carry the new product in order to purchase better established merchandise lines.

Tying arrangements have been found to be in violation of Section 3 of the Clayton Act, Sections 1 and 3 of the Sherman Act, and Section 5 of the FTC Act. The term or concept of tying, however, is not expressly mentioned in any of these Acts. Tying is not viewed as per se violation, but it is generally viewed as illegal if a substantial share of commerce is affected. The courts have noted in recent rulings that it is difficult to prove tying.

> "Even assuming arguments that plaintiff's proof shows that it accepted uneconomic secondary products and that defendant possessed dominant economic power and utilized that power to require plaintiff to buy more of its goods, this is not sufficient a finding of an illegal tying agreement."[60]

FRANCHISE CONSTRAINTS

Since the early 1960s the number of franchised retailers has grown rapidly to the point where United States franchise outlets in 1988 sold $640 billion in goods and services.[61] Associated with this growth have been substantial legal difficulties between franchisors and franchisees.

In principle, a franchise is a relationship between two independent parties, whose rights are determined by the contract existing between them. However, because of the imbalance of power in this relationship (the franchisor has much more), the franchisee should know that certain requirements the franchisor may try to impose may be viewed as illegal in a court of law. Basically, the legal system has attempted to equalize the balance of power between the franchisor and franchisee.

The franchised retailer should keep the following points in mind:

1. Although the franchisor may want the franchisee to set prices at a certain level, generally such agreements will be found in violation of the antitrust laws if tested in court.
2. Requirements that the franchisee purchase materials and supplies from the franchisor when competitive goods of similar quality are available will be viewed as an illegal tying agreement.
3. Geographic limitations may or may not be viewed as unlawful. A rule-of-reason approach will be used.
4. Standards for operating procedures, quality control, and cleanliness are generally legal, since the franchisor has a legitimate interest in maintaining the name or reputation of the franchise.

Thus, the franchisor should not take undue advantage of the franchisee (through tying or price fixing) but the franchisee should also not take advantage of the franchisor (for instance, by not following cleanliness standards).

One way that franchisors could take advantage of franchisees was by unfair franchise termination. Traditionally, a franchise contract ran for a short period (typically a year) and the franchisor had maximal flexibility in cancelling the franchisee. Currently, however, most franchise contracts specify the causes for cancellation (failure to make payments, bankruptcy of franchisee, failure to meet sales quotas). In addition, many franchise contracts now contain an arbitration provision that allows for a neutral third party to make a final and binding decision on whether a breach of contract has occurred and whether it was sufficient to justify cancellation of the franchise. Franchise termination is now quite difficult, because many states have statutes to protect franchisees from arbitrary termination.

Finally, fraud has occurred often in the sale of franchises to unsuspecting potential franchisees. Franchises have been sold to the small investor as get-rich-quick schemes, and the pitches to get franchisees have been based on misleading statements. Because of these practices, several states have enacted franchise investment laws. Under these laws, a franchisee who is deceived by a misleading statement (typically in a prospectus) may sue for damages.[62]

CREDIT CONSTRAINTS

In some lines of retail trade, such as automobiles and furniture, most consumer purchases are on credit. The credit decision is important from both the retailer's and consumer's perspective. To the retailer, the ability to

Illus. 6.2
There are many types of franchise retailers.
Source: Bundy American Corporation

sell on credit represents an attractive sales tool, but it also is an investment of capital that could be used for other purposes (inventory or store expansion). However, the wide use of bankcards has shifted many of these responsibilities to the banks. To the consumer credit is a means of acquiring goods without having the cash to immediately pay for them, but it also involves paying significantly more for the goods than the cash price. The legal aspects of credit decisions relate to two areas: (a) credit disclosure requirements and (b) guidelines for granting credit, collecting, and billing. These are summarized in Exhibit 6.5.

CREDIT DISCLOSURE

The Consumer Credit Protection Act (CCPA), Truth in Lending Act, and Regulation Z of the Federal Reserve Board of Governors attempt to "assure a meaningful disclosure of credit terms so that the consumer will be able to compare more readily the various credit terms available to him and avoid the uninformed use of credit."[63] The CCPA is designed to remedy what Congressional hearings revealed to be unscrupulous and predatory creditor practices throughout the nation. Many of these unscrupulous practices were on the part of retailers attempting to hide the true cost of merchandise in unrealistically high credit terms. For example, the retailer might sell merchandise at a very low price but then tack on a high finance charge. Over the years, many retailers have used this tactic, making their profits on financing, not merchandise. Another common practice was to find out how much the customer could afford to pay per month and then sell the merchandise on monthly payments without revealing the true cost of the merchandise.

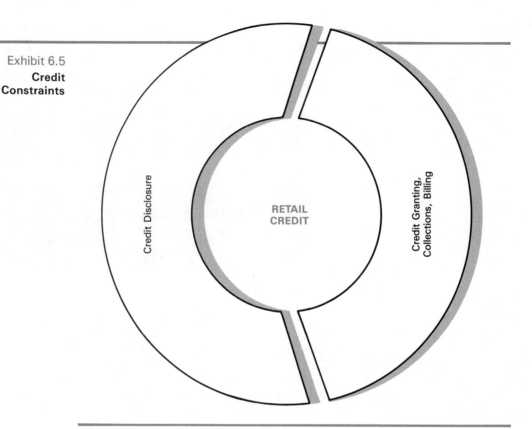

Exhibit 6.5
Credit Constraints

Credit Disclosure

RETAIL CREDIT

Credit Granting, Collections, Billing

To ensure that the consumer can make more informed purchases when using credit, federal laws require that the customer receive information on:

1. the total amount financed,
2. the finance charge as an annual percentage rate (APR),
3. the finance charge in dollars,
4. payments: number, amount, due dates, early repayment, etc.,
5. any other fees or charges (late payment, insurance, etc.)

If the credit agreement involves merchandise bought on time, creditors are also required to provide:

1. a description of the merchandise,
2. the cash price,
3. the deferred payment price (price plus total interest),
4. the amount of any down payment and/or trade-in.

These credit disclosure rules apply not only to in store selling but to all promotional activities of the retailer.

CREDIT GRANTING, COLLECTING, AND BILLING

Retailers are heavily regulated regarding credit granting, collecting, and billing. They must abide by the Equal Credit Opportunity Act, the Fair Credit Reporting Act, the Fair Billing Credit Act, and the Fair Debt Collection Practices Act. For retailers selling on credit, familiarity with these pieces of legislation is of paramount importance.[64]

Equal Credit Opportunity Act.   The Equal Credit Opportunity Act attempts to reduce or eliminate credit discrimination by making it unlawful to discriminate against an applicant for credit on the basis of race, color, religion, national origin, sex, marital status, or age; because all or part of the applicant's income is obtained from a public assistance program; or because the applicant has in good faith exercised any right under the Consumer Credit Protection Act. Furthermore, when a credit application is refused, the retailer must furnish a detailed written explanation to the applicant.[65]

Fair Credit Reporting Act.   Before granting credit, the retailer usually wants to know things about the applicant that may not be on the application form. The retailer will probably purchase the needed information from a private credit bureau. The Fair Credit Reporting Act seeks to protect consumers from potential abuses in the retailer's use of credit bureaus.[66] All customers have the right to see a copy of the report the credit bureau sent the retailer, free of charge if the customer has been denied credit in the previous 30 days. The customer can follow designated procedures to get the error corrected.

Fair Billing Credit Act.   It is not unusual for retailers to make errors in billing their customers. These errors are generally brought to the attention of the retailer by the customer. Under the Fair Billing Credit Act, if the customer that believes an error has been made, certain regulations are imposed on the retailer to ensure fair and prompt handling of the dispute. This act requires retailers to:

1. Include with each monthly bill a statement informing customers of their right to question the bill and giving the address to which all inquiries must be sent.
2. Mail billing statements to the customer at least 14 days prior to payment due date.
3. Settle all disputes within 90 days.
4. Refrain from making adverse reports to credit agencies and/or from turning accounts over to collection agencies prior to settlement of the dispute.
5. Credit all payments, overpayments, and returned merchandise promptly to accounts.[67]

Fair Debt Collection Practices Act.   Improper methods of debt collection are prohibited by the Fair Debt Collection Practices Act and the Consumer Credit Protection Act.[68] Generally prohibited are sending bills that give the impression that a legal action has been taken against the customer and using extortionate methods of collection. In some cases, for instance, the retailer may be prohibited from informing the employer of the customer that the latter owes the retailer money. Retailing in Action 6-3 shows how *not* to go about collecting bad debts.

MERGERS AND ACQUISITIONS

In recent years, a number of retailers were able to achieve explosive rates of growth by acquiring other retail enterprises. Notable examples include Campeau Corp., a Canadian-based real estate firm, acquiring both Allied and Federated Department Stores, American Stores acquiring several Safeway divisions, Macy acquiring Bullock's, Bullock's Willshire, and I. Magnin, May Company's acquisition of Associated Dry Goods, and Dillard's acquisition of Higbee's. Mergers or acquisitions can present legal problems for the retailer. According to Section 7 of the Clayton Act, an

RETAILING IN ACTION   6-3

How *Not* to Collect Bad Debts

What is a retailer, especially a small retailer, to do when customers do not pay their bills? In many cases a collection agency is out of the question due to the amount of money involved. In these situations the retailer is left to his or her own initiative. However, sometimes this retailer's initiative can be considered questionable. Consider the case of a floral shop owner in Illinois. He took to mailing bills that looked like legal papers to customers ninety days late in their payments. These bills, which were in fact not legal documents, had bold headlines reading "Final Notice before Suit" and carried imitation legal seals as well as a statement that the retailer had the right to collect court costs and attorney's fees from the debtor in the event of a suit.

Under pressure from the state Attorney General's office, the retailer dropped this questionable practice, but he was not found guilty or fined any money. No matter what actions a retailer takes, even if legal, it must not be made in an attempt to deceive the customer.

acquisition of stock or assets of a company, where the effect may be to substantially lessen competition or tend to create a monopoly in any line of commerce in any section of the country, is illegal. This section of the Clayton Act was strengthened by the Celler-Kefauver Act (1950).

Mergers or acquisitions are not *per se* violations but rather the courts use a rule of reason. Debate and arguments[69] tend to revolve around two central issues.

1. What is the line of commerce involved? For example, is a women's apparel store in the same line of commerce as a man's apparel store or department store?
2. What is the market involved? Is a shoe retailer in Tucson that acquires a shoe retailer in Phoenix acquiring a firm in the same section of the country?

In each of the preceding issues the concept of competition is crucial. We could restate the two questions thus: Do different types of merchandise compete? Do retailers in different geographic areas compete?

The retail manager might find Exhibit 6.6 helpful in assessing the likelihood of legal problems surrounding a merger or acquisition. In this exhibit we can examine whether the acquisition or merger involved the same or different line of commerce in the same or a different section of the country. At least four distinct possibilities exist. The retailer could acquire or merge with a firm in the same line of commerce and in the same section of the country. A dominant furniture retailer in Seattle, Washing-

Exhibit 6.6

Mergers and Acquisitions

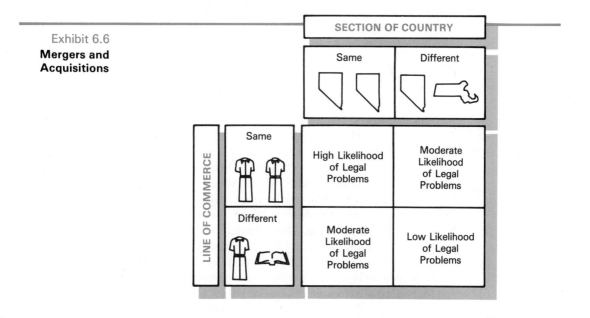

ton, might merge with or acquire another large furniture retailer in Seattle. Such mergers or acquisitions are very likely to be challenged either by existing competitors in that market or by the Justice Department's Antitrust Division. Of course, the challenge is more likely to occur if each firm has a large share of the market. In fact, the larger the market share of the firms involved in an acquisition or merger, the greater the likelihood of antitrust violations, irrespective of other facts surrounding the case.

Another alternative would be the acquisition or merger of two firms that represent different lines of commerce and are currently operating in different sections of the country. For example, a regional department store chain in the Southwest might acquire a petroleum distributor in Oklahoma City and Tulsa. In this situation, the likelihood of violating antimerger provisions of the Clayton or Celler-Kefauver Amendment is relatively small. This example clearly delineates the line of commerce and section of the country. But what if a department store in the Southeast had stores only in cities of over 250,000 in population, and it acquired a chain of drugstores that operated in the Southeast but only in towns of less than 50,000 in population? Are the lines of commerce and sections of the country different? This is more typical of the questions the courts address.

The third and fourth alternatives in terms of acquisition or merger represent a moderate likelihood of antitrust violations. The third option would be to acquire or merge with a firm in the same line of commerce but a different section of the country (a supermarket chain in Colorado acquires a supermarket chain in South Carolina). The fourth option is to acquire a firm in a different line of commerce but in the same section of the country (a supermarket chain in Dallas acquires a retail sporting goods chain in Dallas).

STATE AND LOCAL LAWS

In addition to federal laws, many state and local municipalities have passed legislation regulating retail activities. Zoning laws prohibit retailers from operating at certain locations and require building and sign specifications to be met. Construction, fire, elevator, smoking, parking, and other codes are placed on retailers by state and local governments. Some states regulate prices paid to wholesalers by retailers. New Mexico has a state law requiring that wholesalers sell beer to retailers at the lowest price offered by any wholesaler in the country for that product size. As a result of such legislation, New Mexico beer distributors sell 10½ ounce and 11-ounce cans instead of the customary 12-ounce sizes.

Other states enforce blue laws restricting the sale of certain products on Sundays and unfair trade practices laws regulating the minimum markup a retailer must charge. Various cities have passed laws called Green River Ordinances, restricting door-to-door selling, excessive use of

Illus. 6.3

Construction, fire, elevator, smoking, parking and other codes are placed on retailers by state and local governments.

garage sales, lottery promotions, smoking in certain areas only, sale of obscene materials, and dangerous products. Some states and cities require licenses to operate certain retail businesses. Retailing in Action 6-4 shows that not all laws governing retailing are well thought-out.

RETAILING IN ACTION

6-4

Blue Laws

Many states have "blue laws" which prohibit the sale of certain products on Sundays. However, retailers in cities bordering states without blue laws are at a disadvantage. In view of this situation, the Maryland Legislature recently voted to suspend the blue laws for the four Sundays preceding December 25. This legislation was an attempt to allow retailers in the Baltimore area to compete with Washington, D.C. and Virginia retailers during retailers' busiest seasons, the period between Thanksgiving and Christmas.

Just one problem: what is going to happen the next time there are five Sundays between Thanksgiving and Christmas, which happens 28 times each century?

For further information on these laws a retailer should consult the local Better Business Bureau, the National Retail Merchants Association (NRMA), or state and local regulatory agencies.

One final question must be asked. Where does legal constraint end? In 1988 Sears challenged a New York City law regulating newspaper ads. Sears claimed that as a national advertiser, already under regulation by both the federal and state governments, it should not be subject to regulations by local governments. This issue is extremely important today, as various states are increasing their regulation of business, and particularly retailing.

SUMMARY

The purpose of this chapter was to describe the multifaceted legal environment that confronts retailers in the United States. We identified constraints on retailers' activities in eight broad categories: (1) pricing, (2) promotion, (3) products, (4) channel relations, (5) credit, (6) mergers and acquisitions, and (7) state and local regulations. Within each of these broad categories we summarized some specific activities that are regulated.

For example, with regard to pricing, we discussed horizontal and vertical price fixing, price discrimination, deceptive pricing, below-cost pricing, and predatory pricing. We focused on four areas of promotion constraints—deceitful diversion of patronage, deceptive advertising, bait-and-switch tactics, and substantiation and retraction. When it came to reviewing product constraints, the topics of patents, trademarks, and product safety were discussed as they relate to retailing. Channel relations were also discussed in terms of the legality of territorial restrictions, dual distribution, gray marketing, exclusive dealing, tying arrangements, and franchise distribution. For retailers' credit activities, we focused on regulations dealing with credit disclosure, credit granting, collection, and billing. We discussed potential legal problems in attempting to grow through merger or acquisition by reviewing antitrust provisions. Finally, a brief attempt was made to discuss the impact of the various state and local laws.

QUESTIONS FOR DISCUSSION

1. Do you believe retailers will be more or less constrained by the legal environment in the future? Why?

2. A federal grand jury argues that because all major supermarkets in a town are selling milk at the same price there must be a conspiracy to fix prices. Agree or disagree and explain your reasoning.
3. Retail executives should abide by the philosophy "as long as it is legal, it is ethical." Agree or disagree and explain your reasoning.
4. How could two-way exclusive dealing arrangements be harmful to the consumer and competition?
5. Deceptive advertising and pricing harms not only the consumer but also competition. Agree or disagree and explain your reasoning.
6. Why should a retailer be familiar with the Robinson-Patman Act?
7. Why is sales-below-cost legislation usually ineffective?
8. What is deceitful diversion of patronage? Comment on the legality of it.
9. Discuss the concept of exclusive dealing. Are exclusive dealing arrangements in the retailer's best interest? Are they in the consumer's best interest?
10. Explain how a retailer could minimize its legal problems in mergers and acquisitions.
11. What should a retailer do to ensure that it does not violate the customer's rights under the Magnuson-Moss Warranty Act?
12. When are price discounts legal under the Robinson-Patman Act?
13. How are the retailer's promotional activities affected by current federal regulations?
14. Obtain several recent copies of your local newspaper. Carefully go through the major advertisements and identify the ones you believe to be deceptive. Why are they deceptive?
15. Obtain copies of the last four issues of the *Journal of Marketing* and review the Legal Developments in Marketing section. What cases are discussed involving retailers? What are the major issues in the cases?
16. Is it legal for a manufacturer to tie the sale of one product to the sale of another product? Do the same rules apply to a retailer selling to the final consumer?

SUGGESTED READINGS

Ingene, Charles A. "The Effect of 'Blue Laws' on Consumer Expenditures at Retail." *Journal of Macromarketing* (Fall 1986): 53–71.

Macklin, M. Carole, and Crofford J. Macklin, Jr. "Refuting a Competitor's Advertising Claim." *Journal of Business Strategy* (Summer 1987): 71–75.

Patt, Raymond M. "Promotion Law." *Incentive Marketing* (February 1987): 26–37.

Posch, Jr., Robert J. "How the Law(s) of 'Privacy' Impact Your Business." *Direct Marketing* (October 1987): 74–82, 99–102.

Sheffet, Mary Jane, and Debra L. Scammon. "Resale Price Maintenance: Is It Safe to Suggest Retail Prices?" *Journal of Marketing* (Fall 1985): 82–91.

Stern, Louis W., and Thomas L. Eovaldi, *Legal Aspects of Marketing Strategy.* Englewood Cliffs, N.J.: Prentice-Hall, 1984.

Werner, Ray O. "Marketing and the Supreme Court in Transition, 1982–1984." *Journal of Marketing* (Summer 1985): 97–105.

Wilkie, William L., Dennis L. McNeill, and Michael B. Mazis. "Marketing's 'Scarlet Letter': The Theory and Practice of Corrective Advertising." *Journal of Marketing* (Spring 1984): 11–31.

ENDNOTES

1. "Ohio Wants to Suspend Wine Permits of Three Chains in Price-Fixing Case," *Supermarket News* (May 2, 1982): 21.

2. "Four Supermarket Chains Are Fined A Total of $380,000," *Wall Street Journal*, 27 November 1984, p. 7.

3. "Coupon No-Contest Pleaded by Waldbaum," *Supermarket News* (October 8, 1984): 1.

4. Sherman Act, 26 Stat, 209 (1890) as amended, 15 U.S.C. articles 1–7.

5. For a detailed discussion of fair trade laws, the reader should consult L. Louise Luchsinger and Patrick M. Dunne, "Fair Trade Laws—How Fair?" *Journal of Marketing* (January 1978): 50–53.

6. "A Red Flag for Red Tags," *Business Week* (May 16, 1988): 38.

7. Clayton Act, 38 Stat. 730 (1914), as amended, 15 U.S.C. articles 12–27.

8. Robinson-Patman Act, 49 Stat. 1526 (1936), as amended, 15 U.S.C. article 13.

9. Under the Robinson-Patman Act, references to sellers or suppliers and buyers, purchasers, or customers exclude the ultimate customer, the consumer. Thus, the buyer, purchaser, or customer is the retailer and the seller or supplier is the manufacturer or wholesaler. There is nothing illegal about a retailer charging different customers different prices for identical goods. For example, two households could go to a local Chevrolet dealer to buy an identical automobile and be charged different prices without any legal fault by the dealer. The Robinson-Patman Act protects competitors and not the final consumer.

10. Edwin A. Elias, "Robinson-Patman: Time for Rechiseling," *Mercer Law Review* 26 (1975): 689–736, and Rom J. Markin, Jr., "The Robinson-Patman Act: Regulatory Pariah," in Robert F. Lusch and Paul H. Zinszer, eds., *Contemporary Issues in Marketing Channels* (Norman, OK: Distribution Research Program, University of Oklahoma, 1979): 121–29.

11. Joseph Barry Mason, "Power and Channel Conflicts in Shopping Center Development," *Journal of Marketing* (April 1975): 33.

12. Indian Coffee Corporation vs. The Folger Coffee Company, D.C.W. PA, Sept. 1982.

13. Falls City Industries, Inc., vs. Vanco Beverages, Inc., CCH 65, 282 (U.S.S.C., March 1983).

14. FTC vs. Fred Meyer Company, Inc., 390 U.S. 341 (1968).

15. "GM Ordered to Open Up Car Rental Ad Deals," *Advertising Age* (October 17, 1983): 20.

16. Kate Fitzgerald, "Sears Battles New York Regs on 'Sale' Ads," *Advertising Age* (July 4, 1988): 3, 35.

17. "Lowest-Price Claims in Ads Stir Dispute," *Wall Street Journal*, 12 August 1988, p. 17. For a more complete discussion of this subject, see Sandra L. Schmidt and Jerome B. Kernan, "The Many Meanings (and Implications) of 'Satisfaction Guaranteed,'" *Journal of Retailing* (Winter 1985): 89–108.

18. "Death Among the Pop-Tarts," *Texas Monthly* (August 1982): 90. Jan Jarboe, "What Does H.E.B. Stand For, Anyway?" *Texas Monthly* (April 1988): 102–105, 144–161.

19. "Court, Council KO Kroger Critics," *Progressive Grocer* (May 1979): 32.

20. Willard F. Mueller and Thomas W. Paterson, "Effectiveness of State Sales-Below-Cost Laws: Evidence from the Grocery Trade," *Journal of Retailing* (Summer 1986): 166–185.

21. "Arrival of Discounter Tears the Civic Fabric of Small-Town Life," *Wall Street Journal*, 14 April 1987, pp. 1, 16. and "Not All Small Towns Welcoming Arrival of Giant Wal-Mart," *Lubbock Avalanche-Journal*, 15 March 1988, p. 2.

22. "Companies Are Knocking Off the Knockoff Outfits," *Business Week* (September 26, 1988): 86–88.

23. "On Fair and Foul in 'Big Easy'," *Advertising Age* (August 6, 1984): 12; "Industries Losing Billions of Dollars to Counterfeit Items," *Wall Street Journal*, 2 February 1984, p. 37; "Taiwan Cracking Down on Copycats," *Lubbock Avalanche-Journal*, 25 August 1986, p. A-7.

24. FTC (1983) at 690.

25. Gary T. Ford and John E. Calfee, "Recent Developments in FTC Policy on Deception," *Journal of Marketing* (July 1986): 82–103.

26. Dingell Leads Attack of FTC's New Deception Policy," *Broadcasting* (October 31, 1984): 59.

27. "Pay 'n' Save Loses Supreme Court Appeal," *Chain Store Age Executive* (July 1980): 10.

28. "Sears' Dishonest Ads Draw Ire of FTC," *Chain Store Age-Executive Edition* (April 1979): 43.

29. "Bait-and-Switch Complaints Stir in N.J.," *Advertising Age* (November 23, 1984): 1.

30. Food Store Advertising, Trade Reg. Rpts. 721 and 727.

31. Robert E. Wilkes and James B. Wilcox, "Recent FTC Actions: Implications for the Advertising Strategist," *Journal of Marketing* (January 1974): 55–61.

32. Ray O. Werner, ed., "Legal Developments in Marketing," *Journal of Marketing* (Summer 1978): 120.

33. In re Walgreen Co., FTC File No. 852 3066.

34. Ray O. Werner, ed., "Legal Developments in Marketing," *Journal of Marketing* (Spring 1980): 100.

35. "Borden Sues for New Ad-Claim Remedy," *Advertising Age* (August 6, 1984): 26.

36. When patent laws were developed in the mid-1800s they were designed to grant patents only to processes or products that advanced the welfare of soci-

ety. Since the patent office receives so many applications for patents, they have tended to approve applications as long as the applications have been properly prepared. Thus, this generally leaves it up to the court to decide the worthiness of the product or process. In short, most patents are not worth the paper they are written on.

37. Sears, Roebuck & Co. vs. Stiffel Co., 376 U.S. 225 (U.S. Sup. Ct. 1964).

38. Lanham Act, 15 USC articles 1050–1127.

39. For a more complete discussion of both the legal issues involved in trademark decisions, as well as the effective use of trademark strategies, the reader should consult Dorothy Cohen, "Trademark Strategy," *Journal of Marketing* (January, 1986): 61–74.

40. United States Public Law 92–573, Consumer Product Safety Act (1972).

41. Barnett A. Greenberg, Danny N. Bellenger, and Dan H. Robertson, "An Exploratory Investigation of Retailers Undergoing Implementation of Federal Product Safety Regulations" (Presented to the Southwestern Marketing Association, New Orleans, March 27, 1977.

42. "Fed Aim Probes at Chains," *Chain Store Age Executive* (May 1980): 13.

43. Fred W. Morgan, "Tampered Goods: Legal Developments and Marketing Guidelines," *Journal of Marketing* (April 1988): 86–96.

44. Magnuson-Moss Warranty Federal Trade Commission Act, Public Law 93–637, 93rd. Congress, 1975.

45. Amended Pre-Sale Availability of Written Warranty Terms Rule, 52 Federal Register 7569 (March 12, 1987).

46. Ray O. Werner, ed., "Legal Developments in Marketing," *Journal of Marketing* (Summer 1980): 112.

47. "FTC Still on Retailing's Case," *Chain Store Age Executive* (September 1980): p. 50.

48. **Intrabrand competition** is competition between two retailers selling the same brand, whereas **interbrand competition** would be between retailers selling different brands of the same product class. For example, a Chevrolet dealer engages in **intrabrand competition** with another Chevrolet dealer and **interbrand competition** with a Ford dealer.

49. White Motor vs. U.S., 372, U.S. 253.

50. White Motor vs. U.S., 372, U.S. 253.

51. U.S. vs. Arnold Schwinn and Co., 388 U.S. 365.

52. Continental T.V., Inc. vs. GTE Sylvania, Inc., 433 U.S. 36 (1977).

53. For a suggested approach in vertical restraint cases, see E.F. Zelek, Jr., L.W. Stern, and T.W. Dunfee, "A Rule of Reason Model After Sylvania," *California Law Review* 68 (1980): 801–36.

54. Joe Mendelovitz, d/b/a Eastex Wholesale Beer vs. Adolph Coors Co., and Highland Coors Distributors, Inc., CA-5, Dec. 1982.

55. "Territorial Franchisers Ok'd by House for Soft Drinks," *Supermarket News* (June 30, 1980): 2.

56. U.S. Department of Justice, *Vertical Restraints Guidelines*, (January 23, 1985).

57. "Justice Department Guidelines Support Marketing Restrictions by Makers," *Wall Street Journal*, 24 January 1985, p. 24.

58. Dale F. Duhan and Mary Jane Sheffet, "Gray Markets and the Legal Status of Parallel Importation," *Journal of Marketing* (July 1988): 75–83.

59. "A Red-Letter Day For Gray Marketeers," *Business Week* (June 13, 1988): 30.

60. Unijax, Inc., vs. Champion International Inc., D.C., S.N.Y., May 1981.

61. "Buyer's Guide," *Wall Street Journal*, 10 June 1988, p. 32R.

62. Shelby D. Hunt and John R. Nevin, "Full Disclosure Laws in Franchising: An Empirical Investigation," *Journal of Marketing* (April 1976): 53,62.

63. N.C. Freed Co., Inc., vs. Board of Governors of Federal Reserve System (CA2 NY) 473 F2d 1210.

64. Before entering into retail business an individual would be well advised to check with the FTC or the local office of a Better Business Bureau for an updating of these laws as well as those concerning the issuance and use of credit cards.

65. Equal Credit Opportunity Act, as amended, PL 93–495, PL 94–239, 15 USC article 1691 et seq.

66. PL 91–508, 15 USC article 1681 et seq. adding Title VI to the Consumer Credit Protection Act.

67. Fair Billing Credit Act, PL 93–495, Title III, 15 USC article 1601.

68. Fair Debt Collection Practices Act, added as Title VII to the CCPA, PL 95–109, 91 Stat 874, 15 USC article 1692 et seq.

69. "Antitrust Policy After The Steel Veto," *Fortune* (March 19, 1984): 85–98.

III Part

Location Analysis

7 Chapter

Retail Location Analysis

OVERVIEW

This chapter discusses how the retailer's location decision permeates all the other elements of the retailing mix. It begins with a discussion of how retailers identify the most attractive markets in which to locate, and concludes by studying the various demand and supply factors that must be evaluated in each market area under consideration.

CHAPTER 7
Retail
Location
Analysis

The single most important decision affecting a retailer's success is the store location decision. In fact, a wise retail executive once said that the three major decisions in retailing are location, location, and location.

Unfortunately, as we observed in our discussion of retail planning in Chapter 2, once made, this decision is not easily changed. A retailer can easily adjust prices, promotions, customer services, or even product assortment; but location cannot be easily adjusted because of lease commitments, space requirements of the business, or the unavailability of a better location that is affordable. Often the retailer waits too long to change location because it is difficult to move or because the retailer hopes conditions will improve. Retailers must sometimes watch their market size shrink due to the entry of competitors, changes in population makeup, or the addition of a major traffic artery blocking access to their location. In these situations the retailer will most likely fail because it is unable to make the quick and necessary changes to overcome these disadvantages.

When the retailer does have the opportunity to select a location for a new store or to relocate an old store, time and effort must be taken to make a good decision. The retail location decision involves three sequential steps:

1. Identify the most attractive markets to locate within.
2. Evaluate the density of demand and supply within each market and identify the most attractive sites that are available within each market.
3. Select the best site (or sites) available.

The selection of a store location must be viewed as a process involving each of these three steps. This chapter concentrates on Step 1. Chapter 8 details Steps 2 and 3.

MARKET IDENTIFICATION

The first step toward making a good retail location decision is to identify the most attractive markets in which the retailer could locate. This chapter will cover three theories for identifying the best markets. The first two theories are useful in delineating the size, shape, and total trading area of a potential location decision, while the third theory enables the retailer to evaluate how the demand of this potential trading area is being served by current retail establishments. These first two theories are the retail gravity theory and the central place theory. The third theory is called retail saturation.

RETAIL GRAVITY THEORY

Research on store location started just after World War I. Two groups of social scientists—one theoretical, the other pragmatic—believed that there were underlying consistencies in shopping behavior which would yield to mathematical analysis and prediction, based on the concept of gravity.

Reilly's Law. William J. Reilly, who described himself as a "sometime marketing specialist" as well as a "professor," published the first trading area model in 1929.[1] **Reilly's law of retail gravitation** dealt with how large urban areas attracted customers from smaller communities serving the rural hinterland. As its name implies, Reilly's law had Newtonian gravitational principles as its core: two cities attract trade from an intermediate place approximately in direct proportion to the population of the two cities and in inverse proportion to the square of the distance from these two cities to the intermediate place, or:

$$\left(\frac{Ba}{Bb}\right) = \left(\frac{Pa}{Pb}\right)\left(\frac{Db}{Da}\right)^2$$

where:

Ba = the business which City A draws from the intermediate place.
Bb = the business which City B draws from the intermediate place.
Pa = population of City A.
Pb = population of City B.
Da = distance from City A to intermediate place.
Db = distance from City B to intermediate place.[2]

Mansfield, a small town, is 25 miles from Levelland and 40 miles in the opposite direction from Norwood. Levelland's population is 100,000 and Norwood's is 200,000.

Using Reilly's equations we can see that the retailers in Levelland attract 1.28 times as much business from the citizens of Mansfield as do the retailers in Norwood.

$$\left(\frac{Ba}{Bb}\right) = \left(\frac{100,000}{200,000}\right)\left(\frac{40}{25}\right)^2 = 1.28$$

Since we know that Mansfield's citizens spend 1.28 dollars in Levelland for every dollar spent in Norwood, we can say that Levelland has a 56 percent share of the Mansfield market and Norwood has a 44 percent share:

$$\frac{1.28}{1.28 + 1.00} = 56\% \qquad \frac{1.00}{1.28 + 1.00} = 44\%$$

Converse's Revision.   Two decades later Paul Converse revised Reilly's original law in order to determine the boundaries of a city's trading area or to establish a "point of indifference" between two cities.[3] This **point of indifference** is the breaking point at which shoppers would be indifferent to shopping at either city. Converse's formulation of Reilly's Law can be expressed algebraically as:

$$Dab = \frac{d}{1 + \sqrt{\dfrac{Pb}{Pa}}}$$

where:

Dab = breaking point from City A, measured in miles along the road to
           City B.
  d = distance between City A and City B along the major highway.
Pa = population of City A.
Pb = population of City B.

Referring to our earlier example, the breakpoint of indifference between Levelland and Norwood would be 26.9 miles from Levelland and 38.1 miles from Norwood. This means that if you lived 20 miles from Levelland and 45 miles from Norwood you most probably would choose to shop in Levelland since it is within your zone of indifference and Norwood is beyond your zone of indifference. You might want to figure this out yourself, using Norwood as City A and Levelland as City B:

$$Dab = \frac{65}{1 + \sqrt{\dfrac{200,000}{100,000}}}$$

This formula can also be used with more than two cities. Consider the population and distances separating cities A, B, C, and D in Exhibit 7.1a. City A is the largest, with a population of 240,000, and it is surrounded by three smaller cities. City B is 18 miles away and has a population of 14,000; City D is 5 miles away and has a population of 30,000; and City C is 14 miles away and has a population of 21,000. We will assume that the roads on Exhibit 7.1a are the only ones connecting the smaller cities with the larger City A.

Converse's revision of Reilly's Law will allow us to determine the distances from which each of the smaller cities will be able to attract households. The complement of this is the distances from which City A will be able to attract households in the direction of Cities B, C, and D.

For example, if we consider Cities A and B we would have:

$$D_B = \frac{18}{1 + \sqrt{\dfrac{240,000}{14,000}}} = 3.5 \text{ miles}$$

City B is able to attract households from 3.5 miles in the direction of City A. Since A and B are 18 miles apart, we could also conclude that A could attract customers from 14.5 miles $(18 - 3.5)$ in the direction of B.

Applying the same equation, but using relevant data on Cities C and D, yields:

$$D_C = \frac{14}{1 + \sqrt{\dfrac{240,000}{21,000}}} = 3.2 \text{ miles}$$

$$D_D = \frac{5}{1 + \sqrt{\dfrac{240,000}{30,000}}} = 1.3 \text{ miles}$$

Thus, City C can attract households from 3.2 miles in the direction of City A, and City D can attract households from 1.3 miles in the direction of City A.

In Exhibit 7.1b we show that we can connect the three points that we just determined. The result is City A's **general trading area**, a geographically delineated area that surrounds a community, in which households would generally be willing to travel to the community to purchase goods and services. Once you determine the trading area, you can ascertain the demographic makeup of that area. Thus the retailer now has a clear definition of where its trading area will be and who its customers will be if it elects to locate in City A.

Reilly's Law and Converse's revision rest on two assumptions: that the two competing cities are equally accessible from the major road; and

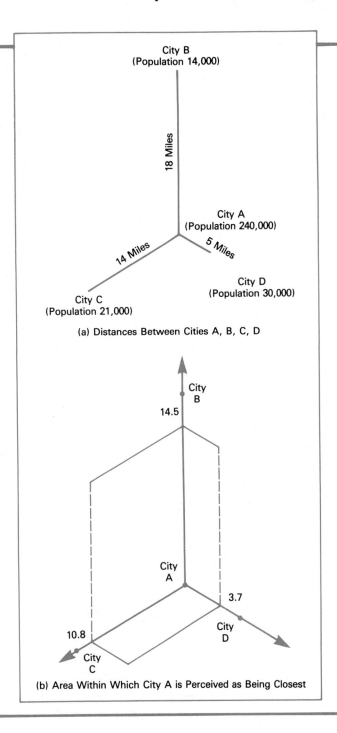

Exhibit 7.1

A Community's General Trading Areas

City B
(Population 14,000)

18 Miles

City A
(Population 240,000)

14 Miles

5 Miles

City C
(Population 21,000)

City D
(Population 30,000)

(a) Distances Between Cities A, B, C, D

City B

14.5

City A

3.7

10.8

City D

City C

(b) Area Within Which City A is Perceived as Being Closest

Exhibit 7.2

New Trading Area for City A after Substituting City E for City B

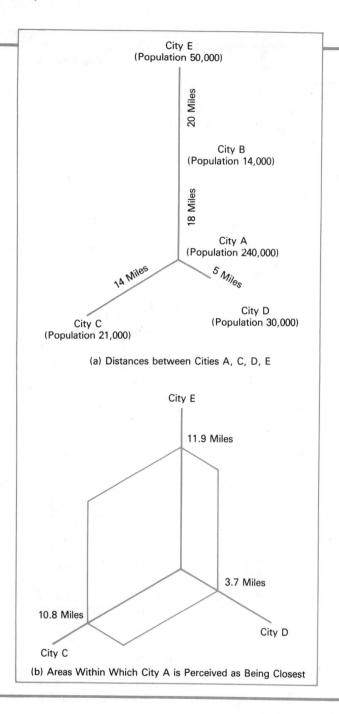

City E
(Population 50,000)

20 Miles

City B
(Population 14,000)

18 Miles

City A
(Population 240,000)

14 Miles

5 Miles

City C
(Population 21,000)

City D
(Population 30,000)

(a) Distances between Cities A, C, D, E

City E

11.9 Miles

3.7 Miles

10.8 Miles

City C

City D

(b) Areas Within Which City A is Perceived as Being Closest

that population is a good surrogate indicator for the differences in the goods and services available in different cities. Consumers are attracted to larger population centers, not because of the city's size, but because of the greater amount of store facilities and product assortment available. The increased selection makes the increased travel time worthwhile.

The law of retail gravitation was an important contribution to trading area analysis because of its ease of calculation. It is easy to use when other data are not available or when the costs of obtaining these data are too high. However, Reilly's Law does have several limitations. First, population doesn't always reflect available shopping facilities. For example, two neighboring cities, each with a population of 10,000 and similar demographics, would not be reflected equally in Reilly's Law if one of the cities had a Wal-Mart-based shopping center and the other didn't. Second, distance is measured in miles, not the time involved for the consumer to travel that distance or the consumer's perception of that distance or time involved. Given our present highway system, this limitation is significant. Traveling 30 miles on an interstate to a mall located at an exit is easier than the stop-start travel involved in going six miles through downtown traffic. Some retailers using Reilly's Law substitute travel time for mileage. Another important limitation is that the size of the trading area is totally dependent on the corner cities selected. If City E, with a population of 50,000, is 20 miles past City B on the same highway from City A as shown in Exhibit 7.2, then City A's trading area will be different. Finally, while the law works satisfactorily in rural areas, where distance is a major decision factor, it isn't as useful in metropolitan areas where consumers typically have a number of shopping choices available within the maximum distance they are willing to travel.

CENTRAL PLACE THEORY

At the same time that Reilly was publishing his work in the United States, Walter Christaller was developing a theoretical model in Southern Germany to evaluate the spatial arrangement of stores required for the distribution of a single good to a dispersed population. Christaller's work was titled *Central Places in Southern Germany*.[4] According to Christaller, a **central place** is a center of commerce—a village, town or city—consisting of a cluster of retail institutions. Central place theory ranks communities according to the assortment of goods available in each. At the bottom of the hierarchy are communities that represent the smallest central places. They provide the most basic assortment of goods and services, the necessities of life. Farther up the hierarchy are larger central places, which carry all of the goods and services found in lower-order central places plus more specialized ones that are not as necessary.

To obtain goods and services, households need to travel to the central places. Thus, consumer travel is crucial in determining the location of cen-

A gas station is an example of a service for which the range of consumer travel is only a short distance.

tral places. Christaller illustrated how central places should be established in a geographic space in order to minimize aggregate travel costs for the consumer. The more basic the good or service, the shorter the distance the consumer should need to travel to purchase it. On the other hand, the typical household could expect to travel a great distance for specialized goods and services, since only the larger central places have them.

Christaller provided central place theory with two important concepts—the *range* and the *threshold* of a good. The **range** is the maximum distance a consumer is willing to travel for a good or service, and as such it determines the outer limit of a store's market area. **Threshold** is the minimum amount of consumer demand that must exist in an area for a store to be economically viable. In spatial terms, this threshold is equal to the radius of the area containing the population that can just support the store. According to Christaller, the range must be greater than the threshold if the store is to be economically feasible. This explains why firms, shopping centers, or communities offering only convenience goods will be more numerous and closer together than firms, shopping centers, or communities offering more specialized but less frequently purchased goods or services that must attract consumers from a much wider geographic area. Consumers also prefer to visit a single location for a variety of needs, rather than traveling to different places for each item. This forces firms to group together as a community of businesses in order to serve as many different needs as possible from a single location. Thus, the communities most centrally located in a region attract the more specialized and largest number of firms.

Although Christaller developed his theory to describe the location of retail activity in Southern Germany in the 1930s, modern retailing experts agree that central place models offer a "powerful explanation of the spatial distribution of retail facilities and market center and the pattern and extent of market areas."[5] The validity of his theory has been tested by at least three independent, empirical studies in the United States over the last three decades.[6] All three studies showed that among the first 20 lines of retail trade to locate in a community, the following nine would appear in this order:

1. Gasoline service station
2. Grocery store
3. Restaurant
4. Physician
5. Insurance agency
6. Beauty shop
7. Real estate agency
8. Auto parts dealer
9. Furniture store

Furthermore, two of the three studies agreed that the following five functions would also locate in the top twenty:

10. Automobile dealer
11. Lawyer
12. Hay, grain, and feed store
13. Women's ready-to-wear
14. Dry cleaner

What are the implications of central place theory for identification of the best markets? There are three:

1. Not all communities will be able to support all types of retailing activity. The more basic or necessity-oriented the goods are that the retailer is selling (gasoline and food), the more communities it can consider as potential markets. If the retailer is selling very specialized goods such as furs and jewelry, then it need only consider the larger communities.

2. Central place theory tells the retailer which types of retail activity a growing community will most likely need in the future. For example, a small community with only a gasoline service station and a grocery store will probably need a restaurant next. Thus, central place theory can help the retailer identify the communities or markets that will be most in need of its type of retailing activity.

3. The theory tells us that a single trip to a higher-order central place will replace the need to make separate trips to several lower-order

centers. This suggests that the larger central places will do a disproportionately larger amount of business. When consumers from small communities travel to a larger central place, they will be able to purchase not only specialized goods and services but also basic ones. The implication is simply that large central places tend to be more attractive in terms of potential demand. This has been demonstrated often in small-town America, where the arrival of a Wal-Mart draws other retailers towards Wal-Mart's location and away from the old downtown business district.

Christaller's work had one major limitation. A number of studies have found that, contrary to the central place assumptions, consumers will sometimes bypass closer shopping opportunities to visit agglomerated centers that are farther away in order to shop for different types of goods on the same trip. Multipurpose shopping trips account for between 30 to 50 percent of all shopping today; however, central place theory ignores the relationship that exists among different types of retail firms.

Ghosh, recognizing that the presence of multipurpose shopping patterns by consumers presented a strong economic incentive for low-order retailers to agglomerate with higher-order ones wherever possible, developed a model of consumer shopping that determines the optimal shopping itinerary of individual consumers. While the actual model developed is beyond the scope of this chapter, it is important to point out that a number of his predictions regarding spatial organization of retailing are consistent with empirical realities. For example, Ghosh predicts that consumers living close to the low-order stores will make more frequent trips to those stores. Ghosh's model provides the underlying rationale for the agglomeration of dissimilar retailing firms in shopping centers and malls and determines the benefits of such actions for both retailers and consumers.[7]

CONTRIBUTIONS FROM REILLY AND CHRISTALLER

Reilly and Christaller looked at the issue of retail location from different perspectives, and each made a significant contribution to its early development. (It should be pointed out that Reilly was probably unaware of Christaller's early work since it was not published in an English translation until 1966.) Reilly's contribution was a statistical model based on empirical observation and Christaller's was a theoretical model showing the relationship of the different ingredients in a location process. It was not until the translation of the work of Losch[8] that a mathematical model of Christaller's theory was produced. Losch argued that since the real price of a good increases with distance travelled, the quantity demanded will decrease correspondingly as we pointed out in Exhibit 5.7 on page 172. Otherwise, Losch's work is of little interest to retailers.

Another important contribution of these pioneers of location studies was that for the first time, retailers were able to predict the shape of their market areas. Based on the work of Christaller, the locations of the various market centers were assumed to be in a hexagonal pattern. Hexagons are the nearest geometrical equivalents to circles that will allow all geographic areas and consumers to be served by a center. A network of circles around a central place would result in some areas being overlapped by two central place cities and/or other areas not being covered. Christaller's argument, however, was only theoretical in nature and could be distorted by natural or man-made barriers to travel, political uncertainites, or nonuniform population patterns.

Given the location of the largest cities, the locations of the next level of communities will occur exactly at the apex of three of the largest cities. Exhibit 7.3 shows that every plan contains two B-level communities for every A-level city. Since the method by which successive orders of com-

Exhibit 7.3

The Arrangement of Trade Centers and Trade Areas According to Christaller's Model of Central Place

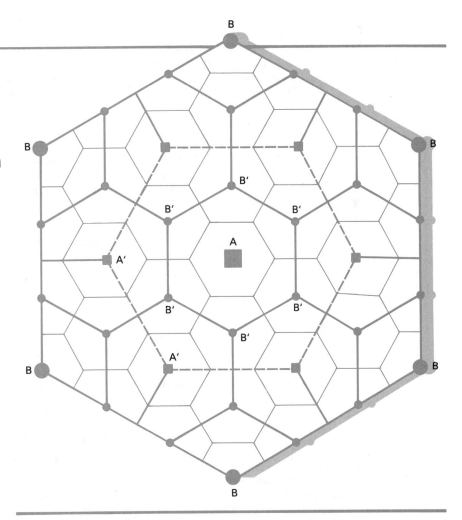

munities are added does not change, it will always be true that the number of communities in a given order will equal twice the number of communities in all higher levels combined. In other words, 1:2:6:18:54:162, etc.

These numbers can be proved by looking closely at Exhibit 7.3 and assuming that A (the central city) is the largest city. At the corners of A's market area are six B-level cities. Each B, however, is located at the junction of the market areas of three A cities, so that each B city may be counted only as 1/1 in calculating the ratio of A to B cities (or 2 to 1).[9]

SATURATION THEORY

A third theoretical concept that can help to determine the attractiveness of different market areas is retail saturation. William Applebaum and Saul Cohen define **store saturation** as follows:[10]

"Store saturation of a market is a condition under which existing store facilities are utilized efficiently and meet customer needs. Saturation exists for a given type of store when a market has just enough store facilities of a given type to serve the population of the market satisfactorily and yield a fair return to the owners on their investments without raising prices to the customer to achieve this return. When a market has too few stores to provide satisfactorily the needs of the customer, it is under-stored. When a market has too many stores to yield a fair return on investment, it is over-stored. Saturation, as defined here, implies a balance between the amount of existing retail store facilities and their use (which in turn is a reflection of need)."

A possible indicator of under- vs. over-stored markets is the **index of retail saturation (IRS).**[11] IRS can be calculated as follows:

$$IRS_1 = \frac{H_1 \times RE_1}{RF_1}$$

where:

IRS_1 = index of retail saturation for area one
H_1 = number of households in area one
RE_1 = annual retail expenditures for a particular line of trade per household in area one
RF_1 = square feet of retail facilities of a particular line of trade in area one (including square footage of proposed store)

When IRS has a high value in comparison with the line of trade in other cities, it indicates that the market is not saturated, and that a potentially attractive opportunity exists. When IRS is a low value, it indicates a saturated market, without significant opportunity.

As an example of how the index of retail saturation is used, consider an individual planning on opening a dry cleaner in either City A or City B. This individual has the following information: Residents of both cities spend $75.36 anually on dry-cleaning. Total households are 17,000 in City A and 22,000 in City B. City A has 2,000 square feet of dry-cleaning facilities, City B has 2,500, and the size of the proposed dry cleaner is 500 square feet. Given this information and using our formula for IRS, we can find the IRS for each city:

$$\text{IRS (City A)} = \frac{17{,}000 \times 75.36}{2500} = 512.45$$

$$\text{IRS (City B)} = \frac{22{,}000 \times 75.36}{3000} = 552.64$$

Thus, based solely on these two factors of demand (number of households and average expenditure for products by each household) and one factor of supply (the number of square feet of retail space serving this demand) the individual would choose to locate in City B.

You should notice two things about the IRS formula. First, IRS informs the retail analyst that market-entry decisions should be based on supply and demand factors. In fact, IRS is simply the ratio of aggregate household demand ($H_1 \cdot RE_1$) to aggregate retail space supply (RF_1). The higher the ratio of aggregate demand to aggregate supply, the more attractive the market opportunity. Second, IRS is essentially a measure of average sales per square foot of the existing retail establishments in the market. With this statistic, the analyst can derive an estimate of profits by working with known gross margin and operating expense ratios for the industry.

The concept of retail saturation forces the retail location decision-maker to assess demand and supply in analyzing various markets. Let us now identify the major demand and supply factors that were not explicitly recognized in IRS.

The computed IRS value can be compared to the sales dollars per square foot needed by the retailer to break even in a new location. Even if one city under consideration has a much higher value than the other cities, if that value isn't greater than the break-even costs of operation, the retailer should reject the city. Some retail scholars have questioned the usefulness of this index, because even markets with a low IRS value may be attractive places to enter if existing retailers are not satisfying consumer desires. Nevertheless, IRS is still widely used in retailing today.[12]

DEMAND FACTORS

The major demand factors that should be carefully analyzed, in addition to retail sales per household (as defined in IRS), are market potential and household and community characteristics. Household characteristics include income, age profile, and size. Community characteristics include life cycle, population density, and mobility.

MARKET POTENTIAL

In analyzing market potential, retailers identify certain criteria which are specific to their product line. The criteria chosen by one retailer might not be of use to a retailer selling a different product line. The major components of market potential to be considered are population and buying behavior.

Population Characteristics.   Population characteristics are the most often used criteria to segment markets. The decennial census of population is the most important source of this data for both large and small communities. The census provides a uniform set of data for intercommunity comparisons. Exhibit 7.4 shows data from the 1980 census. The basic data,

Exhibit 7.4

Population Data Available from 1980 Census

Sample Population Items	100 Percent Population Items
School enrollment	Household relationship
Education attainment	Sex
State or country of birth	Race
Citizenship and year of immigration	Age
Current language and English proficiency	Marital status
Ancestry	Spanish/Hispanic origin or descent
Place of residence 5 years ago	
Activity 5 years ago	
Veteran status and period of service	
Presence of disability or handicap	
Children ever born	
Marital history	
Employment status last week	
Hours worked last week	
Place of work	
Travel time to work	
Means of transportation to work	
Persons in carpool	
Year last worked	
Industry	
Occupation	
Class of worker	
Work in 1979 and weeks looking for work in 1979	
Amount of income by source in 1979	

called "complete count" or "100 percent," comes from the questions asked of every person. Other items are based on sample estimates. In general, the larger the city, the greater the amount of detail there is available in the census reports.

Although total population figures and their growth rates are of primary importance to a retailer in examining potential markets, the executive can get a more detailed profile of a market by examining school enrollment, education, age, sex, occupation, race, and nationality. Retailers should try to match a market's population characteristics to the population characteristics of people who desire their goods and services. Retailing in Action 7-1 examines a chain operation that is extremely successful in matching its offerings to the marketplace.

RETAILING
IN
ACTION

7-1

Ames's Use of Demand Factors in Choosing a Location

Ames Department Stores, operators of 690 discount department stores and variety stores in 21 eastern and midwestern states, is striving to increase its number of stores by 10 percent yearly for the "foreseeable future." Ames's success in the past has been attributed to their philosophy of locating in small- and medium-size towns where they are the dominant retailer. While this strat-

Illus. 7.2
Ames Department Stores, Inc. have been very successful as a result of demographic studies. Source: Ames Department Stores, Inc.

egy has been extremely successful (an Ames store ranges between 50,000 and 80,000 square feet and does nearly $5 million a year in sales), it has resulted in some jokes. Ames's director of research laughs when he recalls the saying that "Ames builds a store whenever it finds more cows than people."

Actually, Ames has made a science out of marketing in the "puckerbrush," and knowing what its trading area is.

To begin, the demographic information on population size, income, number of households, occupations, and education of a proposed new site is compared to the data of existing stores. After comparing this data, a computer model of the new store's trading area is projected. Sometimes the results are surprising. By looking at all these demographic variables, Ames is sometimes able to see success where others have found only failure. Consider the case of a vacant large store near Richmond, Virginia, that Ames purchased in the mid-1980s. Other retailers looked at the demographic indicators and saw only that "the area was 44 percent black." Ames saw that the market area had healthy income levels and only a 3 percent unemployment rate. As a result, they were able to purchase for only $3 per square foot a store that was the most profitable in the chain a year later.

The lesson that can be learned here is simple: knowing just a few key demographics of an area is not enough to know the makeup of the area. No wonder Ames has experienced a 20 percent increase in both sales and earnings over the past decade.

Source: Based on "Ames Profits in the Puckerbrush," *American Demographics* (October 1985): 20–21; "Ames Uses Computer System to Select Store Sites," *Chain Store Age—Executive Edition* (November 1984): 57; September 2, 1988 *Value Line* report on Ames; and August 9, 1988 Standard and Poor's report on Ames.

Buyer Behavior Characteristics.   Another useful criteria for analyzing potential markets is the buying behavior characteristics of the market. Such characteristics include store loyalty, consumer lifestyles, store patronage motives, geographic and climatic conditions, and product benefits sought. This data, however, is not as easy to obtain as population data.

HOUSEHOLD CHARACTERISTICS

Household Income.   The average household income and the distribution of household income can significantly influence demand for retail facilities. Further insights into the demand for retail facilities are provided by **Engel's Laws.** These are generalizations about a household's response to an increase in income. They imply that spending increases for all categories of products as a result of an income increase, but that the percentage

Illus. 7.3

A jewelry store demonstrates Engel's Laws: As average household income rises, the community will exhibit greater demand for luxury goods and more sophisticated demand for necessity goods.

of spending in some categories increases more than for others. According to Engel's Laws, as average household income rises, the community will exhibit a greater demand for luxury goods and more sophisticated demand for necessity goods. Consider the demand for food. Regardless of household income, as long as it is above the poverty level, individuals will consume the same approximate quantity of food. At low incomes, they may consume pinto beans, hot dogs, and bread; at the higher income level they may eat asparagus, sirloin steak, and fancy dinner rolls.

The distribution of household incomes in a community can influence the demand for retail facilities. If all households in a community had an identical income (an unlikely phenomenon), then the same type of retail facility within any given line of trade would probably appeal to all households. There would be no opportunity to segment the market based on income. For example, if all households had relatively low incomes, then an upscale women's apparel store would face little opportunity, even though there might be a need for an additional women's apparel store. On the other hand, if the average household had a low income, but there were also a fair number of households with high incomes, then some potential might exist for such a store.

Household Age Profile. The age composition of households can be an important determinant of demand for retail facilities. In communities where households tend to be young, the preferences for stores may be different than in communities where the average household is relatively old.

For example, in communities with a disproportionate number of young households, the demand for restaurants will be heavily oriented toward fast-food. In communities with a disproportionate number of older households, the demand will be more oriented to leisurely dining. Age will help determine the demand for a wide range of retail facilities such as furniture stores, jewelry stores, and apparel stores.

Size of Household.   If we hold income and age constant and change the average size of households, we will be able to identify another determinant of the demand for retail facilities. Consider two young households with moderate incomes: one household contains a husband and wife and the other, a husband, wife, and three children. For the second household, the moderate income level loses much of its buying power because of the larger household size. This will influence the distribution of retail expenditures between food stores, apparel stores, furniture stores, restaurants, auto dealers, and so on. This will also influence the demand for specific types of retailers (e.g., discount department store vs. full-service, conventional department stores). To illustrate this point further, place yourself as the head of a household with an income of $26,000 and consider how you would spend that money if you had no children and then if you had three children. As Exhibit 7.5 points out, important household data is readily available from census data.

Exhibit 7.5

Housing Data Available from 1980 Census

Sample Items	100 Percent Items
Number of units in structure	Number of housing units at address
Stories in building and presence of elevator	Complete plumbing facilities
Year unit built	Number of rooms in unit
Year moved into this house	Tenure (whether the unit is owned or rented)
Source of water	
Sewage disposal	Condominium identification
Heating equipment	Value of home (for owner-occupied units and condominiums)
Fuels used for home heating, water heating, and cooking	Rent (for renter-occupied units)
Costs of utilities and fuels	Vacant for rent, for sale, etc., and period of vacancy
Complete kitchen facilities	
Number of bedrooms and bathrooms	
Telephone	
Air conditioning	
Number of automobiles	
Number of light trucks and vans	
Homeowner shelter costs for mortgage, real estate taxes, and hazard insurance	

COMMUNITY CHARACTERISTICS

Community Life Cycle. Communities tend to exhibit growth patterns over time. It has been suggested that:

"Over a span of time, growth patterns of communities may be of four major types. These include the pattern of rapid growth, the pattern of continuous growth, the pattern of relatively stable growth and the pattern of decline. The rapid growth pattern can be found largely in communities located along the Gulf Coast, in the Southwest and in the West. The continuous growth pattern is appearing in communities that are developing new industries and expanding established industries. The slow or constant-level growth pattern can be found when a city has developed an established economy that remains in a relatively stable position. The diminished or declining growth pattern is often associated with the exhaustion of resources or a shift in technology."[13]

The retailer should try to identify communities that are in a rapid or continuous growth pattern, since they will represent the best long-run opportunities.

Population Density. The population density of a community can be defined either as the number of persons per square mile or number of households per square mile. In either case, empirical research suggests that the higher the population density, the larger the average store in terms of square feet and thus the fewer the number of stores that will be needed to serve a population of a given size.[14] Therefore, it is important that retailers consider the population density of markets they are evaluating.

Mobility. The easier it is for people to travel, the more mobile they will be.[15] When people are mobile they are willing to travel greater distances to shop, and therefore there will be fewer but larger stores in the community. Thus a community whose households are highly mobile will need fewer retailers than a community whose mobility is low. Mobility cannot be directly determined, but there are surrogate indicators. One popular indicator is the number of automobiles per household. As this number rises, households become more mobile. Other indicators are the availability of public transportation and the amount of traffic congestion. Households may have cars, but if the roadways are inadequate to handle the quantity of traffic, congestion will hamper household mobility. Thus more stores are needed, and they should be closer together.

SUPPLY FACTORS

The IRS formula used an aggregate measure of supply: total square feet of retail facilities by line of trade in a community. Although this is a useful indicator, there are many others—square feet per store, square feet per employee, growth in number of stores, and quality of competition.

SQUARE FEET PER STORE

It is helpful if the retail analyst has data on the square feet per store for the average store in the communities that are being analyzed. This will indicate whether a community tends to have large- or small-scale retailing. This is important in terms of assessing the extent to which the retailer's store would blend with the existing structure of retail trade in the community. This does not mean that a retailer should only consider locating small stores in communities that presently tend to have small stores. But if there currently are only small stores in a community, then before entering with a large store the retailer should make certain that the demand factors would support a large establishment.

SQUARE FEET PER EMPLOYEE

A measure that combines two major supply factors in retailing—store space and labor—is square feet of space per employee. A high number for this statistic in a community is evidence that each employee is able to handle more space. This could be due to either a high level of retail technology in the community or more self-service retailing. Since retail technology is fairly constant across communities, any difference in square feet per employee is most often due to level of service being provided. In communities currently characterized by retailers offering a high level of service, there may be a significant opportunity for new retailers oriented toward self-service.

GROWTH IN STORES

The analyst should look at the rate of growth in the number of stores over the last one to five years. When growth is rapid, then on average the community will have better-located stores with more contemporary atmospheres. Recently located stores will better match the existing demographics of the community. Also their atmosphere will better suit the current tastes of the marketplace and they will tend to incorporate the latest in retail technology. The strength of retail competition will be greater when the community has recently experienced rapid growth in number of stores.

QUALITY OF COMPETITION

These three supply factors have reflected the quantity of competition. Analysts also need to look at the strength or quality of competition. They should attempt to identify the major retail chains or local retailers in each

RETAILING
IN
ACTION

7-2

The Problems Associated With Retail Expansion

Just because a retailer has been successful at one location is no reason to assume that success will follow at other locations. Consider the case of Ralph's. Ralph's, a West Coast grocery chain, is the market leader in Los Angeles and is so highly competitive that Kroger left the L.A. market rather than fight it out with Ralph's and another retailer, Von's.

However, Ralph's Southern California strength did not help it when it tried to enter the Northern California market almost a decade ago. After three years of at-best mixed results, Ralph's management came to the realization that the chain could only operate profitably within a certain radius of its distribution center. When Ralph's got beyond the radius of its ability to distribute merchandise efficiently, its cost went up to such a point that either the additional stores could not be price competitive or profit objectives would have to be reduced. A similar lesson was learned by Joske's of Texas when it expanded into Arizona and by Safeway's Oklahoma City division when it entered the western Texas market.

This doesn't mean that Ralph's, Joske's, or Safeway cannot expand into other market areas; it just means that the management should be aware of the stress that expansion could place on the distribution system. Management must be aggressive upon entering new markets, with a commitment to lots of space and lots of stores over a very short time period. Otherwise, the economies of scale that the retailer is presently enjoying could be lost.

market and evaluate the strength of each. Answers to questions such as the following would provide valuable insights: What is their market share or profitability? How promotion- and price-oriented are they? Are they customer oriented? Do they tend to react to new market entrants by cutting prices, increasing advertising, or improving customer service? A retailer would think twice before competing with Wal-Mart on price, Bloomingdale's on fashion, or Nordstrom's on service. Retailing in Action 7-2 provides an insight into the other problems a retailer might encounter in an expansion program.

SECONDARY SOURCES OF INFORMATION

Our discussion of retail gravity theory, central place theory, saturation theory, and demand and supply factors has provided you with a frame of reference for identifying the most attractive markets to consider for a store site. More complete, statistically-based frameworks are available, but they are beyond the scope of this text. The most important point to keep in mind is that before retailers select a location, they should identify the communities (markets) that represent attractive opportunities. The data necessary to do this type of analysis is available in publications like: *Census of Retail Trades, County and City Data Book, Census of Housing and Population, Sales Management's Survey of Buying Power,* and *Editor & Publisher Market Guide.* Let's look at an example of a retailer using the data from these publications and the tools presented earlier in this chapter.

A SIMPLE EXAMPLE

The XYZ Corporation, a retail chain specializing in general merchandise goods, is considering expansion. The firm is looking at two different trading areas for possible location of their new store. These trading areas were found by using Reilly's Law and are the Alton-Granite City, Illinois and the Hamilton-Middletown, Ohio markets. For each area, the firm will develop a **buying power index (BPI)**, a single-weighted measure combining effective buying income (personal income minus all tax and nontax payments such as social security insurance), retail sales, and population size into an overall indicator of a market's potential. Generally, business firms use the following formula, which was developed by *Sales and Marketing Management* magazine, for BPI.

Buying Power Index = 0.5 (the area's percentage of United States effective buying income)

+ 0.3 (the area's percentage of United States retail sales)

+ 0.2 (the area's percentage of United States population)

This formula can be further refined by breaking these general figures down into more specific figures geared toward a retailer's target market. In XYZ's case, it aims its general merchandise at the 25 to 34 year-old market with incomes over $35,000. Therefore, the 25 to 34 year age group will substitute for population, the general merchandise sales will substitute for total retail sales, and households with income over $35,000 will replace effective buying income.

Using data that can be easily obtained from the above named publications we can develop the BPI for each city.

BPI (Alton-Granite City) = 0.5 (.00026) + 0.3 (.00083) + 0.2 (.00012)
= .000403

BPI (Hamilton-Middletown) = 0.5 (.00032) + 0.4 (.00063) + 0.2 (.000112)
= .000371

As you can see, the BPI of Alton-Granite City is almost 10 percent greater than that of Hamilton-Middletown, although the cities are nearly equal in size. Therefore, XYZ would probably choose to expand its Illinois market rather than the Ohio market.

It must be remembered that BPI is broad in nature and reflects only the demand levels for the two proposed trading areas, not the supply levels. As such, it does not reflect the saturation levels of these two markets. This can be easily addressed by dividing the BPI for each area by the area's percentage of United States retail selling space for general merchandise (the supply factors) to determine each area:

IRS (Alton-Granite City) = .000403 divided by .000432 = .933

IRS (Hamilton-Middletown) = .000371 divided by .000417 = .890

The Illinois trading area is again a better choice. This IRS formula does not reflect the availability of competing products or stores in nearby large cities like Cincinnati and St. Louis.

SUMMARY

Store location decisions are important because of their short-run and long run natures, their investment requirements and their effect on the other elements of the retail mix. The location decision is considered to be uncontrollable; that is, impossible or very difficult to change. Therefore, it is extremely important for a retailer to constantly monitor population shifts, the actions of competitors, and other changes that could affect retail performance.

The choice of retail location involves three decisions: (1) identifying the most attractive markets; (2) evaluating the demand and supply within each market; and (3) selecting the best site (or sites) available. This chapter has concentrated on the first decision.

We began our analysis of market selection by looking at three location theories and how these theories can aid in the location decision. Reilly's Law of Retail Gravitation assumed that the population of a community served as a drawing power for the community and drew customers into its business district. Christaller assumed communities could be ranked by looking at goods and services available within that community. The third theory, the index of retail saturation, compares the total demand for the product under question with the availability of retailers to service or supply that product. We concluded our discussion on market selection by looking into other factors that could influence a community's supply (square feet per store, square feet per employee, growth in stores, and quality of competition) or demand (market potential and household and community characteristics).

1. Explain the importance of the concepts of range and threshold as they relate to retail location decisions.
2. Christaller assumed that the market area surrounding a market center was hexagonal. Based on your own experience do you believe that this is true today?
3. What is the index of retail saturation? How can it be used in making location decisions?
4. What is the buying power index (BPI)? How is it used?
5. Calculate the buying power indexes for the following three cities:

City	Percent of U.S. Effective Buying Income	Percent of U.S. Retail Sales	Percent of U.S. Population
Arkon City	.005	.006	.004
Binghamtown	.006	.004	.005
Cochran	.004	.005	.007

6. Compute the index for retail saturation for the following three markets:

	A	B	C
Retail expenditures per household	$ 510	$ 575	$ 610
Square feet of retail space	600,000	488,000	808,000
Number of households	112,000	91,000	147,000

Which market is most attractive? What additional data would you find helpful in determining the attractiveness of the three markets?

7. Temple is 64 miles from Beckville (population 220,000) and 32 miles in the opposite direction from Waco (population 110,000). Using Reilly's Law, how much money will the citizens of Temple spend in Beckville for every dollar they spend in Waco?
8. If we say that location is an uncontrollable factor for a retailer, does this mean that a retailer with 15 years remaining on his/her lease should make an immediate study of the trends expected 15 years from now or that he/she should do nothing since location is beyond his/her control?
9. Using Reilly's Law, construct a general trading area for your community.
10. For a pair of cities of your choosing attempt to gather as much secondary data on food stores as possible. Consider both supply and de-

mand factors. Collect the following data: (a) average square feet per store, (b) square feet per employee, (c) growth in stores, (d) average household income, (e) average household size, (f) population density, and (g) age profile of population growth over the last five to ten years. Compare these cities on the basis of the data you gather. Identify the opportunities for grocery retailers in each city.

SUGGESTED READINGS

Arnold, Stephen J., Tae H. Oum, and Douglas J. Tigert. "Determinant Attributes in Retail Patronage: Seasonal, Temporal, Regional, and International Comparisons." *Journal of Marketing Research* (May 1983): 149–157.

Ghosh, Avijit, and Gerald Rushton, eds. *Spatial Analysis and Location Allocation Modeling*. New York: Van Nostrand Rheinhold Inc., 1987.

Mahajan Vijay, Subhash Sharma, and D. Srinivas. "An Application of Portfolio Analysis for Identifying Attractive Retail Locations." *Journal of Retailing* (Winter 1985): 19–34.

Riche, Martha Farnsworth. "Computer Mapping Takes Center Stage." *American Demographics* (June 1986): 26–31, 64–65.

ENDNOTES

1. William J. Reilly, "Methods for the Study of Retail Relationships," Research Monograph No. 4 (Austin, TX: Bureau of Business Research, The University of Texas, 1929).

2. Reilly, 48–49.

3. P. D. Converse, "New Laws of Retail Gravitation," *Journal of Marketing* (January 1949): 379–384.

4. Walter Christaller, *Central Places in Southern Germany*, trans. Carlisle W. Baskin (Englewood Cliffs, N.J.: Prentice-Hall, 1966). This is a translation of Christaller's 1935 book.

5. C. Samuel Craig, Avijit Ghosh, and Sara McLafferty, "Models of Retail Location Process: A Review," *Journal of Retailing* (Spring 1984): 6.

6. Brian Berry and William Garrison, "The Functional Bases of the Central Place Hierarchy," *Economic Geography* (April 1958): 146–149; J. Hurlebaus and R. Fulton, "Community Size and the Number of Businesses and Services," *Tennessee Survey of Business*, 1968; and Joseph Barry Mason, "Threshold Analysis as a Tool in Economic Potential Studies and Retail Site Location: An Illustrative Application," *The Southern Journal of Business* (August 1972): 43.

7. Avijit Ghosh, "The Value of a Mall and Other Insights from a Revised Central Place Model," *Journal of Retailing* (Spring 1986): 79–97.

8. A. Losch, *The Economics of Location*, trans. W. Woglam and W. Stopler (New Haven: Yale University Press, 1943).

9. John Urquhart Marshall, *The Location of Service Towns: An Approach to the Analysis of Central Place Systems* (Toronto: University of Toronto Press, 1969), 18–21.

10. William Applebaum and Saul B. Cohen, "Trading Area Networks and Problems of Store Saturation," *Journal of Retailing* (Winter 1961–62): 35–36. Reprinted with permission of the *Journal of Retailing*.

11. Bernard LaLonde, "The Logistics of Retail Location," in William D. Stevens, ed., *Fall American Marketing Proceedings* (Chicago: American Marketing Association, 1961): 572.

12. Charles A. Ingene, "Structural Determinants of Market Potential," *Journal of Retailing* (Spring 1984): 37–64; and Charles A. Ingene and Robert F. Lusch, "Market Selection Decisions for Department Stores," *Journal of Retailing* (Fall 1980): 21–40.

13. Rom J. Markin, Jr. *Retailing Management* 2d ed. (New York: Macmillan, 1977), 150.

14. Charles A. Ingene and Robert F. Lusch, "A Model of Retail Structure," in Jagdish Sheth, *Research in Marketing 5* (1981), 101–64.

15. Mobility can be viewed as either a household characteristic or a community characteristic. We chose to treat it as a community characteristic because the design of the community, the availability of public transportation, and the cost of operating an auto in any given area are determinants of mobility and are themselves characteristic of the community.

Throughout the 1970s and 1980s, retailers focused on increasing the productivity of their retail space. They found that careful planning of layout, design, lighting and merchandise presentation could significantly increase sales.

Store Planning— Merchandise Adjacency, Layout and Circulation

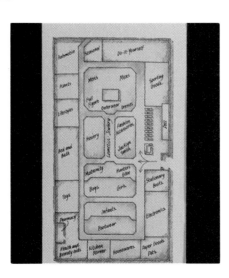

K mart developed a center apparel racetrack layout to encourage shoppers to circulate throughout the entire store. The hardlines departments around the perimeter serve as magnets to draw shoppers past related apparel merchandise cross-aisle in the center core.

K mart's experimental center apparel layout related soft-lines merchandise cross-aisle from destination hardlines categories. Sales have increased and nearly a quarter of K mart shoppers reported buying merchandise they hadn't previously purchased from that retailer.

Source:
Retail Planning Associates, 645 South Grant Avenue, Columbus, OH 43206.

Interior walls, focal points, clearly defined circulation and bold merchandising combine to make K mart's new small–store prototype easier to shop and drive customers to all corners of the store.

To reposition its Mexico City general merchandise stores into full–line upscale department stores, Sears created a dynamic, wide–open store that entices passing shoppers to enter.

A six-floor atrium reiterates the Chicago Bloomingdale's name and announces the store's excitement which has become a Bloomie's trademark.

An enormous video wall anchors an atrium cut into three floors to encourage vertical movement through the Mexico City Sears store.

Bloomingdale's vaulted ceiling and exciting neon strip accentuate "The Main Course" and open up interior space on the narrow sixth floor.

The lower floor, which prior to the remodel of this Mexico City Sears was not used and had a dirt floor, became a highly animated kids world, anchored by Electronica. This consumer electronics core includes a video jockey (VJ) booth, where the more than 400 video screens throughout the store are controlled.

Flexibility

Lazarus, a department store division of Allied/Federated, created a small-town mini-department store to serve outlying towns of 50,000 to 100,000 people. Their goal was to recapture the small-town shopper who no longer has time to travel to the city and shop the downtown flagship store, as well as the young shopper who shops suburban mall speciality stores like The Limited and The Gap. Here the strategy is translated into a colorful, youth-oriented store in which the merchandise itself creates most of the excitment. This technique lengthens the life of the store, since it changes with the merchandise colors and is not locked into a specific design that can become dated in a short time.

Most of the decor elements, such as the columns and yellow pyramid column heads seen here, are inexpensive attachments to the wall panels. They can be moved easily to shrink and expand departments, greatly increasing the flexibility of the store and minimizing construction costs.

Similarly, in the mid 1980s Montgomery Ward abandoned its long history as a general merchandiser to become an operator of specialty stores-within-a-store. This Montgomery Ward "Future Store" conveys this specialty store theme through the use of an extremely flexible grid pattern, seen here in ceiling, wall, floor and fixture systems. By changing and moving the metal "portions" shown at left, Montgomery Ward can quickly change the store to add or delete whole departments. The use of primary colors like red adds visual excitement and prevents the store from becoming dated.

Many retailers have created animated retail environments that seem to have a life of their own, with a retail persona to define or reinforce their merchandising theme. Here Walt Disney Company has created The Disney Store to retail all Disney-licensed products. The store is based on the cartoon and film heritage of Disney and includes hanging animated characters and a cartoon amphitheater complete with an audience of stuffed Disney characters.

The Bloomingdale's jewelry and cosmetics department's subdued, sophisticated color palette reinforces allusions to Frank Lloyd Wright and his Prairie School of Architecture.

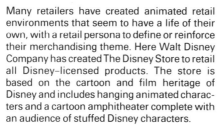

Laura Ashley bedding, dropped ceiling and bedroom vignette create the appropriate atmosphere which announces the department in Bloomingdale's.

Using the store as retail imagery can very effectively give a retailer a distinct image in an otherwise common marketplace. On the right is a typical display of pet food. On the left is The Complete Pet Mart, based on a family theme of animal caricatures, anchored by the store logo with blue dog and yellow cat.

The store interacts with shoppers through animated graphics and informational panels that educate the shopper on pet care. Along the valence are graphic images of life as seen by the pet—hands lowering a food dish, for instance. Small motors actually move creatures in focal points that define each department, such as the Cat Grooming display with moving sunglasses.

Camelot Music has created an "entertainment superstore," resulting in market dominance through a dynamic store that encourages exploration of entertainment options. The bold ceiling with many architectural breaks and flowing neon suggests movement and unpredictability. The large video wall draws customers to the center of the store, from which all departments radiate out. The store is divided into various musical categories (rock, classical, etc.), and the appropriate type of music plays in each area.

HQE, a "high quality electronics" superstore, opened in Canada to offer consumer electronics and computer products with a high level of style and excitement. The store used colored floors, fixtures and ceiling systems to differentiate key departments. Photopanels and informational graphics depict and describe how the merchandise fits into the lifestyle of the customer attracted to this exciting store.

Merchandise imprinted with "Bloomie's" logo helps spread the Bloomingdale's lifestyle message.

Merchandising

Mervyn's re–energized its store by adding primary colors and angles, as well as key merchandising "focal points" called strike zones, as seen at right and below.

Entire collections of merchandise are wheeled into and out of these strike zones weekly, serving as "billboards" to the adjacent departments. In this way, merchandise is given a special home in order to redefine the store's offering.

8 Chapter

Store Site Location

OVERVIEW

This chapter completes the discussion of our retail location decision process. It begins by considering the three basic types of locations available: central business district, shopping center, and free standing units. Next, the chapter looks at how a retailer analyzes the demand and supply alternatives within a given market for the merchandise offerings under consideration, and it concludes with a discussion of retailer locations and descriptions of the various attributes retailers consider as they select a specific site in a target market.

In Chapter 7, we discussed several methods for evaluating and identifying the most attractive markets for a retail location. Once retailers have identified several good markets, the next task is to perform a more detailed analysis of each market. Only after each market is carefully analyzed can the retailer choose the best site (or sites) available. We will refer to these second and third steps in the retail location decision process as the **within-market opportunity analysis**. This analysis should consist of an evaluation of the demand and supply within each market, by census tract or other meaningful geographic area, and should be augmented by an identification of the most attractive sites that currently are available within each market. The third and final step will be the selection of the best possible site.

TYPES OF LOCATION

Before retailers can begin to evaluate the different sites available, they must first decide what type of location is best suited for their product offerings. This type of location decision doesn't have to be made each time the retailer decides to enter a new market. Rather, the decision can be made once, and if market conditions remain unchanged, this same decision can guide all future expansion.

There are three basic types of locations a retailer can select from: the central business district, the shopping center, and freestanding units. No single type of location is always better than the others. Many retailers have been successful in all three location types (e.g., McDonald's, department stores, and furniture stores). Each type of location has its own characteristics relating to the composition of competing stores, parking facilities, affinities with nonretail businesses (such as office buildings, hospitals, universities), and other factors.

CENTRAL BUSINESS DISTRICT

Historically, many retailers were located in the **central business district (CBD)**, usually an unplanned shopping area around the geographic point at which all public transportation systems converge. Many traditional department stores are located in the CBD along with a good selection of specialty shops. The makeup or mix of retailers in a CBD is generally not the result of any planning, but depends on history, retail trends, and luck.

The CBD has several strengths and weaknesses to consider. Among its strengths are easy access to public transportation, wide range of product assortment, variety in images, prices and services, and nearness to commercial activities. Some weaknesses to consider are inadequate (and usually expensive) parking, older stores, high rents and taxes, traffic and delivery congestion, potentially high crime rate, and the general decaying conditions of many inner cities.

This last weakness has resulted in a retail situation known as "inner-city" or "ghetto" retailing, which occurs when only the poorest citizens are left in an urban area. Traditionally product and service offerings in these areas have decreased, while prices held steady or increased. However, good merchandise selection, careful security, and heavy public relations are enabling some retailers, like Stuart's Department Stores, Dollar-General, and Family Dollar Stores, to succeed in inner city areas.[1] These retailers have found success in these markets by tailoring their inventories to the special needs and tastes of these inner city residents.

A newer type of central business district is being created in larger cities by the expansion of secondary business districts and neighborhood business districts. A **secondary business district (SBD)** is a shopping area that is smaller than the CBD and that evolves around at least one department or variety store at a major street intersection. A **neighborhood business district (NBD)** is a shopping area that evolves to satisfy the convenience-oriented shopping needs of a neighborhood. The NBD generally contains several small stores, with the major retailer being either a supermarket or a variety store, and is located on a major artery of a residential area.

The factor that distinguishes these business districts from a shopping center is that they are basically unplanned. Like CBDs, SBDs and NBDs usually evolved partially by planning, partially by luck, and partially by accident. No one planned that there would be two department stores, four jewelry stores, two camera shops, three leather shops, twelve apparel shops, and one theater in an SBD. That happened by chance and there is nothing to stop the camera shop from selling out to a popcorn store. Long-range planning comes about only when the business district is under someone's control.

SHOPPING CENTER

A shopping center is a centrally owned or managed shopping district which is planned, has balanced tenancy (the stores complement each other in merchandise offerings), and is surrounded by parking facilities. A shopping center has one or more anchor stores (a major department store which is expected to draw customers to the center) and a variety of smaller stores. To ensure that these smaller stores complement each other, the shopping center often specifies the proportion of total space that can be occupied by each type of retailer. Similarly, the center's management places limits on the merchandise lines that each retailer may carry. A unified, cooperative advertising and promotional strategy is followed by all the retailers in the center.

A shopping center location can offer a retailer several major advantages over a CBD location. Among them are:

1. Heavy traffic resulting from the wide range of product offerings
2. Nearness to population
3. Cooperative planning and sharing of common costs
4. Access to highways, and availability of parking
5. Lower crime rate
6. Clean, neat environment

Despite these favorable reasons for locating in a shopping center, retailers in shopping centers face several disadvantages. Among the limitations are:

1. Inflexible store hours: the retailer must stay open the hours of the center and can't be open at other times, e.g., Sunday
2. Higher rents
3. Restrictions as to the merchandise the retailer may sell
4. Inflexible operations and required membership in the center's merchant organization
5. Possibility of too much competition and the fact that much of the traffic is not interested in a particular retailer's product offering
6. Dominance of the smaller stores by the anchor tenant

Central place theory assumes that consumers patronize the nearest outlet; however, it has been shown that 30 to 50 percent of consumers tend to make a disproportionate number of trips to large shopping centers. Shopping center image, shopping center preferences, and shopping center personality all attract various subsets of consumers giving retailers located at these centers a competitive advantage over other retailers. Therefore, it is extremely important that a retailer considering a shopping center location be aware of the make-up, image, preferences, and personality of the center under consideration. One study of a specialty apparel chain found that the chain would have lower sales and profits in shopping centers which have Sears, Penney, and/or Ward's stores. This was attributed to the fact that the chain sold moderately priced fashion apparel for the youthful figure which was easily compared to the three general merchandisers with their larger stores and assortments of similar merchandise.[2]

There are four different types of shopping centers, each with a distinct function.

1. A **neighborhood center** provides for the sale of convenience goods (foods, drugs, and sundries) and personal services (laundry and dry cleaning, barbering, shoe repairing, etc.) for the day-to-day living needs of the immediate neighborhood. In the past had a supermarket as the principal tenant; now the supermarkets are often being replaced by home improvement centers or discount department stores. The neighborhood center is the smallest type of shopping center and, as a rule of thumb, has approximately 50,000 square feet in gross leasable space.

2. **Community center** is next in size. In addition to the convenience goods and personal services of the neighborhood center, community centers provide a wider range of facilities for the sale of soft lines (apparel for men, women, and children) and hard lines (hardware and appliances). In addition to a supermarket, community centers are built around a junior department store (not a full-line one), a variety store, or discount department store as the major tenant. The typical size is 150,000 square feet of gross leasable area, but this size may vary. About two-thirds of all shopping centers in the United States are neighorborhood or community types and they account for about one-third of total retail sales.

3. **Regional centers** provide for general merchandise, apparel, furniture, and home furnishings, as well as a range of services and recreational facilities. They are built around one or two full-line department stores of generally not less than 100,000 square feet each. Their typical size is considered to be 400,000 square feet of gross leasable area. The regional center is the second largest type of shopping center. The regional center provides services typical of a central business district, but is not as extensive as a super-regional.

4. **Super-regional centers** provide extensive variety in general merchandise, apparel, furniture, and home furnishings, as well as a variety of services and recreational facilities. They are built around at least three major department stores of generally not less than 100,000 square feet each. The typical size of a super regional is between 600,000 and 1,400,000 square feet of gross leasable area. Super-regionals, while making up only 1 percent of the total number of centers, account for over 10 percent of sales. The *Guinness Book of World Records* ranks the 110-acre West Edmonton Mall (Alberta, Canada) as the world's largest, with over

800 shops, several dozen restaurants, 34 theaters, an 18-hole miniature golf course, a 10-acre waterpark for swimming and sunning under tanning lamps, two dozen amusement rides, and a 360-room hotel for extended stays. It's all indoors, under one roof.[3]

Shopping centers are popular locations for retailers. They first appeared in 1950 and now account for nearly 50 percent of all retail sales, excluding automobile dealers, in the United States.

One of the most exciting developments of the late 1970s and early 1980s was the growth of shopping centers in decaying urban CBDs. Over the last decade the Rouse Co. developed regional or super-regional malls and shopping centers in downtown areas, each one different and each one usually built around some historical landmark of the city (e.g., Faneuil Hall in Boston or Baltimore's Harborplace).

Thus, while the increasing suburbanization of cities has lead to a general decline of the inner cities and their shopping areas, a small number of downtown shopping areas have been growing. Innovations have included modernizing storefronts, developing strong cooperative merchants' associations, closing streets to car traffic, landscaping, providing free parking, improving mass-transit availability, and integrating a commercial and residential environment. However, while the Water Tower Complex in Chicago and Tabor Center in Denver have been hailed across the country as signs of inner-city revival, such is not the case. Many department stores have fled downtown locations and some cities now regret the millions of dollars they spent on building pedestrian-only downtown malls during the last decade.

According to Holly Stabler, vice president of the International Downtown Association, an organization of downtown mall groups based in Washington, "In many places these malls have not worked. The main problem is that people expected too much of the malls and did too little to make them work. The malls didn't prove, in and of themselves, to be a major draw."[4] James Rouse, the man who had early success with inner-city developments, admitted defeat by selling out The 6th Street Marketplace in Richmond and is thinking of "disengaging" from Water Street Pavilion in Flint and Portside in Toledo.[5] In fact, one estimate found that these inner-city malls actually killed business in 80 percent of the cities that put one in.[6]

There are several important, emerging trends in shopping centers. In the late 1980s, a possible conflict of interest regarding shopping centers developed. Robert Campeau, one of the largest real estate developers in North America, took control of both Allied Department Stores (The Bon, Jordan Marsh, Stern's, and Maas Bros.) and Federated Department Stores (Rich's, Bloomingdale's, Abraham & Straus, and Lazarus). Although shopping center developers have owned department stores since 1979, this was by far the largest combination. The major implication was that if Campeau decided to build a new mall, he could have a variety of anchor stores, the large retailers located at the ends of the shopping center and used to attract customers and project images from which to choose. Likewise, if a competitor were to try to build a new mall, Campeau could prevent his retail establishments from being anchors.[7]

Anchor stores are extremely important to the success of a center. They attract customers and project images. Anchors tend to be either mass merchandisers with national reputations and distribution (J. C. Penney, Sears, Ward's, etc.) or branches of national, regional, or local department stores (Bloomingdale's, Dillard's, Robinson's, and Famous Barr). Neighborhood centers typically use a major supermarket chain for anchors. The center's other tenants rely on anchors to draw customers for their target markets to the centers. A high-price women's specialty apparel shop will not do as well in a center anchored by Sears, Penney, and a local department store branch as it would do in one anchored by Marshall Field's, Nieman Marcus, and Jordan Marsh.

However, department stores in shopping centers are the same as the old retail giants of the downtown era and as such, today's department stores are facing another crisis: How do you change a high-volume organization that offers "more of everything" into a much smaller branch anchor? Even the largest branch store is seldom more than 250,000 square feet—less than half the size of its downtown predecessor. In many areas today, we have now seen a decrease in the importance of the center's department stores because, as a group, the center's specialty stores have more space and are far more effective in penetrating specific target markets.[8] Thus, the center or mall of the future will be identified not so much by the anchor but as a single location with combination of stores.

Two other factors will impact the typical mall's appearance over the next decade. Many malls were built in the early 1970s, most with original leases lasting for twenty years. That fact, combined with the advancing age of the population, means changes are sure to occur in shopping centers. Shopping centers and malls in the year 2000 must be ready to respond to these changes. The tenant mix will be changing over the next decade. The number of service-oriented tenants, such as health-care clinics and drive-up services, will probably increase so that shopping, health care, and recreation needs can be met in one place. Also, the architecture and physical layout of the centers will have to consider the needs of the older population.

FREESTANDING LOCATIONS

The last location alternative available to the retailer is to locate as a freestanding retailer. A **freestanding retailer** generally locates along major traffic arteries, without any adjacent retailers selling competing products to share traffic. Freestanding retailing offers several advantages, which include:

1. Lack of direct competition
2. Generally lower rents
3. Freedom in operations and hours
4. Facilities can be adapted to individual needs
5. Isolated area can provide inexpensive parking

Freestanding retailing does have some limitations:

1. Lack of drawing power of complementary stores
2. Difficulties in attracting customer for the initial visit
3. Higher advertising and promotional costs
4. Operating costs that cannot be shared with others
5. Stores may have to be built rather than rented
6. Zoning laws may restrict some activities

The difficulties of drawing, and then holding, customers to an isolated or freestanding store is the reason only large, well known retailers should attempt it. Small retailers may be unable to develop a loyal customer base since customers may be unwilling to travel to a freestanding store that does not have a wide assortment of products and a local or national reputation. K mart and Wal-Mart, as well as many convenience stores and gasoline stations, have used freestanding locations successfully in the past and hypermarkets, discount appliance centers, and wholesale clubs are using it today.

A NOTE ON SERVICE RETAILING

The location decision is just as important to service retailers as it is to the retailers of physical products. Some service retailers are an exception, however, since their products are delivered to the consumer. Some examples of situations where location is not important are plumbers, house painters, repair services, and lawn care firms. In these cases, the retailer's location is the consumer's home or office and travel time to the consumer's location might be the only consideration involved.

Most service retailers, however, are visited by the consumer and location is important. Car washes, dry cleaners, shoe repair stands, and rental retailers are all examples of service retailers who must be concerned about the convenience of their locations. For this reason, many shoe repair stores are beginning to pay a premium to locate in busy shopping malls, just as car rental agencies pay airport managements. Most American consumers do not want to go out of their way to have their shoes repaired, but will have their shoes repaired if it is convenient.

After deciding which type of location is most desirable based on an analysis of existing locations (if available), competitor's actions, and the firm's overall strategy, retailers can begin to evaluate the various sites available in each market.

Illus. 8.2

An electrical contracting firm is a retailer for whom location is not important.

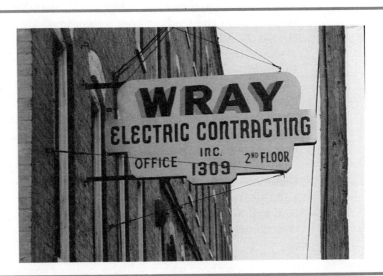

EVALUATION OF DEMAND AND SUPPLY WITHIN THE MARKET

Once retailers have identified the top-ranking market in terms of opportunity and made the decision as to type of location desired, they next need to perform a more detailed analysis of the desired market to determine site location.[9] This analysis consists of evaluating the density of demand and supply of various areas within the chosen market by census tract, ZIP code, or some other meaningful geographic area, and then identifying the most attractive sites available for new stores within each market.[10] One of the advantages of using census tract data is that such data is published by the Census Bureau.

Census tracts are relatively small statistical subdivisions that vary in population from about 2,500 to 8,000 and are designed to include fairly homogeneous populations. They are most often found in cities and in counties of metropolitan areas; i.e., the more densely settled portions of the nation. In addition, about 3,000 census tracts were established in 221 nonmetropolitan counties, along with five states that were entirely tracted: Connecticut, Delaware, Hawaii, New Jersey, and Rhode Island. In all, there are over 43,300 census tracts.

SIZE OF TRADING AREA

In our last chapter we discussed the general trading area of a community. Now we will examine how to determine and evaluate the trading area of specific sites within markets. In short, we will show how to estimate the geographic area from which a store located at a particular site will be able to attract customers.

At the same time that Reilly and Christaller were developing theories to determine the trading area for communities, William Applebaum designed a technique built around *customer spottings* to determine and evaluate trade areas. For each $100 in weekly store sales, a customer was randomly selected or "spotted" for an interview. These spottings usually didn't require much time since the interviewer only asked about demographic information, shopping habits, and some pertinent consumer attitudes toward the store and its competitors. After the home addresses of the shopper were plotted on a map, the analyst could make some inferences about trading area size and the competition.[11]

It is relatively easy to define the trading area of an existing store—all that is necessary is to interview current customers of the store to determine where they reside. For a new store, the task is not so easy. There is conventional wisdom about the correlates of trading area size, which can be summarized as follows:

1. Stores which sell convenience goods have smaller trading areas than those which sell shopping or specialty goods.

2. As consumer mobility increases, the size of the store's trading area increases.
3. As the size of store increases, its trading area increases because it can stock a broader and deeper assortment of merchandise, which will attract households from greater distances.
4. As the distance between competing stores increases, their trading areas will increase.
5. Natural and manmade obstacles such as railroads, rivers, mountains, and freeways can abruptly stop the boundaries of a trading area.

One of the most accepted approaches to defining and estimating a store's trading area was developed by David Huff.[12] Huff defines a **trading area** as "a geographically delineated region containing potential customers for whom there exists a probability greater than zero of their purchasing a given class of products or services offered for sale by a particular firm or by a particular agglomeration of firms."[13] Thus, a trading area can be thought of as a series of demand gradients or zones in which, as the distance from the retailer increases, the probability of a household purchasing or shopping there declines. In Exhibit 8.1, this way

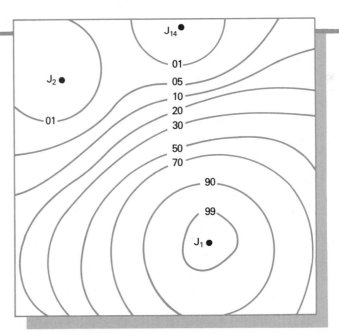

Exhibit 8.1
Retail Trading Area Shown by Probability Contours

SOURCE: Reprinted with permission from David L. Huff, "Defining and Estimating a Trade Area," *Journal of Marketing,* July 1964, 37, published by the American Marketing Association.

of viewing a trading area is graphically presented. The demand gradients or contours are for shopping center J_1. "If the retail trading areas of shopping centers J_2 and J_{14} had also been calculated and superimposed over the trading area of J_1, it would be seen that parts of each shopping center's trading area envelop parts of the others."[14]

The probability of any particular household shopping at a retail site (whether it be a single store or shopping center) can be calculated with the following formula:[15]

$$P_{ij} = \frac{S_j / T_{ij}^{\lambda}}{\sum\limits_{j=1}^{n} (S_j / T_{ij}^{\lambda})}$$

where:

P_{ij} = the probability of a household at a given point of origin i traveling to a particular retail center j

S_j = the size of retail center j (measured in terms of the square footage of selling area devoted to the sale of a particular class of goods)

T_{ij} = the travel time involved in getting from a household's travel base i to a given retail center j.

λ = a parameter which is to be estimated empirically to reflect the effect of travel time on various kinds of shopping trips

n = number of competing retail centers or stores

With this formula, the retailer can calculate the size of its trading area in terms of expected number of households that will be attracted to the retail site.[16] This can be done by summing the number of households in each demand gradient by the probability of their shopping at the retail center. More specifically, the equation is:[17]

$$TA_j = \sum\limits_{i=1}^{n} (P_{ij} \cdot H_i)$$

where:

TA_j = the trading area of the particular firm or agglomeration of firms; that is, the total expected number of households within a given region who are likely to patronize j for a specific class of products or services.

P_{ij} = the probability of an individual household residing within a given gradient i shopping at j.

H_i = the number of households residing within a given gradient i.

The preceding discussion was merely intended to acquaint you with the need to determine the potential trade area of a proposed store at a particular site. Naturally, there are other approaches to determining trade areas, including the buyer behavior of various retail locations.

DESCRIPTION OF TRADING AREA

Local newspapers, as part of their service to advertisers, can often provide retailers with information concerning the trading area for various retail locations, as well as the buyer behavior of the trading area. The following information is based on a 1989 PRIZM study provided retailers in the Los Angeles area by the Marketing Research Department of the *Los Angeles Times*.[18]

The PRIZM system is based on the belief that birds of a feather flock together. In other words, even though the total makeup of the American marketplace is very complex and diverse, neighborhoods tend to be just the opposite. People tend to feel most comfortable living in areas with others who are like them. Think for a moment of the place where you are living now as a student and of your parent's home and you will most likely see the truth of this.

There are many possible reasons consumers usually live in neighborhoods with their own kind. One may be income, because people must be able to afford to live in a particular neighborhood. Factors such as age, occupation, family status, race, culture, religion, population density, urbanization, and housing types also distinguish neighborhoods and thus are important for the retailer to consider.

In distinguishing between neighborhood types, the *Times* uses two basic criteria. First, each type of neighborhood must be different enough from all the others to make it a distinct marketing segment. Second, there must be enough people living in each type of neighborhood to make it a worthwhile segment to retailers. Utilizing Census Bureau data, the study found forty neighborhood types in the United States. These types are distinguished from each other in many ways. Some are based primarily on income, some are family-oriented, some are race-oriented, some are urban, some suburban, and some rural. Most combine two or more distinguishing demographic characteristics. Exhibit 8.2 identifies the forty neighborhood types that PRIZM uses, along with the percentage of United States households each accounts for. They are ranked in socioeconomic order from highest to lowest. Each is identified by a group identifier, an identification number, and a nickname.

The nicknames try to capture the essence of the neighborhood and provide an easy way of remembering distinctions. The identification number is assigned randomly and is used as a reference tool. The group identifier consists of a letter which stands for the degree of urbanization and a number which reflects the level of affluence. An S stands for suburban; U, urban; T, town; and R, rural. Affluence is scaled from 1 (highest) to 4 (lowest). There is more that one neighborhood type for each group identifier.

Exhibit 8.3 provides brief descriptions of several neighborhood types starting with the highest socioeconomic rank Blue Blood Estates and ending with the lowest, Public Assistance. Neiman Marcus would probably locate near Blue Blood Estates and Dollar General would probably choose Norma Rae-Ville.

Exhibit 8.2

Percent Distribution of U.S. Households by PRIZM Neighborhood Types

Neighborhood Types			Households Percent Distribution	Neighborhood Types			Households Percent Distribution
Group	Number	Nickname		Group	Number	Nickname	
S1	28	Blue Blood Estates	0.64%	T2	16	Middle America	4.76%
S1	8	Money & Brains	1.14	U2	36	Old Yankee Rows	1.80
S1	5	Furs & Station Wagons	2.44	T2	29	Coalburg & Corntown	2.55
U1	21	Urban Gold Coast	0.45	R1	19	Shotguns & Pickups	2.53
S2	7	Pools & Patios	3.28	T3	33	Golden Ponds	3.06
S2	25	Two More Rungs	1.03	R1	34	Agri-Business	4.28
S2	20	Young Influentials	3.02	U2	14	Emergent Minorities	2.07
S3	24	Young Suburbia	5.63	U2	26	Single City Blues	2.08
T1	1	God's Country	2.97	T3	22	Mines & Mills	1.85
S3	30	Blue-Chip Blues	5.19	R2	10	Back-Country Folks	4.29
U1	37	Bohemian Mix	0.81	T3	13	Norma Rae-Ville	2.95
S4	27	Levittown, U.S.A.	4.51	T3	18	Smalltown Downtown	1.95
S4	39	Gray Power	2.26	R1	35	Grain Belt	1.43
U1	31	Black Enterprise	1.21	U3	4	Heavy Industry	1.95
U1	23	New Beginnings	4.77	R2	38	Share Croppers	3.65
T2	40	Blue-Collar Nursery	1.70	U3	11	Downtown Dixie-Style	2.30
T1	17	New Homesteaders	5.08	U3	9	Hispanic Mix	1.52
U2	3	New Melting Pot	1.33	R2	15	Tobacco Roads	0.96
T1	12	Towns & Gowns	2.18	R2	6	Hard Scrabble	1.02
S4	2	Rank & File	1.07	U3	32	Public Assistance	2.30
						TOTAL	100.00%

SOURCE: Reprinted with permission of the Los Angeles Times Marketing Research
Department.

Retailing in Action 8-1 provides an example of the factors a service
retailer considers in its location process.

DEMAND DENSITY

The extent to which potential demand for the retailer's goods and services
is concentrated in certain census tracts, ZIP codes, or parts of the community is called **demand density**. To determine the extent of demand density,
retailers need to identify the major variables influencing their potential
demand. One method of identifying these variables is by use of a regression model, a series of mathematical equations that show the relationship
between sales and a variety of independent variables for each existing

RETAILING IN ACTION

8-1

Using Demand Factors in Location

Retailers have long realized that not all locations are equal when it comes to choosing store sites. As a result, some retailers have developed elaborate computer programs to aid in location planning, while other, smaller retailers make their decision by locating near a McDonald's or 7-Eleven. They know that these large franchise operations do an extensive study of traffic patterns and growth projections before deciding on a location. But what about retailers who do not necessarily need to make a location decision based solely on traffic flow: Is one site better than another for them? Consider the case of Kinder-Care Learning Centers, a firm with more than 1,200 day-care centers for children aged 6 weeks to 12 years.

Kinder-Care bases its location decisions on demographic factors. It looks for growth areas, new construction, new homes, and two wage-earning adults. The ideal location is near a new housing development where both husband and wife must work to meet the mortgage payments. The couple is usually in their late twenties or early thirties, earn approximately $30,000 per year, have children, and are planning on having more.

Apartment area locations are out because of the high percentage of singles, as are neighborhoods with a high concentration of older people whose child-rearing years are over.

Illus. 8.3
Kinder-Care bases its location decisions on demographic factors. It looks for growth areas, new construction, new homes, and two wage-earning adults. Source: Kinder-Care Learning Centers, Inc.

Exhibit 8.3
Brief Description of Several Neighborhood Types

TOBACCO ROADS

Cluster 15 is found throughout the South from Virginia to Texas. However, its greatest concentrations are seen in the river basins and coastal, scrub-pine flatlands of the Carolinas, Georgia and Gulf states. It is half Black and a fifth English stock. There is some light industry, but poor,-unskilled labor predominates. Still dependent upon agriculture, Cluster 15 ranks last in white-collar employment.

Number 15 —

NORMA RAE-VILLE

Cluster 13s are concentrated in the South, with their geo-center in the Appalachian and Piedmont regions. They include hundreds of industrial suburbs and mill towns with a great many in textiles and other light industries. The residents are country folk with minimal educations. They are unique among the T3s in having a high index for Blacks and lead the nation in non-durable manufacturing.

Number 13 —

GRAY POWER

This is a new cluster, representing over a million up-scale senior citizens who have chosen to pull up their roots and retire amongst their peers. Primarily concentrated in sunbelt communities of the South Atlantic and Pacific regions, they are the nation's most affluent elderly, retired and widowed neighborhoods. They have the highest concentration of childless married couples living in mixed multi-units, condos and mobile homes with non-salaried incomes.

Number 39 —

PUBLIC ASSISTANCE

With 70% of its households Black, Cluster 32 represents the "Harlems" of America. These are the nation's poorest neighborhoods with twice its unemployment level and five times its share of public assistance incomes. CLuster 32s have been urban-renewal targets for three decades, and show large, solo-parent families in rented, public high-rise buildings interspersed with aging tenement rows.

Number 32 —

BLACK ENTERPRISE

Another new cluster, Black Enterprise is 60% Black with median Black household incomes well above average and consumption behavior to match. A few downscale pockets can be found, exhibiting five-plus person households, divorces and separations, single parents and female breadwinners. However, the majority of these Blacks are educated, employed and solidly set in the upper-middle class.

Number 31 —

FURS & STATION WAGONS

Third in socioeconomic rank, Cluster 5 is typified by "new money," living in expensive new neighborhoods in the green-belt suburbs of the nation's major metros coast to coast. These are well educated, mobile professionals and managers with the nation's highest incidence of teenage children. They are winners—big producers and big spenders.

Number 5 —

Reprinted with permission of the Los Angeles Times Marketing Research Department.

BACK-COUNTRY FOLKS

You can get much farther out than Guntersville, Alabama; Elkins, Arkansas; Saltville, Virginia; or Caribou, Maine. Cluster 10 abounds in such remote, rural towns geo-centered in the Ozark and Appalachian uplands. It is predominantly White and leads the nation in concentration of persons of English ancestry, some of whom are descendents of original colonists and still speak in Elizabethan dialect.

Number 10 —

HARD SCRABBLE

The term "hard scrabble" is an old phrase meaning to scratch a hard living from hard soil. Cluster 6 represents our poorest rural areas from Appalachia to the Ozarks, Mexican border country and Dakota Badlands. With very few Blacks, Cluster 6 leads the nation in American Indians, including many Indian reservations. It also shows a high index for both Mexican and English ancestries.

Number 6 —

MINES & MILLS

Industry is king in Cluster 22, including both light and heavy industry. Cluster 22 gathers hundreds of mining and mill towns scattered throughout Appalachia from New England to the Pennsylvania / Ohio industrial complex and points south. It ranks first in total manufacturing and in total blue-collar occupations. It has very few Black or Hispanic minorities.

Number 22 —

BLUE BLOOD ESTATES

America's wealthiest socioeconomic neighborhoods, populated by super-upper established managers, professionals and heirs to "old money," accustomed to privilege and living in luxurious surroundings. One in ten millionaires can be found in Cluster 28, and there is a considerable drop from these heights to the next level of affluence.

Number 28 —

MONEY & BRAINS

Cluster 8 enjoys the nations's second-highest socioeconomic rank. These neighborhoods are typified by swank townhouses, apartments and condos with relatively few children. Many of these neighborhoods contain private universities and a mix of upscale singles. They are sophisticated consumers of adult luxuries including apparel, restaurants, travel and others.

Number 8 —

LEVITTOWN, U.S.A.

The post-World War II baby boom caused an explosion of tract housing in the late 40's and 50's in brand new suburbs for young white-collar and well-paid blue-collar families. As with "Pools & Patios," the children are now largely grown and gone. Aging couples remain in comfortable middle-class suburban homes. Employment levels are still high, including double incomes allowing for "easy living" in these neighborhoods.

Number 27 —

store. The variables identified should be standard demographic variables, such as age, income, and education, since data will be readily available. Let us construct an example.

A retailer is evaluating the possibility of locating in a community whose geographical boundaries are shown in Exhibit 8.4. It consists of 23 census tracts. The community is bordered on the west by a mountain range, on the north and south by major highways, and on the east by railroad tracks. The retailer has decided that three variables are especially important in determining the potential demand: median household income over $22,000; households per square mile in excess of 1,200; and av-

Exhibit 8.4
Demand Density Map

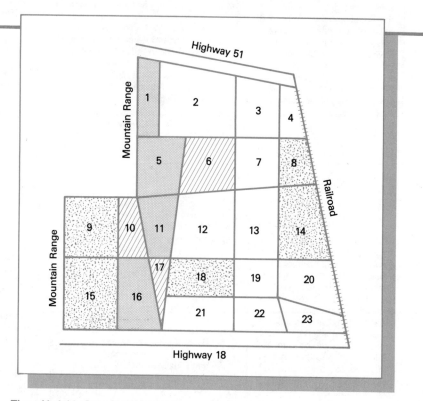

Three Variable Demand Density Map

Variable 1 = Median Income Over $22,000
Variable 2 = Households Per Square Mile Greater Than 1,200
Variable 3 = Average Growth in Population Over Last 3 Years in Excess of 3% Per Year

Number of Variables Met

 0   1   2   3

erage growth in population of at least 3 percent per year over the last three years. Exhibit 8.4 maps the extent to which these three conditions are met for each of the 23 census tracts in the community undergoing evaluation, so the potential demand is readily apparent in each tract. Only three tracts (6, 10, 17) meet all three conditions; four tracts (1, 5, 11, 16) meet two of the three conditions; five tracts (8, 9, 14, 15, 18) meet only one condition; and eleven tracts (2, 3, 4, 7, 12, 13, 19, 20, 21, 22, 23) meet none of the conditions.

Demand density maps similar to the one shown in Exhibit 8.4 are available at modest cost from firms such as DATAMAP, Inc., R. L. Polk and Co., and Urban Decision Systems, Inc. The retail analyst could also construct such maps using data from the Census Bureau.

Another method of looking at potential demand for a retailer's product could be to use the data mentioned earlier when discussing neighborhood types. In this example, suppose a high-fashion women's apparel chain wanted to enter the Los Angeles market. The chain would first determine, from their own records, which neighborhood types accounted for the largest percentage of its sales in comparison to the national average for its product categories. In this case, neighborhood types 5, 28, and 8 would all spend at least three times the average per capita amount for the chain's product line. Neighborhood types 25, 20, and 7 would spend at least twice the average and neighborhood types 1, 3, 23, 37, 24, 39, 12, and 26 would spend up to twice the average. In the remaining 26 neighborhoods, sales for the chain's products would be less than the national average. Exhibit 8.5a provides a map of Los Angeles, highlighting these four groupings by area. Exhibit 8.5b shows only the 5, 28, and 8 neighborhoods.

SUPPLY DENSITY

The demand density map allows you to identify the areas within a community that represent the highest potential demand, but the location of existing retail establishments should also be mapped. This will allow you to examine the **density of supply** or the extent to which retailers are already concentrated in different areas of the market under question.

Exhibit 8.6 shows the density of stores in the community we saw in Exhibit 8.4. Examination of Exhibit 8.6 reveals that two of the three most attractive census tracts (10 and 17) have a lack of stores. Also, in the census tracts with fairly attractive demand density (two of the three conditions met) there are currently no retail outlets (see tracts 1 and 5).

SITE AVAILABILITY

Just because demand outstrips supply in certain geographic locations does not mean that stores should be located in those locations. Sites must be available.

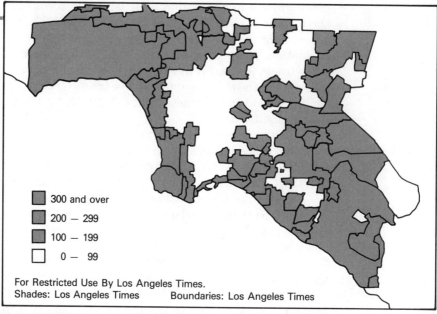

Exhibit 8.5a

Potential for High-Fashion Women's Apparel in Los Angeles and Orange County Zip Code Areas

300 and over

200 — 299

100 — 199

0 — 99

For Restricted Use By Los Angeles Times.
Shades: Los Angeles Times   Boundaries: Los Angeles Times

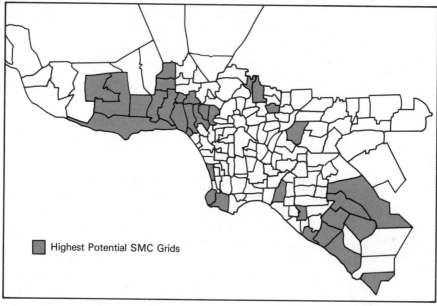

Exhibit 8.5b

Highest Potential Neighborhoods for High-Fashion Women's Apparel

Highest Potential SMC Grids

Exhibit 8.6

**Store Density
and Site
availability Map**

☐ = Current Store   ■ = Available Store Site

A map should be constructed of available sites in each community being analyzed. We have done this in conjunction with the supply density map in Exhibit 8.6. The only available site in the top 6 census tracts (in terms of demand density) is in census tract 10. In tracts 1, 5, and 17, which currently have no retail outlets, no sites are available, which may explain the present lack of stores in these areas; perhaps these tracts are zoned totally for residential use.

Although Exhibit 8.6 seems to show only one good potential site, several more may exist. Census tract 9 borders high-density tract 10, in which there are no stores at present and in which one site is available for a new store. Tract 9 has two available sites. Furthermore, tract 12 has an available site close to the borders of tracts 11 and 17, which are both attractive but lack available sites. This same kind of analysis can be performed by the high fashion chain looking at the Los Angeles market.

SITE SELECTION DECISION PROCESS

After completing the analysis of each segment of the desired market and having identified the best available sites within each market, retailers are ready to make the final decision regarding location: select the best site (or sites) available. Retailers are well advised to use the assistance of a real estate professional in this step. Even if the retailers have done all the analysis to this point, the assistance of a real estate professional should be used now. In fact, more and more large retail firms are setting up separate corporations just to handle their real estate transactions.[19]

THE 100 PERCENT LOCATION

In principle, all retailers should attempt to find a **100 percent location** for their stores: "The essence of this idea is that there is a location that is the best possible (most optimum) site for every store within a given shopping district. Generally, this is the location with the greatest amount of the kind of traffic desired."[20] While this condition for all retailers would be considered the ideal state, Koopmans and Beckman showed that there is no location from which at least one retailer could not improve profitability by moving to a different location.[21] Nonetheless, retailers should strive for the 100 percent location for their product offering. What may be a 100 percent site for one store may not be for another. The best location for a supermarket is not the best location for a discount department store. Further, retailers should realize that if two or more stores view the same site as a 100 percent site, then the retailer willing to pay the highest price for the site will determine its use. This is what is called the highest and best use in resource economics.

How is the 100 percent location or site identified? Unfortunately, there is no best answer to this basic question. There is, however, general agreement on the types of things that the retail location analyst should consider in evaluating sites: the nature of the site, traffic characteristics, type of neighbors, size of trade area, and *pro forma* strategic profit model.

Just being the first retailer to locate a site is no guarantee of success, as the retailer in Retailing in Action 8-2 found out.

RETAILING IN ACTION   8-2

A Good Location Can Be Copied

Just choosing the right location is no guarantee of success. Others might be able to enter your market area and compete for your customers. This is especially true when the retail operation does not require a large initial investment. Consider the case of Sam Mellon. Mellon spent more than two years looking for just the right location for a frozen yogurt shop. He studied the operations of 50 shops in several states. He looked at phone books, trying to find a city with a deficiency in frozen yogurt shops. Finally, he and his wife decided to open

You'd Never Dream It's Yogurt® in Albuquerque. Within months after the Mellons became Albuquerque's first street-side frozen yogurt shop, two franchise frozen chains (I Can't Believe It's Yogurt and This Can't Be Yogurt) opened competing stores nearby. At present, six different operations are competing for the yogurt business in New Mexico's largest city.

This is not a rare case. The same thing happened to other frozen yogurt entrepreneurs across the country. Hundreds of these entrepreneurs have started shops only to watch competitors open establishments nearby. Lured by low start-up costs and tales of fat profits, they hoped to capitalize on the combination of a nationwide fitness kick and sweet tooth. Instead, these entrepreneurs have become mired in a frozen yogurt glut.

What lesson can be drawn here? A simple one. The retailer must remember that retail success is based on more than just location. The strategy must be built on a product or an idea that cannot be easily copied. Frozen yogurt was a low-cost entry business with an easily copied product.

Source: Based on personal correspondence with Sam Mellon and used with his permission.

NATURE OF SITE

Is the site currently a vacant store, a vacant parcel of land, or the site of a planned shopping center? Many available retail sites are by vacant stores. This is because 10 to 15 percent of all stores go out of business each year. Many of the reasons for a retailer's failure at a given location may make that site a bad choice for another store. This is especially true if the prior occupant of the store was in the same line of retail trade. If Supermarket A fails at a particular store site, then the probability is significantly increased that Supermarket B will also fail at that site. Low rent is not the best criteria for site selection.

When the retail site is a vacant parcel of land, the retailer needs to investigate why it is vacant. Why have others passed up the site? Was it previously not for sale? Was it priced too high? Or is there some other reason? For instance, many supermarkets abandon 20,000 square feet locations to move to newer 65,000 square feet sites. These abandoned sites ususally are available at lower costs and are not necessarily bad locations.

Finally, the site may be part of a planned shopping center. In this case, the retailer can usually be assured that it will have the proper mix of neighbors, adequate parking facilities, and good traffic. Sometimes, of course, the center has not been properly planned, and the retailer needs to be on the lookout for these special cases.

TRAFFIC CHARACTERISTICS

The traffic that passes a site, whether it be vehicular or pedestrian, is an important determinant of the potential sales at that site. But more than just traffic flow is important. The retailer must also determine whether the population and traffic are of the type desired. For example, a retailer of fine furs and leather coats may be considering two alternative sites—one in the central business district and the other in a group of specialty stores in a small shopping center in a very exclusive residential area. The CBD site may generate more aggregate traffic, but the small shopping center may generate more of the right type of traffic.

The retailer should evaluate two other traffic-related aspects of the site. The first is the availability of sufficient parking, either at the site or nearby. One of the advantages of shopping centers is the availability of adequate parking close by. If the site is not a shopping center, then the retailer will need to determine if parking will be adequate. It is difficult to give a precise guideline for the space that will be needed. Generally, it is a function of four factors: size of the store, frequency of customer visits, length of customer visits, and availability of public transportation. As a rule of thumb, shopping centers estimate that there should be four and a half spaces for every 1,000 square feet of selling space in medium-sized centers and five spaces per 1,000 square feet in large centers.[22]

A second traffic-related factor the retailer should consider is the ease with which consumers can reach the store site. Are the roadways in good shape? Are there traffic barriers (rivers with limited number of bridges, interstates with limited crossings, one-way streets, or congestion limiting access to the site)? Remember, customers will generally avoid congested

Illus. 8.4
The retailer should evaluate the ease with which consumers can reach the store site. Source: Southern California Visitors Council.

shopping areas and shop elsewhere in order to minimize driving time and difficulties.

TYPE OF NEIGHBORS

What are the neighboring establishments that surround the site? There can be good and bad neighbors. The type of store that one is considering operating at the site determines what a good or bad neighbor is. Suppose you plan to open a children's apparel store and are considering a pair of alternative sites. One site has a toy store and a gift shop as neighbors. The other site has a bowling alley and an adult book store as neighbors. It is obvious who the good and bad neighbors are.

A good neighboring business is compatible with the retailer's line of trade. When two or more businesses are compatible, they can actually help generate business for each other. For example, a paint store, hardware store, and auto parts store located next to one another may increase total traffic and benefit them all.

The **principle of compatibility** has been formalized by Richard Nelson as follows:

> "Two compatible businesses located in close proximity will show an increase in business volume directly proportionate to the incidence of total customer interchange between them, inversely proportionate to the ratio of the business volume of the larger store to that of the smaller store, and directly proportionate to the sum of the ratios of purposeful purchasing to total purchasing in each of the two stores."[23]

This relationship can be more explicitly summarized as follows:

$$V = I\{V_S(P_L V_S + P_S V_L)/V_L\}$$

in which:

V_L = volume of larger store
P_L = purposeful purchasing in larger store
V_S = volume of smaller store
P_S = purposeful purchasing in smaller store
V = increase in total volume of two stores
I = degree of interchange

Consider this example. "If there are two retail stores side by side and one customer in a hundred makes purchases in both, the rule indicates that together they will do 1 percent more business than if separated by such a distance as to make this interchange impossible or unlikely. If one customer in ten makes purchases in both stores, their total increase in business will be about 10 percent. Theoretically, if every customer bought in both stores, their total business volume would double, if both businesses did about the same dollar volume.

"However, a very large store and a very small store would not show the same total increase as two stores of equivalent size. For example, if a department store doing $5,000,000 worth of retail volume a year were next door to a variety store doing $500,000 a year, their total would not double even with a 100 percent interchange of customers. If their customer interchange were on the order of 25 out of 100, the total increase in business for the two establishments would be directly proportionate to the interchange, or 25 percent, but inversely proportionate to the ratio of their volumes, which is 10:1. Thus the total increase would equal one tenth of 25 percent or 2.5 percent. If, however, interviews showed purposeful purchasing at the department store and the variety store to be respectively, on the order of 90 percent and 15 percent of total purchasing, the 2.5 percent increase would have to be multiplied by 105 percent. Thus, these two stores together would show a business increase of 2.5 × 1.05 = 2.625 per cent of the total of $5,000,000, or an additional $144,375. This is not a measure of market potential. All compatibility determinations assume that an adequate market exists."[24]

When Nordstrom entered the Washington, D.C. market in 1988 with a store projected to do a dizzying $100 million in first year sales, the neighboring Hecht's branch had a 35 percent sales increase. Likewise, Marshall Field's enjoyed a double-digit sales increase when Bloomingdale's joined it in downtown Chicago.[25] Retailing in Action 8-3 shows that sometimes compatibility can make a bad situation good.

RETAILING IN ACTION   8-3

Sometimes There's Too Much Compatibility

While the principle of compatibility suggests that two competing retailers are better off when they are located near each other, this competition is not always viewed favorably by all retailers.

Consider the case of the new Burger King and McDonald's restaurants in Lubbock, Texas. Somehow, the local franchisees of these two fast food restaurants opened outlets next to each other at the same time, resulting in the only place in Texas where these two establishments compete side by side. Both operations signed contracts with Outlet Malls of America to provide restaurant service at the main entrance for a mall under construction. Neither fast food operator asked for exclusive rights in its contract with the mall. Both signed their contracts and received building permits the same day. That is when they found out about each other's planned restaurant. Both planned openings for the same month, but Burger King was able to open two months ahead of McDonald's.

Having these two fast food outlets operating so close to each other has benefited the consumer. Burger King's store manager stated that "the closeness in location forces each store to give the customer exactly what he or she wants. And so far there has been enough business for both of us."

The discount mall that both restaurants were so eager to locate near soon faded with the Texas economy. Only a storefront church currently uses the mall. However, both fast-food operations are successful, due to their location on a major highway.

TERMS OF LEASE

A final consideration for the retailer is lease terms. The retailer should review the length of the lease (it could be too long or too short), the exclusivity clause (whether or not the retailer will be the only one allowed to sell a certain line of merchandise), the guaranteed traffic rate (a reduction in rent if the shopping center fails to achieve a targeted traffic level), and an anchor clause (which allows for a rent reduction if the anchor store in a developing center doesn't open on time). Exhibit 8.7 shows some of the highest rents for retail locations.

Exhibit 8.7

The New York City Streets with the Highest Retail Rents

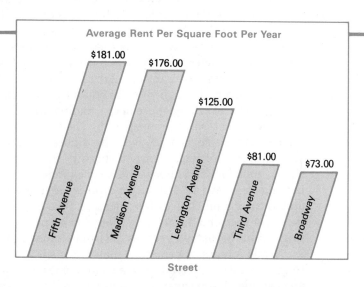

SOURCE: Reprinted with permission from "Space Report Mid-Year 1988" by Garrick - Aug Associates, 99 Park Ave., New York, N.Y. 10016.

PRO FORMA *STRATEGIC PROFIT MODEL*

The final step in site-selection analysis is construction of a *pro forma* strategic profit model for each possible site. The strategic profit model comprises three crucial variables: profit margin, asset turnover, and return on assets.

For the purpose of evaluating sites, the potential return on owner's equity is not important. This is because the financial leverage ratio (total assets divided by owner's equity) is a top-management decision, which represents how much debt the retail enterprise is willing to assume. Most likely, the question of how to finance new store growth has already been answered or at least contemplated. The retailer should already have determined that it has or can obtain the capital to finance a new store. It is therefore reasonable and appropriate to evaluate sites on their potential return on assets and not return on equity.

If the retailer is to evaluate sites on their potential return on assets, it will need at least three estimates: total sales, total assets, and net profit.

Total Sales.   The sales that can be generated from a proposed store at a particular site are not easy to estimate with precision. Quantitative techniques, such as regression, may be employed,[26] but in practice, the estimation is often done less rigorously. Whatever the procedure, the retail analyst should consider all of the factors discussed earlier as part of the within-market opportunity analysis and site-selection analysis. Of the array of considerations under these headings, the most important in estimating sales is the potential trading area of the site.

Given a well-defined trading area, the retailer will know how many potential households are in the area. Next the retailer will seek to determine what percentage of these potential households it will actually serve. One method, used by many small retailers, is to assume that the new store will achieve a percentage of sales equal to its retail selling space as a percentage of total selling space in the trading area. The retailer would divide the proposed store's selling space by the trading area's selling space with the new store's space included. This figure will give the retailer a reasonable estimate of what market share it will achieve. Next, the retailer should multiply total households times market share, and then multiply that figure by the average expenditures per household. This gives the estimated total annual sales for the store. The estimate of average expenditures per household can be developed from past experience in similar settings, from industry averages, or from formal quantitative techniques.[27]

While forecasting can take many forms it must be attempted in order to determine cash, inventory, and employee needs for the future. Consider an example. A supermarket retailer is evaluating a site expected to have a trading area of 36,000 households. The proposed store will have 100,000 square feet of selling space and the other stores in the trading area have a combined selling space of 900,000 square feet. The retailer estimates that annual sales per household will be $1,600. Its expected total annual sales are therefore $5.76 million (36,000 times [100,000 square feet divided by 100,000 square feet plus 900,000 square feet] times $1,600).

Total Assets.   The retail analyst must next estimate total dollar investment needed to conduct business at the site. If the site is to be purchased and a store constructed on it, these costs must be considered. The cost of sites can vary considerably, as can the cost of constructing similar buildings on alternative sites. The costs of inventory, fixtures, lighting, and parking must also be estimated. In addition, if the store is not expected to break even for several months or longer, then anticipated losses should be considered as asset dollars or capital needed to commence operations. In short, the retailer must estimate the total capital needed to begin operations.[28] Generally, the estimate of capital (asset dollars) is much more accurate than the sales estimate, because the retailer can obtain fairly accurate data on what it will cost to acquire various assets.

In the supermarket example, let us assume that the total capital needed to start operations is $1.9 million. This includes the cost of the land, building, fixtures, parking lot, inventory, and other working capital. If the retailer estimated annual sales at $5.76 million, it follows that its expected rate of asset turnover is 3.03 ($5,760,000 ÷ $1,900,000).

Net Profit.   If the retailer has done a good job at estimating total sales and assets, the estimate of net profit should not be too difficult. Net profit equals total sales less fixed and variable costs. Fixed costs are those which remain constant regardless of the level of sales; variable costs change in proportion to sales.

Most fixed costs in retailing are related to the size of the store, which is in turn tied to total assets. As the store becomes larger, it requires more employees, it takes more energy to heat and cool the store, it requires higher interest costs to finance capital, it incurs higher insurance premiums, and it incurs more dollars of depreciation.

The major variable expense will be the cost of merchandise sold. Obviously, as more is sold, the total cost of merchandise becomes higher. There is often a fairly linear relationship between cost of merchandise and sales. If the retailer can estimate how much the goods cost as a percentage of sales, it can easily estimate the total cost of goods sold by multiplying the cost of goods sold percentage by the estimated total sales.

Several other expenses may be expected to vary with total sales (for example, some labor and advertising expenses). Past experience or industry standards can give the retailer a reasonable estimate of operating expenses that vary with sales. These expenses can also be stated as a percentage of sales.

In our supermarket example, we established that the supermarket had expected sales of $5.76 million and would need $1.9 million in assets. Assume that the annual fixed costs of operating the supermarket are estimated to be \$471,000 and the cost of goods sold is expected to be 78.7 percent of sales. In addition, other variable operating expenses are estimated at 9.4 percent of sales. Through analysis of these numbers we can determine the expected net profit:

$$
\begin{aligned}
\text{Net Profit} &= \text{Sales} - \text{Fixed costs} - \text{Variable costs} \\
&= \$5{,}760{,}000 - \$471{,}000 - (0.787 + 0.094)(\$5{,}760{,}000) \\
&= \$214{,}440
\end{aligned}
$$

Thus, the overall profit margin (net profit divided by sales) would be (\$214,440 ÷ \$5,760,000) or 3.72 percent.

Return on Assets.   For each site being evaluated, the expected return on assets should be computed. The computation of return on assets is simple if sales, assets, and net profit have been estimated. The appropriate data can be inserted into the return on assets equation:

$$
\left(\frac{\text{Net profit}}{\text{Total sales}} \right) \times \left(\frac{\text{Total sales}}{\text{Total assets}} \right) = \left(\frac{\text{Net profit}}{\text{Total assets}} \right)
$$

Using our supermarket example, we can compute the expected return on assets as:

$$
\left(\frac{\$214{,}440}{\$5{,}760{,}000} \right) \times \left(\frac{\$5{,}760{,}000}{\$1{,}900{,}000} \right) = \left(\frac{\$214{,}440}{\$1{,}900{,}000} \right)
$$

$$
(0.0372) \times (3.032) = (0.11286)
$$

If the supermarket is located at the site under consideration, it can be expected to have a profit margin of 3.72 percent and a rate of asset turnover of 3.03, which will yield an 11.29 percent return on assets. All of these figures are before taxes. Thus, assuming a 50 percent tax rate, the return on assets would drop to less than 6 percent. This is hardly an attractive return on assets given the cost of capital and rates of inflation facing most supermarket retailers. The retailer should probably search for a better site.

MEASURING PERFORMANCE

At last the site has been chosen and the store is open. In the early weeks of operation, careful attention needs to be given to sales performance. Are sales materializing at the level anticipated? If not, why? Is it a management or merchandising failure, or is it due to having selected a poor site? If the performance is attributable to poor management or merchandising, then corrective action needs to be taken as soon as possible. If a poor site was selected then the retailer can only hope to learn from its error. If retailers carefully plan new locations, then errors in site location should be minimal. Chains can usually learn from their errors, while individual store owners usually go out of business. This is one reason for the high number of retail failures each year.

After the first month or two of operations, retailers will want to analyze not only their sales performance but also their expense performance. If any expenses are not in line with expectations, then an investigation of the deviation will be worthwhile. The cause of the deviation is typically either poor expense control or poor initial planning. Quite frequently, since the expense estimates are approximate (because of no prior experience in operating at the site), the cause will be poor expense planning. But, if the cause is poor management control of the expense item, then corrective action should be taken as quickly as possible.

SUMMARY

This chapter continues the location decision discussion in Chapter 7. We began by reviewing three location alternatives available: the central business district, the shopping center, or a freestanding unit.

The central business district is generally an unplanned shopping area around the geographic point where a city originated and grew up. As cities have grown, we have witnessed an expansion of two new types of central business districts—the secondary business district and the neighborhood business district.

A shopping center is a centrally owned or managed shopping district which is planned, has balanced tenancy, and is surrounded by parking facilities. It has one or more anchor stores and a variety of smaller stores. Because of the many advantages shopping centers offer the retailer, they now account for nearly 50 percent of all retail sales in this country.

A freestanding retailer generally locates along major traffic arteries without any adjacent retailers selling competing products to share traffic.

After reviewing these three location alternatives, we discussed the second of our three steps in the location process: evaluating the density of demand and supply within each market and identifying the sites that are available in the markets under study.

Next, the retail location analyst should conduct a site-selection analysis of the top-ranking sites in each market. The goal is to select the best site or sites. The following factors should be considered: nature of the site, traffic characteristics, type of neighbors, and pro-forma strategic profit model.

After all relevant sites have been analyzed and the best one selected, then the process becomes an ongoing one—measuring sales, expense, and profit performance of the store once it begins operations. Any significant deviations from expectations should be investigated and corrective action taken.

QUESTIONS
FOR
DISCUSSION

1. Identify the factors you would consider most important in locating a fast-food restaurant. Compare them with the factors you would use in selecting a site for a furniture store.
2. Why are discount department stores such as Wal-Mart usually not located in large shopping centers?
3. How can the strategic profit model be used to assist in location decisions?
4. Explain the concepts of demand density and supply density. Why are they important to retail decision making?
5. Compute the expected return on assets for a proposed supermarket with the following characteristics:
   - 4,400 households in trading area
   - 18,000 total square feet of store space
   - Expected annual sales per household of $1,400
   - Land costs of $280,000
   - Construction costs of $40 per square foot
   - Costs to develop land of $38,000
   - Inventory investment per square foot of $10
   - Equipment and fixture costs of $400,000
   - Gross margin of 23.4 percent
   - Operating expenses (variable) of 12.4 percent of sales
   - Fixed operating costs per year (including depreciation) of $340,000
   What other factors, besides expected return on assets, should be considered in deciding whether to build the proposed supermarket?
6. What are the differences among the major location types discussed in this chapter?
7. Nearly 50 percent of all retail sales, excluding automobile dealers, occur in shopping centers. Does this mean that the shopping center's future is bright, or does it face problems in the coming decade?
8. What criteria should a small retailer use in selecting a type of location?
9. What does the principle of compatibility have to say about retail stores locating next to each other?

SUGGESTED READINGS

Davies, R. L., and D. S. Rogers, eds. *Store Location and Store Assessment Research.* New York: John Wiley & Sons, 1984.

Eroglu, Sevgin, and Gilbert D. Harrell. "Retail Crowding: Theoretical and Strategic Implications." *Journal of Retailing* (Winter 1986): 346–363.

Finn, Adam. "Characterizing the Attractiveness of Retail Markets." *Journal of Retailing* (Summer 1987): 129–162.

Green, Howard L. "Retail Sales Forecasting Systems." *Journal of Retailing* (Fall 1986): 227–230.

ENDNOTES

1. "Zayre's Strategy of Ethnic Merchandising Proves to Be Successful in Inner-City Stores," *Wall Street Journal*, 25 September 1984, p. 29; and "The Kings of Discount Dealing," *USA Today*, 7 May 1986, pp. B1-2.

2. Patricia M. Anderson, "Association of Shopping Center Anchors with Performance of a Nonanchor Specialty Chain's Store," *Journal of Retailing* (Summer 1985): 61–74.

3. "Edmonton's Eighth Wonder of the World," *American Demographics* (February, 1986): 20.

4. "Downtown Malls Out of Fashion," *St. Louis Post Dispatch*, 9 August 1987, p. 1C.

5. "Jim Rouse May Be Losing His Touch," *Business Week* (4 April, 1988): 33.

6. *Land Use Digest* (February 15, 1988): 2.

7. "Campeau In Control At Federated," *Chain Store Age Eexcutive* (May 1988): 39-42.

8. George Sternlieb and James W. Hughes, "The Demise of the Department Store," *American Demographics* (August 1987): 3D-33, 59.

9. For a more detailed discussion of site selection, consult Avijit Ghosh and C. Samuel Craig, "Formulating Retail Location Strategy in a Changing Environment," *Journal of Marketing* (Summer 1983): 56–68.

10. Martha Farnsworth Riche, "Computer Mapping Takes Center Stage," *American Demographics* (June 1986): 26-31, 64-65; and Matthew A. Rose, "What's New?" *Direct Marketing* (March 1988): 26. The reader might also want to consult Roland T. Rust and Julia A. N. Brown, "Estimation and Comparison of Market Area Densities," *Journal of Retailing* (Winter 1986): 410–430 for a new method for estimating density of customers around a single retail center. This approach is, however, beyond the scope of our text.

11. The essence of Applebaum's work, plus contributions from several of his students, can be found in "William Applebaum and Other," Curt Korhblau, ed., *Guide to Store Location Research with Emphasis on Supermarkets* (sponsored by Super Market Institute, Addision-Wesley, 1968.

12. David L. Huff, "Defining and Estimating a Trading Area," *Journal of Marketing* (July 1964): 34–38.

13. Huff, 38.

14. Huff, 37.

15. Huff, 26.

16. The Huff model has been extended to include image and other competitive variables. For example, see John R. Nevin and Michael J. Houston, "Image as a Component of Attraction to Intraurban Shopping Areas," *Journal of Retailing* (Spring 1980): 77–93; and Thomas J. Stanley and Murphy A. Sewell, "Predicting Supermarket Trade: Implications for Marketing Management," *Journal of Retailing* (Summer 1978): 13–22, 91, 92.

17. Huff, "Defining and Estimating," 38.

18. Reprinted with permission of the *Los Angeles Times*.

19. "Bonanza Firm to Separate Its Operation," *Lubbock Avalanche-Journal*, 5 July 1983, p. 10A.

20. Rom J. Markin, *Retailing Management* (New York: Macmillan, 1977), 177.

21. Tjalin C. Koopmans and Martin Beckman, "Assignment Problems and the Location of Economic Activities," *Econometrica* (January 1957): 69.

22. "Shopping Habits," *Wall Street Journal*, 21 April 1982, p. 33.

23. Richard L. Nelson, *The Selection of Retail Locations* (New York: F. W. Dodge, 1958), 66. A **purposeful purchase** is one made by a shopper who, when interviewed, states that a visit to the store was a major purpose of the shopping trip. Total purchases, of course, include incidental and impulse purchases as well.

24. Nelson, 67.

25. "Store Wars Break Out All Around the Beltway," *Business Week* (October 10, 1988): 140; and Francine Schwadel, "Bloomingdale's Foray Into Chicago Has Competitors Polishing Their Acts," *Wall Street Journal*, 4 October 1988, p. B-6.

26. G. I. Heald, "The Application of the Automatic Interaction Detector (A.I.D.) Program and Multiple Regression Techniques to the Assessment of Store Performance and Site Selection," *Operations Research Quarterly* (December 1972): 445–57.

27. Charles A. Ingene and Robert F. Lusch, "A New Frame of Reference for Managing Retail Profitability," in *Proceedings of the Sixth International Research Seminar in Marketing* (Gordes, France, 4–8 June, 1979).

28. The retailer might also want to consider leasing a building on the site chosen or other means of financing the building. If so, the retailer might read: "Retailer's Question: Is It Better to Lease or to Own?" *Chain Store Age Executive* (March 1980): 34–35; and "Use of Tax-Exempt Financing for Stores and Other Business Soars, Stirring Critics," *Wall Street Journal*, 8 October 1980, p. 54.

IV Part

Managing Retail Operations

9 Chapter

Introduction to Financial Planning

OVERVIEW

This chapter will introduce the types of financial statements used in retail planning. The discussion revolves around the merchandise budget, accounting statements, and inventory valuation. We will look at how a six-month merchandise budget is prepared and how it is used in making plans for an upcoming merchandise season. Next we will discuss inventory valuation using both cost and retail methods. Finally, we will describe the differences among an income statement, balance sheet, and statement of cash flow as well as how a retailer uses these accounting statements.

**CHAPTER 9
Introduction
to Financial
Planning**

Many people believe that the terms *retailing* and *merchandising* are synonymous. They are not. **Retailing** includes all the business activities necessary to sell goods and services to the final consumer. **Merchandising** refers to the planning and control involved in the buying and selling of goods and services and is only one of the activities in retailing. High-performance merchandising requires total financial planning and control.

This chapter is divided into three sections: the merchandise budget, inventory valuation, and retail accounting statements.

THE MERCHANDISE BUDGET

Successful retailers must have good financial planning and control of their merchandise. In fact, some have said that a retailer is really a financial control officer. The retailer invests money in merchandise for profitable resale to others. A poor choice of merchandise will result in a low or negative return on investment. Therefore, in order to be successful in retailing, as in any other activity, an individual must have a plan of what is to be accomplished. In retailing, this plan of operation is called the merchandise budget. A **merchandise budget** is a plan of projected sales for an upcoming season, when and how much merchandise is to be purchased, and what markups and reductions will likely occur. The merchandise budget forces the retailer to develop a formal outline of merchandising objectives for the upcoming selling season.

In developing the merchandise budget, the retailer must make five major merchandise decisions:

1. What are the anticipated sales for the department, division, or store?
2. How much stock-on-hand will be needed to achieve this sales plan, given the level of turnover expected?
3. What reductions from the original retail price must be made in order to dispose of all the merchandise brought into the store?
4. What additional purchases must be made during the season?
5. What gross margin (the difference between sales and cost of goods sold) should the department, division, or store contribute to the overall profitability of the company?

When preparing the merchandise budget, the high performance retailer must follow four rules.

First, a merchandise budget should always be prepared in advance of the selling season. Since the original plan is often prepared by the buyer for a particular department to be approved by the divisional merchandising manager and/or the general merchandising manager (these job titles will be discussed in detail in Chapter 10), most fashion and hard goods retail firms begin the process of developing the merchandise budget three to four months in advance of the budget period. This is not always the case with specialty stores, like record shops. A buyer only learns about a new record release about a month in advance. These specialty stores don't have to worry about markdowns, because excess quantities can be returned to vendors for full credit or a record can be easily reordered if it goes to the top of the charts. Generally, a firm has only two seasons a year; 1) spring/summer, usually February 1 through July 31 and 2) fall/winter, August 1 through January 31. The buyer for a particular department will usually begin to prepare the merchandise budgets on about September 1 for spring/summer and March 1 for fall/winter.

Second, the language of a merchandise budget must be easy to understand. The merchandise budget illustrated in this chapter has only 11 items, although the number of items contained in a budget may vary by company due to merchandise and market characteristics. Remember, the budget serves no purpose unless it can be understood by all the decision makers and contains all the information needed for that particular retailer.

Third, because the economy today is constantly changing, the merchandise budget must be planned for a relatively short period—six months is the norm for most retailers, although some retailers use a three-month plan. Forecasting future sales is difficult enough without projecting for a period too far in the future. The firm's general management should be concerned with long-term trends and their effects on store and personnel needs. The firm's buyers are more involved in the short-term trends and their effects on the merchandising budget.

Fourth, the budget should be flexible enough that changes are not impossible. All merchandise budgets are plans and estimates of predicted future events. However, competition and consumer preferences are not always that predictable, especially in regard to fashion, and any forecast is subject to error.

A blank six-month merchandise budget for the housewares department of a major department store is shown in Exhibit 9.1. Don't be alarmed if the exhibit is not clear to you now. In the next several pages, as well as in the next two chapters, we will describe why the budget is set up this way. Additionally, we will explain all the analytical tools used by the retailer to calculate the numbers required to develop a six-month merchandise budget or plan.

Exhibit 9.1 appears to be more confusing than it really is because each

Illus. 9.1
When preparing the merchandise budget, the high performance retailer should follow four rules: (1) prepare the budget in advance of the selling season; (2) make the language of the budget easy to understand; (3) plan for a relatively short period; (4) make the budget flexible.

element is broken into four parts: last year, plan, revised plan, and actual. This is merely an effort to provide the decision-maker with complete information. *Last year* refers to last year's sales for the period; *plan* is what the original plan projected; *revised plan* is the result of any revisions caused by changing market conditions after the plan is accepted, and *actual* is the final result.

Exhibit 9.2 presents the same material in a simpler form. Here we will only attempt to show you why and how a retailer develops a six-month merchandising plan. Exhibit 9.2 shows the spring/summer season, February 1 to July 31, for Two-Seasons Department Store, Department 353, with projected sales of $500,000; planned retail reductions of $50,000 or 10 percent of sales; planned initial markup of 45 percent, and a planned gross margin on purchases of $208,750.

DETERMINING PLANNED SALES

The initial step in developing a six-month merchandise budget is to estimate planned sales for the entire season and for each month. The buyer begins by examining the previous year's sales records, along with other relevant data, and then makes adjustments for the upcoming merchandise budget. Retailers often make comparisons to prior years by using a retail reporting calendar as discussed in Retailing in Action 9-1.

Exhibit 9.1

A Sample Six-Month Merchandise Budget

		SIX-MONTH MERCHANDISE BUDGET Housewares Department Fall, 199X						
		FEBRUARY	MARCH	APRIL	MAY	JUNE	JULY	Total
BOM Stock	Last Year							
	Plan							
	Revised							
	Actual							
Sales	Last Year							
	Plan							
	Revised							
	Actual							
Reductions	Last Year							
	Plan							
	Revised							
	Actual							
EOM STOCK	Last Year							
	Plan							
	Revised							
	Actual							
RETAIL PURCHASES	Last Year							
	Plan							
	Revised							
	Actual							
PURCHASES COST	Last Year							
	Plan							
	Revised							
	Actual							
INITIAL MARK-UP	Last Year							
	Plan							
	Revised							
	Actual							
GROSS MARGIN DOLLARS	Last Year							
	Plan							
	Revised							
	Actual							
GROSS MARGIN PERCENTAGE	Last Year							
	Plan							
	Revised							
	Actual							
ON ORDER: END OF MONTH	Last Year							
	Plan							
	Revised							
	Actual							

STOCKTURN: Last Year: _____ Plan _____ Actual ___ _____
ON ORDER – BEGINNING OF SEASON: Last Year _____ Plan _____ Actual _____
EOM INVENTORY FOR LAST MONTH: Last Year _____ Plan _____ Actual _____
REDUCTION PERCENTAGE: Last Year _____ Plan _____ Actual _____
MARKUP PERCENTAGE: Last Year _____ Plan _____ Actual _____

	FEBRUARY	MARCH	APRIL	MAY	JUNE	JULY	TOTAL
1. Planned BOM Stock	$225,000	$300,000	$300,000	$250,000	$375,000	$300,000	– – – –
2. Planned Sales	75,000	75,000	100,000	50,000	125,000	75,000	$500,000
3. Planned Retail Reductions	7,500	7,500	5,000	7,500	6,250	16,250	50,000
4. Planned EOM Stock	300,000	300,000	250,000	375,000	300,000	250,000	– – – –
5. Planned Purchases @ Retail	157,500	82,500	55,000	182,000	56,250	41,250	575,000
6. Planned Purchases @ Cost	86,625	45,375	30,250	100,375	30,937.50	22,687.50	316,250
7. Planned Initial Markup	70,875	37,125	24,750	82,125	25,312.50	18,562.50	258,750
8. Planned Gross Margin	63,375	29,625	19,750	74,625	19,062.50	2,312.50	208,750
9. Planned BOM Stock Sales Ratio	3	4	3	5	3	4	– – – –
10. Planned Sales Percentage	15%	15%	20%	10%	25%	15%	100%
11. Planned Retail Reduction Percentage	10%	10%	5%	15%	5%	21.6%	10%

Exhibit 9.2

A Completed Six-Month Merchandise Budget

Planned Total Sales for the Period $500,000

Planned Total Retail Reduction Percentage for the Period   10%

Planned Initial Markup Percentage   45% .

Planned BOM Stock for August $250,000

After reviewing available data, the buyer for Department 353 forecasted that $500,000 was a reasonable total sales figure for the future season. June, with a projected 25 percent of the season's total sales, and April, with 20 percent, are expected to be the busy months while May, with only 10 percent, is expected to be the slowest month (Exhibit 9.2, Line 10). The remaining months will have equal sales. Since April, May, and June account for 55 percent of total sales, then February, March, and July's total must be 45 percent or 15 percent per month. The buyer is able to determine planned monthly sales by multiplying the planned monthly sales percentage by planned total sales. Since we know February's planned monthly sales are 15 percent of the total planned sales of $500,000, February's planned sales must be $75,000 (.15 × $500,000 = $75,000).

It is important to use recent trends when forecasting future sales. Often, retailers in a no-growth market merely use last season's figure for this season's budget. This method overlooks two major influences on projected sales volume: inflation and competition. If inflation was 10 percent and no other changes occurred in the retail environment, then the retailer planning on selling the same physical volume as the previous year should expect a 10 percent increase in this season's dollar sales. Similarly, if the exit of a competitor across town is expected to increase the number of customer transactions by 5 percent, then this should be reflected in this budget. Suppose last year's sales were $100,000, inflation is 10 percent and you expect your market share to increase by 8 percent. If the total market remains stable, what should your projected sales be? A simple equation used in retail planning is that

$$\text{Total Sales} = \text{Average Sales} \times \text{Total Transactions}$$

In the above example, the average sale would increase by 10 percent (the level of inflation) to 1.10 times last year's average sale, and total transactions would increase by the 8 percent gain in market share to 1.08 times last year's total transactions. This means there will be an increase in total sales of 1.188 times (1.10 × 1.08), or $18,800, for total budgeted sales of $118,800.

DETERMINING PLANNED BOM AND EOM INVENTORIES

Once the buyer has estimated the season and monthly sales for the coming season, plans can be made for **inventory requirements**. In order to achieve projected sales figures, the merchant will generally carry stock or inventory in excess of planned sales for the period, be it a week, month, or season. The extra stock or inventory provides a merchandise assortment deep and broad enough to insure customer sales. A common method of estimating the amount of stock to be carried is the **stock/sales ratio**. This ratio depicts the amount of stock to have on hand at the beginning of each

RETAILING
IN
ACTION

9-1

The Retail Reporting Calendar

Retailers, when comparing this year's sales to last year's sales, don't always compare exact dates (i.e., comparing February 4, 1991 sales to February 4, 1990), since the dates could fall on different days of the week. For instance, February 4 was a Sunday in 1990, when the retailer might be closed, and a Monday in 1991. Instead, retailers use a Retail Reporting Calendar, which divides the year into two seasons, each with six months as shown below. Thus, February 4, 1991, the first Monday of the spring season would be compared to February 5, 1990 and February 3, 1992, which are also the first Mondays of their spring seasons.

By using this calendar, retailers have problems making direct comparisons only once a season. Fashion retailers are affected by the movement of Easter (April 15 in 1990, March 31 in 1991, and April 19 in 1992) when making compari-

SPRING 1991

WEEK	PERIOD	SUN	MON	TUE	WED	THU	FRI	SAT
4	FEB	3	4	5	6	7	8	9
		10	11	12	13	14	15	16
		17	18	19	20	21	22	23
		24	25	26	27	28	1	2
4	MAR	3	4	5	6	7	8	9
		10	11	12	13	14	15	16
		17	18	19	20	21	22	23
		24	25	26	27	28	29	30
5	APR	31	1	2	3	4	5	6
		7	8	9	10	11	12	13
		14	15	16	17	18	19	20
		21	22	23	24	25	26	27
		28	29	30	1	2	3	4
5	MAY	5	6	7	8	9	10	11
		12	13	14	15	16	17	18
		19	20	21	22	23	24	25
		26	27	28	29	30	31	1
4	JUN	2	3	4	5	6	7	8
		9	10	11	12	13	14	15
		16	17	18	19	20	21	22
		23	24	25	26	27	28	29
		30	1	2	3	4	5	6
4	JUL	7	8	9	10	11	12	13
		14	15	16	17	18	19	20
		21	22	23	24	25	26	27
		28	29	30	31	1	2	3

FALL 1991

WEEK	PERIOD	SUN	MON	TUE	WED	THU	FRI	SAT
4	AUG	4	5	6	7	8	9	10
		11	12	13	14	15	16	17
		18	19	20	21	22	23	24
		25	26	27	28	29	30	31
4	SEP	1	2	3	4	5	6	7
		8	9	10	11	12	13	14
		15	16	17	18	19	20	21
		22	23	24	25	26	27	28
5	OCT	29	30	1	2	3	4	5
		6	7	8	9	10	11	12
		13	14	15	16	17	18	19
		20	21	22	23	24	25	26
		27	28	29	30	31	1	2
4	NOV	3	4	5	6	7	8	9
		10	11	12	13	14	15	16
		17	18	19	20	21	22	23
		24	25	26	27	28	29	30
5	DEC	1	2	3	4	5	6	7
		8	9	10	11	12	13	14
		15	16	17	18	19	20	21
		22	23	24	25	26	27	28
		29	30	31	1	2	3	4
4	JAN	5	6	7	8	9	10	11
		12	13	14	15	16	17	18
		19	20	21	22	23	24	25
		26	27	28	29	30	31	1

sons in the spring season. During the fall season, the period between Thanksgiving and Christmas can vary in length by as much as a week. Thanksgiving can fall anywhere between November 22 and 28 and as a result, the number of days in the Christmas shopping season differs from year to year. For example, in 1990 there are five weekends and 32 days between Thanksgiving and Christmas, while in 1991 there are only four weekends and 26 days between Thanksgiving and Christmas.

month to support the forecasted sales for that month. For example, a ratio of 5.0 would suggest that the retailer have $5 in inventory (at retail price) for every $1 in forecasted sales. Planned average beginning-of-month (BOM) stock/sales ratios can be calculated directly from a retailer's planned turnover goals. For example, a retailer wanted a target turnover rate of 3.5. By dividing the annual turnover rate into twelve (the number of months in a year), the average BOM stock/sales ratio for the year can be computed. In this case, 12 divided by 3.5 equals 3.4. 3.4 is the average stock/sales ratio for the season. Generally, these stock/sales ratios will fluctuate monthly because sales tend to fluctuate monthly. Nevertheless, it is important to always review these ratios because if they are set too high or too low, too much or too little inventory will be on hand to meet the sales target.

Other methods of determining opening inventory will be discussed in Chapter 10. From experience, a buyer knows how much stock must be maintained in order to generate planned sales. Retail trade associations such as the National Retail Merchants Association (NRMA) conduct surveys and publish industry average stock/sales ratios. Based on data available, the buyer for Department 353 used a planned stock/sales ratio of 3.0 for February, April, and June, a ratio of 4.0 for March and July, and a ratio of 5.0 for May. The buyer was able to determine that $300,000 worth of merchandise was needed starting March 1 due to a planned stock/sales ratio of 4.0 and planned sales of $75,000 (line 2). Note that stock/sales ratios always express inventory levels using retail, not cost, figures. The beginning-of-month (BOM) inventory for one month is the end-of-month (EOM) inventory for the previous month. This relationship can be easily seen by comparing the BOM figures (Line 1) for one month with the EOM figures for the previous month (Line 4).

DETERMINING PLANNED RETAIL REDUCTIONS

Not all merchandise bought for sale to consumers is sold at the planned initial markup price. Therefore, when preparing the six-month budget, the buyer should make allowances for reductions in the levels of stock not due to sales. Generally, these planned **retail reductions** fall into three types: markdowns, employee discounts, and stock shortages. These reductions must be planned, because as the dollar value of inventory level is reduced, the BOM stock planned to support next month's forecasted sales will be inadequate unless adjustments are made. A buyer must remember that reductions are part of the cost of doing business. A few retailers don't include planned reductions in their merchandise budgets. They treat planned reductions as part of the normal operation of the store and control them without making them part of total budget. This gives management an understated, conservative, planned-purchase figure, and in effect, holds back some purchase reserve. We have included planned reductions as part of the merchandise budget for two reasons. First, to reflect the additional purchases needed in order to have sufficient inventory to begin the next month; and second, to point out that taking reductions is not bad. Too often, inexperienced retailers believe that taking a reduction is a confession of error and therefore fail to mark down merchandise until too late in the season.

Our example has estimated monthly retail reduction percentages on Line 11. To determine planned retail reductions for March (Line 3), planned monthly sales are multiplied by the planned monthly retail reduction percentage to yield the planned monthly retail reduction of $7,500 ($75,000 × .10 = $7,500). Methods available to the retail buyer for minimizing retail reductions caused by retailer mistakes are discussed in Chapter 11. These items are referred to as reductions because they reduce retail inventory values and planned gross margin, unless the **vendor** (the supplier of merchandise to the retailer) makes a corresponding contribution to the retailer.

Reductions are one of the major items subject to constant change in the merchandise budget. One reason is that the planned reductions may prove inadaquate in light of actual conditions encountered by the retailer. Delays in taking reductions may force deeper price cuts later, after style merchandise depreciates even more in value. Alternatively, what happens when the department manager does such an effective merchandising job that not all the reduction money is needed for the period? The answer to both of these situations is found in the rules for developing a budget; namely, that by keeping it flexible it can be intelligently administered.

DETERMINING PLANNED PURCHASES AT RETAIL AND COST

We are now ready to determine whether additional purchases need to be made during the merchandising season. The retailer will need inventory for (1) planned sales, (2) planned retail reductions, and (3) planned EOM inventory. Planned BOM inventory represents purchases that have already been made. In the six-month merchandise budget example, the March planned purchases at retail for Department 353 are $82,500 (Line 5). **Planned purchases at retail** are derived by adding planned sales, planned retail reductions, and planned EOM inventory then subtracting planned BOM inventory.

$$(\$75,000 + \$7,500 + 300,000) - 300,000 = \$82,500$$

Once planned purchases at retail are determined, **planned purchases at cost** can be easily calculated. The retail price always represents cost plus markup. If the markup percentage is given, the portion of retail attributed to cost, called **the cost complement**, can be derived by subtracting the markup percentage from 100 percent. Given a markup percentage of 45 percent of retail for Department 353, the cost complement percentage must be 55 percent (100% − 45% = 55%). Planned purchases at cost for March (Line 6) must be 55 percent of planned purchases at retail, or $45,375 ($82,500 × .55 = $45,375).

DETERMINING THE BUYER'S PLANNED GROSS MARGIN

The last step in developing the merchandise budget is determining the buyer's planned gross margin for the period. As we have seen, a buyer making plans should recognize that the initial selling price for all the products will probably not be realized and that some reductions will occur. The buyer's planned gross margin in Exhibit 9.2 (Line 8) is determined by taking planned initial markup (Line 7) and subtracting planned reductions (Line 3). Thus, for February, $63,375 = $70,875 − $7,500. Notice that the buyer's planned gross margin is not the same as the firm's gross margin for the month as defined in Chapter 2. This is because buyers are only accountable for their own actions. In this case, that means that the buyer is accountable for the purchases made, the expected selling price of these purchases, the cost of these purchases, and the reductions that are involved in selling merchandise the buyer has previously purchased. Thus, in February, the buyer's gross margin is not the result of the $75,000 in sales but of the purchases of $157,500 having an initial markup of $70,875 and the reductions of $7,500. The buyer's planned gross margin of $63,375 ($70,875 − $7,500) therefore reflects the amount of gross margin that the buyer's actions will contribute to the firm when the merchandise is sold.

It might be useful at this time to review some of the definitions from Chapter 2 and to point out again that gross margin is not the same as profit. **Gross margin** is the difference between the total cost of merchandise (including reductions) and net merchandise sales. **Operating profit** is gross margin minus all the operating expenses. **Net profit** is operating profit plus or minus any transactions not directly relating to the firm's retailing activities. Gross margin is considered one of the key measures of a retailer's merchandising success because sales and the cost of goods are essentially controllable by the buying function of the firm, which may have little or no control over the other expenses that affect the profitability of a retailer.

INVENTORY VALUATION

Due to the many different merchandise lines carried, most retail inventory accounting systems are quite complex. These systems must provide the retailer with information such as sales, additional purchases not yet received, reductions for the period, gross margin, open-to-buy, stock shortages, and inventory levels.

Two inventory accounting systems are available to the retailer: (1) the cost method and (2) the retail method. The **cost method** provides a book valuation of inventory based solely on cost including freight. The **retail method** values merchandise at current retail prices. Both of these accounting methods are described below according to the frequency with which inventory information is received, difficulties in completing a physical inventory, difficulties in maintaining records, and the extent to which stock shortages can be calculated.

THE COST METHOD

In the cost method of inventory valuation, the cost of each item is recorded in the accounting records by its inventory code number, or is coded on the price tag. When a physical inventory is taken, all the items are counted, the cost of each item is taken from the records or the price tags, and the total inventory value at cost is calculated.

One of the easiest methods of coding the cost of merchandise is to use the first ten letters of the alphabet to represent the price. Here A = 1, B = 2, C = 3, D = 4, E = 5, F = 6, G = 7, H = 8, I = 9, and J = 0. A product with the code FDIA has a cost of $64.91. Besides being a useful accounting tool, this method works well for retailers who allow price negotiations by customers because dollar markup per item is easy to calculate.

The cost method can be used when one is conducting physical or book inventories. A physical inventory involves an actual count of merchandise, whereas a book inventory relies on bookkeeping entries.

Illus. 9.2
A physical inventory involves an actual count of merchandise, whereas a book inventory relies on bookkeeping entries.

The physical inventory system using the cost method can be illustrated using the income statement for Nowak Company for the spring season 199X, as shown in Exhibit 9.3. The sales amount is from the store's total receipts during the season. Beginning inventory is calculated by a physical count of all merchandise in stock on February 1 and is recorded at cost. Purchases are determined by summing all invoice slips for merchandise received during the season. Ending inventory is the physical count on July 31, at cost.

When using the physical inventory system, gross margin cannot be calculated until after the ending inventory is taken and the cost of goods sold is determined. Because most retailers undertake physical inventories only once or twice a year, the physical inventory method imposes severe limitations on the retailer's merchandise planning. This method also prevents the retailer from calculating inventory shortages resulting from theft or breakage because the ending inventory is only determined by the costing of all items in stock.

The book inventory system (sometimes called the perpetual inventory system) avoids the problem of infrequent financial statements by keeping a running total of the cost value of inventory on hand at a given time. In addition, it allows a retailer to calculate shortages at any point in time. A retailer maintains a perpetual system by continually adding purchases to and subtracting sales from its current inventory value to arrive at the new

Exhibit 9.3

A Sample Income Statement

The Nowak Company
Income Statement
Feb. 1–July 30, 199X

Sales		$500,000
Less: Cost of Goods Sold:		
Beginning inventory (at cost)	$400,000	
Purchases (at cost)	150,000	
Goods available for sale	$550,000	
Ending inventory (at cost)	325,000	
Cost of goods sold		225,000
Gross Margin		$275,000
Less: operating expenses		
Salaries	$125,000	
Utilities	25,000	
Rent	40,000	
Depreciation (fixtures + equipment)	35,000	
Total Operating Expenses		225,000
Net Profit Before Taxes		$ 50,000

current value of the inventory at cost. Exhibit 9.4 shows how the perpetual inventory system would have worked for our example with the Nowak Company.

Exhibit 9.4 contains the same financial information (beginning inventory, total purchases, total cost of goods sold, and ending inventory) for the Nowak Company as the income statement in Exhibit 9.3. If sales and operating expenses were given, one could determine the income for the period using the perpetual inventory data.

As shown above, the book inventory system is superior to the physical inventory system in two ways. First, it enables the retailer to know end-of-month inventory levels without taking a physical count, allowing frequent financial statements to be developed. Second, a book inventory value can be compared with the physical count to determine shortages.

Both cost methods of inventory valuation share several limitations, however. These limitations include:

1. daily inventories (or even monthly inventories) are impractical,
2. the difficulties involved in costing out each sale,
3. the problems involved in allocating freight charges to the cost of goods sold
4. the difficulty of adjusting inventory values to reflect changes in the demand for the product at the retail level.

The cost method is generally used by retailers with big-ticket items, where there are few lines, infrequent price changes, and low turnover rates, such as jewelry or furniture stores. Due to the limitations of the cost method, most retailers today use the retail method of inventory valuation, which was created in the early 1900s.

Exhibit 9.4

The Nowak Company Perpetual Inventory System

Date	BOM Inventory (at Cost)	+	Purchases (at Cost)	−	Sales (at Cost)	=	EOM Inventory (at Cost)
2/1	$400,000		$ 30,000		$ 45,000		$385,000
3/1	385,000		20,000		40,000		365,000
4/1	365,000		40,000		35,000		370,000
5/1	370,000		10,000		25,000		355,000
6/1	355,000		25,000		40,000		340,000
7/1	340,000		25,000		40,000		325,000
TOTAL			$150,000		$225,000		

THE RETAIL METHOD

The retail method of inventory valuation overcomes the disadvantages of the cost method by keeping detailed records of inventory based on the retail value of the merchandise. The fact that the inventory is valued in retail dollars makes it a little more difficult for the retailer to determine the cost of goods sold when computing the gross margin for a time period.

There are three basic steps in computing an ending inventory value using the retail method: calculation of the cost complement, calculation of reductions from retail value, and conversion of the adjusted retail book inventory to cost.

Calculation of the Cost Complement.   Inventories (beginning and ending) and purchases are recorded at both cost and retail levels when using the retail method. Exhibit 9.5 shows an inventory statement for Spengel's Sporting Goods for the fall season.

In Exhibit 9.5, the beginning inventory is shown at both cost and retail. Net purchases, which are total purchases less merchandise returned to vendors, allowances, and discounts from vendors, are also valued at cost and retail. Additional markups are the total increases in the retail prices of merchandise already in stock, due to inflation or heavy demand. Freight-in is the cost to the retailer for transportation of merchandise from the vendor.

Using the information from Exhibit 9.5, the retailer can calculate the average relationship of cost value to retail value for all merchandise available for sale during the fall season. This calculation is called the cost complement:

$$\text{Cost complement} = \text{Total cost valuation/Total retail valuation}$$
$$= \$270,000/\$560,000 = .482$$

Since the cost complement is .482, or 48.2 percent, 48.2 cents of every retail sales dollar is merchandise cost.

Exhibit 9.5

Spengel's Sporting Goods Inventory Available for Sale, Fall Season, 199X

	Cost	Retail
Beginning inventory	$199,000	$401,000
Net Purchases	70,000	154,000
Additional Markups		5,000
Freight-in	1,000	
Total inventory available for sale	$270,000	$560,000

Calculation of Reductions from Retail Value.   During the course of day-to-day business activities, the retailer must take reductions from inventory. The retail inventory level can be decreased by sales or by retail reductions. These reductions include: sales; markdowns (reduced prices on end-of-season, discontinued, or shopworn merchandise); discounts (employees, senior citizens, students, religious, and other customer groups); and stock shortages (employee and customer thefts, breakages). Markdowns and discounts can be recorded throughout an accounting period, but a physical inventory is required to calculate stock shortages.

Exhibit 9.5 shows that Spengel's had a retail inventory available for sale of $560,000. This must be reduced by sales of $145,000, markdowns of $12,000, and discounts of $2,000. This results in an ending book value of inventory at retail of $401,000. This is shown in Exhibit 9.6.

Once the ending book value of inventory at retail is determined, a comparison can be made to the physical inventory to compute stock shortages. If the book value is greater than the physical count, a stock shortage has occurred; if the book value is lower than the physical count, a stock overage has occurred. Shortages are due to thefts, breakages, over-shipments not billed to customers, and bookkeeping errors—the most common cause. These bookkeeping errors result from the failure to properly record markdowns, returns, discounts, and breakages. Many retailers can greatly reduce their original shortage estimate by reviewing the season's bookkeeping entries. A stock overage is usually the result of bookkeeping errors, either miscounting during the physical inventory or improper book entries.

Exhibit 9.7 shows the results of Spengel's physical inventory and the resulting adjustment.

Since a physical inventory must be taken in order to determine shortages (overages), and retailers only take a physical count once or twice a year, shortages (overages) are often estimated in merchandise budgets, as shown in Exhibits 9.1 and 9.2. As a rule of thumb, convenience stores use a 1 to 2 percent of sales figure while furniture stores use a half percent of sales to estimate monthly shortages.

Exhibit 9.6

Spengel's Sporting Goods Ending Book Value at Retail, Fall Season, 199X

Inventory available for sale at retail		$560,000
Less reductions:		
Sales	$145,000	
Markdowns	12,000	
Discounts	2,000	
Total reductions		159,000
Ending book value of inventory at retail		$401,000

Exhibit 9.7

Spengel's Sporting Goods, Stock Shortage (Overage) Adjustment Entry, End of Fall Season, 199X

Ending book value of inventory at retail	$401,000
Physical inventory (at retail)	398,000
Stock shortages	$ 3,000
Adjusted ending book value of inventory at retail	$398,000

Conversion of Adjusted Retail Book Inventory to Cost.   The final step to be performed in the retail method is to determine the closing inventory at cost by converting to cost the adjusted retail book inventory figure. Simply multiply the adjusted retail book inventory value ($398,000 in the case of Spengel's) by the cost complement (.482).

$$\begin{aligned} \text{Closing Inventory at Cost} &= \text{Adjusted Retail Book Inventory} \\ &\quad \times \text{Cost Complement} \\ &= \$398,000 \times .482 \\ &= \$191,836 \end{aligned}$$

While this equation does not yield the actual closing inventory at cost, it does provide a close approximation of the cost figure. Now that closing inventory at cost has been determined, the retailer can determine gross margin, as well as net profit before taxes if operating expenses are known. In the Spengel's example, let's use $12,000 for salaries, $1,000 for utilities, $9,000 for rent, and $2,200 for depreciation. This is shown in Exhibit 9.8.

The retail method of inventory valuation has several advantages over the cost method. Among these advantages are:

1. Accounting statements can be drawn up at any time. Inventories need not be taken for preparation of these statements.
2. Physical inventories using retail prices are less subject to error and can be completed in a shorter amount of time.
3. The retail method provides an automatic, conservative valuation of ending inventory as well as inventory levels throughout the season. This is especially useful in cases where the retailer is forced to submit insurance claims for damaged or lost merchandise.

A major complaint about the retail method is that it is a method of averages. Closing inventory is valued at the average relationship between cost and retail, even though large retailers have many different classifications and lines with different relationships. This disadvantage can be

Exhibit 9.8
Spengel's Sporting Goods, Income Statement, Aug. 1–Jan. 31, 199X

Sales		$145,000
Less: Cost of Goods Sold:		
Beginning inventory (at cost)	$200,000	
Purchases (at cost)	70,000	
Goods available for sale	$270,000	
Ending inventory (at cost)	191,836	
Cost of goods sold		78,164
Gross Margin		$ 66,836
Less: operating expenses		
Salaries	$ 12,000	
Utilities	1,000	
Rent	9,000	
Depreciation (fixtures + equipment)	2,200	
Total Operating Expenses		24,200
Net Profit Before Taxes		$ 42,636

overcome by breaking down the total inventory into smaller, homogeneous subsections with similar averages.

Another limitation of the retail method is the heavy burden it places on the bookkeeping activities. The true closing book inventory value can be correctly calculated only if there are no errors in recording beginning inventory, purchase, freight-in, markups, markdowns, discounts, returns, transfers between stores, or sales. As noted earlier, many stock shortages have later been determined to be bookkeeping errors.

RETAIL ACCOUNTING STATEMENTS

Successful retailing requires sound accounting practices, although the number and types of accounting records needed depend upon management's objectives. Large retailers generally require more detailed information based on merchandise lines or departments, while smaller retailers may be able to make firsthand observations on sales and inventory levels and make decisions before financial data is available. However, small retailers should consult accounting records to confirm personal observations.

Properly prepared financial records provide a record of all transactions and a measurement of profitability and retail performance within a given period. These financial records provide the manager not only with a look at the past but also a look into the future so the manager can plan. Financial records indicate whether a retailer has achieved high-performance results and what growth potential and problem areas lie ahead. For example:

1. Is some merchandise line outperforming or underperforming the rest of the store?
2. Is inventory level adequate for the current sales level?
3. Is the firm's debt level too high?
4. Are reductions as a percentage of sales too high?
5. Is gross margin adequate for the firm's profit objectives?

These are just a few of the questions that financial data can answer for the retailer. In one retail firm, Product X was generating an annual profit of $800,000 and Product Y was losing money at the rate of $600,000 per year. Management was totally unaware of the situation—just happy to be making $200,000! They were astounded when a little accounting work revealed the truth.[1]

INCOME STATEMENT

Probably the most important financial statement a retailer prepares is the income statement, also referred to as the profit and loss statement. The **income statement** gives a retailer a summary of the sales and expenses for a given period, usually a month, a quarter, a season, or a year. Comparison of current results with prior results allows the retailer to notice trends or changes in sales, expenses, and profits. Many financial institutions base loan decisions on a retailer's income statement. Retailers, as pointed out in Retailing in Action 9-2, have learned how to improve their income statements. Because income statements can be subdivided by departments, divisions, branches, etc., the retailer can evaluate each subunit's operating performance for the period. Exhibit 9.9 shows the basic format for an income statement and Exhibit 9.10 shows the income statement for TMD Furniture.

**RETAILING
IN
ACTION**   **9-2**

Better-Looking Financial Statements?

Retailers, especially small retailers, learned long ago that lenders judge the worth and creditworthiness of a business by the firm's financial statements. Thus, common sense suggests that retailers make their statements look as good as possible. Listed below are a number of perfectly legitimate things retailers can do to achieve these objectives.

As you have learned, ratio analysis is the most common way lenders analyze a balance sheet. The current ratio (current assets divided by current liabilities) can be improved by paying off current debt before the review. For example, suppose a retailer has $45,000 in cash, $5,000 in other current assets, and $25,000 in current liabilities, for a current ratio of 2:1. If $10,000 of the cash is used to reduce debt, however, the ratio improves significantly to 2.7:1. The same principle can be used when a retailer exchanges long-term debt for short-term debt.

Another tool available to retailers is to borrow against receivables from a bank or a finance company. Retailers normally issue a payment to the lender for any collection on these receivables. As a result, one day (the day the retailer collects from a customer) the retailer's bank balance is impressive, the next day it is anemic. A common method to improve the balance sheet is to have the lending financial institution agree to a slower repayment schedule, enabling the retailer to build up its cash balance.

Still no matter how much window dressing a retailer does, the ultimate question is, "Does the firm pay its debts on time?" If the retailer has a history of being a late pay, no amount of financial statement repair will make the lender happy.

Exhibit 9.9
Retailers' Basic Income Statement Format

Gross Sales		$ _____
— Returns and Allowances	$ _____	
Net Sales		$ _____
— Cost of Goods Sold	$ _____	
Gross Margin		$ _____
— Operating Expenses	$ _____	
Operating Profit		$ _____
± Other Income or Expenses	$ _____	
Net Profit Before Taxes		$ _____

Gross sales are total retail sales, whether the sales were for cash or credit. Returns and allowances are reductions from gross sales. In Exhibit 9.10, the retailer made adjustments to customers because the customers returned merchandise to the retailer. Since these reductions represent cancellations of previously recorded sales, the gross sales figure must be reduced to reflect these cancellations.

Net sales, gross sales minus returns and allowances, represent the amount of merchandise the retailer actually sold during the time period.

Cost of goods sold is the store's cost of merchandise sold during the period. While this concept is easy to understand, the exact calculation of the cost of goods sold is somewhat complex. For example, retailers may

Exhibit 9.10
A Sample Income Statement

TMD Furniture, Inc.
Six Month Income Statement
July 31, 199x

			Percentage
Gross Sales		$393,671.79	
Less: Returns and Allowances		16,300.00	
Net Sales		$377,371.79	100%
Less: Cost of Goods Sold			
Beginning Inventory	$ 98,466.29		
Purchases	218,595.69		
Goods Available for Sales	$317,061.98		
Ending Inventory	103,806.23	213,255.75	56.5%
Gross Margin		$164,116.04	43.5%
Less: Operating Expenses			
Salaries & Wages:			
Managers	$18,480.50		
Selling	17,755.65		
Office	7,580.17		
Warehouse & Delivery	6,685.99		
	$ 50,502.31		
Advertising	15,236.67		
Administration and Warehouse Charge	800.00		
Credit, Collections and Bad Debts	1,973.96		
Contributions	312.50		
Delivery	1,434.93		
Depreciation	5,398.56		
Dues	23.50		
Employee Benefits	566.26		
Utilities	3,738.74		
Insurance	3,041.75		
Legal and Auditing	1,000.00		
Mds. Service & Repair	1,439.16		
Miscellaneous	602.00		
Rent	9,080.00		
Repairs & Maintenance	1,576.99		
Sales Allowances	180.50		
Supplies, Postage	1,135.40		
Taxes:			
City, County & State	$ 2,000.00		
Payroll	3,902.90	5,902.90	
Telephone		1,520.09	
Travel		404.92	
Warehouse Handling Charges		12,216.86	118,088.00	31.3%
Operating Profit		$ 46,028.04	12.2%
Other Income:			
Carrying Charges	$ 3,377.48		
Profit on sale of parking lot	740.47	4,117.95	1.1%
Net Profit Before Taxes		$ 50,145.99	13.3%

get some return privileges or receive some allowances from vendors. Also, there is the problem of establishing inventory costs.

Two methods of costing inventory are **FIFO (first in-first out)** and **LIFO (last in-first out)**. The FIFO method assumes that the oldest merchandise is sold before recently purchased merchandise. During inflationary periods, this method allows inventory profits (caused by selling less expensive, earlier inventory rather than more expensive, newer inventory) to be included as income.

The LIFO method is designed to cushion the impact of inflationary pressures by matching current costs against current revenues. Cost of goods sold is based on the costs of the most recently purchased inventory, and older inventory is regarded as unsold inventory. The LIFO method results in the application of a higher unit cost to the merchandise sold and a lower unit cost to inventory still unsold. In times of inflation, most retailers use the LIFO method, resulting in lower profits on the income statement and lower income taxes. Most retailers also prefer to use LIFO for planning purposes, since it accurately reflects replacement costs. The IRS restricts switching back and forth so the retailer must stick with one method.

Let's compare the effects of LIFO and FIFO on the firm's financial performance. Suppose you began the year with a total inventory of 15 typewriters which you purchased on the last day of the preceding year for $300 each. If the typewriters were the only merchandise you had in stock, your beginning inventory was $4500 (15 × $300). During the year you sell 12 typewriters for $700 each for total sales of $8,400. In June you purchase eight new typewriters (same make and model as your old ones) at $325. In November you buy four more at $350. Thus, your purchases were $2,600 in June and $1,400 in November, for a total of $4,000. You still have fifteen typewriters in stock at the end of the year.

Using the LIFO method, your ending inventory would be the same as it was at the beginning of the year—$4,500—since the LIFO method assumes the 12 typewriters sold were the 12 purchased during the year. The FIFO method assumes that 12 of the original $300 typewriters were sold and three were left. These three, along with June's and November's purchases, resulted in an ending inventory of $4,900 [(3 × $300) + (8 × $325) + (4 × $350)]. Now let's see how these two approaches can affect gross margins.

	LIFO		FIFO	
Net Sales		$8,400		$8,400
Less: Cost of Goods Sold				
Beginning Inventory	$4,500		$4,500	
Purchases	4,000		4,000	
Goods available	$8,500		$8,500	
Ending Inventory	4,500		4,900	
Cost of Goods Sold		4,000		3,600
Gross Margin		$4,400		$4,800

Once the retailer makes a determination of cost of goods sold, gross margin can be computed. **Gross margin** is the difference between net sales and cost of goods sold, or the amount available to cover operating expenses and produce a profit. In our example, using LIFO inventory valuation results in $4,400 in gross margin dollars vs. $4,800 when FIFO inventory valuation is used. This is why LIFO results in lower profits during inflationary times.

Operating expenses are those expenses the retailer incurs in operation of the business (e.g., payroll, rent, utilities, advertising, depreciation, supplies, taxes, interest paid, repairs, insurance, etc.). The cost of merchandise sold is not an operating expense.

Operating profit is the difference between gross margin and operating expenses.

Other income or expenses is income or expense items that the firm incurs, though not in the course of its normal retail operations. For example, a retailer might have purchased some land to use for expansion and after careful deliberation, postponed the expansion plans. Now the retailer rents out that land. Since renting land is not part of normal retail operations, the rent received would be considered other income.

Net profit is operating profit plus or minus other income or expenses. Net profit is the figure upon which the retailer pays taxes and thus it is usually referred to as net profit before taxes.

Most retailers divide the income statement into two sections: the top half, above the gross margin total, that includes sales and cost of goods sold, and the bottom half, below the gross margin total where expenses are included. Sales and cost of goods sold are essentially controllable by the buying functions of the retail organization which are becoming increasingly separated from the operating expenses that take place below gross margin. A number of retail organizations now include the cost of personnel responsible for the acquisition of merchandise in the cost of goods sold. This practice, however, drastically distorts the firm's gross margin figures when compared to retailers who don't include those costs as part of cost of goods sold.

BALANCE SHEET

The second accounting statement used in financial reporting is the balance sheet. A **balance sheet** shows the financial condition of a retailer's business at a particular point in time, as opposed to the income statement, which reports on the activities over a period of time. The balance sheet identifies and quantifies all the firm's assets and liabilities. The difference between assets and liabilities is owner's equity or net worth. Comparison of a current balance sheet with a previous balance sheet enables a retail analyst to observe changes in the firm's financial condition.

A typical balance sheet format is illustrated in Exhibit 9.11. It shows the basic equation for a balance sheet:

Exhibit 9.11
Retailers' Basic Balance Sheet Format

Current Assets		Current Liabilities	
Cash	$ _____	Accounts Payable	$ _____
Accounts Receivable	$ _____	Payroll Payable	$ _____
Prepaid Expenses	$ _____	Current Notes Payable	$ _____
Inventory	$ _____	Taxes Payable	$ _____
Total Current Assets	$ _____	Total Current Liabilities	$ _____
Fixed Assets		Fixed Liabilities	
Building (less depreciation)	$ _____	Long-term Notes Payable	$ _____
Fixtures and Equipment		Mortgage Payable	$ _____
(less depreciation)	$ _____		
Total Fixed Assets	$ _____	Total Fixed Liabilities	$ _____
Goodwill	$ _____	Net Worth	
		Capital Surplus	$ _____
		Retained Earnings	$ _____
		Total Net Worth	$ _____
TOTAL ASSETS	$ _____	TOTAL LIABILITIES and NET WORTH	$ _____

$$\text{assets} = \text{liabilities} + \text{net worth}$$

The two sides must always be in balance with each other. Exhibit 9.12 shows the balance sheet for TMD Furniture.

An **asset** is anything of value that is owned by the retail firm. Assets are of two types—current and fixed.

Current assets include cash and other items which the retailer can easily convert into cash within a relatively short period of time, generally a year. Besides cash, current assets include accounts receivable, prepaid expenses, and inventory. Accounts and notes receivable are amounts that customers owe the retailer for goods and services. Frequently, the retailer will reduce total receivables by a fixed percentage (based on past experience) to take into account those customers who may be unwilling or unable to pay. Prepaid expenses are goods and services, such as trash collection, that the retailer has paid for but has not yet received. Retail inventories are comprised of merchandise that the retailer has in the store or in storage and that is available for sale. Earlier we discussed the effect that the LIFO and FIFO methods of retail valuation have on profits. They have the same effect on the current asset section of the balance sheet. In times of rising prices, the LIFO method reduces the value of the firm's inventory and the FIFO method increases the value of the firm's inventory. Most retailers favor the more conservative LIFO method, so as to not overstate assets or profits.

Fixed assets are those assets that cannot be converted into cash in a

Exhibit 9.12
A Sample Balance Sheet

TMD Furniture
Balance Sheet
July 31, 199x

Current Assets			Current Liabilities		
Cash	$ 11,589		Accounts Payable	$57,500	
Accounts Receivable	71,517		Payroll Payable	$ 1,451	
Inventory	103,806		Current Notes Payable	$14,000	
			Taxes Payable	$ 1,918	
Total Current Assets		186,912	Total Current Liabilities		$ 74,869
Fixed Assets			Fixed Liabilities		
Building (less depreciation)	$ 61,414		Long-term Notes Payable	$52,750	
Fixtures and Equipment			Mortgage Payable	$38,500	
(less depreciation)	$ 11,505				
Total Fixed Assets		72,919	Total Fixed Liabilities		$ 91,250
Goodwill		100	Net Worth		$ 93,812
TOTAL ASSETS		$259,931	TOTAL LIABILITIES and		
			NET WORTH		$259,931

short period of time in the normal course of business. These long-term assets include buildings, parking lots, fixtures (e.g., display racks) and equipment (e.g., air conditioning system). These items are carried on the books at cost minus accumulated depreciation. Depreciation is necessary because fixed assets have a limited useful life. Subtracting depreciation provides a more realistic picture of the value of the retailer's assets and prevents an overstatement of these assets.

Some retailers also include goodwill as an asset. Goodwill is an intangible asset, like customer loyalty, that a retailer pays for when buying an existing business. Usually the dollar value assigned to goodwill is minimal.

Total assets equal current assets plus fixed assets plus goodwill.

The other part of the balance sheet reflects the retailer's liabilities and net worth. A **liability** is any legitimate claim against the retailer's assets. Liabilities are classified as either current or fixed.

Current liabilities are short-term indebtedness, payable within a year. Included here are accounts payable, notes payable which are due within a year, payroll payable, and taxes payable. **Accounts payable** is money owed vendors for goods and services. **Payroll payable** is money due employees on past labor. Taxes due the government (local, state, or federal) are also considered a current liability. Another current liability is interest due within the year on long-term notes or mortgages.

Fixed liabilities are long-term indebtedness. Mortgages, notes, and bonds which are not due within the year are the most common examples of

Illus. 9.3
Fixed assets include buildings, parking lots, fixtures (like display racks) and equipment (like the air conditioning system).
Source: Retail Planning Associates

fixed liabilities. **Total liabilities** is the sum of current and fixed liabilities.

Net worth is the difference between the firm's total assets and total liabilities, and represents the owner's equity in the business. Net worth might also be described as the owner's original investment plus any profits reinvested in the business, less any losses incurred and any funds that the owners have taken out of or added to the business over time.

The balance sheet doesn't really reflect all the firm's assets and liabilities. Some items, such as personnel, can be an asset or a liability to the business. These items might not appear on the balance sheet but are extremely important to the success of a high-performance retailer. Other items which could be either assets or liabilities are goodwill, customer loyalty, and vendor relationships. Each of these items contributes to the success or failure of a retailer, even though they cannot be quantified.

STATEMENT OF CASH FLOW

A third financial statement available to the retailer is the **cash flow statement**. A cash flow statement lists in detail the source and type of all revenues (cash inflows) and the use and type of all expenditures (cash outflows) for a given period. When cash inflows exceed cash outflows, the retailer is said to have a positive cash flow; when cash outflows exceed cash inflows the retailer is said to have a negative cash flow. The purpose of the cash flow statement is to enable the retailer to project the cash needs of the firm. Based on these projections, plans can be made to seek additional financing if a negative flow is projected, or make other investments if a positive flow is anticipated. A retailer with a projected positive cash flow might be able to take advantage of closeouts or other good deals from vendors.

A cash flow statement is not the same as an income statement. In a cash flow statement, the retailer is only concerned with the movement of cash into or out of the firm. An income statement pertains to the profitability of the retailer after all revenue and expenses are considered. Consider the statement of cash flow for TMD Furniture for the month of August, 19xx, as shown in Exhibit 9.13.

August is a slow month for furniture sales because many customers are taking vacations. As a result TMD is expecting sales of only $40,000 for the month. However, only $15,450 of that amount will be for cash and TMD expects to collect $24,998 on its account receivables. Along with a tax refund check due from the state for $97, TMD has projected a cash inflow of $40,545 for August. However, because August is the month that several notes and accounts payable are due, TMD Furniture is expecting

Exhibit 9.13
A Sample Cash Flow Statement

TMD Furniture
Statement of Cash Flow
August, 199x

Cash Inflow		
Cash Sales	$15,450	
Collection of Accounts Receivable	24,998	
Refund on State Taxes	97	
Total Cash Inflow		$40,545
Cash Outflow		
Rent	$ 1,513	
Purchases at Cash	5,750	
Salaries	8,483	
Utilities	1,450	
Advertising	2,300	
County Taxes	173	
Supplies	921	
Telephone	150	
Paying Off Accounts Payable	20,632	
Paying Off Notes Payable	7,000	
Total Cash Outflow		$48,372
TOTAL CASH FLOW		($7,827)

to have to pay out $48,372 during August. This will result in a negative cash flow for the month of $7,827. TMD has prepared for this by having cash on hand (as reported on the July 31, 199x balance sheet) of $11,589. However, many retailers forget about cash and realize the difference between cash flow and profit only after the coffers are empty. In our example, TMD Furniture's paying off the notes and accounts payable had no effect on the income statement. Likewise, the statement of cash flow only considered that part of purchases that were paid for with cash, not those placed on account. These credit purchases had no direct effect on the cash flow. Exhibit 9.14 graphically depicts typical cash inflow and outflow items.

Exhibit 9.14   **Typical Cash Inflow and Outflow Categories**

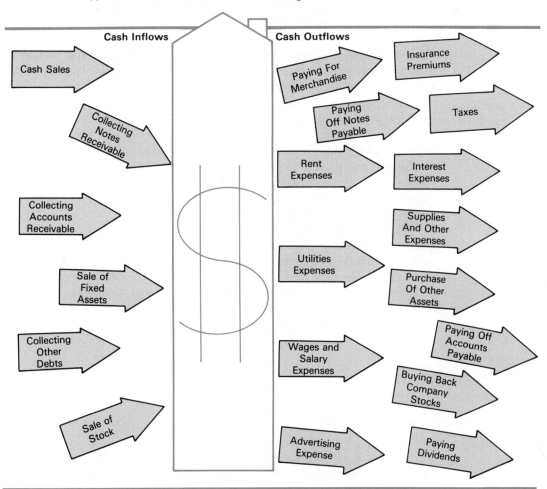

SUMMARY

This chapter has introduced the different financial statements used in retail planning and their importance. We began our discussion with the six-month merchandising budget. This statement projects sales, when and how much new merchandise should be ordered, what markup is to be taken, what reductions are to be planned, and the target or planned gross margin for the season. The six-month merchandising budget does several important things for the retailer:

1. It controls the amount of inventory and forces management to control markup and reductions.
2. It helps determine how much merchandise should be purchased so that inventory requirements can be met.
3. It can be compared with actual or final results to determine the performance of the firm.

We concluded our discussion of the six-month merchandising budget by showing how to determine estimated sales, inventory levels, reductions, purchases, and gross margin.

The second section of this chapter described two different methods of inventory valuation: the cost method and the retail method. The cost method is the simplest to use, but the retail method is the most widely used. Either method can be employed with physical or book inventory systems. The physical inventory system involves the actual counting of inventory at stated intervals, while the book inventory system relies on accurate bookkeeping and a reliable information exchange between the selling floor and bookkeeping office.

The final part of this chapter explains how the retailer uses three important accounting statements: the income statement, the balance sheet, and the cash flow statement. The income statement gives the retailer a summary of income and expense over a given period. A balance sheet shows the financial condition of the retailer at a particular point in time. The cash flow statement lists in detail the source and type of all revenue and expenditures for a given period.

QUESTIONS FOR DISCUSSION

1. What are the components of a merchandise budget?
2. What rules should be followed in developing a merchandise budget?

3. Retailers must carry inventory in excess of planned sales for an upcoming period. Why?
4. List the advantages and disadvantages the retail method of inventory valuation has over the cost method.
5. Define FIFO and LIFO and the reasons for using one or the other.
6. What is a stock/sales ratio?
7. What is the difference between the balance sheet and the income statement?
8. Why is it difficult to determine the exact value of inventory when preparing financial statements?
9. What is the cost method of inventory valuation and when is it most appropriate to use this method?
10. Dena's Deli is trying to determine net profit before taxes. Use the following data to assist Dena in her endeavor.

Rent	$25,000
Salaries	$40,000
Purchases	$100,000
Sales	$300,000
Beginning Inventory	$20,000
Utilities	$30,000
Ending Inventory	$18,000

11. The Antique Shoppe has planned $65,000 in sales for the coming fall season. Given the supply and demand for antiques, the manager believes a high initial markup of 60 percent can be sustained by the market. Based on past sales reports, it is expected that 25 percent of the season's sales will occur in November, 35 percent in December, and 40 percent equally dispersed over the remaining four months. From the records, it has also been determined that (1) planned stock/sales ratios of 4.8 can be used for each month except January, where a 14.0 ratio is anticipated, (2) planned retail reductions should be 15 percent for the first four months and 30 percent for the last two months and, (3) inventory of $87,500 needs to be on hand to start the spring season. Complete the following six-month merchandise budget for the Antique Shoppe.

SIX-MONTH MERCHANDISE BUDGET	Kinder Korner				Date	March 1	
					Season	Fall/Winter	

	AUG	SEPT	OCT	NOV	DEC	JAN	TOTAL
1. Planned BOM Stock							– – –
2. Planned Sales							
3. Planned Retail Reductions							
4. Planned EOM Stock							– – –
5. Planned Purchases @ Retail							
6. Planned Purchases @ Cost							
7. Planned Initial Markup							
8. Planned Gross Margin							
9. Planned BOM Stock/Sales Ratio							– – –
10. Planned Sales Percentage							
11. Planned Retail Reduction Percentage							

Planned Total Sales for the Period   _____

Planned Total Retail Reduction Percentage for the Period   _____

Planned Initial Markup Percentage   _____

Planned BOM Stock for February   _____

12. Complete the following six-month merchandise budget.

SIX-MONTH MERCHANDISE BUDGET	Bernhardt Department Store Dept. 353				Date March 1 Season Fall/Winter		
	AUG	SEPT	OCT	NOV	DEC	JAN	TOTAL
1. Planned BOM Stock	30,000	45,000	40,000	60,000	40,000	30,000	— — —
2. Planned Sales	15,000	15,000	20,000	20,000	20,000	10,000	100,000
3. Planned Retail Reductions	1,500	1,500	4,000	2,000	2,000	2,500	13,500
4. Planned EOM Stock							— — —
5. Planned Purchases @ Retail							
6. Planned Purchases @ Cost							
7. Planned Initial Markup							
8. Planned Gross Margin							
9. Planned BOM Stock/Sales Ratio	2	3	2	3	2	3	— — —
10. Planned Sales Percentage	15%	15%	20%	20%	20%	10%	100%
11. Planned Retail Reduction Percentage	10%	10%	20%	10%	10%	25%	13.5%

Planned Total Sales for the Period	$100,000
Planned Total Retail Reduction Percentage for the Period	13.5%
Planned Initial Markup Percentage	40%
Planned BOM Stock for February	$45,000

NOTE: All dollar signs have been deleted from the merchandise budget grid.
All dollar figures have been rounded to the nearest dollar.
All percentages have been rounded to the nearest tenth of a percent.

13. Complete the following six-month merchandise budget.

SIX-MONTH MERCHANDISE BUDGET	Shirley's Sport Haus					Date	March 1	
						Season	Fall/Winter	
	AUG	SEPT	OCT	NOV	DEC	JAN	TOTAL
1. Planned BOM Stock							— — —
2. Planned Sales							
3. Planned Retail Reductions							
4. Planned EOM Stock							— — —
5. Planned Purchases @ Retail							
6. Planned Purchases @ Cost							
7. Planned Initial Markup							
8. Planned Gross Margin							
9. Planned BOM Stock/Sales Ratio	2	3	3	4	3	2	— — —
10. Planned Sales Percentage	10%	10%	20%	20%	20%	20%	100%
11. Planned Retail Reduction Percentage	15%	15%	15%	15%	15%	15%	15%

Planned Total Sales for the Period $250,000

Planned Total Retail Reduction Percentage
for the Period   15%

Planned Initial Markup Percentage   30%

Planned BOM Stock for February $100,000

NOTE: All dollar signs have been deleted from the merchandise budget grid.
All dollar figures have been rounded to the nearest dollar.
All percentages have been rounded to the nearest tenth of a percent.

14. Complete the following six-month merchandise budget.

SIX-MONTH MERCHANDISE BUDGET	The Jewel Shop					Date	March 1	
						Season	Fall/Winter	
	AUG	SEPT	OCT	NOV	DEC	JAN	TOTAL
1. Planned BOM Stock							— — —
2. Planned Sales	20,000	20,000	20,000	30,000	60,000	50,000	200,000
3. Planned Retail Reductions							
4. Planned EOM Stock							— — —
5. Planned Purchases @ Retail							
6. Planned Purchases @ Cost							
7. Planned Initial Markup							
8. Planned Gross Margin							
9. Planned BOM Stock/Sales Ratio	3.0	3.0	3.2	3.4	3.8	3.5	— — —
10. Planned Sales Percentage	10%	10%	10%	15%	30%	25%	100%
11. Planned Retail Reduction Percentage	10%	10%	10%	10%	20%	25%	

Planned Total Sales for the Period   __ $200,000 __

Planned Total Retail Reduction Percentage
for the Period   _____

Planned Initial Markup Percentage   ____ 50% ____

Planned BOM Stock for February   __ $140,000 __

NOTE: All dollar signs have been deleted from the merchandise budget grid.
       All dollar figures have been rounded to the nearest dollar.
       All percentages have been rounded to the nearest tenth of a percent.

15. Kinder Korner in Modesto anticipates planned sales of $300,000 for the fall season based on a planned initial markup of 50 percent. Within the season, planned monthly sales are projected to be as follows: 20 percent in August, 17.5 percent in September, 12.5 percent in October, 20 percent in November and December, and 10 percent in January. To ensure a profitable season, past store records were consulted. The records indicated: (1) the stock/sales ratios need to be 3 for October and November; 2.5 for August, September, and December; and 3.5 for January; (2) reductions can be planned at 10 percent for the first four months, 20 percent for December, and 30 percent for January; and (3) an inventory of $150,000 is necessary to begin the spring season. Complete the six-month merchandise budget for Kinder Korner.

SIX-MONTH MERCHANDISE BUDGET	Antique Shoppe				Date: March 1	Season: Fall/Winter	
	AUG	SEPT	OCT	NOV	DEC	JAN	TOTAL
1. Planned BOM Stock							— — —
2. Planned Sales							
3. Planned Retail Reductions							
4. Planned EOM Stock							— — —
5. Planned Purchases @ Retail							
6. Planned Purchases @ Cost							
7. Planned Initial Markup							
8. Planned Gross Margin							
9. Planned BOM Stock/Sales Ratio							— — —
10. Planned Sales Percentage							
11. Planned Retail Reduction Percentage							

Planned Total Sales for the Period _____

Planned Total Retail Reduction Percentage for the Period _____

Planned Initial Markup Percentage _____

Planned BOM Stock for February _____

ENDNOTE

1. Patrick M. Dunne and Harry I. Wolk, "Marketing Cost Analysis: A Modularized Contribution Approach," *Journal of Marketing* (July 1977): 83–84.

10 Chapter

The Merchandise Buying and Handling Process

CHAPTER 10
The
Merchandise
Buying and
Handling
Process

OVERVIEW

This chapter explores the roles of various personnel involved in the merchandise selection process. Emphasis will be placed on planning and controlling the amount of merchandise purchased by the retailer. The selection of, and negotiations with, vendors will also be discussed, as well as security measures when handling merchandise. Finally, various merchandise performance measures will be evaluated.

Retailers often say that "goods well bought are half sold." This chapter will examine merchandise management, or the merchandise buying and handling process, and its effect on a store's performance.

Merchandise management is the analysis, planning, acquisition, handling, and control of the merchandise investments of a retail operation. *Analysis* is included in the definition because retailers must be able to correctly identify their customers before they can ascertain consumer desires and make a good buying decision. *Planning* is important, because merchandise to be sold in the future must be bought now. The term *acquisition* is used because the merchandise needs to be procured from others, either distributors or manufacturers. *Handling* involves seeing that the merchandise is where it is needed and in the proper condition to be sold.

Finally, *control* of the large dollar investments in inventory is important to ensure an adequate return on the retailer's merchandise investment.

No one in retailing can completely avoid contact with merchandising activities. Merchandising is the day-to-day business of all retailers. As inventory is sold, new stock needs to be purchased, displayed, and sold. Merchandising is the heartbeat of retailing. In fact, a retailer's investment in inventory is second only to building and equipment in terms of percentage of total dollars invested. Exhibit 10.1 dramatizes this point by showing that, on average, more than 25 percent of all retailers' assets are invested in inventory.

In 1986, more than 65 billion dollars were invested by United States retailers in inventory alone.[1] Retailers that manage this massive inventory investment will make substantial progress toward achieving their desired high-performance objectives. Now you know why business journals take such an interest in retail inventory levels as different seasons approach, especially Christmas. The Christmas season normally accounts for 30 to 40 percent of a department store's annual sales, and can be ruined by a lack of inventory. Conversely, the costs involved in carrying ex-

Exhibit 10.1

The Composition of Assets in Retailing

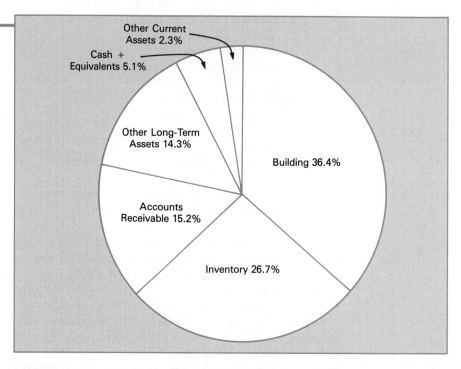

SOURCE: United States Census Bureau, *Quarterly Financial Report on Manufacturing, Mining, and Trading Companies,* (Washington, D.C.: U.S. Government Printing Office, 4th Quarter 1986).

cess inventory can result in a poor retail performance if the retailer is forced to take many markdowns.

In retailing, high-performance results are produced not just by investments in buildings and fixtures (though they help), but also by wise investments in inventory. Location and display do contribute to retail success, but merchandise must be available to produce a financial return.

MERCHANDISE MANAGEMENT PERSONNEL

The personnel responsible for performing the merchandise management function in a large retail department store chain are depicted in Exhibit 10.2. In most smaller, independent stores buying is not treated as a separate function. Instead, the owner or manager is usually in charge of buying and all other facets of the retail operation. Often, small retailers use **resident buying offices**, specialists who are in continuous contact with vendors and other retailers and thus are able to provide retailers with accurate and timely information about fashion trends, expected price changes, and product movement in regional market cities. Small retailers also rely on the assistance of manufacturer's sales reps who visit on a regular basis.

Although this chapter discusses the buying pattern of a large department store chain, buying patterns will vary a good deal among the department store chain, large supermarket chains, specialty apparel chains, convenience store chains, etc. However, to discuss all of these would be beyond the scope of our text.

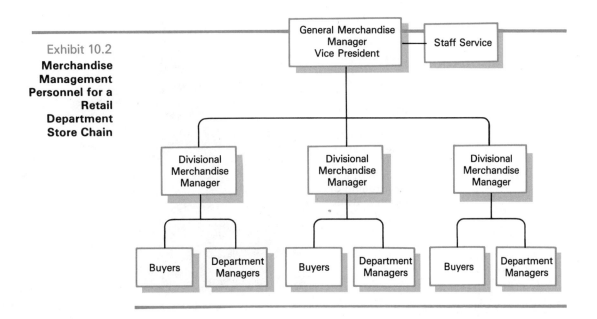

Exhibit 10.2

Merchandise Management Personnel for a Retail Department Store Chain

GENERAL MERCHANDISE MANAGER

In most large retail firms there is a **general merchandise manager (GMM)** who probably holds the rank of vice president. Because this executive has a high position in the organizational hierarchy, he or she does not get involved in many day-to-day merchandise management problems. Rather, the GMM is likely to be involved with quarterly, seasonal, or annual planning; budgeting; and the control of merchandising activities.

DIVISIONAL MERCHANDISE MANAGER

Reporting to the GMM are several **divisional merchandise managers (DMMs)**. These DMMs are responsible for particular lines of merchandise. For example, in a department store there may be DMMs for menswear, furniture, appliances, women's wear, china, children's, and so on.

Divisional merchandise managers, regardless of the retailer's size, have four basic duties:

1. Forecasting sales for the forthcoming budget period. This involves estimating consumer demand and the impact of changes in the retail environment. Charles Lazaurus, founder and CEO of

Illus. 10.1
Rather than becoming involved in the day-to-day merchandise management problems, the General Merchandise Manager is more likely to be involved with quarterly, seasonal, or annual planning, budgeting, and controlling of merchandising activities.

Toys 'R' Us Inc., is said to be one of the most successful forecasters in the business, "not because he guesses the winners right, but because he rarely guesses at all." He is quick to spot trends before others see them and to drop products before these trends play out.[2] Another highly successful DMM credited her success in the late 1980s to not letting her buyers load up on the same merchandise everybody else was getting (miniskirts and other youthful clothing). Her reasoning was that as American women were getting older, their figures no longer permitted them to wear such clothing, despite a desire to retain a youthful appearance. Successful retailers must base their decisions not on intuition, but on market research and information.

2.   Translating the sales forecast into dollar inventory levels. To do this effectively, the DMM needs to know what inventory levels are necessary to support the level of forecasted sales.

3.   Inspiring commitment and performance on the part of the buyers and department managers. The buyers need to procure the right types of merchandise and the DMM can assist by providing the buyer with lists of those vendors that must be seen and those that should be avoided. The DMM must also assist the department manager in moving the merchandise after it reaches the store.

4.   Assessing not only the merchandise performance, but also the buyer's performance, in order to provide control and maintain high-performance results. While most retail organizations have conducted detailed post-season performance evaluations of vendors and products for years, few have looked closely at buyers. There have always been some buyers who accepted kickbacks from vendors, but the practice was never widespread. With the recent surge of imports in the clothing industry, many retailers are changing their review process. In many foreign countries, kickbacks are a way of life.[3] Retail buyers today are exposed to temptations that may not have been present when the DMM was a buyer. So far, no major scandals have developed involving kickbacks to retail buyers.

BUYER

The buyer has three primary duties.[4] By doing them well the buyer can significantly contribute to overall store profitability. These three tasks are:

1.   To purchase merchandise that can be sold effectively to the target customers. To procure the merchandise, buyers must visit the marketplace to purchase goods in the colors, sizes, patterns, and assortments needed by their customers and to negotiate terms such as backup stock, guaranteed sales, distinctive products,

brands, product features, exclusivity, sales help, price maintenance, price protection against a drop in price by the supplier, special values, closeouts, advertising money, service arrangements,
credit, price, return privileges, markdown money, training of retail sales help, freight, and fixtures.[5]

2. To work with the divisional merchandise manager in arriving at
   dollar inventory levels. The buyer has considerable insight into
   the market and should share this insight with the DMM.
3. To convert the dollar inventory plans into unit plans. Specifically,
   the buyer needs to decide what mix of merchandise to procure
   with the dollars that have been allocated.

DEPARTMENT MANAGER

The final players in the merchandise management process are the department managers. They are responsible for certain merchandise lines on the
selling floor, and they have five central tasks:

1. To work with the buyer on the unit inventory plan, especially regarding merchandise assortments. Since department managers
   are closer to the customer than buyers are, they should have a better feel for what types of merchandise will sell well.
2. To lead, motivate, and guide the sales personnel. The sales personnel need to know their merchandise and how to present and sell it
   to the customer.

Illus. 10.2
**One of the
responsibilities
of the
department
manager is to
monitor
changing
customer tastes.**

3. To monitor changing consumer tastes and wants for the merchandise lines being sold. On a recurring basis, the department manager needs to examine what the customer wants.
4. To make certain that customers are properly served. Customer complaints, suggestions, questions, or praise must be properly handled.
5. To work with the store's display staff so that the department's displays are coordinated with the merchandising plans.

If the department manager does a good job of performing these tasks, the retailer will be better able to achieve good merchandise management.

MERCHANDISE SUPPORT STAFF

The merchandise management personnel will often require special assistance in performing their tasks. In a small retail organization they often have to do without it. This may even be the case in some large retail organizations. However, in an increasing number of large retail organizations, staff personnel and resident buying offices are available to facilitate the merchandise management cycle. They generally provide six types of services.

1. **Comparative data services** offer merchandise managers, buyers, and department managers comparisons of other stores' offerings in their respective trade area. The most frequent comparisons are for price, service, style, quality, and assortment.
2. **Consumer research services** offer tailored research based on consumer responses or behavior patterns. Such research includes trading area delineation studies, store image studies, competitive store ratings, and segmentation research.
3. **Fashion research and analysis services** can help coordinate buying and selling efforts by providing seasonal fashion forecasts, techniques for identifying dead fashions early, advice on fashion portrayal in advertising and display, and direction for the development of fashion shows for customers.
4. **Sales and inventory analysis services** typically are provided by the accounting or controller's office and provide timely information on product movement, markdowns, returns and allowances, and gross margins. This information is crucial in determining whether merchandising objectives are being achieved. Some stores have moved this data out of accounting and onto the buyers' personal computers. This allows buyers to develop their own product movement reports.
5. **Product testing services** are provided in some of the largest retail chains. This service allows the buyer to assess the performance of a product before making a commitment for more substantial pur-

chases. This service helps to ensure that the customers are receiving the best merchandise for their dollars.

6. **Training services** allow for the training of new merchandise management personnel (assistant buyers and assistant department managers). There is also continuing education for existing personnel, to prepare them for more responsible positions within the merchandise management cycle.

Not all retailers provide all these services to their buyers, but the underlying principle, that merchandise management needs specialized services in many areas, cannot be ignored.

PLANNING AND CONTROL

Merchandise management revolves around planning and control. Because it takes time to buy merchandise, have it delivered, record the delivery in company records, and properly display the merchandise, it is essential to plan. Merchandise managers need to decide what their stock requirements will be several weeks, months, merchandising seasons, or even a year in advance.

Control must be exercised over the merchandise dollars or units that the retailer plans on purchasing. A good control system is vital if the retailer is to obtain high-performance results. The remainder of this chapter will discuss the various decisions facing the merchandise manager: the dollar amount of inventory needed for stock requirements, the dollar amount available to be spent, the unit or type of goods to be purchased, choosing and evaluating merchandise sources, handling vendor negotiations, handling the merchandise in the store, and evaluating merchandise performance.

DOLLAR MERCHANDISE PLANNING

Although divisional merchandise managers may get input from buyers and department managers, they alone are ultimately responsible for the dollar planning of merchandise requirements. The sales forecast is the first step in determining inventory needs. Once the sales forecast has been made, DMMs can use any one of four different methods for planning dollars invested in stock: basic stock, percentage variation, week's supply, or stock/sales ratio.

The same basic principles apply to retailers who sell physical goods and to service retailers with one exception. Goods are first produced, then sold, then consumed. Services are first sold, then produced and consumed simultaneously.[6] Thus, service retailers cannot stockpile their inventories in anticipation of future demand. Still, service retailers must be able to forecast demand and make preparations, most likely with regard to personnel, to satisfy that demand.

BASIC STOCK METHOD

The **basic stock method** (BSM) of dollar merchandise planning, is used when retailers believe that it is necessary to have a given level of inventory available at all times. It gets its name because it requires the retailer always to have a base level of inventory investment regardless of the predicted sales volume. In addition to the base stock level, there is a variable amount of inventory that will increase or decrease at the beginning of each sales period (one month in our example) by the same dollar amount that the period's sales are expected to increase or decrease. The BSM can be calculated as follows:

Average monthly sales = total planned sales for the season/
for the season   number of months in the season

Average stock for the = total planned sales for the season/
season   estimated inventory turnover rate
                      for the season

Basic stock = average stock for the season − average
              monthly sales for the season

BOM stock = planned monthly sales + basic stock

To illustrate the basic stock method, let's look again at the planned sales for Two-Seasons Department Store's Department 353, shown in Exhibit 9.2. Assume that the inventory turnover rate for the season, or the number of times the average inventory is sold, is 2.0.

Average monthly sales for
the season   = Total sales/number of months
                          = $500,000/6 = $83,333

Average stock for the = Total sales/inventory turnover
season   = $500,000/2 = $250,000

Basic stock = Average stock − average monthly sales
            = $250,000 − $83,333 = $166,667

BOM (Feb) = Planned monthly sales + basic stock
          = $75,000 + 166,667 = $241,667

BOM (Mar) = $75,000 + 166,667 = $241,667

BOM (Apr) = $100,000 + 166,667 = $266,667

$$\text{BOM (May)} = \$50,000 + 166,667 = \$216,667$$

$$\text{BOM (June)} = \$125,000 + 166,667 = \$291,667$$

$$\text{BOM (July)} = \$75,000 + 166,667 = \$241,667$$

As you can see, $166,667 of basic stock is added to each month's planned sales to arrive at the BOM stock. When actual sales exceed or fall short of planned sales for the month, the retailer can easily bring the next month's BOM inventory back in line by buying more or less stock.

The basic stock method of planning dollar inventory levels fails to perform adequately when the turnover is greater than once every two months. In that situation, the basic stock level calculation for each month would be negative. Thus, when inventory turnover is greater than three times per season, or six times per year, another method of planning dollar inventory levels should be used.

PERCENTAGE VARIATION METHOD

A second method for determining planned stock levels is the **percentage variation method (PVM)**. This method is used when the retailer doesn't desire to have a given level of inventory available at all times, but does face fluctuations in sales. It assumes that the percentage fluctuations in monthly stock from average stock should be half as great as the percentage fluctuations in monthly sales from average sales.

BOM stock = Average stock for season $\times$ ½ [1+(Planned sales for the month/Average monthly sales)]

Since PVM utilizes the same components as BSM, we can use the data from the previous example.

$$\text{BOM (Feb)} = \$250,000 \times \tfrac{1}{2}[1+(\ \$75,000/83,333)] = \$237,500$$
$$\text{BOM (Mar)} = \$250,000 \times \tfrac{1}{2}[1+(\ \$75,000/83,333)] = \$237,500$$
$$\text{BOM (Apr)} = \$250,000 \times \tfrac{1}{2}[1+(\$100,000/83,333)] = \$275,000$$
$$\text{BOM (May)} = \$250,000 \times \tfrac{1}{2}[1+(\ \$50,000/83,333)] = \$200,000$$
$$\text{BOM (Jun)} = \$250,000 \times \tfrac{1}{2}[1+(\$125,000/83,333)] = \$312,500$$
$$\text{BOM (Jul)} = \$250,000 \times \tfrac{1}{2}[1+(\ \$75,000/83,333)] = \$237,500$$

A seasonal turnover rate of 2.0 is equal to an annual turnover rate of 4.0. When the annual turnover rate is 6, PVM and BSM will produce the same results. When the turnover is less than 6, PVM will have a greater fluctuation, and when turnover is higher than 6, PVM will fluctuate less. Thus, PVM should be used when the annual turnover rate is greater than 6.0, and BSM should be used when the annual turnover rate is less than 6.0.

WEEKS' SUPPLY METHOD

A third method for planning inventory levels is the **weeks' supply method (WSM)**. The WSM formula is used by retailers such as grocers, who plan inventories on a weekly, not monthly, basis and whose sales do not fluctuate substantially. WSM states that the inventory level should be set equal to a predetermined number of weeks' supply. The predetermined number of weeks' supply is directly related to the stock turnover rate desired. In WSM, the stock level in dollars varies proportionally with forecasted sales. If forecasted sales triple, inventory in dollars will also triple.

To illustrate WSM, return to our earlier problem and use the following formulas:

Number of weeks to be stocked = the number of weeks in the period/ stock turnover rate for the period

Average weekly sales = estimated total sales for the period/ the number of weeks in the period

BOM Stock = average weekly sales x number of weeks to be stocked

Thus,
Number of weeks to be stocked = 26/2 = 13
Average weekly sales = $500,000/26 = $19,231
BOM Stock = $19,231 × 13 = $250,000

Having determined the number of weeks' supply to be stocked (13) and the average weekly sales ($19,231), stock levels can be replenished on a frequent or regular basis to guard against stockouts. The major problem with this method is that during weeks in which there is a below-average turnover, there will be a buildup of inventory, which will increase costs. Therefore, unless a business is marked by stable sales and a stable turnover, use of this method is not advisable.

STOCK-TO-SALES METHOD

The final method for planning inventory levels, and the one used in Chapter 9, is the **stock-to-sales method (SSM)**. This method is very easy to use but requires the retailer to have a beginning-of-the-month stock/sales ratio. This ratio tells the retailer how much inventory is needed at the beginning of the month to support that month's estimated sales. A ratio of 2.5, for example, would tell retailers that they should have 2½ times that month's expected sales on hand in inventory at the beginning of the month.

Stock/sales ratios can be obtained from internal or external sources. The statistics can be obtained internally if the retailer has a good accounting system and has stored historical data so that it can be readily retrieved. Externally, the retailer can often get the data from retail trade associations such as the National Retail Merchants Association or the Menswear Retailers Association. These and other trade associations collect stock/sales ratios from participating merchants and then compile, tabulate, and report them in special management reports or trade publications. Exhibit 10.3 is an example of beginning-of-the-month stock/sales ratios that the National Retail Merchants Association releases to the department store industry.

Inventory turnover is a key factor in a retailer's financial performance. Planned, average, beginning-of-the-month stock/sales goals can be easily calculated using turnover goals. If you divide the number of months in the season by the desired inventory turnover rate, an average BOM stock/sales ratio for the season can be computed. For example, if you desired an inventory turnover rate of 1.8 for the upcoming six-month season (3.6 annually), your average BOM stock/sales ratio would be 3.3 (6 divided by 1.8 = 3.3).

DOLLAR MERCHANDISE CONTROL

Once the dollar amount of inventory needed at the beginning of each month or season is planned by the merchandise manager, it is essential that the buyer not make commitments for merchandise that would exceed the dollar plan. In short, the dollars planned for merchandise need to be controlled. This control is accomplished through a technique called open-to-buy. The **open-to-buy (OTB)** represents the dollar amount currently

Exhibit 10.3

Beginning-of-the-Month Stock/Sales Ratios for Stores

Store Volume (millions $)	Feb	Mar	Apr	May	Jun	Jul	Aug	Sept	Oct	Nov	Dec	Jan
Department Stores												
2-10	6.48	5.51	6.00	6.87	5.86	6.57	6.51	5.48	6.65	5.12	3.07	7.22
10-50	5.31	4.19	4.76	5.03	4.04	4.88	5.11	4.31	5.30	4.79	2.40	5.84
Specialty Stores	7.11	7.69	7.11	6.66	6.97	8.71	7.27	6.04	7.12	6.26	3.86	7.01

SOURCE: National Retail Merchants Association, *Department Store and Specialty Store Merchandising and Operating Results of 1987,* New York: Financial Executives Division, National Retail Merchants Association, 1988, p. xxix and xxx. Reprinted by permission of the National Retail Merchants Association.

available to a buyer to spend on merchandise without exceeding planned dollar stocks. When planning for any given month (or season) the buyer will not necessarily be able to purchase a dollar amount equal to the planned dollar stocks for that month (or season). This is the case because there may be some inventory already on hand or on order but not yet delivered. Let's see how to compute open-to-buy for an upcoming month; open-to-buy is computed in the following manner:

1. End-of-month planned retail stock
2. Plus planned sales for month
3. Plus planned reductions for the month
4. Minus stock on hand at retail
5. Equals planned purchases at retail
6. Minus commitments at retail for current delivery
7. Equals open-to-buy at retail

If the merchandise manager or buyer in Department 353 for the Two-Seasons Department Store had merchandise on order but not yet received of $15,000 retail on February 1, 199x, the open-to-buy for the month would be $142,500 at retail.

1.	EOM planned retail stock	$300,000
2.	Plus planned sales for February	75,000
3.	Plus planned reductions for February	7,500
4.	Minus BOM stock	225,000
5.	Equals planned purchases at retail	157,500
6.	Minus commitments at retail for current delivery	15,000
7.	Equals open-to-buy	$142,500

The OTB figure should not be thought of as a fixed quantity that cannot be exceeded. Consumer needs are more important. If sales of a product line, department, or store exceed planned sales, quantities should be ordered in addition to those scheduled for purchase on the merchandise budget. This should not, however, be a common occurrence. Buyers must get permission from their divisional merchandise manager to purchase additional inventory of fast-moving merchandise. If this happens too often, the sales planning process is wrong. Either the buyers are too conservative in estimating sales or they are buying the wrong merchandise. In any case, management should always determine the causes of OTB adjustments. Some common buying errors include:

1. Buying merchandise that is priced too high or too low for the store's target market.
2. Buying the wrong classification or product line.
3. Having too much basic stock on hand.
4. Buying from too many vendors.

5. Failing to identify the season's hot items early enough in the season.
6. Failing to let the vendor assist the buyer by adding new items and/or new colors to the mix. Too often, an original order is repeated without careful analysis, resulting in a limited selection.

Merchandise planning is a dynamic process subject to many changes. Consider the implications of the following to planning stock levels: a) sales for the previous month lower or higher than planned, b) reductions higher or lower than planned, and c) shipments of merchandise delayed in transit.

UNIT STOCK PLANNING

The dollar merchandise plan is only the starting point in merchandise management. Once the merchandise manager has decided how many dollars can be invested in inventory, the dollar plan needs to be converted into a unit plan. It's not dollars that are sold, but items. The assortment of items that will comprise the merchandise mix must be planned.[7]

Designing the optimal merchandise mix is a complex process for which there exists no standard solution. The final mix will be determined by a combination of creative and analytical thought processes. Consider, for example, a grocery store manager attempting to allocate $250,000 in inventory dollars among 8,000 to 10,000 individual items. On a strict analytical basis, the manager might try to allocate the $250,000 to the thousands of possible items in order to maximize the combined contribution of all the items to total store overhead and profits. But without knowledge of the demand functions for each item, the preceding task could not be accomplished using only analytical techniques. Thus, creative thought processes must accompany analytical thinking in attempting to design the optimal merchandise mix.

WHO WILL PLAN?

The unit plan should be developed with the input of several parties. The divisional merchandise manager sets dollar limits for the plan, but the buyer and department manager will do most of the detail work. The buyer knows what merchandise is available from competing vendors. The department manager is closest to the consumer. An optimal merchandise mix cannot be developed unless these three parties cooperate and share their knowledge and insights. Of course, in the small, one- or two-person store, the unit plan is developed by probably only one individual. That person will need to question his or her own decisions, since others will not be on hand to check the consistency of logic and the assessment of supply and demand.

OPTIMAL MERCHANDISE MIX

Exhibit 10.4 shows the three dimensions of the optimal mix: variety, breadth, and depth. Each of these dimensions needs to be defined; however, we need first to define merchandise line. A **merchandise line** consists of a group of products that are closely related because they are intended for the same end use (televisions); are sold to the same customer group (junior miss womens' wear); or fall within a given price range (budget womens' wear).

Variety.   The **variety** of the merchandise mix refers to the number of different lines the retailer stocks in the store. For example, department stores have a great variety of merchandise lines. Some have more than 100 departments, carrying such lines as menswear, women's wear, children's clothing, infants, toys, sporting goods, appliances, cosmetics, and

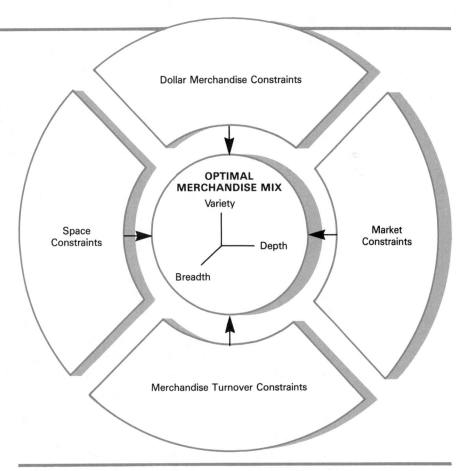

Exhibit 10.4
Dimensions of and Constraints on Optimal Merchandise Mix

Dollar Merchandise Constraints

OPTIMAL MERCHANDISE MIX
Variety
Depth
Breadth

Space Constraints

Market Constraints

Merchandise Turnover Constraints

household goods. One the other hand, Foot Locker, a specialty chain, carries only one basic merchandise line—athletic shoes.

Breadth.   **Breadth**, also called **assortment**, refers to the number of merchandise brands in the merchandise line. For example, a supermarket will have a great amount of breadth, or assortment, in the number of different brands of mustard that it carries: six or seven national or regional brands, a private brand, and a generic brand.[8] A 7-Eleven convenience store, however, will offer very little breadth. It will generally carry only one or two brand(s) in any merchandise line.

Depth.   Merchandise **depth** refers to the average number of SKUs (stock-keeping units) within each brand of the merchandise line. For instance, the supermarket manager must decide on which sizes and types of French's mustard to carry. The convenience store will probably only carry a 9-ounce jar of French's.

CONSTRAINING FACTORS

With these definitions in mind, look again at Exhibit 10.4 to identify the four constraining factors that influence design of the merchandise mix.

Dollar Constraint.   The dollars available for investment in inventory can be expended to increase merchandise variety, depth, breadth, or some combination thereof. Seldom will there be enough dollars to emphasize all three dimensions. If the decision is made to emphasize variety, it would be unrealistic to also expect a lot of breadth and depth.

For instance, assume you are the owner/manager of a local gift store. You have $30,000 to invest in merchandise. If you decide that you want a lot of variety in gifts (jewelry, crystal, candles, games, cards, figurines, ashtrays, clocks, and radios) then you obviously could not have much depth in any single item, such as crystal.

Space Constraint.   The retailer must also deal with space constraints. Depth, breadth, and variety all require space. If variety is to be stressed, it is also important to have enough empty space to separate the distinct merchandise lines. For example, consider a long counter containing cosmetics, candy, fishing tackle, women's stockings, and toys. This would obviously be an unslightly and unwise arrangement. As more variety is added, empty space is necessary to allow the consumer to clearly distinguish among distinct product lines.

Turnover Constraint.   As depth is increased, the retailer will be stocking more and more variations on the product to serve smaller and smaller segments. Consequently, inventory turnover will decrease and the chances of being stocked out will increase. It is important to think about how various merchandise mixes affect inventory turnover.

Market Constraints.   Market constraints also affect decisions about the variety, breadth, and depth of the merchandise mix. These three dimensions of the merchandise mix have a profound effect on how the consumer perceives the store, and what kinds of consumers the store will attract. The consumer perceives a specialty store as one with limited variety and breadth in terms of merchandise lines but considerable depth within the lines handled. An individual searching for depth in a limited set of merchandise lines such as formal menswear will thus be attracted to a menswear retailer specializing in formal wear. On the other hand, the consumer perceives general merchandise retailers like Penney's or Sears as having lots of variety and breadth in terms of merchandise lines, but less depth. Someone who needs to make several purchases across several merchandise lines, and who is willing to sacrifice depth of assortment, would be more attracted to the general merchandise retailer.

Comment.   The constraining factors make it almost impossible for a retailer to emphasize all three dimensions. Even Marshall Fields' flagship store in downtown Chicago, with more than 2 million square feet and more than $50 million in inventory, is not able to offer the broad and deep assortments within certain merchandise lines (e.g., jewelry, luggage) that some specialty stores are able to offer. Recently, Marshall Fields closed out all its furniture departments. Saks Fifth Avenue carries nothing but clothing. These retailers learned that they cannot be all things to all people and instead have decided to concentrate on areas of merchandising where they can provide adequate coverage. Some customers will walk out of a store empty-handed because a store doesn't have what they want or can afford. No retailer can avoid this completely. However, if a store is going to lose customers, it is better to lose the less profitable ones by properly mixing merchandise in terms of variety, breadth, and depth within given dollar, space, turnover, and market constraints.

Nowhere is this problem more evident than in the supermarket industry. In an industry where the average retailer stocks 22,000 to 25,000 SKUs, the supply of new products vs. the capability of the store to handle them poses many problems. In 1987, 7,866 new food products and 2,316 nonfood items were introduced to the supermarket trade. One study reported that the average chain buyer would give fewer than 40 percent of these new offerings a five-month trial period. Existing products have to be dropped to make way for the new items. The reasons cited for deciding which items got a five-month trial were, in order of importance, introductory terms, including ad/display allowances and discounts; consumer ad plans; consumer promotions; and perceived consumer demand.[9]

MODEL STOCK PLAN

After a retailer has determined what emphasis to place on the three dimensions of the merchandise mix, the next task is to decide what merchandise lines and items to stock. This can be an overwhelming task for

Illus. 10.3
Saks Fifth Avenue carries nothing but clothing, having learned that they enjoy greater success by providing adequate coverage in a limited area of merchandising.

the novice; it is time consuming and often frustrating for even an experienced retailer. Units are planned using a model stock plan. The **model stock plan** gives precise items and quantities that should be on hand for each merchandise line. A model stock plan needs to be compiled for each line of merchandise.

Exhibit 10.5 shows part of a hypothetical menswear retailer's unit plan for men's shirts. The retailer has already formulated a dollar plan and has allocated $25,000 at retail for men's shirts. Since the average retail price of a shirt for the store is $25, 1,000 shirts will need to be stocked. The model unit plan will reveal how many shirts of each kind the retailer should keep in stock. The exhibit shows the breakdown only within one attribute (casual shirts), but the same procedure would be followed for all types.

The first thing the menswear retailer should do is attempt to identify what attributes the customer considers in purchasing shirts. Exhibit 10.5 shows that the retailer has identified six attributes: (1) type of shirt (dress, casual, sport, or work), (2) size, (3) sleeve length, (4) collar type, (5) color, and (6) fabric. Are any key attributes left out? What about price? If customers shop for shirts by price, then price should also be a product attribute.

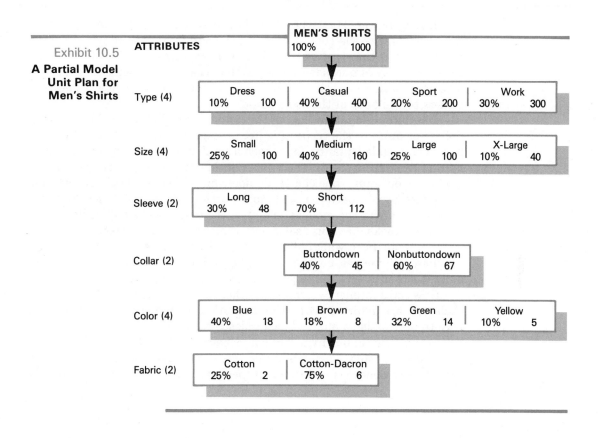

Exhibit 10.5

A Partial Model Unit Plan for Men's Shirts

ATTRIBUTES	MEN'S SHIRTS
	100% 1000

Type (4)

Dress	Casual	Sport	Work
10% 100	40% 400	20% 200	30% 300

Size (4)

Small	Medium	Large	X-Large
25% 100	40% 160	25% 100	10% 40

Sleeve (2)

Long	Short
30% 48	70% 112

Collar (2)

Buttondown	Nonbuttondown
40% 45	60% 67

Color (4)

Blue	Brown	Green	Yellow
40% 18	18% 8	32% 14	10% 5

Fabric (2)

Cotton	Cotton-Dacron
25% 2	75% 6

The second step is to identify the number of levels under each attribute. The retailer in Exhibit 10.5 has selected four types of shirts, four sizes, two sleeve lengths, two collar types, four colors, and two fabrics to stock.

An important fact is that stocking requirements grow explosively as more product attributes and expanded levels are offered for each attribute. If the retailer offers four shirt types, four sizes in each type, two sleeve lengths, two collar styles, four colors, and two fabrics, it will have to stock 512 shirts ($4 \times 4 \times 2 \times 2 \times 4 \times 2$) just to stock one unit of each. More importantly, if the retailer now decides to offer two prices in each category instead of one, the stocking requirements double to 1,024 items. But this example assumes that only 1,000 shirts can be stocked. Obviously the retailer has a problem if it wants to feature six or seven attributes and several levels on each attribute.

The preceding discussion illustrates the ever-present trade-off in merchandise management. As more attributes are featured, the probability is increased that a product on hand will match the customer's needs and purchasing power. However, there is a cost associated with increasing this probability—the cost of carrying the additional inventory. At some point, the carrying cost of the additional inventory required to increase the probability of purchase is greater than the profit obtained from those additional unit sales. Ultimately, every retailer has to allow some customers to walk out of the store empty-handed.

The third step in developing the model stock plan is to allocate total dollars or units to the respective item categories. If the model unit plan has recommended quantities for each item that are in direct proportion to market demand patterns, there is an optimum allocation. If the plan reflects this optimum, one can easily determine whether the stocks are out of balance by comparing actual stocks with model stocks. The closer actual stocks are to the model stock plan, the more stocks will be balanced. Balanced stocks maximize sales potential. Stocks that are out of balance cause customers to walk out of the store without the item they came to purchase. Worse yet, customers might walk out with a product not well suited to their needs, hurting the retailer's long-run business.

How can a retailer determine whether the recommended quantities for each item are in direct proportion to market demand patterns? The best way to do this is to analyze past sales records. Exhibit 10.6 shows the sales experience of our hypothetical menswear retailer in reference to the last 500 shirts sold. This exhibit, derived from past sales records, shows the demand density for different types and sizes of shirts. This simple

Exhibit 10.6

A Sales Analysis of Men's Shirts

TYPE	Small	Medium	Large	X-Large
Dress	XX	XXXX	XXX	X
Casual	XXXX XXXX XX	XXXX XXXX XXXX XXXX	XXXX XXXX XX	XXXX
Sport	XXXX X	XXXX XXXX X	XXXX X	X
Work	XXXX XXXX	XXXX XXXX XXX	XXXX XXX	XXXX

KEY: Each X = 5 Shirts

analysis forms the basis of planning unit stocks in the model plan. Changing the data in Exhibit 10.6 to percentage form, we can see that 10 percent of shirt sales were dress; 40 percent, casual; 20 percent, sport; and 30 percent, work. Furthermore, of the casual shirts, 25 percent were small; 40 percent, medium; 25 percent, large; and 10 percent, extra large. The percentages derived from such a sales analysis can be used in the model stock plan (Exhibit 10.5). Thus, in this example, of the 1,000 shirts the retailer plans to stock, 100 will be dress; 400, casual; 200, sport; and 300, work. These numbers are obtained by multiplying the 1,000 shirts by the percentage obtained in the sales analysis. In the past, 10 percent of the shirts sold were dress shirts, so the retailer will plan to stock 100 dress shirts, which is 10 percent of 1,000. How many shirts to stock in each size, sleeve length, collar type, color, and fabric is determined the same way.

One should not always allow past sales results to determine future stocking patterns. In the past, quantities not in proportion to demand patterns may have been stocked and perhaps sold—but probably at a loss. Pure sales statistics will not reveal this. In addition, new products that come into the market may feature attributes previously not stocked, and the demand for these may be so great that the item must be stocked in order to compete. Strict analysis of past statistics cannot dictate a model stock plan. Insight and creative power must also be applied. Retailing in Action 10-1 provides an insight into the process the retail buyer goes through in merchandise selection.

RETAILING IN ACTION   **10-1**

The Retail Buyers' "Black Box" Process

A study was recently conducted to compare the way senior buyers evaluated the saleability of an apparel product (a basic misses' blouse) to the way assistant buyers from the same store and retailing undergraduates did the task.

Each participant was given a case that described a blouse having eight cues, each representing information which might be used by retail buyers in evaluating saleability. The first five cues represented qualitative information, reflecting product characteristics: (1) fiber content; (2) cut; (3) color; (4) brand and (5) country of origin. The remaining cues represented quantitative information: (6) markup; (7) selling history; and (8) promotional strategy. In addition each buyer was provided the following background information:

a. Consumer confidence is relatively high. The inflation rate is 4 percent. Your open-to-buy is 4 percent higher than last year's.

b. No major new competitors are scheduled to open stores in your trading area this season.

c. The vendor is reputable. Delivery is good, and the terms of sale are 8/10 E.O.M.

d. Conditions within the store are identical to last year's. Department location, square footage, fixtures, and promotional plans have not changed.

In evaluating saleability, all three groups considered quantitative information to be more important than qualitative information. All three groups found selling history to be most important, but senior buyers placed greater emphasis on this cue than either the assistant buyers or the students. Senior buyers also differed in their use of markup and advertising allowance.

The senior buyers were more likely to include markup. Two possible explanations are: (a) senior buyers may be more sensitive to the importance of pricing strategies, since they are generally judged by the profitability of their departments and (b) the relationship between markup and merchandise saleability is too complex for inexperienced decision makers. This may also account for why the assistant buyers, with some experience, were more sensitive to markup than the students.

The senior buyers were also less likely to include advertising allowance in their evaluations. Maybe experience has taught them that sales promotions, no matter how extensive, are unlikely to influence saleability unless demand for the merchandise already exists.

The final finding was that senior retail buyers evaluate the saleability of merchandise more systematically than their less-experienced counterparts.

Source: The above is based on Richard Ettenson and Janet Wagner, "Retail Buyers' Saleability Judgements: A Comparison of Information Use Across Three Levels of Experience," *Journal of Retailing* (Spring 1986): 41-63.

So far, we have ignored the problems of individuals opening their first store. These individuals have no past sales records to rely on. Should they use only gut feelings and creativity in developing a model stock plan? Certainly not! New retailers should consult trade or other external sources about consumer purchasing patterns. For example, in the food industry, the Towne-Oller Index measures the actual sales and sales rank of each product, and shows the number of different products needed to meet the demand of a certain percentage of the buying public for that particular product line. For instance, if a retailer's goal is to meet 80 percent of the demand preferences for mouthwash, the four leading brands would need to be stocked.

CONFLICTS IN UNIT STOCK PLANNING

Unit stock planning involves compromise and conflict. The conflict which is multidimensional is due to the fact that not everything can be stocked. The dimensions of conflict are presented in Exhibit 10.7. The conflicts are summarized below.

1. Maintain a strong in-stock position on new items while avoiding the 90 percent of new products that fail in the introductory stage. The retailer wants to stock those new products that customers will be satisfied with. If the consumer is sold a poor product, it hurts the retailer as much as the manufacturer. The challenge is to screen out poor products before they reach the customer. Any screening device, however, has error; sometimes losers will be stocked and winners will be turned down. Because of this basic conflict, even the best of buyers will make a mistake sometimes and be forced to use markdowns.

2. Maintain an adequate stock of the basic popular items while having sufficient inventory dollars to capitalize on unforeseen opportunities. Sometimes, if the model stock is filled out with recommended quantities, there is little if any money available for the super buy that may present itself. If some money is held in reserve and basic stock is cut back, customers may be lost, or that super buy may never surface.

3. Maintain high merchandise turnover goals while maintaining high margin goals. This is perhaps the most obvious conflict. Almost always, items that turn over more rapidly have smaller

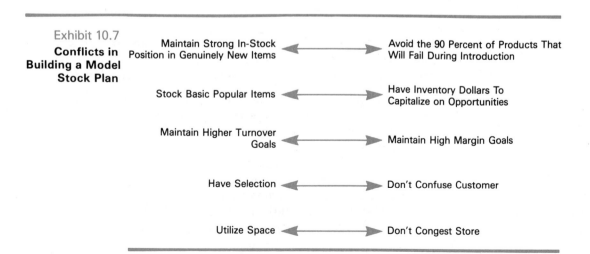

Exhibit 10.7
Conflicts in Building a Model Stock Plan

Maintain Strong In-Stock Position in Genuinely New Items ⟷ Avoid the 90 Percent of Products That Will Fail During Introduction

Stock Basic Popular Items ⟷ Have Inventory Dollars To Capitalize on Opportunities

Maintain Higher Turnover Goals ⟷ Maintain High Margin Goals

Have Selection ⟷ Don't Confuse Customer

Utilize Space ⟷ Don't Congest Store

profit margins. Trying to build a unit plan that will accomplish both objectives will surely be frustrating.

4.   Maintain adequate selection for customers without confusing them. If customers are confronted with too many close alternatives, they may not be able to make up their minds and may leave the store empty-handed and frustrated. The customer will also leave the store empty-handed if the selection is inadequate. A delicate balance needs to be struck between too little and too much selection.

5.   Maintain space productivity and utilization without congesting the store. Take advantage of buys that will utilize the available space, but avoid buys that cause the merchandise to spill over into the aisles. Unfortunately, some of the best buys come along when space is already occupied.

It should be evident at this point that unit stock planning is no easy task.

SELECTION OF MERCHANDISING SOURCES

After deciding on the type and amount of inventory to be purchased, the next step is to determine the source. Many people have misconceptions about how retailers choose and negotiate with vendors. Many people perceive the job of a retail buyer as glamorous. Many people say, "I'd love to be a buyer. After all, I have been told I have good taste and I love to travel." But buying isn't that simple. With the proper planning and control, it can be very rewarding, especially when your customers react positively to your merchandise selection. However, no matter how rewarding buying experience is, it is also grueling. A buyer not only determines what merchandise lines to carry, but must select the best possible vendor to supply these items and then negotiate the best deal possible with that vendor.

When selecting a merchandise source, the merchandise manager must consider many criteria. While one study lists 27 possible retailer supply criteria,[10] the following six criteria should always be considered:

1.   the target market's desire for the product. Resaleability of the merchandise should be the primary consideration for the buyer.
2.   the product's or company's reputation.
3.   the vendor's reputation.
4.   the reliability and rapidness of delivery.
5.   whether the product is manufactured in the United States. More logistical problems occur with imports.
6.   whether a seasonal buying discount (a discount for buying merchandise out of its normal season) is available.

One of a retailer's greatest assets when dealing with a vendor is past experience with that vendor. Whether you are a small retailer doing all the

Illus. 10.4
A merchandise manager must select the best possible vendor to supply the desired items and then must negotiate the best deal possible with that vendor.

buying yourself or a new buyer for a large chain, you should always go to market with two important resources: the vendor profitability analysis statement and the confidential vendor analysis. The **vendor profitablity analysis statement** (see Exhibit 10.8) is a record of all purchases the retailer made from a particular vendor last year, the discount granted by the vendor, transportation charges paid, the original markup, markdowns, and the season-ending gross margin on that vendor's merchandise. The **confidential vendor analysis** (see Exhibit 10.9) lists the same companies as the profitability analysis statement but also provides a three-year financial summary with the names, titles, and negotiating points of all the vendors' sales staff. This last information is based on the notes the buyer made after the previous season's buying trip.

After selecting vendors, the retailer must decide on the specific merchandise to be bought. Some products, such as the basic items for the particular department in question, are easy to purchase. Other products, especially new items, require more careful planning and consideration. Retailers should concern themselves with several key questions, such as:

1. Where does this product fit into the strategic position that I have staked out for my department within my firm?
2. Will I have an exclusive with this product or will I be in competition with nearby retailers?
3. What is the estimated demand for this product in my target market?

Exhibit 10.8
Two-Seasons Vendor Profitability Analysis Period Ending 01/03/9X Dept. 135

Vendor Name	Purchases		Discount and Anticipation %	Freight %	Markup % Landed Loaded	Markdown		Gross Margin Percentage	Vendor No.
	Cost	Retail				$	%		
Anderson Sports	62,481	129,861	7.1	1.4	50.7	20,211	15.6	46.2	273359
Jack Frost, Inc.	26,921	53,962	8.0	1.3	49.4	3,233	6.0	50.5	818922
Sue's Fashions	25,572	51,930	8.1	1.8	49.9	6,667	12.8	47.1	206284
Jana Kantor Asso.	14,022	29,434	8.0	.8	52.0	481	1.6	55.1	050187
Pierce Mills	12,761	25,438	9.5	1.7	49.8	7,858	30.9	33.1	132886
Ray, Inc.	2,196	4,416	8.0	1.8	49.4	754	17.1	43.8	148296
Dusty's Place	2,071	4,332	8.0	1.3	51.6			55.4	662411
Lady Carole	1,050	2,100	8.0	2.1	48.9			52.9	676841
Jill Petites	740	1,584	10.4	.5	54.2	640	40.5	29.2	472977
Andrea's	198	410	8.0	.8	51.1			55.0	527218

Cost: your cost
Retail: your original selling price
Discount and anticipation %: discount received for early payments
Freight %: your shipping expenses
Markup % Landed Loaded: [Retail selling price − (Cost + Freight)]/Retail Selling
Markdown: Amount original selling price is reduced
Gross Margin %: [Actual selling price − (Cost + Freight)]/Actual Selling

Exhibit 10.9   **Confidential Vendor Analysis, Retail**

Trip Dates ___Fall Market___ City ___Dallas___ Buyer's Name ___Cooper___ Dept. Name ___Women's Wear___ Dept. No. ___491___

Vendor/Address/ Phone No./Floor No.		Volume History 199X 199X 199X			Markup History 199X 199X 199X			Markdown History 199X 199X 199X			Vendor Executives & Title	Remarks
West Texas Blouse	Spring	590.5	719.4	330.8	47.5	47.7	46.7	2.4	5.3	4.4	Name: Larry Wilcox (VP)	
	Fall	1002.8	706.7		47.3	47.5		3.4	7.8		Julie Davin	Prone to co-op
	Year	1593.3	1426.1		47.4			3.1			Ted Rombach	
	Objectives:											
	Results: As of 5/22											
Flatland Fashions	Spring	224.5	230.2	210.8	47.7	50.0	47.2	6.5	8.5	3.8	Name: Joe Hall (P)	
	Fall	175.8	230.5		47.3	47.6		17.0	9.0		Richard Reel	Will deal on
	Year	400.3	460.7		47.5	48.8		11.1	8.7			transportation
	Objectives:											
	Results: As of 5/22											
Southern	Spring	—0—	42.3	50.7		48.4	45.4	—0—	9.1	4.2	Name: Jackie Poteet (SM)	
	Fall	37.0	69.2		47.1	42.3		7.7	7.8		Boonie Hanley	"Quantity"
	Year	37.0	112.5		47.1	44.7		7.7	8.2		Carol Little	
	Objectives:											
	Results: As of 5/22											
Gallo	Spring	21.7	195	55.6	46.9	50.0	48.3	1.3	0.2	1.2	Name: Ruth Wilson (P)	
	Fall	—0—	13.9		—0—	46.7		—0—	2.0		John Murphy	Easier of
	Year	21.7	33.4		46.9	48.6		1.3	0.9			the two
	Objectives:											
	Results: As of 5/22											

4. What is my anticipated gross margin for this product?
5. Will I be able to get reliable, speedy replacement stock?
6. Can this product stand on its own, or is it merely a "me too" item?
7. What is my expected turnover rate with this product?
8. Does this product complement the rest of my inventory?

VENDOR NEGOTIATIONS

The climax of a successful buying plan is active negotiation with those vendors that have been identified as suitable supply sources. The effectiveness of the buyer-vendor relationship depends on the negotiation skills of the buyer and the economic power of the firms involved.

The retail buyer must negotiate price, delivery dates, discounts, shipping terms, and return privileges. All of these factors affect the firm's profitability and cash flow.

Vendors, as well as retailers, are becoming increasingly aware of the cost of carrying excess inventory. Likewise, both parties are becoming more concerned with the time value of money and its resulting effect on the firm's cash flow. Since both parties to the negotiation process are aware of these factors and are trying to shift these costs to the other party, most negotiations produce some conflict. However, successful negotiation is usually accomplished when buyers realize that the vendors are really their partners in the upcoming merchandising season, since both the buyer and vendor are striving to satisfy the retailer's customers better than anybody else. They should remember that negotiation is a two-way street and a long-term, profitable relationship is the goal. After all, the vendor wants to develop a long-term relationship with the retailer as much as the retailer does with its customers.

There are many factors to be negotiated: prices, freight, delivery dates, method of shipment, shipping costs, exclusivity, guaranteed sales, markdown money, promotional allowances, return privileges, and discounts, and life is simplest when there aren't surprises. Therefore, the smart buyer leaves nothing to chance and discusses everything with the vendor. The vendor and buyer, together, work out the upcoming merchandising plans using the buyer's merchandise budget and planned turnover. The vendor and buyer should seek to make negotiations a win-win situation, where both sides win and neither feels like a loser. The essence of negotiation is to trade what is cheap to you but valuable to the other party, for what is valuable to you but cheap to the other party.[11]

The smart buyer puts all the upcoming areas of negotiation and previous agreements in letter form and sends it out to the vendors before going to market. This helps to prevent any misunderstandings.

Price, of course, is probably the first factor to be negotiated. Buyers should attempt to purchase the desired merchandise at the lowest possible net cost. The buyer should not expect unreasonable discounts or price concessions, but can try to induce any type of price discrimination that is legal under the Robinson-Patman Act.

The buyer must be familiar with the prices and discounts allowed by each vendor. This is why past records are so important. However, the buyer must remember that his or her bargaining power is a result of planned purchases from the vendor. A large retailer may be able to purchase goods from a vendor at a lower price than a small mom-and-pop retailer. There are five different types of discounts to be negotiated.

TRADE DISCOUNT

A **trade discount**, sometimes referred to as a functional discount, is a form of compensation which the buyer may receive for performing certain services for the manufacturer. Inasmuch as this discount is given for the performance of some service, the size of the discount will vary according to the service. Variations in trade discounts are legally justifiable on the basis of the different costs associated with doing business with various buyers.

Trade discounts can either be a single discount (e.g., 20 percent off list) or as a chain applied to the list price in successive order. For example, a discount of 20, 10, 5 would be calculated as 20 percent off list price, 10 percent off the balance, and 5 percent off the second balance, for a total of 31.6 percent off list.

QUANTITY DISCOUNT

A **quantity discount**[12] is price reduction offered as an inducement to purchase large quantities of merchandise. There are three types of quantity discounts available:

1. **noncumulative**: a discount based on a single purchase.
2. **cumulative**: a discount based on total amount purchased over a period of time, and
3. **free merchandise**: a discount where merchandise is offered in lieu of price concessions.

Quantity discounts can be legally justified by the vendor if its costs are reduced because of the quantity involved or if the vendor is meeting a competitor's price in good faith.

Recent research has shown that quantity discounts might not always be in the seller's best interest and should always be viewed by the buyer as an invitation for further negotiations. Consider this price schedule published by IBM for an AT computer.

Quantity	Unit Price
1–19	$5,795
20–49	$5,099
50–149	$4,636
150–249	$4,486

Let's say that a buyer for a retail chain wants 18 of these computers, and the cost is $104,310 (18 × $5,795). But 20 would only cost $101,980 (20 × $5,099). What should the retailer do? It has four choices: a) tell IBM to ship 20 computers at $5,099, and keep the extra two, b) tell IBM to ship you 18 computers at $5,099 and have them keep the other two, c) order 20 but tell IBM to ship only 18 and issue a credit for two computers at $5,099 each or d) negotiate a purchase price.[13] Whenever quantity discounts are offered, the buyer should check to see whether by ordering more, the total purchase price may be lower.

PROMOTIONAL DISCOUNT

A third type of discount is a **promotional discount**, given when the retailer performs an advertising or promotional service for the manufacturer. For example, a vendor might offer a retailer 50 extra pairs of jeans if a) the retailer purchases 1,250 jeans during the season and b) runs two newspaper advertisements featuring the jeans during the season. The use of promotional discounts has enabled Campbell Soup Co. to sometimes sell as much as 40 percent of its annual chicken noodle soup production to wholesalers and retailers in just six weeks.[14] Promotional discounts encourage the retailer to use a strategy known as *forward buying*. Many times, also, retailers can make a quick profit on special promotional deals or the excess products resulting from utilizing quantity discounts by selling the extra merchandise to a diverter. The diverter, who is not an authorized member of the marketing channel, purchases these goods from the retailer for less than it can from the manufacturer, then sells the merchandise to other retailers. Consider the retailer who needed only 18 computers but purchased 20. The retailer could sell the two extra computers to a diverter for $3,500 each and would be better off by $9,330 than if it bought only eighteen computers at $5,795 each. (18 × $5,795 = $104,310; 20 × 5,099 = $101,980 minus $7,000 = $94,980; $104,310 − 94,980 = 9,330.) The diverter could profit by selling these two computers to another retailer for $4,000 each. No wonder diverters are becoming respectable members of the retailer's channel.[15]

SEASONAL DISCOUNT

A **seasonal discount** can be earned by the retailers if they purchase and take delivery of the merchandise in the off season; e.g., buying swimwear in October. (Not all seasonal discounts result in the purchase of merchandise out of season. Retailers in resort areas often take advantage of these discounts since swimwear is never out of season for them.)

CASH DISCOUNT

The final type of discount available to the buyer is a **cash discount** for prompt payment of bills. Cash discounts are usually stated as 2/10, net 30, which means a 2 percent discount is given if payment is received within ten days of the invoice date and the net is due within thirty days.

The cash discount encourages early payment. Another negotiating tool involves delaying the payment due date. The most common forms of future dating are:

a. **End-of-Month (EOM) Dating** allows for cash discount and full payment period to begin on the first day of the following month instead of invoice date. End-of-month invoices dated after the 25th of the month are considered to be dated on the first of the following month.

b. **Middle-of-Month (MOM) Dating** is similar to EOM except the middle of the month is used as the starting date.

c. **Receipt-of-Goods (ROG) Dating** allows the starting date to be the date goods are received by the retailer.

d. **Extra Dating** allows the retailer some extra or free days before the period of payment begins.

e. A final discount form, not widely used today, is **anticipation**. It permits a retailer to pay the invoice in advance of the expiration of the cash discount period and earn an extra discount. However, anticipation is usually figured at an annual rate of 7 percent, which is below the current cost of money.

Many vendors have eliminated the cash discount since retailers, especially department stores, have been taking 60 to 120 days to pay and still deducting the cash discount. Many vendors require new accounts to pay up front until credit is established.

DELIVERY TERMS

Delivery terms are another negotiating tool. **Delivery terms** specify where title to the merchandise passes to the retailer, whether the vendor or buyer will pay the freight charges, and who is obligated to file any damage claims. The three most common delivery terms are:

a. **FOB (Free on Board) Factory**. The buyer assumes title at the factory and pays all transportation costs from the vendor's factory.
b. **FOB Shipping Point**. The vendor pays the transportation to a local shipping point. The buyer assumes title there and pays all further transportation costs.
c. **FOB Destination**. The seller pays the freight and the buyer takes title on delivery.

IN-STORE MERCHANDISE HANDLING

Every retailer needs some means of handling incoming merchandise. For some types of retailers (a grocery store, for instance), this need will be significant and frequent; for others (as for a jeweler), it will be relatively minor and infrequent. A retailer with a frequent and significant amount of incoming merchandise needs to do considerable planning to receive merchandise and handle space. For example, a full-line grocery store will need to build receiving docks for forty- to sixty-foot semitrailers. Space may be needed for a forklift to drive between the truck and the merchandise receiving area to unload the merchandise. The merchandise will need to be moved from the receiving area, where it may be counted and marked, to a storage area, either adjoining the selling floor or in a separate location.

The point at which incoming merchandise is received can be a high-theft point. The retail manager needs to design the receiving and handling area in order to minimize this problem. Several frequently used theft methods that take place in the back room are mentioned below. Some involve the retail employees, others involve outsiders.

Vendor collusion refers to the types of loss that occur when the merchandise is being delivered. Typical losses involve the delivery of less merchandise than is paid for, removal of good merchandise disguised as old or stale merchandise, and stealing other merchandise from the stock room or off the selling floor while making delivery. This type of theft often involves both the delivery people and the retail employees who sign for the delivery, with the two splitting the profit.

Employee theft is when retail employees steal merchandise while they are on the job. Some employees believe that free merchandise is part of their pay. Although some of the stolen goods come from the selling floor, a larger percentage is pilfered from the stockroom. This type of theft is most prevalent in food stores, department stores, and discount stores. Considering that these types of stores are usually larger in size, sales volume, and number of employees, the lack of close supervision might contribute to this problem.

Customer theft can also be a problem where merchandise is received. Stealing merchandise from the stockroom or receiving area may be easier

Illus. 10.5
Employee theft can be a significant problem where merchandise is received.

than taking it from the selling floor for several reasons. First, much of the back-room merchandise is not ticketed, so it is easier to get it through electronic antishoplifting devices. Second, once the thief enters the stock area, there is very little antitheft security, because most security guards watch store exits and fitting rooms. Third, there is usually an exit near the stockroom through which the thief can carry out the stolen goods. Today, most of these exits are wired to set off an alarm when opened without a key, helping to reduce thefts somewhat.

The retailer must be aware that there is plenty of opportunity for receiving, handling, and storage thefts to happen. Therefore, steps should be taken to reduce these crimes.[16] The retailer cannot watch employees every minute, but some surveillance is helpful.

The amount of storage space the retailer will need is related to the physical dimensions of the merchandise and the stock level needed to maintain the desired rate of stock turnover. For example, furniture is bulky and requires considerable storage space; grocery items turn over frequently, so more merchandise is needed than can be displayed on the shelves. This excess inventory means retailers have to stack boxes and cartons on the floor of the stockroom. In most cases, however, this scenario would be fairly inefficient and also costly when the retailer is probably paying those stockroom employees anywhere from five to fifteen dollars per hour. Thus, in most cases, some type of equipment will be used to increase productivity in this area. Instead of having cartons and boxes stacked directly on the floor of the stockroom where they must remain packed and risk being damaged, the merchandise should be unpacked,

10-2

A Different Type of Theft

A great deal has been written about employee theft and shoplifting, but what about the new trend of retailers stealing from suppliers? This is not rare. However, few suppliers are willing to talk about it for fear of hurting customer feelings. One supplier or vendor who *is* willing to talk about it is Julie Davis of Seville Industries. Seville is a manufacturer, importer, and distributor of high quality tabletop lines, including Dark's Silk Flowers. Most of Seville's customers are small- to medium-size gift shops.

According to Davis, a customer orders some flowers and after receiving the order, calls to inform Seville that the wrong order was sent. The customer states that he or she doesn't know what was sent and cannot identify the color(s). After Seville issues a pickup sticker, they find that the customer has sent back merchandise that was discontinued one to two years ago. Seville has no recourse but to drop the customer from the active file, and will probably never receive payment (usually $800 to $1,200 is owed). Or, Seville can issue another pickup sticker only to find that merchandise originally packed in 20 boxes is crammed into two boxes. This returned merchandise is unusable and the supplier has no recourse.

This is only the tip of the iceberg. Retailers are beginning to rip off vendors for many of the same reasons customers steal from retailers: they are so big; they will never miss it; they will never catch me; what can they do to me?

It is no wonder that many suppliers long for the good old days, when the only thing they had to worry about was a late paying retailer taking the cash discount.

Source: Based on data supplied by Julie Davis, Seville Industries.

checked, inventoried, ticketed, then placed on shelves or in bins until needed. This increases the amount of merchandise stored per square foot and is less tempting to dishonest employees.

Retailing in Action 10-2 is an example of another means of theft in a retailer's channel, this time by the retailer.

EVALUATING MERCHANDISE PERFORMANCE

So far we have ignored the important task of evaluating the merchandising function's performance. To address this, we need to introduce several new concepts.

In retailing, inventory turnover, which may also be called *inventory or merchandise stockturn* or just *turnover,* is a key to performance. **Inventory turnover** measures how long inventory is on hand before it is sold. Items that are on hand a short time have a high turnover; those that are on hand longer have a low turnover.

Retailers calculate inventory turnover several ways:

1. Net sales/average inventory at retail
2. Cost of merchandise sold/average inventory at cost
3. Units sold/average units in inventory

Methods 1 and 2 are the most frequently used. Method 3 can be misleading unless units are measured in homogeneous groups. The other methods are better for combining heterogeneous groups of items, because each item can be weighted by its dollar value.

The relationships between turnover and sales and turnover and inventory levels can be shown by analyzing Method 1 in more detail. For example, it can be shown that:

4. Net sales = turnover $\times$ average inventory at retail
5. Average inventory at retail = net sales/turnover

Method 4 shows that if a retailer is capable of achieving a given turnover—say six—and has an average retail inventory of $100,000, then that retailer has the capacity to generate $600,000 in annual sales (6 $\times$ $100,000). Method 5 could be used to determine inventories needed to support an expected sales volume with a fixed turnover goal. If the retailer has forecasted sales of $500,000 and experience has shown that a turnover of four is reasonable to expect, then the retailer would need to have average inventories at retail of $125,000 ($500,000/4 = $125,000).

Turnover is a key to high performance, which means profits, in retailing. However, higher turnover will not indefinitely increase profits, and the lowest turnover will not necessarily result in the lowest profits. This point can be better understood by examining the advantages and disadvantages of rapid turnover, outlined in Exhibit 10.10.

Rapid turnover enables the retailer to reduce certain expenses. Central to this proposition is the relationship demonstrated in Method 5—the more rapid the turnover, the lower the average inventory required. Lower inventories will obviously require less capital, and thus the retailer's interest expense will be lower. Also associated with lower inventories will be lower levels of required insurance coverage, lower inventory taxes on year-end inventories, and lower cost of space to store the inventory. On the other hand, rapid turnover can increase expense. With smaller average inventories on hand, the retailer must order more frequently and in smaller quantities, resulting in higher clerical costs, lost quantity discounts, and higher transportation rates. The costs of correspondence and handling will also increase, since more orders will need to be processed over a season or year.

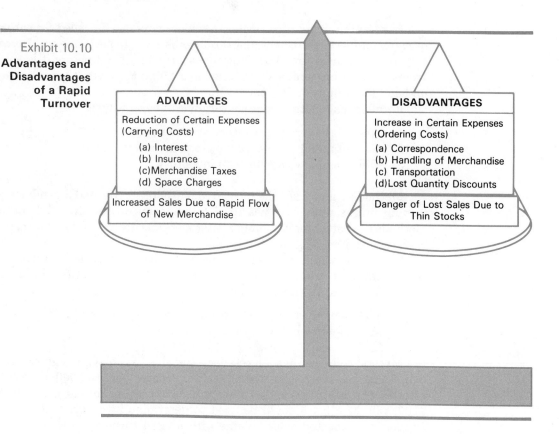

ADVANTAGES
Reduction of Certain Expenses (Carrying Costs)
(a) Interest
(b) Insurance
(c) Merchandise Taxes
(d) Space Charges
Increased Sales Due to Rapid Flow of New Merchandise

DISADVANTAGES
Increase in Certain Expenses (Ordering Costs)
(a) Correspondence
(b) Handling of Merchandise
(c) Transportation
(d) Lost Quantity Discounts
Danger of Lost Sales Due to Thin Stocks

If the retailer places one large order per year, order placement costs will be low, but inventory carrying costs will be high. If the retailer orders every week, the ordering costs will be high, but inventory carrying costs will be relatively low.

The rate of turnover influences not only the supply side of retailing (cost functions), but also demand (sales or revenue functions).[17] A rapid turnover can increase sales, or result in lost sales due to decreased stocks and customers not being able to find the merchandise desired.

Programming a store to operate on the optimal rate of turnover is a difficult, but necessary, task in propelling the retailer toward the goal of high-performance results. However, turnover is not the only measure of performance. Exhibit 10.11 shows the turnover rate by all merchandise lines for large department stores.

PROFIT MEASURES

The ultimate test of merchandising performance should not be a productivity measure such as inventory turnover, but a profit measure. The re-

Exhibit 10.11

Inventory Turnover for All Department Stores with Sales Over $2 Million, 1987 Operating Results

Shoes	1.9
Female Apparel	3.2
Adult Female Accessories	2.6
Mens & Boys Apparel	2.5
Infants & Childrens Clothing and Accessories	2.9
Cosmetics & Drugs	2.1
Recreation	2.1
Home Furnishings	1.7
All Other Merchandise	4.8

GM% for All Department Stores with Sales Over $2 Million

Shoes	41.4%
Female Apparel	42.3%
Adult Female Accessories	46.5%
Mens & Boys Apparel	40.5%
Infants & Childrens Clothing and Accessories	41.5%
Cosmetics & Drugs	38.6%
Recreation	39.8%
Home Furnishings	37.8%
All Other Merchandise	33.2%

GMROI for All Department Stores with Sales Over $2 Million

Shoes	$1.8
Female Apparel	$2.8
Adult Female Accessories	$2.6
Mens & Boys Apparel	2.0
Infants & Childrens Clothing and Accessories	2.5
Cosmetics & Drugs	1.4
Recreation	1.4
Home Furnishings	1.2
All Other Merchandise	2.7

Since GM% and GMROI reported here are median numbers, not averages, the reader should be careful in performing calculations using these numbers. Therefore, while the GMROI and GM% would be $1.3 using the median inventory turnover, it actually was $1.8 since NRMA used real figures, which more closely represented averages, in computing its figures.

SOURCE: National Retail Merchants Association, *Department Store and Specialty Store Merchandising and Operating Results of 1987* (New York: Financial Executives Division, National Retail Merchants Association, 1988): 5. Reprinted by permission of the National Retail Merchants Association.

tailer could have excellent turnover by giving the merchandise away, but that defeats the purpose of retailing. The role of the retail executive is to manage demand and supply factors in order to achieve a return on investment sufficient for survival and future growth. We have already said that inventory investments influence supply (cost) functions and demand (sales) functions. We need to see how inventory can help the retailer achieve profit objectives.

How profitable are a retailer's merchandising decisions? To answer this, we need to define profit. Merchandise managers may use three measures of profitability when assessing merchandising performance.

1. **Gross margin** is net sales less the cost of goods sold. This measure is good if there are no expenses other than the cost of merchandise that can be directly related or traced to the merchandise. For example, it may not be possible to directly tie any advertising or sales expenses to particular lines of merchandise.
2. **Contribution profit** is net sales less the cost of goods sold and any expenses that are directly traceable to the goods. In this case, items such as advertising expense can be related to specific product lines.
3. **Operating profit** is net sales less the cost of goods sold, direct expenses, and a share of all indirect expenses the retailer incurs. This method is not good unless the indirect expenses can be equitably allocated. Typically, however, they cannot, since it is difficult to allocate such expenses as the president's salary or clerical and office expenses to merchandise lines without doing it on an arbitrary basis.

All three profit figures can be related to a sales base, to obtain profit measures like these:

Gross margin percentage = gross profit/net sales
Contribution margin percentage = contribution profit/net sales
Operating margin percentage = operating profit/net sales

Of the available profit measures, gross margin percentage is the most widely used to assess merchandising performance. There are two reasons for this. First, it is the most accurate, since both sales and the cost of merchandise sold can be measured with minimal error. This is a significant advantage over the contribution margin and operating margin percentages—both of them require decisions as to which expenses, besides cost of merchandise, should be subtracted from net sales. Second, many industry trade associations regularly report data using gross margin percentage, making it possible for the retailer to compare its performance to the experience of others. Consider Exhibit 10.11, which gives gross margin data by merchandise line for large department stores.

GROSS MARGIN RETURN ON INVENTORY

Gross margin return on inventory (GMROI) incorporates both inventory turnover and profit into a single measure.[18] It can be computed as follows:

(Gross margin/Net sales)(Net sales/Average inventory at cost)
= (Gross margin/Average inventory at cost)

In this simple model, the gross margin percentage (gross margin/net sales) is multiplied by the sales/stock ratio[19] to obtain a gross margin return on inventory. Thus, if a particular merchandise line has a gross margin of 35 percent and an inventory turnover rate of 3.9, its sales/stock ratio would be 6.0 [3.9 divided by (100 percent minus 35 percent)] and a GMROI of $2.10 ($.35 × 6). That is, for each dollar invested in inventory, the retailer obtains $2.10 in gross margin annually. These gross margin dollars can be used to pay store operating expenses and help yield a profit for the retailer. Exhibit 10.11 lists the median GMROI for large department stores by merchandise lines.

The GMROI model is not complex but it does tell us three things:

1. The principal goal in managing merchandise investments should be a return on investment goal—specifically, gross margin return on inventory investment. Gross margin and inventory turnover are not goals; they are worth pursuing only to the extent that they enhance GMROI.
2. There are two principal decision-making criteria in merchandise management. The first is gross margin management and the second is inventory turnover management.
3. Merchandise managers who can effectively interrelate gross margin management and inventory turnover management will be able to achieve high-performance results.

DIRECT PRODUCT PROFIT

Direct product profit (DPP) was first used in the retail food industry as a means to reduce costs and control the product proliferation. DPP focuses on the contribution profit of individual retail items in individual stores. **Direct product profit (DPP)** equals an item's gross margin dollars, plus discounts and allowances earned, less direct handling, selling, and inventory holding costs. DPP enables the retailer to develop results for brands, categories, departments, stores, etc., thus forming the basis for merchandising decisions.

Because DPP is a much more accurate measure of retail profit than gross margin, it is replacing gross margin in making merchandising decisions, not only in the retail food industry, but also for mass and general merchandisers. Exhibit 10.12 shows how DPP is more accurate than traditional measures (dollar sales, sales per square foot, gross margin percentage, and GMROI) because it includes all of the variable costs of handling a product. By including these costs, the retailer can arrive at the product contribution, or DPP, of each individual product, in our example $9.19 or $35.51 per square foot per week.

By expressing DPP against a common unit of measure (floor space) retailers can compare the performance of products of different physical proportions. Since retail space is usually limited, DPP can be used for:

1. item selection (high DPP items should generally be added, low ones reviewed with an eye toward pruning),
2. store/shelf location (high DPP items should be given prime location), and
3. promotion (total DPP can be improved by increasing the sales of high DPP products).

Recently several authors have recommended that the GMROI concept be replaced by residual income analysis.[20] These authors have argued that the GMROI concept has two weaknesses: first, GMROI does not reflect accounts receivable and payable in the cost of inventory or the cost of financing that inventory; second, GMROI bases decisions on the short-

Exhibit 10.12

Computing Direct Product Profit for an Individual Product

Retail price	$ 25.00
Less: Cost	12.50
Equals: Gross margin dollars	12.50
Plus: Discounts and allowances earned	
Payment discount	.45
Merchandise allowances	1.10
Equals: Adjusted gross margin	$ 14.05
Less: Direct handling costs	
Freight in	.11
Promotion expenses	.38
Retail direct labor	2.13
Retail inventory expense	.16
Retail operating expense	.97
Distribution center direct labor	.78
Distribution center inventory expense	.14
Distribution center operating expense	.19
Equals: DPP per unit	$ 9.19
Times: Number of units/week	51
Equals: DPP per week	$468.69
Divide: Square feet used	13.2
Equals: DPP per square feet per week	$ 35.51

run, rather than long-run, profits. Though their arguments make sense, the residual income analysis concept has not yet been adopted by the retail industry.

SUMMARY

Merchandise management is the analysis, planning, acquisition, and control of inventory investments and assortments in a retail enterprise. An understanding of the principles of merchandise management is essential to good retail management.

In a small retail enterprise, one person will typically perform all activities related to the analysis, planning, acquisition, and control of merchandise. However, in a large retail organization, such as a chain store, several parties will be involved. There may be a general merchandise manager, divisional merchandise manager, buyer, department manager, and merchandise support staff.

A major part of merchandise management is planning. The retailer needs to plan, first, the dollars to invest in inventory and, second, the units of merchandise to purchase with these dollars. These two forms of planning are called dollar merchandise planning and unit stock planning. In the section on dollar merchandise planning, we discussed the basic stock, percentage variation, weeks' supply, and stock-to-sales inventory methods. In the section on unit stock planning, we discussed the conflicts between the optimal level of inventory and the various constraints deterring this level.

In addition to deciding what and how much to purchase, successful retailers must also consider vendor selection and negotiations as part of merchandise management. We reviewed what factors are important in the selection of a vendor, how a merchandise manager prepares for a buying trip and what factors can be negotiated. We concluded the chapter by pointing out that good merchandising management cannot occur unless the retailer's merchandising performance can be evaluated. Evaluative techniques include inventory turnover and profit measures. Useful formulas for combining these measures are GMROI (gross margin return on inventory) and DPP (direct product profit).

QUESTIONS FOR DISCUSSION

1. Why is merchandise planning so important to a retailer's success?
2. How does the retail buyer interface with the divisional merchandise manager and the department manager?

3. A retailer has a target GMROI for a particular merchandise line of $2.40 and believes that it can be achieved with a sales/stock ratio of 6.0. What must its target gross margin be?

4. If your annual turnover rate is 15, which inventory stock level method would you use and why? If the annual inventory turnover rate was 4 would your answer be the same? Why?

5. What is the difference between *inventory turnover rate* and *sales/ stock ratio*?

6. What is the difference between the *sales/stock ratio* and the *stock to sales method* when discussing inventory?

7. What does the term *open-to-buy* mean? How can it be used to control merchandise investments?

8. Do you think it would be more difficult to make a merchandise plan for a supermarket or a dress shop? Why?

9. How can a merchandise line have too much breadth, yet not enough depth?

10. Would it require more inventory to support a supermarket doing $10 million in annual sales or a furniture store with the same amount of annual sales? Why?

11. Can you think of any unique problems in merchandise planning and control that nonstore retailers might face?

12. Why are both dollar merchandise planning and unit stock planning necessary?

13. What type of personnel can the buyer use to facilitate his or her job performance?

14. What are the major constraining factors in the design of the optimal merchandise mix?

15. Herb's Hardware is attempting to develop a merchandise budget for the next twelve months. To assist in this process, the following data have been developed. The target inventory turnover is 4.8 and forecasted sales are shown below:

Month	Forecasted Sales
1	$27,000
2	26,000
3	20,000
4	34,000
5	41,000
6	40,000
7	28,000
8	27,000
9	38,000
10	39,000
11	26,000
12	28,000

Develop a monthly merchandise budget using the basic stock method (BSM) and the percentage variation method (PVM).

16. Compute the ratios in the GMROI model for the three merchandise lines identified below.

Merchandise Line	Sales	Average Inventory at Cost	Gross Profit
A	$120,000	$35,000	$31,000
B	$130,000	$34,000	$42,000
C	$115,000	$50,000	$38,000

17. A buyer is going to market, and has this relevant data: planned stock at end of March is $319,999 (at retail prices); planned March sales are $149,999; current stock on hand (March 1) is $274,000; merchandise on order for delivery is $17,000; planned reductions are $11,000. What is the buyer's open-to-buy?

18. A retailer has a target GMROI for a particular merchandise line of $1.44 and believes that it can competitively price the line to obtain a gross margin of 32 percent. What must its target sales/stock ratio on this line be?

19. If the inventory turnover rate is 4 and the gross margin 50 percent for a given line of merchandise, what is the sales/stock ratio?

SUGGESTED READINGS

Allen, Randy L. "Merchandise Planning: By the Numbers." *Chain Store Age: General Merchandise* (April 1982): 103–4.

Dunn, William. "In Pursuit of the Downscale Market." *American Demographics* (May 1986): 26–33.

Ettenson, Richard, and Janet Wagner. "Retail Buyers' Saleability Judgments: A Comparison of Information Use Across Three Levels of Experience," *Journal of Retailing* (Spring 1986): 41–63.

Gilman, Hank. "Wholesalers Caught in a Squeeze by Retailers," *Wall Street Journal*, 29 May 1986, p. 6.

Lusch, Robert F. "The New Algebra of High Performance Retail Management," *Retail Control* (September 1986): 15–35.

ENDNOTES

1. *U.S. Bureau of Census, Quarterly Reports*, 4th. Quarter 1986, p. 142.
2. "Where the Dollars R," *Fortune* (June 1, 1981): 45.

3. "Bribery of Retail Buyers Is Called Pervasive," *Wall Street Journal*, 1 April 1985, p. 6.

4. David J. Rachman, "The Organization Structure of the Retail Firm: The Buyer's Role," in R. Patrick Cash, ed., *The Buyer's Manual* (New York: National Retail Merchants Association, 1979), pp. 29–42.

5. Roger Dickinson, "Supplier-Retailer Negotiations: The Negotiation Ratio" (Proceedings of a Joint Conference of the American Collegiate Retailing Association and Academy of Marketing Science, Charleston, 1988), 28–33.

6. For a complete discussion on service strategies, the reader should consult Valarie A. Zeithaml, A. Parasuraman, and Leonard L. Berry, "Problems and Strategies in Services Marketing," *Journal of Marketing* (Spring 1985): 33–46.

7. Frank Burnside, "Merchandise Assortment Planning," in R. Patrick Cash, ed., *The Buyer's Manual* (New York: National Retail Merchants Association, 1979), 245–71.

8. "Food Items Proliferate, Making Grocery Aisles A Corporate Battlefield," *Wall Street Journal*, 17 August 1984, p. 1.

9. "Life in the Food Chain Becomes Predatory," *Advertising Age* (May 9, 1988): p. S2.

10. James R. Brown and Prem C. Purwar, "A Cross-Channel Comparison of Retail Supplier Selection Factor," 1980 AMA Educators' Conference, 217–220.

11. Dickinson, p. 29.

12. For a look at the sophisticated use of these discounts, see Ashok Rao, "Quantity Discounts in Today's Markets," *Journal of Marketing* (Fall 1980): 44–51.

13. Roy Howell, Robert Britney, Paul Kuzdrall, and James Wilcox, "Unauthorized Channels of Distribution: Gray Markets," *Industrial Marketing Management* (1986): 257–263.

14. "Retailers Buy Far In Advance To Exploit Trade Promotions," *Wall Street Journal*, 9 October 1986, p. 31.

15. "Diverting Gets Respectable," *Supermarket Business* (April 1988): p. 23.

16. Warren A. French, Melvin R. Crask, and Fred H. Mader, "Retailer's Assessment of Shoplifting Problem," *Journal of Retailing* (Winter 1984): 108–115.

17. John T. Mentzer and R. Kirshnan, "The Effect of the Assumption of Normality on Inventory Control/Customer Service," *Journal of Business Logistics* 6, no. 1 (1985): 101–120.

18. Daniel J. Sweeney, "Improving the Profitability of Retail Merchandising Decisions, *Journal of Marketing* (January 1973): 60–68.

19. The sales/stock ratio is similar to inventory turnover except the average inventory is expressed at cost rather than retail. Sales/stock ratio is used in GMROI instead of inventory turnover, since the denominator of a return on investment measure should reflect the cost of the investment. Inventory turnover is obtained by multiplying (net sales/average inventory at cost) by (100 − gross margin percent).

20. Michael Levy and Charles A. Ingene, "Residual Income Analysis: A Method of Inventory Investment Allocation and Evaluation," *Journal of Marketing* (Summer 1984): 93–104.

11 Chapter

Pricing Merchandise

OVERVIEW

In this chapter, we will examine the retailer's need to make pricing decisions. Both demand- and supply-oriented theories of pricing will be discussed. We will look at why initial markups and maintained markups are seldom the same. We will also discuss how a retailer establishes an initial markup. The chapter concludes with a discussion of why and how a retailer takes markdowns during the normal course of business.

I. Interactive Price Decisions
   A. Merchandise
   B. Location
   C. Promotion
   D. Credit
   E. Customer Services
   F. Store Image
   G. Legal Constraints
II. Demand-Oriented Pricing
   A. Population Density
   B. Consumer Travel Costs
     1. Actual Dollar Transport Cost
     2. Opportunity Transport Cost

Perhaps the most common question facing retailers today is, "What is the correct selling price for this product?" Yet, this really should *not* be a difficult decision if retailers have been performing their other activities correctly. Pricing[1] is an interactive decision made in conjunction with the firm's mission statement, its goals and objectives, its strategy, and the other elements of operations management (e.g., merchandise planning, promotional mix, building and fixtures, and level of service), as well as the element of administrative management.

Pricing is more difficult for service retailers than it is for retailers selling physical products. This is because services are intangible, not easily stored and because service retailers cannot return their excess inventory to the vendor for credit. A movie theater will have the same fixed costs for being open the night of a blizzard as it would on any other night. The theater manager cannot sell the empty seats at a later date or increase attendance on the night of the blizzard by reducing ticket prices. Before going into a detailed discussion of pricing decisions, two basic concepts—positioning and price points—must be understood.

Positioning refers to managing retail operations to shape the way consumers view the firm's products or stores relative to the competition. Positioning is a key point in any retail strategy. It is not merely a pricing strategy. Pricing has to be coordinated and integrated with merchandise selection, promotion, personal selling, and service to establish and reinforce the firm's position as perceived by the consumer.

One of the best ways for retailers to create a position for themselves is by making use of price points. **Price points** are when goods are separated into several groupings according to their quality, image, fabric, or cost and offered at specific prices (e.g., neckties may be displayed in four groups and sold at $10, $15, $17.50 and $24). The retailer selects these particular price points in the belief that they are the prices customers prefer to pay for the different grades of ties. (Price points are sometimes called *price zones* although the term *price points* usually refers to specific prices and the term *price zones* refers to a price range). For example, assume a linen buyer in a discount department store has noticed that consumers have concentrated their buying of hand towels around three retail price points: $3, $5, and $8. On the other hand, the main volume prices for hand towels in a high fashion department store may be around $8, $11, and $18. In each case there would usually be some additional towels priced outside of these three main prices, but these are the main prices around which the department's merchandising and selling efforts would be concentrated. Price points have a tremendous impact on the way the store is perceived by its target customers. As you might expect, Neiman-Marcus has higher price points than J. C. Penney's for similar merchandise lines, and Penney's has higher price points than K mart.

Let's look now at how pricing may impact other strategic decisions. Consider a retailer whose strategy is aimed at the entire middle class market with the goal of achieving a market share of 30 percent, a sales/stock ratio of 9.0, and a GMROI of 3.00. It is easy to see that this retailer should not use high price points to capture a large market share and have a high turnover rate. Rather, the retailer should probably use price points below the competition's. This strategy is called **below market pricing** and is used when customers are highly sensitive to price. Low prices can also discourage competition. Alternatively, consider the retailer who wants a highly specialized, prestige image. This retailer will use **above market pricing**, which is appropriate when the target market is insensitive to price and little or no competition is at hand. These retailers attract customers who value status more than price.

There are many examples of retailers failing to consider the importance of price in the overall strategy of the firm. One of the more interesting involves fair trade laws (resale price maintenance laws). These laws were originally enacted as a way to protect small retailers from the pricing policies of the larger chain stores. Small independent retailers felt secure in charging the manufacturer's suggested list price, knowing that everyone was charging the same price. Pricing became a non-decision.

In fact, these laws, which enabled some ineffective retailers to weather the depression, gave impetus to discount stores.[2] These fair trade laws allowed consumers to compare the discounters' prices with those of the traditional retailers, and led to the introduction of the discounting form of retailing. And it was all because retailers did not want to be concerned with pricing decisions or failed to see the importance of pricing in the overall development of a firm's strategy. Research indicates that marketing decision-makers—retailers included—rate pricing decisions as one of their two most important functions. Yet they spend less time working with pricing decisions, and have lower levels of confidence in these decisions, than on those involving other business functions.[3]

INTERACTIVE PRICE DECISIONS

Pricing decisions should be interactive with other retail decisions. Specifically, the decision to price an item at a certain level should interact with the retailer's decisions on lines of merchandise carried, location, promotion, credit, customer services, the store image the retailer wishes to convey, and legal constraints.

MERCHANDISE

You should not set prices without carefully analyzing the attributes of the merchandise being priced. Does your merchandise have attributes that differentiate it from similar merchandise?[4] What is the value of these attributes to the consumer? Consider, for example, the menswear retailer who has purchased 100 men's suits for the fall selling season. What are the attributes of these suits (sizes, colors, type of fabric, cut or style, brand label, quality of workmanship, quality of fabric)? How does the consumer value these attributes? Is a Hickie Freeman label more valuable than a Stanley Blacker label or a Hart-Shafner Marx label? Is good workmanship worth more? Are better quality fabrics worth more? The answers to these questions are not obvious; they depend on the market the retailer is serving. In Tucson, Arizona, 100 percent wool fabrics would have little value to the typical menswear customer; in Boston they would. In Grosse Pointe, Michigan, a suburb of Detroit, the value of the Hickie Freeman label would be high, but in poorer sections of Detroit the value would be zero.

Merchandise selection presents the retailer with an opportunity to consider the range of price points to be made available to the consumer. Remember, the retailer's controllable element of price can be either the cost of goods sold or the gross margin that is added to the cost. The retailer, in deciding to buy to a particular price point, may purchase lower cost merchandise and have a high gross margin, or purchase more expensive goods and reduce the gross margin to achieve the same price point. For this reason, retailers try to educate their customers to move up to a higher price point. This enables the retailers to maintain their gross margin percentage, buy a better grade of merchandise to be sold at a higher price, and increase both total sales and profits.

LOCATION

A retail store's location has a significant effect on what prices can be charged. The closer the store is to competitors with identical or similar merchandise, the less pricing flexibility it will have. The distance between the store and the customer is also important. Generally, if the retailer wants to attract customers from a greater distance, it must lower the prices it establishes on its merchandise lines. This is because of the increased travel costs (in both time and dollar amounts) consumers incur when they are located farther from the store. These high travel costs cut into the amount the customer is able or willing to pay for the merchandise, causing the retailer to lower prices to attract those customers. Two recent studies support the contention that travel costs affect demand. One study found that distance from the retailer (a restaurant) had the expected negative influence on sales.[5] The other study found that the retailer's gross margin percentage is, in general, higher in higher population areas.[6] The findings prove that retailers are not forced to reduce gross margin as a means to attract customers in high population density areas where travel time would be minimal; in fact, higher gross percentages were generally necessary in these areas to offset higher costs (rents, crime, etc.).

PROMOTION

This chapter concentrates on how pricing generates demand. Promotion, too, can be a significant demand-generator, and it is important to realize that pricing and promotion decisions are not independent.[7] If the retailer promotes heavily and is also very price competitive, it may get a cumulative increase in demand greater than the high promotion and lower price strategies would produce independently. Imagine, for example, the retailer establishing low prices but not promoting them in the marketplace. Or, imagine heavy promotion but no cut in prices. Obviously, each strategy would generate demand, but the cumulative effect of both would be much greater.

CREDIT

For a given price level on merchandise, the retailer selling on credit will often be able to generate greater demand than the retailer not selling on credit. Likewise, the retailer selling merchandise on credit may be able to charge a slightly higher price than the retailer not selling on credit and still generate the same demand as the noncredit retailer. Credit-granting retailers often charge higher prices, as shown by the recent move by some retailers to offer special discounts for cash-paying customers. This move is an attempt by the retailer to eliminate the 1.5 to 4.5 percent bankcards charge retailers for credit card purchases, and shift the credit costs back onto the customers actually using the credit.

CUSTOMER SERVICES

Retailers that offer many customer services (delivery, gift wrapping, alterations, more pleasant surroundings, sales assistance) tend to have high prices. A decision to offer many customer services will automatically increase operating expenses yet this policy still might result in higher profits. Consider the case of women's dresses. Customer service used to be common in department stores which took 60 to 65 percent initial markups, but price pressure by discounters caused department stores to respond by cutting markups and service. Many smaller stores have picked up on this and as a result offer the consumer greater assistance in selecting and trying on a dress, something unheard of in many department stores. Many women are willing to pay more for this extra service. It is important to remember that customer service decisions interact heavily with pricing decisions.

STORE IMAGE

One of the most influential cues the customer receives from a store is its prices. Prices help the customer (either consciously or unconsciously) de-

Illus. 11.1
Many consumers are willing to pay more for dresses sold at specialty stores that provide greater customer assistance.

velop an image of the store. If an exclusive women's apparel store started to discount the merchandise heavily, its customers would revise their opinion of it. The merchandise, store decor, and personnel may remain unchanged, but the change in price strategy would significantly alter the overall store image. Price policies and strategies interact with store image policies and strategies.

LEGAL CONSTRAINTS

Pricing decisions must only be made after examining the impact of the legal environment, especially if state laws are involved and the retailer wants to operate in more than one state. A retailer may not set a price in conjunction with a competitor, sell below cost, or claim or imply in any ads that a price has been reduced unless it really has. However, the retailer can sell below the manufacturers' suggested retail price, or offer different prices to different retail customers.

The other environmental factors we discussed in Part 2 of this book (conflict in the channel, consumer behavior, competitor behavior, the socioeconomic environment, and the technological environment) should also be considered when the retailer is developing its overall pricing and market strategy. Retailing in Action 11-1 provides an insight into how one group of retailers (restaurant owners) responded to an environmental change (a move toward a more restrained use of alcoholic beverages) that impacted their most profitable product line.

RETAILING IN ACTION **11-1**

Reacting to an Environmental Demand Variable

Retailers have come up with many different approaches to meet the changing conditions of the marketplace. Let us look at an example of how one class of retailers, restaurants, have turned what could have been disaster into an opportunity for expansion and growth.

Only a few years ago, restaurant owners didn't mind selling food at little more than cost as long as customers were guzzling beer and cocktails, typically priced at three or four times cost.

Now, however, restaurants that serve alcoholic beverages are facing a changing consumer attitude toward drinking. Tougher drunk-driving laws, active campaigns by various civic and religious groups, and changing tastes have eroded liquor sales. It is not uncommon for a restaurant to have experienced a 20 percent drop in alcoholic beverage sales over the past couple of years. Furthermore, restaurants' bottom line has been further impacted by soaring insurance rates because of the rising number of lawsuits filed against restaurants and bars by victims of drunken patrons who caused car accidents.

As a result of pressure on profit caused by this reduction in alcoholic beverage sales, restaurants have expanded the sales of two product lines, desserts and nonalcoholic drinks.

Employees are being trained to push high-markup items, such as Chocolate Mousse Cheesecake. Restaurants that never served desserts before are adding new products either from their own kitchen or from wholesalers. One Texas steakhouse found a high profit item in Baskin-Robbins ice cream. Others have added more exotic products than ice cream and pie. Pastries, which traditionally carry 80 percent markups on selling price, are the most popular of these new exotic items. The Texas steakhouse owner claims to make as much off a dessert as she does from the entree.

Nonalcoholic drinks, which generally sell for the same price as their alcoholic counterparts at a third of the cost, have also become big sellers. Faced with the choice of raising food prices or introducing "mocktails" the restaurants went with the latter. Restaurant managers have been flabbergasted by the profits in nonalcoholic ice cream drinks. It is not uncommon to charge $4 for an ice cream drink which would cost less than a dollar at a fast-food restaurant. Yet, it is one of the best selling after-dinner drinks.

DEMAND-ORIENTED PRICING

When establishing prices, retail decision-makers should be demand oriented. They should conscientiously take into account customers—their wants, needs, preferences, and ability to purchase the merchandise.

A frame of reference for the demand-oriented retailer is the three dimensional demand model in Exhibit 5.7. That model suggested that the retailer pay particular attention to population density, consumer travel costs, and maximum demand price.

POPULATION DENSITY

Since retailers attract customers from a spatial area, they should be concerned with the number of potential customers in that area. In high population density areas, the retailer will not have to draw customers from as great a distance in order to generate a given level of total revenue. There will be less need to lower prices to attract customers from greater distances. Of course, a low price strategy may still be profitable.

Assume you are a retailer operating in a city with a population density of 3,000 households per square mile and you are currently attracting patrons from a two-mile radius of your store. The area within your trading area would be equal to πr^2 (the formula for the area of a circle) or (22/7)4, which equals 12.57 square miles. Therefore, the potential number of households in your trading area is $12.57 \times 3,000$, or 37,710. Assume now that you could lower prices sufficiently to attract households from a 2.5-mile radius; then your trade area would be 19.64 square miles, and the number of potential households in the trade area would be 58,920. Notice that by increasing the radius by a half a mile, the number of potential households in the trade area rose by more than 50 percent.

CONSUMER TRAVEL COSTS

The three-dimensional demand model tells us that consumer travel costs are important determinants of shopping at retail stores. In terms of retail shopping behavior, consumer travel costs consist of the actual dollar costs of transporting oneself to the store and back, the time involved (related to opportunity costs—what else could you be doing with your time and what would be the value you would attach to those alternative activities?), and the psychological costs of traveling to the store and back. The retailer needs to know that lower prices can offset all three of these travel costs. Let us explore the demand implications of each type of travel cost.

Actual Dollar Transport Cost.   Consumers demand goods that offer form, possession, and place utility. To obtain the possession utility, the customer needs to travel to the store. To obtain the place utility, the customer usually needs to transport the goods home. Assume that the customer would be willing to pay $25 for the item in order to obtain the total package of form, place, and possession utility. If the customer is 5 miles from the store (10 miles round-trip) and the cost per mile of travel is 20 cents, then the actual travel cost would be $2.00. Thus, if the retailer had a price on the item more than $23, this consumer would not purchase the item.

Opportunity Transport Cost.   Travel takes time, and time is money to an increasing number of households in the United States. As the number of two-income households increases, time will become more scarce for even more households. Consumers dislike waiting to purchase merchandise because waiting prevents them from engaging in other leisure-time activities. Thus, households attach an opportunity cost to their time.[8] Consider again the consumer who is willing to pay $25 for an item. The round-trip distance to the store is 10 miles and it takes an hour to visit the store and purchase the item. Actual travel costs are 20 cents per mile and the opportunity cost per hour is $4.75. In this case, the highest price the customer would pay would be $18.25.

Psychological Travel Costs.   Traveling may also involve psychological costs or benefits. On the cost side, travel may be punishing. For example, travel to a store in a metropolitan area where the traffic arteries or public transportation is very congested may be annoying or even dangerous. On the other hand, the travel may yield net psychological benefits. Consider, for example, the first warm day after a dreadfully cold winter on which the consumer decided that an afternoon drive to a regional shopping mall, on a quiet back country road, would actually be enjoyable. These psychological travel costs and benefits are difficult to measure, but they influence how much the consumer is willing to pay to acquire an item.

Pricing Implications.   All of these components of consumer travel costs have implications for retail price policies. Consider the following suggestions, to minimize the costs of travel and maximize its benefits:

1. Offer customers "shop and park" or "shop and ride" coupons. These effectively lower the price of merchandise and can be a strong force attracting customers to the store.
2. Offer to pay the customers' gasoline cost to the store and back if they come from far away to shop at the store. An appliance and stereo retailer in Madison, Wisconsin offers customers who present a driver's license from Milwaukee $5 for gasoline expenses.
3. Offer special discounts for multiple-item purchases, since this encourages the customer to economize on time—a scarce resource.
4. Try to design the store so that there is a net psychological benefit to visiting it. This is the logic behind the theatrical atmosphere of department stores such as Neiman-Marcus. Department stores, specialty shops, and large banks have opened special clubs or lounges for high-volume customers. These customers get special privileges not available to other customers. For example, Neiman-Marcus has a gold card for customers who spend a certain amount per year. It's called the "In Circle Club" and members get a monthly newsletter and invitations to special events.

A Note on Nonstore Retailing.   From the customer's perspective, one of the most significant advantages of nonstore retailing (catalogues, cable television shopping channels, direct sellers, etc.) is the absence of travel costs. Thus, nonstore retailers should be able to demand a higher price for merchandise similar to that offered by traditional retailers. This assumes that, on all other dimensions, the customer would view the nonstore and traditional retailer the same way. Some consumers might want immediate possession, something nonstore retailers are not able to provide. These consumers would incur a higher cost in using nonstore settings. Since nonstore retailers tend to have lower operating costs than traditional retailers, and since the customer would be willing to pay at least the same as in a traditional retail store, nonstore retailers have the potential of increasing their market share during the rest of this century. Offsetting this advantage, however, is the fact that direct sellers such as Tupperware,

Illus. 11.2
One of the most significant advantages of nonstore retailing from the customer's perspective is the absence of travel costs.

Avon, and Mary Kay have found that economic conditions can drastically affect the supply of part-time sales people available. Likewise, the "party sales" concept is on the verge of change. Many consumers don't want, or have the time, to attend a party in order to make a purchase. More and more of these sales now result from phone orders or orders received from parties held in offices during lunch hours.

MAXIMUM DEMAND PRICE

The **maximum demand price** is the highest price (inclusive of all transportation costs) a consumer would be willing to pay for one unit of a product. What factors tend to make the consumer willing to pay a higher maximum demand price for an item? There are three basic determinants. The first is the utility or satisfaction the customer expects to get from the product. This boils down to the attributes of the product and the value the consumer attaches to each attribute. The second is the consumer's income or budget. How much money does the consumer have to allocate to the purchase of goods and services? The third factor influencing the maximum demand price is the price at rival stores. Is a competitor offering the same merchandise for a lower price?

These three basic determinants of maximum demand price can be influenced by three types of variables: environmental, household and managerial.

Environmental Demand Variables. Demand variables that are beyond the control of the individual household and the individual retailer are called environmental. Examples include traffic congestion, weather patterns, and population density. Environmental demand variables can have either a positive or a negative effect on demand, depending on the product type and the direction of change in the demand determinant. Consider, for example, weather patterns and the demand for snow tires, swimsuits, or overcoats. Weather can have a major effect on the demand for almost all goods, because bad weather keeps people indoors and makes shopping trips less likely. Many retailers subscribe to weather forecasting services to help them plan for downturns or upturns in demand.

Household Demand Variables.   Variables that characterize the household can effect demand. Typical household characteristics are income, education, and sex of the household head. For example, two-income households have higher income levels, but often have little time to make purchases; thus, these households place heavy reliance on brand names. The education level of the household, while often similar to the income level, has a significant influence on the way consumers spend their leisure time. Finally, as more and more men are becoming single heads of households, retailers and manufacturers alike are developing special marketing programs for them. Consider department stores that run special cooking classes for men only. Consider what the change in demand for a record store might be if more households with teenage children moved into the trade area.

Managerial Demand Variables.   Any variable that is under the control of the retailer and can influence demand is a managerial demand variable. Some of the more common are promotion, credit, customer services, and price. An important concept to understand is **demand elasticity of price**. This is the percentage change in quantity demanded divided by the percentage change in price. Formally, it can be defined as follows:

$$E_p = -(\Delta Q/Q)/(\Delta P/P) = -(P/Q)(\Delta Q/\Delta P)$$

where:
E_p = demand elasticity of price
$\Delta Q/Q$ = percentage change in quantity demanded
$\Delta P/P$ = percentage change in price

Since quantity demanded and price vary inversely, a positive change in price will be accompanied by a negative change in quantity demanded. Thus, in order to make the coefficient of price elasticity positive, a minus sign is added to the equation.

Assume that a retailer has an item priced at $10 and sells 100 units a month; this would result in sales of $1,000 ($10 × 100). If demand elasticity of price is 1.5 and if price is cut by 10 percent, what will happen to total sales? Using the above equation we could determine that the percentage of change in quantity demanded would be 15 percent (10 percent $\times$ 1.5). As a result, the quantity demanded would rise from 100 to 115 when the price fell from \$10 to \$9. The new sales volume would be \$1,035 (\$9 $\times$ 115), which is an increase from the previous month's sales volume of \$1,000. However, just because the retailer experienced a \$35 increase in sales doesn't mean that profits increased by \$35. Assume that the retailer's cost was \$5 per item. In previous months this resulted in a gross margin of \$500 (sales minus cost, or \$1000 minus \$500); now the retailer's gross margin is only \$460 (\$1,035 − \$575). Thus, while price elasticity is important as a tool for analyzing the relationship between sales and price changes, the retailer must not overlook the effect of a price change on gross margin. A retailer should not get very excited about a huge increase in total sales if the new selling price is not sufficient to cover costs.

If demand elasticity of price is less than 1.0, then demand is price inelastic. That means a 1 percent change in price results in less than a 1 percent change in quantity demanded. If demand is price inelastic, a cut in price will yield a drop in total revenues, and an increase in price will yield an increase in total revenue. On the other hand, if demand elasticity of price is greater than 1, demand is price elastic. A 1 percent change in price results in more than a 1 percent change in quantity demanded. Thus, a drop in price will raise total revenues and a price increase will lower total revenues.

SUPPLY-ORIENTED PRICING

Up to this point we have considered how demand influences price. Now, let's consider the influence of supply on price.

Retail decision-makers should analyze their supply or cost curves when establishing and changing prices. Typical cost curves for a retail store were presented in Exhibits 5.8 and 5.9; take a moment to review them. For our purposes we can view costs in retailing as fixed and variable.

COST CURVES

Fixed costs are those which do not change over the short run as a result of an increase in volume. Most retailers have relatively high fixed costs, which include telephone, heat, light, cooling, insurance, taxes, rent, and wages for most types of employees. The presence of high fixed costs in retailing suggests that retailers have high break-even points. A store opening each morning needs to have a staff or employees on hand, the lights and heating or air conditioning operating, and so on. All of these costs must be incurred regardless of whether any customers enter the front door.

Variable costs are those which change in proportion with volume. The major variable cost in retailing is that of the merchandise sold. Another might be some portion of wages, since salesclerks are often paid on commission. Another example could be promotional expenses.

PROFIT

In a sense, desired profit is a cost. The profit the retailer desires can be viewed as a cost on the use of its capital and as a payment for taking risks. In other words, profit incurs an opportunity cost. If a retailer took its capital and invested it in a relatively safe fashion (United States Treasury securities) how high a return could it obtain? Desired profit from the retail store should equal this return plus a premium for taking risk.

The retailer cannot use its capital or that provided by stockholders or creditors without programming into its supply function a fair return on that capital. In short, profit is a necessary cost of doing business.

MARKUP EQUATION

Using supply-oriented pricing, the retailer should begin with the following basic markup equation.

$$P = C + M$$

where:
 C = dollar cost of merchandise per unit
 M = dollar markup per unit
 P = selling price per unit

Thus, if the retailer has a cost per unit of $16 on a pen set and a dollar markup of $14, then the selling price per set is $30.

In other words, **markup** is the difference between the cost of the merchandise and the selling price. This markup should cover all operating expenses (wages, rent, utilities, promotion, credit, etc.) incurred in the sale of the product and still provide the retailer with a profit. Occasionally, a retailer will sell a product without a markup high enough to cover the cost of the merchandise, in order to generate traffic or build sales volume. This product is called a loss or price leader and the laws in many states carefully regulate this type of activity. This chapter will be concerned only with using markup to produce a profit on the sale of each item.

MARKUP METHODS

Markup may be expressed as either a dollar amount or as a percentage of the selling price. It is most useful when expressed as a percentage of the selling price because it can then be compared to other financial data, such as last year's sales, reductions in selling price, or the firm's competition. The equation for expressing markup as a percentage of the selling price is:

$$\% \text{ markup on selling price} = (P - C)/P = M/P$$

Some businesses, usually manufacturers or small retailers, express markup as a percentage of cost, but this method is not widely used in retailing because everything else the retailer does is expressed as a percentage of selling price. The equation for expressing markup as a percentage of cost is:

$$\% \text{ markup on cost} = (P - C)/C = M/C$$

Several problems occur when we attempt to compare markup as a percentage of selling price to markup as a percentage of cost. Because the two methods use different bases, we really are not comparing the same thing. However, there is an equation that can be used to find percentage markup on selling price when we know percentage markup on cost.

$$\% \text{ markup on selling price} = (\% \text{ markup on cost})/$$
$$(100\% + \% \text{ markup on cost})$$

Likewise, when we know percentage markup on selling price we can easily find percentage markup on cost.

$$\% \text{ markup on cost} = \% \text{ markup on selling price}/$$
$$(100\% - \% \text{ markup on selling price})$$

These equations are conversions; they convert percentage markup on cost to percentage markup on selling price, or vice versa. Exhibit 11.1 shows a conversion table for markup on cost and markup on selling price. Let's go back to the pen set example and see how easy it is to determine markup on selling price when we know the markup on cost and vice versa.

The retailer purchased the pen set for $16 and sold it for $30. The difference between the selling price and the cost is $14. This $14 as a percentage of selling price (markup on selling price) is 46.7 percent ($14/$20). This same $14, however, represents 87.5 percent ($14/$16) of the cost (markup). In this example, if all we knew was that the calculator had a 87.5 percent markup on cost, we could determine that this was the same as a 46.7 percent markup on selling price: % markup on selling price = (% markup on cost)/(100% + % markup on cost) = 87.5%/(100% + 87.5%) = 46.7%. Likewise, if we knew we had a 46.7 percent markup on retail, we could easily determine percentage markup on cost: % markup on cost = (% markup on selling price)/(100% − % markup on selling price) = 46.7%/(100% − 46.7%) = 87.5%.

Exhibit 11.1
Markup Conversion Table

Markup Percent of Selling Price	Markup Percent of Cost	Markup Percent of Selling Price	Markup Percent of Cost	Markup Percent of Selling Price	Markup Percent of Cost
4.8	5.0	18.0	22.0	32.0	47.1
5.0	5.3	18.5	22.7	33.3	50.0
6.0	6.4	19.0	23.5	34.0	51.5
7.0	7.5	20.0	25.0	35.0	53.9
8.0	8.7	21.0	26.6	35.5	55.0
9.0	10.0	22.0	28.2	36.0	56.3
10.0	11.1	22.5	29.0	37.0	58.8
10.7	12.0	23.0	29.9	37.5	60.0
11.0	12.4	23.1	30.0	38.0	61.3
11.1	12.5	24.0	31.6	39.0	64.0
12.0	13.6	25.0	33.3	39.5	65.5
12.5	14.3	26.0	35.0	40.0	66.7
13.0	15.0	27.0	37.0	41.0	70.0
14.0	16.3	27.3	37.5	42.0	72.4
15.0	17.7	28.0	39.0	42.8	75.0
16.0	19.1	28.5	40.0	44.4	80.0
16.7	20.0	29.0	40.9	46.1	85.0
17.0	20.5	30.0	42.9	47.5	90.0
17.5	21.2	31.0	45.0	48.7	95.0
				50.0	100.0

Exhibit 11-1 gives a total picture of the relationships between markup on cost and markup on selling price. In Exhibit 11-2 you can see that dollar markup does not change as the percentage on cost or selling price changes. Dollar markup is simply presented as a percentage of a different base—cost or selling price.

USING MARKUP FORMULAS

The basic markup formulas will enable you to determine more than the percentage of markup on a particular item. Let us work with the markup on selling price formula to illustrate how a frequently asked question might be answered. If you know that a particular item could be sold for $8 per unit and that you need a 40 percent markup on selling price to meet

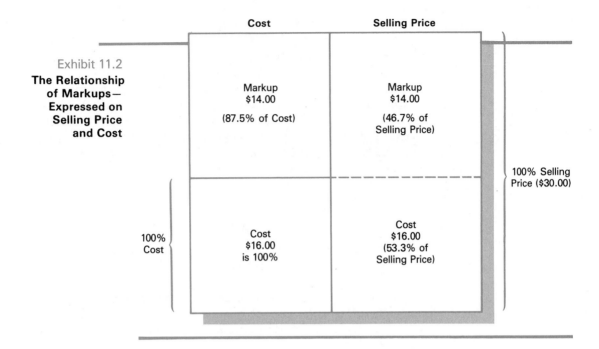

Exhibit 11.2

The Relationship of Markups— Expressed on Selling Price and Cost

your profit objective, then how much would you be willing to pay for the item? Using our equation for markup on selling price, we have:

$$\% \text{ Markup on selling price} = (P - C)/P$$

$$40\% = \$8 - C/\$8$$

$$C = \$4.80$$

You would be willing to pay $4.80 for the item. If the item cannot be found at $4.80 or less, it is probably not worth stocking.

Likewise, if a retailer purchases an item for $12 and wants a 40 percent markup on selling price, how would the retailer determine the selling price? Returning to our original equation ($P = C + M$) we know that $P = C + .40P$ since markup is 40 percent of P. If markup is 40 percent of selling price, cost must be 60 percent, since cost and markup are complements. Thus if:

$$60\% \; P = \$12.00$$

$$P = \$20.00$$

INITIAL VS. MAINTAINED MARKUP

Up to this point we have assumed that we have been able to sell the product at the price we initially put on it when it arrived at the store. We have assumed that the **initial markup** (the markup placed on the merchandise when the store receives it) is equal to the **maintained** or **achieved markup** (the actual selling price minus the cost). Since in many cases the actual selling price for all of the firm's merchandise is lower than the original retail price, the firm's maintained markup is usually lower than the initial markup. Thus, maintained markup differs from initial markup by the amount of reductions.

$$\text{Initial markup} = (\text{Original retail price} - \text{Cost})/ \text{Original retail price}$$

$$\text{Maintained markup} = (\text{Actual retail price} - \text{Cost})/ \text{Actual retail price}$$

There are five reasons for this difference between initial and maintained markups. First is the need to balance demand with supply. Since most markup formulas are cost-oriented, rather than demand-oriented, adjustments in selling prices must occur. This is especially true when consumer demand changes and the only way for retailers to sell their merchandise is by taking a markdown. A second reason is stock shortages. Shortages can occur because of thefts by employees or customers or because of mismarking the price when the merchandise is received or sold. In either case, the selling price received will be less than the price carried in the inventory records. In fact, clerical error probably accounts for more stock shortages than theft does. Third are employee and customer discounts. Employees are usually given some discount privileges after they have worked for the firm for a specified period of time. Also, certain customer groups (i.e., religious and senior citizen groups) may be given special discount privileges. Fourth is the cost of alterations. Some clothing requires alterations before the product is acceptable to the customer. Men's clothing usually includes free alterations, and there is usually a small charge for women's wear. Still, this charge doesn't cover all alteration costs and therefore alterations actually contribute to the cost of the merchandise. The final reason that initial markup may be different from maintained markup is cash discounts. Cash discounts are offered to retailers by manufacturers or suppliers to encourage prompt payment of bills. Cash discounts reduce the cost of merchandise and therefore make the maintained markup higher than the initial markup. This has just the opposite impact of the first four factors.

Some retail buyers ignore cash discounts in calculating initial markup because they have little control over whether or not the discount is taken. Achieving discounts through prompt payment is thought to be the result of financial operations, not merchandising decisions.

PLANNING INITIAL MARKUPS

INITIAL MARKUP EQUATION

Retailers do not casually arrive at an initial markup percentage. The initial markup percentage is the result of careful planning. Markups must be great enough to cover all operating expenses and provide a reasonable profit. In addition, markup must provide for markdowns, shortages, employee discounts, and alteration expenses (all of these together are referred to as total reductions) which reduce net revenue. Likewise, cash discounts, which increase net revenue, must be included.

To determine the initial markup, use the following formula:

Initial markup percentage = (operating expenses + net profit + markdowns + stock shortages + employee and customer discounts + alteration costs − cash discounts)/(net sales + markdowns + stock shortages + employee and customer discounts)

This equation can be simplified if we remember that markdowns, stock shortages, and employee and customer discounts are all reductions from stock levels. Likewise, gross margin is the sum of operating expenses and net profit. This produces a simpler formula:

Initial Markup Percentage = (gross margin + alteration costs − cash discounts + reductions)/net sales + reductions

Since many retailers record cash discounts as other income, not as a cost reduction, in determining initial markup, the formula can be simplified even more:

Initial Markup Percentage = (gross margin + alteration costs + reductions)/(net sales + reductions)

Regardless of which formula is used, the retailer planning initial markup must always remember the effect of each of the following items: operating expenses, net profits, markdowns, stock shortages, employee and customer discounts, alterations costs, cash discounts, and net sales.

Assume a retailer plans to achieve net sales of $1 million and expects operating expenses to be $270,000. The net profit goal is $60,000. Planned reductions include $80,000 for markdowns, $20,000 for merchandise shortages, and $10,000 for employee and customer discounts. Alteration costs are expected to be $20,000, and cash discounts from suppliers are expected to be $10,000. What initial markup percentage should be planned? What is the cost of merchandise to be sold?

The initial markup percentage can be obtained by using the first equation:

Initial markup % on retail = ($270,000 + $60,000 + $20,000 − $10,000 + $80,000 + $20,000 + $10,000)/ ($1,000,000 + $80,000 + $20,000 + $10,000) = 40.54%

The cost of merchandise sold can also be determined. We know that gross margin equals operating expenses plus net profit ($330,000). Gross profit is equivalent to net sales less cost of merchandise sold, where cost of merchandise sold includes alteration costs and where cash discounts are subtracted. Thus, in the problem at hand, we know that $1 million less cost of merchandise sold (including alteration costs and subtracting cash discounts) is equal to $670,000. Since the alteration costs are planned at $20,000 and cash discounts at $10,000, the cost of merchandise is equal to $660,000 (670,000 − 20,000 + 10,000).

We can verify our result by returning to the basic initial markup formula: original retail price minus cost divided by original retail price. Original retail price is the planned net sales of $1 million plus planned reductions of $110,000 ($80,000 for markdowns, $20,000 for shorts, and $10,000 for employee and customer discounts). Cost is the cost of merchandise before the alteration costs and prior to cash discounts, or $660,000. Using the basic initial markup formula, we obtain ($1,110,000 − $660,000)/$1,110,000, or 40.54%. This is the same result we achieved earlier.

The preceding computations yielded a markup percentage on retail selling price for merchandise lines storewide. Obviously, not all lines or items within lines should be priced by unilaterally applying this markup percentage. All retailers would like to increase the demand by shifting the three-dimensional demand curve (Exhibit 5.7) outward and attracting more customers from a wider area who are willing to pay more. However, this does not always happen. The actions of competitors affect what prices a retailer is able to charge for each merchandise line. The mix of merchandise lines should be priced in such a fashion that a storewide markup percentage is obtained. Some lines may be priced with considerably higher markups and others with substantially lower markups than the storewide average that was planned. Let's explore some of the common reasons for varying the markup percentage on different lines or items within lines.

PRICE LINING

Price lining is a custom whereby retailers only sell merchandise at given price points. For example, the original variety stores were called "Five

Illus. 11.3
During the first half of the century, five and dime stores sold only merchandise priced at either a nickel or a dime. Source: F. W. Woolworth Co.

and Ten Cent Stores'' because all their merchandise was priced either at a nickel or a dime. One of the major reasons for deviating from the average storewide markup is that potential customers may fall into different price points or zones. For example, a customer for a men's suit might be willing and able to purchase one in a high ($400+), moderate ($185 to $345), or low (below $185) price zone. A **price zone** is a range of prices for a particular merchandise line that appeals to customers in a certain demographic group. The demographic groups can be either psychographic or socioeconomic. A **price point** is a specific price within a price zone.

A menswear retailer might carry two lines of men's suits in the high price zone (one at $459 and another at $529); two lines in the moderate price zone (one at $219 and one at $299); and two lines in the low price zone (one at $99 and another at $159). You can see that once the retail price has been established it is difficult to ensure that the storewide average markup will occur in every situation. Take for example a desired storewide average markup of 50 percent and the $219 price line. The mathematics of this example would imply that the cost of the $219 suits should be $109.50. But, as you might expect, it will be next to impossible for buyers to buy all the suits that will be priced at $219 for exactly $109.50. Some suits can be purchased for less than the $109.50 and others for somewhat more. Therefore you will want to establish a **cost range** for each retail price line. Thus, for the price line of $219 men's suits, the cost range might be from $100 to $120, which represents markups between 54.3 percent and 45.2 percent. It is possible for the average markup to be much higher than planned. For example, if the buyer finds a super buy on men's suits (they could sell at $219 but cost $78), then the markup would be 64.4 percent.

Price lining as an element of price policy has much to offer. Perhaps foremost is the ease that it offers for setting prices on merchandise. The retailer needs to decide which price line the purchased merchandise falls into; once this is done, the price has been established. Price lining also offers advantages in inventory and promotion management. With price lining, fewer stocks need to be carried, and inventory turnover will be higher. Also, the consumer will quickly learn what the retailer has to offer, and therefore promotional dollars will be more effective. The salesperson's job is made easier because price coordination of merchandise in different lines is facilitated. For example, the man purchasing a suit from the $219 price line can quickly be shown dress shirts in a moderate price range.

Price lining can also benefit the consumer. The consumer's decision-making process is simplified because the number of alternative price lines to consider is minimized.

Price lining is not without drawbacks. It offers the buyer less flexibility, because price lining coupled with percentage markup targets mean that the buyer must buy in established cost zones. Also, in a market with rapidly rising or falling prices, the established price lines may become quite unrealistic. If prices increase drastically, it may become impossible to find a man's suit at $99, regardless of whether there exists a strong demand at the $99 price or not.

Another problem with price lining is that it may be difficult for the customer to trade up if the price jumps between price lines are sizable. In the example we gave earlier, the customer who is not satisfied with the quality of a $159 suit must take a $60 jump to get to the $219 price line. For many customers, this jump may be too large. The customer may leave in hope of finding a suit elsewhere that is better than the $159 suit, but does not cost $219. Sears, Roebuck has recognized the importance of establishing price lines that allow the customer to move easily up the spending scale and allow Sears to minimize its inventory investment.

Where a leading department store will stock 250 to 300 china patterns, Sears . . . simply can't afford the duplication. A mere 25 to 30 designs, from traditional down to plastic at $10.99 a set, must do the job. But the limited selection is carefully planned on a system of price points or levels that will cover the whole range and gently, but inexorably, encourage the customer to step up in the spending scale . . . In the words of Sears' jargon, the customer is moved from "good" to "better" to "best."[9]

Without exception, retailers agree that price lines must be competitive with the offerings of other retailers. Next, most retailers agree that the greatest unit volume for a merchandise category is enjoyed at a middle price zone. Thus, stocking should be heaviest at the middle price zone. In fact, if a retailer discovers that the high price zone is selling the best, there is compelling evidence that an even higher price zone should be established. Retailers also agree that the dollar jumps between price lines in the high price zones should be greater than those in the medium and low price zones. Finally, it is generally agreed that price lines carried in related departments should be correlated, since this will allow customers to put together assortments within their purchasing range. In other words, a store carrying $219 suits should have $25 shirts and $15 ties, and a store carrying $99 suits should have $15 shirts and $7 ties.

LEADERSHIP PRICING

Many retailers use a technique called **leadership pricing,** establishing a price on an item at a markup significantly lower than the demand warrants for that item. In short, these retailers are establishing a price below the one that would allow profits to be maximized on that item. There is compelling logic behind this technique. The retailer anticipates that the low price on the item will increase store traffic and generate sales of related items. Although the profits on the leadership-priced item may be low, profits storewide are expected to increase, because of the increased sales of related items.

There are several keys to the successful use of leadership pricing. First, there must exist the possibility that low-markup goods will attract customers who will make related purchases. This possibility does not exist in all retail settings. If a jewelry retailer promotes a line of diamonds at a 10 percent markup, it will probably sell a large quantity of diamonds; but it will not be very likely to sell other items to the bargain-hunting purchaser of diamonds. On the other hand, the supermarket pricing milk and eggs at low markups will likely sell other items, since many grocery purchases are made on impulse. Thus, the more traffic in the store the greater sales will be.

A second key to successful leadership pricing is the lead item's appeal to a large proportion of the potential clientele. It must be an item that most of the retailer's clientele are interested in. A supermarket using pickled pigs' feet as a lead item would meet with dismal results since most people are not regularly in the market for pickled pigs' feet.

Third, the lead item must be visible enough to potential customers to appear as a bargain. Thus, the potential customers should have a general idea of the regular price of the item or else they will have little basis on which to judge whether it is a bargain. Also, the lead item will need to be advertised so that potential customers will be aware of the low price. To be highly effective, leadership pricing cannot involve only in-store promotion. Since the goal is to build store traffic, out-of-store promotion is necessary. That means advertising in the mass media.

Finally, potential savings must be great enough to attract customers to the store. As we know, travel costs are a significant factor in determining whether a consumer will visit a store. To increase the number of people willing to visit the store, prices need to be cut sufficiently to offset the travel costs that are keeping customers from visiting the store. Many supermarkets do this with double coupons, although evidence suggests that much of the consumer response to double couponing comes from the store's present customer base and not customers attracted to the store from competing retailers.[10]

If the retailer follows the preceding suggestions, it is likely to use leadership pricing successfully. However, leadership pricing is not without its drawbacks. Of primary concern to the retail manager should be the effect of aggressive leadership pricing on channel relations. Manufacturers and wholesalers put a lot of effort into developing high-quality brand images. If a retailer prices the brand at rock bottom, manufacturers' marketing efforts have been diluted. Manufacturers become especially concerned, because once their brand is used as a lead item by a single retailer, the practice will spread within that city or trading area very rapidly. As a result, relations between manufacturers, wholesalers, and retailers become strained, and less channel cooperation is likely. This happened with Waterford Crystal. Now that discounters have started handling Waterford, many traditional retailers have become infuriated and dropped the line.

As a result of the headway discount retailers have made selling manufacturer brands, many traditional retailers are developing their own private labels. A private label item contains the retailer's name or some other brand name which only the retailer can sell. These private labels offer the

Illus. 11.4
Private labels offer the retailer several advantages.

retailer several advantages: (1) they can be priced below the normal price of manufacturer's brands and above the discounters, (2) they have a higher gross margin percentage than manufacturer brands, (3) they cost less than the manufacturer brands, (4) they can ensure the retailers that they will have a product for every price zone, (5) only one retailer can sell that particular brand in a given market, thus ensuring that not every store in the mall will have the same brands, and (6) the retailer will have a higher GMROI because of lower price and higher gross margin. In addition, by using private labels, the retailers can ensure product quality because the products are made to their specifications.[11]

For example, Marshall Field's has a multi-label strategy for its menswear departments:

"Club Fellow" is a combat line, opening price range, heavy-volume line.
"Field Standard" is for prestige and basic wear.
"New Traditions" for goods at the peak of, or felt to be in advance of, acceptance by trend-aware customers.
"Field Sport" is for active and active-styled sportswear.
"Field Gear" is for rugged wear.[12]

Mass merchandisers like Sears, Roebuck and A & P long have relied on private labels. More recently, specialty chains like Gap Inc., Limited Inc., and Benetton have adopted the private label concept. In fact, the Limited's own Forenza brand is now second only to Liz Claiborne as the best-selling women's label in the country.[13]

Another problem with leadership pricing involves ethical or legal issues. Sometimes a retailer will purchase an item to sell at one price but have the package printed with a higher price on it. While the firm had no intention of selling it at the higher price, more than half the consumers in one area associate the manufacturer's suggested list price with that charged by a majority of stores in the local area.[14] Likewise, retailers sometimes use leadership pricing to bring customers into the store and then instruct salespeople to bad-mouth the lead item (which the retailer has no intention of selling), and try to switch the customer to a higher-priced item. This bait-and-switch technique is not to be confused with trading up, a technique where the retailer is willing to sell the lower price item but does try to lead the consumer to a higher price product. A final possible legal problem with leadership pricing is that it might violate certain state below-cost selling acts if markups are too low.

ODD-EVEN PRICING

A perusal of newspaper ads will reveal that many retailers price items either slightly below an even dollar figure ($4.97 vs. $5.00) or just below an even denomination ($495 vs. $500). If you were to query retailers about the rationale behind these odd numbered prices they would suggest that they create significantly higher sales. Supposedly the consumer views these odd numbered prices as substantially lower than the even numbered prices. That is, the $495 seems more like $400 than like $500, and the $4.97 seems more like $4.00 than $5.00. Whether this is indeed true is debatable. In fact, the empirical research is inconclusive.[15] Nevertheless, the use of this pricing technique results in a markup percentage that may deviate slightly from what the store might otherwise use. For example, a furniture retailer might buy a sofa at $254 and might typically have a markup of 50 percent on such items—which would yield a price of $508. But if the retailer believes in using odd numbered pricing, it might price the item at $497, which would yield a markup of 48.9 percent. Retailing in Action 11-2 provides an insight into the early development of odd-even pricing as a means to reduce employee theft.

RETAILING
IN   **11-2**
ACTION

The Origin of Odd Numbered Pricing

Some retailers favor odd numbered prices, based on the belief that $9.99 sounds much less formidable to the customer than $10. Other retailers believe that the use of an odd price signals the consumer that the price is at the lowest level possible, thus encouraging the customer to purchase more units. Neither theory has ever been conclusively proven.

Odd numbered pricing goes back to the early part of this century, before there were sales taxes. In those days, merchandise was priced at even dollars, and it was very easy for retailers to pocket an occasional five or ten dollar bill since they didn't have to ring up the sale in order to make change for the customer.

When Marshall Field caught on to this, he devised the first odd numbered pricing system to stop the practice. Field ruled that "We'll charge 99 cents instead of even dollars. This will force the clerks to ring up the sales, open the cash register, put the money in and give the customer a receipt and change."

Maybe this explains why despite the lack of supportive research, odd numbered pricing is standard in retailing today.

MARKUP DETERMINANTS

In planning initial markups, it is useful to know some of the determinants of the magnitude of markups. These are summarized below.

1. As goods are sold through more retail outlets, the markup percentage decreases. Goods being sold through few retail outlets have a greater markup percentage.
2. The higher the handling and storage costs of the goods, the higher the markup should be.
3. The greater the likelihood of a price reduction due to the seasonality of the goods, the greater the magnitude of the markup percentage early in the season.
4. The higher the demand inelasticity of price for the goods, the greater the markup percentage.

Although these determinants are common to all retail lines, there are others that are unique to each line of trade and are only learned through experience in the respective lines, such as how much to mark up produce in a supermarket during different seasons.

MARKDOWN MANAGEMENT

In order to determine the actual percentage markup achieved for a period, retailers must calculate their maintained markup. This is the most important markup percentage for retailers, since maintained markup determines the operating profit of the store. The maintained markup percentage is vital to determine the operations efficiency of the store's merchandising practices.

While retailers would like to have their initial markup (the markup placed on the merchandise when the store receives it) equal the maintained markup (the actual selling price minus the cost), this seldom happens. Markdowns and other reductions result in a firm getting a lower price for its merchandise than originally asked. Maintained markup (sometimes referred to as gross) is the key to profitability, because it is the difference between actual selling price and the total cost of that merchandise. Exhibit 11.3 shows the maintained markup or gross margin, for a large department store chain by department for a recent year.

For effective retail price management, markdowns need to be planned. Pricing is not a science with a high degree of precision, but an art form with considerable room for error. If the retailer knew everything it needed to know about demand and supply factors, it could use the science of economics to establish a price that would maximize profits and ensure the sale of all the merchandise. Unfortunately, it does not possess perfect

Exhibit 11.3

Maintained Markup or Gross Margin for A Large Department Store Chain

Department Description	Gross Margin Percentage	Department Description	Gross Margin Percentage
Better Coats	43.0	Inexpensive coats	46.2
Better Dresses	36.4	Suits	44.5
Women's Dresses	42.9	Special Occasion	36.2
Petite Sportswear	43.9	Moderate Dresses	41.4
Ms. Budget Separates	48.1	Petite Dresses	42.4
Ms. Active & Status	40.9	Contemporary	44.7
Better Sportswear	37.5	Ms. Sweaters	44.1
Ms. Better Blouses	44.7	Budget Coordinates	44.7
Jewelry	49.8	Bridge Jewelry	46.1
Fashion Accessories	50.9	Small Leather Goods	47.5
Footwear & Bodywear	47.7	Fragrance	39.2
Men's Fragrance	38.7	Cosmetic Accessories	38.6
Junior Tops	45.6	Junior Bottoms	45.6
Junior Budget Dresses	46.8	Daywear Lingerie	53.9
Young Juniors	43.4	Lamps	40.6
Sleepwear	48.8	Junior Lingerie	46.8
Foundations	53.4	Loungewear	46.3
Girls Wear (7 to 14)	45.6	Young World Accessories	44.3
Girls Wear (4 to 6X)	45.6	Girl's Lingerie	46.6
Boys Wear (4 to 7)	43.7	Toddler (2 to 4)	44.1
Newborn	45.5	Boys Furnishings	44.1
Boys Clothing	40.2	Mens Outerwear	43.7
Mens Suits	27.5	Mens Active Wear	43.3
Updated Mens Wear	30.3	Mens Shirts and Sweaters	43.3
Young Mens	41.6	Mens Better Sportswear	35.5
Mens Sport Clothing	45.5	Mens Underwear & Hosiery	49.3
Mens Furnishings	51.2	Mens Neckwear	55.1
Mens Dress Shirts	45.3	Stationery	42.8
Toys	36.4	Electric Floor Care	24.6
Gift Housewares	39.6	Candy	38.2
Cookware	39.6	Towels and Rugs	44.4
Table Tops	48.3	Blankets	41.5
Sheets and Pillow cases	37.8	Pillows and Accessories	44.3
Curtains and Drapes	36.6	Occasional Furniture	42.9
Notions	43.5	Casual Furniture	37.1
Television	19.2	Bedding and Accessories	45.7
Upholstered Furniture	42.4	Furniture Accessories	34.5
Dining and Bedroom Furniture	38.4	Lamps	44.1
Rugs	44.3	Silverware	41.2
Luggage	43.4	Glassware	42.5
		Gift Shop	43.8

information about supply and demand factors. As a result, the entire merchandising process is subject to error, which makes pricing difficult. Four basic errors can occur: (1) buying errors, (2) pricing errors, (3) merchandising errors, and (4) promotion errors.

BUYING ERRORS

Errors in buying occur on the supply side of the pricing question. The retailer may buy the wrong merchandise, or the right merchandise in too large a quantity. The merchandise purchased could be in the wrong styles, sizes, colors, patterns, or price range. Too large a quantity could have been purchased because demand was overestimated or a recession was not foreseen. Whatever the cause of the buying error, the net result is a need to cut price to move the merchandise. Often price cuts reduce the price of the merchandise to below cost. Thus, buying errors can be quite

Exhibit 11.4

Some Common Buying Errors

1. Failure to analyze previous year's merchandise results before going to market or making purchases.
2. Failure to have kept records from the previous year.
3. Determining only the quantity and leaving the merchandise selection to the vendor, especially size and color selections.
4. Using too many vendors.
5. Merchandise whose sizes and/or colors were wrongly bought or in too large a quantity or were wrongly delivered and proved to be disproportionate to customer demand at regular price.
6. Not helping out inexperienced buyers.
7. Failure to know the selling season for your market.
8. Buying too many items rather than just a few styles.
9. Buying too many hot, new items.
10. Failure to make small initial purchases, that can be followed up by reorders.
11. Failure to determine if buyer can deliver on time the merchandise ordered or accepting changes by the manufacturer.
12. Buying too broad of a product line.
13. Failure to cancel past due orders.
14. Making the last re-order once too often. The last one may arrive just in time to be marked down.
15. Failure to negotiate all possible discounts from the vendor.
16. Failure to study the market sufficiently so as to know the best quality merchandise and best price.
17. Failure to ask one of the following questions during negotiations: a. "Does your company substitute ship?" b. "Does your company backorder often?" c. "How long has your company been in business?"
18. Failure to shop the competition so as not to buy identical items.
19. Failure to talk with the central office (where applicable) in order to see what other buyer services are offered.
20. Failure to buy enough merchandise, resulting in lost sales volume.
21. Buying your personal preferences, instead of the market's preferences.

costly. As a consequence, you might expect that the retail manager would wish to minimize buying errors. However, this is not the case. The retailer could minimize buying errors by being extremely conservative. It could buy only what it knew the customer wanted and what it could be certain of selling. Buying errors would be minimized, but at the expense of lost profit opportunities on some riskier types of purchase decisions. Remember, the more likely the potential price reduction, the higher the markup percentage. This is simply another way of recognizing that taking a gamble on some purchases can be profitable if initial markups are high. Exhibit 11.4 lists some of the most common buying errors made by buyers.

PRICING ERRORS

Errors in pricing merchandise can be another cause of markdowns. They occur when the price of the item is too high to move at the speed and in the quantity desired. The goods may have been bought in the right styles, at the right time, and in the right quantities, but the price on the item may simply be too high. This would create purchase resistance on the part of the typical customer.

A price is often judged to be high relative to the pricing behavior of competitors. Perhaps in principle, the price would have been optimum, but if competitors price the same item substantially lower, then the original retailer's price becomes too high.

MERCHANDISING ERRORS

Many retailers believe that carrying over seasonal or fashion merchandise into the next merchandising season is the most common merchandise error, but it isn't. Failure by the buyer to inform the sales staff how the new merchandise relates to the current stock, ties in with the store's image, and satisfies the needs of the store's target market is the most common merchandising error. A key point in this error category is the failure to keep store employees informed about new merchandise lines so that they can be more knowledgeable to customers. Too many times, new merchandise is left in the storeroom or the salespeople are not informed about key features of the new item and thus the customer will never be able to get excited about the new merchandise. Another merchandising error is the improper handling of the merchandise by the sales staff or ineffective visual presentation of the merchandise. Failure to stock the new merchandise behind old merchandise or misplacing the merchandise are examples of merchandising errors. All too often an item is a slow seller because it is a "lost" bundle of merchandise.

PROMOTION ERRORS

Sometimes the right goods are purchased in the right quantities and are priced correctly, but the merchandise fails to move as planned. This is most often due to a promotion error. The consumer has not been properly informed or prompted to purchase the merchandise. The advertising, personal selling, sales promotion activities, or in-store displays were too weak or sporadic to elicit a strong response from potential customers.

MARKDOWN POLICY

Retailers should develop a **markdown timing policy**. In almost all situations, retailers will find it necessary to take markdowns; but the crucial decision is when and how much of a markdown to take.[16] There are two extreme markdown timing policies—early and late.

Early Markdown Policy.   Most retailers who concentrate on high inventory turnover pursue an early markdown policy. Markdowns taken early speed the movement of merchandise and also generally enable the retailer to take less of a markdown per unit to dispose of the goods. This will allow the dollars obtained from selling the merchandise to be used to help finance more salable goods. At the same time, the customer seems to benefit, since markdowns are offered on goods that some consumers still think of as fashionable. Another advantage of the early markdown policy is that it allows the retailer to replenish lower-priced lines from the higher ones

Illus. 11.5
Retailers should develop a markdown timing policy.

that have been marked down. For instance, many women's apparel retailers regularly take slow-moving dresses from higher-priced lines and move them down to the moderate-or lower-priced lines. Other retailers mark down goods at regular intervals until the merchandise is sold. This represents a markdown, even though it is not recognized as such by the consumer.

Late Markdown Policy.   Allowing goods to have a long trial period before a markdown is taken is called a late markdown policy. This policy avoids disrupting the sale of regular merchandise by marking goods down too frequently. As a consequence, customers learn to look forward to a semiannual or annual clearance sales, when all or most merchandise is marked down. Thus, the bargain-hunters or low-end customers will be attracted only at infrequent intervals.

Regardless of which timing policy a retailer follows, these reductions must be planned. Remember, when preparing a merchandise budget the retailer must estimate reductions for that time period. Exhibit 11.5 shows the monthly markdown totals for department and specialty stores for the year ending January 1988.

Markdown and GMROI.   The profit effect of varying markdown policies on merchandise can be analyzed in relation to the gross margin return on inventory (GMROI) model that was introduced in the last chapter. The GMROI model suggests that inventory investments be gauged in terms of the gross margin percentage and the sales/stock ratio. It is important to recognize that the more quickly merchandise is marked down, the more rapidly inventory will sell, but at the expense of lower gross margins. If markdowns are postponed, gross margins will remain high but inventory will sell slowly.

Exhibit 11.5

Monthly Markdowns (% of Monthly Total) For Fiscal Year Ended January 1988

Store Volume (millions $)	Feb	Mar	Apr	May	Jun	Jul	Aug	Sept	Oct	Nov	Dec	Jan
Department Stores												
2–10	13.89	8.21	8.70	10.81	17.07	16.34	12.23	7.93	8.02	8.11	13.71	39.53
10–50	17.84	12.43	10.51	13.60	17.27	23.89	14.02	10.92	14.32	13.88	13.52	29.60
Specialty	13.74	12.63	8.67	11.93	21.17	30.46	11.96	7.25	15.21	17.17	14.67	25.42

SOURCE: National Retail Merchants Association, Department Store and Specialty Store Merchandising and Operating Results of 1987, pp. xxix and xxx. Reprinted by permission of the National Retail Merchants Association.

Assume that a retailer purchases $40,000 in merchandise and expects to be able to sell the merchandise in twelve weeks, without using any markdowns, at a retail value of $50,000. The average investment in inventory annually is:

Average inventory investment = [(Beginning inventory + Ending inventory)/2](Inventory turnover in weeks/52 weeks)
= [($40,000 + 0)/2](12/52)
= $4,615

The annual sales/stock ratio is sales divided by average inventory investment ($50,000/$4,615), or 10.83. Given a gross margin of 20 percent, one would obtain a GMROI of (20% × 10.83) or $2.17. Now assume that instead of not marking down the merchandise, it is marked down by $3,000 after three weeks and liquidated in another three weeks. Consequently, average inventory investment annually would be:

($40,000 + 0/2)(6/52) = $2,308

Sales/stock would be ($47,000/$2,308), or 20.36. The gross margin would be ($7,000/$47,000), or 14.89 percent. GMROI would thus be (14.89% × 20.36), or $3.03. Thus, the markdown of $3,000 was profitable, since it bolstered GMROI from $2.17 to $3.03.

Amount of Markdown.   An issue related to the timing of markdowns is their magnitude. If the retailer waits to use a markdown at the last moment, then the markdown should probably be large enough to move the remaining merchandise. This, however, is not the case with an early markdown. Then, the markdown only needs to be large enough to stimulate sales. Once sales are stimulated, the retailer can monitor merchandise movement; when it slows, the retailer can give sales another stimulant by again marking the merchandise down. Which strategy is more profitable depends on the GMROI effect. One rule of thumb for markdowns is that prices need to be marked down at least 20 percent for the consumer to notice.[17] However, the markdown percentage should vary with the type of good, time of season, and competition.

Retailing in Action 11-3 describes how retailers can sometimes regain part of their markdowns from suppliers.

MAINTAINED MARKUP PERCENTAGE

Now let's look at how the maintained markup percentage is determined. A retailer purchases the pen set used in an earlier example for $16, with the intent of selling it for $25 (an initial markup of 36 percent). However, the

11-3

Markdowns Aren't Always Totally the Retailers' Loss

Many times retailers are able to have their suppliers supplement their markdown losses with markdown money, or some other type of price reduction. This markdown money can be in the form of cash payment or a discount on future purchases.

Here's how it works: Let's say the Acme Clothing Company delivers 100 sweaters to Judy's Dress Shop at the wholesale price of $40 each. Judy plans to take her customary markup of 50 percent on selling price and sell each sweater for $80, thus producing a gross margin of $4,000.

After three months, Judy still has 50 of the sweaters in stock and puts them on sale for $50. After selling the remaining sweaters, Judy's gross margin was only $2,500 (50 × $80) + (50 × $50) − (100 × $40).

The following month Judy went to market and visited the Acme showroom. Judy wanted Acme to pay her the $1,500 she lost in taking the markdowns on their sweaters. Judy threatened Acme with a loss of future orders if they didn't cover her losses. Does this sound fair to you?

Actually, this scenario occurs quite frequently. Buyers maintain that manufacturers should share in the responsibility when the merchandise doesn't sell as promised. They claim that if a supplier cannot deliver the gross margin they want, there is no reason to reorder from them. From the retailers' point of view, when a manufacturer contributes markdown money, the manufacturer is really asking for a second chance to prove the salability of its line.

pen set did not sell at $25 and the retailer reduced it to $20 in order to sell it. This would result in a maintained markup of 20 percent.

$$\text{Maintained Markup} = (\text{Actual Selling Price} - \text{Cost})/\text{Actual Selling Price}$$

$$= \$4/\$20$$

$$= 20\%$$

The following formula can also be used to determine maintained markup percentage.

$$\text{Maintained markup \%} = \text{Initial markup \%} - [(\text{Reduction \%})(100\% - \text{initial markup\%})]$$

Where
Reduction % = Amount of reductions/Net sales
In the above example,
Maintained Markup % = 36% − [($5/$20)] × [(100% − 36%)]
$$= 36\% - 16\%$$
$$= 20\%$$

SUMMARY

Price decisions are among the most frequent a retailer must make. It is important to understand pricing concepts and techniques. Price decisions cannot be made independently; they interact with the merchandise, location, promotion, credit, customer service, and store image decisions.

Retail decision-makers should be demand-oriented when establishing prices. A useful frame of reference is the three-dimensional demand model. This model suggests that the retailer pay particular attention to several important demand variables: population density, consumer travel costs, and the maximum demand price. Demand elasticity is product-specific and refers to the change in quantity demanded due to a change in a demand determinant. Demand variables may be environmental, household, or managerial.

Retailers should also be supply-oriented when setting prices. They should know both their fixed and variable cost curves and recognize their need for profit. The profit needed can be viewed as the cost for the use of the retailer's capital and payment for taking risks.

A useful frame of reference for supply-oriented pricing is the markup equation, which states that the retail selling price per unit is equal to the dollar cost plus the dollar markup. Since the initial price may not be attractive enough to sell all of the merchandise, a markup may need to be taken. When we talk of actual selling prices vs. initial prices, we are discussing the difference between an initial price and the maintained markup.

Markups should be planned. The initial storewide markup percentage can be determined by using operating expenses, net profit, alteration costs, cash discounts, markdowns, stock shortages, employee and customer discounts, and sales. The retailer must recognize that not all items can be priced by unilaterally applying this initial markup percentage. Some lines will need a considerably higher markup and others, a substantially lower markup. Some concepts that help explain varied markup are price lining, leadership pricing, and odd-even pricing. The initial markup is seldom equal to the maintained markup because of three kinds of reductions: markdowns, shortages, and employee and customer discounts.

Because the retailer does not possess perfect information about supply and demand, markdowns are inevitable. Markdowns are usually due to errors in buying, pricing, merchandising, or promotion. Since markdowns are inevitable, the retailer needs to establish a markdown policy. Early markdown speeds the movement of merchandise and allows the retailer to take less of a markdown per unit to dispose of the merchandise. Late markdown avoids disrupting the sale of regular merchandise by too-frequent markdowns. The best policy from a profit perspective depends on how it influences GMROI.

QUESTIONS FOR DISCUSSION

1. What is the relationship between a household's travel cost and a retailer's pricing decisions?
2. Explain how markdowns can be profitable.
3. A buyer buys 28 raincoats at $342/dozen. If the department markup on selling price is 52.5 percent, what should be each raincoat's retail price?
4. Why may an initial markup be equal to the maintained markup?
5. In a practical sense, how should retailers establish price levels?
6. Compute the markup on selling price for an item that retails for $19.95 and costs $11.20.
7. If an individual would be willing to pay $28 for an item and a local retailer has it priced at $26, but the consumer must travel 17 miles to purchase the item, should the individual purchase the item? Assume the travel costs for the individual are 18 cents per mile.
8. An item has a markup on cost of 53 percent; what is its markup on retail?
9. Assume that a retailer plans to achieve a net sales of $1.5 million and expects operating expenses to be $375,000. The net profit goal is $100,000. Planned reductions include $88,000 for markdowns, $38,000 for merchandise shortages, and $14,000 for employee and customer discounts. Cash discounts from suppliers are expected to be $30,000. At what percentage should initial markups be planned?
10. A buyer plans to achieve net sales of $500,000 with operating expenses of $95,000, total retail sales reductions of $40,000 and a profit goal of $55,000. What should the average initial markup be?
11. How can location and promotion decisions influence the demand for a retailer's product line?
12. A retailer hopes to make $50,000 on sales of $600,000 next year. If operating expenses are estimated to be $115,000 and planned total retail sales reductions are $25,000, what should the average initial markup be?
13. Why should a retailer plan on taking markdowns during a merchandising season?

14. Complete the following:

	Dress Shirt	Sport Shirt	Belt
Selling Price	$30.00	$24.95	$12.50
Cost	$18.00	$14.35	$ 7.50
Markup in Dollars	_____	_____	_____
Markup Percentage on Cost	_____	_____	_____
Markup Percentage on Selling Price	_____	_____	_____

15. You have just purchased some blouses for $26.00 each and you want to sell them at a 56 percent markup on selling price. What should the selling price be?

16. The selling price is $14.95 and the markup is 40 percent on selling price. What is the cost and markup in dollars?

17. The markup is 45 percent on selling price and the cost is $437.50. What is the selling price?

18. Complete the following:

Selling Price	_____	_____	$75.00	$80.00	$44.00
Cost	$15.00	$25.00	_____	_____	$33.00
Markup in $	$10.00	_____	_____	$20.00	_____
Markup on Selling Price Percentage	40%	50%	33$\frac{1}{3}$%	_____	_____

19. Sportswear wants to produce a 12 percent operating profit this year on sales of $460,000. Based on past experience, the owner made the following estimates:

Net Alteration Expenses $	800	Employee Discount	$ 3,400
Markdowns	27,000	Operating Expense	215,000
Stock Shortages	4,200	Cash Discounts Earned	2,100

Given these estimates, what average initial markup should be used for the coming year?

20. A retailer wants to produce a 10 percent operating profit on sales of $380,000. Based on past experience, the owner made the following estimates.

Alteration Revenues	$ 325	Customer Discounts	$450
Alteration Expenses	1425	Operating Expenses	128,000
Stock Shortages	2150	Markdowns	40,000
Employee Discounts	1100	Cash Discount Earned	150

Given these estimates, what average initial markup should be used for the coming season?

SUGGESTED READINGS

Cobb, Cathy J., and Wayne D. Hoyer. "Planned Versus Impulse Purchase Behavior." *Journal of Retailing* (Winter 1986): 384–409.

Curry, David J., and Peter C. Riesz. "Prices and Price/Quality Relationships: A Longitudinal Analysis." *Journal of Marketing* (January 1988): 36–51.

Kirby, Gail Hutchinson, and Rachel Dardis. "A Pricing Study of Women's Apparel in Off-Price and Department Stores." *Journal of Retailing* (Fall 1986): 321–330.

Mazursky, David, and Jacob Jacoby, "Exploring the Development of Store Images." *Journal of Retailing* (Summer 1986): 145–165.

Mueller, Willard F., and Thomas W. Paterson. "Effectiveness of State Sales-Below-Cost Laws: Evidence From the Grocery Trade." *Journal of Retailing* (Summer 1986): 166–185.

Tellis, Gerald J. "Consumer Purchasing Strategies and the Information in Retail Prices." *Journal of Retailing* (Fall 1987): 279–297.

Zeithaml, Valarie A., "Consumer Perceptions of Price, Quality, and Value: A Means-End Model and Synthesis of Evidence." *Journal of Marketing* (July 1988): 2–22.

ENDNOTES

1. The classic work in the area of pricing is Alfred R. Oxenfeldt, *Pricing For Marketing Executives* (San Francisco: Wadsworth Publishing Co., 1961).

2. L. Louise Luchsinger and Patrick M. Dunne, "Fair Trade Laws—How Fair?", *Journal of Marketing* (January 1978): 50–53.

3. Patrick Dunne and Rajaram Baliga, "Pricing Decisions: Who Makes Them and How?", working paper, 1989.

4. For a more complete discussion of differential pricing see Roger Dickinson, "Differential Pricing At Retail," *Retailing: Its Present and Future*, Proceedings of ACRA, AMS Conference, 1988, 90–94.

5. Randall G. Chapman, "Assessing the Profitability of Retailer Couponing with a Low-Cost Field Experiment," *Journal of Retailing* (Spring 1986): 19–40.

6. Ben Bode, Johan Koerts, and A. Roy Thurik, "Research Note: On Storekeepers' Pricing Behavior," *Journal of Retailing* (Spring 1986): 98–110.

7. Joseph N. Fry and Gordon H. McDougall, "Consumer Appraisal of Retail Price Advertisements," *Journal of Marketing* (July 1974): 64–67.

8. See Zarrel V. Lambert, "An Investigation of Older Consumers' Unmet Needs and Wants at the Retail Level," *Journal of Retailing* (Winter 1979): 35-57; Leonard L. Berry, "The Time-Buying Consumer," *Journal of Retailing* (Winter 1979): 58–69; and Rebecca H. Holman and R. Dale Wilson, "Temporal Equilibrium as a Basis for Retail Shopping Behavior," *Journal of Retailing* (Spring 1982): 58–81.

9. "Why Sears Stays the Number 1 Retailer," *Business Week* (January 20, 1968): 66.

10. Rockney G. Walters and Heikki J. Rinne, "An Empirical Investigation into the Impact of Price Promotions on Retail Store Performance," *Journal of Retailing* (Fall 1986): 237–266.

11. For more information on private labels see Walter J. Salmon and Karen A. Cmar, "Private Labels Are Back In Fashion," *Harvard Business Review* (May/June 1987): 99–106.

12. "Private Label on National Brand Men's Wear," *Stores* (March 1983): 39.

13. "Clothing Retailers Stress Private Labels," *Wall Street Journal*, 9 June 1988, p. 31.

14. A. A. Ahmed and M. Gulas, "Consumer's Perception of Manufacturer's Suggested List Prices," *Psychological Reports* (1982): 517.

15. Zarrel V. Lambert, "Perceived Prices as Related to Odd and Even Price Endings," *Journal of Retailing* (Fall 1975): 13–21, 78; and "Strategic Mix of Odd, Even Prices Can Lead to Increased Retail Profits," *Marketing News* (March 7, 1980): 24.

16. Phillip G. Carlson, "Fashion Retailing: The Sensitivity of Rate of Sale to Markdown," *Journal of Retailing* (Spring 1983): 67–76.

17. Stewart Henderson Britt, "How Weber's Law Can be Applied to Retailing," *Business Horizons* (February 1975): 24.

12 Chapter Retail Promotion

OVERVIEW

Promotion is the major generator of demand in retailing. This chapter focuses on the role of advertising, sales promotion, and publicity in the operation of a retail business. Retail selling, another important element of promotion, will be discussed in Chapter 14, "Servicing the Retail Customer." Our discussion will have a managerial orientation; that is, it is directed not at how to design and create successful promotional campaigns, but how to manage a firm's promotional resources.

CHAPTER 12
Retail
Promotion:
Advertising,
Sales
Promotion,
and Retail
Selling

Retailers can generate some sales without spending any money on promotion. Sales could come from households close to the retailer who frequent it because of its location. This is especially the case for retailers selling convenience goods. Or, sales could be derived from passersby who visit the store for an impulse purchase. Many other retailers use a combination of location and promotion as a means to generate store traffic and sales. Specifically, stores such as The Limited and The Gap that operate out of prime mall locations will trade off unspent advertising dollars against rent dollars and use, in addition to their own promotional campaigns, the promotional campaigns of other mall merchants that will increase total mall traffic. Direct promotional expenditures are not a prerequisite to generating sales. Rather, they are a means of generating sales above those which could be obtained merely from location and traffic flow.

THE RETAIL PROMOTION MIX

Retailers need to manage at least four basic promotion components: advertising, publicity, personal selling, and sales promotions. Collectively, these components comprise the retailer's promotion mix. Each component is defined below and will be discussed from a managerial perspective.

1. **Advertising** is "any paid form of nonpersonal presentation and promotion of ideas, goods, and services by an identified sponsor."[1] This is the official definition of advertising by the American Marketing Association. The definition proposed by Wilkes and Wilcox describes the purpose of advertising by retailers in a more managerial perspective: "Advertising's function is primarily to inform potential buyers of the problem-solving utility of a (retailer's) market offering, with the objective of developing consumer preferences for a particular (retailer)."[2] Common retail advertising vehicles are newspapers, radio, television, and printed circulars.
2. **Publicity** is any "nonpersonal stimulation of demand for a product, service, or business unit by planting commercially significant news about it in a published medium or obtaining favorable presentation of it upon radio, television, or stage that is not paid for by the sponsor."[3] Popular examples are Macy's Thanksgiving Day Parade and 7-Eleven's sponsorship of the Jerry Lewis Telethon on Labor Day.
3. **Personal selling** is an "oral presentation in a conversation with one or more prospective purchasers for the purpose of making a sale."[4] Many retail employees are involved in personal selling. Personal selling will be discussed in detail in Chapter 14.
4. **Sales promotions** are those "marketing activities, other than personal selling, advertising, and publicity that stimulate consumer

Illus. 12.1

Macy's Thanksgiving Day Parade is a good example of publicity. ©Alan Oransky/STOCK, BOSTON.

purchasing and dealer effectiveness, such as display, shows and exhibitions, and demonstrations."[5] The most popular sales promotion tools in retailing are point-of-purchase displays and consumer premiums, such as free gifts, trading stamps, and games.

All four components of the retailer's promotion mix need to be managed in a systems perspective. That is, they need to be mixed to achieve the retailer's promotion objectives. Each must reinforce the others. If advertising conveys quality and status, so must personal selling, publicity, and sales promotion. Otherwise, the consumer will receive inconsistent messages about the retailer, which will result in confusion and loss of patronage.

INTEGRATED EFFORT

Promotional efforts must figure in the retailer's overall plan. Promotion decisions relate to, and must be integrated with, decisions about location, merchandise, credit, cash, building and fixtures, price, and customer service. Consider the following facts:

1. There is a maximum distance consumers will travel to visit a retail store; thus, a retailer's location will help determine who to pro-

mote to. The most effective promotion dollars are those directed toward households in the retailer's trading area.

2. Retailers need high levels of store traffic to keep their merchandise turning over rapidly. Promotion helps build traffic.

3. A typical retailer's credit customers are more loyal and purchase in larger quantities; thus, they are an excellent target for increased promotional efforts.

4. A retailer confronted with a temporary cash flow problem can use promotion to increase short-run cash flow by having a special event like "Midnight Madness" or "Summer Bargain Days".

5. A retailer's promotional strategy must be reinforced by its building and fixture decisions. Promotional creativity and style should complement building and fixture creativity and style. If the ads appeal to a particular target market, so should the building and fixtures.

6. A retailer will seldom push product features, because manufacturers typically do that. However, a retailer with an exclusive line will talk features, service, and image rather than price. Consequently, most retailers feature price in their advertising. Obviously, price management and advertising management should be highly interrelated.

7. Promotion provides customers with more information, which helps them make better purchase decisions. Promotion, therefore, can be viewed as a major component of customer service.

The retailer that systematically integrates its promotional programs with other retail decision areas will be better able to achieve high-performance results.

PROMOTION AND THE MARKETING CHANNEL

The retailer is not the only marketing channel member that uses promotion. Suppliers (wholesalers and manufacturers) also invest in promotion for many of the same reasons retailers do—to move merchandise more quickly, speed up cash flow, better serve customers, and so on. However, the promotional activities of the retailer's channel partners may not be in harmony with the promotional objectives of the retailer.

For example, automobile manufacturers in any given model year want to sell as many units as possible, because they have an extremely high investment in fixed costs. Therefore, as unit volume increases, the average cost per automobile drops rapidly. In contrast, an automobile dealer faces a relatively constant cost per automobile. The dealer wants to sell as many cars as possible without drastically cutting the retail price. But manufacturers who want to sell a large number of cars will put pressure on retail dealers to heavily promote price. In many cases, it would be more profitable for the dealer to sell fewer cars at a higher price per unit. However, this would cut into the profits the manufacturer could achieve by producing more cars. The dealer and manufacturer can have serious disagreements over promotional programs because of these incompatible goals.[6]

As we discussed in Chapter 3, perceptual incongruity can be another source of supplier-retailer conflict. Let us relate this to promotion using our automobile example. Assume that the general rate of real economic growth has slowed considerably and that industry-wide auto sales are off 21 percent from last year. The manufacturer believes that the recession will be short lived and therefore does not want to offer any price rebates or special promotions from the factory. However, the automobile dealer believes that the recession will be prolonged and therefore feels that advertising by the manufacturer should be hyped and that special allowances should be given for increased local advertising. The dealer would also like to see the manufacturer offer an $800 rebate from the factory. Because the manufacturer and dealer have different beliefs about the future, there are serious conflicts between them.

Another source of conflict among channel members over promotional policies is when the manufacturer seeks, through the use of promotion, to attract a high-quality, high-price, status image to its brand, while the retailer wants to be known as the price leader and advertises "We will not be undersold!" In this case the manufacturer's and the retailer's promotional strategies are not complementary and a serious conflict could develop between them.

LAW, ETHICS, AND PROMOTION

Retail managers need to be familiar with the legal constraints on promotion. In addition, a strong ethical philosophy about what is right and wrong in retail promotion should be developed by retail managers early in their careers. Promotion decisions are probably the most ethically-oriented decisions that a retailer will encounter. A few examples will show some of the legal or ethical issues that can develop in promotion.

One important ethical consideration is customer deception. Customers can be deceived in several ways, but two common ways are to advertise sale prices that are not actually special prices or to claim in the advertising that items are being marked down more than they actually are. Remember the example in Chapter 6 of a national retail chain being charged with continually advertising carpet cleaning services at a special "sale price" if ordered by the end of the month, only to run the same "special" for six consecutive months.[7]

This deception could occur because consumers typically only look at advertisements on the day they are considering cleaning their carpets. Thus, consumers are likely to believe that there is a significant savings to be made by buying during the "sale." In reality, the service frequently sells at the advertised price or perhaps an even lower one. Unfortunately, this practice occurs often in retailing and is causing retailers to lose credibility with the consumer who realizes how difficult it is to determine the "true" price of any product or service.

Regarding the practice of claiming that items are marked down more than they really are, consider a clothing retailer who offered customers coupons stating that the coupons would be accepted as cash payment of $20 to $50 on certain garments. However, the usual price of the garments was increased by the amount of the coupons, and this practice was found to be deceptive.[8] Other retailers have been known to mark up the regular selling price before a sale by the amount of the "sale". Such deception occurs when the stated "regular" price is not really the usual price of the merchandise, and the actual savings passed on to the consumer are less than advertised.

Another facet of promotion ethics is the advertising substantiation issue: is what we say about the product really the whole truth?[9] The FTC has primarily policed manufacturers to control this problem, but FTC regulations have implications for retailers as well. The retailer is well advised to review the current FTC interpretation of advertising substantiation. The reader might also want to review the difference between deceptive ad practices and puffery, which were discussed in Chapter 6.

PROMOTION AND CREATIVITY

Promotional programs and decisions cannot totally be determined by analytical and scientific methods. On the contrary, promotion offers the opportunity for highly creative thought. By using creativity a retailer can differentiate itself from competitors. Usually, however, where the retailer has the greatest opportunity for being creative, it somehow misses that opportunity.

One needs only to read the daily newspapers from several large metropolitan areas to quickly notice that retailers copy one another. Within the same city and across the United States, most retail advertising looks the same. In addition, retailers mimic each other in deciding which items to promote. When one department store has a sale on designer jeans, the other department stores in town follow suit. One appliance retailer has a sale on color TVs, so other stores in town do, too. Imitation applies to other facets of the promotional mix as well. One bookstore will have a noted author visit the store to sign books, so other bookstores in town will have authors visit (probably different authors). One shopping center will have an arts and crafts show in its mall, so other shopping malls have competing shows.

The reason for this is that not all retailers take the time to think of means to differentiate their wares. Original promotion is not the product of hurried executives trying to meet deadlines. If division merchandise managers (DMMs) decide on Tuesday afternoon that they want to move more merchandise this weekend and need to get an advertisement to the newspaper by noon on Wednesday, that ad will not be creative. Creativity requires time to think without worrying about other problems. This is idealistic, and retailers may argue that the pressures and fast pace of retailing do not allow time to think and be creative. But if retailers want a good return on their promotional expenditures, then each promotional event must be different and creative; it must attract traffic to the store and be talked about by the consuming public.

Another reason for this lack of creativity has to do with the difference between large retailers and their smaller counterparts. Large retailers have their own advertising staff which strives for some level of creativity. They attempt to generate ads with consistent design elements, so the ads for a particular store are recognized as being from that store, even if the logo is missing from the ad. Small retailers, on the other hand, generally have no advertising personnel and tend to rely on the advice and assistance of the media salesperson in the preparation of their ads. Also, small retailers make more use of the materials and copy supplied by the manufacturer.

A final reason for the lack of creativity in retail ads is that it is difficult to be creative when using only a price appeal, which many retailers are doing today.

PROMOTION STRATEGY

The retailer's promotion strategy is just a part of the total company's strategy. While a retailer's promotion program cannot totally be determined by analytical and scientific methods, it is a process that must contain several important steps:

1. Determine the promotion objectives;
2. Determine a means of differentiating the offering in order to provide a promotional opportunity or advantage;
3. Select the target;
4. Select the message;
5. Set a budget;
6. Allocate promotional dollars;
7. Measure the performance; and
8. Organize the firm to perform the promotional functions.[10]

These steps are common to all promotion strategies.

PROMOTION OBJECTIVES

To devise an effective promotion mix, the retail manager must first establish promotion objectives. These objectives should be the natural outgrowth of the retailer's operations management plan. All promotion objectives should ultimately improve the retailer's financial performance, and this is what strategic and administrative plans are intended to accomplish.

In Exhibit 12.1 we attempt to show how promotion objectives should relate to financial performance objectives. As this exhibit shows, promotion objectives can be established to help improve both long- and short-term financial performance.

LONG-RUN OBJECTIVES

The retailer can establish two major types of promotion objectives to improve long-run financial performance: store image and positioning objectives, and public service objectives.

Store Image and Positioning.   The first type of objective is intended to reinforce in the consumer's mind the store image and position the retailer wants to convey. For example, when the consumer thinks of the Elegant Jewelry Shoppe, the retailer may want the customer to perceive an elegantly designed store, featuring the top names in jewelry, backed by an excellent service and sales staff. Promotion directed at fulfilling this objective will have its major effect on improving the retailer's long-run financial performance. However, as you might expect, this type of promotion will also assist the retailer in the short run, such as when a consumer is seeking to purchase a gift. The promotional efforts of a store have been found to be a key predictor of store choice when gift shopping.[11] Image

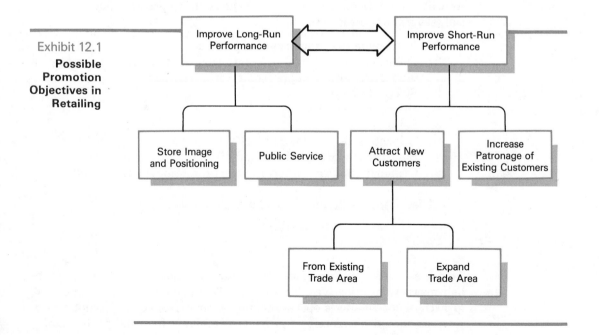

Exhibit 12.1

Possible Promotion Objectives in Retailing

Illus. 12.2
Holiday Inns
Inc. changed its
neon signs in
the mid-eighties
"in order to
project a con-
temporary im-
age that better
reflects the
chain's current
quality of prod-
uct, customer
base, and range
of property
types." Source:
Holiday Inns,
Inc.

was the reason Holiday Inns, Inc. changed its neon signs in the mid-eighties "in order to project a contemporary image that better reflects (the)
chain's current range of property types, customer base, and product quality." Gone were the green, yellow, and orange signs with the flashing arrow and star. In were the more modern, rectangular signs in green and
white.[12]

Other retailers who turned to image advertising in the late 1980s included K mart and Dayton Hudson. K mart, in an effort to shed the image
of its "blue light specials," dropped one of its two weekly newspaper circulars in favor of a humorous television campaign that emphasized the
variety and quality of its merchandise, rather than simply sale items.
K mart also upgraded its merchandise lines and hired Martha Stewart, a
well-known author of cookbooks and home entertainment guides. Michael
Wellman, vice president of K mart, was quoted as saying "what we're trying to do with our TV ads is to project an image of what the store is and
stands for while at the same time promoting specific K mart products.
It's a waste of time not to do both." Dayton Hudson launched its first
image campaign in nearly a decade, declaring that "Dayton's (or Hudson's) Knows You."[13]

Public Service Promotion.   The second type of long-run objective is getting the consumer to perceive the retailer as a good citizen in the community. Retailers may sponsor public service advertisements to honor local
athletes and scholars. For example, some retailers offer meeting rooms for
local civic organizations to meet; some supermarkets have begun publishing consumer newsletters with health, cooking, safety, and beauty tips;

and other retailers provide public service announcements and sponsor programs on public television stations.

SHORT-RUN OBJECTIVES

In Exhibit 5.7 we introduced the three-dimensional demand model, which showed the three ways demand for a product could be increased. In the chapter on pricing we discussed one of the ways of increasing demand; now we are going to relate the other two ways to short-run promotional objectives. The first way, increasing patronage of existing customers, is related to the maximum quantity demanded. The second way, attracting new customers, relates to the maximum distance a customer is willing to travel or effort a customer is willing to expend to shop. In the short run, the retailer can establish two major promotional objectives to improve financial performance: increased patronage of existing customers and attraction of new customers.

Increased Patronage from Existing Customers.   Increased patronage is one of the most common promotion objectives in retailing. This strategy directs promotion expenditures at current customers in order to encourage them to make more of their purchases at the retailer. In other words, it attempts to make present customers more store-loyal. For example, if the typical family of four spends $2,800 a year on groceries and if Supermarket A's average customer (that represents a family of four) currently spends 37 percent of its food dollar at Supermarket A, then the family's yearly expenditures at Supermarket A are $1,036. If, with a good promotional program, the retailer can increase the 37 percent to 43 percent, average expenditures per household at Supermarket A will increase from $1,036 to $1,204—an increase of $168 per year. Thus, if the supermarket was serving 2,100 four-person households, the net increase in the retailer's annual sales would be 2,100 × 168, or $352,800. There is, however, some question about the advantages of catering only to the loyal shopper. Research has shown that consumers who regularly shop more than one supermarket spend up to 50 percent more for groceries than the loyal shopper.[14]

Attraction of New Customers.   A second major short-run promotion objective may be to increase the number of customers attracted to the store. One way is to try to attract new customers from the retailer's existing trading area. There are always some households within the existing trading area that, for a variety of reasons, do not patronize the retailer. Perhaps they do their shopping at a retailer close to their place of employment or perhaps they simply do not find the retailer's store attractive. A second approach is to attempt to expand the trading area by attracting customers from outside the existing trade area. In this situation the retailer might want to consider the selection of different media to expand the geographic coverage of its promotional efforts. A third way to attract new customers is to target customers just moving into the retailer's trading area. Mobile consumers are generally more prone to use national retailers, unless local retailers use promotions to inform them of their offerings.

INTERDEPENDENCE

Exhibit 12.1 shows that although promotion objectives are established primarily to improve either long- or short-run financial performance, programs designed to achieve either objective will benefit the other as well. This is shown in Exhibit 12.1 by the arrow connecting the short- and long-run objectives. What is done promotionally to build long-run financial performance will begin to have an effect almost immediately, but also will have a cumulative effect over time. Similarly, what is done to promote short-run financial performance will carry over to affect the long-run results of the retailer.

RETAIL ADVERTISING MANAGEMENT

The discussion that follows develops a perspective for managing the advertising component of the retailer's promotional mix. Throughout the discussion, remember that advertising decisions should be integrated with other promotional decisions.

TYPES OF RETAIL ADVERTISING

Retail advertisements can be classified in several ways, but the most popular system categorizes retail advertisements as institutional or promotional. Institutional advertisements are most beneficial in increasing long-run retailer performance. They attempt to sell the store rather than the merchandise in it by building a store image and creating a unique position for the retailer in the consumer's mind. Promotional advertisements attempt to bolster short-run performance by advertising product features or price as a selling point.

   Although dividing retail advertising into institutional and promotional ads is useful, it is also somewhat artificial. All good retail advertisers know that all advertising should have institutional overtones; after all, any ad for merchandise that does not place the store in a favorable image is a mistake.

SPONSORSHIP

At the start of this chapter, we defined advertising as a paid form of nonpersonal presentation. The actual sponsor of the advertising can be the retailer, supplier, or several retailers. Most retail advertising is paid for solely by the retailer. If manufacturers or vendors pick up part or all of the cost of advertising, it is called **vertical cooperative advertising**. If several retailers share the cost of advertising, it is called **horizontal cooperative advertising**. Let us elaborate on each of these.

Vertical Cooperative Advertising.   This form of cooperative advertising allows the retailer and other channel members to share the advertising burden. For example, the manufacturer may pay up to 40 percent of the cost of the retailer's advertising of the manufacturer's products, up to a ceiling of 4 percent of annual purchases by the retailer from the manufacturer. If the retailer spent $10,000 on advertising the manufacturer's products, then it could be reimbursed 40 percent of this amount, or $4,000, as long as the retailer purchased at least $100,000 from the manufacturer during the last year.

The responsibilities of each party in a vertical cooperative advertising arrangement are typically specified in a contract. In Exhibit 12.2 a typical contract is shown. The manufacturer has significant control over the general content of the advertising, considerably constraining the distinctiveness of the retailer's advertising. To illustrate, consider the relatively high possibility that in a large city (over 250,000 in population), two or more retailers in the same area of the city would cooperate with the same manufacturer on a particular merchandise line. In such a situation, their advertisements would look very similar to the consumer.

There is a strong temptation among retailers to view vertical co-op advertising money as free. Retailers must remember that even if the supplier is putting up 50 percent of the money, they must put up the other 50 percent. Another way to look at it is that since the supplier exercises considerable control over the content of the advertising, retailers are actually paying 50 percent of the supplier's cost of advertising.

Retailers must ask themselves whether they can get a better return on their money with vertical co-op dollars or with total sponsorship of the advertising. Assume you are considering the possibility of advertising two alternative merchandise lines. You have $5,000 to spend on advertising either Line A or Line B. With Line A, you have been offered a co-op deal from a supplier, which roughly translates into the supplier paying 50 percent of the cost of the advertising. This would allow you to purchase $10,000 of advertising for a $5,000 investment. No co-op deal is being offered by the supplier of Line B, but Line B is increasingly popular among consumers, and you believe it could benefit substantially from $5,000 in advertising. What should you do?

The answer depends on two major factors. First, how much will the sales of Line A increase with $10,000 in advertising vs. how much the sales of Line B will increase with the $5,000 in advertising that can be spent on it? Second, what is the gross margin percentage for each line? Generally, any given merchandise line will be a more attractive candidate for increased advertising if its sales are more responsive to increased ad-

Exhibit 12.2 **Example of Vertical Cooperative Advertising Contract**	MICROCOOK Cook Electronics, Inc. 1331 Queen Street The Cook Building Queensboro, AZ 86201

Cook Electronics, Inc.
Thomas C. Cook, President
Roy P. Cook,
    Vice President

COOPERATIVE ADVERTISING CONTRACT

The dealer _____ has read the terms of this contract and wishes to enter into a cooperative advertising agreement with MICROCOOK, a division of Cook Electronics, Inc.

TERMS OF CONTRACT

1. MICROCOOK will allow to an authorized dealer 5% of the dealer's gross purchases of microwave ovens (based on distributor costs) to be used for the cooperative advertising of MICROCOOk microwave ovens.
2. Coop funds apply only to nationally recognized local media and will be paid at the standard rate for local advertisers.
3. The coop fund is not to be used for production costs. It applies only to payment of media space, radio time costs, or special promotional material.
4. Cooperative advertising funds are figured by computing the 5% of the dealer's MICRO-COOK purchases for a 6-month period and applying it to 50% of the cost of the dealer's advertising of MICROCOOK microwave ovens. Cooperative funds not used during each 6-month term will expire.
5. Only MICROCOOK microwave ovens are eligible for coop funds and the dealer must show adequate stock and prominent in-store display of MICROCOOK products.
6. The MICROCOOK trademark must be prominently displayed in all advertisements.
7. The dealer shall not use MICROCOOK microwave ovens in any advertisements in which a competing microwave oven appears.
8. Dealers will be supplied with newspaper advertisements of MICROCOOK microwave ovens by Cook Electronics, Inc. The copy and layout of any ads other than those supplied by MICROCOOK or Cook Electronics must be cleared before use.
9. To receive credit the following must be sent to the Advertising Manager, MICROCOOK:
   a. a completed copy of form #A-216 "Cooperative Advertising Claim"
   b. a full-page tearsheet of all printed advertisements
   c. a verified copy sheet of all radio or TV advertisements
   d. a receipted copy of the media invoice
   e. the dealer's invoice claiming 50% of the total cost of the MICROCOOK advertising.
10. All claims will be checked against purchases and media advertising dates.

_____   _____
      dealer   MICROCOOK

_____   _____
      date   date

Mail to: Advertising Manager, MICROCOOK, Cook Electronics, Inc., 1331 Queen Street, The Cook Building, Queensboro, AZ 86201

vertising expenditures and its gross margin percentage is higher. Let's examine some specific figures. Line A has 50 percent gross margin and Line B has 60 percent gross margin. Currently, Line A has sales of $80,000, and it is expected that a $10,000 advertising program would push sales up to $110,000. Line B has sales of $18,000 and it is expected that a $5,000 advertising program would increase the sales volume to

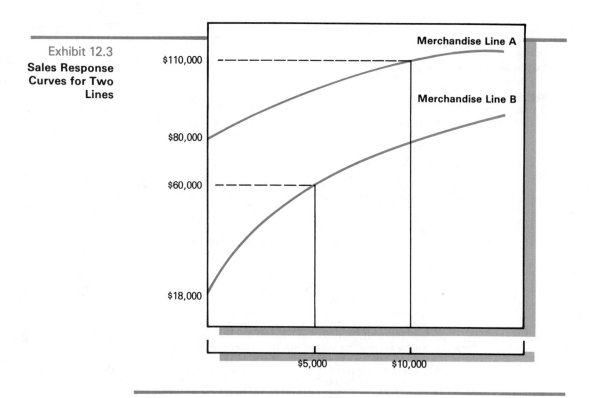

Exhibit 12.3

Sales Response Curves for Two Lines

$60,000. Exhibit 12.3 shows the sales response functions for Lines A and B.

Notice that Line B, although its current sales are relatively low, is more responsive to advertising expenditures than Line A. Below we present the numerical analysis that will help you determine which line to advertise.

	Line A		Line B	
	Before	After	Before	After
Sales	$80,000	$110,000	$18,000	$60,000
Cost of merchandise	40,000	55,000	7,200	24,000
Gross profit	40,000	55,000	10,800	36,000
Advertising (net cost to retailer)	0	5,000	0	5,000
Contribution profit	$40,000	$ 50,000	$10,800	$31,000

This analysis suggests that it would be more profitable to pass up the co-op deal on Line A and spend $5,000 on advertising Line B.

Horizontal Cooperative Advertising.   With horizontal cooperative advertising, two or more retailers band together to share the cost of advertising. This tends to give small retailers more bargaining power in purchasing advertising than they would have alone. Also, if properly conducted, horizontal cooperative advertising can create substantially more store traffic. For example, retailers in shopping malls will often jointly sponsor multiple-page spreads in newspapers promoting special sales events such as "George Washington's Birthday Sale Days" or "Moonlight Madness" sales, while downtown merchants usually gather and jointly sponsor "Sidewalk Days" or "Downtown Days" sales. These events are good traffic generators. They pull significantly more people to the shopping area than any individual merchant's advertising could expect to, and all retailers benefit from the increased traffic in the shopping area. Exhibit 12.4 shows the various horizontal cooperative campaigns planned for one shopping mall for an upcoming year. Sometimes these horizontal co-op programs can produce unexpected negative results, as the letter to a mall manager in Retailing in Action 12-1 shows.

RETAILING IN ACTION   **12-1**

A Mall's Sales Promotion Backfires

Sometimes even the best plans can go astray. Consider a mall's plan for an Easter Egg Hunt. The hunt was supposed to generate traffic, sales, and goodwill for the mall, but the result was the following letter to the mall's marketing director.

Last Saturday I took my 3-year-old on her first Easter Egg Hunt. We went to your mall. For each child in the 1-to-5-year-old group there were three adults.

At 9 a.m., someone said "go." Suddenly my daughter's hand was pulled out of mine and she was knocked down and stepped on, not by eager children, but by adults stampeding to pick up eggs for their children, most of whom were left standing at the starting line, while moms, dads, aunts, uncles, and grandparents pushed and shoved to get at the eggs.

The "race" lasted only about two minutes. At the end of that time my daughter, who hadn't even gotten to see an egg, asked with tears in her eyes if we were leaving now. On our way back to the starting line, we saw many, many children with empty sacks and tearful eyes, and others with three or four sacks full of eggs, hurrying to get them open to see if they had a winning ticket inside.

One man asked my daughter what was wrong. Upon hearing she didn't get anything, he gave her an egg. Her face lit up and she was perfectly happy with one egg.

I talked to the workers in charge of the hunt. They said it is unfortunate these things happen, but the parents were not supposed to participate in the race . . .

I think that by having parents in the hunt, pushing, shoving, and grasping, they are teaching not only their child to be greedy and self-centered, but mine also. What are you going to do about this?

Source: Based on "The Easter Egg Hunt" in Doral Chenoweth, *Media Primer* (Columbus: USA Network Publishers, 1985). Printed with permission.

ADVERTISING OBJECTIVES

A retailer's advertising objectives should flow from the promotion objectives but be more specific, because advertising is a specific element of the promotion mix. The advertising objectives will suggest how advertising will help retailers achieve their overall promotional objectives.

Not a Panacea.   Before we explore specific advertising objectives, we need to stress that advertising will not cure all the retailer's financial performance problems. Many retailers falsely believe that heavy doses of advertising can cure their minor as well as major problems. Advertising, regardless of its quality, cannot do the following:

1. Advertising cannot sell merchandise that people do not want to buy.
2. Advertising cannot sell merchandise in profitable quantities without the backing of every other division of the store (credit department, janitorial services, etc.).
3. Advertising cannot succeed to its fullest extent unless it is used continuously.[15]

What Advertising Can Accomplish.   Although advertising is not a panacea, it can be powerful if properly used. The terms *institutional* and *promotional* do not describe the more specific objectives of advertising. The objectives advertising can accomplish are many and varied. Examples of advertising objectives include:

- Increase traffic during slow periods
- Move old merchandise at the end of a selling season

19XX		
January	**February**	**March**
Thou$and Dollar $ale (Coupon) Misspelled Word Contest Christmas Card Return Mad Hatter Sale	Washington's Birthday Sale (One Day) Open Market Health Fair	Do It Yourself Sale (Demos/Paint/Clean/Fix) Go Fly Your Thing Art Show — Easter is March 30
April	**May**	**June**
Fashions in the Mall Midnight Madness The Great Trade-In Sale Funny Bunny Munny	Mother's Day Free Gift Wrapping Sports Show (Exhibition) Safety Town (Tots) (Bikes)	Pop's Our Pet Senior Citizen Salute Craft Show
July	**August**	**September**
Dog Days (Sale/Dog Show/Trade-In Sale)	Back to School Coupon Days Girl Scout Camp-In/Show	Fall Music Festival (4 Weeks) Harvest Sale (Farm Group Exhibition) Open Market Safety City (Law Enforcement Show) High School Football Night (Intros)
October	**November**	**December**
Birthday Sale (Sidewalk/Clowns/Music) Oktoberfest (Costumes/Travel Exhibits) Spook Parade Midnight Madness	Detroit City (New Car Show) Gobbler Give-Away (Silver $$) Gift Guide (Tabloid) Santa Arrival (Day After Thanksgiving)	Last Minute Gift Guide (Tabloid) Santaland Caroling for Charity

Exhibit 12.4

Next Year's Promotional Campaign for a Large Shopping Mall

SOURCE: Doral Chenoweth, "12/12 Program" *in Media Primer,* (Columbus: USA Network Publishers, 1985). Reprinted with permission.

- Explain store policies
- Attract newcomers in the community to the store
- Strengthen the store's image or reputation
- Identify the store with nationally advertised brands
- Reposition the image of the store in the minds of consumers
- Cultivate new customers

Creative advertising was used by Mazzio's Pizza to successfully reposition itself in the minds of consumers. The pizza chain carried products similar to those carried by Pizza Hut and Domino's. Rather than compete head-on with Pizza Hut and Domino's on price appeal, Mazzio's, a midwestern pizza chain, sought to position itself as the premium alternative to the other chains. TV ads were created to position Mazzio's as the pizza retailer that offered real value for the price with the theme "Mazzio's means more." The chain not only increased traffic and sales but gained more than a 50 percent market share in key markets.[16]

SETTING A BUDGET

A well-designed retail advertising program requires capital that could be spent on other areas (more consumer credit, more merchandise, higher wages for employees). The retailer hopes that the dollars spent on advertising will bring back many more dollars, which can be used to finance these other areas of the retail enterprise. The decision on how much to spend on advertising in any given budget period should be made only after the retailer considers several factors that will influence not only the advertising budget, but the promotion budget as well. These factors are:

1. **Age of store.** New stores or stores seeking to rebuild a lost image need more advertising.
2. **Store location.** Poor store locations need more advertising.
3. **Types of goods sold.** High-fashion goods generally require more advertising than convenience goods. Discounters will need greater selling support in order to increase turnover.
4. **Level of competition.** The greater the level of competition, the more advertising and other promotional activities are needed.
5. **Market area size.** The size of the retailer's ADI (Area of Dominant Influence: that geographic area from which the majority of a retailer's customers come) will often dictate the type and extent of the media used. Also, the larger the ADI the greater the need for promotional (i.e., advertising) activities.
6. **Supplier support.** Suppliers may provide advertising and other promotional support that will enable the retailer to reduce its expenditures for those activities.[17]

After considering these factors, the retailer can use one of the following three methods to determine the amount to be spent on advertising.

Affordable Method.   Many small retailers allocate whatever funds they can afford to advertising in a given budget period. They view advertising as a residual. This approach presumes that advertising does not stimulate sales or profit, but rather is supported by sales and profit. However, many small retailers have little choice but to use this approach. A small retailer usually cannot borrow $100,000 to spend on advertising. This is not to suggest that banks will not lend to small retailers—they will; but they tend to loan funds only for tangible property (inventory, fixtures, equipment), not intangibles such as advertising. This is unfortunate, since the small retailer might benefit more from advertising than it would from more inventory or equipment. The affordable method may not be ideal, but it is certainly defensible given the capital constraints that confront small retailers.

Percentage of Sales.   In the **percentage of sales method** of budgeting for advertising, the retailer targets a specific percentage of forecasted sales to be used for advertising. How do retailers decide what percentage to use? First, it could be the percentage of sales the retailer has traditionally spent on advertising. Second, the percentage budgeted for advertising could be obtained from studies done by retail trade associations. Exhibit 12.5 shows the average percentage of sales and the average percentage of gross margin that retailers spend on advertising. It also shows the annual growth for advertising expenditures by various retail groups.

Advertising budgets based on the percentage-of-sales method do not require great analytical skill and can be developed quickly. However, this method has several limitations.

1.   It bases advertising on sales, ignoring the fact that sales are derived (in part at least) from advertising.
2.   It assumes that the percentage that was appropriate a year or two ago is appropriate for a future budgeting period.
3.   If an average industry ratio of advertising to sales is used, it may be inappropriate for a particular store. New businesses require a larger advertising budget than established stores.
4.   It fails to provide the flexibility to consider changing economic conditions. One very successful retailer once claimed that he never worried about economic slowdowns because when they came, his competitors would cut down on their advertising and he could gain market share by increasing his ad budget. His increased budget and their decreased budgets caused his ads to make a significant impression on the target market.
5.   If the ad budget is based on a sales forecast that is too optimistic, the store may end up overspending early in the season and not have the finances available for advertising in the latter part of the season.
6.   It does not allow a retailer to differentiate itself if all its competitors do the same thing.

Exhibit 12.5

Exhibit 12.5

Advertising as a Percentage of Sales and Gross Margin by Retailers, 1988

Industry	SIC Code	Ad/ Sales	Ad/ Margin	Annual Growth Rate
Bldg Matl, Hardwr, Garden-Retl	5200	4.5	11.1	−8.4
Lumber & Oth Bldg Matl-Retl	5211	2.2	7.9	9.1
Mobile Home Dealers	5271	1.6	5.1	25.5
Department Stores	5311	2.9	11.8	7.2
Variety Stores	5331	2.2	8.7	9.3
Catalog Showrooms	5334	3.7	15.5	2.8
Food Stores	5400	.6	2.3	−47.4
Grocery Stores	5411	1.4	5.7	5.6
Convenience Stores	5412	1.6	5.3	−3.5
Auto Dealers, Gas Stations	5500	.5	1.8	5.5
Auto and Home Supply Stores	5531	2.6	7.3	20.5
Apparel and Accessory Stores	5600	2.3	5.6	12.4
Women's Ready-to-Wear Stores	5621	2.7	7.8	9.7
Family Clothing Stores	5651	2.0	6.3	12.5
Shoe Stores	5661	3.2	8.2	−10.9
Furniture, Home Furnish Store	5700	5.0	10.4	11.7
Furniture Stores	5712	7.2	16.0	6.3
Radio, TV, & Music Stores	5730	1.9	6.0	13.2
Radio and Television Stores	5732	5.3	22.2	20.2
Music Stores	5733	1.2	3.0	12.5
Eating and Drinking Places	5810	5.6	44.4	10.3
Eating Places	5812	3.4	18.8	7.0
Miscellaneous Retail	5900	5.3	13.5	11.5
Drug & Proprietary Stores	5912	1.6	5.6	10.7
Jewelry Stores	5944	3.9	8.6	−5.8
Hobby, Toy, and Game Shops	5945	1.5	4.6	10.5
Sewing, Needlework Stores	5949	3.9	8.1	5.6
Mail Order Houses	5961	6.6	26.8	14.2
Auto Mdse Mach Operators	5962	1.7	2.9	8.5
Fuel and Ice Dealers	5980	N/A	N/A	N/A
Computer Stores	5995	1.0	4.0	18.3

SOURCE: ©1988 Schonfield & Associates, Inc., 2550 Crawford Ave., Evanston, IL 60201 (312) 869-5556. Reprinted with permission.

The percentage of sales method does, however, allow retailers to work toward their objectives in an affordable, controlled manner. Most retailers, especially smaller ones, do not use ad agencies and lack the sophistication to adequately implement the task and objective method (see below). If the dollars are carefully applied in appropriate amounts over the year in such a way that they relate to expected sales percentages in each month, the percentage of sales method can work well.

Task and Objective Method. With the affordable method and the percentage of sales method, advertising follows sales results. With the **task and objective method**, the logic is reversed; advertising leads to sales or some other measure of financial performance. The retailer establishes its advertising objectives and then determines the advertising tasks that need to be performed to help achieve those objectives. Associated with each task is an estimate of the cost of performing the task. The retailer's advertising budget is the sum of all these costs. In short, this method begins with the retailer's advertising objectives and then determines what it will cost to achieve those objectives.

Exhibit 12.6 is an example of the task and objective method. Notice that the retailer has five major advertising objectives and eleven tasks to

Exhibit 12.6
The Task and Objective Method of Advertising Budget Development

Objective and Task	Estimated Cost
Objective 1: Increase traffic during dull periods.	
Task *A:* 15 full-page newspaper advertisements to be spread over these dates: February 2–16; June 8–23; October 4–18	$22,500
Task *B:* 240, 30-second radio spots split on two stations and spread over these dates: February 2–16; June 8–23; October 4–18	4,320
Objective 2: Attract new customers from newcomers to the community.	
Task *A:* 2,000 direct-mail letters greeting new residents to the community	1,000
Task *B:* 2,000 direct-mail letters inviting new arrivals in the community to stop in to visit the store and fill out a credit application	1,000
Task *C:* yellow-page advertising	1,900
Objective 3: Build store's reputation.	
Task *A:* weekly 15-second institutional ads on the 10 P.M. television news every Saturday and Sunday	20,800
Task *B:* one half-page newspaper ad per month in the home living section of the local newspaper	9,500
Objective 4: Increase shopper traffic in shopping center.	
Task *A:* cooperate with other retailers in the shopping center in sponsoring transit advertising on buses and cabs	3,000
Task *B:* participate in "Midnight Madness Sale" with other retailers in the shopping center by taking out 2 full-page newspaper ads—one in mid-March and the other in mid-July	3,000
Objective 5: Clear out end-of-month, slow-moving merchandise.	
Task *A:* run a full-page newspaper ad on the last Thursday of every month	18,000
Task *B:* run 3, 30-second television spots on the last Thursday of every month	14,000
Total advertising budget	$99,020

perform to accomplish these objectives. The total cost of performing these tasks is $99,020. While the task and objective method of developing the advertising budget is the best of the three methods from a theoretical and managerial control perspective, it is not adopted by all retailers.

ALLOCATION OF ADVERTISING DOLLARS

No matter which method a retailer uses to determine its budget, it subsequently needs to decide how to allocate its advertising dollars. It would probably not be profitable to advertise all merchandise lines or departments very heavily. Even if it were, most retail advertising budgets would not be large enough to do so. Some conscious decision on where to spend advertising dollars is always necessary.

Deciding which lines or departments to spend advertising dollars on is not easy. Obviously, the retailer's limited advertising funds should be allocated to products or departments so as to maximize the retailer's overall profitability. But because of uncertainty and inadequate information, this rule is extremely difficult to implement. The retailer must settle for an allocation that is approximately correct.

It is important for a retailer to be familiar with the factors that indicate a merchandise line or department is a candidate for a high advertising allocation. These factors are summarized in Exhibit 12.7.

Gross Margin Percentage. Merchandise lines or departments that have a high gross margin percentage are better able to benefit or produce a profit from high levels of advertising. If a merchandise line has a gross margin of 20 percent, then $5 in merchandise needs to be sold to pay for each dollar of advertising. If a merchandise line has a gross margin of 50 percent, then only $2 in sales have to be created for each dollar of advertising.

Advertising Elasticity of Demand. A product's **advertising elasticity of demand** is the percentage change in unit sales as a result of a percentage change in advertising. For example, an advertising elasticity of demand of 3.8 suggests when advertising is increased by 1 percent, sales will increase by 3.8 percent. When the advertising elasticity of demand is high, the product is a better candidate for a high advertising expenditure.

Market Share Dominance. There is a close correlation between market share by merchandise classification and profit.[18] Retailers with large market shares enjoy an unusually large consumer franchise that can be protected only with high levels of advertising. Thus, retailers with dominant market-share merchandise lines or departments should allocate a disproportionate share of advertising to those lines or departments. The same

Exhibit 12.7

Factors in Allocating Advertising Dollars

HIGH ADVERTISING ALLOCATION

High Gross Margin Percentage

High Advertising Elasticity of Demand

Dominant or Potentially Dominant Market Share in Department or Merchandise Line

Good Backup Resources (Space, Inventory, Accounts Receivable, People)

Willingness to Allocate Enough to Achieve "Critical Mass"

LOW ADVERTISING ALLOCATION

Low Gross Margin Percentage

Low Advertising Elasticity of Demand

Low Market Share and Limited Potential for Being Dominant Market Share Department or Line

Poor Backup Resource, (Space, Inventory, Accounts Receivable, People)

Unwillingness to Allocate Enough to Achieve "Critical Mass"

applies to lines or departments that are growing rapidly and have the potential of becoming dominant in terms of market share.

Sales Displacement and Substitution.   Retail promotions, including price reductions, have been shown to increase current period sales substantially. However, retail promotions may also reduce sales of the brand during subsequent, nonpromotional periods (sales displacement) and reduce current and future demand for competitive brands (substitution effect). If a promoted brand causes extensive substitution effects, for example, a retailer may be worse off, because consumers may switch from high-margin unpromoted brands to low-margin promoted ones. Likewise, sales displacement may have deleterious effects on a retailer's sales if consumers switch from a potentially high-margin time period to low-margin promotional periods.[19]

Backup Resources.   A merchandise line or department should not receive a heavy dose of advertising unless it is supported sufficiently by other resources. Adequate inventory needs to be in stock to handle sales generated from the advertising. There needs to be sufficient space to display the goods and enough employees to serve the customers when they visit the store. If the type of merchandise that is being advertised is often sold on credit, the retailer should have adequate funds to finance the consumer credit or some method by which to get the needed funds quickly.

Critical Mass.   The retailer needs to have sufficient funds to allocate to a
department or merchandise line so that the advertising funds can really
make a difference in the line's or department's performance. Even if a retailer decides a merchandise line or department should receive a high proportion of the advertising budget, it must ensure that the proportion is
high enough in absolute dollars to make things happen. Otherwise, the
dollars are better spent on another line or department that does not require as much in absolute advertising dollars to make things happen.

MEDIA ALTERNATIVES

The retailer has many media alternatives from which to select. Each medium has strengths and weaknesses that are shown in Exhibit 12.8.

Newspaper Advertising.   The most frequently used retail advertising
medium is the newspaper for many reasons. First, most newspapers are
local; that is, they circulate in a well-defined community. This is advantageous since most retailers appeal to a local market or trading area. Second, a low skill level is required to create advertisements for newspapers.
This is helpful because the majority of retailers are small and relatively
unsophisticated in the design and creation of ads. Third, newspaper ads
take only a short time from when they are submitted for publication until
they appear. Since most retailers do a poor job at planning their advertising program over a prolonged period, and since they tend to use advertising to respond to crises (poor cash flow, slackening of sales, need to move
old merchandise), the short lead time for placing newspaper ads is a significant advantage.[20]
    Retail newspaper advertising also has its disadvantages. Just be-
cause a consumer was exposed to an issue of a newspaper does not mean
the consumer read or even saw the retailer's ad.[21] In addition, the life of
any single issue of a newspaper is short—it's read and subsequently dis-
carded. The typical person spends relatively little time with each issue,
and the time spent is spread over many items in the newspaper. Newspapers have poor reproduction quality, which means most ads have little
appeal. Finally, if a retailer has a small target market, much of its newspaper advertising money will be wasted, since newspapers tend to have a
broad appeal. In fact, a retailer's ADI seldom matches the circulation of
any newspaper—it is either larger, in the case of small communities, or
smaller, in the case of large metropolitan newspapers. The exception to
this is chain stores which do much of their advertising using pre-planned
newspaper copy. Retailers such as Mervyn's, Wal-Mart and K mart rely
almost exclusively on newspaper inserts. Mervyn's media plans call for 53
tabloid inserts a year in each market area—one for each Monday of the
year and an extra for Thanksgiving Day.
    The recent shift toward image advertising could lead large retailers to
rely less on newspapers and more on television, radio, magazines, and

Advantages	Media Alternative	Disadvantages
Local, well-defined distribution Low technical skill required for design and creation of ads Short time required between copy and deadline and appearance of ad	Newspaper	Low attention value Short life Poor reproduction quality Wasted coverage when market is small Short exposure
Ability to segment audiences Can effectively employ sound and volume to create distinction and appeal	Radio	Low attention due to passive nature of media Clutter Short life Limited to sound (no visual appeal)
Offers both sight and sound Broad coverage Local cable offers competitive prices for local retailers	Television	High cost Greater coverage than required by local advertisers Clutter
High reproduction quality Longer life than newspaper Longer exposure than newspaper Specialized vehicles can create appropriate mood for purchase	Magazine	Long lead time prevents use of price advertising
Good audience selection Offers means of personal contact Does not directly compete with competitors' messages Results are easily measured	Direct Mail	High cost per contact Dependence on quality of mailing list Junk mail perception

Exhibit 12.8

Advantages and Disadvantages of Media Alternatives

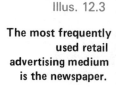

Illus. 12.3

The most frequently
used retail
advertising medium
is the newspaper.

even billboards to get their message across. This is evidenced by K mart's recent decision to move $45 million from newspaper inserts into television.[22] The combination of the shift to other media and the wave of retail buyouts caused department stores to spend only $556.1 million on newspaper ads during the first quarter of 1988, a decline of 13 percent from the previous year.[23]

Radio Advertising.   Many retailers prefer to use radio because it can target select groups. In most communities there are 5 or more radio stations, each appealing to a different demographic group. Radio is also good for developing distinctive and appealing messages through the use of proper variations in volume and types of sounds. In short, there is a lot of flexibility. Also, many radio audiences develop strong affection and trust for their favorite radio announcers. When these announcers endorse the retailer, the audience is impressed.

Radio advertising also has its drawbacks. It is frequently listened to during work hours or driving to and from work (drive time) and tends, over time, to become part of the background environment. After a time, active listeners become passive listeners as the blare of the radio blends into what they are doing. Also, radio is increasingly suffering from too many ads. People listen to radio for the music or programming, not for the ads. They get disturbed when ads are too frequent and block them out. When people do perceive an ad, their memory of it is rather short, and because of the nature of radio, they can't go back and check an ad again. Another disadvantage is that since radio is nonvisual, it is impossible to effectively demonstrate or show the merchandise being advertised. Finally, radio signals tend to cover an area much larger than a retailer's trading area. Therefore, a good portion of the retailer's advertising dollars may be wasted.

Television Advertising.   More and more retailers are turning to television advertising as a way to create an image or position in the marketplace. Research suggests that, over time, pictures retain their effect on consumer memory to a greater extent than the verbal messages from media such as radio.[24] However, a half-dozen well-designed television ads may use up the total ad budget. In addition, for the small or even intermediate retailer, a television ad would reach well beyond its trading area. A final disadvantage of television advertising is that competition for the viewer's attention is great. During commercials, the viewer may leave the room or may be exposed to several ads, one right after another—often advertising different brands of the same product or different retailers in the same line of trade.

In spite of these drawbacks, television advertising can be a powerful tool for generating higher sales. The American public spends more time in front of the television than in any other recreational activity. Television has broad coverage; more than 98 percent of homes in the United States

Illus. 12.4
In spite of some disadvantages, television advertising can be a powerful tool for generating higher sales. Photo reproduced by permission of Albertson's, Inc.

have at least one television set. Many of these sets are color and offer the retailer an even better vehicle for creating a significant perceptual and cognitive effect on the consumer.

Cable TV has made television even more attractive to local retailers. Local cable operators have been selling retailers advertising on channels reserved for local programming. The cost of advertising on such channels is competitive with that of newspaper advertising. However, retailers just starting to use TV advertising may be hard-pressed to find a niche since so many others have already been seeking to fill these niches. Remember, it is important to sell both the products and store image at the same time.

Magazine Advertising.   Relatively few local retailers advertise in magazines, unless the magazine has only a local circulation. National retailers such as Sears or Penney's will allocate some of their advertising budget to magazines, but most of the ads in magazines are institutional.

Magazine advertising can be quite effective. Magazines outperform newspapers, the other major print medium, in several categories. They have a better reproduction quality; they have a longer life per issue; and consumers spend more time with each issue. A very specific market can be targeted through magazines. Featured articles in the magazine can put people in the mood for a particular product class. For example, an article on home remodeling in *Better Homes and Gardens* can put people in a frame of mind to consider purchasing wallpaper, carpeting, tile, draperies, paint, and other home improvement items. The major disadvantage of using magazines is that the early deadlines prevent price appeal advertising.

Direct Mail.   With direct mail, the retailer can precisely target its message at a particular group as long as a good mailing list of the target population is available. Direct mail can be a powerful addition to the retailer's promotional strategy. Topol and Gable have listed nine specific uses for direct mail:[25]

1. To cultivate new customers
2. To minimize or reduce inventory investment
3. To advertise unique, but limited, merchandise offerings
4. To intensify cross-selling
5. To convert infrequent purchasers to frequent purchasers
6. To help develop, maintain, or alter store image
7. To derive an additional source of revenue
8. To bring customers into the store
9. To secure sales leads

While these can be achieved using other media, direct mail provides retailers personal contact with individual consumers who share certain valued characteristics. Also, these messages can be timed to reach the consumer at a specific time without being noticed by the competition. Fi-

RETAILING
IN
ACTION

12-2

How a Retailer Minimized Inventory Using Direct Mail

One of the most overlooked benefits of direct mail is that it can be used to minimize inventory and at the same time, gain important sales. For example, a department store chain might consider selling a line of expensive men's sport shirts that retail between $75 to $100 because the gross margin is high for these items. However, the demand for them is likely to be low, and therefore they may be difficult for the chain to handle effectively in its stores.

If the buyer has a database of the customers who have purchased such items in the past, a mailing can be designed to reach this small, select audience; an audience with a willingness and ability to pay. The database the retail buyer develops is the key to the success of this kind of marketing effort.

An executive of a department store chain with 30 units related the following incident regarding how his firm was able to reduce inventory investment. The buyer of women's handbags had an opportunity to purchase a line of high-quality, high-fashion handbags retailing at over $350 each. The store was interested in carrying four handbags from the line, but stocking an adequate assortment of this merchandise in each of the 30 stores would have represented a very sizable inventory investment, especially considering color choices. Rather than make such a commitment to inventory, a direct mail campaign was initiated. Customers who had purchased a handbag at a retail price of $300 or more during the preceding 18 months were identified. This information was secured from customer credit records and was used to assemble the mailing list.

A mailing piece featuring only these handbags was created and sent only to customers whose purchase history met the criteria established for this mailing. These handbags could be purchased only by mail or by calling a toll-free number, and were *not* available at any of the 30 stores. Sales totaling more than $100,000 were generated within a few weeks, and because stock was maintained only at one location, total inventory requirements were greatly reduced. There was a maintained gross margin exceeding 50 percent, and no markdowns were necessary. In this case, all the ordered inventory was sold. If inventory had remained, it could have been transferred to one of the stores and, if necessary, marked down there for clearance.

Retailers desiring to introduce new lines of merchandise or who have spatial or financial constraints can make excellent use of direct mail to reduce inventory investment *and* reach market segments interested in these new lines.

Source: Martin T. Topol and Myron Gable, "A Teaching Module: Introducing Direct Marketing Into The Retailing Course" in *Retailing: Its Present and Future,* 1988 AMS and ACRA Proceedings, 155–160. Used with permission.

nally, direct mail results can generally be easily measured, providing the retailer with important feedback information. Retailing in Action 12-2 is an example of how one department store chain was able to reduce investment inventory with a direct mail campaign.

On the negative side, direct-mail advertising is relatively expensive per contact or message delivered. Also, the ability to reach the target market depends entirely on the quality of the mailing list. If the list is not kept current, advertising dollars will be wasted. A related problem is the incidence of unopened or unexamined mail, especially when it is addressed to "occupant" or mailed using third-class postage.

Miscellaneous Media.   There are other advertising media available to retailers: the Yellow Pages; outdoor advertising; transit advertising (on buses, cabs, subways), electronic information terminals, shopping guides (newspaper-like printed material, but with no news), and specialty firms such as Welcome Wagon. Each of these is usually best used to reinforce the other media and should not be relied on exclusively unless the retailer's advertising budget is minimal. Most retailers consider these media vehicles as more suited to particular product advertising by manufacturers. However, some supermarkets have used outdoor advertising very successfully.[26]

MEDIA SELECTION

To select the best media, the retailer needs to determine the coverage, reach, and frequency of each medium being considered. The strengths and weaknesses of each medium were summarized in Exhibit 12.8.

Coverage refers to the theoretical percentage of a retailer's target market that can be reached by a medium, not to the percentage actually reached. For example, if a newspaper is circulated to 70 percent of the 20,000 households in a retailer's trading area, then the theoretical coverage is 14,000 households.

Reach, on the other hand, refers to the actual coverage of an advertising medium. If, on any given day, only 90 percent of those households that receive a newspaper have time to read it, the reach of the newspaper is $0.90 \times 0.70 \times 20,000$, or 12,600 households. Another useful term is **cumulative reach,** the actual coverage that is accumulated over time. Using the newspaper example, if 90 percent of the households read the paper on the day they receive it, 8 percent read it on the second day after receiving it, and another 1 percent on the third day after receipt, then the cumulative reach is $0.99 \times 0.70 \times 20,000$ or 13,860.

Frequency is the average number of times each person who is reached is exposed to an advertisement during a given time period. If the newspaper advertisement that we have been using as an example is run for five days straight and if the average person sees three of the ads, the frequency is three.

Media can be evaluated by comparing the cost of ads, the reach, and the cumulative reach for each type of media. The most common way to do this is the **cost per thousand method (CPM)**. The most appropriate way to compute the CPM is to take the cost for an ad or series of ads in a medium and divide by the reach or cumulative reach. If the newspaper ad we discussed previously cost \$500 and the cumulative reach was 13,860, then the cost per thousand was \$36.08 [(\$500/13,860) $\times$ 1000)]. The newspaper may have actually reached 38,200 households in the community, but if only 13,860 of those reached were in the retailer's trading area, then that is the relevant statistic.

CPM is good for comparing similar-size advertisements in the same media type; for example, two local newspapers. But when comparing different media (TV vs. newspapers) CPM can be misleading. A medium such as television may cost more on a CPM basis, but if it has a significantly greater impact, it may be the better buy. **Impact** refers to how strong an impression an advertisement will make and how well it will ultimately lead to a purchase.

Many retailers, especially smaller ones, make little or no effort to evaluate the effectiveness of their advertising, because they believe that there are no good ways to measure advertising's effectiveness. Several methods are available to retailers of all sizes.

One simple method is to check the sales of the advertised products. A common practice is to track unit sales of the featured items for a limited time after the ad runs. However, this method fails to reflect the future loss of sales for the featured item if consumers view the sale as an opportunity to stockpile the featured item or substitute it for another brand not on sale.

Another, more advanced, method is to make use of the new scanning technology available. For example, A. C. Nielsen has developed a system to relate purchase decisions to stimuli, measure the competitive impact, and evaluate advertising and promotion effectiveness. In evaluating the relative results of each promotional event Nielsen seeks to define the

- net extra cases sold as a result of each ad or promotion
- net extra gross margin and cost per each event
- consumption/inventory impact of the promotion schedule

Nielsen's analysis procedures are logical and straightforward. The actual results of the promotional event are compared to an estimated volume for the event period and post-event period assuming that the promotion did not occur.[27]

SCHEDULING OF ADVERTISING

When should a retailer time its advertisements to be received by the consumer? What time of day, day of week, week of month, and month of year should the ads appear? No uniform answer to these questions is available for all lines of retail trade, but there are some general guidelines:

1.   Ads should appear on, or slightly precede, the days when customers are most likely to purchase. If most people shop for groceries on Thursday through Saturday, then grocery store ads might appear on Wednesday and Thursday.
2.   Advertising should be concentrated around the times when people receive their pay checks. If they get paid at the end of each month, then advertising should be concentrated at that point.
3.   If the retailer has limited advertising funds, it should concentrate its advertising during periods of highest seasonal demand. For example, a lawn and garden retailer should concentrate its advertising in the spring and early summer months and perhaps early fall. Along similar lines, a muffler repair shop should advertise during drive time on Thursday and Friday, when the consumer is aware of his problem and has Saturday available for the repair work.
4.   The retailer should try to minimize advertising during periods of bad weather, since poor weather keeps people indoors and sales are not very successful at bringing them out. For this reason, some retailers subscribe to weather forecasting services.
5.   The retailer should time its ads to appear during the time of day or day of week when the best CPM will be obtained. Many small retailers find it advantageous to use late-night television.[28]
6.   The higher the degree of habitual purchasing of a product class, the more the timing of the advertising should precede the purchase time.[29]
7.   The greater the carryover effect (i.e., the more the ad is remembered and influences sales in the future), the more the timing of the advertising should precede the purchase time.[30]

Many retailers use advertising to react to crises, and if this is the situation, the timing of ads is not planned in advance. This is a very ineffective method of retail advertising.

ADVERTISING RESULTS

Will the advertising produce results? It depends on how well the advertising decisions have been made and how well the ads are designed. Good retail advertising happens only if the retailer effectively plans its advertising program.

Some retailers will try to systematically assess the effectiveness and efficiency of their advertising. **Advertising effectiveness** refers to the extent to which the advertising has produced the desired result (i.e., helped to achieve the advertising objective). **Advertising efficiency** is concerned with whether the advertising result was achieved with the minimum cost and effort.

Certain quantitative or statistical tools are used to assess the effectiveness and efficiency of advertising. These tools include multiple regression, experimental design, and computer simulation. Developments in electronic point-of-sale terminals and universal product codes have significantly increased the retailer's ability to obtain valid and timely data. Recently a supermarket discovered a brand new "breed" of customers after analyzing its scanning data. Increases in multiple-wage-earning families, single-person households, and increasing career opportunities for women have swelled the ranks of the after 5 p.m. shopper. This shopper wants one-stop shopping advantages and prepared foods, seldom uses coupons or reads newspaper ads, and hates a crowded check-out line. The media solution to reaching this customer group—drive time radio—was not the most effective for other target groups.

The effectiveness or efficiency of a retailer's advertising can also be assessed on a subjective basis. Simply ask yourself: Are you satisfied with the results produced? Do you believe you got those results at the least cost? Most, but not all, ineffective advertising is due to ten common errors:

1. The retailer may be bombarding the consumer with so many messages and sales that any single message or sale tends to be discounted. A retailer that has a major sale every week will tend to wear out its appeal.
2. The advertising may not be creative or appealing. It may be just more "me too" advertising in which the retailer does not effectively differentiate itself from the competition.
3. The advertisement may not give the customers all the information they need. The store hours or address may be left out because the retailer assumes that everyone already knows this information. Or, information about sizes, styles, colors, and other product attributes may be missing.
4. Advertising dollars may have been spread too thin over too many departments or merchandise lines.
5. There may have been poor internal communication between salesclerks, cashiers, stockclerks, and management. For example, customers may come to see the advertised item, but salesclerks may not know the item is on sale or where to find it, and cashiers may not know the sale price.
6. The advertisement may not have been directed at the proper target market.
7. The retailer didn't consider all media options. A better buy was available, but the retailer didn't take the time to find out about it.
8. The retailer made too many last-minute changes in the advertising copy, increasing the cost of the ad.
9. The retailer took co-op dollars just because they were free, without considering whether they were a good deal.

10. The retailer used a medium that reached too many people outside the target market. Thus, too much money was spent on advertising to people who were not potential customers.

SALES PROMOTION MANAGEMENT

The most popular sales promotions in retailing are consumer premiums such as gifts or trading stamps, games of chance, product demonstrations, and samples. In-store displays, another type of sales promotion, will be discussed in Chapter 13.

ROLE OF SALES PROMOTIONS

Sales promotion tools are excellent demand generators. Many can be used on relatively short notice and can help the retailer achieve its overall promotion goals. Furthermore, sales promotions can be significant in helping the retailer differentiate itself from competitors. A noted authority has suggested:

> "It takes more than merchandise to make a store take wing and rise above others, and some of that buoyancy is the excitement of in-store happenings. Chop them out, chop the stuff that makes them happen, and you've chopped visibility. You've chopped some of the very things that lift one store above and beyond all others."[31]

In the retailer's overall promotion mix, the role of sales promotion is large and often represents a larger expenditure than advertising. Many retailers do not recognize this because of poor record-keeping systems. They know the cost of advertising because most of that is paid to parties outside the firm. However, the cost of sales promotion includes the cost of end-of-aisle displays, product demonstrations, increased energy consumption, etc. The cost of sales promotions includes many in-store expenses that the retailer does not trace to promotion activities. If these costs were properly traced, many retailers would discover that sales promotion represents a sizable expenditure. Therefore, promotions warrant more attention by retail decision-makers than is typically given.

The role of sales promotion in the retail organization should be consistent with and reinforce the retailer's overall promotion objectives. Most sales promotions are not institutional although they do have institutional overtones. They tend to be directed at improving the retailer's short-run performance. As we saw in Exhibit 12.2, short-run performance can be improved by increasing the patronage of existing customers or by attracting new ones, either from within the existing trading area or from an expanded trading area. The retailer should attempt to develop sales promotion objectives that relate to the overall promotion objectives. With well-designed sales promotion, all of the overall objectives can be achieved. In fact, it has been empirically demonstrated that sales promotion can expand a retailer's trading area by a substantial amount—at least temporarily.[32]

SALES PROMOTION TOOLS

We will discuss the more frequently used sales promotion tools: consumer premiums, games of chance, and product demonstrations and samples.

Consumer Premiums.   Premiums typically involve a tie-in arrangement: customers get a free gift or a discount on a gift if they purchase a particular product or quantity of merchandise. For example, a grocery retailer may offer a four-piece table setting at $1.99 each time the consumer accumulates $20 in purchases. Or an appliance retailer might offer a free twelve-inch television with each complete stereo system purchased.

One can give single- or multiple-transaction premiums. With a **single transaction premium**, the consumer will receive or qualify for the premium through a single transaction (e.g., the free TV with the purchase of a stereo). With a **multiple transaction premium**, the consumer will receive or may qualify for the premium through more than one transaction (the tableware example could be a multiple transaction premium, since it may take several purchases for the customer to accumulate $20 in purchases).

The most popular multiple-transaction consumer premium is the trading stamp. **Trading stamps** are given to the customer in proportion to purchases made. For example, the consumer may receive ten stamps for each dollar in purchases. These stamps can be accumulated and be traded for merchandise—usually durable goods—at a redemption center. The value of the merchandise received by the customer is typically more than the cost of the stamps to the retailer. That is, if the retailer were to give a cash discount instead of the stamps, the customer would receive less value.

Trading stamps peaked in 1969, with sales totaling $821 million and more than 75 percent of the nation's supermarkets participating. The economic downturn of the 1970s saw many of these retailers drop stamps and cut prices to keep customer loyalty. Having gone through price discounting, cash prize games, and double coupons, the grocery industry is now trying to return to trading stamps to redevelop the customer loyalty that price wars have destroyed. One study found no evidence whatsoever that double couponing increased market share or resulted in increased store loyalty or traffic. Rather, the use of the double coupons was contained within the store's present customer base.[33] Retailers hope that customers today will look at stamps as a way to acquire items that are desired but not needed.

To use trading stamps effectively as a consumer premium, Duncan, Hollander, and Savitt state that the retailer should meet four criteria:[34]

1.   Enough unused capacity to permit a 10 to 20 percent increase in sales without an appreciable change in total overhead costs.

2. A location reasonably close to a group of stores that do not provide harmful competition but do use the same consumer needs.
3. A willingness to promote the stamps, (i.e., a willingness to encourage customers to take them, save them, and redeem them.)
4. The ability to meet competitors in terms of convenience of location, prices, selection and quality of merchandise, courteous and friendly service, cleanliness of housekeeping, and type and quality of services.

Strict adherence to these criteria implies that trading stamps may not be the most effective consumer premium for the majority of retailers. However, trading stamp programs can produce good results for select retailers if they meet the preceding criteria.

Games of Chance.   Games give the customer a chance of winning a gift. The major difference between games and premiums is the fact that with a consumer premium, everyone who meets the requirement gets a gift, whereas only a few patrons receive a gift with games. The gifts can be large (a free automobile, television, or vacation) or small (a free bath towel or record album). Naturally, the larger the gift, the less likely a customer is to win. At the same time, the large gifts elicit the most excitement and fanfare. A delicate balance between these factors needs to be achieved. The retailer wants to create excitement but also wants to have enough winners to provide incentive for the customer to try to win.

Most games are relatively short-run in their appeal and thus are best used for building short-run market share. In the long run, if games are continually used and are successful, competitors will act to offset the re-

Illus. 12.5

In-store demonstrations are designed to encourage impulse purchasing.

tailer's advantage with games of their own. Another problem that dilutes the effectiveness of games is the antilottery laws in most states. Because of these laws, some retailers must offer anyone over 18 a chance to win regardless of whether they make a purchase at the store or not. Still other states prohibit all such games.

Product Demonstrations and Samples.   Some retailers use in-store demonstrations and samples to help generate demand for a product. Many times, in-store demonstrations and samples are paid for, in whole or in part, by suppliers.

In food stores, free taste samples may convince consumers to decide to purchase the item. In apparel stores, the product demonstration may be a fashion show. In appliance stores, the product demonstration may consist of a person demonstrating how to prepare foods with a microwave oven. Whatever its form, the product demonstration is designed to encourage impulse purchasing.

EVALUATING SALES PROMOTIONS

Since sales promotions are intended to generate short-run increases in performance, they should be evaluated in terms of their sales- and profit-generating capability. Like advertising, sales promotions can also be evaluated with sophisticated mathematical models. However, the development and use of such models is usually not cost effective.

A simpler approach is to monitor weekly unit volume before the sales promotion and compare it to weekly unit volume during and after the promotion. The before measure provides the retailer with a benchmark that can be compared to results during the sales promotion. This comparison should be adjusted by measures taken after the promotion, since the sales promotion may have borrowed sales from future time periods.

Consider a grocery store retailer that featured Tide detergent in an end-of-aisle display for two weeks. Before the display, typical weekly movement of Tide was 8 cases. During the display, movement accelerated to 13.2 cases per week. But for the four weeks after the sales promotion, movement was 4.8, 5.3, 6.7, and 7.1 cases per week. In the fifth and subsequent weeks, movement returned to 8 cases per week. Thus, the net impact of the sales promotion was to move only 2.3 more cases of Tide over the two-week display period than would normally have been moved. (The 2.3 cases are obtained by the following computation: movement during promotion period minus normal movement during period if there had been no promotion minus sales borrowed from future periods; numerically, $(13.2 \times 2) - (8 \times 2) - (8 - 4.8) - (8 - 5.3) - (8 - 6.7) - (8 - 7.1) = 2.3$.) Most of the gross increase in sales during the two-week display period was due to customers buying for future needs. This illustrates an important point about sales promotions: for staple and necessity items, sales promotions will generally encourage people to stock up but seldom encourage them to consume more. Thus, the value of sales promotions for these goods rests on their ability to expand the retailer's trading area and capture customers that would have purchased these items elsewhere. Selling more to existing customers at the expense of their buying less in the future will not economically justify the promotion.

PUBLICITY MANAGEMENT

Publicity was defined at the beginning of this chapter as any "nonpersonal stimulation of demand for a product, service, or business unit by planting commercially significant news about it in a published medium or obtaining favorable presentation of it upon radio, television, or stage that is not paid for by the sponsor."[35] In a way, this definition is misleading. Although the retailer does not directly pay for publicity, it can be very expensive to have a good publicity department to plant commercially significant news in the appropriate places. It may be even more expensive to create the news that is worth reporting. For example, Hudson's Thanksgiving Day Parade in Detroit, 7-Eleven sponsoring a car in the Indianapolis 500 race, and McDonald's Ronald McDonald Houses represent significant dollar expenditures. They create favorable publicity, but they are expensive. Whether the money could be better spent in other ways is debatable.

We will not pursue a detailed discussion of publicity management, since most retail enterprises do not have a formal publicity department or even a person in charge of publicity. But it is important to recognize that publicity, like all forms of promotion, has its strengths and weaknesses. Its major advantages are that it is objective, credible, and appeals to a mass audience. Its major disadvantages are that publicity is difficult to control and time. Publicity-related events are hard to plan, and the cost of planning can be exorbitant.

If publicity is formally managed in the retail enterprise, it should be integrated with other elements of the promotion mix. In addition, all publicity should reinforce the store's image.

SUMMARY

Retail promotion is comprised of advertising, sales promotions, publicity, and personal selling. These four components must be integrated with each other and with other retail decision areas such as location, merchandise, credit, cash, building and fixtures, price, and customer service. Using the retail management model, the retailer should establish promotion objectives that are either directly or indirectly related to improving financial performance.

Retail advertisements can be institutional (attempting to sell the store) or promotional (attempting to bolster short-run performance by advertising product features or price). All good retail advertising has institutional overtones: any ad that does not give the store a favorable image is a mistake.

When budgeting advertising funds, retailers tend to use the affordable method, the percentage-of-sales method, or the task and objective method. Once the budget is established, it should be allocated in such a way that it maximizes the retailer's overall profitability. Retailers can choose from a variety of media alternatives, primarily newspapers, radio, television, magazines, and direct mail. Each medium has its own advantages and disadvantages. To choose among the media, the retailer should know their strengths and weaknesses, coverage and reach, and the cost of an ad. After the retailer selects a medium, it must decide when its ad should appear.

The ability of advertisements to produce results depends on how well the retailer plans its advertising program. Advertising results should be assessed in terms of efficiency and effectiveness. Effectiveness is the extent to which advertising has produced the desired result. Efficiency is concerned with whether the result was achieved with minimum cost.

Sales promotion is a second component of the retail promotion mix. The most popular forms are consumer premiums, games of chance, and product demonstrations and samples. They can be used to help the retailer bolster its short-run performance. As with advertising, the retailer should evaluate the effectiveness and efficiency of sales promotions.

Publicity is the final component of the retail promotion mix discussed in this chapter. Retail selling will be discussed in Chapter 14. Although the retailer may not directly pay for publicity, the indirect cost can be quite significant. Most retail enterprises do not have formal publicity departments or directors, but some of the more progressive retailers do. The major advantage of publicity is that it is objective, credible, and appeals to a mass audience. The major disadvantage is that publicity is difficult to control and schedule.

QUESTIONS FOR DISCUSSION

1. What is the relationship between retail promotion decisions and the marketing channel?
2. How should advertising and sales promotions be evaluated?
3. What methods should a retailer use in selecting the media for advertising?
4. What is sales promotion? How is it different from advertising?

5. Do you agree or disagree with the following statement: "A retailer should always make use of every dollar of co-op advertising available." Explain your answer.
6. Define the term *publicity*. How does publicity fit into a retailer's promotional efforts?
7. Visit a local retailer that offers trading stamps. What do you think of the status of trading stamps in your community? What do you think is the future for trading stamps nationally, over the next decade?
8. What is the first thing a retailer should do when developing its promotion strategy? Why?
9. Explain how a long-run promotional objective can effect the firm over the short run.
10. What are the two different types of retail advertising?
11. What is cooperative advertising? When should it be used?
12. Describe the three methods available to the retailer for determining the amount to spend on advertising.
13. A retailer is offered a co-op advertising deal from a major supplier. The supplier will pay 60 percent of the retailer's advertising expense as long as the advertising features the supplier's product line. The retailer is considering spending $8,000 on advertising the supplier's line, since the supplier will pick up $4,800. The product line has a gross margin of 64 percent, and the retailer expects the advertising to increase sales by 30 percent. Current sales are $100,000. Should the retailer participate in this program?

SUGGESTED READINGS

Blasko, Vincent J., and Michael P. Mokwa. "Creativity in Advertising: A Janusian Perspective," *Journal of Advertising* (1986): 43–50.
Dhebar, Anirudh, Scott A. Neslin, and John A. Quelch, "Developing Models for Planning Retailer Sales Promotions: An Application to Automobile Dealerships," *Journal of Retailing* (Winter 1987): 333–364.
Golden, Linda L., Gerald Albaum, and Mary Zimmer, "The Numerical Comparative Scale: An Economical Format for Retail Image Measurement," *Journal of Retailing* (Winter 1987): 393–410.
Higie, Robin A., Lawrence F. Feick, and Linda L. Price, "Types and Amount of Word-of-Mouth Communications about Retailers," *Journal of Retailing* (Fall 1987): 260–278.
Mazursky, David, and Jacob Jacoby, "Exploring the Development of Store Images," *Journal of Retailing* (Summer 1986): 145–165.
Piercy, Nigel, "The Politics of Setting an Advertising Budget," *International Journal of Advertising* (1986): 281–305.

ENDNOTES

1. Ralph S. Alexander et al., *Marketing Definitions: A Glossary of Marketing Terms* (Chicago: American Marketing Association, 1960), 9. Reprinted with permission of the American Marketing Association.

2. Robert E. Wilkes and James B. Wilcox, "Recent FTC Actions: Implications for the Advertising Strategist," *Journal of Marketing* (January 1974): 55.

3. Alexander et al., *Marketing Definitions*, 19. Reprinted with permission of the American Marketing Association.

4. Alexander et al., *Marketing Definitions*, 20. Reprinted with permission of the American Marketing Association.

5. Alexander et al., *Marketing Definitions*, 20. Reprinted with permission of the American Marketing Association.

6. Louis Bucklin, "A Theory of Channel Control," *Journal of Marketing* (January 1973): 39–47.

7. "Sears Battles New York Regs on 'Sale' Ads," *Advertising Age* (July 4, 1988): 3, 35; and "Sears Drops Suit, Agrees to Change Ads in New York," *Wall Street Journal*, 10 January 1989, B6.

8. Dorothy Cohen, "Couponing and Sampling Can Entail Numerous Legal Problems," *Marketing News* (September 24, 1984): 14.

9. John S. Healey and Harold H. Kassarjian, "Advertising Substantiation and Advertisers Response," *Journal of Marketing* (Winter 1983): 107–117.

10. This list was adapted from John J. Burnett, *Promotion Management* (St. Paul: West Publishing Company, 1984), 41–48.

11. Bruce E. Mattson, "Situational Influences on Store Choice," *Journal of Retailing* (Fall 1982): 46–58.

12. Based on information supplied by Holiday Inns, Inc.

13. "Retailers Turn to Image Advertising, Hoping to Win Over Jaded Customers," *Wall Street Journal*, 8 June 1988, 26.

14. It's Worth Wooing 'Disloyal' Shopper; She's Big Spender," *Supermarket News* (August 1980): 1.

15. Charles M. Edwards, Jr., and Russell A. Brown, *Retail Advertising and Sales Promotion*, 3d ed. (Englewood Cliffs, N.J.: Prentice-Hall, 1959), 14.

16. "Mazzio's Positions Itself in New Market," *Advertising Age* (August 3, 1987): 24.

17. David L. Hurwood and James K. Brown, *Some Guidelines for Advertising Budgeting* (New York: Conference Board, 1972).

18. Bert C. McCammon, Jr., et al., "The New Parameters of Retail Competition: The Intensified Struggle for Market Share," in Ronald W. Stampfl and Elizabeth Hirschman, eds., *Competitive Structure in Retail Markets: The Department Store Perspective* (Chicago: American Marketing Association, 1980), 108–18.

19. Mark M. Moriarty, "Retail Promotional Effects on Intra- and Interbrand Sales Performance," *Journal of Retailing* (Fall 1985): 27–48.

20. William O. Bearden, Donald R. Lightenstein, and Jessee E. Teel, "Comparison Price, Coupon, and Brand Effects on Consumer Reactions to Retail Newspaper Advertisements," *Journal of Retailing* (Summer 1984): 11–34.

21. Lawrence C. Soley and William L. James, "Estimating the Readership of Retail Newspaper Advertising," *Journal of Retailing* (Fall 1982): 59–76.

22. "K mart Hacks Insert-ad Funds," *Advertising Age* (November 16, 1987): 3, 106.

23. "Lackluster Sales Affect Ad Plans," *Advertising Age* (July 11, 1988): 12.

24. Meryl P. Gardner and Michael J. Houston, "The Effects of Verbal and Visual Components of Retail Communications," *Journal of Retailing* (Spring 1986): 64–78.

25. Martin Topol and Myron Gable, "A Teaching Module: Introducing Direct Marketing Into The Retailing Course," in *Retailing: Its Present and Future*, 1988 AMS and ACRA Proceedings, 155–160.

26. "Advertising In The Great Outdoors," *Progressive Grocer* (August 1983): 123–128.

27. "Customer Needs," in *The Role of Media in Nielsen Scantrack* (A. C. Nielsen Co., 1987): 16, 17; "Supplementing the Value of Nielsen Data Through Computer Technology," *The Nielsen Researcher*, 4 (1982): 8–11 and "Scan Data Quality: The Nielsen Approach," *The Nielsen Researcher* 2 (1987): 2–9.

28. "Big Advertisers Are Waking To Benefits of Late-Night TV," *Wall Street Journal*, 9 February 1984, 27.

29. This principle is discussed in more detail in Lawrence Jacobs, *Advertising and Promotion for Retailing: Text and Cases* (Glenview, IL: Scott, Foresman, 1972), 92.

30. Jacobs, *Advertising and Promotion*, 92.

31. M. Seklemaian, *Sek Says* (New York: Retail Reporting Bureau, 1979), 71.

32. Arno K. Kleimenhage, Donald G. Leeseberg, and Bernard A. Eilers, "Consumer Response to Special Promotions or Regional Shopping Centers," *Journal of Retailing* (Spring 1972): 2–29, 95.

33. Rockney G. Walters and Heikki J. Rinne, "An Empirical Investigation into the Impact of Price Promotions on Retail Store Performance," *Journal of Retailing* (Fall 1986): 237–266.

34. Delbert J. Duncan, Stanley C. Hollander, and Ronald Savitt, *Modern Retailing Management*, 10th ed. (Homewood, IL: Richard D. Irwin, 1983), 475.

35. Alexander, et al., *Marketing Definitions*, 19.

13 Chapter

Store Design and Atmosphere

OVERVIEW

This chapter will examine how retailers plan and manage their largest fixed asset—the store building and fixtures. It begins with a look at the major factors to be considered in selecting a building and the elements that influence the building's image. Next, it analyzes the effect of store layout and design on the productivity of the store's selling space. The chapter concludes with a discussion of the importance of nonselling space to a store's performance.

Retailers have always needed a place to transact business and display merchandise to prospective customers. This place could be a department store in a regional shopping mall, complete with aisles, plush carpet, and beautiful light fixtures. It could be a small roadside stand that sells fireworks for the two weeks prior to the Fourth of July. In fact, the place need not even be a retailer's building; consider the Tupperware parties that are held in customers' homes or the catalogues that offer merchandise through the mail or over the phone. Since most retailers do require a building, however, this chapter will focus on retailers that use a building to transact their business.

The layout and the use of in-store fixtures are attempts by the retailers to direct traffic around the store to increase sales. Typically, the retailer attempts to have the consumer visit as many areas of the store as possible, with particular emphasis on visiting the departments having high gross margin merchandise. Retailers have discovered that the store layout and fixtures are as important as couponing and promotions in attracting customers.[1] For example, all Payless Cashways stores are designed to route shoppers through aisles of high-margin tools and gadgets before they get to the bargain items such as lumber, roofing materials, insulation, and plywood. According to a company survey, this has resulted in 40 percent of all customers making unplanned purchases.[2]

The purpose of this chapter is to provide you with an appreciation and understanding of the challenges and problems retail managers incur in managing their building and fixtures.

A CAPITAL ALLOCATION PROBLEM

Capital allocation is the distribution of the total funds a retailer has decided to commit to a store among the available options. The number of available dollars is limited and usually there are more places to use those dollars than there are dollars to go around. All of us know the problem of trying to pay all the bills, put money into savings, and still have some discretionary funds. The problem is the same for retailers who have to distribute their funds to several need areas and still have enough to cover the day-to-day business expenses. In making this allocation decision, retailers will need to choose between the following alternatives: fixed vs. current assets, store space vs. parking space, selling space vs. nonselling space, and store space vs. fixtures.

FIXED VS. CURRENT ASSETS

Building and fixture decisions in retailing require capital allocation decisions. The total capital available to the retailer must be allocated between current assets (cash, inventory, and accounts receivable) and fixed assets (building, land, fixtures, and equipment). The allocation is necessary because no retailer has an unlimited source of capital and because the potential sales a retailer can generate in a trading area will justify only a certain level of capital investment. For example, if the potential sales in the trading area of a furniture store in Atlanta, Georgia are $3.8 million, it would be unwise for the retailer to invest $30 million, $10 million, or even $5 million to capture that sales level. The level of capital that can be invested in retailing has some limit and this limit is dependent on expected sales, net (not gross) margin, and the cost of capital. For example, in the above illustration, the retailer would invest $2 million in Atlanta if the store's net margin exceeded 5.3 percent of sales and cost of capital was 10 percent. 5.3 percent of $3.8 million ($210,400) would be greater than the cost of servicing the debt (10% × $2.0 million or $200,000). Even after deciding to go ahead with the store, the retailer must still decide on the amount to invest in fixed vs. current assets.

Obviously, if 100 percent of capital is devoted to fixed assets, the retailer will have no merchandise to sell or cash to facilitate transactions.

On the other hand, if the retailer has invested 100 percent of the capital in current assets, then it will have merchandise and cash to facilitate transactions, but no buildings or fixtures to store and display the goods and conduct sales transactions. A balance needs to be set between these two extremes. Should the ratio of current to fixed assets be 50/50, 40/60, 60/40, or something else? The answer will be different for each line of trade and for each firm, since each will derive different marginal revenues for increases in both fixed and current assets. However, one general rule is that current assets should be greater than the fixed assets. This is primarily because the retailer is in business to sell merchandise, not its fixed assets. In fact, it is not unusual in retailing for 70 to 75 percent of assets to be current assets.

Even when the retail executive has decided how much to invest in fixed assets, the capital allocation decision is not complete. The retailer still needs to determine the mix of current assets (cash and inventory) and the mix of fixed assets (space and fixtures). Inventory levels were discussed in Chapter 10. The remainder of this chapter will focus on the retailer's fixed assets.

STORE SPACE VS. PARKING SPACE

The larger the square footage of a store, the more people will be attracted to that store. In most (but not all) areas of the country, customers travel to a store by automobile. Consequently, adequate parking facilities should be made available. If, for example, a 38,000-square-foot supermarket is constructed in suburban Dallas on a 60,000-square-foot piece of land, then regardless of how good its location is, business will be dismal. The reason? There will not be enough space for customers to have a place to park, so they will not be able to patronize the store. Again we see the continual retail balancing act: the size of the building, the size of the piece of land, and the amount of parking space all have to be compatible.

If too much land is allocated to parking, too much money is being spent on land that isn't being used. On the other hand, if there are too few parking spaces, building space will fail to achieve its potential because inconvenienced customers will patronize another retailer. You can probably recall driving to a store or shopping center only to become frustrated because you could not find a place to park. What was your reaction when this happened? Most of us would develop a negative attitude toward that store or shopping center and then drive on to a store or shopping center that had adequate parking. The negative attitude toward the first store would then influence future patronage. As a rule of thumb, the Urban Land Institute recommends four parking spaces for every 1,000 square feet of retail space for small shopping centers and up to five spaces per 1,000 square feet for large centers.[3]

SELLING SPACE VS. NONSELLING SPACE

Just as the piece of land needs to be divided into store space and parking space, the store needs to be divided into selling and nonselling space. Typically, nonselling space will be required for offices, merchandise receiving, employee lounges, restrooms, and storage. The question is, how much of the total space should be committed to such uses? In answering this question, we must keep in mind that nonselling space does not stimulate or create sales. It is used only to support sales. Any sales volume requires a certain amount of nonselling space to support it but this space does not stimulate or create sales. Retailers need to allocate enough space to support activities such as receiving and marking merchandise, clerical or office work, and inventory storage that the work can be done efficiently. However, once the point of efficiency is passed, valuable store space is being wasted. Again, the retailer is confronted with a balancing decision that is not simple to make. Typically, 65 to 85 percent of a retailer's total space is available for selling.[4] The large difference in nonselling space requirements can be accounted for by a number of factors: distance from warehouse (supermarkets generally can be restocked overnight, clothing stores cannot), need for preparation or service area (tire dealers need more space for service than do gift shops), and storage needs (furniture and home improvement centers need more space for warehousing and storage than do jewelry stores).

STORE SPACE VS. FIXTURES

Large amounts of store space require not only a large investment in space, but also a large investment in capital to pay for fixtures for the space. If a retailer were to spend all its dollars on space, the building will be of little use because there would be no shelves, counters, or racks to display the merchandise, or even a cash register in case a sale was made. Accounting would have to be done by hand rather than by computer or other mechanical system. This sounds ludicrous, but it highlights the importance of allocating funds for fixtures. Many retailers have built stores that were larger than they could afford to fit with fixtures and equipment, resulting in inefficiency. Other retailers have over-fixtured stores by cramming so many fixtures and so much equipment into the floor space that the store looked crowded and unkempt. This allocation is also inefficient and unprofitable.

THE BUILDING DECISION

The building a retailer selects is a key determinant in the achievement of high-performance results. In fact, the building is so important to success that it can make or break an otherwise average retailer. This does not mean that the building alone can create a retailer's image. No, the building is only one set of attributes related to the development of a retailer's image. Personnel, merchandise, price, advertising, and service are also key image factors.

IMAGE DIMENSION

Although most retailers pay special attention to location decisions, these same retailers often ignore the way the building's interior affects the store image. Martineau found more than 30 years ago that "different class and different types of shoppers have different psychological outlooks on the world and different ways of life. Each segment of the market looks for a different emphasis" when shopping. Lower-status shoppers look for goods in a functional sense: they want the store image to reflect their values of concreteness, practicality, and economy. This consumer group is concerned with the quality of merchandise and dependability of the store. Upper-status consumers are, however, more interested in whether the symbolic meaning of the store reflects their status and life-style.[5] For both groups, the building is more than just bricks and mortar. Although location is of prime importance, the actual building and its characteristics must also be considered. For instance, studies might indicate that the perfect spot for a new children's clothing store is the northeast corner of Tenth Avenue and Park Place. All location theory may point to this corner as being right, so such a store opens in the big red building already on the site. The retailer is pleased to have found a site with an existing building. Since the location theory points to that location, seemingly the store is certain to be a big success. However, it fails within just a few months due to lack of customers. What went wrong? There are a lot of possible explanations, but perhaps the big red building had the wrong image for a

Illus. 13.1

While lower-status shoppers frequent stores whose images reflect their values of correctness, practicality, and economy, upper-status consumers are more interested in whether the symbolic meaning of the store reflects their status and life-style.

children's store. Was it barnlike or warehouse-like? Was it old and shabby? Was it dirty and smelly? Or had a gang of drug dealers been found using the big red building as a front several months earlier? Whatever the cause, the building itself could have contributed to the failure.

A retail building projects an image. The image of a building is its character *as perceived in the mind of the public*. The image as perceived by the retailer may be quite different from the image perceived by the public. In our example, for instance, the retailer viewed the big red building as an ideal children's clothing store. However, the customers obviously saw it as something else, something out of character with children. Without a doubt, the character or image of a building can be a selling tool.

The building's image includes the external appearance of the structure and its compatibility with contiguous buildings and parking areas. If given the choice, most of us would buy food at a supermarket that is new, brightly lighted, and sparkling clean rather than an old, run-down, dimly lit store with a dark, dirty parking lot. It might be fun to visit a flea market to enjoy the carnival-like atmosphere and search for bargains, but most of us would not purchase diamonds, works of art, or major appliances at flea markets. Instead, we seek out retailers whose stores convey an image of trust and stability. Retailers must remember that these virtues can be conveyed through the building.

Bolen captures the importance of the building as a selling tool: "The store is the package which contains the merchandise. If that package does not attract, entice, or at least interest the customer, the product will not sell. A good design helps the product. A poor design will not."[6]

In recent years our nation's largest department store chains have paid special interest to the images their stores convey to customers. Dayton's Department Stores, for example, "has developed a national reputation for innovative merchandising techniques and strong visual display presentations". Andrew Markopoulos, the winner of the first Visual Merchandiser of the Year award from the National Retail Merchants Association, says his job at Dayton's is to present merchandise through visual design so that it creates a pleasing environment for customers.[7]

What these chains have attempted to do is to create an atmosphere conducive to the merchandising of their product offerings. The **atmosphere** of a building is its tone, mood, or psychological environment. The atmosphere can be controlled to build the image. Seldom does a successful atmosphere happen by accident. Consider, for example, the Jax Brewery Mall in New Orleans, Faneuil Hall in Boston, Water Tower Place in Chicago, the Galleria in Houston and Dallas, or Union Station in St. Louis. All were very carefully planned. According to James Levi, president of Oppenheimer Properties, Inc., the 91-year-old Union Station had elegant historical features that had to be retained in order to develop the overall atmosphere. The entire project was well planned and totally coordinated—even down to placing two hotel structures beneath the iron train shed.[8] The overall atmosphere is quite elegant, and its image most favorable. Creating the right atmosphere will be discussed later in this chapter in the section on selling space layout.

SIZE REQUIREMENTS

How large a building does the retailer need? In general, the size requirements of a store depend on location, type of merchandise handled, and amount of capital available to invest in a building.

Location.   When speaking of size in relation to location, one can typically expect buildings in cities to be smaller than buildings in suburban areas. In a city, especially in the central business district, land is very expensive and the amount of space that can be devoted to an average retail outlet will be smaller than it would be if the land cost less. For example, in a city of 250,000, it is not unusual for an acre of land in the CBD to cost $1 million. This high cost of land creates pressure to use land efficiently. Stores that are oversized in relation to their trading area quickly become unprofitable.

Also, because of cost and the availability of land, stores located in the Northeast are, on average, smaller than stores in the West or Southwest. In the Northeast, almost all of the prime land is already developed, some with buildings that have been standing for more than 100 years. Thus, to build a large, new store not only requires the cost of construction, but the cost of moving or tearing down the existing buildings. In some cities, like Boston, buildings have been standing for centuries. Rather than removing them, it has been the practice to renovate them, as mall developers in New Orleans, Baltimore, and St. Louis have done.[9] In other cities, the central business district has been completely razed and rebuilt, creating a new, modern CBD. Another solution to this space problem is to build up rather than out. Using a multistory building, a retailer can get enough square footage without using a large amount of land. This practice will probably continue as the cost of land increases and the amount of usable land decreases. Water Tower Place in Chicago is an excellent example of this concept.

Size may also be determined by whether the building is located in a shopping mall or is freestanding. Space in a shopping mall is much more expensive because of the services the mall provides shoppers, such as air conditioning and heating, lounge areas, public restrooms, shopping lockers, and public display space for shows and civic groups. The retailer cannot afford as much space in a mall because of all these added costs. However, the mall retailer may not *need* as much space as the freestanding retailer because of these added services. For example, parking facilities are shared, each store doesn't need to provide restrooms and janitorial services, and low-profit, low-volume departments can be eliminated with-

Illus. 13.2

Water Tower Place in Chicago is an example of building up rather than out. Photo by Kee Chang, Chicago Association of Commerce and Industry.

out upsetting the customer if the merchandise is carried elsewhere in the mall.

Finally, retailers with several outlets in the same metropolitan area can have, on average, smaller stores because they can consolidate such things as accounting services, purchasing, and merchandising storage.

Type of Merchandise.   It takes considerably less room to display and sell $1 million of diamonds than $1 million of furniture or appliances. Some merchandise, such as appliances, stereos, TVs and electronic games, and cameras, require demonstration space. Other merchandise, such as frozen food or cut flowers, might require a controlled environment. Clothing requires fitting rooms and shoes need a lot of storage space.

The type of merchandise carried affects not only the amount of space needed to display the goods, but also the space needed for aisles and checkout areas. Supermarkets, discount stores, and home improvement centers generally need to devote more space to these areas than bookstores, tobacco shops, or record stores.

Capital Available.   The final influence on the size of a building is the retailer's capital constraint. Retailers need to realize that when borrowing money for a building, lenders are generally less concerned with the building itself than with its location. As we pointed out in Chapters 7 and 8, the three most important principles in real estate are location, location, and location. Lenders are very concerned with the resale prospects in case the retailer does not succeed. Also, lenders look at the selling space rather than total space, because it is the selling space that will generate the profits to pay back the loan.

NEW VS. OLD BUILDING

Retail executives must decide between constructing a new building and occupying an old building. A new building may be ideal in terms of enabling the retailer to design a total atmosphere into the building, construct the proper amount of space in the desired form, and have energy efficiency. However, a new building is usually much more expensive than an existing building.

Even with an old building, a retailer can't just move in. It usually needs to be renovated or at least remodeled to take on the right character, fill the retailer's specific needs, and meet building codes. Sometimes this renovation is more expensive than a new building would have been. Some governmental agencies will only require the retailer to meet the intent, if not always the letter of the codes. Others have been known to put so much red tape in the retailer's path that they postpone the entire project by making the renovation and remodeling costs more expensive than a new building. Careful planning and assessment of the alternative costs and opportunities are required before committing to either an old or new building.

The following insights on renovating an old building for retail use are offered by Mel Kaufman:[10]

1. The structure of an old building may yield interesting and sometimes unexpected opportunities such as 12-inch thick floors, steam heat radiators which can be electronically controlled, and unique display possibilities.
2. Old buildings are, on the average, not as mechanically sound as new ones.
3. Sometimes entire systems (heating, cooling, plumbing, etc.) have to be replaced because of obsolescence. It may be difficult to get new systems to fit an old building.
4. Old buildings are difficult to air condition unless they were originally built with that capability because there is rarely enough space for duct systems and central plants. This can lead to inadequacy, hot spots, and high utility bills.

These are some of the risks involved in renovating old buildings. However, there are sometimes tax advantages available to the retailer who renovates an older building. Therefore, before making a final decision, a retail executive should check with a tax expert. Oppenheimer Properties has stated that without a tax credit, it never would have developed its Union Station project in St. Louis and the same can be said of most of these other downtown renovations.[11]

LEASE VS. BUY

Since the capital outlay required for construction can be substantial, many retailers choose to lease space. During periods of inflation, high interest rates and high construction costs have made ownership almost impossible for small retailers. Generally, specialty stores that seek only mall locations haven't any choice; they must lease. Department stores, on the other hand, are more able to construct their own building. According to some developers, bankers, accountants, and retailers it may be advantageous, in the long run, to build, because of depreciation write-off and property appreciation. In the short run, however, leasing allows a retailer the opportunity to evaluate market conditions and relocate if necessary without incurring any major financial losses. Some malls even offer to cancel leases for retailers whose sales do not meet expectations, since the entire mall will benefit by replacing the unprofitable retailer with a more competitive one.[12]

Some large retailers build new stores and then sell them back to real estate investment trusts (REITs), who then lease the building back to the retailers on a long-term agreement. The advantages of these sale-lease-back agreements for retailers are a store built to their specifications, a reduction in fixed assets, and a bargaining advantage in settling lease terms.

One of the pitfalls of leasing space in new malls or recycled buildings is that the retailer has to build its own interiors, even though the finished product is owned by the landlord. Many retailers have had to install their own floors and walls before they could put in fixtures. Granted, this is why leasing is usually cheaper and the store interior is customized to the retailer's needs, but if the retailer leaves after the lease expires, everything except the portable fixtures must be left behind. It all belongs to the landlord, for the retailer has no equity in the floors and walls it builds.

Most rates for the lease of a building for retail use involve a fixed dollar charge per year that is usually based on square footage. In addition, a charge is usually made on a specified percentage of sales volume with a guarantee from the retailer of some minimum sales volume. For example, a discount sporting goods retailer may lease a 22,000-square-foot building for $70,000 annually plus 1.25 percent of annual retail sales with minimum guaranteed sales of $2 million. Thus, on retail sales up to $2 million, the annual rent would be $95,000, and for any volume above $2 million, the retailer would pay 1.25 percent of the volume.

If the retailer chooses a mall location, lease costs may be more than expected. Costs of a mall lease often include minimum rent, merchants association dues, maintenance charge for the common area, real estate taxes, HVAC (heating and cooling of common area), a sprinkler system charge, and a percentage of sales charge. In addition, if taxes are raised, tenants in the mall usually pay the increase on a pro-rata basis. The decision of whether to lease or buy is important and should be thoroughly studied by the retailer before a commitment is made.

SELLING SPACE LAYOUT

The space within the store must be efficiently and effectively utilized. To accomplish this a retailer must design a store layout. Davidson and Doody define **layout** as: "the arrangement of selling and nonselling departments, aisles, fixtures, displays, and equipment in the proper relationship to each other and to the fixed elements of the building structure."[13]

TRAFFIC PATTERNS

Traffic is the most important aspect of selling space layout decisions. By stimulating more traffic within the store, retailers expose shoppers to more merchandise and cause them to purchase more. The basic idea of a good layout is to route customers through the entire store in their search for goods, while keeping the goods they are looking for easy to locate. The area near the store entrance will get the heaviest consumer traffic, thus it is the store's most valuable space. In supermarkets, 50 percent of all profits should come from the first third of a store's selling space, 33 percent should come from the next third, and the remaining 17 percent of profits should come from the least accessible third of selling space. Payless Cashways, as we mentioned in our introduction to this chapter, compares its strategy to that most used by supermarkets, which will direct shoppers through the produce department first. This is because produce has a high markup, and the consumer is usually hungry and still rich.[14] Retailers have long sought to move shoppers through their stores in a planned manner so that they come in view with as many product categories as possible. Redinbaugh has stated:

> "Traffic should be deliberately routed through the areas which will induce the most merchandise comparison and stimulate purchases. Usually higher-priced items are placed near the rear of the store so that the customer must walk past all the goods. By putting the high priced things at the back, the customer has already seen the lower-priced goods and is more ready to appreciate the features of the higher-priced goods."[15]

A study by the Point-Of-Purchase Advertising Institute (POPAI) found that more than a third of all drugstore purchases were unplanned.[16] Other retailers have taken advantage of this finding. It is no accident that supermarkets have recently expanded to include service departments (delis, bakeries, fish sections, and pharmacies), health and beauty aids (HBA), and general merchandise sections. The logic for these actions is that the gross margins for these lines are a good deal higher than those on groceries, and depending on the level of turnover, their GMROI may be excellent.[17] This forced traffic pattern is applied with good results in high-fashion apparel, furniture and appliances, and gift stores.

Here are some other basic principles of retail layout as related to traffic flow:

1. Aisles need to be wide enough that they are easy to get through, even when customers stop to examine merchandise. Remember, consumers today have less time for purchase planning. There is a general trend toward decision-making in the store environment by consumers with intent to purchase a product category but not a particular brand.[18]

2. Aisles need to be short enough that the customers aren't forced to go through a maze of goods to reach a specific item at the end of the aisle.

3. The store entrance should be free of obstacles or clutter that may interfere with the flow of customers into or out of the store; this could cause "crowding stress".[19]

4. Try to visualize how the traffic should move to reach the entire store, then arrange the fixtures, displays, and aisles to help route the traffic this way.

5. Place staple goods in more remote areas of the store, because the traffic patterns will move to them.

6. Place impulse goods in high-traffic areas.

7. Place frequently purchased goods in easy-access areas.

8. Remember that your target market, especially the elderly, might have special needs that must be considered in developing traffic patterns.[20]

9. Remember that no amount of promotion or selling expertise will overcome a poorly designed store layout. If the product category is in the wrong place, the sale is usually lost.[21]

STORE DISPLAYS

Store displays are of two major types—window and interior. Window displays have actually declined in importance since the early 1960s. In many new suburban stores, there is very little, if any, window display space. In regional shopping malls, the outside perimeter typically has no windows. All windows are on the inside, but even then each store has a very small storefront and window displays are kept to a minimum. In downtown department stores, window displays are still dominant. In downtown shopping, there is considerable foot traffic as people walk from store to store.

Illus. 13.3
Window displays are still dominant in downtown department stores.

This sidewalk traffic can be intercepted with good window displays that urge people to stop and enter the store.

Interior displays are much more widespread than window displays in contemporary retailing. One study found interior displays to be the most powerful competitive strategy for short-term sales and market share gain.[22] Most are point-of-purchase merchandise displays, which have been shown to be significant demand generators.[23] Technically, interior displays include store signs and banners, which can, if properly designed, help generate demand. In some lines of retailing, such as groceries, up to half of all purchase decisions are made after entering the store. Thus, interior displays can be significant aids in helping the consumer make purchase decisions. Another study showed that interior displays played a significant role in redemption rates of coupons for price elastic products in supermarkets. Consumers were found to save coupons for highly price-sensitive product categories until the retailer prompted the consumer to use the coupons by means of a special display and a good price.[24] Retailing in Action 13-1 provides an interesting insight into the use of POP signs as opposed to displays.

As a potential retail manager, you should appreciate the potential return to be achieved from well-designed displays. You should also know that most of your advertising budget may be wasted if the displays don't reinforce the advertising. Advertising may bring people to the store, but displays are needed to prompt people to make the purchase decision.

The characteristics of a good display are:

1. The display is *distinctive and dramatic*. This means that the attention and interest of the consumers are aroused by the dramatic

RETAILING
IN
ACTION

13-1

The Effect of Nutrition POP Signs

Despite the fact that interior displays are highly effective for producing short-term sales gains and that the Food Marketing Institute found that 36 percent of supermarket shoppers indicated that "providing nutrition and health information is a supermarket's responsibility," actual purchases shift very little on the basis of using POP nutrition signs. Even when there is a shift in purchases because of sign usage, the switching is only between brands within a product class.

In a study involving more than 300 supermarkets nationwide, Achabal, et al., showed that commodity sales did not differ between stores using nutrition signs and regular signs. Thus, nutritional programs are probably not good sales-generating programs. The study did find, that while the nutrition signs were noticed by surprisingly few consumers, they did significantly enhance consumers' evaluations of the stores for those who noticed the signs.

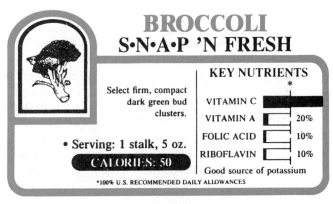

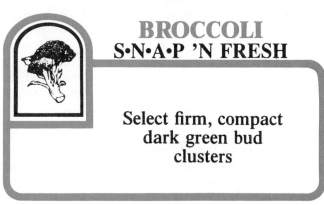

The authors presented three possible explanations for the lack of sales support for the signs.

1. The signs were only used on six of the more than 50 produce items available in each store.
2. The shoppers tend to look down at the produce, not up at the signs.
3. The produce itself may have had a much stronger visual impact than the signs.

Source: Dale D. Achabal, Shelby H. McIntyre, Cherryl H. Bell, and Nancy Tucker, "The Effect of Nutrition POP Signs on Consumer Attitudes and Behavior," *Journal of Retailing* (Spring 1987): 9-24.

interplay of such forces as color, lines, props, accessories, lighting arrangements, and motion.

2. It is *pleasing and appropriate*. All the elements must be in agreement so that the effect produced is one of unity.
3. It is *simple*. Simplicity means that the display message can be quickly received and understood.
4. It generally has a *dominant theme*. The display problem is simplified when merchandise is featured alone and without any special theme, but attention and interest are enhanced when a central theme is used. In many merchandise lines, for example, events commonly used for special displays are Easter, Mother's Day, Valentine's Day, Halloween, Christmas, and Back to School.
5. It emphasizes the *merchandise in use*. Arrangements, pictures, mannequins, and demonstrations that show or suggest the goods in use add greatly to the effectiveness of displays and also afford an opportunity to promote related items and accessories. When practicable, motion or movement adds to the realism and appeal of the display.
6. The display is *clean and neat* in appearance. This aspect of effective display frequently is overlooked or neglected. Nothing detracts so promptly and completely from the value of the display as dirty windows, dusty floors and backgrounds, soiled merchandise, or shabby-looking props and fixtures.[25]

SHOPLIFTING PREVENTION

Store managers should lay out their selling space in order to help prevent shoplifting. Although shoplifting may not seem to be a major problem at first glance, statistics show otherwise. Approximately $22 billion worth of merchandise is shoplifted annually, a figure that nearly equals Sears, Roebuck's annual gross sales. Yet, given this enormous figure, very little is known about the shoplifter. Some experts, like Gary Curtis, manager of the Greater Washington D.C. Board of Trade's retail bureau, feel that the greatest damage is done by amateurs who, as a whole, steal more merchandise in dollars than professionals.[26]

William "Dick" Deal, an ex-professional shoplifter, claims that this assumption is based on wrong information—the arrest records of those caught shoplifting. According to Deal, a professional is seldom or never caught in the act, and can easily steal $6,000 to $8,000 worth of merchandise a day.[27] There is no agreement as to month or day of the week when shoplifting is most likely to occur although the *Wall Street Journal* reports that 35 percent of supermarket thefts occur between 3 and 6 p.m.[28] Bob Curtis, a security specialist, suggests that in self-service stores, shoplifting creates 35 to 45 percent of total inventory shortages. In department stores, 25 to 35 percent of total losses may be attributed to shoplifting and the remaining 70 percent losses are due to employee theft.[29] These figures refer to actual thefts and not mis-rings by cashiers or mis-marking of merchandise.

Some layouts can minimize shoplifting. One of the most important considerations when planning the layout of a retail store is visibility of the merchandise. Most shoplifting takes place in fitting rooms, blind spots, aisles crowded with extra merchandise, or behind high displays. As a general rule, display fixtures should be no taller than eye level, so employees can see over them into the next aisle. Fitting rooms should not give the dishonest customer a secure place to steal. Instead, they should be designed so that employees can easily keep an eye on everyone and everything that goes into or comes out of the area. The manager's office is often stuck in a dark, unused corner—out of sight and out of mind. However, this office can be an excellent deterrent to shoplifting in a one-story building if it is placed in an obvious area above floor level, where the manager can easily see the entire store. Sometimes shoplifting deterrents present retailers with new problems; for example, record manufacturers now use blister packs for cassettes, which require more retail space, thus higher rents.

Another consideration when planning the general layout of a retail store is merchandise characteristics. Small, expensive items that are easily palmed or pocketed should be placed in locked display cases rather than on open displays. Items near stockrooms, fitting rooms, public restrooms, or exits should be less attractive to the average shoplifter.

The checkout area should be located where it is most efficient and where the employees can watch the exit. The checkout also needs to be speedy, because the customer left waiting in a long, slow line is more likely to pocket a few items and walk out. Exhibit 13.1 lists the most commonly used devices to control stock shrinkage, as well as those judged to be the most effective.

Exhibit 13.1

Commonly Used Antishoplifting Devices and Their Effectiveness

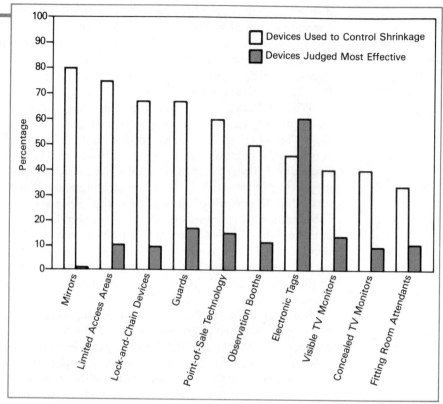

SOURCE: A study conducted for the National Mass Retailing Institute by Arthur Young as reported in *Chain Store Age-Executive Edition,* (February 1985), pp. 55 and 56. Reprinted with permission.

ATMOSPHERE

We have already mentioned the building must be designed to project an image. Similarly, the layout of the space within the store should reinforce the image projected by the building. If the external appearance of the building invites the customer to enter but the internal layout doesn't reinforce the projected image, the customer may immediately turn around and exit. To prevent that, the retail manager needs to develop an understanding of how the image of a store is determined through the atmosphere of the selling space. We call this **atmospherics**—the conscious designing of space and its various dimensions to evoke certain effects in buyers. Some of the main components of selling space atmosphere are the type and density of employees, merchandise, fixtures, sound, and odor, which combine with the visual factors to create the store atmosphere.

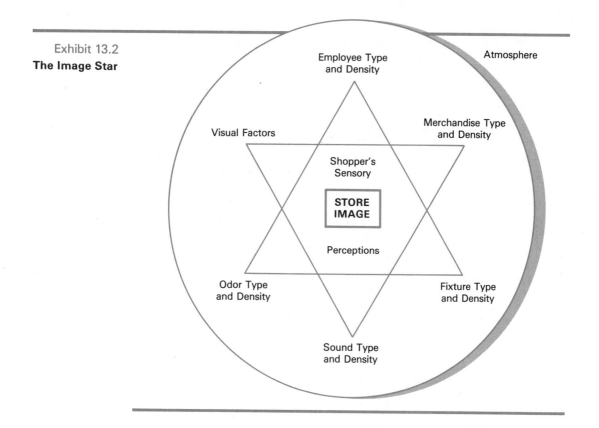

Exhibit 13.2
The Image Star

This relationship is shown in Exhibit 13.2. These factors help to create the store atmosphere, which in turn determines the customers' sensory perceptions and the image the store projects.

Research by King and Ring[30] has shown that shoppers' perceptions differ from one type of retail outlet to another. Exhibit 13.3 shows the perceptions that shoppers have of discounters, department stores and middle- and high-style fashion chains as sources of menswear. Arnold, Sylvia, and Tigert found consumers patronized a supermarket based on location and low price, but selected fashion clothing outlets based on best value, largest overall assortment, and highest quality.[31] It is extremely important that retail store managers are aware of the store image demanded by their chosen target market, their own store image, and the store image of the competition.

Employee Type and Density.   A major determinant of store atmosphere and image is employee type and density. The type of employee refers to the employees' general character. For example, are they neat and well dressed? Old or young? How compatible are the employees with the merchandise? Employers need to be careful not to discriminate in hiring prac-

Exhibit 13.3
Evaluations of Store Types on Determinants of Patronage by Shoppers Who "Last Shopped" at Each Store Type for Menswear

Determinant of patronage	(type of store last shopped for menswear)			
	Discounter/ mass merchandiser	Department store	Midrange fashion specialty chain	High- fashion specialty chain
1. Easiest to get to from home	41%*	48%	32%	14%
2. Lowest prices	60	30	26	12
3. Highest quality	2	17	34	51
4. Best value for the money	47	54	50	43
5. Most knowledgeable, helpful salesclerks	21	38	50	65
6. Largest overall assortment/selection	27	43	33	20
7. Most exciting display	14	31	29	52
8. Best advertising	18	39	18	28
9. Best for conservative everyday menswear	31	43	35	27
10. Best for current, up-to-date menswear	21	29	31	63
11. Best for very latest most fashionable menswear	9	19	26	58

*On the average, among those respondents who "last shopped" at a discounter/mass merchandiser, 41 percent also said the discounter/mass merchandiser was the "easiest to get to from home," and 60 percent said the discounter/mass merchandiser had the "lowest prices."

SOURCE: Charles W. King and Lawrence J. Ring, "Market Positioning Across Retail Fashion Institutions: A Comparative Analysis of Store Types," *Journal of Retailing* (Spring 1980) p. 50.

tices, but they should try to match the employees with the merchandise, store atmosphere, and customer characteristics. Employees can be outfitted to help reinforce an atmosphere; they can wear western clothing in a western wear store, or sportswear in a sporting goods store. Employees with special characteristics can enhance the overall atmosphere of a store. Some maternity shops have found success in hiring pregnant women to supplement the regular sales force. Sears uses larger-sized models in its catalog to show larger-sized clothing. This appeal could carry over to the store sales force as well. As a rule, the type of employee should be consistent with the atmosphere and the image the retailer is trying to project.

Density of employees refers to how many store employees there are per 1,000 square feet of selling space. Self-service stores such as Target and K mart have fewer employees per 1,000 square feet of selling space, which promotes their atmosphere of self-service and casualness. If the retailer has too low an employee density, shoppers will develop a negative opinion of the store. But, if there is too high an employee density, the customer may get the impression that the employees are waiting to prey on the customers. Customers don't like to feel like they are walking into a den of wolves. The key is to have just enough employees to give the level of service desired. By doing so, the retailer is usually projecting the right image.[32]

Merchandise Type and Density.   Type and density of merchandise also determines a retailer's image. If a furniture retailer wants to project a high-quality, high-status image, the merchandise lines must reinforce this. The merchandise density (the amount of merchandise displayed or shelved per 1,000 square feet) is also crucial. Our furniture retailer could not project the high-quality and high-status image if the furniture was packed into the store so that only one person could squeeze down an aisle. High quality can be connoted by arranging furniture in room settings, a low-density use of space. Merchandise density can be increased by stacking merchandise very high, possibly even right up to the ceiling. This does not project a high-quality, high-status image. Similarly, the retailer does not want to clutter the aisles with in-store merchandising displays. Merchandise displays must attract the attention of shoppers, provide proper balance, be constructed in proper proportion, and quickly convey a message to the shopper. The National Retail Merchants Association estimates that more than 25 percent of all fashion merchandise is sold primarily because of how it is displayed.[33]

Fixture Type and Density.   Fixture type refers to the physical makeup of the fixtures. Are they chrome and smoked-glass showcases, standard metal shelves, antique wooden buffets, or old, cast-iron bathtubs? Fixtures should be consistent with the overall theme or atmosphere. For instance, if a retailer wants the store to look like an old English pub, the fixtures should be made of wood and brass rather than chrome or Chinese lacquer. The type and density of fixtures depends largely, but not entirely, on merchandise type. Sometimes, retail executives take advantage of good deals on fixtures that don't complement the decor. These good deals can wreck the continuity needed to achieve a high-status image. Retailers nationally spend about $8 per square foot on fixtures alone and around $19 per square foot on store remodeling.[34]

Decorator pieces can add immeasurably to the store's atmosphere if they are wisely selected. This is especially true in specialty stores, such as using Scandinavian furniture and lights in a shop that specializes in Scandinavian housewares and gifts. In addition, flooring sets the tone and image of a store; e.g., the carpeted floors of Macy's vs. the tiled floors of a Wal-Mart.

Often retailers lack imagination when planning for fixtures. For example, while most chains report an earnings increase of 7 percent per square foot after remodeling,[35] poor planning can jeopardize such an increase. Motherhood, a Santa Monica-based maternity chain, failed to align itself with the needs and taste levels of pregnant women when it remodeled in the early 1980s. The remodeled fixtures had a traditional dark wood finish, heavily accented with brass and mirrors. This decor appealed more to men than to pregnant women, and had to be replaced with another complete remodeling.[36]

Retailers should explore options other than traditional, ready-made store fixtures. Not only can the cost be less, but the result can be the difference between an average store and a unique one. Some sources to explore are local cabinetmakers, metalworkers, welders, and antique and second-hand dealers. Large retailers and chain stores, however, usually find it necessary to rely on standardized fixtures to obtain consistency throughout the country. But even these retailers can add a bit of local atmosphere through a few special accent pieces. When necessary, retailers should use commercial interior designers.

The density of fixtures refers to the number of fixtures per 1,000 square feet of selling space. Stores can be over- or under-fixtured. If the store is over-fixtured, the customer may become confused as to what the retailers' business actually is. Picture, for example, a menswear retailer using the following for display: antique dressers and tables on which shirts and sweaters are piled; a display of antique pipes and guns on two walls; antique books in shelves bordering the other two walls, the shelves also containing merchandise such as cufflinks, ties, and belts; and a turn-of-the-century bicycle flanked by mannequins dressed in 1890s attire in the front display window. The density of antique fixtures and accents is so great that the customer may wonder if the retailer is selling men's clothing or antiques.

On the other hand, stores can be under-fixtured. Picture a hardware store with all the merchandise sitting on the selling floor in crates, boxes, and a few old wooden tables. Such a store tends to look old, run-down, and highly inefficient. It would be difficult for the do-it-yourself shopper to find desired items. Imagine having to search through all the boxes to find 30 finishing nails, #001 sandpaper, a small can of walnut stain, and a paintbrush. Think how much easier it is to find these items in a hardware store with adequate fixtures for displaying the merchandise. The proper density and type of fixture can turn a disorganized, inefficient store into the opposite.

Sound Type and Density.   The type of sound and its density can influence the atmosphere of a store positively or negatively. Sounds can be pleasant or unpleasant. An unpleasant or wrong sound (the shrill pitch of a dentist's drill or the roar of jet planes) can detract from, and even destroy, the atmosphere the retailer is trying to build. Noises like these are usually from external sources over which the retailer has little control beyond installing sound-deadening insulation or producing sounds internally to muffle the unpleasant noises. Wrong noises in one place, however, can be considered pleasant in other circumstances or places. For example, the sound of balls rolling, pins falling, and people laughing and joking are all pleasant inside a bowling alley; but these same sounds inside Neiman-Marcus or a jewelry store would be inconsistent with the desired atmosphere.

A pleasant sound can draw attention to the merchandise. Clocks ticking and chiming, wind chimes blowing in the breeze, music boxes playing, and the sound of television sets being demonstrated can all be right sounds that will draw the customer's attention to the merchandise when used in the proper places.

Counter-noise is background sound piped into the store to cover up other sounds and to overcome dead quiet, which can also be distracting. The most widely used counter-noise is Muzak, a programmed music service that reaches over 80 million people a day in elevators, retail stores, offices, and restaurants. Muzak, which began in Cleveland in 1934, produces a fresh program of 486 songs each day.[37]

Sound density refers to the strength or the volume of the sounds. Since background music is used so much by retailers, it is one of the most important sounds for the retailer to control. It helps to eliminate unwanted sounds and pace employees. However, music can be so loud that it is irritating or so soft that it is useless. Thus, the volume of the music must be appropriate for the in-store environment the retailer is trying to create.

Milliman has found that, holding sound density constant, lower tempo background music increases sales nearly 40 percent more than fast tempo music. The fast tempo music increased the pace of in-store traffic flow over the slower tempo background. No significant differences were found between slow tempo music and the lack of background music although slow tempo did produce a slower pace.[38]

Odor Type and Density.   Odor is also important in creating an atmosphere and making the selling space maximally productive. If the space does not smell right, the merchandise will not sell to its true potential. The right type of odor makes the customer anxious to purchase the product. The taste buds react to some odors to the point that people can actually taste some things just by smelling them. Examples are chocolate, fresh bread, oranges, popcorn, and coffee. Other odors stimulate other reflexes; musk oil, used in perfume and after-shave, is supposed to be sexually arousing. Odors can create a pleasant mood. The smell of flowers in a florist, perfume at a cosmetic counter, cookies at a bakery, fudge and nuts at a candy store, scented candles in a gift shop, leather in a leather goods department, or tobacco in a pipe store, all are consistent with the merchandise and can stimulate a desire for it.

Just as there can be wrong sounds, there can also be wrong odors, which can actually drive the customer away from making a purchase. Examples of wrong odors include musty carpets, cigarette smoke, strong fabric dyes, rodent and insect repellents, lingering fire damage odors, gasoline, or even paint and cleaning supplies if improperly located. Next-door odors, like outside sounds, can also be a problem for the retailer. These odors need not be unpleasant, just inconsistent—such as the smell of chocolate and nuts drifting into a health food store, or the overly medicated scent of a doctor's or dentist's office in a bakery. The odor must be the right one to be conducive to a purchase. It was not surprising that when K mart sought to upgrade its image in the mid-1980s, one of its first steps was to remove the popcorn stand from its entrances.[39]

As with other influences on atmosphere, the density (strength) of the odor must be considered along with the type. If the odor is the wrong type, the retailer should try to diminish its density with air filtration systems. For the right odors, density should be high enough to stimulate the purchase of merchandise but not so high that it distracts or irritates the customer. For example, the scent of perfume around a cosmetic counter may stimulate the demand for perfume or cosmetics, but too strong a scent may be overpowering or may irritate allergies, thus driving customers from the area.

Visual Factors. Visual factors also help determine atmosphere. Most important is overall appearance as seen through the eyes of the customer. This will be the combined effect of several factors we have discussed—employee type and density, fixture type and density, and merchandise type and density—as well as of several factors still to be discussed—color combinations, lighting, and floor covering.

Color can create a mood and focus attention. For example, displaying diamonds on blue, red, or black velvet shows them better than putting them against pink, yellow, or white velvet.

Colors themselves have moods which it is helpful to understand. Red, yellow, and orange are considered warm colors, and as such they are used when a feeling of warmth and closeness is desired. Many restaurants use these colors along with candlelight and fireplaces to help create a mood. Blue, green, and violet are considered cool colors and are used to open up closed places and create an air of elegance and cleanliness. These colors do well in dark hallways, restrooms, infant departments, and other areas the retailer wishes to make appear larger or lighter. Browns and golds are considered earth tones, and blend with everything. They also convey a warmth to the surroundings.

Studies involving the affects of color in retail surroundings are limited. One study suggests that color has customer drawing power as well as image-creating potential in store design. Warm colors are better than cool colors for drawing shoppers into a store. Cool colors were found to be more relaxing and positive; warm colors were felt to make the shopper feel pressured into a quick decision.[40]

The degree of lighting can also change the atmosphere. Consider a well-lighted gift shop compared with one that is dimly lit. On examining trade journals, you will readily notice numerous ads for different types of lighting. Each type has its purpose and retailers need to determine what their lighting needs are then seek the fixtures to fill those needs. For example, jewelry, especially diamonds and other precious stones, is best displayed under high-intensity spotlights, and cosmetics under no-glare natural lighting. Some lighting may cause colors to look different than they do in natural sunlight; a customer may purchase a pair of navy blue socks only to discover, when they take them home, that the socks are really black.

The type and colors of floor coverings are also important to the overall appearance and atmosphere of a retail store. Do the other atmosphere determinants indicate a subdued, functional flooring, a shiny parquet, or plush carpeting? The floor covering must be consistent with the desired customer perception, without using too much capital.

Demand Stimulation.   Proper investments in buildings and fixtures can actually be investments in stimulating demand. The building is more than a place to store the merchandise and fixtures are more than vehicles for displaying the merchandise. The building and fixtures should bring the customer and the retailer closer together. They can be strong motivators in getting potential customers to make a purchase by inviting them into the store to look around.

LAYOUT TYPES

After the retail manager has made atmospheric decisions regarding colors, floor covering, and fixtures, the type of layout must be chosen. This refers to the actual arrangement of the fixtures, merchandise, stockroom, and other features of the store's interior. Remember, the store layout and the individual department configurations must logically move customers through more areas of the store. Supermarkets have long known that the three most commonly purchased items in their stores are dairy products, produce, and bread and have arranged their stores accordingly. Sometimes the ideal store layout arrangement is not always possible, as shown in Retailing in Action 13-2.

There is a paradox in planning retail layout. Sound store layout planning is one of the foundation stones for retail success. To reach its high-performance financial goals and achieve its growth expectations, the retailer must plan store openings and renovations wisely. Store layout planning is made a top priority in every retail chain and receives attention

RETAILING IN ACTION

13-2

Sometimes the Ideal Floor Plan Just Won't Do

Sometimes retailers are prevented from using an ideal layout plan by "act of God." Consider the case of Joske's downtown department store in San Antonio. This store, the second started by the Joske brothers, was built in 1876 between the San Antonio River and the Alamo. Next to the store was St. Joseph's Catholic Church. As Joske's grew into one of Texas's most highly respected retailers (it had more than 30 stores in Texas when it was acquired by

Illus. 13.4

Joshe's Department Store was forced to expand to a U-shape around St. Joseph's Catholic Church. Source: Kathy Bacon

Dillard's in 1987), so did its downtown San Antonio store. Unfortunately, so did church membership—to the point where Joske's was forced to expand its downtown location by building in a U-shape around the church.

from senior management. Tremendous amounts of capital are invested. Why then is this activity approached with such a low level of sophistication? The reason is that most retailers have ignored the computer. Though retail executives use the computer in all other areas of merchandising and control, they still typically plan stores the old-fashioned way—in longhand, with a pencil. A few retailers do use computers to plan store layouts and merchandise locations.[41]

Perhaps, because so few retailers have used computer systems to design store layouts, other retailers feel safe. Yet, John Morrissey, senior vice-president for Super Valu, states "If you're not in graphics today, you won't be around tomorrow.'' Super Valu's engineering and architectural division, Planmark, was able, in less than half an hour, to show a retailer how to increase the size of shops in the front of his store by moving them all out by 20 feet.[42] This failure to use all the available technology will keep many retailers from achieving high-performance results.

There are basically two types of layout, grid and free-flow, as well as several variations on these two basic types.

Grid Layout.   The **grid layout** is one in which all the counters and fixtures are at right angles to each other, forming a maze. This type of layout is most often used in supermarkets, drug stores, variety stores, and discount department stores. Exhibit 13.4 shows a grid layout for a supermar-

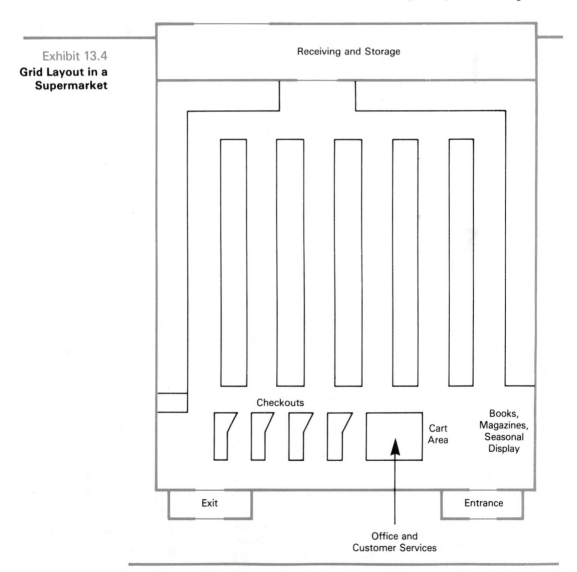

Exhibit 13.4
Grid Layout in a Supermarket

ket. Notice how the layout moves the customer through the maze of merchandise from the entrance to the exit.

Free-Flow Layout.   The second type of layout is the **free-flow layout**, in which the fixtures and merchandise are grouped into patterns or left freestanding, creating an unstructured traffic pattern. Many of the fixtures in a free-flow layout are irregularly shaped, such as circles, horseshoes, arches, and triangles. The aisles are usually wide and curving and leave little more than walking areas between merchandise displays.

Exhibit 13.5
The Free-Flow Layout

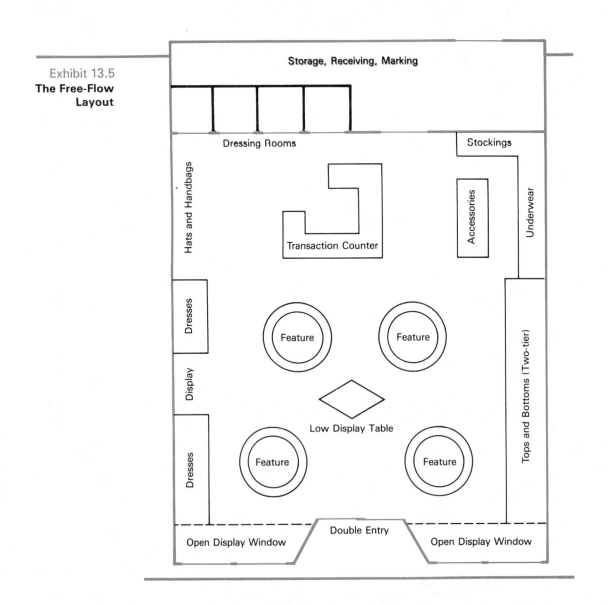

The free-flow layout is often used in specialty stores, boutiques, gift stores, and some apparel stores. Exhibit 13.5 shows a free-flow layout for a junior apparel shop.

A chart highlighting the advantages and disadvantages of the grid and the free-flow types of layout is shown in Exhibit 13.6.

Some Variations.   There are two common subtypes of layout. The first is used mainly for fast-food chains, ticket agencies, and other businesses whose major concern is moving customers in and out rapidly. It is called the **standard layout** and consists of an entrance, a counter, a checkout area, and an exit. The second subtype, which is gaining support from retailers, is the **boutique layout**. A form of free-flow layout, the boutique layout creates mini-stores within a larger store. Each of the mini-stores is aimed at a specific target group and is often a grouping of merchandise from a single designer or company. The boutique layout works best for gift shops, high-status department stores, and any field where specific designers or names are known. Exhibit 13.7 shows a women's apparel store using the boutique layout arranged according to designer. A variation of this boutique layout has been introduced in grocery retailing by Furr's

GRID

ADVANTAGES		DISADVANTAGES
1. Low cost	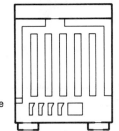	1. Plain and uninteresting
2. Customer familiarity		2. Limited browsing
3. Merchandise exposure		3. Stimulation of rushed shopping behavior
4. Ease of cleaning		4. Limited creativity in decor
5. Simplified security		
6. Possibility of self-service		

Exhibit 13.6

Advantages and Disadvantages of Grid and Free-Flow Layouts

FREE FLOW

ADVANTAGES		DISADVANTAGES
1. Allowance for browsing and wandering freely	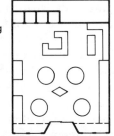	1. Loitering encouraged
2. Increased impulse purchases		2. Possible confusion
3. Visual appeal		3. Waste of floor space
4. Flexibility		4. Cost
		5. Difficulty of cleaning

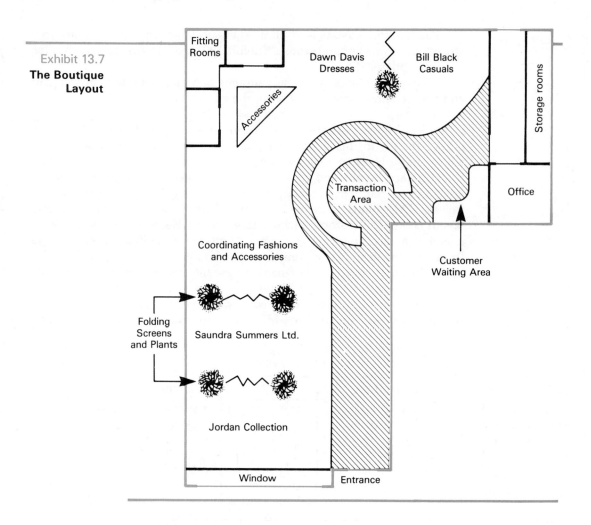

Exhibit 13.7

The Boutique Layout

Incorporated. Exhibit 13.8 shows the layout of a Furr's Food Emporium. This 65,000-square-foot model has a shopping environment similar to a shopping mall, with specialty shops located along the outer walls. Thus, the convenience shops (cheese, deli, bakery, floral, pharmacy, photo, cafe, and customer service) can be seen from virtually any part of the store. Realizing that the natural tendency of supermarket shoppers is to enter the store and go towards the right, Furr's has put cosmetics and other high gross margin categories at the right front area of the store along with the produce.

There is no right or wrong layout for every retailer or retail classification. The layout must depend on other variables, like the type of merchandise, size and shape of the building, and the atmosphere desired by the retailer.

Exhibit 13.8
Layout of Furr's Food Emporium

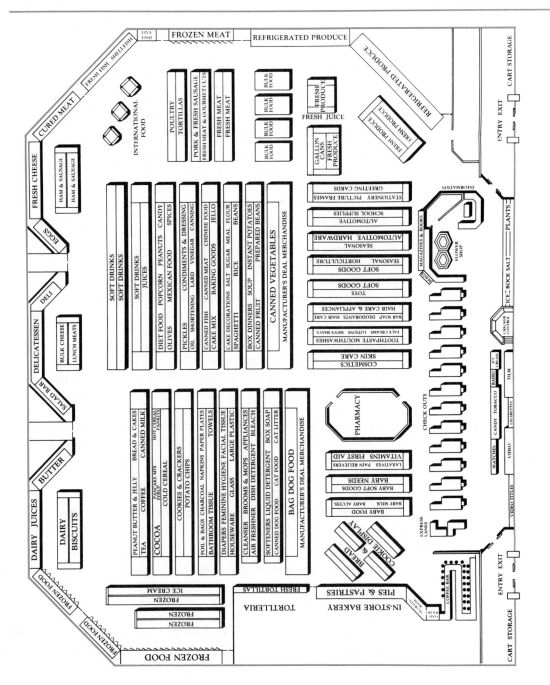

SELLING SPACE PRODUCTIVITY

Retailers cannot achieve high-performance results unless selling space is used productively.[43] To ensure selling space productivity, retail managers must assess selling space performance.

Productivity Measures.   Any productivity measure relates output to input. In the case of selling space productivity, the input is the amount of selling space, which is typically measured in square feet. Output can be measured a variety of ways. The most common measures of output are net sales, gross margin, contribution profit, and operating profit.

1. **Net sales** reflects total dollar sales (less any returns and merchandise allowances) created in the selling space.
2. **Gross margin**, also referred to by retailers as **gross profit**, equals net sales less cost of goods sold. This measure is good if no expense other than the cost of merchandise can be directly related to the selling space. For example, it may not be possible to directly tie advertising expenses to any particular selling space areas within the store.
3. **Contribution profit** is net sales less cost of goods sold and any expenses that are directly traceable to the space in which the goods were sold. In this case, items such as advertising and labor expenses can be directly related to specific selling areas. For instance, department store ads for bowling balls can be directly allocated to the sporting goods department.
4. **Operating profit** is net sales less cost of goods sold, direct expenses, and a share of all indirect expenses that the retailer incurs. This method is not good unless the indirect expenses can be equitably allocated to the respective selling areas within the store. Typically, only the cost of renting or maintaining the selling space can be equitably allocated according to the square footage occupied by each selling area; other expenses, such as salaries, can be allocated only on an arbitrary basis.

Utilizing these output measures and accepting square footage of selling space as the appropriate input measure, we can identify four measures of selling space productivity:

1. **Sales per square foot of selling space** equals net sales divided by square feet of selling space. This ratio shows, on average, how much in annual net sales dollars the retailer generated for each square foot of selling space.
2. **Gross margin per square foot of selling space** equals total gross profit divided by square feet of selling space. This simple measure reflects how many gross margin dollars a retailer generates, on average, for each square foot of selling space.
3. **Contribution profit per square foot of selling space** equals total

contribution profit divided by square feet of selling space. A more stringent measure of space productivity than the previous two measures, it reveals how many contribution profit dollars were generated, on average, for each square foot of selling space.

4. **Operating profit per square foot of selling space** equals total operating profit divided by square feet of selling space. The most stringent measure of space productivity, this measure reveals the dollars of operating profit that were generated, on average, for each square foot of selling space.

The most accurate measure of selling space productivity is contribution profit per foot of selling space. However, sales per square foot and gross profit per square foot are used more frequently, because many retail trade associations regularly publish these measures in their studies. For example, Exhibit 13.9 profiles selling space productivity measures for several high-performance retailers. These statistics from company reports, and others published by the various trade associations, provide the retail manager with useful benchmarks by which to gauge selling space productivity.

Determinants of Space Productivity.   Since space productivity is so essential to a retailer's success, it is important to understand its primary determinants. Remember the discussion in Chapter 10 about the importance of turnover management to the success of a retail enterprise. In that chapter you learned that higher inventory turnover, everything else being equal, results in higher financial performance for the retail enterprise. Turnover management is important to retail space productivity because space is required to merchandise and store inventory, and the higher the turnover, the less space required. Imagine an apparel store of 10,000 square feet with annual sales of $1,000,000 and an average inventory of $200,000. The store has a sales/stock ratio of 5. If this retailer doubled this ratio to 10 and held sales at $1,000,000, it would only need half as much inventory ($100,000 vs. $200,000). With half as much inventory, it would not need nearly as much retail space. Another way to look at this would be to assume that with a sales/stock ratio of 10 and the ability to store $200,000 in inventory the retailer would have the capacity to increase sales to $2,000,000 without an increase in space.

Another determinant of space productivity is **merchandise density** which can be measured by the inventory investment per square foot. The higher the merchandise density, the higher the space productivity (everything else being equal). Using our hypothetical apparel retailer, we can compute inventory investment per square foot at $20 ($200,000/10,000). If this apparel retailer is able to increase its merchandise density by 50 percent, from $20 to $30, and maintain the same sales/stock ratio, its space productivity (sales per square foot of selling area) would increase by 50 percent.

Exhibit 13.9

Space Productivity Profile of Leasing High Performance Retailers

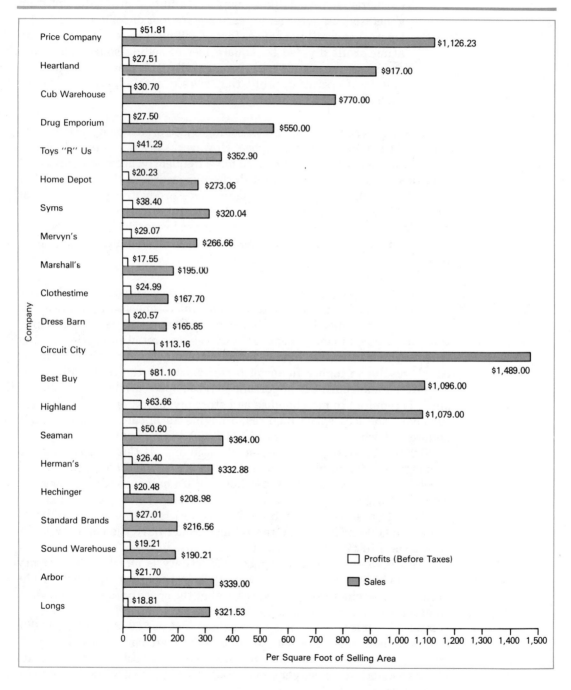

SOURCE: Company annual reports and Distribution Research Program,
The University of Oklahoma, 1988.

To summarize, two primary determinants of space productivity are inventory turnover and merchandise density. Inventory turnover reflects the velocity of merchandise moving over the floor space and merchandise density reflects how densely inventory has been poured into the limited space available.

Algebraically this relationship can be depicted as:

(Net sales/Average Inventory at cost) (Average Inventory at cost/Square Feet of Selling Space) = Net Sales/Square Feet of Selling Space

or

Sales to Stock Ratio × Merchandise Density = Sales per Square Foot of Selling Space

From this simple algebraic relationship it can be seen that our apparel retailer with a sales/stock ratio of 5 and merchandise density of $20, has $100 sales per square foot of selling space. A 50 percent increase in merchandise density, from $20 to $30, when multiplied by the sales to inventory ratio of 5, results in a sales per square foot of selling area of $150, a 50 percent increase from the prior $100 level.

The third primary determinant of space productivity is the *gross margin percent*. A retailer with a higher gross margin percent has more money left per dollar of sales to pay for occupancy costs such as rent, light, heat, insurance, cooling, etc. We can show the impact of the gross margin percent by the following simple algebraic relation:

(Net Sales/Square Feet of Selling Space) × (Gross Margin/New Sales) = Gross Margin/Square Feet of Selling Space

For example, if the preceding apparel retailer had a gross margin percent of 35 percent, then its $100 in sales per square foot of selling area would yield $35 in gross margin per square foot of selling space.

Exhibit 13.10 summarizes the algebra of the determinants of retail space productivity. Retail managers must attempt to engineer and design their stores to have respectable levels of sales and inventory turnover, merchandise density, and gross margin percentage, if their stores are to have high levels of space productivity.

NONSELLING SPACE LAYOUT

The efficient design and layout of nonselling space is as important as the design of selling space. Unfortunately, many retailers ignore this fact, believing that the only stimulator of space productivity is selling space layout. *All* space must be properly allocated and designed in order to maximize space productivity. Selling and nonselling space are interdependent.

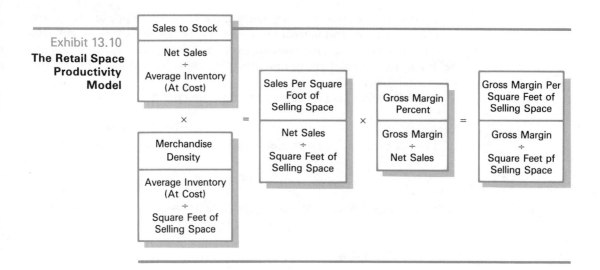

Exhibit 13.10

**The Retail Space
Productivity
Model**

Consider, for example, storage space for reserve stock. In general, the reserve stock should be located near the selling area, because customers don't like to be left alone for a long time while the employee searches for items from stock. If left alone too long, the customer will leave, the sale will be lost, and sales per square foot of selling space will suffer.

In addition to merchandise receiving and handling space requirements, the retail manager requires space for three other nonselling needs: office space and equipment, storage or warehousing space, and equipment and space for customer service. For all three areas, the key is to allocate adequate space so the job to be done in that space can be performed efficiently without wasting space.

OFFICE SPACE AND EQUIPMENT

The design of office space is a science in itself. Many consulting firms specialize in the efficient layout of the office. These firms also can assist retailers in selecting the proper type of equipment for performing clerical functions. With today's sophisticated office equipment (computerized typewriters, copying machines, mail sorters, and minicomputers), most retailers need the professional advice of someone other than the equipment salesperson.

Office space, like selling space, has an atmosphere. The retail executive should try to create a work atmosphere that stimulates productivity. An office could be bare of carpet, wall decor, background music, and efficient lighting. It could consist of a dark, drab corner with a few metal desks, chairs, and filing cabinets. However, such an atmosphere would make the office so unpleasant that the staff would spend as much time as possible away from their desks. Employees are hardly efficient when they are in the employee lounge or restroom, running personal errands, making personal phone calls, or wandering around the stockroom or selling space. They are productive only when they are working. The retailer needs to create an office atmosphere that is cheerful, yet subdued enough to promote a work atmosphere.

STORAGE OR WAREHOUSING

The amount of storage space the retailer needs is related to the physical dimensions of the merchandise and the stock level needed to maintain the desired rate of turnover. For example, furniture is bulky and requires considerable storage space; grocery items turn over frequently, so more merchandise is needed than can be displayed on the shelves. The safety stock level is not specific to the line of merchandise. It depends more on the retailer's willingness to lose a sale if merchandise is out of stock.

Retailers also need to decide what equipment to use to store merchandise. The manager could have employees carry the merchandise from delivery trucks and stack the boxes and cartons on the floor of the stockroom. In most cases, however, this would be inefficient, because the retailer is probably paying those employees $3 to $15 per hour. In most cases, some type of equipment facilitates receiving. For instance, rather than having the employees carry incoming merchandise, there are carts specially made for this purpose. Instead of stacking the cartons and boxes

Illus. 13.5

Merchandise can be checked, inventories, and ticketed, and then placed on shelves or in bins until needed. Source: Sears, Roebuck and Co.

directly on the floor of the stockroom where they must remain packed and risk being damaged, the merchandise can be unpacked, checked, inventoried, and ticketed, then placed on shelves or in bins until needed. This can increase the amount of merchandise stored per square foot by decreasing the amount of packing materials and, as noted earlier, a tidy, well-ordered stock area is less tempting to dishonest employees. Trash compactors can be used to compress the packing clutter.

CUSTOMER SERVICES

Space needs to be allocated to customer service functions as well. This includes space for restrooms, check cashing, dressing rooms, elevators, stairways, gift wrapping, handling of complaints, processing of credit applications, and payment of bills, among other things. Space devoted to customer services can stimulate or reinforce selling efforts, but its primary purpose is not for selling. For example, well-designed restrooms give a favorable impression, which can help reinforce future selling efforts. A dirty restroom can cloud a customer's perception of the entire store.

It is important for retail executives to realize that they are not in the business of providing customer services. Some customer services are necessary, but they are not the reason a retailer exists. Therefore, the space devoted to them should be in proportion to how these services support the selling efforts; the executive should decide how much space is actually necessary.

The customer's perception of the store depends on, among other things, its visual effect. Therefore it is important to blend customer service areas with the desired atmosphere of the store. For example, a discount department store might get by very well using barren fitting rooms with small mirrors and flimsy curtains. But putting those same fitting rooms into a bridal shop would be inconsistent with the store's image and would adversely affect the consumer's perception of the store.

SUMMARY

In this chapter we dealt with the building and fixture decisions the retailer must make. Since the building can be a demand stimulator, it is more than just a place to transact business. It is a vehicle for bringing the customer and retailer together.

Whenever the retailer decides how to allocate funds for building and fixtures, it has to perform a balancing act between such factors as fixed assets vs. current assets, store space vs. parking space, selling space vs. nonselling space, and store space vs. fixtures. Generally, the retailer will allocate more funds to current assets (cash, inventory, and accounts receivables) than to fixed assets (building, land, fixtures, and equipment), because its business is selling goods. However, it needs enough fixed assets to ensure efficiency. This ratio varies considerably among retailers.

The retailer should make adequate parking facilities available for its customers. Since nonselling space does not directly stimulate sales, it needs to be allocated wisely. The retailer needs to determine how much space is needed to accomplish the nonselling tasks efficiently and allocate only that amount of space to them. There should be enough fixtures to efficiently display the merchandise, but not so many that the store becomes crowded.

A poor image can damage the retailer. Besides the building's image, the retailer must also consider size, location, merchandise, the amount of capital available, the building's age, and whether to lease or buy it.

Store layout is the arrangement of selling and nonselling departments and their merchandise, fixtures, and equipment. Selling space layout was discussed in terms of traffic patterns, shoplifting prevention, and atmosphere. The main determinants of the selling space atmosphere are the type and density of employees, merchandise, fixtures, sound, and odor, which combine with the visual factors to create the store's atmosphere and image.

There are two main methods of laying out the store's interior. The grid layout—often used by grocers, drugstores, variety stores, hardware stores, and discount department stores—is characterized by counters and fixtures at right angles, forming rows. The free-flow layout allows the fixtures and merchandise to be artistically grouped, creating an unstructured traffic pattern. It is successful in department stores, apparel stores, and gift stores. Two subtypes of layout are the standard layout and the boutique layout.

Selling space productivity is one means of achieving high-performance results. Four output measures were defined: net sales, gross profit, contribution profit, and operating profit. Using those measures, we identified four productivity measures: sales per square foot of selling space, gross profit per square foot of selling space, contribution profit per square foot of selling space, and operating profit per square foot of selling space. We concluded our discussion with our Retail Space Productivity Model based on turnover, merchandise density, and gross profit percentage.

The discussion of nonselling space highlighted the arrangement of office space and equipment, storage space and equipment, and customer service space and equipment.

1. How does store layout influence shoplifting?
2. What factors influence store atmosphere?
3. How is the building and fixture decision in retailing an exercise in capital allocation?
4. What is traffic and how is it important in the store layout decision?
5. How should a retail manager evaluate selling space productivity? How is it important to the retailer?
6. How would building and fixture decisions be different for nonstore retailers than for conventional retailers?
7. Discuss the interrelationships among the retailer's building, image, and atmosphere.
8. Evaluate the space productivity of the following four departments in a department store.

	A	B	C	D
Sales	$394,000	$611,000	$304,000	$791,000
Square feet	5100	7200	6000	9400
Gross margin percent	31%	29%	42%	34%
Advertising	21,000	54,000	11,000	24,000
Wages	30,000	50,000	18,000	81,000

9. Fred's IGA Supermarket is considering allocating 800 additional square feet to frozen foods, taking the space from dry groceries. These are the changes Fred expects to occur after this change:

	Dry Groceries		Frozen Foods	
	Before	After	Before	After
Square feet	7,000	6,200	1,200	2,000
Sales	$1,210,000	$1,108,000	$250,000	$360,000
Gross profit	278,000	265,000	77,580	100,400
Contribution profit	208,300	199,700	46,548	58,232

Should Fred allocate more space to frozen foods? What other factors should be considered?

10. Distinguish between the grid layout and the free-flow layout. In what types of stores is each pattern most useful? Why?
11. What conditions or factors might cause a retailer to want to change the image of a store? How could a retailer go about changing a store image?

12. How can store layout and design be used to reduce shoplifting?
13. Considering the variables discussed in this chapter (building size, fixtures, parking space, selling vs. nonselling space, building image, traffic patterns, layout arrangements, and selling space productivity), suggest a store design for your campus bookstore.

SUGGESTED READINGS

Donovan, Robert J., and John R. Rossiter, "Store Atmosphere: An Environmental Psychology Approach," *Journal of Retailing* (Spring 1982): 34–57.

Hirschman, Elizabeth C., and Melanie R. Wallendorf, "Characteristics of the Cultural Continuum: Implications for Retailing," *Journal of Retailing* (Spring 1982): 5–21.

Korgaonkar, P. K., Daulat Lund, and Barbara Price, "A Structural Equations Approach Toward Examination of Store Attitude and Store Patronage Behavior," *Journal of Retailing* (Summer 1985): 39–60.

Malhotra, Naresh K., "Modeling Store Choice Based on Censored Preference Data," *Journal of Retailing* (Summer 1986): 128–144.

Thurik, Roy, and Peter Kooiman, "Modeling Retail Floorspace Productivity," *Journal of Retailing* (Winter 1986): 431–445.

Zimmer, Mary R., and Linda L. Golden, "Impressions of Retail Stores: A Content Analysis of Consumer Images," *Journal of Retailing* (Fall 1988): 265–293.

ENDNOTES

1. "Supermarket Design Takes Bold Strides," *Chain Store Age Executive* (May 1985): 37.
2. "Payless Profits By Prompting Impulse Buys," *Wall Street Journal*, 13 July 1983, p. 29.
3. "Shopping Habits," *Wall Street Journal*, 21 April 1982, p. 33.
4. Adolph Novak and James Tolman, *Store Planning and Designs* (New York: Lebhar Friedman Books, 1977), 76.
5. Pierre Martineau, "The Personality of the Retail Store," *Harvard Business Review* (January–February, 1958): 47–55.
6. William H. Bolen, *Contemporary Retailing* (Englewood Cliffs, N.J.: Prentice-Hall, 1978): 99.
7. "The Visual Connection," *Home Furnishing Daily*, 8 August 1983, p. 7.
8. "Tax Credit Is the Ticket For St. Louis Station Rebirth," *Wall Street Journal*, 12 June 1985, p. 31.
9. "Real Estate," *Wall Street Journal*, 19 June 1985, p. 33.
10. "Mel Kaufman and His Rules on Rehab," *Buildings* (June 1979): 63–66.
11. "Tax Credit. . . ," *Wall Street Journal*.
12. "Mall Protocol," *St. Petersburg Times*, 11 March 1985, p. 20E.
13. William R. Davidson and Alton F. Doody, *Retailing Management*, 3d ed. (New York: Ronald Press, 1966): 163.
14. "Payless Profits . . . ," *Wall Street Journal*.

15. Larry Redinbaugh, *Retail Management* (New York: McGraw-Hill, 1979), 187–88.

16. "Pilot Study Finds Final Product Choice Usually Made In Store," *Marketing News* (August 6, 1982): 5; and "In-Store Merchandising Is Attracting More Marketing Dollars With Last Word in Sales," *Marketing News* (August 19, 1983): 1, 12.

17. "View Store Layout From the Shopper's Viewpoint," *Progressive Grocer Mid-Year Executive Report*, 1984: 8–11.

18. Cathy J. Cobb and Wayne D. Hoyer, "Planned Vs. Impulse Purchase Behavior," *Journal of Retailing* (Winter 1986): 384–409.

19. Sevgin Eroglu and Gilbert D. Harrell, "Retail Crowding: Theoretical and Strategic Implications," *Journal of Retailing* (Winter 1986): 346–363.

20. James R. Lumpkin, Barnett A. Greenberg, and Jac L. Goldstucker, "Marketplace Needs of the Elderly: Determinant Attributes and Store Choice," *Journal of Retailing* (Summer 1985): 75–105.

21. For a new approach to determining what product categories should be placed next to each other, the reader should see the Harris and Rose article above.

22. J. B. Wilkerson, Christie H. Paksoy and J. Barry Mason, "A Demand Analysis of Newspaper Advertising and Changes in Space Allocation," *Journal of Retailing* (Summer 1981), 45.

23. Wilkerson, Paksoy, and Mason, "A Demand Analysis of Newspaper Advertising . . .," 30–48; and Gary F. McKinnon, J. Patrick Kelly and E. Doyle Robinson, *Journal of Retailing* (Summer 1981): 49–63.

24. "New Light on Ad Readership and Impact," *Progressive Grocer—Executive*, (mid-year 1984), 17.

25. Davidson and Doody, *Retailing Management*, 658–659.

26. "When You Least Expect It. . . ," *Chain Store Age—Executive* (February 1985): 18.

27. "Confessions of An Ex-shoplifter," *Chain Store Age—Executive* (February 1985): 17.

28. "Crime Time," *Wall Street Journal*, 21 July 1987, p. 29.

29. "Hotlines and Heavy Rewards: Retailers Step Up Efforts to Curb Employee Theft," *Wall Street Journal*, 17 September 1987, p. 31.

30. Charles W. King and Lawrence J. Ring, "Market Positioning Across Retail Fashion Institutions: A Comparative Analysis of Store Types," *Journal of Retailing* (Spring 1980): 37–55.

31. Stephen J. Arnold, M. A. Sylvia, and Douglas J. Tigert, "Comparative Analysis of Determinant Attributes in Retail Store Selection," 1978 *Proceedings of Advances in Consumer Research*, 665–666.

32. David Mazursky and Jacob Jacoby, "Exploring the Development of Store Image," *Journal of Retailing* (Summer 1986): 145–165.

33. Ray Marquardt, "Merchandise Displays are Most Effective When Marketing, Artistic Factors Combine," *Marketing News* (August 19, 1983): 3.

34. "Remodeling Pays Off in Higher Profits," *Chain Store Age—Executive* (April 1985): 27–29.

35. "Remodeling Pays Off . . .," 27.

36. "Motherhood Adopts a Fashion Look for the Eighties," *Chain Store Age—Executive* (April 1985): 31.

37. "Elevator Music Celebrates Anniversary," *Lubbock Avalanche-Journal*, 9 July 1984, p. 6A.

38. Ronald E. Milliman, "Using Background Music to Affect the Behavior of Supermarket Shoppers," *Journal of Marketing* (Summer 1982): 86–91.

39. "K mart: The No. 2 Retailer Starts to Make an Upscale Move—At Last," *Business Week* (June 4, 1984): 50–51; "K mart Assumes New Posture," *Chain Store Age—Executive* (August 1984): 25–29; and "K mart Stores Trying New Look to Invite More Spending," *Wall Street Journal*, 26 December 1980, p. 29.

40. Joseph A. Bellizzi, Ayn E. Crawley, and Ronald W. Hasty, "The Effects of Color in Store Design," *Journal of Retailing* (Spring 1983): 21–45.

41. "What's Ahead?" *Discount Merchandiser* (December 1987): 26, 27.

42. "The Store Designer's New Best Friend," *Progressive Grocer* (October 1984): 83.

43. For a detailed review of the issues involved in retail productivity the reader should consult the *Journal of Retailing* (Fall 1984).

14 Chapter

Servicing the Retail Customer

OVERVIEW

The purpose of this chapter is to demonstrate how customer services generate additional demand for the retailer's merchandise. It discusses how customer service, including retail selling, can be used in conjunction with other operational functions of the firm to increase demand. It also covers the determination of an optimal customer service level. The chapter concludes with a look at the unique managerial problems service retailers must address.

CUSTOMER SERVICE

During the 1980s the forces of inflation and the intense competition from discounters caused many traditional retailers to reduce customer service levels as a means of staying price competitive. It was the contention of these retailers that reduced service levels would lower cost, allowing lower gross margins and increased competitiveness. This was similar to another retail phenomenon that occurred after the economic depression of the 1930s. As labor costs increased (or as labor became scarce during World War II), self-service retailers appeared, offering lower prices and lower service. This movement grew from supermarkets and five-and-dime stores to include discount department stores, gasoline retailers, and even to the restaurant's salad bars. However, in recent years, traditional department stores and many specialty stores have come to realize that customer service is their strong suit.[1] Instead of frustrating the customer by not having the necessary stock on hand or the proper sales support[2] resulting in the customer doing more shopping elsewhere, high-performance retailers of the 1990s realize that customer service is a major demand factor for their merchandise.

Customer service consists of all those activities performed by the retailer which influence (1) the ease with which a potential customer can shop or learn about the store's offering, (2) the ease with which a transaction can be completed once the customer attempts to make a purchase, and (3) the customer's satisfaction with the service or merchandise after the transaction. These three elements are the pretransaction, transaction, and posttransaction components of customer service. Some common services include alterations, delivery, gift wrapping, and layaway.

Retailers should design their customer service program around pretransaction, transaction, and posttransaction elements in order to obtain a differential competitive advantage. Because of mass distribution, most retailers today have access to the same merchandise and, therefore, retailers can seldom differentiate themselves from others solely on the basis of merchandise stocked. The same can be said regarding locational and store design advantages. Retailers can, however, obtain a high degree of differentiation through their customer service programs.[3] Customer service in retailing can be a significant dimension on which to build a strong and unique competitive strategy. In fact, service excellence is a hallmark of America's most successful retailers. Service excellence pays off in greater customer loyalty, and service can actually insulate retailers from price, merchandising, locational, and design competition.[4]

DEMAND GENERATION

Serving the customer before, during, and after the transaction can attract new customers and strengthen the loyalty of present customers. If customer service before the transaction is poor, there is a decreased probability of the transaction occurring. If customer service is poor at the transaction stage, the customer may back out of the transaction. And, if customer service is poor after the transaction, the probability of a repeat purchase at the same store decreases.

Illus. 14.1

Service excellence pays off in greater customer loyalty, and service can actually insulate retailers from price, merchandising, locational, and design competition.

Many retail executives now realize that customers expect product service and have identified different strategies for meeting those needs in order to influence demand.[5] Refer back to the three-dimensional demand model (Exhibit 5.7 on page 172) and consider the effects of good customer service programs on these dimensions. Good customer service can increase the price the consumer is willing to pay, the quantity demanded, or the distance the consumer is willing to travel to obtain the products.

TRANSIENT CUSTOMERS

The customer who visits a store and finds the service level below expectation or the product out of stock will become a **transient customer**. This transient customer will seek a store with the level of customer service he or she feels is appropriate. At any given moment, for all lines of retail trade, there are a good number of transient customers. The retailer with a superior customer service program will have a significant advantage in intercepting these transients and converting them into loyal customers. Thus, customer service can play a significant role in building a retailer's sales volume.

RESEARCH STUDIES

Let us review four research studies that will illustrate the role of customer service in generating demand. The first study deals with grocery retailing, the second with department store retailing, the third with service retailing, and the fourth with handling customer complaints at both retailers and governmental agencies.

The first study was conducted by *Progressive Grocer* and the Home Testing Institute.[6] In this study consumers were asked to weigh 37 store characteristics. Eleven of these characteristics were found to be crucial in determining store-switching behavior. In other words, when a customer's present store didn't score well on those 11 points, the consumer tended to switch grocery stores. Of these 11 characteristics, 7 were directly related to customer service: (1) open late hours, (2) new, advertised items are available, (3) good assortment of nonfood merchandise, (4) check-cashing service, (5) short wait at checkout, (6) good parking facilities, and (7) adequate supply of items on special. In grocery retailing, good customer service is a crucial variable in attracting and retaining customers. In other words, customer service is a demand generator.

The second study was conducted by R. H. Braskin Associates, a market research firm, for ten major retailers in New York including Macy's and Saks.[7] The study examined consumer attitudes and perceptions about department store shopping. Results indicated that shoppers have ten common complaints about department store shopping for women's clothing:[8]

1. "Every time you want to try on a new item, you have to get dressed and leave the fitting room."
2. "The department store sells clothes too far in advance, such as selling winter clothes at the end of summer."
3. "When they have a big sale, they don't have enough help and you have to wait too long."
4. "If I need a different size while I'm in the fitting room, there are no salespeople to get it for me."
5. "You're not allowed to bring enough garments into the fitting room."
6. "Department stores have fewer and fewer people to serve me."
7. "The lines to pay at department stores are too long for me to shop during lunch hour."
8. "There's no way of telling which size will best fit me without trying the garment on."
9. "You have to go from place to place all over the store to get a refund or exchange."
10. "When they have a clothing sale, they don't have enough stock in the most popular items."

These findings suggest that department stores can gain a major competitive advantage by upgrading their customer service levels, especially in fitting rooms.

The third study, which focused on service retailing, was conducted by the American Hotel and Motel Association and asked business travelers what their biggest complaints about hotel service were. Their major complaints were poor attitude of employees; rooms not ready, worn facilities/ poor maintenance; no record of reservation, and problems checking in and checking out.[9]

The final study was conducted by the Technical Assistance Research Programs Institute (TARP). The study involved a survey of how complaints were handled in various businesses and governmental agencies. The study found that the proper handling of complaints by retailers could increase return on investment in service programs by 35 to 400 percent, because 70 percent of consumers who have had their complaints addressed satisfactorily became the retailers' most loyal customers.[10]

While these four studies dealt with different industries, their conclusion—good customer service generates demand and builds customer loyalty—is true for all lines of retail trade. In fact, Gimbels Midwest has also proven the positive effects of a good customer service program. Using the acronym CARE (Customers Are Really Everything), Gimbels Midwest instructed its sales force not to take inventory counts, fill in stock, or talk to buyers for one day. Instead they were told to concentrate on the customer and offered a $5 bill to anyone who made an extra sale that day. The sales research staff supplied the historical sales figure of $24,000 for the day and Gimbels hoped to increase this to $28,000 using CARE. The final sales figure was $42,000 for the day, and as a result Gimbels inaugurated a new service program. The sales force still did nonselling functions—stocking, counting, talking with buyers—but not at the customer's expense. Top management realized the importance of customer service.[11]

CUSTOMER SERVICE AS INTEGRATIVE

A customer service philosophy should be integrated into all aspects of retail management. Customer service cannot happen all by itself, but must involve all aspects of the retail enterprise.

MERCHANDISE MANAGEMENT

One of the most significant ways a retailer can serve a customer is by having on hand the merchandise that the customer wants. There are few things more disturbing to a customer than to make a trip to a store for a specific item only to discover that the item is out of stock. The better the store is at allocating inventory in proportion to customer demand patterns, the better the customer will be served.

BUILDING AND FIXTURE MANAGEMENT

Management decisions regarding building and fixtures can have a significant effect on how well the customer can be served. For example, consider the following building and fixture dimensions and how they might influence customer service:

- Heating and cooling levels
- Availability of parking space
- Ease of finding merchandise
- Layout and arrangement of fixtures
- Placement of restrooms and lounge areas
- Location of check cashing, complaint, and returns desks
- Level of lighting
- Width and length of aisles

This list is not comprehensive; it is merely intended to show that customer service considerations need to be taken into account in building and fixture decisions.

PROMOTION MANAGEMENT

Promotion provides customers with information that can help them make purchase decisions. Therefore, retailers should be concerned with whether the promotion programs they develop help the consumer. The following questions can help a retailer assess whether its promotion is serving the customer:

1. Is the advertising informative and helpful?
2. Does the advertising provide all the information the customer needs?
3. Are the salespeople helpful and informative?
4. Are the salespeople friendly and courteous?
5. Are the salespeople easy to find when needed?
6. Are sufficient quantities of sales promotion items available?
7. Do salespeople know about the ad and what's being promoted and why?

This list also is not comprehensive, but shows that customer service issues need to be considered in designing promotional programs.

PRICE MANAGEMENT

Price management will also influence how well the customer is served. Are prices clearly marked and visible? Is unit pricing available? Is pricing fair, honest, and not misleading? Are customers told the true price of credit? The pricing decision should not be isolated from the retailer's customer service program.

CREDIT MANAGEMENT

The management of credit should also be integrated into the customer service program. Credit is a significant aid in helping the customer purchase merchandise. It helps to generate and facilitate transactions. Retailers' in-house credit policies will influence the customers' perception of how well they are being serviced. Many retailers do not use credit management properly. They look at in-house credit as an expense or a loss leader. Since it is a necessary cost of doing business, many just provide the service and pray to break even.[12] However, more and more retailers today are realizing that credit is a potential profit generator, just as merchandising is. Eaton's, with 117 stores in Canada, has developed the *mop-cop* (*m*erchandise *op*erating *p*rofit and *c*redit *op*erating *p*rofit) concept in which the credit department is responsible for producing an operating profit just as merchandising is.[13]

American consumers carry 165.2 million VISA cards and 144.6 million MasterCards.[14] Most retailers accept these as an alternative to in-house credit. There are also 20 million Sears' Discover cards in circulation, and many retailers accept them as well as American Express or Diner's Club cards.[15] Many department stores and gasoline producers also issue their own credit cards, bringing the total number of credit cards issued in the United States to more than 700 million. However, the increased popularity of credit cards has presented retailers with a dilemma: should the costs associated with the granting of credit be passed on to all customers or just to those customers who use credit? Ingene and Levy have pointed out that retailers incur two costs in each credit card transaction: the discount or factoring fee paid to convert the charge slip into cash and the interest expense arising from the time lag between the sale and collection of funds.[16] Grant[17] disagreed with some of their economic assumptions, but Ingene and Levy estimated that an optimal cash discount should be 1 percent for $25 purchases and 2.25 percent for $100 purchases.

The Cash Discount Act of 1981 permits businesses to give discounts to consumers paying cash so as not to burden them with financial expenses involved in credit card sales. Oil company retailers AMOCO, EXXON, ARCO, Sohio, and Mobil were among the first retailers to try discounts for cash in lieu of credit card sales. However, because of the drop in interest rates during the late 1980s, retailers are presently encouraging the use of credit cards. High-performance retailers would be well advised to take the following steps now to prepare for the time when interest rates and factoring fees make credit card sales a high-cost operation. By taking these steps now, the retailer will be able to develop a policy for determining the use or nonuse of cash discounts.

1. Determine what proportion of total sales is made by cash and credit card. If most sales are for cash, retailers don't need cash discounts.
2. Determine whether the cash-credit proportion fluctuates during different times of the week, month, or season. For example, if cash sales are high around normal pay periods and credit sales are higher during other time periods, retailers might be advised to use other promotions or discounts, rather than a regular cash discount which will cut into profits during the times customers would use cash anyway.
3. Determine what your customers' reactions to a policy change will be. Maybe the ill will associated with a charge will overcome any cash benefits.
4. Determine what additional expenses will be incurred by implementing a policy change. The extra time and paperwork involved may offset any advantages.
5. If retailers have more than one store, they might measure the results of a cash discount policy by testing different approaches in different locations.

A RECAP

Integration is important when retailers develop their customer service programs. Much of what has been discussed in this book relates directly or indirectly to one of the three broad categories of customer service: pretransaction, transaction and posttransaction. By devoting a chapter to customer service, we hope to reinforce the notion that customer service is a key demand generator and a dimension on which retailers can build a strong competitive advantage.

COMMON CUSTOMER SERVICES

Much of the discussion on merchandise, fixed assets, pricing, promotion, and store layout in previous chapters had implications for serving the customer. However, many of the more popular types of customer service have not been mentioned or have received sparse coverage. Let us review some of them.

PRETRANSACTION SERVICES

The most common pretransaction services are convenient hours, information aids, and food service. Each of these makes it easier for the potential customer to shop or to learn about the store's offerings.

Convenient Hours. The more convenient the operating hours of the store are, the easier it is for the customer to visit the store. Convenient operating hours are one of the most basic but essential services that a retailer can provide to its customers.

The operating hours often depend on competition. If a competitor is willing to stay open until 9 p.m. six nights a week, it would probably not be wise to close every night at 6 p.m. unless a lease requires it. The exception would be if not enough revenue were generated to stay open late six nights per week. For example, a large grocery chain recently discontinued its 24-hour-a-day policy when it discovered that in certain locations, the shoplifting that occurred more than offset the sales gained by being open those hours. A convenience store/gasoline retailer in the same neighborhoods offers 24-hour service successfully. According to the owner, "the 24-hour operation is really a matter of perception. People drive by at 2 a.m. and notice we are open. Maybe they don't come in then, but they'll come by in the daytime. There's a psychological factor there that we haven't quite been able to figure out. All we know is that it works. No wonder our suppliers have been telling us for years that round-the-clock was the way of the future."

Therefore, customer service programs, as all retail management decisions, should be assessed on the basis of profit impact. This requires a retailer to assess its target market and that market's shopping habits to estimate how customers would respond to a change in store operating hours. The target market may flock to an all-night drug store but stay away from a dress shop opening at 8 a.m. Retailers must ascertain what their customers want and weigh the cost of providing those wants against the additional revenues that would be generated.

Information Aids.   As we already mentioned, the retailer's promotional efforts help to inform the customer. Many retailers offer customers other information aids to help them make intelligent transactions. For example, some retailers offer lessons that instruct the customer in how to use, operate, or care for a product. Not surprisingly, many stores that offer these lessons can increase their market shares because many customers are afraid to buy a new item (such as a microwave, videotape machine, home computer, or electric wok) without first knowing how to use it. If the store offers classes or specific instruction on the use of a product, the customer will be less resistant to purchasing the product. The customer will tend to buy items that are technologically sophisticated from the retailer who teaches.

Some firms also offer booklets that provide useful consumer information. Sears' *How To Choose and Use Retail Credit* has been very popular among consumers and educators. Other consumer information booklets published by Sears include *Floor Coverings: Their Selection and Care; Kitchen Planning Basics; How to Select Furniture; How to Select Hand and Power Tools*; and *Fabric Care Manual.* Consumer information booklets can be important sources of pretransaction information to the consumer. Retailers that provide such booklets are not only serving customers, but are also building goodwill.[18]

Another example of the retailer providing the customer with information before the sale is shown in Retailing in Action 14-1.

RETAILING IN ACTION 14-1

Educational Programs Lead to Success for Car Dealerships

Given that most consumers, especially women, would rather visit the dentist than take their car back to the dealer for repairs, one group of west Texas car dealers has developed an educational program to change this feeling.

Tom King, the service manager for the lead dealer, developed a program featuring education (pretransaction), high quality service (transaction) and follow up (posttransaction) called Sterling Care. The name is meant to reflect the attitude that the car dealers have toward the customer's car. The program has been so successful that the dealers using this concept are all at the top of the service ranking conducted by the automobile manufacturers.

The success of the program revolves around the educational seminars the dealers provide women. The seminars, promoted with direct mail and ads in the women's section of the newspaper, are advertised as no pressure seminars covering the various aspects of car care, including how the engine works, how to do simple spot maintenance such as checking tire pressure, fluid levels, and belts, and even a visit to the service area of the dealership.

More than 500 women attended the seminars the first year, and most attendees rated the service department higher than before. A great deal of confusion was cleared up by the seminars and, even more important, several new car sales were directly attributed to the seminars.

Source: Used with permission of Tom King and Gene Messer Ford.

Food Service.   Many times shopping trips are an all-day event. These long trips create a need for convenient and easy-to-consume food. Many retailers provide restaurants within their stores, thus enabling customers to eat without leaving the store.

Regardless of its impact on sales of other products, the provision of food service itself can be profitable. Some retailers, however, will design their food service to just break even by offering good food at a low price. This actually helps to bring more traffic into the store, which can stimulate sales.

TRANSACTION SERVICES

The most important transaction services are credit, layaway, wrapping and packaging, check cashing, personal shopping, merchandise availability, personal selling, and the sales transaction itself. These services facilitate transactions once customers have made a purchase decision.

Credit.   One of the most popular transaction services offered by retailers is consumer credit. Credit can be a very expensive customer service, but if handled correctly, it can increase profits substantially.

Offering credit in one or more forms can be of great service to the customer because it enables shopping without the need to carry large sums of money. It allows the customer to buy now and pay later. Credit can benefit the retailer, too: it increases sales by increasing impulse buying and sales of expensive items. Of course, in-house credit can decrease profits if the credit policy is too lenient.

Layaway.   With a layaway service, a customer can place a deposit (usually 20 percent) on an item, and in return the retailer will hold the item for the customer. The customer will make periodic payments on the item and, when it is paid for in full, can take it home. In a sense, a layaway transaction is similar to an installment credit transaction, but the retailer retains physical possession of the item until it is completely paid for. Successful retailers such as Hill's Department Stores have placed layaway on-line with their computer system. This allows the retailer to know at any time exactly where any customer stands in terms of payments. The database can also be used to judge product demand. This is especially useful at the approach of the Christmas season, when layaways can provide a good sales indicator.[19]

Wrapping and Packaging.   Customers are better served if their purchase is properly wrapped or packaged. The service may be as simple as putting the purchase into a paper bag or as complex as packaging crystal in a special shatterproof box to prevent breakage.

The retailer must match its wrapping service to the type of merchandise it carries and its store image. A discount grocer or hardware store does quite well by simply putting the merchandise into a paper sack. Specialty clothing stores often have dress and suit boxes that are easy to carry home. Some upscale retailers put merchandise in decorated shopping bags or prewrapped gift boxes. This reduces considerably the number of packages that must be gift wrapped.

Many larger department stores and most gift shops offer a gift wrapping service. Usually there is a fee for gift wrapping unless the purchase price exceeds some limit, usually $10 to $25. Many stores also offer a courtesy wrap, which consists of a gift box and ribbon, or a store paper that identifies the place of purchase. This type of wrap is not only a customer service, but a form of advertising.

Check Cashing.   Most retail stores offer some form of check-cashing service. The most basic type of check-cashing service allows qualified customers to cash a check for the amount of purchase. A **qualified customer** is one who has applied to and been accepted by the retailer for check-cashing privileges. Often these customers are provided with an identification card that entitles them to pay for merchandise with a personal check. More liberal check-cashing services allow qualified customers to cash checks for amounts in excess of the purchase price. This practice has

Illus. 14.2

Stores usually have set policies regarding their transaction services.

made some supermarket chains become the biggest check-cashing operators in some cities, bigger than the banks.

Some retailers provide payroll check cashing services for recognized local employers. This develops goodwill and usually results in increased sales, since many customers feel guilty asking a retailer to cash their payroll checks without purchasing anything. Stores that do a significant amount of payroll check cashing will need to plan to have ample cash on hand to coincide with payroll dates of local employers.

Personal Shopping.   Personal shopping is the activity of assembling for a customer an assortment of goods. This can be as varied a service as picking out clothing, filling a telephone order, assembling a supply of groceries and sending them to the customer's home, or selecting a wedding gift. Personal shopping services are usually found in stores with a high-status image and affluent customers. However, even department stores serving middle-class America are offering this service.[20] Exhibit 14.1 is a letter promoting Dillard's personal shopping service.

Merchandise Availability.   Merchandise availability refers to whether the customers can find the items they are looking for in the store. Two reasons exist for the customer being unable to find an item: the item may be out of stock[21] or the customer may not be able to locate it. The retailer can minimize out-of-stock conditions by good merchandise management, although some out-of-stocks are inevitable. The customer's ability to locate an item in the store can be increased by having good in-store signing, layout, and displays and helpful employees.

Merchandise availability is an element of customer service that many retailers take for granted, but they shouldn't. When customers can't find the items they are looking for—whatever the reason—they will remember their bad experience.

Personal Selling.   Another important transaction service that retailers can offer is a strong, customer-oriented sales force. A good job of personal selling resulting in a need satisfying experience, or even suggestive selling if done well, will greatly enhance customer satisfaction. Personal selling will be discussed in detail later in this chapter.

Sales Transaction.   The final service is the sales transaction itself. Mason has noted that in spite of the headway being made by discounters and department and specialty stores, most retailers do little to improve sales transaction service. Most retailers view service as a cost to be controlled, not a demand generator. Albertson's promise to have all express checkouts open between 4 p.m. and 7 p.m. and Zayre's promise to open a new checkout whenever more than three people were waiting in line were met with positive disbelief on the part of consumers. Such logical responses to customer needs go a long way toward building customer loyalty.[22]

Exhibit 14.1
**Letter
Promoting
Dillard's
Personal
Shopping
Service**

Dillard Department Stores, Inc.

SOUTH PLAINS MALL • 6002 SLIDE ROAD • LOOP 289 • LUBBOCK, TEXAS 79414

Mr. Ned Jones
312 Clifford Court
Anytown, US   54321

Dear Mr. Jones:

Because of today's fast paced lifestyles and busy work
schedules, we realize that professionals like yourself cannot
always afford the time to shop for your business attire. Proper
dress is essential in the business place, and we want to assist
you by bringing clothing selections to your home or office.

This service has been well received by the professional
community in other Dillard's markets. It provides a relaxing
shopping environment without the inconvenience of shopping mall
outings. You will appreciate the individual attention from one of
our clothing associates in the privacy of your home or office.

Please complete the enclosed card and drop it in the mail.
This will enable us to determine your clothing needs for each
season and let us know when an appointment would best fit your
schedule. Many enjoy our program, and there is no charge for this
unique service - we just think you deserve the service you have
always wanted.

Sincerely,

Mark Lawson
Buyer - Sales Manager

 Dillard's

POSTTRANSACTION SERVICES

The relationship between the retailer and the consumer has become more complex in today's service-oriented economy. The nature of many products, like computers, automobiles, and travel and financial services, requires an extended relationship between the retailer and consumer. The longer this period of time can be extended by ensuring the customer's satisfaction after the transaction is completed, the greater the chances are that future sales will result.[23] Servicing the customer after the sale is called **posttransaction service** and the most common services are com-

One key to effective merchandising presentation is understanding how shoppers view a store. As shown at the right, shoppers' sightlines generally extend ahead at a 45-degree angle to the circulation path and, as shown below, move up and down searching for visual cues.

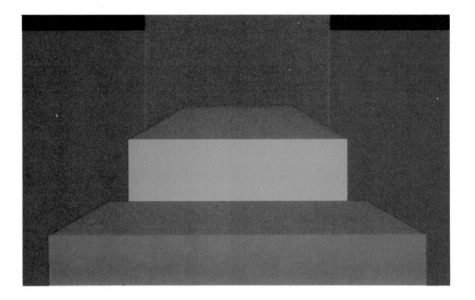

In Bloomingdale's, vistas framed by architectural elements and focal points created by lighting and video wall draw customers visually through the store.

Clover, a discount store chain in Philadelphia, maximizes the impact of merchandise in its housewares department through careful choice of fixturing, angling fixtures to face oncoming traffic and carefully planning fixture and merchandise heights to fully utilize the shopper's sightline into the department.

Minimalist design enhances merchandise exclusivity in Bloomingdale's women's designer shops.

Towers in Canada employs large, front-lit photopanels to define departments and turn the store into a "living map," which guides customers through their shopping trip.

Many retailers adopt a "power format" intended to create a price or merchandise assortment so dominant that it pre-empts competition in the consumer's mind. This power image must be forcefully conveyed through the architecture of the store itself. Hypermart USA, the hypermarket developed by power retailer Wal-Mart, uses the very scale of its 220,000 square feet to create a dominant price image that isn't soon forgotten.

The barrel-vaulted roofline is reminiscent of Grand Central Station and establishes the store on that scale.

Mass displays of enormous quantities of merchandise and large, conversational sign-age reinforce the store's price dominance.

The 170,000 square feet of visible ceiling are painted soft rose to complement the merchandise and create an exciting atmosphere. The color neither attracts eyes upward away from merchandise (as would too light a color) nor creates a cavelike feeling (as would a dark color).

Toys R Us was one of the dominant power formats to come on the scene in the 1980s. Its tremendous assortment of toys is reinforced by large in-store quantities of goods presented in mass displays. Once inside a Toys R Us, it is hard to imagine where else one would go for toys—an example of pre-emptive dominance.

Undoubtedly, Wal-Mart is the epitome of pre-emptive dominance. Generating 20–30 percent sales increases yearly and still reaching less than two-thirds of the nation, Wal-Mart threatens to surpass K mart and Sears as the world's largest retailers by the early 1990s. Its formula for success is clearly communicated in the store through mass displays that climb the walls, promotional aisles touting tremendous values, and prominently displayed gondola endcaps that constantly reinforce Wal-Mart's commitment to delivering value. The store is as straightforward as Wal-Mart itself, and this clarity of mission extended through the entire operation has created a seemingly unstoppable retail machine.

Similarly, The Limited takes a simple formula and implements it with near flawless clarity. The store reflects this discipline, creating a highly structured platform from which the merchandise can exhibit a strong presence. While The Limited's success is largely predicated on distribution efficiency which delivers cost control and uncannily quick response to consumer fashion trends, the store becomes a flexible and inexpensive stage for this offering and allows The Limited to grow quickly.

Another successful new format whose mission is reinforced through the retail environment is the warehouse store, such as Price Club. Often restricted to "member shoppers," warehouse stores offer retail customers and small business operators merchandise at very low margins, often in quantity packaging, in a no–frills environment.

While the warehouse format has been highly successful, other formats have borrowed from the low–price image of the warehouse motif to create their own low–price image, as seen here in a Good Guys home electronics clearance center. The open ceiling, grid system tying into fixturing and visible ductwork add a level of aesthetic styling to the basic warehouse elements, and appeal to customers who want a low price but feel uncomfortable shopping in a warehouse.

Lighting is one of the most critical but frequently overlooked factors in the retail environment. Here Victoria's Secret, a division of The Limited, creates a sense of intrigue by significantly lowering the ambient lighting within the store, then spotlighting specific merchandise focal points.

Fluorescent and incandescent lighting produce distinct effects on interior design materials and merchandise, actually making colors appear differently. Retailers must carefully plan the proper lighting to create the desired store atmosphere and enhance the appearance of the merchandise, particularly food and apparel.

Lighting can also be used to influence the movement of the shopper's sightline. Here lower (ambient) general illumination permits the use of brighter spotlights, which are strategically set on focal points and feature areas to draw the customers' eyes to a specific "editorial statement" the retailer wishes to make.

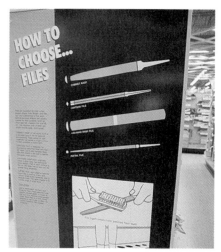

Many retailers use informational panels to describe the role merchandise plays in the shopper's life. This home center in Canada provides "how to" instructions.

Today good customer service is defined not so much by a store clerk being available to give assistance, but by a store that is so easy to shop that a clerk isn't needed at all. Bell Canada created a self-service phone center that uses visual communications to greatly improve its previous "human service" store, where the average wait to ask a clerk about phone service was 45 minutes. By creating visual focal points such as the "Application Centre," Bell Canada allows customers to see for themselves the available options, learn about the various services, and initiate the ordering process. Contact with the clerk is reserved for the final transaction, which reduces the average waiting time to less than 15 minutes, increases the shopper's sense of control over the retail experience, and exposes shoppers to more goods and services.

Similarly, financial service retailers are employing visual communications to merchandise the more than 120 services available at the typical bank branch. Unfortunately, customers who come in the branch to use checking and savings services are usually unaware of the other service options. This Bank One branch places the teller line at the back of the "store," then draws the customer past many stations that represent and describe available services visually.

CoreStates bank makes heavy use of visual communications to tell how it is "a better bank." Brochure racks reinforce this message and offer take home evidence, and merchandising stations tell the story of specific services available.

plaint handling, return policies, merchandise repair, and servicing and delivery.

Complaint Handling. Customer dissatisfaction occurs when the customer's experience with a retailer or a product fails to live up to expectations.[24] The proper handling of customer complaints can mean the difference between surviving or failing. Dealing with customers is tricky: it involves employees who make human errors dealing with customers who make human errors. This doubles the chance of misunderstanding and mistakes between the two parties. Unfortunately, these mistakes and misunderstandings often lead to a poor image of the retailer. It is essential that retail executives try to solve customer complaints. If retailers solve the customer's problem, then the customer is being served.

There are several ways of handling and solving customer complaints. For a large retailer, a central complaint department is most efficient. Here, all customer complaints are handled by a staff specially trained for this task. This method leaves the sales force free to do its job and allows the customer to deal with someone who has the authority to act on most complaints. Many large retailers even use an 800 number so that these complaints can be handled with little effort on the part of the customer. One such result of using this system is shown in Exhibit 14.2. For a small retailer, however, this system is usually not necessary; the owner, store manager, department head, or salesperson can handle what few complaints the average small retailer would get. If there are more than a few complaints, retailers should attempt to find out why and make the necessary corrections.

Other retailers are taking a lesson from their industrial goods counterparts and looking at the advantages of using the individual salesperson in handling the complaint. They believe that a friendly, sympathetic attitude exhibited by the salesperson will have a positive effect on future sales, especially if the complaint is about a product, rather than the retailer or salesforce. This method does, however, have several disadvantages. First, the individual salesperson often does not have the authority to settle the problems. The salesperson usually has to call someone else to take care of the problem and the customer has to state the problem again. Second, a salesperson who is listening to a customer complaining cannot serve other customers who, incidentally, are overhearing complaints. Many manufacturers, as a part of their marketing programs, are now actively soliciting complaints from the customer.

Regardless of the complaint-handling system, three things are important when handling complaints. The customer deserves courteous treatment, fair settlement, and prompt action. Even if a sale is lost, the customer need not be lost. The proper handling of complaints has substantial paybacks for the retailer.[25]

Merchandise Returns. The handling of merchandise returns is an important customer service—it can even make the difference between mak-

PEOPLES DRUG STORES, INCORPORATED
AND SUBSIDIARY CORPORATIONS
District Offices ● 29238 North 7th Street, Harrisburg, Pennsylvania 17110
(717) 238-1376

December 7, 1989

Dr. Ned Jones
312 Crowell Rd.
Anytown, US   54321

Dear Dr. Jones:

We received notice here in our District Office regarding a call you
made to our Divisional Corporate Office in Northumberland, PA. Your
call related to an experience you had while shopping in our Peoples
Drug Store, Shippensburg, PA.

According to the report, you were obviously not treated well nor was
proper customer service given to you. For that and for the lack of
courtesy which is quite obvious according to our Customer Service
Representative, we certainly apologize. I will speak to the manager
of this store, Mr. Gregory Antoon, and his assistant, Robert Quigley,
and reiterate our customer service policies. Peoples Drug Stores
nor I will tolerate this kind of action which you described to our
Customer Service Representative.

We appreciate the time you took in calling to inform us of this situation; however, we would encourage you to call here to the District
Office collect to inform us of any future concerns. If I am not here,
my Secretary, Mrs. Susan Gallion, will be most happy to help you
resolve any problems you may have regarding any of our stores.

Enclosed please find a merchandise gift certificate good in any Peoples
Drug Stores. This is just a token of our appreciation of your concern.

May you and your family have a most joyous Holiday Season!

Sincerely,

John B. Campbell, R.Ph.
District Manager #33

---

ing a profit and losing money. The return policy can range from "no returns, no exchanges" to "the customer is always right." A retailer needs
to choose these extreme policies or a more moderate one. Few services
build customer goodwill as effectively as a fair return policy. On the other
hand, the return service is widely abused by American consumers. It is
important that the store's return policy must be consistent with the
store's image.

Exhibit 14.3 identifies the key cost elements of a return. Because of
its size, some merchandise has to be picked up by a delivery service when
it is returned, which can become costly. Also, the amount of time spent by
the bookkeeping department is increased because records must be made
on every item that is returned, and often earlier records on the item must
be changed. In addition, there is a restocking cost, especially if all price
and code tags have been removed.

Depending on the item returned, there can be a substantial loss due to

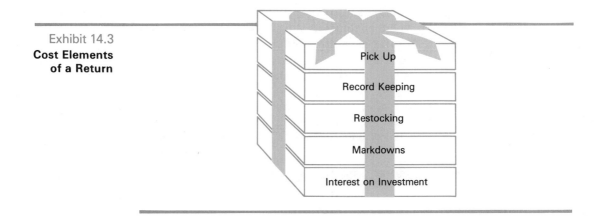

Exhibit 14.3
**Cost Elements
of a Return**

Pick Up

Record Keeping

Restocking

Markdowns

Interest on Investment

the time the item was out of stock. Beach or patio furniture, for example, wouldn't sell as well in the winter, and a returned snow shovel would be in low demand in the summer. Because of this delay, returned merchandise is often stored until the proper season or sold at a reduced price. Reducing the price is also common practice if the merchandise has been used. There is also an opportunity cost—the foregone interest or return on investment dollars. Money gets tied up in merchandise that is in the possession of the customer but hasn't been paid for and will be returned.

Retailing in Action 14-2 describes how one of the nation's most out-

RETAILING IN ACTION   14-2

This Store's Return Policy is Unbeatable

In the highly competitive world of department stores, Seattle-based Nordstrom has turned exacting standards of customer service into something legends are made of. Nordstrom, an apparel, shoe, and soft good retailer since 1901, recently entered the East Coast market with two stores in the Washington, D.C. area.

A major ingredient in Nordstrom's success (1988 sales of $2.3 billion from 59 stores) is the quality of the salesforce. They are better paid and trained than the competition and are encouraged to do almost anything within reason to satisfy customers. One salesclerk personally ironed a customer's newly purchased shirt so it would look fresher for an upcoming meeting.

However, the big part of the legend is the firm's return policy laid down by the president, James Nordstrom: "replace anything on demand, no matter how expensive, no questions asked." Although the policy is sometimes abused by shoppers (who may, for example, order an expensive dress, wear it to a party, and then return it), it made Nordstrom's a symbol of customer satisfaction. There is even a story—which the company doesn't deny—about a customer who got his money back on a tire. Since Nordstrom doesn't sell tires, it was a testament to James Nordstrom's dictum of "no questions asked."

Source: "Why Rivals Are Quaking As Nordstrom Heads East," *Business Week* (June 15, 1987): 99 and 100; "Where the Customer Is Still King," *Time* (February 2, 1987): 56 and 57; and "Spoiling for Success," *U.S. News & World Report* (December 5, 1988): 52-54.

standing retailers has built its reputation on providing outstanding services, including its return policy. Many other retailers have reevaluated their policies in recent years in order to use this service to generate demand. There has been a shift to cash refunds vs. exchange only so as not to offend good customers.[26] However, this policy can result in some abuse. For example, one large department store retailer in the Southwest took back more food processors in exchange after Christmas one year than it sold during the Christmas season. It seems a discount competitor had the item on special and the store did not want to offend customers who got it in a department store gift box and were told by their friends that they had purchased the gift at the department store.

Another possibility of employee abuse is the refund system. Most retailers operate on the theory that the average employee does not steal. Maybe one or two in a hundred employees steal, but most do not and thus the store rarely sets up complete safeguards for the employee who does steal. One large department store found an employee who issued more than 400 fraudulent refunds, all with legitimate authorization signatures. The problem was that the authorizers failed to look at the merchandise or the customer; they just signed the refund slip. As a result of this incident the former employee got eight consecutive life sentences and the authorizers now question why a refund is being made. Shortages at the store have now been reduced by more than 75 percent.[27]

To best serve customers, the retailer should plan to conduct business in such a way that customers will not need to return merchandise. This requires that delivery people be trained so they will not damage merchandise in transit and that salespeople be instructed not to push unsuitable merchandise on the customer.

Some customers are more prone to return merchandise than others. Exhibit 14.4 provides an analysis of the differences between customers who are prone to returning goods and those who aren't.

Servicing and Repair.   Any product with at least one moving mechanical part is a candidate for future servicing or repair. In fact, even items

Exhibit 14.4

Some Significant Differences Between Heavy Returners and Nonreturners

HEAVY RETURNERS

- Liberal
- Opinion Leader
- Swinger
- Bargain Seeker
- Action Oriented
- Some College Education
- Large Household Size
- Marrieds
- High Income

NON-RETURNERS

- Conservative
- Dependent Decision Making
- Home Oriented
- Cautious Buyer
- Less Than High School Education
- Small Household Size
- Singles
- Low Income

SOURCE: Adapted from Barnett Greenberg, Danny Bellenger, Dan Robertson and Ravi Parameswaran, "An Analysis of Return-Prone Consumers," *Proceeding of 1979 Southern Marketing Association Meetings,* pp. 254. Adapted with authors' permission.

without moving parts such as clothing, coffee tables, and paintings are candidates for repair. Retailers who offer merchandise servicing and repair to their customers tend to generate a higher sales volume. If the work they perform is good, they also can generate repeat business. For example, if the service department of a TV and appliance store has a reputation for doing good work at fair prices, customers will not only purchase TVs at the store but will also purchase radios, stereos, and washers.

Retailers who might receive substantial benefit from offering repair and servicing of merchandise are TV and appliance stores, jewelry stores, bicycle stores, auto dealers, clothing stores, lawn mower and small engine shops, furniture stores, and computer stores.

Repair and servicing is perhaps one of the most difficult customer services to manage. While good repair and servicing can stimulate additional sales, the reverse is also true. When customers get substandard repair and service work, they do not return to the same retailer for future purchases of merchandise. These disgruntled customers will tell their friends, relatives, and acquaintances of the retailer's poor work.

Retailers who perform service and repair work will find it advantageous to behave ethically. The National Business Council for Customer Affairs has a Code of Responsible Practices that retailers should openly embrace. The key components of this code are:

1. Customers should be offered an estimate of cost in advance of services to be rendered.
2. Customers should be promptly notified if service appointments cannot be kept.
3. Only repairs authorized in writing by the customer should be performed, except where other arrangements have been made to the customer's satisfaction.
4. A written itemized invoice for all parts, labor, and any other charges should be given to the customer on completion of the work.
5. All repair services should be guaranteed for a reasonable length of time.
6. Appropriate records of services performed and materials used should be maintained by the service company for at least one year.
7. Service technicians should not be paid according to the size of the customer's repair bill.
8. The service dealer should maintain insurance coverage adequate to protect the customer's property while it is in custody.
9. Service dealers should cooperate with consumer protection agencies at all levels of government to ensure satisfactory resolution of customer complaints.
10. Customers should be treated courteously at all times, and all complaints should be given full and fair consideration.[28]

Delivery.   Delivery of merchandise can be a very expensive service, but the benefits derived from providing delivery may be worth the expense if the store, merchandise, and customer characteristics warrant it.

Retailers can offer free delivery (which is actually absorbed in slightly higher prices) or they can charge the customer a small fee to help offset the cost of delivery. There are three types of delivery service: the store-owned system, the co-op system, and the independent contractor system.

The **store-owned delivery system** consists of a store employee delivering merchandise in a store-owned or -leased vehicle. It could involve a sole proprietor using a car or a fleet of drivers in trucks. Advantages of this system include control over employees, tailored delivery routes for individual customer purchases, and advertising created by displaying the store's logo on the vehicle. The main disadvantage of the store-owned system is its relatively high cost.

With a **co-op delivery system,** several retailers jointly own and operate the delivery service. This system offers significant economies of scale because the number of deliveries in a geographic area can be increased and the cost per unit of delivery can be significantly decreased. Exhibit 14.5 shows how goods to be delivered to each retailer's customers are consolidated by a delivery company and grouped into delivery areas or zones to be delivered on certain days or at certain times. One of the major disadvantages of this system is fitting customers into a delivery timetable that is convenient to them. A delivery to Area Z in Exhibit 14.5 will be inconvenient if the customer is not available on Tuesday afternoons to receive the delivery. A second problem with the system is a lack of control over the delivery employees, because the delivery personnel are not store employees.

A third delivery alternative is the use of an **independent contractor.** A good example of this system is United Parcel Service. Charges for this service may be made on a per parcel rate based on size or weight of the package, a flat rate per week, or a combination of both. The main advantage of this system is that the retailer doesn't incur the expense of owning and operating the delivery service and is still able to reap the benefits of consumer approval for offering delivery service. The main drawback is the lack of control over the quality of delivery service and the inability to customize delivery to fit customer wants.

Exhibit 14.5
**Co-op Delivery
System**

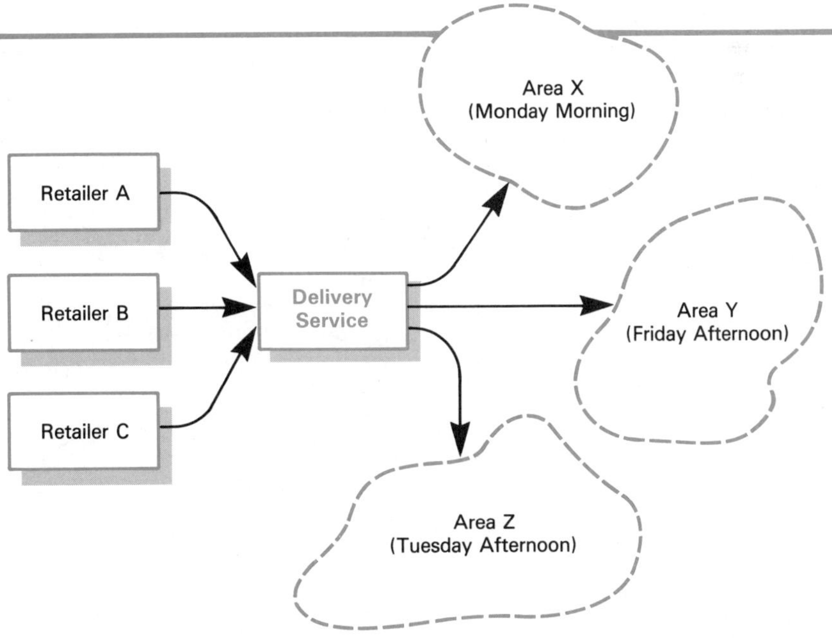

DETERMINING CUSTOMER SERVICE LEVELS

It is not easy to determine the optimal number and level of customer services to offer. Theoretically, a retailer should add customer services until the incremental revenue generated by higher service levels is equal to the incremental cost of providing those services. This would establish the level of customer services where profit is maximized. In the short run, profits can usually be increased by cutting back on costly customer services, but the effect on long-run profits should be the overriding consideration.

It is difficult to decide what specific customer services to offer to increase sales volume. Exhibit 14.6 lists six pointers to help determine which customer services to offer: store characteristics, services offered by the competition, type of merchandise handled, price image of the store, income of the target market, and cost of providing the service. It is the retailer's job to study these six factors to arrive at the service mix that will increase long-run profits by keeping present customers, enticing new customers, and projecting the right type of store image. Above all, retailers must be realistic and not expect to satisfy the wants and needs of all customers. No strategy could be less profitable than trying to satisfy everybody.

Exhibit 14.6

Pointers for Determining Customer Service Mix

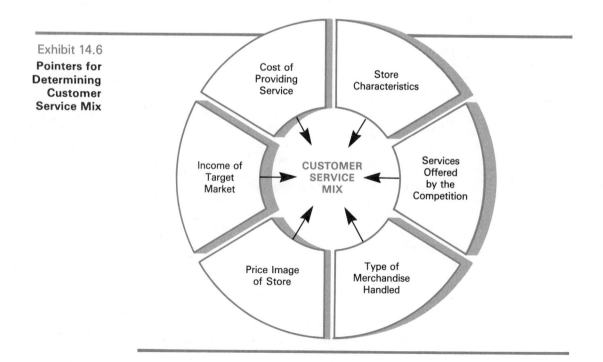

STORE CHARACTERISTICS

Store characteristics include store location, store size, and store type. It is especially important to look at these three store characteristics when considering adding a service.

Services offered in the downtown area of a large city would probably be different from those offered by a similar store in a rural shopping center. For example, a drugstore in the downtown area might offer free delivery of prescriptions as a service to its clientele. This service would be of great benefit to city dwellers without cars and businesspeople who don't want to spend time waiting at the drugstore for a prescription. This same service in a rural community shopping center would not be as important. Rural residents usually drive to most stores they visit, travel greater distances, and make many multiple-purpose trips. Therefore, the rural druggist might get a better return on investment by offering check cashing, credit, and free parking, rather than free delivery of prescriptions.

The size and type of store also determine which services to offer. A major department store would offer a different assortment of services than a grocery or hardware store. There would also be a difference between a large and a small store of the same type. The customer would expect more services from a large retailer, and fewer but more personalized services from the small retailer.

COMPETITION

The services offered by competitors have a significant effect on the level and variety of customer services offered. A retailer must either offer these services or suitable substitutes, or offer lower prices.

Suppose there are three clothing stores of the same general type, price range, and quality within a given area. Store A and Store B offer free gift wrapping, standard alterations, bank card credit, and a liberal return policy. Store C, on the other hand, offers only store credit and has an exchange-only return policy. Customers who are shopping for gifts generally frequent Stores A and B over C because they feel confident that whatever they purchase will ultimately be just right. It can even be gift wrapped at the store. If the gift isn't suitable, the receiver can have it altered to fit, exchange it, or even get a cash refund. Store C must do one of two things to compete: add services or lower prices.

TYPE OF MERCHANDISE

The merchandise lines carried can indicate the types of services to offer. Certain merchandise lines benefit from complimentary services: bicycles and free assembly; major appliances and delivery; men's suits and alterations; and sewing machines and free instructions.

PRICE IMAGE

Generally, customers will expect more services from a store with a high-price image than from a discount retailer. When a customer perceives a store as having high prices, it also sees the store as possessing an air of luxury. Therefore, the services rendered by a high-price store should carry the image of luxury or status. Some of the typical high-price image services are elegant food service, personal shopping, a home design studio, free gift wrapping, free delivery, and free alterations.

Discount stores needn't offer luxury services because customers who shop there are seeking low prices, not fancy customer services. A discount retailer or one with a low-price image might offer such basic services as free parking, layaway, bank card credit, and convenient store hours.

TARGET MARKET INCOME

The higher the income of the target market, the higher the maximum demand prices that consumers will pay. The higher the prices consumers will pay, the more services the retailer can profitably provide. Some customers may expect more services than they are able to afford, but retailers must avoid the temptation of providing costly services to such consumers. In the long run, the retailer will have to raise prices to pay for the services and will lose its share of low-income customers.

Young mothers, for example, usually have low discretionary income. If the retailer's target market is young families, it needs to gear the customer service program to their purchasing power level. Although these young mothers may want free delivery, gift wrapping, elegant food service, and many other services, the retailer would have to raise prices to provide them. And, by raising prices, it will lose a portion of the target market.

COST OF SERVICES

It is imperative for a retailer to know the cost of a service so that it has an idea of how much in additional sales would need to be generated to pay for the service. Customer services should be evaluated in a manner similar to promotional expenditures. The key criterion is the financial effect of adding or deleting a customer service. For example, if a customer service were expected to increase costs by $20,000 per year, and the store operated on a gross margin of 25 percent, the service would have to increase sales by at least ($20,000/0.25) or $80,000 in order to be profitable.

Exhibit 14.7 lists the services most commonly offered by conventional department stores and the percentage of stores offering these services. Not all stores offer every service.

Another way of evaluating the cost of customer service is to examine what costs would be if you didn't have good service. If a 100-store super-

Exhibit 14.7

The 25 Services Most Offered by Conventional Department Stores' Main Downtown Store (N = 214)

	Respondent Firms Offering	
	Number	Percent
1. Altering of men's clothes bought in store	121	57
2. Gift wrapping	121	57
3. Delivery, local	119	56
4. Alteration of women's clothes bought in store	118	55
5. Fashion shows	113	53
6. Personal shopping	100	47
7. Pay telephones	98	46
8. Layaway	98	46
9. Bridal registry	89	42
10. Car-parking facilities	86	40
11. Wrapping for mailing	86	40
12. Custom-made draperies	80	37
13. Delivery, out of local area	78	36
14. Suburban calls free	75	35
15. Decorating consulting	70	33
16. Restaurant	68	32
17. Carpet laying	59	28
18. Beauty salon, women	59	28
19. Monogramming, embossing soft goods	58	27
20. Shopping for merchandise not in stock	56	26
21. Wig salon, women	53	25
22. Accessory repairs	52	24
23. Fur storage	51	24
24. Jewelry/watch repairs	51	24
25. Baby strollers available	49	23

SOURCE: Saul Diamond and Hoyt Wilson, "A Survey of Some Services Offered by Traditional Department Stores" (Cedar Falls: University of Northern Iowa, 1980), mimeo. Reprinted with permission.

market chain alienated only one customer per day per store, the chain would lose $94.9 million in annual revenue. This is based on the assumption that the grocery business is repeat business and that the real cost is the $50 a customer spends weekly.[29]

RETAIL SELLING

Retail salespersons and the service they provide are a major factor in consumer purchase decisions. For example, when the retail salesperson is busy helping someone else, is rude, or is not helpful, customers often walk

out of the store empty-handed. The salesperson is a major determinant of store image. When the salesperson is available, friendly, and helpful, customers will often be influenced to enter into a transaction with the retailer. The management of the retail sales force plays a crucial role in demand generation for retail enterprises.

The importance of personal selling is even greater in service retailing, since consumers of services seldom know exactly what they want or need—they can't see the final product before purchasing like consumers of tangible products can. These consumers generally don't know what they are really purchasing until they don't get it. If the homeowner's rugs were cleaned properly, that's fine. This is a passive satisfaction—something that's expected. However, if the rugs still have the stain from last weekend's party, the customer will not be passive. It is extremely important for the sales personnel of a service retailer to a) understand exactly what the customer expects, b) explain what the retailer is able to provide, and c) balance these two expectations together at the completion of the service to see that the promises made to gain the sale were fulfilled. Sales staffs of tangible product retailers generally don't need to be this involved in a retail transaction.

TYPES OF RETAIL SELLING

In many retail settings, the employees that are called salespeople are order takers. For example, consider the role of salespeople in a discount department store like a K mart or Target. The employees might show the customer where the merchandise is located or go to the storeroom to get an item that is not on the shelf, but seldom, if ever, attempt to sell the merchandise. In fact, according to Target's president, it is his firm's "policy to provide next-to-no sales help." Target, and other discounters, "don't want to get into the business of person-to-person selling." These stores are appealing to customers who want value instead of service.[30] Whether these employees should be called salespeople is debatable; perhaps they should be referred to as retail clerks. Nevertheless, these order takers can influence demand, especially in a negative manner. If you are in a store like Target and cannot find a retail clerk to assist you when you need help, you may get frustrated and leave the store without making a purchase.

Retail employees that are most appropriately labeled **salespeople** are order getters as well as order takers. **Order getters** are involved in conversation with prospective purchasers for the purpose of making a sale. They will inform, guide, and persuade the customer in order to close a sale either immediately or in the future.

How much emphasis a retailer places on its employees being order getters depends on the line of retail trade and the retailer's strategy. Lines that concentrate on the sale of shopping goods (e.g., automobile dealers, furniture retailers, computer retailers and appliance retailers) will want their salespeople to be both order getters and takers. In lines of retail trade where convenience goods are predominantly sold (gasoline service stations and grocery retailers) the role of the salesperson or retail clerk will simply be that of an order taker. Retailers with high margins and high levels of customer service generally place more emphasis on order getting. Those with low margins and a low customer service policy tend to emphasize order taking.

Regardless of the line of retail trade or the retailer's strategy, all retail enterprises must carefully evaluate the role of the salesperson in helping to generate demand.

LABOR FORCE MANAGEMENT

There has been debate recently about how to measure the productivity of retail labor.[31] No matter how it is measured, retail labor productivity has been declining over the past two decades. Retailers are caught in a vicious circle—the relatively low wages they offer salespeople have attracted low-quality employees, which tends to perpetuate the low wage-low quality cycle. It might even be argued that "Americans have developed utter contempt for the retail clerk."[32]

Let us elaborate on this point further. Retail salespeople are not motivated by low wages and thus quickly lose morale. Consequently, many of them become disgruntled. Employee turnover rises and productivity falls. This decline in productivity and the prospect for continued high turnover prompts retailers to keep wages low. It is not surprising that in some retail stores the sales force today is entirely different from the sales force last year or the sales force next year. In some retail establishments, such as fast-food restaurants, more than 50 percent of the labor force is between 16 and 20 years old.

The profit impact of increased salesforce productivity can be dramatic. Retailers operate very close to their break-even point. A 10 to 15 percent increase in salesforce productivity (measured in sales per employee hour, gross margin per employee hour, value-added per employee hour, or gross margin minus sales commission per employee hour) would directly translate into a proportionate increase in store profits. All retail managers should accept as a priority the need to increase salesforce productivity.

To do this, a retailer needs to focus on the following salesforce decision areas: selection, training, compensation, size, scheduling, and evaluation. This chapter will discuss the selection, training, and evaluation of the retail salesforce. Chapter 16, *Retail Personnel Management*, will discuss the other topics in detail.

SALESPERSON SELECTION

Selecting retail salespeople should involve more than casually accepting anyone who answers an ad or walks into the store seeking employment. The casualness with which many retailers select people to fill sales positions is one reason for poor productivity.

Criteria.   To select salespeople properly, retailers must first decide what their criteria will be. What is expected from retail salespeople? Low absenteeism? The ability to generate a high volume of sales? Some combination? Unless a retailer knows what it is looking for in salespeople, it will not be able to acquire a salesforce that possesses the proper qualities.

High-performance results are dependent not just on the salesperson's characteristics, but also on how satisfied the salesperson is with the job[33] and what the sales job entails. One study has shown that retail selling jobs should be designed to have high levels of variety (the opportunity to perform a wide range of activities), autonomy (the degree to which an employee determines the work procedures), task identity (the degree to which an employee is involved in the total sales process), and feedback from supervisors and customers.[34] An earlier study indicated that the retail salespersons were more satisfied when they were closely supervised and in highly structured positions.[35]

Predictors.   Next, retailers must identify potential predictors to meet the chosen criteria.[36] The most common predictors used in selecting retail salespeople are demography, personality, knowledge, intelligence, and prior work experience.

Demography.   Depending on the line of retail trade, demographic variables can be important in identifying good retail salespeople. For example, a record and stereo store appealing to teens will probably benefit from retail salespeople under thirty. A high-fashion women's apparel store appealing to 30- to 50-year-old, career-oriented, upwardly mobile women would probably not want to hire 18-year-old salespeople from lower social class backgrounds. A motorcycle shop would probably not want 60-year-old women selling motorcycles. Obviously, there are exceptions to these rules, but the essential point is that retailers can use demographic variables to screen applicants for sales positions. One study found that convenience store employee turnover was related to experience and age. The study concluded that convenience store executives could reduce turnover by hiring older and more experienced individuals.[37] Other demographic variables to consider are length of time at current address, military service, current employment record, and education.

Personality.   A person's personality can reflect his or her potential as a retail salesperson. Most retailers prefer salespeople who are friendly, confident, stable, and empathetic. These personality traits can be identified either through a personal interview with the applicant or by computerized personality inventories.[38] In most lines of retail trade, a personal interview will be sufficient.

Knowledge and Intelligence.   Many products that retailers sell, like microcomputers, solid-state televisions, microwave ovens, 35 mm cameras, and ten-speed bicycles, are technically complex. Salespeople with knowledge of these products will be better able to sell them. To be able to respond to customer inquiries in a logical fashion, retail employees will need to possess some level of intelligence as well as an educational level compatible with the job description.

Experience.   One of the most reliable predictors of success as a salesperson is prior work experience, especially selling experience. If applicants have performed well in prior jobs, there is a good chance that they will perform well in the future. The correlation, however, is not perfect. Many applicants for retail selling jobs are young and have no prior work experience. These applicants can be assessed on their personal character and apparent ambition, drive, and work ethic.

The above discussion pertains to selection of candidates for sales positions, not for managerial trainees. This topic will be covered in a later chapter.

SALESPERSON TRAINING

After salespeople are selected, they need to be trained. This is true even if they have selling experience. In these training programs, retailers need to explain store policies to the trainees. In addition, new salespeople need to become familiar with and knowledgeable about the retailers' merchandise, the different customer types they may have to deal with, and the selling strategies available for different customer choice criteria. Even order takers need training in greeting customers, thanking customers, and using a POS terminal. Some retailers consider themselves fortunate if they retain 50 percent of new salespeople for two to three years, since employee training and turnover costs can range from $1,000–$2,000 per salesperson.

Store Policies.   The retail salesperson is a spokesperson for the retailer. Most interaction between the customer and retailer takes place through the salesperson. It is important for the salesperson to become familiar with those store policies that involve the customer directly. Some of these policies relate to merchandise returns and adjustments, shoplifting, credit terms, layaway, delivery, and price negotiating.

In addition, the retail salesperson should become knowledgeable about work hours, rest periods, lunch and dinner breaks, commission and quota plans, nonselling duties, and standards for periodic job evaluation. It might also be useful to inform sales employees about criteria used for promotion and advancement within the retail enterprise.

Merchandise.   If the merchandise includes shopping goods, the retailer should train its salespeople to be familiar with the strengths and weaknesses of the merchandise. This will allow salespeople to assist customers in shopping for the best goods to meet their needs. Salespeople should also become knowledgeable about the competitor's merchandise offerings and their strengths and weaknesses.

Increasingly, retail salespeople need to be familiar with the warranty terms and serviceability of the merchandise. This requires that the salesperson know something about the reputation of each manufacturer the retailer represents. Exhibit 14.8 lists in greater detail the specific information a retailer generally expects its salesperson to know about its products.

Customer Types.   Retail salespeople can be taught to identify and respond to certain customer types. The basic customer types are described in Exhibit 14.9. By knowing how to handle each of these customers the salesperson can generate added sales.

Customer Choice Criteria.   The retail salesperson should also learn how to identify the customer's choice criteria and how to respond to them.[39] The four potential choice criteria situations are described in the following sections. For each situation there is an appropriate selling strategy that the salesperson can learn.

No Active Product Choice Criteria.   The best sales strategy when the customer does not have a prior criteria is to educate the customer on the best choice criteria and possibly how to weigh them. For example, a

Exhibit 14.8

Summary of Merchandise Information Needed by Salespersons

Uses of The Product
Primary and Secondary Uses
Suitability
Versatility

How The Product Will Perform
Durability
Degree of Color Performance
Shrinkage or Stretchage (In Case
 of Textiles)
Breaking Strength
Resistance to Water, Wind, Wear,
 Heat, Light
Cost of Upkeep

How To Use The Product
How To Operate It, Wear It, Prepare It,
 Eat It, Apply It, Assemble It, Display
 It, Place It

How The Product Is Made
Size
Weight
Weave (In Case of Textiles)
Finish
Handmade or Machine Made
Pressed, Molded, Stamped,
 Inlaid, etc.
Conditions Under Which Goods
 Are Made
Packaging

What The Product Is Made Of
Kinds of Materials Used
Quality of Materials Used
Cost of Materials Used
Sources of Materials Used
Available Supplies of Materials Used

How To Care For The Product
How To Handle and Adjust The Product
How To Clean The Product
How To Store The Product
How To Oil and Grease The Product
How To Refrigerate The Product

Background Of The Product
History Of The Article
History Of The Manufacturer
History Of Its Uses
History Of Competing Articles
Rarity
Prestige

Appearance Of The Product
Beauty
Style
Ensemble Possibilities

Services Available With The Product
Credit Terms
Shipping Terms
Speed and Cost of Delivery
Transportation Methods

SOURCE: Kenneth H. Mills and Judith E. Paul, *Successful Retail Sales* (Englewood Cliffs, NJ: Prentice Hall, 1979), pp. 82-83. Reprinted with permission of the publisher.

Exhibit 14.9

How Salespeople Should Handle the Various Types of Customers

Characteristics	Basic Types	Recommendations
Doesn't trust any salesperson. Resists communication as they have a dislike of others. Generally uncooperative and will explode at slightest provocation.	 **Defensive**	Avoid mistaking their silence for openness to your ideas. Avoid any arguments. Stick to basic facts. Tactfully inject product's advantages and disadvantages.
Intense, impatient personality. These impulsive types often interrupt salespersons and have a perpetually "strained" expression. Often driven and successful people who want results fast.	 **Interrupter**	Don't waste time, move quickly and firmly from one sales point to another. Avoid overkill since they know what they want.
Confident in their ability to make decisions and stay with them. Open to new ideas but wants brevity. Highly motivated by self-pride.	 **Decisive**	No canned presentations. The key is to assist. Don't argue or point out errors in their judgment.
They worry about making the wrong decision, therefore, they tend to postpone all decisions. Want salesperson to make decision for them.	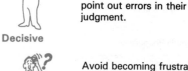 **Indecisive**	Avoid becoming frustrated yourself. Determine as early as possible the need and concentrate on that. Avoid presenting customer with too many alternatives. Start with making decisions on minor points.
Friendly, talkative types who are enjoyable to visit with. Many have excess time on their hands (e.g., retirees). They usually resist the close.	 **Sociable**	You may have to wait out these customers. Listen for points in conversation where you can interject product's merits. Pressure close is out. Subtle friendly close needed.
Quick to make decision. Impatient, just as likely to walk out as they were to walk in.	 **Impulsive**	Close as rapidly as possible. Avoid any useless interaction. Avoid any oversell. Highlight product merits.

Illus. 14.4

If the customer does not have a prior criteria, a car salesperson should educate a customer about best choice criteria and possibly how to weigh them.

prospective customer enters an automobile dealership to purchase a used automobile but does not know what criteria to use to select the best car. The car salesperson may present convincing arguments on why the customer should consider four criteria in the following order of importance: warranty, fuel economy, price, and comfort. Once the salesperson and customer agree on this list, they can work together at finding the used car that best fits the criteria.

Inadequate or Vague Choice Criteria.   When the criteria are vague, the range of products that will satisfy them is often wide. The easiest thing for the salesperson to do is to show that a particular product fits a customer's choice criteria. Since the choice criteria are vague, this would probably not be difficult and little actual selling would be involved. But since the criteria are vague, the customer may have trouble believing that the product the salesperson selected is the best one to meet his or her needs, and may therefore choose to shop around at other stores.

If the salesclerk is interested in repeat business and customer goodwill and has a wide range of products to sell, a preferable strategy would be to help the customer define his or her problem in order to arrive at a set of choice criteria. The customer and salesclerk should work together in defining the criteria and then select the product that best fits the criteria.

Choice Criteria in Conflict.   Prospective customers with choice criteria that are in conflict frequently have trouble making the purchase decision. There are two basic ways choice criteria can be in conflict. First, the customer may want a product to possess attributes that are mutually exclusive. For example, a person purchasing a ten-speed bicycle may want high quality and low price, when these two attributes do not exist in common. The best strategy in this situation is for the salesperson to play down one of the attributes and play up the other. A second way the choice criteria could be in conflict is if a single attribute possesses both positive and negative aspects. Consider a person thinking of purchasing a high-performance automobile. High-performance automobiles have both positive aspects (status, speed, and pleasure fulfillment) and negative aspects (high insurance and low mileage per gallon). For this type of conflict, the best selling strategy is to enhance the positive aspects and depreciate the negative aspects.

Explicit Choice Criteria. When the customer has well-defined, explicit choice criteria, the best selling strategy is for the salesperson to illustrate how a specific product fits their criteria. "The salesclerk guides the customer into agreeing that each attribute of his product matches the attributes of the customer's specification. If, at the end of the sales talk, the customer does not agree to the salesclerk's proposition, he appears to be denying what he has previously admitted."[40]

THE SELLING PROCESS

There are several basic steps which occur during the retail selling process. The length of time a salesperson should spend on each of these steps depends upon the product type, the customer, and the selling situation. Exhibit 14.10 details the process model we will now discuss.

Prospecting.   **Prospecting** is the search process of finding customers who have the ability and are willing to purchase your product. Prospecting is particularly important when the store is full of customers. A salesperson should be aware that good prospects generally display more interest in the products than poor prospects who are "just looking." Salespeople should take advantage of the behavioral cues in Exhibit 14.9.

Approach.   The salesperson may meet hundreds of customers a day, but the customer is only going to meet the salesperson once that day. The first 15 seconds should set the mood for the sale. Never begin a sales presentation with "May I help you?," or any other question to which the customer may respond negatively. A simple "good morning," or any other greeting acknowledging the customer's presence, should do.

Discover as early as possible what the customer's needs are. Discovering begins with listening. What the salesperson hears about the customer's problem or need is more important than anything the salesperson can possibly contribute at this point. Ask a few well chosen questions to find out more about the need or problem to be solved. The salesperson should also find out whether the user will be a different individual than the customer. Remember the salesperson should ask only as many questions as needed and let the customer do most of the talking.

Exhibit 14.10

**Selling Process
in the Retail
Environment**

Step 1 - Prospecting
Who can benefit from your product

a. Finding prospects.

b. Qualifying prospects.

Step 2 - Approach
The first 15 seconds is the is the key as it sets the *mood* for the sale.

a. Never say "May I help You?".
A single "hello," "good morning" or "what may I show you?" makes the customer realize that you are glad they are in your store.

b. Determine as early as possible the customer's needs.
Listen - *What you hear* is more important than anything you could possibly tell your customer. Ask a few well-chosen questions - What do I need to know.
1. Product needed or problem to be solved.
2. User of the product (tell me about so-and-so).

Step 3 - The Sales Presentation
Getting the customer to want to have your product / service

a. Pick the right price level.
If uncertain - ask "Is there a price range you have in mind?" Remember, you can't pick out the *right product"* for the uncertain customer if the price is wrong.

b. Pick the right product.
Match user and need with product. Show the customer at least two items.

c. Show the merchandise in an appealing manner.
Make the merchandise stand out.
Show the item so that its good points will be seen.
Get the customer to handle the merchandise.
Stress the features of the product.
Explain the benefits of these features.
Appeal to the customer's emotions.

e. Help the customer to decide.
Handle objections.
Replace unneeded items.
Watch for unconscious clues.
Stress features and benefits of "key" product

Step 4 - Closing The Sale
Reaching an agreement

a. What is going on in the customer's mind.

b. Five effective ways to close.
1. Make decision for the customer.
2. Assume the decision has already been made.
3. Ask the customer to choose.
4. Turn an objection around.
5. Throw-ins.

Step 5 - Suggestion Selling

Follow-up lead to other sales.

Sales Presentation.   Once the initial contact has been established, the salesperson is in a position to present the merchandise and sales message correctly. How the salesperson presents the product or service depends on the customer and the situation. The key is to get the customer to want to buy your product or service. Begin by determining the right price range of products to show the customer. A price too high or too low will generally result in a lost sale. If uncertain, ask the customer about the price range desired.

Next, the salespeople, because they know the merchandise and where it is located in the store, should pick out what they believe will be the right product or service to satisfy the customer's needs. The salespeople should be careful not to show the customer so many products that the customer is confused.

The salesperson should tell the customer about the merchandise in an appealing way, stressing the features that are the outstanding qualities or characteristics of the product. Let the customer handle the merchandise.

Help the customer decide on the product or service that best fulfills the customer's needs. Handle any objection that the customer might have, replace the rejected items, and continue to stress the features and benefits of the product the customer seems most interested in.

Closing The Sale.   Closing the sale is a natural conclusion to the selling process. However, for most salespersons, closing the sale is the most difficult part of the selling process. Remember the salesperson is there to help the customer solve a problem, so the salesperson should not be afraid to ask for the sale. The key to closing the sale is to determine what is going on in the customer's mind. If the salesperson waits too long to do this step, or is too impatient, the customer will leave. There are four effective ways to close a sale: 1) make the decision for the customer, 2) assume that the decision has been made and ask if it will be cash or charge, 3) ask the customer to choose which product or service she or he wants, and 4) overcome objections by stressing that, though the product's initial cost is high, its longer life span will reduce total cost.

Suggestion Selling.   A good salesperson continues to sell after the sale has been completed. There is always the possibility of an additional sale. The salesperson should find out if the customer has any other needs or if the customer knows of anybody else with needs that can be solved with the salesperson's product line. A good example of the follow-up would be the salesperson selling a Valentine's gift to a college student for his girlfriend and, asking if she can be of help with a gift for his mother.

SELLING IN THE SERVICE SECTOR

Proper selling techniques are even more important in service retailing. It is difficult to get new customers since they can not try the product, inspect it, or test it. Once they have purchased the service, they only know if it *didn't* satisfy or solve their problem. They are generally not pleased with good service, only dissatisfied if the service was not what they were lead to believe it would be.[41]

Gelb has concluded that first, the retailer of services needs to understand what benefit the customer is really buying. It is important for the salesforce to understand that hospitals market health care, not operations, and that colleges market educational attainment, not classes.

Second, the provider must consider how to help the customer achieve that benefit—a different task than simply providing the service. For example, a plumber is not merely selling the ability to unclog sink pipes, but also informing consumers as to what they can do to keep the sink draining properly. This enables consumers to become involved and to feel a sense of accomplishment.

Third, the retailer should determine how to change the product so as to produce customer satisfaction. A consumer might not feel positive if the security firm guarding the household property is merely checking the property daily with routine inspections and nothing bad happens. However, consider the customer satisfaction that could be gained if the security firm also involved the customer in the process with a self-defense class.

Finally, remember that with services the goal is to preclude dissatisfaction. It is important for the sales staff to be aware that the result should match the customer's expectation, so as to preclude any customer unhappiness. Consumers never forget a poor service job.[42]

SALESPERSON EVALUATION

Salesperson evaluation seeks to determine each salesperson's value to the firm. It is the basis for salary adjustments, promotions, transfers, terminations and sales reinforcement. Rather than subjectively evaluating performance, the retailer should develop a systematic method for evaluating individual salespeople and the total sales staff.

Performance Standards.   Several standards can be used to measure a salesperson's performance. Some of them apply only to individual effort, whereas others assess both individual and total salesforce effort.

Conversion Rate.   The conversion rate is computed by dividing the total number of customers who walk out of the store with a purchase by the total number of customers who entered the store. The measure reflects the percentage of shoppers who were converted into customers and the overall performance of the salesforce. This is a measure of the total staff's performance, not an individual's.

A poor conversion rate can be caused by a variety of factors. Perhaps there were not enough clerks on hand when customers needed them. This could have resulted in many customers making unassisted searches and long waiting times for other customers. Or the number of salesclerks could have been adequate, but the salesclerks may not have been doing a good selling job. A poor selling job could be caused by clerks giving inadequate product information to the customer, disagreeing or arguing with the customer, demonstrating the product poorly, having an unfriendly attitude, or giving up too early. All of these factors are really related to *poor training*, which is the underlying reason for poor sales. A low conversion rate may also be due to factors beyond the salesperson's control, such as inadequate merchandise levels. When a substandard conversion rate exists, the retailer should try to identify the causes and attempt to remedy the situation.

Sales per Hour. Perhaps the most common measure of a salesperson's or sales force's performance is sales per hour, which is computed by taking total dollar sales during a particular period and dividing by total salesperson or salesforce hours. With a well-designed record keeping system, a retailer can compute this simple measure for each salesperson, any group of salespeople, or the entire sales force.

When employing this measure, remember that standards should be specific to the group or person being evaluated for a particular time period. For example, in a department store the sales per hour cannot be expected to be the same for the toy department as for the jewelry department. Nor would sales per hour be the same during July as in December, because of the heavy Christmas demand for toys and jewelry.

Use Of Time. Standards can be developed for evaluating how salespeople spend their time. A salesperson's time can be spent in four ways:

1. *Selling time* is any time spent assisting customers with their needs. This could be time spent talking, demonstrating, writing sales receipts, or assisting the customer in other potentially revenue-generating ways.
2. *Nonselling time* is any time spent on the nonselling tasks such as rearranging and straightening up the merchandise, taking inventory, etc.
3. *Idle time* is time the salesperson is on the salesfloor but is not involved in any productive work.
4. *Absent time* is the time the salespeople are not on the sales floor. They may be at lunch, in the employee lounge, in another part of the store, or in some inappropriate place.

The retailer may develop standards for each of these types of time. For example, the evaluation standard may be that salespeople spend 60 percent of their time selling, 28 percent of their time on nonselling activities, 5 percent idle, and 7 percent absent. Any deviation from these standards should be investigated and corrective measures should be taken if necessary.

Data Requirements.   To establish proper standards of performance the retailer needs data. What are good standards for the conversion rate? Sales per hour? Time allocation? Only data will help answer these questions. The data can come from retail trade associations, consulting firms, or the retailer's own experience.

Once the retailer obtains the data on which to base standards, it must collect additional data on actual performance continually, or at least periodically. The actual conversion rate, sales per hour, and time allocation must be contrasted to their respective standards. If the actual data differ significantly from the standard, an investigation is warranted. Both favorable and unfavorable variances should be investigated—because there is just as much to be learned from unusually good performance as from unusually poor performance.

GEOGRAPHICALLY DISPERSED RETAILERS

Stores operating in several different geographic areas need to be especially careful in designing the correct mix of customer services. Many geographically diversified retail organizations try to standardize operations in an attempt to achieve better control and scale economies. Unfortunately, if they try to standardize customer services, they may not be responsive to local needs. The best strategy is to offer a core of services at all locations and allow store or regional managers to tailor other services to the needs of their trading areas.

Tandy has designated certain stores "computer centers." These stores have service personnel not present at regular Radio Shacks. While all Tandy outlets offer credit, returns, and other basic customer services, only the computer centers offer extensive on-site and in-store service for the computer users.

SERVICES RETAILING

Many retailers are in the business of selling only services. Examples are barber and beauty shops, health spas, laundry and dry cleaners, movie theaters, and amusement parks. When retailers sell services rather than tangible products, the management of customer service becomes more important. There is simply more service to manage. This section explores some of the problems of managing a service-oriented retail enterprise.

GOODS VS. SERVICES

The key difference between a retailer of goods and a retailer of services is that the product offered by the retailer of goods is tangible and can be inventoried, and the product offered by the retailer of services is intangi-

Illus. 14.5
When retailers sell services rather than tangible products, the management of customer service becomes more important.
Source: Rick Norton/Kings Island.

ble and cannot be stored. Almost all retailers provide both services and goods.[43] For example, the convenience food store selling a quart of milk is selling more than milk (a tangible item) but also place and time utility (intangible attributes). In other words, the customer is paying for convenience as well as for the milk. The beautician who styles hair is also selling goods, since he or she must use materials such as hair spray, shampoo and water.

All retailing involves services, the degree of service can vary considerably. For instance, in a self-service grocery, almost all the purchase price goes for goods, whereas in a motel almost all the price of a room goes for services.

MANAGEMENT PROBLEMS

For retailers that sell almost totally services (motel, maid or house cleaning, movie theater, barber shop, etc.), five major management problems must be addressed: competitive differentiation, inventory, demand forecasting, heavy dependence on people, and creation of tangibility.

Competitive Differentiation.   Services, unlike tangible products, are easy to replicate. In a service there seldom can be any hidden technology, and obtaining a patent on a service is impossible. Consequently, services have short life cycles. For instance, if TWA comes up with a new service such as seat assignments in advance, United Airlines can quickly follow suit. If Avis develops a quick check-in procedure for returning a rental car to an airport, Hertz can quickly copy it. Retailers must constantly modify their services in order to differentiate themselves from competitors. It should be pointed out, however, that a high-service image is difficult to duplicate.

Inventory.   Because services cannot be inventoried, it is very difficult to meet fluctuations in consumer demand. If an airline seat or a classroom seat is not occupied, the potential revenue from that seat at that time is lost forever. "In essence, the service manager is without an important 'shock absorber' available to most of his counterparts in the manufacturing sector to absorb fluctuations in demand."[44]

Forecasting Demand.   Since services cannot be inventoried, it is crucial that the demand for them be accurately forecast. If demand is accurately forecast, then the proper number of service employees can be on hand to meet demand. If too many employees are on hand to service demand, employee productivity will fall; if there are too few employees, customers will leave dissatisfied.

Forecasting of demand is also crucial for determining the quantity of other service resources to have available. For example, the forecast of demand will determine how large an airplane to schedule for a particular flight, or how large a classroom to schedule for a public lecture.

People Dependence.   The greatest means of differentiation in service retailing is people. People are perceived to *be* the service. Service employees can be categorized into four types, all of whom can have a positive or negative effect on the performance of the service. These employees may be either visible or invisible to the customers, and they may or may not have contact with customers. We will use the car rental industry to give examples of the four types of service employees:

1. *Visible/contact.* A counter clerk is visible and has contact with customers. If the clerk is rude, the customers will feel angry.
2. *Visible/no contact.* Service personnel who bring the car to the office are visible to customers but do not have direct contact with them.
3. *Invisible/contact.* A telephone reservation clerk has voice contact with customers but is not visible. Obviously, the reservations clerks' physical appearances do not affect the service, but their telephone etiquette and knowledge are very important. Since these employees cannot be seen, the customer will form an evaluation solely on the basis of what is said and how it is said. If the clerk is rude or mistakenly books the customer in the wrong car, the overall image of the rental firm will be damaged.
4. *Invisible/no contact.* The members of the maintenance staff are invisible to customers and have no contact with them. If they do not perform their jobs competently, the result could be lawsuits or at the very least the loss of a customer.

To ensure that a service firm's personnel reinforce the desired standards, four things should be emphasized.[45] First, high priority should be placed on the careful selection, training, and proper compensation of service personnel. Investments in these areas are time and money well spent. Many service firms attempt to cut costs in these areas, a mistake that actually results in low service performance and profitability, which serves as further justification for additional cost cutting. Second, a firm should emphasize internal marketing. Employees as well as customers should be the target of promotional efforts. Third, practices should be developed to obtain consistency of job performance. For example, telephone personnel should follow set procedures in greeting callers and thanking them for calling. Also, personnel should be monitored to ensure these procedures are being followed. Finally, all employees who are visible to the customer should have a consistent appearance. For example, desk clerks and bellhops at fine hotels wear uniforms that distinguish them as hotel personnel with particular tasks and duties.

Creation of Tangibility.   Since services are intangible, it is difficult for the consumer to compare the offerings of service retailers. To help consumers compare competitive service offerings, service retailers attempt to make their service offerings tangible by packaging them.[46] Airlines, for instances, will paint their airplanes with distinguishable colors, upholster their seats in leather, or outfit their cabin attendants attractively. Beauty and barber shops will carefully arrange the shop decor to be attractive, will pipe in music to relax customers, or will give free hair grooming samples or booklets. By creating a tangible aspect of their offering, service retailers can more easily position themselves in the minds of consumers.

SUMMARY

The purpose of this chapter was to demonstrate that customer service is a key revenue-generating variable in retail decision making. To properly manage the customer service decision area, the retailer needs to integrate customer service with merchandise management, promotion management, building and fixtures management, price management, and credit management. Only an integrated customer service program will allow the retailer to achieve maximum profits.

This chapter classified customer services into pretransaction, transaction, and posttransaction services. Pretransaction services make it easier for a potential customer to shop at a store or learn about its offering. Common examples are convenient hours, informational aids, and food service. Transaction services make it easier for the customer to complete a transaction. Popular transaction services are consumer credit, wrapping and packaging, check cashing, personal shopping, merchandise availability, personal selling, and the transaction itself. Posttransaction services influence the customer's satisfaction with the merchandise after the transaction. The most frequently encountered posttransaction services are handling of complaints, merchandise returns, servicing and repairing, and delivery.

Customer service should be evaluated by the retailer with a long-run profit perspective, because in the short run, retailers bottom-line performance can always be increased by reducing services. In the long run, however, a significant number of customers may switch their patronage to another retailer that offers a more satisfactory service mix. In establishing the mix of customer services the retailer should consider six factors: store characteristics, competition, type of merchandise, price image, target market income, and cost of the service.

This chapter also illustrated the role of the retail salesperson in generating demand. Regardless of whether salesclerks are primarily order getters or order takers, they play an important role in creating demand for retail products. However, the role played by the order getter was obviously more important in this regard.

The productivity of retail salespeople has been stagnant the past two decades. This problem has been traced to low wages, poor morale, high turnover, and a general inability of retailers to properly manage their salespeople. The chapter discussed the criteria to be used in the selection of a selling staff and its training program. The section concluded by reviewing how this staff should be evaluated.

Retailers that operate stores in geographically dispersed areas should not attempt to standardize customer services at all their stores. Each geographic area will have customers with different needs and wants, so some flexibility has to be designed into customer service programs to allow the tailoring of the customer service mix to each area.

This chapter concluded with a discussion of some of the management problems that services retailers confront. The major management tasks of service retailers are competitively differentiating their services, inability to inventory services, forecasting demand in order to schedule service resources, heavy dependence on people and creating tangibility of services.

QUESTIONS FOR DISCUSSION

1. Retailers with high levels of customer service operate on higher gross margins than retailers with low levels of customer service. Agree or disagree and defend your point of view.
2. Could a retailer segment its market according to consumer preferences for customer service?

3. How is a retailer's customer service policy related to other retail management decisions?
4. How should a retailer determine its optimal customer service level?
5. Identify some of the major management problems that service retailers face.
6. How can it be that while other retailers are adopting or extending their self-service operations, it may be profitable for a retailer to offer more customer services?
7. Some discount stores have "no checks," "no returns" and "no layaways" policies. Will this hinder the stores in the marketplace? Is the trend moving toward increasing or decreasing service by these types of retailers?
8. Exhibit 14.7 listed the most commonly offered services provided by department stores. How would this list be different for a supermarket, sporting goods store, and university bookstore? List and explain what you believe would be the five most common services for each of these retailers.
9. What are the significant differences between heavy returners and nonreturners? What do you feel accounts for these differences?
10. What should retail salespeople know about consumer behavior?
11. A major discount department store chain has analyzed the annual sales per salesperson in 20 of its stores nationwide. Sales per salesperson range from a low of $91,000 to a high of $134,000. Develop the list of factors that might help to explain this wide variation.
12. Is it possible to increase expenditures on salespeople as a percentage of sales and increase the overall profitability of the firm?
13. What should retail salespeople know about customer choice criteria?
14. Develop a list of predictor variables you would use to screen applicants for a sales position in (a) the jewelry department in a high-prestige department store, (b) a used-car dealership, (c) a health club, (d) an antique shop.
15. Someone once said that "selling is selling regardless of the product being sold." Do you agree with this statement? How would your answer change if we were to compare the selling of services to the selling of physical products?

SUGGESTED
READINGS

Fox, Richard J. and Ellen Day. "Research Note: Enhancing the Appeal of Service Contracts: An Empirical Investigation of Alternative Offerings." *Journal of Retailing* (Fall 1988): 335–352.

Heskett, James L. *Managing in the Service Economy.* Boston: Harvard Business School Press, 1986.

Parasuraman, A., Leonard L. Berry, and Valarie A. Zeithaml. "Service Firms Need Marketing Skills." *Business Horizons* (November–December 1983): 28–31.

Schmidt, Sandra L. and Jerome B. Kernan. "The Many Meanings (And Implications) of 'Satisfaction Guaranteed.'" *Journal of Retailing* (Winter 1985): 89–108.

Zeithaml, Valarie A., A. Parasuraman, and Leonard L. Berry. "Problems and Strategies in Services Marketing." *Journal of Marketing* (Spring 1985): 34–46.

Zeithaml, Valarie A., Leonard L. Berry, and A. Parasuraman. "Communication and Control Processes in the Delivery of Service Quality." *Journal of Marketing* (April 1988): 35–48.

ENDNOTES

1. Douglas M. Lambert and M. Christina Lewis, "Managing Customer Service to Build Market Share and Increase Profit," *Business Quarterly* (Fall 1983): 50–57.

2. "Many Stores Abandon 'Service With a Smile,' Rely on Signs, Displays," *Wall Street Journal*, 16 March 1981, pp. 1, 20.

3. Robert A. Westbrook, "Sources of Customer Satisfaction with Retail Outlet," *Journal of Retailing* (Fall 1981): 68–85.

4. Leonard L. Berry, "Delivering Excellent Service in Retailing," *Retailing Issues Letter* (April 1988).

5. Milind M. Lele and Uday S. Karmarker, "Good Product Support Is Smart Marketing," *Harvard Business Review* (November–December 1983): 124–132.

6. "37 Things You Can Do to Keep Your Customers—Or Lose Them," *Progressive Grocer* (June 1973): 59–64.

7. "10 Commandments Aid Department Stores," *Chain Store Age Executive* (September 1980): 10.

8. "10 Commandments Aid Department Stores," *Chain Store Age Executive* (September 1980): 10. Reprinted with permission.

9. "Hotel Hassles," *Wall Street Journal*, 27 June 1985, p. 21.

10. Philip Z. Dolen, "Technology Can Be The Consumer's Best Friend," *Retailing Issues Letter* (April 1988): 4.

11. "Gimbels to Sales Staff: Function Is Selling," *Stores* (October 1984): 50–51.

12. "In-House Credit," *Stores* (February 1983): 30–36.

13. "In-House Credit," 34.

14. "MasterCard Fee to Retailers is Increased 29%," *Wall Street Journal*, 19 September 1988, p. 2.

15. "K mart to Honor Sears Roebuck's Discover Cards," *Wall Street Journal*, 29 October 1987, p. 30.

16. Charles A. Ingene and Michael Levy, "Cash Discounts to Retail Customers: An Alternative to Credit Card Sales," *Journal of Marketing* (Spring 1982): 92–103.

17. R. M. Grant, "On Cash Discounts to Retail Customers: Further Evidence," *Journal of Marketing* (Winter 1985): 145–146; and Charles A. Ingene and Michael Levy, "Further Reflections on Cash Discounts," *Journal of Marketing* (Winter 1985): 147–148.

18. "Getting Consumers to Read All About It," *Progressive Grocer* (October 1983): 105–110.

19. Dolen, 4.

20. "Retailers Turning to Personal Shoppers To Boost Sales, Win Customer Loyalty," *Wall Street Journal*, 23 December 1988, p. B1.

21. For a discussion of how retail stockouts can be modeled, see C. K. Walter and John R. Grabner, "Stockout Cost Models: Empirical Tests in a Retail Situation," *Journal of Marketing* (July 1975): 56–58; and Philip B. Schary and Martin Christopher, "The Anatomy of a Stock-Out," *Journal of Retailing* (Summer 1979): 59–70.

22. Joseph Barry Mason, "Redefining Excellence In Retailing," *Journal of Retailing* (Summer 1986): 115–119.

23. Theodore Levitt, "After the Sale is Over. . . ," *Harvard Business Review* (September–October 1983): 87–93.

24. J. Barry Mason and William O. Bearden, "From the Editors," *Journal of Retailing* (Fall 1981): 2. Since this special issue of the *Journal of Retailing* was devoted to the topic of "Consumer Satisfaction/Dissatisfaction: Theory and Implication for Retailing," the more advanced student interested in complaint handling might consult this important source of information. In particular the student should see Jacob Jacoby and James C. Jaccard, "The Sources, Meaning and Validity of Consumer Complaints: A Psychological Analysis," 4–25; Richard Oliver, "Measurement and Evaluation of Satisfaction Processes in Retail Setting," 25–48; John Swan and I. Frederick Tarwick, "Disconfirmation of Expectations and Satisfactions with a Retail Service," 49–67; Ralph S. Day, Klaus Grabicke, Thomas Schaetzel and Fritz Stauback, "The Hidden Agenda of Consumer Complaining," 86–106; Kenneth S. Bernhardt, "Consumer Problems and Complaint Actions of Older Americans: A National View," 107–123; and Michael Etzel and Bernard I. Silverman, "A Managerial Perspective on Directions for Retail Customer Dissatisfaction Research," 124–136.

25. Dolen, 4.

26. "Note To Refund Abusers: The Check is in the Mail," *Chain Store Age Executive* (May 1982): 57–58.

27. "Back to Basics," *Stores* (June 1983): 49–50.

28. National Business Council for Consumer Affairs, Sub-Council on Performance and Service, *Product Performance and Servicing* (Washington, D.C.: U.S. Government Printing Office, 1973), 39–40.

29. "The Real Cost of Losing Customers," *Incentive* (May 1988): 8.

30. "Many Stores Abandon . . . ": 1, 20.

31. A special issue of the *Journal of Retailing* (Fall 1984) under the guest editorship of Dale Achabal was devoted to the issue of productivity in retailing. The reader should review: Charles Ingene, "Productivity and Functional Shifting in Spatial Retailing: Private and Social Perspectives;" Robert Lusch and Soo Young Moon, "An Exploratory Analysis of the Correlates of Labor Productivity in Retailing;" Roy Thurik and Nico van der Wijst, "Part-time Labor in Retailing;" and Dale Achabal, John Heineke, and Shelby McIntyre, "Issues and Perspectives on Retail Productivity."

32. "Many Stores Abandon . . . ": 1.

33. Charles M. Futrell and A. Parasuraman, "The Relationship of Satisfaction and Performance to Salesforce Turnover," *Journal of Marketing* (Fall 1984): 33–40.

34. Alan J. Dubinsky and Steven J. Skinner, "Impact of Job Characteristic on Retail Salespeople's Reactions to their Jobs," *Journal of Retailing* (Summer 1984): 35–62.

35. R. Kenneth Teas, "A Test of Model of Department Store Salespeople's Job Satisfaction," *Journal of Retailing* (Spring 1981): 1–22.

36. For a good discussion of how data can be systematically used to select retail salespeople, see J. N. Mosel and R. R. Wade, "A Weighted Application Blank for Reduction of Turnover in Department Store Salesclerks," *Personnel Psychology* (1951): 177–184; and Robert F. Hartley, "The Weighted Application Blank Can Improve Retail Employee Selection," *Journal of Retailing* (Spring 1970): 32–40.

37. William R. Darden, Ronald D. Hampton, and Earl W. Boatwright, "Investigating Retail Employee Turnover: An Application Of Survival Analysis," *Journal of Retailing* (Spring 1987): 69–88.

38. "Computer Takeover," *Wall Street Journal*, 15 July 1986, p. 1.

39. Much of the following is based on John O'Shaughnessy, "Selling as an Interpersonal Influence Process," *Journal of Retailing* (Winter 1971–72): 32–46.

40. O'Shaughnessy, "Interpersonal Influence Process," p. 41.

41. Theodore Levitt, "Marketing Intangible Products and Product Intangibles," *Harvard Business Review* (May–June 1981): 100.

42. Betsy Gelb, "How Marketers of Intangibles Can Raise The Odds For Consumer Satisfaction," *The Journal of Consumer Marketing* (Spring 1985): 60.

43. Leonard L. Berry, "Retail Businesses Are Service Businesses," *Journal of Retailing* (Spring 1986): 3–6.

44. W. Earl Sasser, R. Paul Olsen, and D. Daryl Wyckoff, *Management of Service Operations: Text, Cases and Readings* (Boston: Allyn and Bacon 1978), 16.

45. Donald Cowell, *The Marketing of Services* (London: William Heinemann Ltd., 1984), 207.

46. G. Lynn Shostock, "Breaking Free From Product Marketing," *Journal of Marketing* (April 1977): 73–80.

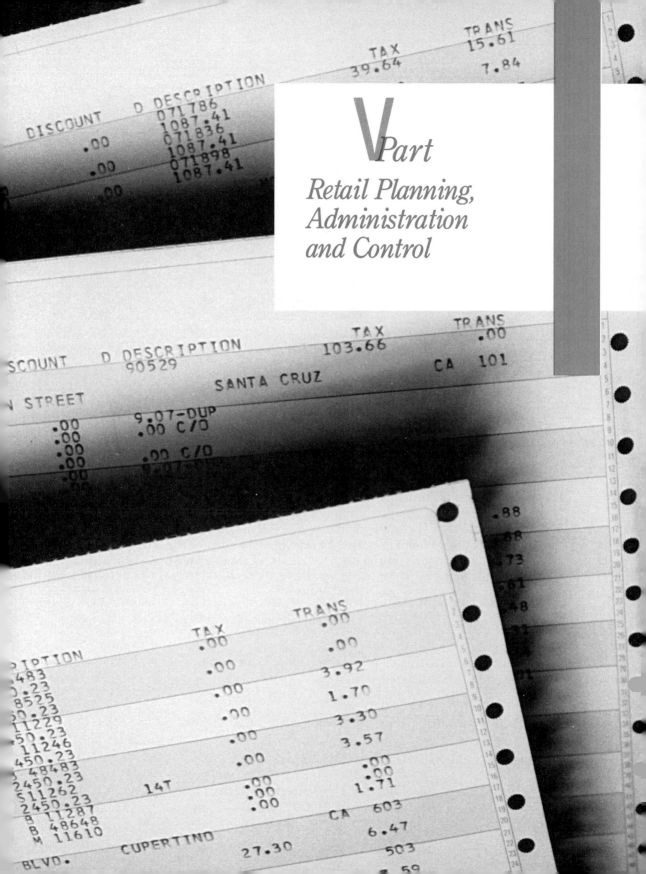

V Part

Retail Planning, Administration and Control

15 Chapter

Retail Planning and Control

OVERVIEW

The purpose of this chapter is to outline, in detail, the strategic planning process. The retail strategic planning process consists of five interrelated steps: definition of a firm's statement of mission, definition of the firm's objectives, analysis of opportunities, generation of a strategy, and the control of the strategic plans. We will also discuss the extent to which strategic planning is used by retailers. The chapter will be concluded with a look at some of the key mistakes that retailers have made in strategic planning.

Chapter 2 presented an overview of the retail planning and management process. It emphasized the need for good strategic planning as well as good management of the operation and administrative sectors of the firm. Chapters 3 through 6 looked at the environmental factors which could affect a retailer's strategic planning process. Chapters 7 and 8 were devoted to the selection of a store site location. The part you just completed, Chapters 9 through 14, dealt with the day to day decisions facing retailers. This chapter will discuss in detail how to develop strategic plans in retailing.

We have positioned this discussion of strategic planning after operations management because you now have an understanding of what operations management entails, and are in a better position to conceptualize strategic planning from the retailer's point of view. Ideally, strategic planning should take place before operations management, but by putting it here, you can understand the influence of strategic decision making on the operations side of the business.

THE STRATEGIC PLANNING PROCESS

Strategic planning is the process of determining the general direction the retailer will take over a period of several years. This process begins with the development of a *statement of purpose or mission* for the firm and a definition of the *specific goals and objectives* for the firm. Next the retailer must be able to *analyze the marketplace* for opportunities. The retailer must then *develop a basic strategy* to capitalize on the most attractive opportunities. When the retailer's strategy is well matched with opportunities in the marketplace so as to maximally achieve its mission and objectives, the retailer will have obtained a *strategic fit*. Finally, the retailer's strategy will need to be assessed periodically to ensure that the strategic fit is in *control*. This brief overview of the strategic planning process is summarized in Exhibit 15.1.

Strategic planning in business has been receiving increased attention over the last decade; however, until recently, little of this attention was devoted to strategic planning in retailing. Two factors contributed to this lack of strategic planning in retailing. First, retailers tend to place a great deal of importance on flexibility—the ability to quickly adapt to a changing environment. They point out that such factors as the unpredictability of changes occurring in the retail market, the fluid nature of the industry's competitive structure, the ever-changing life cycle for retail institutions, and an unstable economic climate make a high degree of flexibility mandatory to secure a high profit. For this reason they have dismissed strategic planning. How can you be concerned about problems and opportunities five years from now when you have an inventory shortage today on products that are in tomorrow's ad? Retailers want and need a strategic planning process that will enhance rather than inhibit their ability to

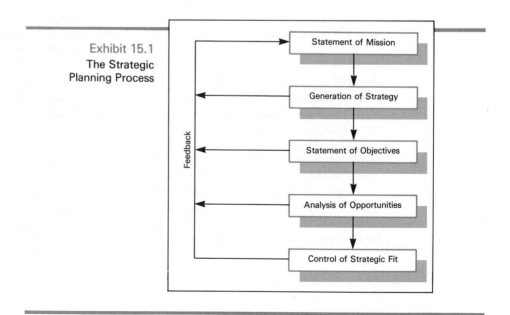

Exhibit 15.1
The Strategic Planning Process

Statement of Mission

Generation of Strategy

Statement of Objectives

Analysis of Opportunities

Control of Strategic Fit

Feedback

be flexible. Strategic planning processes that call for rigid long-term commitments are not favored by retailers.

Arnold Becker, in a presentation to the Retail Research Society, said:

"Most retailers are not strategic thinkers, they are action oriented; wanting to see real results in a short time frame. . . . There is no commitment by management to strategic planning. In most, but not all, retail companies, the time of top management is used inappropriately. Too often, it is devoted to short-term, firefighting, crisis management activities."[1]

A second argument used by retailers to dismiss strategic planning is that, because retailers must focus on different decision areas than other businesses, traditional strategic planning models are useless for them. Retailers are typically more concerned than other businesses about decisions concerning store location, store image, need for local input on merchandise selection, and organization structure. Some larger retailers have recently discovered the importance of some of the frequently overlooked facets of business, such as real estate. Remember, more than 36 percent of a retailer's assets are tied up in buildings and fixtures. Land is usually carried at cost, which is usually much less than present value, and can be used to finance other business functions. Carson Pirie Scott and Co., Sears, and several Campeau units recently sold property for large profits and are studying the disposition of other properties they rent or own. Retailers are devoting more attention to their real estate than ever before.

Without strategic planning, retailers lose their vision of where they are headed. Therefore, let us turn to an in-depth discussion of the strategic planning process in retailing and its current use.

STATEMENT OF MISSION

The retailer's **statement of mission** is its overall justification for existing. A retailer with a mission will find it much easier to survive and prosper than one without a mission. A retailer's mission should not be time- or merchandise-dependent. The statement of mission should be generic. That is, it should be stated so that it will be just as applicable in five, ten, or twenty years as it is today. It should not be stated as selling specific merchandise lines or brands.

The retail customer does not patronize a retail establishment to purchase products or services, but to buy need fulfillment. The automobile dealer's mission is not to sell Chevrolets or even necessarily to sell automobiles. Rather, it is to help fulfill some basic needs of the customer— probably a need for personal transportation. Most beauty shops are patronized not to get one's hair cut, but to acquire a feeling of beauty. The supermarket is not patronized to purchase food but to provide substance to satisfy physiological and often psychological needs.

A mission statement does not have to be as long or as detailed as the one of Sears, Roebuck and Company which is shown below.

"We are the premier distributor of durable goods—and we intend to keep it that way. We are valued by our customers for our integrity, for a reputation for fair dealing, for service, and for our guarantee. We also are a premier distributor of nondurable goods—but nondurable goods which are purchased primarily for their uses rather than their fashions. In fact, Sears' balance of sales between durable and nondurable goods is nearly identical to the way a vast majority of Americans allocate their purchases. We are not a high-fashion store; we are not a specialty store, a discounter, or an avant-garde department store.

"In the pursuit of our merchandising strategy, we intend to commit ourselves to substantial and consistent increases in the quality of our goods, in the belief that the best way to achieve increased profits is through a commitment to quality merchandise.

"We plan to achieve this end by committing our buying strength to those sources who share our concern for intrinsic quality and adherence to rigid product specifications."[2]

A mission statement can be short and very general in meaning. Exhibit 15.2 contains several examples of how retailers might use a very general statement of mission. These are not intended to illustrate how all retailers in these respective lines of trade should view their missions. They only help to convey that a retailer's mission can be stated generically. When its mission is stated generically, the retailer will not need to change its mission statement every time the environment changes. The mission statement will provide a long-run perspective and guiding force for all strategic plans. This is how Sears was able to decide in late 1988 to sell the Sears Tower, sell the commercial division of its real estate subsidiary, and lower

Exhibit 15.2

Some Examples of a Firm's Statement of Mission

Our mission is to help make ordinary women feel beautiful.
— Retail apparel chain

Our primary mission is to help people of all ages experience and enjoy literature.
— Retail book chain

Our primary mission is to help people better express their feelings toward others.
— Retail card and gift store

Our primary objective is to help households protect their investments in transportation.
— Automotive repair shop

the price points of its merchandise. None of these actions affected Sears' mission statement of offering true value to middle-class America. These changes represented changes in strategy, not mission.

STATEMENT OF OBJECTIVES

The second stage in our planning process is to define specific *objectives*. These objectives should derive from and give precision and direction to the retailer's mission statement. They should identify the performance results that the retailer intends to bring about through the execution and control of its major strategies. The statement of objectives serves two purposes. First, it provides direction and guidance to the firm in the formulation of its strategy. Second, it provides a standard against which the firm can measure and evaluate its performance results. In addition to the market performance and financial performance objectives that retailers may set for themselves, retailers may also establish societal objectives and personal objectives. Retail objectives can be categorized into four groups:

1. **Market performance objectives** are those which compare your position in the marketplace to that of the competition.
2. **Financial performance objectives** are those which can be stated in monetary or economic terms. These are objectives that directly relate to the dollars and cents of retailing.
3. **Societal objectives** are phrased in terms of helping society fulfill some of its needs.
4. **Personal objectives** relate to helping people employed in retailing fulfill some of their needs.

Let us examine each type of objective in more detail.

MARKET PERFORMANCE OBJECTIVES

Market performance objectives establish the amount of dominance the retailer has in the marketplace. The most popular measures of market performance in retailing are sales volume and market share. **Market share** is the proportion of total sales in a particular market that the retailer has been able to capture. It is calculated by dividing the retailer's total sales by total market sales. In measuring market share, it is important to pay particular attention to delineation of the geographic and line-of-trade markets. For instance, if we desire to compute the market share of a supermarket chain in Cincinnati, Ohio, we would not state the total sales of that chain in the Cincinnati area in relation to total retail sales in the state of Ohio, but in relation to total food store sales in the Cincinnati area.

In most cases, a strong market position is correlated to profitability. Research conducted by the Strategic Planning Institute for 12 of the top retailers in the United States has shown that profitability is clearly and positively related to market share.[3] Thus, market objectives are not pursued for their own sake but because they are a key profit path.

FINANCIAL PERFORMANCE OBJECTIVES

Retailers can establish many financial performance objectives, but they can all be conveniently fitted into categories of profitability and productivity.

Profitability Objectives. Profit-based objectives deal directly with the monetary return a retailer desires from its business. The most frequently encountered profit objectives in a retail enterprise are:

1. **Gross Margin Return on Sales.** Gross margin return on sales, also called gross margin, is defined as gross margin divided by net sales. A retailer's gross margin return on sales depicts what percentage of the average dollar of sales is available to pay fixed and operating expenses and produce a profit.
2. **Return on Assets.** A retailer's return on assets is defined as net profit divided by total assets. This ratio depicts what percentage of the average dollar invested in assets is returned in profit.
3. **Return on Net Worth.** Return on net worth (also called return on equity) is net profit divided by owner's or stockholder's equity. It shows the percentage profit return on each dollar invested in equity.
4. **Earnings per Share.** This ratio is defined as total earnings available to common stockholders divided by shares of common stock outstanding. It shows the profit that each share of common stock has earned.
5. **Operating Profit Margin.** Operating profit margin is the retailer's operating profit divided by net sales.

All retail enterprises establish some form of profit objective. The specific profit objectives adopted will play an important role in evaluating potential strategic opportunities.

Productivity Objectives. Productivity objectives state how much output the retailer desires for each unit of resource input. The major resources at the retailer's disposal are space, labor, and merchandise; and productivity objectives for each may be established.

1. **Space productivity.** Space productivity is defined as net sales divided by total square feet of retail floor space. (In this discussion,

whenever we refer to net sales we are talking about annual net sales.) A space productivity objective states how many dollars in sales the retailer wants to generate for each square foot of store space.

2. **Labor productivity.** Labor productivity is defined as net sales divided by number of full-time equivalent employees. A labor productivity objective reflects how many dollars in sales the retailer desires to generate for each full-time equivalent employee.

3. **Merchandise productivity.** Merchandise productivity is net sales divided by average dollar investment in inventory. This measure is also known as the sales/stock ratio. Specifically, this objective states the dollar sales the retailer desires to generate for each dollar invested in inventory.

Productivity objectives are vehicles by which a retailer can program its business for high-profit results. For instance, it would be impossible for a supermarket chain to achieve a respectable return on assets while experiencing dismal space, labor, and merchandise productivity. In short, productivity is a key determinant of profit in retailing.

This might be a good time to examine the basic return on investment model (Exhibit 15.3) to see how the profitability and productivity objectives are interrelated. Space productivity is reflected in Boxes 13, 14, 15, 16, and 19. If retailers fail to fully utilize their space, the amount in Box 13 will be overstated. This in turn will overstate total assets (Box 14), causing the rate of asset turnover to be lower or unproductive (Box 15) and lowering both the return on assets (Box 16) and return on net worth (Box 19).

Labor productivity is reflected in Boxes 4 and 5, the cost of labor plus other expenses. If retailers pay too much for labor, total expenses (Box 6) will be too high, thus lowering operating profit (Box 7), net profit margin (Box 8), return on assets (Box 16) and return on net worth (Box 19).

Finally, we can look at merchandise productivity, starting with Box 9. If retailers have too large an average inventory then total current assets (Box 12) and total assets (Box 14) will be too high, thereby reducing the rate of asset turnover (Box 15), return on assets (Box 16), and return on net worth (Box 19).

Research by Gifford and Stearns has shown that department store executives rank operating profit margin, gross margin return on sales, and space productivity as the three most important indicators of financial performance. Specialty store executives ranked, in order of importance, operating profit margin, merchandise productivity, and gross margin return on sales. Retailing faculty members ranked merchandise productivity, operating profit margin, and gross margin return on sales in that order.[4]

Exhibit 15.3a

Basic Return on Investment Model

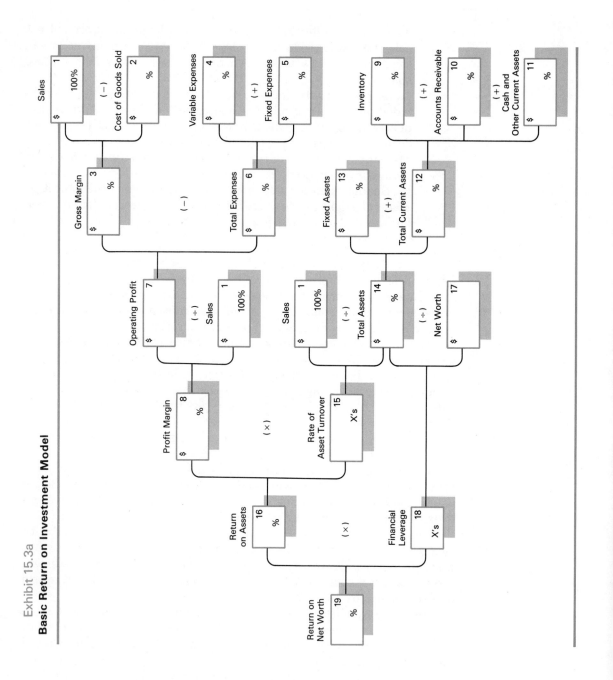

Exhibit 15.3b

Definition of Terms in the Basic ROI Model

Item and Calculation	Source Statement
1. **Sales:** all revenues from exchange of merchandise and/or services	Income
2. **Cost of goods sold:** cost value of merchandise sales which are made during a period.	Income
3. **Gross Margin:** subtract Cost of Goods Sold from Sales.	Income
4. **Variable Expenses:** all expenses which change with changes in sales volume; short run concept.	Income
5. **Fixed Expenses:** all expenses that stay the same over a wide range of sales volume and a long time period.	Income
6. **Total Expenses:** add Variable Expenses and Fixed Expenses.	Income
7. **Operating Profit:** subtract Total Expenses from Gross Margin.	Income
8. **Net Profit Margin:** operating profit divided by sales.	
9. **Inventory:** value of merchandise in stock.	Balance Sheet
10. **Accounts Receivable:** money owed retailer by customers.	Balance Sheet
11. **Cash and other Current Assets:** Cash and any asset other than Accounts Receivable or Inventory which can easily be converted into cash.	Balance Sheet
12. **Total Current Assets:** add Inventory, Accounts Receivable, Cash and other current assets.	Balance Sheet
13. **Fixed Assets:** assets which are depreciated over time.	Balance Sheet
14. **Total Assets:** add Current Assets and Fixed Assets.	Balance Sheet
15. **Rate of Asset Turnover:** divide Sales by Total Assets.	
16. **Return on Assets:** multiply Rate of Asset Turnover times Net Profit Margin.	
17. **Net Worth:** subtract total Liabilities (debt) from Total Assets.	Balance Sheet
18. **Financial Leverage:** divide Total Assets by Net Worth.	
19. **Return on Net Worth:** multiply Return on Assets by Financial Leverage.	

SOCIETAL OBJECTIVES

Sometime in the early 1970s, a significant number of retailers began to establish societal objectives. Societal objectives are generally not as specific or as quantitative as market or financial objectives, but they do highlight the retailer's concern with broader issues in our world. There is no agreed-upon list of societal objectives in retailing. The following list includes the most frequently encountered objectives.

1.   **Employment objectives.** Employment objectives relate to providing employment opportunities for the members of the retailer's community. Many times these objectives are more specific, relating to hiring the handicapped, ethnic minorities, or students.

2.   **Payment of taxes.** By paying taxes, the retailer is helping finance societal needs that the government deems appropriate. One retailer had as his stated objective to have the privilege of paying

Illus. 15.1
Retailers may act as benefactors, underwriting performing arts or providing scholarships. Source: H. Armstrong Roberts.

taxes in the highest possible tax bracket. He was implicitly saying that if he could be so successful that he had to pay high taxes, then he wouldn't mind it.

3. **Consumer choice.** A retailer may have as a societal objective to compete in such a fashion that the consumer will be given a real alternative. A retailer with such an objective desires to be a leader and innovator in merchandising and provide the consumer with choices that previously were not available in the trading area.

4. **Equity.** An equity objective reflects the retailer's desire to treat the consumer fairly. The consumer will not be gouged in case of merchandise shortages. Consumer complaints will be handled quickly, fairly, and equitably. The retailer will inform the consumer, to the extent possible, of the strengths and weaknesses of its merchandise.

5. **Benefactor.** The retailer may desire to underwrite certain community activities. For example, many department store retailers make meeting rooms available for civic groups. Other retailers help underwrite various performing arts. Still others provide scholarships to help finance education. Centers for the study of retailing at colleges and universities are all supported in part by the generous contributions of retailers, large and small.

PERSONAL OBJECTIVES

The final set of objectives that retailers may establish is personal. The personal objectives may relate only to the owners or top-level executives in the firm, or they may reflect all employees of the retail establishment. No standard list of personal objectives exists, but retailers tend to pursue three types of personal objectives.

1. **Self gratification.** Self-gratification has as its focus the needs and desires of the owners, managers, or employees of the firm to pursue what they truly want out of life. For example, an individual may have opened up a sporting goods store because she enjoyed being around athletically oriented people. This individual is also an avid amateur golfer and skier, and by operating a sporting goods store she is able to combine pleasure with work. Basically, this individual is living the life she really wants, even though the profit potential may have been higher in another line of trade.

2. **Status and respect.** All humans strive for status and respect. In stating this type of objective, the retailer recognizes that the owners, managers, or employees need status and respect in their community or within their circle of friends. The retailer may, for example, give annual awards to outstanding employees. Or when promotions occur, press releases may be sent to local newspapers or trade journals such as *Stores* or *Chain Store Age.*

3. **Power and authority.** Objectives based on power and authority reflect the need of managers and other employees to be in positions of influence. Retailers may establish objectives that give buyers and department managers maximum flexibility to determine their own destiny. They are given the power and authority to allocate scarce resources such as space, dollars, and labor to achieve a profit objective. Having the power and authority to allocate resources makes many of these managers feel important and gives them a sense of pride when they excel because they know they controlled their own destiny.

Exhibit 15.4 is a synopsis of the market performance, financial performance, societal, and personal objectives that retailers can establish in the strategic planning process. All retail objectives, of whatever type, must be consistent with the overall mission of the retailer. The retailer's objectives must reinforce its mission.

THREE RECOMMENDATIONS

Philip Kotler has stated that, as a general rule, an organization's objectives be realistic, quantitative, and consistent.[5] Retail organizations are no exception to this general rule.

Realistic.   Objectives should be developed so that they are within the realm of reason. To state during a recessionary year that a moderately successful supermarket chain in Detroit, Michigan, is going to increase

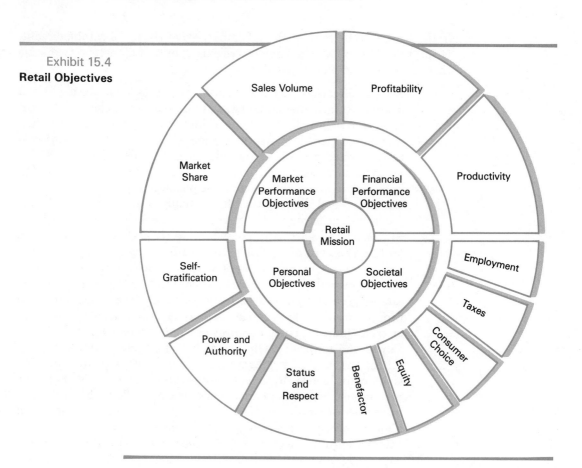

Exhibit 15.4
Retail Objectives

sales by 50 percent is unrealistic. Some overstatement may help stimulate managers and employees, but an unrealistic objective will tend to frighten them off rather than motivate them. Furthermore, if the retailer continually states unrealistic objectives, employees will quickly begin to discount *any* objectives that are established for them. Objectives that are established should have a reasonable chance of being achieved if the environment does not change significantly.

Quantitative.   Objectives that are quantitative are better than those that are nonquantitative. Performance can be more accurately measured if specific quantities are stated as part of the objectives.

Assume a retailer stated that one of its primary objectives was to increase return on net worth over the next three years. At the close of the three-year period, financial statements show that return on net worth increased from 10 percent in the first year to 10.4 percent in the third year. Did this retailer attain its objective? Mathematically it did, because 10.4 percent is greater than 10 percent. But what if the retailer really had in mind a much more significant increase—say, an increase of 14 to 16 percent? Then the objective was not achieved. Unless a precise quantitative goal to be achieved within a given period of time is established, the degree of achievement of that objective will be difficult to assess.

Of the three types of retail objectives, financial objectives are the easiest to state in quantitative terms. Societal and personal objectives are much more difficult, but not impossible, to state quantitatively. See if you can develop quantitative measures of some of the personal and societal objectives that were discussed earlier in this chapter.

Consistent.   A third criterion of good retail objectives is consistency. A retailer will state not one, but many, objectives. The potential exists for some of these objectives to be internally inconsistent. Early in the strategic planning process, the retailer must ensure consistency.

For example, the retailer who states a financial objective of maximizing return on assets and a societal objective of maximizing consumer choice introduces a glaring inconsistency. If the retailer truly wanted to maximize consumer choice, it would need to offer many brands or product lines, and these would not generate high enough margins or rates of inventory turnover to aid the retailer in maximizing its return on assets. Clearly these two objectives, like many others, can exist only in tradeoff relationships. Maximizing both of them is not possible.

Eight basic trade-offs confronting any company are:[6]

1. Short-term profits vs. long-term growth.
2. Profit margin vs. competitive position.
3. Direct sales effort vs. market development.
4. Penetration of existing markets vs. the development of new markets.
5. Related vs. nonrelated new opportunities as a source of long-term growth.
6. Profit vs. nonprofit goals (that is, social responsibilities and personal goals).
7. Growth vs. stability.
8. Riskless environment vs. high-risk environment.

Each of the trade-offs needs to be explicitly considered in the retailer's attempt to develop strategic plans. The relative emphasis to be placed on each of these conflicting objectives needs to be decided early in the strategic planning process. If these conflicts are not resolved early, there will be problems in implementation and execution of retail plans.

ANALYSIS OF OPPORTUNITIES

Once retailers have firmly established their mission and objectives, they must attempt to identify and analyze opportunities on which they can develop strategy. The key to identifying opportunities is analysis of external forces. This can be facilitated by futures research. **Futures research,** which will be discussed in greater detail in Chapter 18, is the analysis of future environments.

The external forces that need to be carefully examined were discussed in Chapters 3 through 6. These forces, which retailers have little control over, are the behavior of members of the marketing channel, the behavior of consumers, the behavior of competitors, the socioeconomic environment, the technological environment, and the legal environment. Retailers need to analyze these forces for two reasons. First, because they are all largely uncontrollable, retailers will have to be able to adapt to them. Second, retailers need to translate threats emanating from these external forces into opportunities and subsequently into strategies.

The notion that environmental threats can be translated into opportunities is highlighted in Retailing in Action 15-1, which shows how specific trends in the legal, socioeconomic, technological, and competitive environments were changed from threats to specific lines of retail trade into

**RETAILING
IN
ACTION** **15-1**

Environmental Threats Can Be Retail Opportunities

Trend	Threatened Retailer	Opportunity
Increasing proportion of households eating food out of the home (social-environmental trend)	Grocery stores	Grocery store managers should view this as an opportunity to develop in-store delis, expanded frozen food departments, and an increased assortment of food items that are easy and quick to prepare but that compare favorably to food sold at fast-food restaurants.
Decline in birth rate (social-environmental trend)	Toy stores	Toy store managers should view this as an opportunity to broaden their market base to appeal to adults by adding sophisticated toys and games.

Casual wear for wide variety of occasions (social-environmental trend)	Formal wear store	The manager of the retail formal wear store should view this as an opportunity to put increased emphasis on rental vs. purchase of formal wear.
Increasing costs of personal transportation (economic-environmental trend)	Regional shopping centers	This presents the manager of a regional shopping center with the opportunity to use the shopping center as a regional recreational area in order to attract people for social motives; for instance, having an art show or boat show in the mall.
Increasing minimum wage (legal-environmental trend)	All retail stores	Presents the retail manager with increased incentive to explore new methods and techniques for improving labor productivity.
In-home ordering of merchandise via computer (trend in technological environment)	General merchandise retailers	Presents the traditional general merchandise retailer with the opportunity to offer both in-home and in-store shopping services and therefore obtain a significant advantage over the new retail firms that offer only in-home purchasing services.
Growth of low-cost warehouse food stores	Grocery stores	Offers the manager of a traditional grocery store the opportunity to strongly differentiate itself on nonprice variables such as friendliness of employees, store decor, and customer service.

Illus. 15.2
Most grocery
store managers
turned the trend
for households
to eat food out-
side the home
into an opportu-
nity by develop-
ing in-store
delicatessens,
expanding fro-
zen food depart-
ments, and
increasing the
assortment of
food items that
are easy and
quick to pre-
pare.

opportunities. For example, one trend in the social environment was the increasing proportion of households eating food outside the home. Most grocery store managers perceived this as a threat to their livelihood. But astute and adaptive managers viewed this trend as an opportunity to develop in-store delicatessens, expand frozen food departments, and increase the assortment of food items that are easy and quick to prepare.

Retailers should be able to generate many attractive opportunities. The difficult task is deciding which to pursue. The opportunities must be narrowed down, since all retailers have limited resources and cannot pursue all opportunities. Retailers must select the opportunities that offer the best prospects for fulfilling their mission and accomplishing their objectives.

THE GENERATION OF STRATEGY

We have addressed how the retail planner might assess and adapt to external forces, but not how the retail planner develops good retail strategies. Good retail strategy must be based on the information that was gathered on the external forces.

Generating ideas on which to build a retail strategy can be the most demanding part of planning. This is because the generation of ideas cannot usually be accomplished through a precise series of scientific steps; it is a creative process. However, this does not mean that the development of ideas cannot be approached in an orderly manner.

Sometimes ideas pop spontaneously into the head of the retailer, but more often they are developed through conscious and deliberate procedures. There are at least five techniques for facilitating the generation of new and innovative strategies: (1) brainstorming, (2) attribute listing, (3) morphological synthesis, (4) checklist, and (5) synetics. These techniques are useful in most of the stages of the creative problem-solving process outlined in Chapter 1. For a brief discussion of each of these techniques, refer to Exhibit 15.5. Let's look at how this strategy generation process occurs.

A DETAILED EXAMPLE

White Knight Supermarkets, Inc., is holding a planning meeting to develop a list of as many alternative long-range strategies as possible. This is the third such meeting; the first two yielded little more than jangled nerves. This meeting promises to be different because the company president has brought in Sharon Riley, an expert in creative problem-solving techniques, to lead the discussions. In addition, at the request of Riley, the president has brought in three households that are representative of White Knight customers—a young married couple with no children in which both husband and wife have professional careers; a couple in their late thirties with two teenage daughters and the wife not employed outside the home; and a retired couple living on a small pension and social security payments.

Riley was introduced to the group. The top management of the White Knight Supermarkets, Inc., eyed her suspiciously, wondering how an outsider could possibly help them. She began the meeting by using a technique called **brainstorming**. Riley got the ball rolling by posing the following questions: "What will a supermarket be like in 2000?" After a long pause (because nobody wanted to be first) the responses shown below emerged:

- Supermarkets in 2000 won't be any different than they are now.
- They will be larger.
- They will be fully automated, with the shopper having only to push buttons and pay.
- They will handle no cash, since purchases will be automatically deducted from the customer's bank account.
- They will be smaller and more specialized.
- They will be almost nonexistent, because consumers will shop by cable TV and have groceries delivered to their homes.
- We won't need supermarkets because people will use vitamins and food pills for nourishment.
- Stores will be life-style oriented—there will be convenience markets catering to the person on the go, back-to-nature stores that sell only fresh foods or pure ingredients with no preservatives, low-cal stores for people on diets, and low-sodium stores for people with salt restrictions.

Exhibit 15.5
Techniques of Creative Thinking

Morphological-Synthesis

The purpose of this technique is to produce as many combinations of attributes as possible. To do this, two or more attributes are chosen, then specific values of these attributes are listed and combined in different ways to potentially yield a new or better combination.

Checklist

In this procedure the group members consider each item on a prepared list as a possible source of innovation in respect to a given problem. By discussing the given solutions, the group members have an opportunity to expand the list with other possibilities.

Brainstorming

In this technique the participants freely toss out ideas, which are recorded but not discussed by the group as they are suggested. The purpose is to obtain the greatest number of ideas possible, even wild ones, for the greater the number of ideas, the greater the chance of obtaining one or more that is innovative.

Attribute Listing

This method is used to improve something that already exists. It involves listing or itemizing the important attributes of the item needing change, then considering each separately as a source of potential change or improvement.

Synetic

This method uses metaphors and similes, especially those drawn from nature. There are three types of synetic problem solving:

1. *Personal analogy:* Group members imagine themselves to be one of the problem objects, then try to figure out how they would change to solve the problem.
2. *Fantasy analogy:* Members are encouraged to propose ideal, although sometimes far-fetched solutions such as using insects, animals, or machines to solve problems.
3. *Free-association word meaning:* Group members are asked to react to a specified stimulus word before they are told about the specific problem they need to solve, thus preparing the subconscious mind for the problem.

Many ideas emerged from this brainstorming session, and creative juices really began to flow.

As the number of new ideas began to taper off, Riley broke in with the following questions: "It is difficult for us to visualize the future, isn't it? You're right, we may not even have supermarkets in the future, but then again, we might. What are the attributes that make a supermarket what it is?" (Now Riley was using the technique called **attribute listing**.) The attributes that the group members listed were

- Prices
- Quality of meats
- Parking
- Personnel
- Atmosphere
- Hours of operation
- Product mix
- Layout
- Services
- Location

After this list of attributes was generated, Riley asked the group how each attribute could be modified to make supermarkets better in the future. Most of the suggestions were in reference to product mix and layout.

The third technique, **morphological synthesis**, was then introduced to the group. "We've got a list of attributes, now we need the specific values for those attributes," announced Riley. "If, for example, I asked you what services were important to the grocery shopper, what would you reply?" The participants answered: check cashing, package pick-up, speedy check out, coupon and food stamp acceptance, and ease of locating merchandise.

"Ok then, you need to come up with the specific values that are important to you for each of the attributes named earlier. Then combine these attributes and values in as many combinations as possible and maybe a new combination of attributes or values will emerge as being superior to all the others. It is sometimes helpful to list the attributes and values in a grid," Riley instructed.

After a break, the group reassembled, thinking they had already come up with all possible new ideas, but Riley wasn't through with them yet. "Remember the list of store attributes we developed earlier?" she asked as she held up a long list. "Well, from it I have compiled a **checklist of attributes** that we will examine." "We're looking for sources of change and innovation," she said as she handed each of the group members a questionnaire like the one shown in Exhibit 15.6. A short discussion followed as each participant's response was read.

The **synetic technique** was introduced next, and enthusiasm began to build. Riley introduced three types of synetic techniques. The **personal**

Exhibit 15.6

**White Knight
Checklist**

Question: We want to make some improvements in our existing stores in the areas of convenience and atmosphere. What suggestions can you make for each item on the checklist?

Checklist	Convenience	Atmosphere
1. Aisles	_____	_____
2. Checkouts	_____	_____
3. Services	_____	_____
4. Lighting	_____	_____
5. Personnel	_____	_____
6. Layout	_____	_____
7. Decor	_____	_____
8. Parking	_____	_____

analogy is used to stimulate the thought process. Riley began, "I am a White Knight Supermarket. How can I be better or more efficient?" Everyone laughed. "No, really," she replied, "How can I change? Put yourselves in my position. You are supermarkets; or better yet, let's divide into smaller parts. There are twelve of you; each of you will become one of these things and design yourself to be better. Here is the list: main entrance, meat counter, checkout counters, frozen foods cases, fresh fruit and vegetable display, canned foods area, specialty goods and foods section, and bakery. Now get to work and improve yourselves." The person who "became" the checkout area pictured a self-unloading shopping cart which plugged into a computer terminal register, that totaled the sale and automatically subtracted it from the customer's bank account. The groceries would then be packaged by a robot and sent out via conveyer belt to the customer's auto.

"What about the store personnel? Picture the ideal worker and tell me what this employee is like," Riley asked, introducing the **fantasy analogy**. Someone answered, "The ideal worker would always be on time, friendly, energetic, reliable, and willing to work without being paid. For that matter, why have *people* work at all? Why not train animals to do it, or machines? That's it! We should have robots do all the labor-intensive jobs such as stocking, marking, checkout, and packing. That way people wouldn't have to do those things."

The third type of synetic method, **free-association word meaning**, proved to be a real eye-opener. Riley asked the group members to free associate to the word *Mexico*. The group responded with the following list: warm, sunny, bright colors, cactus, good food, big hats, burros, mariachi bands, handicrafts, friendly people. The group members, however, were confused. "What does Mexico have to do with a supermarket?" someone asked. Riley replied, "You need to develop a new atmosphere for your foreign food department." "Let's build a foreign market area within our supermarket and put all the Mexican things together, all the Oriental, all the French, and all the German, and build little stalls for each and decorate them to look like the country."

"We could even sell the plants and notions that go with the particular atmosphere," added another.

"I've got it!" a third chimed in, "but it would take some doing. Rather than just stalls for each country, we could create 'atmospheres.' For example, a Mexican food section could play mariachi music, be painted bright colors, be decorated with cactus and big straw hats, and have a warm, sunny dry climate. A German area might play polka music, feel cool, smell like German chocolate cake, and be surrounded by mountain peaks and window boxes full of geraniums."

"I understand," added another. "You're right, that would take a lot of work, but it's worth looking into. Can you imagine how much more exciting grocery shopping could become?"

The synetic technique was so successful at generating new ideas that the group did not want to quit. The group members were excited with the results of their meeting, but more important, they realized that the skills they had learned could be used in all their problem-solving situations.

As the final step in the process, Riley asked each participant to write a scenario of the White Knight Supermarket of the future based on the ideas that had been generated during their meeting and send it to her. When all are received, the group will be called together once again to read and discuss their scenarios. The White Knight executives will then strategically plan the future of their company.

The White Knight example has been presented as a detailed example of the various methods of creative thinking and how they can be applied. It does not mean that in order to solve problems and plan future strategies all these techniques should be used, or that they should be used in the manner described here. It is up to retail managers to decide which technique to use and how to use it.

CORE AND CONTINGENCY STRATEGIES

In the strategy generation stage, a mainstream strategy should be developed, which will become the core strategy. This **core strategy** should blend with the configuration of external forces that management anticipates. This involves making assumptions about future environments—a necessary process, not only for the development of the core strategy, but also for the selection of contingency strategies. A **contingency strategy** is one that the firm has on hand, ready in case the most likely configuration of environmental factors does not occur.

Each contingency strategy is designed for a different set of environmental factors. Contingency strategies are important because it is difficult to predict the most likely set of environmental events. If expectations do not materialize, contingency strategies can be quickly implemented. The retailer avoids future shock if an alternative scenario occurs.

Consider a general merchandise retailer who has carefully assessed the environment and concludes that the most important elements in the environment that could affect business are population and income trends. In looking at the future, the retailer feels that while the population base will probably level off over the next ten years, the real income level of the population will increase because the high-tech industries are expected to locate in its market.

As a result, a type core strategy referred to as incremental positioning has been developed, and this is shown in Exhibit 15.7. This strategy consists of maintaining present market position in terms of geographical areas and income groups served, but incrementally positioning the firm in the marketplace to attract people with higher incomes from a larger geographical area.

The company has developed three contingency strategies, as follows:

1. *Contingency Strategy A* is to be implemented if population remains stable as expected but the high-tech industries fail to materialize, resulting in a stable income level. In this scenario, the retailer expects fierce competition, since markets would not be experiencing growth. Here the firm would adopt a market protec-

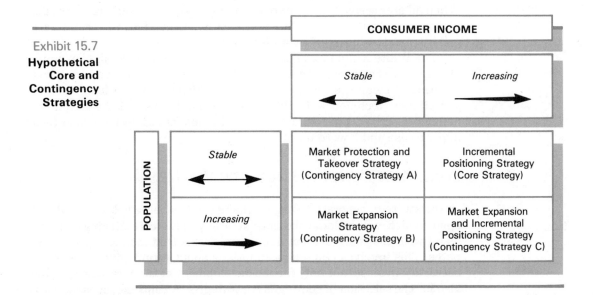

Exhibit 15.7

Hypothetical Core and Contingency Strategies

tion and takeover strategy, consisting of defending present market position while preying on and finally taking over weaker competitors that cannot weather the increased pressure.

2. *Contingency Strategy B* is to be implemented if population increases as expected but income remains stable. This scenario would call for a market expansion strategy consisting of opening additional outlets to serve an increased population.

3. *Contingency Strategy C* is to be implemented if income increases as expected but population increases unexpectedly. Under this favorable scenario the retailer would pursue a market expansion and incremental positioning strategy. The company would open new outlets to serve an increasing population and incrementally position its stores to appeal to a slightly higher income group while still being careful not to lose their core market.

Because this retailer has identified several alternative futures, it should be able to change quickly from its core strategy to a contingency strategy if the need arises. It should not need to waste time wondering about how best to operate in an unanticipated environment. In today's turbulent environment, contingency strategies are extremely important. Retailers should develop these contingency strategies to ensure themselves flexibility at all points, not just at the beginning. The manager should have contingency strategies that spin off the core at various points, so that once the manager has begun implementing the core strategy and finds the environment changed, the manager needn't go back to the beginning to start implementing a contingency strategy. Visualize the future as a road with many forks at different points—the object is to maintain flexibility along the road, not just at the beginning.

THE ROLE OF MARKET SEGMENTATION

Market segmentation is the process of dividing a heterogeneous group of consumers into smaller, more homogeneous groups. The smaller groups will be quite different from one another but members within any given group will be quite similar. Ideally, the members of the different market segments respond differently to a retailer's merchandise and service offering. This implies that their demand elasticities for different retail decision variables will be different. For example, the retailer might find that respective segments vary in how responsive they are to lower prices, increased advertising, or higher levels of customer services.

Whatever strategy the retailer develops, it will need to decide which group of consumers to focus its efforts on. Consumers are not homogeneous in their wants and preferences. The retailer needs to focus its efforts in order to use its resources more efficiently and better achieve its financial objectives. Wendy's, McDonald's, and Steak and Ale seek to focus their efforts at different groups of consumers. Wendy's seeks the over-25, childless, fast-food consumer. McDonald's seeks the couples with children, as well as the under-19 crowd, and Steak and Ale targets the upper and upper-middle income groups desiring non-fast food dining. These retailers have realized that marketplaces are becoming more heterogeneous, with great diversity in life-styles and values.[7] Eleanor May, a leading retail academician states, "A long-established goal of being 'all things to all people' is not possible in today's consumer market. A store must decide which segments of the market it is serving, or wants to serve, and then attempt to match the store to the need of these consumers."[8] The retail manager must develop an effective market segmentation strategy that will complement its overall retail strategy.

Demographic Segmentation.   Retailers can segment their market by using **demographic variables**, which describe the population characteristics of the market. Common demographic variables used to segment retail markets are age, ethnic group, income, education, sex, geography, family life cycle, and social class.

Age is a good variable to segment many retail markets. For instance, most records are purchased by people between ages 12 to 24. Stereo retailers receive a disproportionate amount of their business from people in the 18 to 30-year-old bracket.

Ethnic group is another useful segmentation variable. Grocery stores, especially, may cater to local ethnic groups, designing their merchandise assortment to cater to the ethnic dishes these groups frequently prepare. Occasionally clothing stores or restaurants will focus their efforts on certain ethnic groups. For example, in El Paso and San Diego, there are clothing stores that appeal primarily to Mexican-Americans, while many restaurants in the Midwest and East Coast cater to the Catholic market by offering nonmeat specials on Fridays during Lent.

Income can also be used as a segmentation variable. Exclusive restaurants often cater to high-income households. However not all retailers should aim at the higher income segments. Retailers like Dollar General, Family Dollar Stores Inc., and Stuart's Department Stores primarily target lower-income shoppers and have experienced tremendous growth during the last decade.[9] Another example of an income segment is the professional woman who, with her higher income level, has different shopping habits than her nonprofessional counterpart.[10]

Education level is occasionally used to partition the retailer's market. Consumption of most products or retail services is not a function of educational attainment, but there are notable exceptions. For example, book stores generally cater to more educated individuals, and consumers with lower levels of education comprise the largest market for fishing and camping equipment. Also, college graduates eat out nearly 50 percent more often than people with less education.

Sex, when used to segment a retailer's market, can be approached from two perspectives. First, merchandise appeal can be based on one sex.

This would be applicable to bridal stores, for example. Second, regardless of the product's appeal, the market could be segmented on the basis of whether women or men make the most purchase decisions. Thus, a menswear store might try to appeal to females if a significant number of wives made clothing decisions for their husbands.

Geography can also be approached from two perspectives. First, the retailer must decide which area of the country to focus its efforts on. Major geographic areas include Pacific, Mountain, West North Central, West South Central, East North Central, East South Central, South Atlantic, Middle Atlantic, and New England. Second, the retailer must decide where to concentrate its efforts within an area. Options include the central business district, the non-CBD central city, and the suburbs. All retailers must explicitly or implicitly focus on some geographic segment. Every time a store location decision is made, the retailer is making a decision to cater to a geographic market.

Family life cycle refers to the changes in family composition that, over time, substantially alter family needs, decision making, and market behavior. The three stages of the family life cycle suggested by Murphy and Staples[11] are:

1. Young
   a. Single without children
   b. Married without children
   c. Single with children
   d. Married with children
2. Middle-aged
   a. Single without children
   b. Married without children
   c. Single with children
   d. Married with children
   e. Single without dependent children
   f. Married without dependent children
3. Older
   a. Single
   b. Married

Households in each of these stages exhibit different wants and preferences for such basic items as housing, home furnishings, food, automobiles and recreational equipment. This system enables retailers to identify which groups are the heaviest users, and thus the best customers, for its products.

Social class refers to relatively permanent and homogeneous divisions in a society in which individuals or families share similar values, lifestyles, interests, and behavior. In the United States, six social classes (based on income source, wealth, education, and occupational prestige) are typically identified: upper-upper, lower-upper, upper-middle, lower-middle, upper-lower, and lower-lower. Retailers can direct their overall retail

Illus. 15.3

Stores such as Bergdorf Goodman and Neiman Marcus focus their retail strategy on the lower-upper and upper-middle social classes.

strategy to a particular social class. For instance, K mart and other discount department stores tend to target efforts on the lower-middle and upper-lower social classes. Bergdorf Goodman and Neiman-Marcus focus on the lower-upper and upper-middle classes.

Effective Segmentation.   Philip Kotler notes that, regardless of the variables used to segment the market, there are three requirements for effective segmentation:

1. **Measurability**, or the "degree to which the size and purchasing power of the resulting segments can be measured."
2. **Accessibility**, or the "degree to which the resulting segments can be effectively reached and served."
3. **Substantiality**, or the "degree to which the resulting segments are large and/or profitable enough to be worth considering for separate marketing attention."[12]

Some of these variables produce segments that are much easier to measure than others. Consider age vs. life-style. Using census data, the retailer can easily determine how many people within its trading area are in various age brackets. But if the retailer wanted to know how many people in its trading area pursued a "casual" life-style, no ready source of data would be available. There is not even an agreed-upon definition of what a "casual" life-style is. Therefore, segmenting on this variable would be more difficult than segmenting according to age.

Some segmentation variables produce segments that are easier to gain access to than others. For example, 12 to 18-year-olds can be reached by advertising on popular radio stations. But how does a store manager direct its advertising at upper-middle class households? Do they tend to watch different TV programs, or read different parts of the newspaper?

Unless the retailer can readily obtain access to a market segment, the segmentation strategy will not be totally effective.

Finally, the retailer needs to be concerned with the substantiality or size of the segment. Does it offer sufficient profit potential? A menswear retailer could decide to focus its retailing efforts on extra large or tall men but the number of these men in its trading area might not justify such a segmentation strategy.

CONTROL OF STRATEGIC FIT

Strategic planning is useless unless the retailer has a systematic process for monitoring the firm's environment and performance. One system for doing this is the Retail Information System, which will be discussed in Chapter 17. If the retailer develops a strategy that is in tune with the contemporary retail environment and implements that strategy, but then fails to monitor the retail environment, the strategy may, over time, become inappropriate. As the environment slowly changes, retailers occasionally need to alter their strategy so that it stays in tune with the environment. McDonald's initially focused its strategy on providing low-cost, quick, and tasty lunches for workers and low-cost dinners for families. Over time, more households had two working spouses and McDonald's realized that it had some excess capacity available—a restaurant not open in the morning. Thus McDonald's expanded its strategy to appeal to working families that need quick, low-cost, nutritious breakfasts.

THE IMPLEMENTATION OF STRATEGIC PLANNING CONTROL SYSTEM

Now you know why it is so important for retail executives to constantly review their strategic plans—markets change and environments change. We will now discuss how a retailer should review its strategic plans and make adjustments to them. After all, plans without control are useless in the ever-changing retailing world.

THE CONTROL REVIEW PROCESS

There are several steps that must be performed by retail executives when implementating a control process review of the firm's strategic plans. They are:

1. Determining who should perform the review.
2. Determining when and how often the review should take place.
3. Determining what areas of the strategic plan should be reviewed.
4. Conducting the review.
5. Reacting to the review's findings.

Who Should Perform the Review. Any one of three different groups can perform the reviews: a special group of internal staff, outside consultants, or department or store managers.

The special internal staff group has the advantage of being an on-going operation which is able to make use of the data provided by the Retail Information System (RIS) we will discuss in Chapter 17. In addition, they will be knowledgeable about operations of the retailer. The disadvantage of this source is that many small retailers cannot afford to have a full-time review staff and some large retailers question the independence of an internal staff.

Outside consultants have independence but are expensive, and while they have broad experience, they lack familiarity with the firm.

The third group—department and store heads—is the source most commonly used. The process is inexpensive and they have familiarity with the firm's operations. However, this process takes managers away from their main duties and sometimes results in a lack of objectivity.

When and How Often to Review. The most logical time for conducting a review is at the end of a retailer's fiscal year when a physical inventory is taken. The date can vary, but the review should be conducted at least once a year. Some firms may want to review even more frequently. However, for meaningful comparisons, the same dates should be used each year.

What Areas Should Be Reviewed. A review of the strategic plan is more than an audit of the firm's financial affairs by a Certified Public Accountant. It should be used to examine all aspects of a firm's strategy and operations. However, circumstances may prevent retail executives from examining in-depth more than one or two areas of operations. An **overall review** is an analysis of the overall performance of the retailer to see if the objectives are reasonable and if the strategy is workable. A **segmental review** is an in-depth analysis of only one area's performance (e.g., credit or promotion).

Conducting the Review. Some questions should be answered when conducting the review itself. Should the firm's employees be made aware that the review is being conducted? It is always desireable to have complete employee cooperation when doing a review. However, if a particular area, such as credit or sales personnel, is being examined it might be better not to inform them of the review.

Management Reactions. The most important element of any review process is management's reactions to the findings. If the firm's objectives are unobtainable or the strategy is ill-conceived it would be unwise to continue with the current strategy. High-performance results can be attained only if management uses the review process to control operations. This is why a retailer must have some type of Retail Information System. A seri-

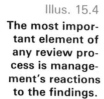

Illus. 15.4

The most important element of any review process is management's reactions to the findings.

ous error could be made if the findings of the review are downplayed by management. Long-term success comes from control, which is based on evaluating the present and adapting to the future.

REVIEW PROCESS PROBLEMS

There are several potential pitfalls in performing a review. They are:

1. The process involves a considerable amount of expense, especially if outside consultants are used.
2. The process ties up top management's time.
3. Management might choose the wrong source to conduct the review.
4. Incorrect data and information might be obtained.
5. The wrong conclusions may be drawn from the review.
6. A reluctant management may ignore the findings.[13]

In spite of its problems, the review process is worthwhile and it is a major contributor to high-performance results. Just imagine what could have happened if the auto dealers discussed in Retailing in Action 15-2 had conducted a review earlier, when self-service gas first appeared.

EXTENSIVENESS OF STRATEGIC PLANNING IN LARGE RETAILING FIRMS

Earlier in this chapter we mentioned that even though other industries were adopting the strategic planning process, retailers were slow to endorse it. Retailers claimed that flexibility and focus hindered their use of

RETAILING
IN
ACTION

15-2

Car Dealers Fail to Respond to Changing Market Conditions

Few retailers are quick to perceive the far-reaching consequences of actions taken by retailers in other lines of business. Consider the case of automobile dealers and their reactions to the shift by many gasoline dealers to self-service.

During the late 1970s and early 1980s, many oil companies began closing their service station dealerships and opening self-service outlets. Many of these new outlets did not provide restrooms or even air for tires. At the same time, many convenience stores began adding gas pumps, further reducing the demand for full-service gas dealerships. It was no wonder that these lower-price self-service outlets forced many full service operations to either adopt self-service and reduce their profit margins or go out of business. Census Bureau data shows that there were 226,500 service stations in 1972, compared to fewer than 125,000 in 1988, and that many survivors had cut back on services offered.

This presented the automobile dealerships with an enormous market opportunity. Consumers were no longer having their service station operator tend to their car's needs. Car service and repair could now come from the remaining full-service stations and automobile dealerships. *Business Week* reported in 1983 that automobile dealerships were hoping that increased profits from the service department would offset the slowdown in new car sales. In short, dealerships were beginning only then to realize the lasting effects of a trend that began more than a decade earlier. But the dealers' new reverence for the consumer had come too late. While many consumers were forced to take their car back to the dealership for simple repairs and maintenance work, they do not like it. In fact, in 1985 the *Wall Street Journal* reported on a research study that found that 38 percent of Americans would rather have a tooth extracted than take their car back to the dealership for repairs. No wonder another change has since taken place in this retail environment: the birth of the quick service oil change, tune-up and brake service retailers (especially franchises) during the late 1980s.

strategic planning. This is not true today. Since the beginning of the 1980s, many large retailers have adopted the strategic planning process as wholeheartedly as their counterparts in other businesses. William A. Andres, former chairman and CEO of the Dayton Hudson Corporation, states:

"We manage change at Dayton Hudson through our comprehensive strategic planning process. That process, which, incidentally, is a continuous one (rather than a once-a-year exercise), forces us to examine, and reexamine, our 'niche' in the marketplace. It causes us to reexamine our 'reason for being.'

"Strategic planning helps us identify and respond to how the world is changing: how the customer is changing, how the market and the competition are changing, and, most of all, how we must change to capitalize on these opportunities.

"Our five-year strategic plan becomes the blueprint for how we change the business to respond to the trends we foresee continuing and becoming more important. After all, it does little good to analyze trends if we're not willing to *act* on the basis of that analysis."[14]

A study of retailers with annual sales over $100 million by Rosenbloom and Tripuraneni[15] found more than 90 percent of these retailers have, at least occasionally, engaged in strategic planning and that more than half have done so frequently. Top management devoted 5 to 10 percent of its time to strategic planning. The functional areas with the highest participation level were, in order, finance, merchandising, operations, promotion, and personnel. The major external environmental factors considered were, in order, competition, consumer behavior, economy, technology, and government regulations. Finally, Rosenbloom and Tripuraneni found that only 23 percent of the large retailing chains used a time frame of one year or less and that more than half used a time frame of two or more years.

Research conducted on the smaller retailers found that while smaller retailers generally don't commit their plans to writing, 30 percent of them claim to plan and include the firm's goals and strength and weakness in their plans.[16] However, it may be assumed that because of the smaller retailers' lack of expertise in this area, lack of necessary resources, or failure to realize the need for strategic planning, they have not yet advanced to the level of their large-scale counterparts. Nevertheless, that day is drawing near.

KEY MISTAKES IN STRATEGIC PLANNING

Of course, mistakes can be made in strategic planning. Most retailers who have failed at strategic planning focused on the trappings of strategic planning rather than its substance. This is the conclusion of Allan Pennington, the former vice president of corporate development at Dayton-Hudson Corporation, who has identified seven key mistakes that retail executives make in strategic planning:[17]

1. Thinking that strategic plans are an extension of financial plans. . . . Strategic plans and financial plans must be linked, but in the right sequence. Financial plans should follow the strategic

plans and be merely the quantitative expression of the overall strategy.

2. Confusing strategy and objective. What we want to accomplish is not the strategy. The statement that "our strategy is to operate on a 20 percent gross margin" is not a strategy, but an objective. The strategy tells how to accomplish what we want to accomplish.

3. Expecting consultants to plan. . . . Consultants can play a very important role. They can help define the process of planning, interpret the external environment, serve as a devil's advocate, and provide research and perspective. But they cannot assume the responsibility for the content of a company's strategy. This must fall upon the shoulders of those accountable for the execution of the plan—top management.

4. Reliance on staff experts. . . . Staff experts can't provide any better plans than outside consultants, and for the same reasons.

5. Reliance on quantitative tools. . . . Just as financial plans can obscure the quality of strategic plans, so can formulas, models, and other mechanistic devices which take the focus off direction, commitment, and execution. These tools, if they are used at all, should be employed as an adjunct to the effective planning process, not as the core of it.

6. Too many retailers focus too sharply on expansion and diversification and ignore their base business in the strategic planning process.

7. Taking too narrow a perspective. . . . Placing planning in too narrow a perspective results in strategic inconsistencies that are difficult or expensive to correct. A common example is the development of a rapid expansion program that is inconsistent with the financial structure of the company.

These mistakes are the central causes of strategic failure in retailing.

SUMMARY

While other industries adopted the strategic planning process a couple of decades ago, it has only recently been implemented by retailers. Two possible explanations for this delay were suggested. Retailers (1) wanted a process that would enable them to become more flexible in responding to their environment and (2) felt that they focused on different decisions than other businesses.

The strategic planning process consists of the retailer's matching its mission and objectives to external opportunities. From these opportunities, strategies must be generated. These strategies must be controlled to ensure that they stay in tune with the external environment.

Futures research can help the retailer identify significant trends in the external environment. Once the environment has been assessed for significant trends and opportunities, the retailer must generate possible strategies. Techniques that can be used to facilitate the generation of retail strategies include brainstorming, attribute listing, morphological synthesis, checklist, and synetics.

Whatever retail strategy is pursued, the retailer must focus on well-defined consumer segments. For this reason, we discussed market segmentation as it applies in a retail setting. The retailer also needs to control its strategic fit by regularly monitoring the external environment and adjusting the strategy as the environment warrants.

Next, we focused on the extent to which strategic planning is used today by large-scale retailers and made an assumption on its use by smaller retailers. The chapter concluded by pointing out the major causes of failure by retailers using strategic planning.

QUESTIONS FOR DISCUSSION

1. Does strategic planning become more or less important as uncertainty in the external environment increases?
2. The retailer could simplify the strategic planning process if it stated only profit objectives. Agree or disagree and explain why.
3. In analyzing opportunities, the retailer should develop a strategy for the opportunity which offers the highest expected return on investment. Agree or disagree and explain why.
4. Is strategic planning or operations management of the store more important?
5. How many contingency strategies should a retailer develop?
6. To what extent should the retailer analyze the legal environment when developing strategic plans?
7. Strategic planning is an exercise in creative thinking vs. analytical problem solving. Agree or disagree and explain why.
8. Identify and briefly discuss the steps in the strategic planning process.
9. Why are quantitative objectives preferable to qualitative objectives? Should a retailer have no qualitative objectives?
10. If you were the manager of an independent fast-food restaurant next to a campus, how would you conduct your strategic planning review process? How often would you have a review?
11. Retailers have been slow in adopting the strategic planning process. Why do you think this is so?

SUGGESTED READINGS

Achrol, Ravi Singh, and David L. Appel. "New Developments in Corporate Strategy Planning." *AMA Educators' Proceedings*. P. E. Murphy et al., eds. (American Marketing Association, 1983): 305–10.

Dodge, H. Robert, and E. Terry Deiderick. "Retail Metamorphosis: A Fundamental Change in Strategic Orientation." *Retailing: Its Present and Future*. (Proceedings of 1988 AMS/ACRA Conference), 12–16.

File, Karen M., Ben B. Judd, and Frank E. Moriya. "New Breed of Retailers? Business Values of Natural Food Store Owners." *Retailing: Its Present and Future*. (Proceedings of 1988 AMS/ACRA Conference), 45–49.

Meloche, Martin S., C. Anthony diBenedetto, and Julian E. Yudelson. "A Framework for the Analysis of the Growth and Development of Retail Institutions." *Retailing: Its Present and Future*. (Proceedings of 1988 AMS/ACRA Conference), 6–11.

Robinson, R. B., Jr., J. E. Logan, and M. Y. Salem. "Strategic Versus Operational Planning in Small Retail Firms." *American Journal of Small Business* (Winter 1986): 7–16.

ENDNOTES

1. Arnold Becker, "Development of Retail Store Strategies" (Paper presented at Retail Research Society meeting, New York, June 29, 1977).

2. Edward R. Telling, Sears, Roebuck and Co. report to Investment Analysts Society (Chicago, November 16, 1978), 2.

3. Sidney Schoeffler, "Nine Basic Findings on Business Strategy," *PIMS Letter, No. 1*, The Strategic Planning Institute, 1977.

4. John B. Gifford and James M. Stearns, "Perceived Importance of Financial Ratios as Indicators of Corporate Health and Vitality in the Retail Industry" (Paper presented at 1985 A.C.R.A. Spring Conference).

5. Philip Kotler, *Marketing Management: Analysis, Planning and Control*, 4th ed. (Englewood Cliffs, N.J.: Prentice-Hall, 1980), 69–70.

6. Robert Weinberg, "Development Management Strategies for Short-Term Profits and Long-Term Growth" (Presented in a seminar sponsored by Advanced Management Research, Inc., New York City, September 29, 1969).

7. Roger D. Blackwell and W. Wayne Talarzyk, "Lifestyle Retailing: Competitive Strategies for the 1980s," *Journal of Retailing* (Winter 1983): 10 and 13.

8. Eleanor G. May, "Practical Applications of Recent Retail Image Research," *Journal of Retailing* (Winter 1974–75): 19.

9. "Selling to the Poor: Retailers That Target Low-Income Shoppers Are Growing Rapidly," *Wall Street Journal*, 24 June 1985, pp. 1 and 8.

10. Mary Joyce and Joseph Guiltiman, "The Professional Woman: A Potential Market Segment for Retailers," *Journal of Retailing* (Summer 1978): 59–70.

11. Adapted from Patrick E. Murphy and William A. Staples, "A Modernized Family Life Cycle," *Journal of Consumer Research* (June 1979): 16.

12. Kotler, *Marketing Management*, 205–6.

13. Adapted from Martin J. Bell, *Marketing Concepts and Strategy* (Boston: Houghton Mifflin Company, 1979), 474.

14. William A. Andres, "Managing Change: A Challenge for Retailers," (Texas A&M Center for Retailing Studies Lecture Series, April 21, 1983).

15. Bert Rosenbloom and Ravi V. Tripuraneni, "Strategic Planning In the One Hundred Million Club," (Proceedings of the Research and Teaching in Retailing Conference, San Antonio, TX, February and March 1984), 18–23.

16. Myron Gable and Martin T. Topol, "Planning Practices of Small-Scale Retailers," *American Journal of Small Business* (Fall 1987): 19–32.

17. Allan L. Pennington, "Do's and Don'ts of Retail Strategic Plans," *Marketing News* (March 7, 1980): 5. Reprinted with permission.

16 Chapter

Management of Human Resources

OVERVIEW

This chapter will examine the role that human resources play in retail enterprises. It will show that to successfully carry out a retail strategy, it is necessary to have the proper number and mix of human resources. Retail managers must plan for human resources, evaluate the employees' performances, acquire human resources, train and develop human resources, compensate human resources, improve the job environment, and finally, organize their human resources for maximum efficiency.

602

C. Organizing Around Functions
  1. One-Function Organization
  2. Two-Function Organization
  3. Three-Function Organization
  4. Four-Function Organization
  5. Complex Structures
D. Organizing Around Merchandise
E. Organizing Around Location
F. Multi-Mode Organizations
G. Branch-Store Organization
  1. Brood Hen and Chick
  2. Separate Store
  3. Equal Store
H. Chain Store Organizations
  1. Coordination and Control
  2. Buying and Selling
  3. Ownership Groups

In the retail planning and management model (Exhibit 2.2) the role of administrative management was defined as "acquiring, maintaining, and controlling retail resources." This chapter will examine one of the, if not the, most important of these retail resources—human resources. Human resources make things happen; they propel the firm into achieving high-performance results. Since good human resources are in short supply, proper planning and management of these resources is a key correlate of a retailer's ultimate performance level.

Retailers use different methods for planning and managing human resources. Nevertheless, there is a core of knowledge regarding planning and managing human resources in retailing, and that core will be the focus of this chapter.

HUMAN RESOURCE MANAGEMENT

There has been debate recently on how to measure the productivity of retail labor but no one will argue with the fact that no matter how it is measured, retail labor productivity has been declining over the past two decades. Retailers are caught in a vicious circle in which the relatively low wages they offer salespeople have attracted low-quality employees, perpetuating the low wage-low quality cycle. It might even be argued that "Americans have developed utter contempt for the retail clerk."

Retail salespeople are not motivated by low wages and thus quickly lose morale. Consequently, many of them become disgruntled, and employee turnover rises and productivity falls. The decline in productivity and the prospect for continued high turnover prompts retailers to keep wages low. In short, retailers have created a self-fulfilling prophecy. It is not surprising, therefore, that in some retail stores the salesforce you see today is totally different from the one you would have seen last year or the one you will probably see next year, or that in some retail establishments, such as fast food restaurants, more than 75 percent of the labor force of 3.5 million is in the age group of 16–20 years old.

The profit impact of increased salesforce productivity in retailing is dramatic. For example, the use of suggestion selling, a lost art, can often be the difference between success and failure for many retailers. Retailers operate very close to their break-even point due to the relatively high costs of opening the store doors each morning. Therefore, a 10 to 15 percent increase in salesforce productivity, be it measured in sales per employee hour, gross margin per employee hour, value-added per employee hour or gross margin minus sales commission per employee hour would, in most part, directly translate into a proportional improvement in store profits. Consequently, retail managers should accept a major performance imperative to increase human resource, especially salesforce, productivity in the future.

PLANNING FOR HUMAN RESOURCES

Planning is deciding today what to do in the future. Planning for human resources involves deciding now what human resources will be needed later to satisfy the customer's needs and wants. Existing retailers as well as those wishing to establish a retail enterprise must engage in human resource planning. The importance of this was highlighted when Carson Pirie Scott & Co. changed the title of its vice president of human resources to "vice president of customer satisfaction through people involvement."[1]

TASK ANALYSIS

The starting point for human resources planning in retailing is task analysis. **Task analysis** involves identifying all tasks the retailer needs to perform and breaking those tasks into jobs. Three steps should be followed: *identifying the functions* within the marketing system that retailers need or wish to perform; *identifying the tasks* that need to be performed within each function; and *mapping the tasks into jobs*.

Marketing Functions.   Retailers need to view themselves as a part of a larger marketing system. Retailers are but one institution in a marketing channel which, as a system, must perform eight marketing functions: buying, selling, storing, transporting, sorting, financing, information gathering, and risk taking. Since the eight functions can be shifted and divided, no single institution in the marketing channel will typically perform all of the functions.

The starting point for good human resource planning is for the retailer to decide which and how much of the eight marketing functions it will perform. As retailers assume more functions, they will require more human resources. For instance, the large chain store may:

1. Perform more of the buying function by having buying offices in major cities throughout the world.
2. Perform more of the selling function by heavily advertising and promoting merchandise on TV and radio and in newspapers and magazines.
3. Perform more of the storage function by operating its own warehouse.
4. Perform more of the transportation function by having its own trucks.
5. Perform more of the sorting functions by buying in large quantities and breaking bulk and in some cases doing its own packaging.
6. Perform more of the financing function by establishing a subsidiary to finance consumer purchases or by helping to finance small manufacturers.
7. Perform more of the information gathering function by developing a department of consumer research and long-range planning.
8. Perform more of the risk-taking function by designing and developing specifications for products and then contracting with manufacturers to produce them.

Identifying Tasks.   Once retailers have established the amount of each marketing function to perform, they must identify all of the tasks that will need to be performed. Functions are broad classifications of activities; tasks are specific activities. For example, selling is a function that may involve the tasks of customer contact, customer follow-up, advertising in newspapers, and pricing merchandise.

Exhibit 16.1 provides a list of tasks that retailers typically perform—ranging from transporting goods to cleaning the floor of the store.

Mapping Tasks into Jobs.   The final step in task analysis is mapping the tasks into jobs. Retailers want a job to be comprised of a relatively homogeneous set of tasks. Since the tasks are heterogeneous, retailers will need to find those which are most similar and group them together. The smaller the retail organization, the less this will be possible. In a mom-and-pop store, the owner does everything from purchasing supplies and merchandise, preparing financial statements, and contacting customers to washing the windows.

As stores grow and add more employees, specialization can occur. As a retailer grows, the tasks of granting credit, billing customers, paying bills, and preparing financial statements will be placed in the hands of an accounting or financial clerk. Similarly, the tasks of handling customer

Exhibit 16.1
Typical Tasks Retailers Perform

Searching for merchandise	Following up on customers	Contacting customers	Doing customer research
Packaging	Handling customer complaints	Transporting inbound merchandise	Preparing press releases
Gift wrapping	Cleaning store	Transporting outbound merchandise	Preparing financial statements
Advertising	Controlling inventory	Paying bills	Storing merchandise
Purchasing supplies	Hiring and firing employees	Handling cash	Preparing merchandise statistics
Purchasing merchandise	Training employees	Altering merchandise	Maintaining the store
Granting credit	Selling	Repairing merchandise	Providing store security
Billing customers	Supervising employees	Forecasting sales	
Building merchandise assortments	Displaying merchandise		
Pricing merchandise			

complaints, repairing and altering merchandise, and gift wrapping may be placed in the hands of a director of customer services. When a retailer is small, these two sets of tasks may be handled by the same person, even though they are heterogeneous. If the retailer gets large enough, each task may be performed by a separate individual and ultimately there may be an entire department handling a single task. For instance, Sears needs hundreds of employees to bill customers, and thousands more to purchase merchandise.

LONG-RANGE ANALYSIS

In the long run (two to five years), the driving force behind human resource requirements will be the retailer's projected growth in sales volume and number of stores. This is not to suggest that human resource requirements are unilaterally a function of growth in sales and number of stores. Frequently, growth in sales and number of stores depends on the availability of good human resources. This is especially true when a chain store retailer's growth is constrained, not by its capital or market opportunities, but by the availability of qualified assistant store managers to promote to the position of store manager. Every new store that is opened by a chain store retailer needs not only a store manager but an assistant manager and a multitude of other supervisory employees. In analyzing long-range growth trends, retailers should pay particular attention to the speed and predictability of growth, the geographical dispersion of growth, and the amount of growth related to line-of-trade diversification. Each of these has significant implications for human resource planning.

Speed and Predictability of Growth.   The more rapid the growth, the more difficult it will be to manage human resources. Fast-growing retail enterprises create both opportunities and problems in regard to human resource planning. Rapid growth creates many opportunities for existing retail employees, because possibilities for promotion and advancement are numerous. At the same time, rapid growth can create a host of problems. Naturally, for every retail employee promoted, another individual has to take over the promoted employee's job. In addition, not every employee who thinks they deserve a promotion will receive one, creating tension in the organization. In some situations, no employee may be ready for the promotion, and an outsider may be hired—again possibly creating internal tension and hostility. The more rapid the growth, the more such problems there will be.

To a considerable extent, these problems can be avoided if the retailer knows with some certainty that strong growth will occur over the next two to five years. The retailer can start early to groom its current employees for increased responsibility, and recruit new people for the organization. Of course, there is some risk to this process: what if the expected growth does not occur? In that case, the retailer has prepared a select group of employees for significant increases in authority and responsibility but has no new positions for these employees. An employee who has been prepared for a key management position and doesn't get it will most likely seek such a position elsewhere.

Geographic Diversification.   If growth is expected to occur through geographic diversification, then a problem arises in regard to the frequent necessity of transferring employees and their families to stores in different geographical areas. Consider a retailer that has saturated one city with its stores and begins to build stores in other cities or towns. Each new store will need managers. A potential pool for these new managers is the employees in existing stores. However, not all talented employees will jump at a promotion if it involves a geographic move. This is especially true if the area is perceived as an unattractive place to live or raise a family, or if the employee's spouse has a good job and doesn't want to move.

Diversification into a new geographic area may also be accompanied by a different labor environment. For instance, in large cities and on the West Coast, retail employees are more likely to be unionized. Furthermore, wages may be significantly higher in large cities due to more intense competition from other industries (manufacturing, wholesaling, and banking, to name a few).

Line-of-Trade Diversification.   Retailers that plan to diversify into other lines of retail trade will face additional problems. Especially important will be the problem of deciding which, if any, of the present employees can adapt to a different line of retail trade. Although the basics of retailing are constant across lines of trade, the specifics are quite different. There is no assurance that a manager of a supermarket can manage a women's apparel store or a jewelry store. In general, the higher the position in the organization, the less this will be a problem. The controller or president of a supermarket chain should be able to perform similar functions for a women's apparel chain or jewelry chain. But, for more day-to-day operations, like reordering, this is more likely be a problem.

Once the speed and predictability of growth, geographic diversification, and line of trade diversification have been identified, a human resources audit should be performed.

Human Resources Audit.   A **human resource audit** is a careful examination, by top management or an outside consultant, of the strengths and weaknesses of all employees. Lower-level employees such as salesclerks, janitors, and delivery persons might be placed in groups and evaluated as a whole. Or a small retailer may want to carefully evaluate the prospective management abilities of *each* employee. Many salesclerks, janitors, delivery persons, and other low-level employees have moved on to become store managers, vice presidents, and presidents or owners of their own stores.

An individual evaluation of each person holding a middle- or top-management position should be made. Where does each excel, perform poorly, and need improvement? What are the desires and goals of each manager? What are their track records? How fast have they progressed, and how motivated and talented are they? Do they desire to continue to move up in

Illus. 16.1

Many salesclerks and other low-level persons move on to become store managers, vice presidents, presidents or owners of their own stores.

the organization? How flexible are they (are they willing to make a geographic move for a promotion)? These are only a sampling of the questions
that the audit should answer.

From this audit, management should be able to develop a profile of
the number and quality of employees in the organization that are potential first-line managers, and the number of managers at each subsequent
stage in the organizational hierarchy who have potential for advancement. By comparing this profile with long-range growth needs, the retail
executive should be able readily to identify the human resource areas that
need the most attention.

The retailers that identify their weak points through a human resource audit, can begin to correct the situation by training and developing
existing employees. For example, by foreseeing a significant need for
more store managers within the next two to five years, a retailer could
start today to train and develop those employees who exhibit the drive
and potential to advance to the rank of store manager.

SHORT-RANGE ANALYSIS

Human resources need to be planned not only on a long-range basis, but
also over the short run. The short run horizon is usually less than a year
and may be weekly, monthly, or seasonal. Retailers should forecast any
short-run swings in sales and adjust human resource inputs appropriately. For instance, if retailers forecast a recession in the next few quar-
ters, they might stop hiring now, so that no employees will need to be fired
or laid off.

It is wise to analyze recurring seasonal trends. If a retailer always
does a strong business during the Christmas season, plans should be
made to have adequate human resources during this period each year. If a
retailer always experiences more traffic on Friday and Saturday, it should
plan to have the increased staff on hand on these days.

Periodic and predictable increases in the short-run demand for human
resources can be handled by part-time employees or by having existing
employees participate in job sharing. Part-time employees for peak periods such as Christmas or weekends can help retailers serve more customers. One way to attract good part-timers is to send statement stuffers
to charge account holders who already use and probably like your store,
offering part-time employment for the Christmas season with standard
employee discount privileges. However, the peak business can often be
handled by having existing employees share jobs, such as having managers wait on customers, or having some employees work overtime.

HUMAN RESOURCE ACQUISITION

Few retailers will be able to operate indefinitely without sooner or later
needing additional human resources. Present employees may retire, quit,
be fired, become terminally ill, or die. Also, retailers may need additional

employees because of growth. The source of these new employees, especially at entry level, will present some problems for retailers in the 1990s. The baby boomers have reached middle-age and there is a birth dearth. These factors have resulted in a lack of high schoolers to fill entry–level retail jobs. Two possible solutions are:

- Change the people hired. McDonald's "new kid," the elderly and handicapped, is a good example of a new source of labor.
- Change the job. Many fast-food places have switched to salad and drink bars, relying more on self-service, and some specialty shops have started using direct mail as a labor substitute.

COMPETITION

Human resources are acquired in a competitive marketplace. Good employees are not waiting around to be hired, and seldom will they come pounding at your door. When good workers or managers are looking for employment, they seldom think of contacting retail firms, because retailers have a reputation for low starting wages. Therefore, retailers have to aggressively recruit good employees; that is, they must compete for labor resources.

SOURCES

What are the sources from which retailers can obtain human resources? The following six are the most common: walk-ins, employment agencies, schools and colleges, former employees, advertisements, and recommendations.

Walk-ins.   During periods of high unemployment, retailers have many walk-ins seeking employment. These walk-ins can be a source for clerical,

Illus. 16.2
During periods of high unemployment, retailers have many walk-ins seeking employment.

sales, and custodial positions, but seldom are they a source for managerial or supervisory employees. Also, it is when walk-ins are most frequent—during periods of high unemployment—that retailers need additional human resources least. Still, it is good practice to file applications filled out by walk-ins, since it is a low-cost method of acquiring a list of prospective employees.

Employment Agencies.   Using the services of public or private employment agencies is another possibility. All states provide public employment services, which are typically available free of charge to both job seekers and employers. The ability of these public services to provide a good pool of prospective managerial or white-collar employees is generally poor. They can, however, be a reasonable source for unskilled employees. They are an excellent source for minority, handicapped, and veteran employees. This can help retailers achieve a specific policy of equal employment opportunity.

Private employment agencies are generally a much better source for managerial and white-collar employees. The reputations and skills of these agencies, however, vary widely. All of them charge a fee to either the retailer or the job applicant when the applicant is hired. Retailers should be careful of agencies more interested in getting a fee than in achieving a good fit between applicant and employer.

Some private employment agencies specialize in recruiting retail executives. Two examples are Retail Executive Search, Inc., based in Chicago and Retail Recruiters based in New York City. Both are good sources for suitable candidates for top-management retail positions.

Schools and Colleges.   Many candidates for potential employment may be completing formal educational programs. They could be completing high school, junior college, college, or even graduate school. All graduates are potential candidates, but they possess differing levels of talent, skills, knowledge, and expectations.

Many high schools have Distributive Education Clubs of America (DECA) chapters. High school students who belong to DECA take courses that relate to retailing, such as bookkeeping and merchandising. They also, while in school, work part-time for local retailers. These students are an excellent source for operating-level employees. Many of them have the basic talent, skills, and ambition to become shift managers or assistant department managers within one or two years. High schools do not have placement bureaus; the best way to attract good high-school graduates with an interest in retailing is to develop a good working relationship with the teachers of business-related courses or with advisors of the local DECA chapter.

Graduates of junior college business administration or retailing programs are another source of human resources. Recruiting these graduates is somewhat easier, because almost all junior colleges have a placement bureau that facilitates the interviewing and selection process. Many junior college graduates have some retail experience and, because of their college training, can begin in a low-level supervisory role, such as assistant night manager of a store.

Retailers can also recruit graduates of four-year college programs. If the retailer decides to move in this direction, it should be willing to make a significant commitment in terms of financial resources to attract and hire a given number of employees. Not only do four-year college graduates expect and receive higher starting salaries, but the cost of recruiting them can be significant. Not every city or town has a four-year college, and if there is a college in town it may not train the type of graduates the retailer desires. Thus, the retailer will need to send a representative (recruiter) to screen candidates on campus. Once all candidates are screened, a few will be selected to visit the retailer, with the retailer picking up the travel and lodging cost. If things go well, the retailer will extend an offer to one or several applicants. Probably, not all will accept, because top college graduates will have several offers. All of the costs of recruiting should be related to the number of hires. Suppose a retailer has openings for three people in a management training program and visits two campuses for two days to interview a total of thirty students. The retailer then invites five prospects to company headquarters and subsequently hires two of them. If the cost of all of this recruiting was $5,600, then the cost per hire was $2,800—not an insignificant amount. Incidentally, nearly 60 percent of a new employee's annual salary is spent to locate, interview, screen, hire, train, and retain that employee.

Some retailers are experimenting with hiring MBA graduates. The available evidence suggests that results have been mixed. Too often these graduates expect to advance quickly through the organization and become vice presidents or presidents of retail organizations within a few years. This is most often not possible—but given the right candidate and the right retail organization, it is not impossible.

Former Employees.   Retailers should keep a tab on former employees who performed well. These may have been employees the retailer valued, but did not have the ability to promote. Since retail organizations are always changing, there may be a time when a position is open for which a former employee would be excellent. It is not unusual for a person to leave one retail organization as an assistant buyer, take a job as a sales rep for a supplier or as a buyer at another retail organization, and return to the first retailer several years later as divisional merchandise manager.

Advertisements.   Obviously, a retailer can get a pool of applicants for a particular job by placing advertisements in the classified section of the local newspaper. Retailers often advertise for salesclerks, cashiers, and janitors, and occasionally they seek buyers and managers this way. This is especially true when a retailer is entering a new geographic area and wants to make sure that employees at other retail firms in the area are aware that the new retailer is really interested in obtaining personnel with knowledge of the local market and not merely transferring in existing personnel. Ads can also be placed in retail trade journals such as *Chain Store Age* or *Stores* or in magazines with a more specific orientation, such as *Hardware Retailing* or *Progressive Grocer*. Trade journal advertising is most useful if the search is for a middle- or top-management position, because it is a low-cost means of reaching retail executives across the nation.

Recommendations.   A final source of prospective employees is the recommendations of current employees and vendors. These people may have acquaintances or friends with an interest in applying for the jobs that are open. This source is good for filling jobs at all levels in the organization. Salesclerks, store managers, vice presidents, and sales reps may all know of good people seeking employment at a variety of ranks or positions.

SCREENING

Regardless of the specific source from which they're obtained, all job applicants should be subject to a formal screening process to sort the potentially good from the potentially bad employees. As with any type of screening, some degree of error is unavoidable. That is, the retail personnel manager may classify an applicant as a potential loser when in reality the applicant would be excellent for the job, or vice versa. But fewer errors should occur with screening than with no screening at all.

Retailers tend to vary in the amount of screening they use. Five screens that the applicant can be put through are displayed in Exhibit 16.2. The applicant pool for a particular job is progressively reduced as the applicants are subjected to each screen. This process will be illustrated as each screening device is briefly discussed.

Application Blanks.   As a matter of procedure, all applicants should be asked to fill out an application blank. The application blank should try to capture conveniently and compactly those aspects of an individual's personality and history that will impact on his or her performance of the job tasks. Federal law prohibits the retailer from discrimination on the basis of race, color, religion, sex, age, or national origin. Thus, the employer is prohibited from asking any questions related to these areas. Exceptions may be made where religion, sex, or national origin (but not race or color), is a **bona fide occupational qualification (BFOQ)**. An example of a BFOQ might be a French restaurant's hiring a French cook.[2] Similarly, a retailer seeking a night security guard to protect its property is allowed to eliminate individuals with physical disabilities that would prevent them from effectively performing the tasks of a night security guard.

Exhibit 16.2
**Employee
Screening
Process**

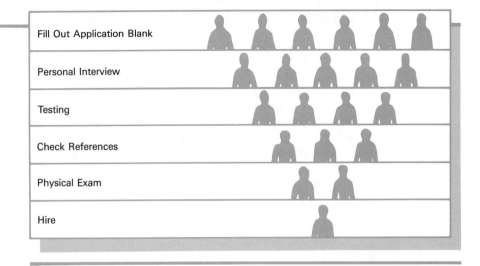

| Fill Out Application Blank |
| Personal Interview |
| Testing |
| Check References |
| Physical Exam |
| Hire |

From the list of qualified applicants who filled out applications the retailer must select the best possible candidates for each job. In selecting the best possible candidates to personally interview, retailers have several methods to evaluate the applications. Some retailers have developed weighted application blanks.[3] These have statistical weights assigned to different types of information that reflect how well the respective pieces of information predict success on the job. Two advantages accrue in the use of such applications. First, the retailer can better process the information on the application blank to determine which of the applicants are most likely to be successful on the job and to stay for some time. Second, adhering to a weighted system ensures that the retailer does not unfairly discriminate against individuals because of personal characteristics.

One study provided evidence that it is possible to make some predictions about employee turnover, which is 50 percent higher in retailing than in all other business, based on information included on the application blank.[4] Managerial trainees who had prior military experience were more likely to leave a training program than those who did not. Trainees who earned income to finance college, who had a clear understanding of job responsibilities, or who had some prior retail experience were more likely to stay.

Retailing in Action 16-1 lists some questions that retailers may and may not use on their application blanks.

Personal Interview.   Applicants who possess the basic characteristics needed to perform the job should be personally interviewed. This important step allows the retailer to assess how qualified the applicants are for the job. By its very nature, an interview is subjective; but in a well-struc-

Legal and Illegal Questions To Be Asked of Prospective Employees

Here is a list of legal and illegal questions that retailers might ask a prospective employee. Remember, retailers may not ask any questions that would lead to discrimination on the basis of race, color, religion, sex, age or national origin. What is involved in these questions is not always clear as there are no questions at all that are specifically banned by federal law. Thus, while a question about, say, ethnic origin or religious affiliation *could* be illegal (as well as in poor taste), it need not necessarily be so.[1] However, the following lists should serve as a guideline for retailers.

LEGAL

Are you over 18?

Is there anything that would prevent you from being transferred to another city?

Do you, or have you in the past, used another name?

What do you feel are your major strengths (weaknesses)?

What languages do you speak fluently?

Do you have any relatives working for the firm?

Are you a U.S. citizen? (If not, do you intend to become a U.S. citizen?)

Where do you live?

Do you have any physical disability that would prevent you from performing this job?

How long have you lived at your current residence?

Where have you worked previously?

ILLEGAL

Do you prefer *Miss, Mrs.* or *Ms.*?

What is the name of your pastor?

Are you married?

What social organizations are you currently a member of?

Other than the usual holidays, would you be absent for any religious holidays?

How old are you?

Where does your spouse work?

Of what country are you a citizen?

What is your birthplace?

Do you have a disability?

Have you ever been arrested?

Have you ever had a serious illness?

[1] Arthur A. Sloane, *PERSONNEL: Managing Human Resources* (Englewood Cliffs: Prentice Hall, 1983), 130.

tured interview one can obtain information about the attitudes, personality, motives, and job aspirations of the interviewee.

The interview should be a two-way communication process. Not only does the retailer want to gather information about the applicant, but the applicant will probably want information about the retailer. Allowing time for the applicant to ask questions is essential if the retailer is competing for highly recruited applicants. In fact, part of the interview time may actually be used by the interviewer to try to sell the applicant on the retailer as well as honestly explaining what the job entails so as not to lead to job dissatisfaction.

Testing.   Sometimes formal tests are administered to applicants who received favorable ratings in their personal interviews. These may be skill tests for jobs that require proficiency in certain tasks; e.g., the retailer hiring clerical staff may be concerned with typing or shorthand skills. Other characteristics, such as intelligence, interests, leadership potential, personality traits, or honesty, may also be measured with tests. For example, the Ghiselli Self Description Inventory has been administered to applicants for store management positions.[5] This test measures a variety of individual traits such as supervisory ability, initiative, self-assurance, perceived occupational level, decision-making approach, and sociometric popularity. Bloomingdale's has for several years asked entry-level sales, stock, and clerical candidates to sit down with a computer and answer multiple-choice questions about their background. Bloomingdale's has found that people are more at ease talking to a computer and that their answers are more accurate. Marriott Hotels found that workers screened by computers tend to stay with Marriott longer.[6]

When tests are used in screening, the retailer needs to be especially careful about any bias or discrimination inherent in the tests. The Equal Employment Opportunity Commission (EEOC), which enforces the Civil Rights of Act of 1964, has been concerned about some tests used in employment screening. For example, many intelligence and interest tests are culturally biased and can result in discrimination against racial minorities. Since 1989, retailers have not been permitted to use lie detector tests. While most retailers never used polygraph tests, some, especially in the jewelry business, relied heavily on their results. Marshall Field's, in 1989, switched to more credit checks and drug tests as a substitute.[7]

References.   Employers should not ask for or check the references the applicant has provided until the applicant has been screened or filtered through the preceding stages. It would be too expensive to obtain and verify references for all applicants. It is more cost-effective to obtain and check references after most applicants have been eliminated from consideration.

References should be used to assess the honesty and reliability of the applicant. The reason for leaving the prior place or places of employment should also be investigated. The retailer should try to find out what type of person will vouch for the prospective employee. Finally, although most references provided by the applicant will give a favorable recommendation, the reference check does give the retailer a means to verify the accuracy and completeness of the application. Many retailers have had greater success using telephone interviews than asking for written replies. This enables retailers to gather more complete and honest evaluations than letters, especially to notice what the reference *doesn't say* about the applicant.

Many retailers admit that this is one area of the screening process where they are weak. While they acknowledge the need to check with a borderline applicant's previous employer, they seldom check educational references. One retailer was stunned when he found out that two of his valued employees never graduated from college before entering the firm's training program.

The retail executive confers with the firm's legal staff annually to determine the firm's and the applicant's legal rights. The courts have recently set new guidelines about what questions may be asked of prospective employees.[8]

Physical Examination.   The final step in the screening process is the physical examination. The retailer wants some information on the applicant's physical capabilities as related to the physical tasks of the job, and will also want to have on file any preexisting medical problems. This will minimize expensive liability claims in the future by preventing employees from claiming that a preexisting medical condition was in fact job-related. If the retailer can show that the condition existed before the present job, there will be less risk of legal liability.

If an individual passes all of the screens, he or she might be offered the job, but not necessarily. Several applicants may pass all the screens, but there may only be one vacancy. In this case, the retailer will need to match each of the remaining applicants to the job description in an attempt to identify the best candidate. This candidate will be offered the job.

Retailing in Action 16-2 shows the information sources used by three different types of retailers for the three different classifications of retail employees.

SOME COMMON MYTHS ABOUT EMPLOYEES

Every retailer knows that employee theft—just like consumer theft—of money, merchandise, and time erodes profits. But few know how to spot these bad traits in applicants, or even in existing employees. Supermarkets are said to measure profit margins in pennies and dimes and employee theft losses in dollars because they believe in three common myths.[9]

16-2

How Various Types of Retailers use Different Information Sources

Table 1 shows the information sources used by three different types of retailers for three different classifications of retail employees. These classifications are:

1. **Exempt Employees.** Those not covered by the minimum wage and overtime provisions of the Federal Labor Standards Act (e.g., store managers, lawyers, merchandise managers, other executives).
2. **Full-time Nonexempt Employees.** Those covered by the minimum wage and overtime provisions of the Federal Labor Standards Act and considered by the respondent to be full time (e.g., sales clerks, store clerks, office workers).
3. **Part-time Nonexempt Employees.** Those covered by the minimum wage and overtime provisions of the Federal Labor Standards Act and considered by the respondent retailer to be part time.

Table 2 breaks down the use of these sources by store dollar volume.

Table 1

Information Sources by Type of Store (Percentage reporting usage)

Method	Department store	Specialty store	Discount store
Exempt Employees			
Interview	91.2	71.1	82.6
Application blank	88.7	61.5	87.0
Business references	78.9	58.5	78.3
Personal references	59.3	52.6	47.8
Credit report	36.8	26.7	47.8
Police check	21.6	12.6	39.1
Physical examination	15.7	10.4	17.0
Testing	11.3	5.2	13.0
Polygraph	3.4	5.9	4.3
Assessment center	3.9	2.2	8.7
Handwriting analysis	1.0	0.0	0.0
Full-time Nonexempt			
Interview	97.1	92.6	91.6
Application blank	96.1	85.9	95.7
Business references	78.4	66.7	91.3
Personal references	62.7	61.5	60.9

Table 1   *Continued*

Method	Department store	Specialty store	Discount store
Credit report	26.0	25.2	39.1
Police check	26.0	13.3	30.4
Physical examination	17.2	8.9	17.4
Testing	17.2	8.9	43.5
Polygraph	6.9	8.9	0.0
Assessment center	2.0	0.7	0.0
Handwriting analysis	1.0	0.7	0.0
Part-time Nonexempt			
Interview	94.6	90.4	95.7
Application blank	95.1	81.5	95.7
Business references	69.6	59.3	78.3
Personal references	57.4	59.3	56.5
Credit report	18.1	18.5	30.4
Police check	23.5	12.6	26.1
Physical examination	12.7	6.7	4.3
Testing	14.2	7.4	30.4
Polygraph	5.9	6.7	0.0
Assessment center	0.5	0.0	0.0
Handwriting analysis	1.0	0.7	0.0

SOURCE: Charles J. Hollon and Myron Gable, ''Information Sources in Retail Employment Decision Making Process,'' *Journal of Retailing* (Fall 1979): 66.

Table 2

Information Sources by Annual Sales Volume (Percentage reporting usage)

Method	Less than $1,000,000	$1,000,000 to 9,999,999	$10,000,000 to 99,999,999	$100,000,000 to 499,000,000	$500,000,000 or more
Exempt Employees					
Interview	52.5	82.2	94.5	95.2	93.3
Application blank	42.6	76.3	92.7	97.6	93.3
Business references	37.7	65.9	84.5	90.5	93.3
Personal references	42.6	65.9	57.3	42.9	66.7
Credit report	19.7	37.0	39.1	35.7	26.7
Police check	1.6	17.0	27.3	26.2	26.7
Physical examination	3.3	5.2	12.7	52.4	33.3
Testing	0.0	7.4	14.5	9.5	20.0
Polygraph	3.3	1.5	8.2	4.8	13.3
Assessment center	0.0	1.5	3.6	7.1	26.7
Handwriting analysis	0.0	0.7	0.0	0.0	0.0

Table 2 *Continued*

Method	Less than $1,000,000	$1,000,000 to 9,999,999	$10,000,000 to 99,999,999	$100,000,000 to 499,000,000	$500,000,000 or more
Full-Time Nonexempt					
Interview	90.2	94.8	97.3	97.6	100.0
Application blank	72.1	94.8	97.3	97.6	100.0
Business references	52.5	68.9	83.6	90.5	100.0
Personal references	65.6	73.3	55.5	47.6	66.7
Credit report	19.7	31.1	26.4	28.6	26.7
Police check	3.3	19.3	30.9	28.6	26.7
Physical examination	1.6	7.4	11.8	52.4	33.3
Testing	3.3	14.1	19.1	26.2	40.0
Polygraph	3.3	3.7	10.0	14.3	13.3
Assessment center	0.0	0.7	1.8	2.4	6.7
Handwriting analysis	0.0	2.2	0.0	0.0	0.0
Part-time Nonexempt					
Interview	91.8	92.6	97.3	92.9	80.0
Application blank	68.9	94.8	96.4	92.9	80.0
Business references	42.6	61.5	76.4	78.6	80.0
Personal references	62.3	65.9	54.5	45.2	60.0
Credit report	16.4	21.5	20.9	16.7	20.0
Police check	3.3	16.3	30.0	23.8	26.7
Physical examination	0.0	4.4	8.2	38.1	20.0
Testing	3.3	11.9	14.5	21.4	33.3
Polygraph	3.3	3.0	8.2	14.3	6.7
Assessment center	0.0	0.7	0.0	0.0	0.0
Handwriting analysis	0.0	2.2	0.0	0.0	0.0

SOURCE: Charles J. Hollon and Myron Gable, "Information Sources in Retail Employment Decision Making Process," *Journal of Retailing* (Fall 1979): 70 and 71.

1. "They're not really taking much"
2. "None of my people would steal"
3. "There's no way to tell who is honest"

Regarding the first myth, evidence now indicates that employee theft exceeds $10 billion a year, not including loss of time due to employees arriving late, leaving early, or goofing off. Even worse, drug usage is costing American industry nearly $50 billion a year in absenteeism and employee turnover.[10]

Regarding the second myth, it is just wishful thinking for retailers to say none of their employees would steal from them. For example, a supermarket chain was recently sold. One of the first things the new management did was to investigate internal security. The results were shocking. Thirty-one of the chain's 63 store managers were fired within one year for theft. Some took merchandise, some took cash, and others substituted manufacturers' coupons for cash. The average loss was nearly $1,000 per week, per store. All but three of the fired employees had been with the chain for more than ten years.

Regarding the third myth, there *are* ways to determine an applicant's or employee's honesty. One way is to use a test such as those marketed by the Stanton Survey, Charlotte, NC.; John E. Reid & Company, Chicago; or London House Management Consultants, Chicago. However, based on the information presented in Retailing in Action 16-2, this procedure is not commonly used. Therefore, it is important for the person doing the hiring to look for other clues about what to expect later. Among them are:

Physical Appearance—Lack of concern about appearance is a red flag. A low-risk candidate will appear on time, dressed properly, with whatever materials are expected.

Vagueness—Beware of an applicant who doesn't know answers to specific questions. The applicant could be trying to cover up something.

Reasons for leaving—Answers such as "personal reasons" or "I quit" often indicate potential risks. They may signal that a person was "allowed to resign." Be sure to check for gaps in an applicant's previous work history.

Blame Shifting—A potential problem worker is one who is likely to blame everyone but himself for past failures.

Personal habits—A personnel director said that, based on the information she has seen on applications, 40 percent of this country's population never drink alcohol and the other 60 percent are social drinkers; that is, they have fewer than two drinks a week. The personnel manager should be on the lookout for a person who is too good. These people are usually hiding something.

TRAINING AND DEVELOPMENT

Retailers who are serious about wanting a good return on their investment should provide training and development for both new and existing human resources. Training and development are consistent with the concept of human resource planning. The importance of proper training and development was shown in a report by a B. Dalton executive. B. Dalton reported a 20 percent reduction in store manager turnover as a result of more realistic job previews in the training process, as well as increasing salaries and providing managers with opportunities to gain recognition.[11]

Training and development is an area where retailing has traditionally lagged behind other forms of business. Previously, retailers used either the **sink or swim method**, where the new employee was thrust into the job and had to learn in any way possible or else get fired, or the **sponsorship method**, in which training consisted of assigning the new employee to a senior employee for on-the-job instruction. Today, however, retail personnel directors are developing more sophisticated approaches to meet their human resource needs. These approaches are geared to transforming college graduates into assistant buyers and area managers, then into buyers and store managers. These new programs teach hands-on skills like operations and merchandising, and make extensive use of training manuals, classroom sessions, computer-based simulation games, video tapes, role-playing, and cases.

Training is not a one-time happening, however. Retailers today view training as a process of continuing education. As an individual's responsibilities increase, so does the training and development. Employees are taught not just technical skills but administrative and people skills as well. Each phase of development is built on the training that has proceeded it and includes training in merchandising, operations management, motivation, decision-making, problem analysis, and time management.

In addition to developing a pool of future managers and assisting employees with present duties, training and development programs enable the employees to know where they are and how they are doing. Remember, a career in retailing is different than careers in other businesses. In the beginning, opportunities for advancement are like a pyramid, with the employee becoming increasingly specialized, as he or she advances toward the goal of being a buyer, the ultimate specialist. Afterwards, the goal is to increase breadth, not specialty, so as to become a store or division manager.

Retailers should view their salespeople as a strategic resource and invest resources in their training and development. This involves providing new salespeople with information about the company and its goals, plans, and policies. The more they understand the firm's objectives and policies, the better prepared are they to communicate to customers the message that the retailer wants its customers to hear. Training and development for salespeople is an ongoing process and should include such topics as: product knowledge, different selling approaches, code of ethics, communication theory, planning and problem-solving skills, and self assessment and understanding.

Finally, the results of all training programs should be evaluated. The reasons for conducting this evaluation are to:

1. Determine whether the program is accomplishing its objectives.
2. Identify the program's strengths and weaknesses.
3. Calculate the cost/benefit ratio of the program.
4. Establish a reference point for future decisions about the program.

Training programs can be evaluated with a variety of methods. The most popular method is to analyze questionnaires completed by the trainees after the program. In the case of salespeople, professional shoppers could pose as customers and report on their experience with a sales trainee.

The best training and development program devised is useless unless management adopts a philosophy of complete support. Many retail executives become so tied up in merchandising concerns that they forget about human resources.

PERFORMANCE APPRAISAL

Performance appraisal and review is the formal, systematic assessment of how well employees are performing their jobs in relation to established standards and the communication of that assessment to employees. The employees place a lot of importance on appraisals and the performance system affects morale and organizational climate in significant ways. Moreover, the appraisal system has an impact on other human resource processes, like training and development, compensation, and promotion.

Informal appraisals take place on an ongoing basis within the retail firm as supervisors evaluate their subordinates' work on a daily basis and as subordinates appraise each other and their supervisors. However, the formal, systematic appraisal of an individual is likely to occur at certain intervals throughout the year or when the employee is being considered for a wage increase, a promotion, a transfer, or additional training and development.

There are several keys to conducting equitable performance appraisals. First, the process should be an ongoing affair, not just a periodic review. Regularly scheduled review times should not keep supervisors from appraising or coaching their subordinates whenever necessary. Second, feedback on how well employees are doing their jobs should be provided to them on a timely and relevant basis. Third, the same appraisal system should not be used for two different functions; e.g., for a wage increase

Illus. 16.3

Employee appraisals should be ongoing, not just periodic, and feedback should be provided to employees on a timely and relevant basis.

and improvement of job performance at the same time. Fourth, the person doing the review should know what the job being reviewed entails and what the performance standards are. Employees get upset when a reviewer is not aware of the problems and limitations of the job under review. Retailers have found success using various types of measures. The most commonly used are rating scale, checklist, free-form essay, and rankings.

EMPLOYEE MOTIVATION

Human resource management goes beyond selecting, training, and compensating employees. It also involves motivating employees to improve performance. A high-performance retailer today must constantly motivate the salesforce, as well as other employees, to strive for higher sales figures, to decrease expenses, to communicate company policies to the public, and to solve problems as they arise. This is achieved through the proper use of motivation.

Motivation is the drive within a person to excel either individually or corporately. Several theories on motivation have been developed. These theories can be divided into **content theories**, which ask what motivates an individual to behave and **process theories**, which are concerned with how to motivate an individual. Among the content theories we will discuss are Maslow's hierarchy of needs model, Herzberg's two-factor theory of motivation, and McGregor's Theory X and Theory Y. We will then look at two of the most widely used process theories: expectancy theory and goal-setting.

CONTENT THEORIES

Maslow's Hierarchy of Needs.   Maslow's model suggests that people have different levels of needs, and that they satisfy needs on lower levels before moving to higher levels. The first level is the basic physiological needs which are satisfied by the employee's cash wages. Once the salesforce becomes content at this level, they become concerned with safety and security needs. Retailers can satisfy these needs with such benefits as patrolled parking areas. The third level of needs, that of belongingness and social needs, can be satisfied with employee or salesperson of the month awards. Retailing in Action 16-3 is an example of how one retailer provides just such a need satisfier. A similar approach can be used for the fourth level of needs, esteem, by providing fancier offices and job titles. The highest need level is self-actualization, or becoming all you can be. Here retailers could provide seminars to help broaden the horizons of salespeople. Maslow's hierarchy can be used by retailers to appeal to the basic needs of their salespeople.

Herzberg's Two-Factor Theory.   Herzberg offers another perspective on motivation. Herzberg states that two factors operate as motivators: hy-

16-3

A Very Special Parking Place

One retailer who has done an outstanding job of recognizing the achievements of its employees is Mervyn's. Not only does the firm honor each employee's birthday, wedding, birth of a child, graduation, or other special event with a card and sign on the employee bulletin board, but it even reserves the parking place nearest the main entrance for its employee of the month.

Mervyn's corporate philosophy stresses that the store's success is the result of team effort. In an effort to reward outstanding contributions of the past month, Mervyn's gives the employee of the month use of a special parking

Illus. 16.4
Mervyn's em-
ployee of the
month has use
of the parking
space nearest
the front door.
Photo by Neils
Neilsen.

place (the one nearest the front door.) This employee award is open to all non-management personnel and is voted on by the department managers based on nominations received from any employee. The award is based on the employee's leadership, enthusiasm, productivity, team contribution, and doing that little something extra for fellow workers and customers.

giene factors and motivators. Hygiene factors are extrinsic to the individual and can cause dissatisfaction but not produce satisfaction. Examples of hygiene factors in a retail setting are pay, verbal praise, and special name badges. Motivators, in contrast, are intrinsic to the individual and include a feeling of self-accomplishment or the desire to excel.

Maslow's and Herzberg's theories about what motivates an individual are quite similar. Herzberg's hygiene factor basically comprises Maslow's two lower levels of need (physiological and safety) and Herzberg's motivators are Maslow's top two levels (esteem and self-actualization). Maslow's third level of need, belonging, can fit into either of Herzberg's two categories.

Theory X and Theory Y.   McGregor divides employers' attitudes into two categories: Theory X and Theory Y. Theory X assumes that employees must be closely supervised and controlled and that economic inducements (salaries and commissions) are the best means of influencing employees to perform. Theory X assumes that employees need to be induced or coerced to work since they are inherently lazy. Theory Y, on the other hand, assumes that employees are self-reliant and enjoy work and can be trusted with authority and responsibility. Over the past decade, many employee groups have foregone wage increases for a share of management. These employee-managed retail stores generally experience increased organizational effectiveness, supporting Maslow's, Herzberg's and McGregor's Theory Y contention that money alone is not a primary motivator.

The problem with content theories is that they do not tell you how to motivate people. Also, these theories don't account for individual differences.

PROCESS THEORIES

Process theories are concerned with how to motivate a salesperson to behave in the retailer's best interest. This discussion will cover two process theories: expectancy and goal setting.

Expectancy Theory.   Expectancy theory addresses the relationship between effort, performance, and organizational outcome. It assumes that the employees understand this relationship and that this understanding influences them to behave in one way or another. More specifically, expectancy theory states that a salesperson's motivation to increase effort on some task depends on whether (1) the salesperson expects that the effort will lead to a sale (performance), (2) the sale will likely lead to a bonus (outcome), and (3) the bonus is desireable (valued). The critical consideration is how much importance the salesperson attaches to the bonus, be it cash, prizes, a promotion, a fancier office, increased job status, better conditions, or a greater sense of achievement.

Expectancy theory appears to provide a logical explanation for answering the question of how to motivate a sales staff. If a salesperson likes to travel and thinks he or she can reach the quota, he or she will work hard to win a trip.

Goal Setting.   Goal setting is a way to achieve the firm's objectives that results in inducing a person to behave in the desired manner. The goals must be attainable; too difficult a goal, such as an increase in sales of 50 percent, will not motivate a salesperson because the chances of achieving this target are slim. Likewise, too easy a goal, like a 1 percent increase, is often demotivating and unchallenging. The time frame is important, too. Too long a time frame is generally unmotivating. Just as you would put off a term paper due in four months, the salesperson will put off a year-long sales goal. A 10 percent increase in yearly sales might be broken down into either the two seasons or twelve months, with changes being made at stated intervals based on market conditions.

Remember, it is the retail manager's job to motivate employees in a manner that yields job satisfaction, low turnover, low absenteeism, and high-performance results.

HUMAN RESOURCE COMPENSATION

As all businesspeople know, human resources are not free. They are expensive, and in retailing their cost typically represents 50 percent of operating expenses. This discussion will not focus on how to control labor expenses, but merely highlight some important facts about compensating human resources.

Compensation is a major variable in attracting, retaining, and motivating human resources. The quality of employees that can be attracted, as salesclerks or executives, is directly proportional to the compensation package offered. The better the human resource, the higher the price. Naturally, other things besides compensation are important to employees, but compensation stands out as the most important aspect in most employees' feelings of job satisfaction. A study by the Hay Group reported that knowledge about the employee benefit program and about pay policies and procedures was more important than any other type of information the employer could give the employee.[12]

It is impossible to retain good employees unless they receive competitive compensation. The retailer needs to realize that if it invests more money in training and developing employees, these employees will increase in value, not only to the retailer, but also to competitors who may try to hire them. Thus, as the retailer invests money to train and develop employees, it must also make a commitment to provide them with more compensation, or the retailer will be training and developing employees for its competitors.

In this book **compensation** includes direct dollar payments (wages, commissions, bonuses) and indirect payments (insurance, vacation time, retirement plans) to the workers. A discussion of compensation packages should also cover collective bargaining with union negotiators, since most lower level retail employees are members of unions. For example, almost 70 percent of all supermarket chains have unionized personnel.[13]

Compensation plans in retailing can have up to three basic components: a fixed component, a variable component, and a fringe benefit component. The **fixed component** typically is composed of some base wage per hour, week, month, or year. The **variable component** is often composed of some bonus that is received if performance warrants it. Salesclerks may be paid a bonus of 10 percent of sales above some established minimum; department managers may receive a bonus based on the profit performance of their department. Workers in restaurants often receive tips, a variable component that the retailer does not control. Finally, a **fringe benefit package** may include such things as health insurance, disability benefits, life insurance, retirement plans, automobiles, and financial counseling.

Each of the three components can help the retailer achieve a different human resource goal. The fixed component helps ensure that employees have a basic source of income to meet their most basic financial obligations. As such, it helps to fulfill the employees' need for safety. The variable component allows the retailer to offer its employees an incentive for higher levels of effort and commitment. As such, it helps to fulfill a need among employees for special recognition in return for high performance. The fringe benefit component allows the retailer to offer employees security and prestige. Retail employees have a need to be protected and cared for when they are faced with difficult times or when they become too old to provide for themselves. Also, certain employees (especially executives) have a need for prestige and status.

The best combination of fixed, variable, and fringe benefits components depends on the person, the job, and the retail organization. There is no set formula. Some people prefer mostly salary, others thrive on bonuses, still others would rather have more pension benefits. Therefore, the compensation package needs to be tailored to the individual. The following discussion will focus on compensation of the salesforce, but the same principles apply to managers.

COMMON TYPES OF COMPENSATION PROGRAMS FOR SALESFORCE

Retail salesforce compensation programs can be conveniently broken into three major types, each with advantages and disadvantages: (1) straight salary, (2) straight commission, and (3) salary plus commission.

Straight Salary.   In a straight salary program, the salesperson receives a fixed salary per time period (usually per week) regardless of the level of sales generated or orders taken. However, over time, if the salesperson does not generate sales or take enough orders, he or she will likely be fired for not performing adequately. If, over time, the salesperson generates more than a proportionate share of sales or fills more than a proportionate number of orders, the retailer will be unable to retain the employee without a raise.

Many small retailers use this compensation method, because they typically assign stock rearranging, merchandise display, and other non-selling duties to their salespeople. If the employees were paid on a commission basis they would spend little or no time on their nonselling duties, and the entire organization would suffer. Many promotional and price-oriented chain stores whose salespeople are merely order-takers use the straight salary method because the salesperson is not much of a factor in generating sales. Most clerks and cashiers, as well as other lower-level retail personnel are usually paid straight salaries.

The salesperson may find straight salary attractive because it offers income security or unattractive because it gives little incentive for extraordinary effort and performance. For this method to be effective, it must be combined with a periodic evaluation so that superior salespeople can be identified and singled out for higher salaries.

Straight Commission.   Income of some salespeople is limited to a percentage commission on each sale they generate. The commission could be the same percentage on all merchandise or it could vary depending on the profitability of the item. Retail salespeople working on a straight commission typically receive commissions of 2 to 9 percent of the selling price.

The straight commission plan provides substantial incentive for retail salespeople to generate sales. But when the general business climate is poor, retail salespeople may not be able to generate enough income to meet their basic needs (mortgage payment, auto payment, food expenses). For that reason, most retailers slightly modify the straight commission plan to allow the salesperson to draw wages against future commissions up to some specified amount per week. For instance, the employee may be able to draw $200 per week, which will be paid back with future commissions.

In this plan, quotas must be established. Developing the quota-based commission plan involves four steps:

1. Determining the department's or store's quota for a given period. This is usually based on past sales, with adjustments for changed conditions and for seasonal fluctuations. If $5,000 has been the average weekly sales in the past, this figure may be used as the quota. To be a sales stimulus, the quota should remain within the reach of practically all the salespeople. Yet it cannot be too low or everyone will reach it without much effort.

2. Establishing a base salary. Base salary is usually determined on the basis of the past wage/cost ratio; that is, if the ratio in the past had been about 9 percent, the base salary might be established at 9 percent of the quota; that is $450 on a $5,000 quota.

3. Setting the commission rate for sales in excess of the quota. In

practice, this commission rate is usually set considerably below the store's average wage cost, frequently about 3 percent.

4. Deciding whether each time period involves a fresh start (noncumulative plans) or whether salespeople who fail to make their quota in one period have to fill the deficiency before becoming eligible for a bonus in the next period (cumulative plans). This type of plan tends to discourage employees who, for reasons beyond their control, fail to reach quota two periods in a row. Most plans today are noncumulative.[14]

A major problem with the straight commission plan is that it may provide the retail salesperson with too much incentive to sell. The straight-commission employee may use pressure tactics to close sales, hurting the retailer's image and long-run sales performance. Also, the employee may not be willing to perform other duties such as helping customers with returned merchandise or setting up displays, because compensation is paid to sell and not to handle customer complaints or displays.

Generally, sales personnel for high-price merchandise such as automobiles, real estate, jewelry, and furniture, as well as those sales personnel who have to prospect or seek out potential customers (e.g., insurance and door to door salespeople), are paid straight commission.

Salary Plus Commission.   Sometimes a salesperson is paid a fixed salary per time period plus a percentage commission on all sales or on all sales over an established quota. The fixed salary is lower than that of the salesperson working on a straight salary plan, but the commission struc-

Illus. 16.5

A commission plan provides substantial incentive for retail salespeople to generate sales.

ture gives the salesperson the potential to earn more than the straight salary plan. In fact, most salespeople on the salary plus commission program earn more than their counterparts on a straight salary program.

This plan gives employees a stable base income—and thus incentive to perform nonselling tasks—but it also encourages and rewards superior effort. It's a good compromise between the straight salary and the straight commission programs. In many cases, top management receives a salary and a bonus based on overall store or department performance.

SUPPLEMENTAL BENEFITS

Retail employees, in addition to receiving regular wages (salary, commission, or both) also can receive three types of supplementary benefits: employee discounts, insurance and retirement benefits, and PMs or spiffs.

Employee Discounts.   Almost all retailers offer their salespeople discounts on merchandise they purchase for themselves or their immediate family. About the only line of trade where these discounts are not offered is grocery retailing. This is because grocery retailers operate on relatively thin gross margins. In other lines of retail trade the discounts range from 10 to 40 percent.

Insurance And Retirement Benefits.   Historically, retail salespeople were not provided any insurance or retirement benefits. In some situations this is still the case; however, many retailers are providing their salespeople with either free or low-cost group health and life insurance. Others are making profit-sharing, stock ownership, and retirement programs available to long-tenure salespeople. These benefits amount to between $50 and $90 a month per salesclerk.

Child Care.   In an effort to attract employees from two-income families, some United States businesses have started to provide child care for employees during working hours. While most retailers do not yet provide child care for their employees, experts agree that it will be a necessity in the 1990s.[15]

PM.   A final type of supplementary benefit available to salespeople is the PM, which stands for *push money, prize money*, or *premium merchandise*; in retailing it is commonly called *spiffing*.[16] The PM is paid to the salesperson in addition to the base salary and regular commissions. It is said to encourage additional selling effort on particular items or merchandise lines.

PMs can be sponsored by either the retailer or the supplier. A retailer may give a PM in order to get salespeople to sell old or slow-moving merchandise. The salesperson who sells the most may win a trip to Hawaii or some other prize. Or possibly everyone who sells an established quantity of merchandise may get a prize or premium. Or the retailer may simply offer a $10 bonus for the sale of a specific product; e.g., a dining table. Suppliers may offer PMs to retail salespeople for selling the top-of-the line or most profitable items in the suppliers' product mix. These supplier-offered PMs are common in the appliance, furniture, jewelry, and floor covering lines.

Occasionally there may be a conflict between the supplier and retailer over PMs. This conflict arises because the supplier may be offering the retailer's salespeople an incentive to push an item or merchandise line that may not be the most profitable line for the retailer or best for the customer. Some retailers prefer to keep all PMs for themselves, since they believe they are already paying a fair wage to their salespeople.

COMPENSATION PLAN REQUIREMENTS

Regardless of what method a retailer uses in compensating its employees, the method should meet the following general requirements:

1. *Fairness.* The plan should not favor one group or division over any other group or division or enable such a group to gather a disproportionate amount of reward. It must also keep wage costs under control so that they do not put the store at a competitive disadvantage.
2. *Adequacy.* The level of compensation should enable the employee to maintain job satisfaction and a standard of living commensurate with position.
3. *Prompt and regular payments.* Payments should be made on time and in accordance with the agreement between employer and employee. In incentive plans, greater stimulation is provided when reward closely follows the accomplishment.
4. *Customer interest.* The plan should not reward any actions by an employee that could result in customer ill-will.
5. *Simplicity.* The plan must be easy to understand so as to prevent any misunderstanding or bad feeling. This should also enable management to minimize the man-hours needed to determine compensation levels.
6. *Balance.* Pay, supplemental benefits, and other rewards must provide a reasonable total reward package.
7. *Security.* The plan must fulfill the employee's security needs.
8. *Cost-effectiveness.* The plan must not result in excessive payments given the retailer's financial condition.

While none of the three plans discussed satisfies all of these requirements to the maximum level, awareness of these requirements will help the retailer to select the best plan given individual circumstances. It is not uncommon for the same retailer to use more than one plan in the same store, as different divisions or departments have different needs.

JOB ENRICHMENT

A type of planned program for enhancing job characteristics is job enrichment. **Job enrichment** is the process of enhancing core job characteristics for the purpose of increasing worker motivation, productivity, and satisfaction. According to Hackman and Oldham, there are five core job characteristics which should be increased:

1. Skill variety: The degree to which an employee can use different skills and talents.
2. Task identity: The degree to which a job requires the completion of a whole assignment that has a visible outcome.
3. Task significance: The degree to which the job impacts on other employees.
4. Autonomy: The degree to which the employee has freedom, independence, and discretion in achieving the outcome.
5. Job feedback: The degree to which the employee receives information about the effectiveness of his or her performance.[17]

Job enrichment programs have their roots in Maslow's need hierarchy theory and Herzberg's motivation-hygiene theory. These theories suggested that job factors themselves—such as job challenge, independence, and responsibility—are powerful motivators.

Retail management has long recognized that paying attention to job descriptions, work scheduling, job sharing, and employee input will have a positive effect on employee productivity and satisfaction.

ORGANIZING HUMAN RESOURCES

An owner-manager of a retail organization cannot merely plan for and hire human resources and then let them run loose. Rather, human resources need to be organized to work efficiently toward the organization's objectives and goals. This requires an organization structure.

An **organization structure** is an arrangement of human resources in terms of lines of authority and responsibility. There are, of course, formal and informal organization structures. The **formal organization structure** represents the way employees *should* behave in terms of lines of authority and responsibility. The **informal organization structure** depicts how the employees within the retail organization *actually* behave in terms of lines of authority and responsibility. All retail enterprises have both formal and informal organization structures—and both are useful.

ORGANIZING MODES

Retailers tend to organize their human resources around three modes: functions, merchandise line, and geography. Organizing around function involves delineating the functions the retailer performs (buying, selling, transporting, storing) and structuring the human resources so that there are specific tasks, responsibilities, and lines of authority for the performance of the functions. Organizing around merchandise lines would involve a similar process. What are the major merchandise lines to be handled (produce, meats, etc.)? How should the human resources be structured to perform tasks related to each of the lines? What are appropriate levels of responsibility and authority? To organize around geography one might ask: What are the major geographic areas in which tasks need to be performed? Which human resources should perform these tasks in each geographic area?

WHICH MODE?

How does one decide which mode is best for a specific retail enterprise? The answers to three questions will help answer this fundamental question.

1. What is the target market?
2. Where do decisions need to be made?
3. What is best for employees?

Target Market.   All retail organizations serve certain markets. The customers in these markets provide the transactions that make the retailer profitable or unprofitable. Whether human resources are organized around functions, merchandise, or geography, the human resources ultimately have to be concerned with retaining present customers and attracting new customers to the retail enterprise. The retailer must carefully define its target market in order to organize human resources in a way that is customer-oriented.

Decision-Making.   Where will most of the decisions in the organization be made? In a 200-unit women's apparel chain with units spread over 30 states, most decisions will probably be made at the local or regional level. Such a retailer might organize around geographic regions. On the other hand, decision making in a local department store may center on departments and merchandise lines. Such a store might organize around merchandise lines. A retailer whose decisions most often center on functions might organize around functions.

Employees.   Which organizing mode would be best for employee morale and productivity, thus protecting the retailer's investment in human resources? Assume that a local sporting goods retailer is growing rapidly and expects to open five stores in nearby cities over the next three years. If this retailer is organized around merchandise lines, then it may not be developing its human resources so that middle managers (merchandise managers) can become store managers in the near future. This retailer needs to develop a group of managers who understand all of the functions within the retail enterprise. A merchandise line organization may not be its best organization structure.

Or consider a retailer that divides its salesclerk function into greeting customers, assisting customers, persuading customers, and collecting payment from customers. If a separate clerk was employed for each sub-function, the practical problems of employee boredom and morale would block any theoretical productivity gains.

ORGANIZING AROUND FUNCTIONS

Regardless of how retailers organize around functions, there are basic tasks that need to be performed in retailing. For example, assume you are the owner/manager of a local hardware store. In your organization you may formally recognize only one function—to manage the store. In principle, however, you have as many tasks and related functions to perform as some of the largest retail organizations in the world.

Illustrations will be provided of one-, two-, three-, four-, and five-function retail organization structures. There is a direct correlation between the size of the retailer and the number of functions formally recognized in the organization structure.

One-Function Organization.   Exhibit 16.3 shows a typical organizational structure for a small, single-unit retailer. The two- to four-employee hardware store, record store, drugstore, gasoline station, or floral shop are good examples of the one-function retail organization. As illustrated in Exhibit 16.3, these organizations are headed by a store owner or manager, who is most often the same person. Reporting directly to the manager/owner is a head salesperson; this reflects the fact that the major function in this type of retail organization is to sell merchandise. Reporting to the head salesperson are two employees, labeled the second and third salespeople (obviously, there could be more). Almost all small retail enterprises initially organize around the selling function.

In a typical one-function retail organization, the selling function appears to be dominant and pervasive. This is somewhat misleading, though, because all retail organizations, regardless of size, must perform the same basic tasks and jobs. If we were to examine the duties assigned to each of the individuals in a basic one-function retail organization, we would see this more clearly. Refer to Exhibit 16.3 to examine the duties of each employee.

Two-Function Organization.   As retail organizations grow, they usually find that the basic one-function organization structure has become obsolete. With an increase in size, a modest degree of specialization can be obtained by establishing a two-function organization structure. Typically,

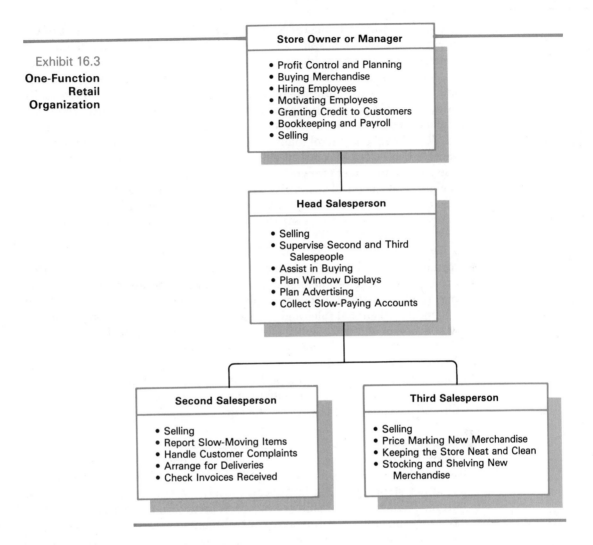

Exhibit 16.3
**One-Function
Retail
Organization**

Store Owner or Manager

- Profit Control and Planning
- Buying Merchandise
- Hiring Employees
- Motivating Employees
- Granting Credit to Customers
- Bookkeeping and Payroll
- Selling

Head Salesperson

- Selling
- Supervise Second and Third Salespeople
- Assist in Buying
- Plan Window Displays
- Plan Advertising
- Collect Slow-Paying Accounts

Second Salesperson

- Selling
- Report Slow-Moving Items
- Handle Customer Complaints
- Arrange for Deliveries
- Check Invoices Received

Third Salesperson

- Selling
- Price Marking New Merchandise
- Keeping the Store Neat and Clean
- Stocking and Shelving New Merchandise

the two functions that are formally delineated are merchandising and operations.

Each function is handled by units headed by managers. Reporting to both the merchandise and operations manager are a set of subordinates, each of whom is assigned certain duties. In general, the merchandise manager is responsible for all activities related to the buying and selling of merchandise, and the operations manager is responsible for activities related to maintaining the store in good working order (paying utility bills and purchasing display units) and serving customers (delivery and stocking merchandise). With the two-function organization, the owner/manager still retains primary responsibility for profit control and planning but probably has some assistants to help with record keeping.

Three-Function Organization.   As the retailer grows, the amount of paperwork and record keeping grows more than proportionately. Tighter financial controls are needed as the number of employees grows, because the opportunity for embezzlement and theft of merchandise grows rapidly. It is not surprising, therefore, that the next function to be formally added to most retail enterprises is financial control, performed under the supervision of the financial control manager.

The financial control manager relieves the owner/general manager of much of the work associated with profit planning and control; however, the general manager or owner is still responsible for the overall profit performance of the retail enterprise. By delegating some authority to a financial control manager, the general manager/owner will have more time to concentrate on long-range strategic planning and growth goals.

Four-Function Organization.   When retailers become large enough to formalize a fourth function in their organization structure, it is most often promotion. Large retailers spend a lot of money on promotion (advertising, public relations, window displays). A local department store doing $10 million in annual sales and spending $3\frac{1}{2}$ percent of sales on promotion would be spending $350,000 annually. Such an expenditure might warrant the addition of a promotion manager to the organization structure. The four functions—financial control, merchandise, operations, and promotions—are now each being performed by separate units, with each unit headed by a manager. The four managers, all with equal status, report directly to the owner or general manager.

Complex Structures.   Our preceding discussion has intentionally been simplistic to allow you to visualize how retail enterprises change their organization structures as they grow. Exhibit 16.4 presents a complex organization structure for a large, corporately owned, general merchandise store. The skeleton of this organization structure is the basic four-function organization: the financial control manager, merchandise manager, promotion manager, and operations manager head the four functions and each reports to the general manager. At this point, however, the organization becomes more complex.

The general manager is not the owner, because we are dealing with a corporately owned organization; the stockholders are the owners. Between the stockholders and the general manager are a board of directors, president, and vice president. The president and vice president concentrate on strategic and administrative planning matters, with a staff to assist and advise. The president's staff includes an executive secretary, a legal counselor, and a treasurer. The vice president has an executive secretary, research director, and director of planning.

There is also complexity in the number of subordinates reporting to each of the four functional managers. The reality of a retail organization is even more complex than Exhibit 16.4 shows. For example, the accounts

Exhibit 16.4
Complex Organization for a Large, Corporate-Owned, General-Merchandise Store

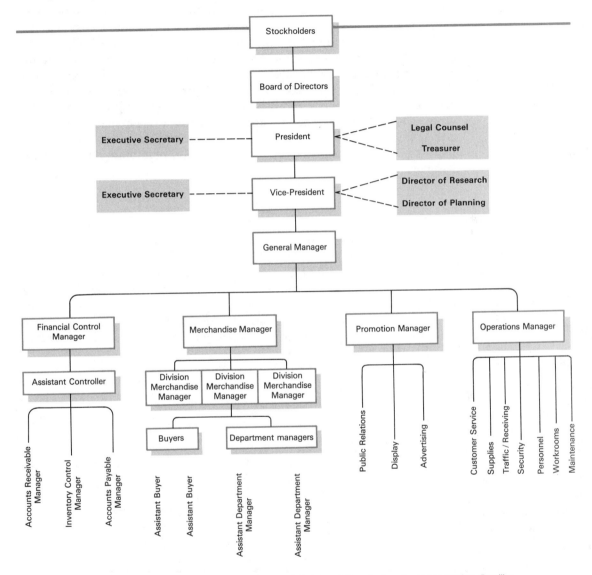

SOURCE: Parts of this exhibit are adapted from Paul M. Mazur, *Principles of Organization Applied to Modern Retailing* (New York: Harper, 1927), frontispiece.

payable manager who reports to the assistant controller has a staff—Sears has more than a hundred accounts-payable clerks. And Exhibit 16.4 shows the subordinates for only one division merchandise manager, whereas each would have a number of buyers and department managers reporting to her.

ORGANIZING AROUND MERCHANDISE

Retailers who offer a wide variety and assortment of goods sometimes organize their enterprise around the merchandise categories they handle. By organizing around distinct merchandise categories, the retailer is recognizing that separate merchandise categories require unique managerial skills, and that these skills are more crucial than skills in managing specific functions. Exhibit 16.5 shows a basic, merchandise oriented, retail organization for a home improvement center. Reporting directly to the store owner or general manager are a lawn and garden manager, a lumber and building materials manager, a paint and wall covering manager, a hand and power tool manager, and a hardware, plumbing, and electrical supplies manager.

ORGANIZING AROUND LOCATION

A retail enterprise that has a large number of stores spread over a broad geographic area will often find it advantageous to structure its organization around geographic locations. It does this in order to be able to quickly address operating problems on a regional or local level. Having good managerial talent in each region, with the appropriate amount of responsibility and authority, means that decisions can be made more rapidly. The basic, location oriented retail organization structure is shown in Exhibit 16.6.

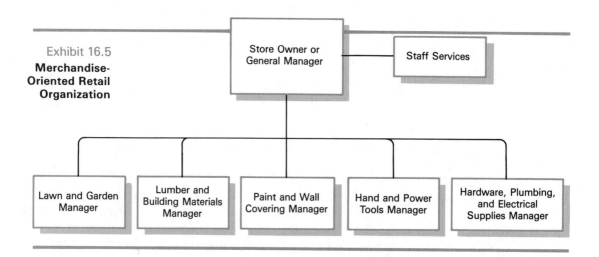

Exhibit 16.5
Merchandise-Oriented Retail Organization

Store Owner or General Manager — Staff Services

Lawn and Garden Manager | Lumber and Building Materials Manager | Paint and Wall Covering Manager | Hand and Power Tools Manager | Hardware, Plumbing, and Electrical Supplies Manager

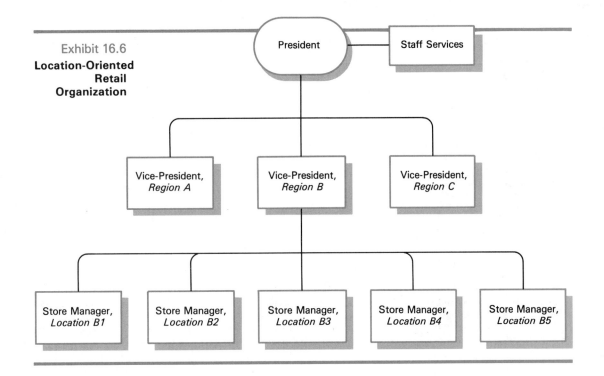

Exhibit 16.6
**Location-Oriented
Retail
Organization**

MULTI-MODE ORGANIZATIONS

Retailers need not only organize around a single mode—functions, locations, or merchandise categories—but may organize their human resources around several modes. Two examples are the functional-location organization structure and the locational-merchandise organization structure. These two examples are depicted in Exhibit 16.7 and Exhibit 16.8.

BRANCH-STORE ORGANIZATION

When a single-unit retailer decides to add a second store in the same city, it typically refers to this as a branch store. The first several stores usually present coordination and control problems. There is no best way to handle these problems in terms of organization structure, but several alternatives are available. Duncan, Hollander, and Savitt call these alternatives the *brood hen and chick organization*, the *separate store plan*, and the *equal store structure*.[18]

Brood Hen and Chick.   When a retailer first begins to expand by opening new stores, and when these new stores are substantially smaller than

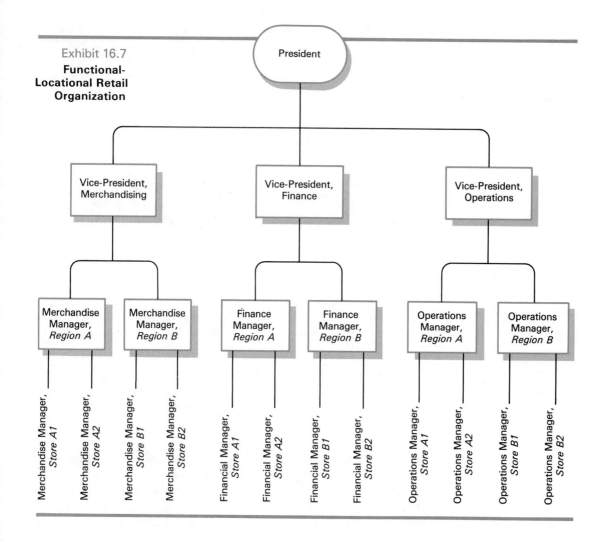

Exhibit 16.7
**Functional-
Locational Retail
Organization**

the parent store, the brood hen and chick plan is often followed. In principle, the parent store operates the branch. Each key executive at the parent store performs or supervises the functions of related personnel in the
branch. For example, the financial control manager of the parent store is
also the controller of branch operations.

Separate Store.   If too many branches are added or if the branch becomes too large, the workload on the executives at the parent store will
become too heavy. At this point, the retailer may create a separate management group and staff for the branch. However, if each branch has its
own management group and staff, there may easily be duplication of efforts and inefficient use of human resources.

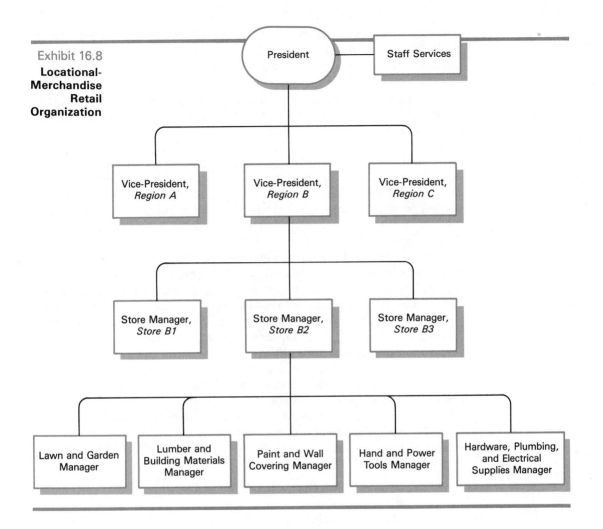

Exhibit 16.8
Locational-Merchandise Retail Organization

Equal Store.   Under this plan, the management group and staff at head-quarters treat all stores as equal in terms of organizational status. The first store is not given special treatment or attention merely because it was the parent. The major problem with this plan is that many of the unique problems of the individual stores cannot be given special attention, because most decisions are centralized and made at headquarters.

CHAIN STORE ORGANIZATIONS

Most of the concepts already discussed apply to chain store organizations. Chains that have many outlets have problems of coordination, and control becomes more crucial. However, there is not a precise pattern for organizing chain store enterprises. The structure developed by a particular chain depends on the organizational philosophies of top management, merchandise lines carried, and whether the chain is national, regional, or local.

In organizing chain store enterprises, two special problems should be considered: how to coordinate and control decisions, and how to separate buying and selling.

Coordination and Control.   The central problem in organizing chain store organizations is one of coordination and control of individual stores. In fact, what we want to do with the organization structure is to create a system in which a network of stores, each with human and economic resources, will work smoothly. As the chain store grows in size, this becomes a more difficult feat.

Most chain stores have an extremely centralized organization structure in which all major decisions for all stores are made at chain headquarters. In short, the store managers merely make sure that policies, procedures, and directives from headquarters are followed. The system becomes a bureaucracy, with store managers responding to memos from headquarters and filling out numerous reports (daily, weekly, monthly) to keep headquarters informed of the store's performance. Obviously, chain stores vary in the degree to which they are centralized. But all have to be more centralized than decentralized in order to cope with the major problems of coordination and control.

In order to facilitate coordination and control in a chain store enterprise, the central management will often have a large number of staff personnel who are specialists in various functional decisions. Staff personnel could include:

- Consumer research specialists
- Merchandise statistics specialists
- Real estate specialists
- Legal counselors
- Public relations specialists
- Tax planning specialists
- Pension plan specialists
- Consumer advocate advisors

Obviously, only chain store enterprises, with their considerable size and complexity, can justify this degree of management specialization and investment in human resources.

Buying and Selling.   The second major problem in designing chain store organization structures is whether to separate buying and selling. In other words, should buying be totally centralized, with headquarters buying all the merchandise for all the stores, while the stores are responsible for selling the merchandise? By centralizing all buying, the chain store can purchase in large quantities and obtain significant buying economies. The problem with this approach is that all stores get a standard merchandise mix that will not be tailored to the trading area of each store. This is obviously less of a problem for supermarkets than for fashion apparel chains. But in either situation, it is a problem.

Some chain store organizations have responded to this problem by allowing local stores to purchase up to a certain percentage (say, 20 percent) of their own merchandise. This gives each store, regardless of location, a core of standard merchandise, but it allows some tailoring of the merchandise mix to local demands and preferences. The major problem is that as each local store is allowed to buy a greater percentage of its own merchandise, the presentation of a consistent image for the chain's stores becomes increasingly difficult. For example, a person who generally shops at a chain store in Georgia may not recognize the chain's store in Michigan.

It is still the dominant industry practice in chain store retailing to centralize decisions, doing 100 percent of the buying at headquarters and most of the selling on a local level. Any selling at headquarters relates to designing or placing national or regional advertisements and occasionally managing local advertising.

Ownership Groups.   Ownership groups are retail enterprises that have purchased previously independent retailers or other retail chains. The ownership group allows individual stores to maintain their prior image and management and merchandising procedures. Any changes that are made typically relate to centralizing certain staff services, such as legal services or long-range planning. Examples of ownership groups are Campeau Corporation U.S., Carter Hawley Hale Stores, May Company, Cities Stores Company, Dayton-Hudson Corporation, and Mercantile Stores Company. Campeau Corporation, in addition to being one of the largest shopping center developers in North America, owns Abraham & Straus, Lazarus, Bloomingdale's, Burdine's, The Bon, Stern's, Rich's, Maas Brothers, Jordan Marsh, and Goldsmith's.

Ownership groups, as opposed to chain store organizations, allow their stores to be relatively autonomous. One important area in which they are not autonomous is expansion—opening new outlets, adding additional space, or remodeling. All positive cash flow goes to headquarters and the top management of the ownership group allocates capital back to the respective divisions according to need and long-range plans that each division has developed in consultation with the ownership group. Some divisions will receive more financial capital than they generated, and others less. This is because some divisions, based upon their location, image, or strategic advantage, will be better positioned for profitable growth opportunities. This is why it was such a major news item in the mid-1980s when Federated's top management decided to let Bloomingdale's expand into Foley's Texas market. Federated based its decision on the facts that with 11 major department store chains operating in Texas, and with

Bloomingdale's and Foley's projecting different images, there was room for both operations. Since then, Campeau Corporation has acquired Federated and sold Foley's to the May Company.

SUMMARY

Our discussion of human resource planning and management focused on five major dimensions: planning for human resources, human resource acquisition, training and development, human resource compensation, and organizing human resources.

To properly plan for human resources, the retailer should first identify the myriad tasks that need to be performed. A useful frame of reference is the eight basic marketing functions. Which functions, and how much of each, does the retailer desire to perform? Each function can then be broken into tasks, and the tasks into jobs.

In long-range planning, the retailer should carefully examine its projected speed of growth and the predictability of this growth. It should also carefully examine its plans to diversify geographically or by line of trade. Finally, it should conduct a human resource audit. In short-run human resource planning, the retail executive should attempt to forecast weekly, monthly, or seasonal swings in sales activity and adjust human resources appropriately.

Human resources acquisition occurs in a competitive labor market. There are many available sources of applicants; the more common include: walk-ins, employment agencies, schools and colleges, former employees, advertising, and recommendations from existing employees. Once the applicants are obtained, they must be properly screened. We suggested a five-step screening process: application, personal interview, testing, reference check, and physical examination. We then explored several myths about employee honesty.

Expenditures on training and development are an attempt by the retailer to increase the productivity of human resources. These programs are on-going: the employees' responsibilities first become specific (the buyer), then increase in breadth (the store manager).

The employee's performance should be subjected to an ongoing, formal systematic review process. This process will enable the employer to make better decisions concerning wage increases, promotions, transfers, or improvement in job skills.

Employee motivation is also a topic of great importance. Two schools of thought, the content models and the process models, were discussed. While the content models are older, retailers have made more use of the process models in that they have tried to link together the task, outcome, and reward.

Compensation is crucial to attracting, retaining, and motivating retail employees. A good compensation program includes a fixed component to provide income, a variable component to motivate employees, and a fringe benefit component to provide security and prestige. Special attention was paid to the advantages and disadvantages of the three types of compensation plans: straight salary, straight commission, and salary plus commission.

Job enrichment is the process of increasing the skill variety, task identity, task significance, autonomy, and feedback of a job in an effort to improve motivation, productivity, and satisfaction.

Retailers can organize their enterprises around functions, merchandise lines, or geographic location. Some large retail enterprises organize around more than one. In deciding which way to organize, the retailer should ask, What is my target market? Where do decisions need to be made? and What is best for my employees?

We discussed alternatives for organizing branch stores, including the brood hen and chick organization, the separate store plan, and the equal store structure. We also commented on chain store organization and ownership groups.

QUESTIONS FOR DISCUSSION

1. What are the various methods of compensating retail employees?
2. Discuss the alternative methods for organizing branch stores.
3. Can retailers increase the productivity of their employees if they pay them higher wages? Explain your answer.
4. How can better organization of human resources increase labor productivity?
5. What are the major problems in centralizing the buying function in a chain organization?
6. What are the advantages and disadvantages of paying salespeople in a furniture store strictly on a commission basis?
7. Are the problems facing a personnel manager in a retail institution different from the problems confronting a personnel manager in a factory? How?
8. Why is it so important for a retailer to screen an applicant before hiring the individual?
9. If you were a personnel director for a large department store chain, what traits or characteristics would you look for in a college senior under consideration for your management training program?
10. Compare the organization needs of a department store chain and a local bookstore.
11. The annual turnover rate in retailing is about 20 percent. Is this good or bad?

12. Why must training be an on-going operation?
13. Obtain an employment application form from a local retailer. What questions are asked on this form? Why do you think these questions are asked?
14. Find out from your campus placement office which retailers interview college students on campus. What do these retailers have in common? Write to each company for a copy of its annual report to stockholders. Which companies look like the type you might like to work for when you graduate?
15. Interview a friend or acquaintance that works for a retailer. How do the formal and informal organizations vary? In other words, are there people who have more influence than their position on the organization chart would suggest? What lines of communication have developed outside the formal organization chart?

SUGGESTED READINGS

"Athlete's Foot Steps on Theft; Pencil-and-Paper Honesty Cuts Shrinkage." *Chain Store Age Executive* (July 1987): 103 & 106.

Fisher, Wayne H. "Bud," The Cautious Approach To Firing." *Progressive Grocer* (May 1985): 159-162.

Good, Linda K., Grovalynn F. Sisler, and James W. Gentry. "Antecedents of Turnover Intentions Among Retail Management Personnel." *Journal of Retailing* (Fall 1988): 295-314.

Hampton, Ron, Alan J. Dubinsky, and Steven J. Skinner, "A Model of Sales Supervisor Leadership Behavior and Retail Salespeople's Job-Related Outcomes." *Journal of the Academy of Marketing Science* (Fall 1986): 33-43.

Hollinger, Richard C., and John P. Clark, *Theft By Employees*. Lexington, MA: Lexington Books, 1983.

Jacoby, Sanford M., "Employee Attitude Testing at Sears, Roebuck and Company, 1938-1960." *Business History Review* (Winter 1986): 602.

James, Donald L., Philipp A. Stoeberl, and Marc J. Schniederjans, "Copy Strategies for Managing: The Ineffective Subordinate in Retailing Management." *Akron Business and Economic Review* (Fall 1986): 7-23.

"Relaxing Hiring Procedures Often Proves Costly for Retailers." *Discount Store News* (January 19, 1987): 11.

"Retailers Slow to Develop AIDS Policies: Some Fear Customer Reaction, But Time to Prepare For Crisis is Now." *Chain Store Age Executive* (June 1988): 27-29.

ENDNOTES

1. "Odds and Ends," *Wall Street Journal*, 5 June 1986, p. 29.
2. Mack A. Player, *Federal Law of Employment Discrimination* (St. Paul: West Publishing, 1976), 116.

3. Robert F. Hartley, "The Weighted Application Blank Can Improve Retail Employee Selection," *Journal of Retailing* (Spring 1970): 32–42.

4. Myron Gable, Charles J. Hollon, and Frank Dangello, "Predicting Voluntary Managerial Trainee Turnover in a Large Retailing Organization from Information on an Employment Application Blank," *Journal of Retailing* (Winter 1984): 43–63.

5. Jan P. Muczyk, T. H. Mattheiss, and Myron Gable, "Predicting Success of Store Managers: A Force Choice Personality Text Refined by Discriminant Analysis," *Journal of Retailing* (Summer 1974): 44.

6. "Computer Takeover," *Wall Street Journal*, 15 July 1986, p. 1.

7. "Polygraph Restraints," *Wall Street Journal*, 11 January 1989, p. A1.

8. "Uniform Guidelines on Employee Selection Procedures," *Federal Register*: August 25, 1978; and Clifford M. Koen, Jr., "Application Forms: Keep Them Easy and Legal," *Personnel Journal* (May 1984): 26–29.

9. This section is based on "An Ounce of Prevention Can Offer Profit Protection," *Progressive Grocer* (October 1983): 85–88.

10. "Privacy," *Business Week* (March 28, 1988): 61–68.

11. Frederick Ford, "An Analysis of Store Manager Turnover" (Paper presented at the National Retail Merchants Association meeting, New York, 1983).

12. "Tell Me More," *Wall Street Journal*, 9 August 1985, p. 17.

13. "Labor and Productivity," *Progressive Grocer* (August 1981): 134.

14. Delbert J. Duncan, Stanley C. Hollander, and Ronald Savitt, *Modern Retailing Management*, 10th ed. (Homewood, IL: Richard D. Irwin, 1983), 195.

15. Rena Cheskis-Gold, "Child Care: What Parents Want," *American Demographics* (February 1988): 46–47 and Carol Dilks and Nancy L. Croft, "Child Care: Your Baby?" *Nation's Business* (December 1986): 16–24.

16. Dale Varble and L. E. Bergerson, "The Use and Facets of PMs—A Survey of Retailers," *Journal of Retailing*, (Winter 1972–73), 40–47.

17. J. Richard Hackman and Greg R. Oldham, *Work Redesign* (Reading, MA: Addison-Wesley, 1980), 77–80.

18. Delbert J. Duncan, Stanley C. Hollander, and Ronald Savitt, *Modern Retailing Management*, 10th ed. (Homewood, IL: Richard D. Irwin, 1983), 159–161.

17 Chapter

Retail Information Systems

OVERVIEW

The purpose of this chapter is to illustrate the role of information in retail planning and management. Information plays a role in all types of retail planning and management, and the chapter will show that information and its availability in a useable form is a pervasive force in retail decision making.

Successful retailers have their ideas and strategies quickly imitated by their competitors. Therefore, success in retailing can only come from having a better understanding of the whys and hows of the marketplace. Unless retail decision-makers have all possible relevant information, their decisions might not be successful in today's highly competitive retail environment. Decisions based on the absence of information will cause disaster. Good ideas can, and will, be copied, but a strategy based on a detailed understanding of the environment can produce high-performance results before competition is able to react. This chapter will focus on how a retailer can use a retail information system (RIS) to gather the necessary knowledge about the marketplace in order that strategic plans can be made and executed. Also, a RIS should be used to monitor existing operations so that they may be modified as necessary.

INTRODUCING THE RIS

A RIS can consist of a store owner regularly reading retail trade association magazines, talking to customers to determine how satisfied they are with merchandise and service, and regularly studying quarterly income statements and balance sheets. Or a RIS can be much more extensive, by using vendor reports, market research, and charge account records. However, we do not wish to define a RIS in terms of what it might be in a typical retail enterprise, but in terms of what it should be in a model retail enterprise; that is, we want to give a normative definition. Thus, a **retail information system (RIS)** will be defined as a blueprint for the continual and periodic systematic collection, analysis, and reporting of relevant data about any past, present, or future developments that could have influenced or already have influenced the retailer's performance. Several prominent features of a RIS are:

1. Both *continual* and *periodic collection* of relevant data should occur. Data should be continually collected on those activities that are always in a state of flux, such as the retailer's financial performance or competitor behavior. Data should be periodically collected when a nonrecurring problem arises, such as a capital budgeting or an inventory productivity problem.

2. The data collection activities should be *systematic* and *relevant*. The world is drowning in data. Retailers must decide what information they need and collect only that information in an orderly fashion.

3. *Analysis* and *reporting* of data are important parts of the RIS. The data cannot merely be dumped on the executive's desk: it must be analyzed and put in a reportable format. A computer tape with 300,000 bits of data is not usable information. Data is not information until it is analyzed and placed in a reportable format that the executive can understand.

4. The data can be about the *past*, *present*, and/or *future*; all of which can be relevant for retail decision making. Most accounting information is historical: it tells where the retailer has been (in the past). However, point of sale (POS) terminals provide data on what is happening now (present), and six-month monetary projections by the Federal Reserve System tell what will likely happen to interest rates in the future.

This is an ideal definition of a RIS, but it is one a retailer should strive for.

One of the most sophisticated retail information systems in use today is the one developed by Dillard's Department Stores. Dillard's goal was to design a system with on-line ability to enter and update data, as well as to inquire at the needed level of detail, about all the firm's operations. The following shows how Dillard's uses this system for planning, tracking, and controlling.

1. *Planning.* Management is able to develop operating and merchandise plans on-line to determine projected net profit. This planning includes historical data from several years prior to the planning period: actual expenses, sales, merchandise levels, turnover rates, markup percent, shrinkage, and ROI. Management planning also includes simulating various environmental change data to test alternative plans.

2. *Tracking.* Actual performance tracking is reported for expenses, sales, merchandise levels, and compared with planned expenses, sales to inventory levels, markup dollar and percent, markdowns, freight expenses, shrinkage, and gross margin dollar and percent. Actual reporting is daily and weekly. Operating expense tracking includes monitoring of payroll, receivables, collections, credit scoring, and even the phone system. As part of its merchandise tracking system, Dillard's uses magnetic tickets to capture the department, description, quantity and price of all sales. Current daily sales are reported by division, department, and store on "flash sales" reports. Orders are placed on-line, instantly updating open-to-buy, or are automatically generated by the inventory system. Receiving discrepancies between orders and receipts are resolved by the receiving system. Invoices are entered on-line and matched to the receipts in batch processing.

3. *Controls.* The register audit system validates the previous day's sales including Dillard's charge card and bankcards. This system processes only the exceptions, so that by 3 p.m. the next day management knows the audited sales for the entire chain and payments on Dillard's accounts. Audited sales data are then passed to billing clerk production, sales and stock, inventory systems, general ledger, manpower planning, merchandise planning, and bankcard receivables. Inventory sales data are analyzed to identify early trends in order to reorder merchandise before unnecessary stock-outs occur, either by repeating the merchandise on-line order and receiving cycles, or by marking down the merchandise through the retail price change system. Merchandise assortment plans are monitored at the department level so that Dillard's can better assess vendor, department, and item profitability. This results in the ability to reduce inventory levels while improving level of service and sales.

Exhibit 17.1 shows a comparative sales report for a specialty chain store. This type of a report enables the chain's management to see which stores may be experiencing sales difficulties and which stores are doing well. As shown in Exhibit 17.1 the chain's total sales for the week were $527,800, up 9.1 percent from the year before. However, since two of the stores were only opened recently, sales for the stores in operation last year were only $494,700 for the week, or up only 2.3 percent over the previous year for the same week.

This chapter will elaborate on what an ideal RIS should look like. It will not, however, discuss the many procedures for the systematic collection and analysis of data. These topics are best covered in many of the fine books on marketing research, accounting and management information systems.

THE NEED FOR INFORMATION

Previous chapters have demonstrated repeatedly the need managers of retail business have for information. The fact can clearly be seen by referring to the retail planning and management model, reproduced here as Exhibit 17.2. As this model clearly shows, (1) strategic planning can only be accomplished after all information on the environment is obtained; (2) operations management relies on information concerning the efficient use of resources and (3) administrative management needs information on acquiring, maintaining, and controlling these resources.

Assume that you are the general manager of a local chain of three apparel stores called "Leslie's." You need to develop a new strategy. Could you develop it without information? Perhaps, but you could develop a better strategy by obtaining information about your competitors, consumers in your trading area, the local economic climate, recent technological developments in retailing, etc. Now place yourself in other decision-making roles—needing to adjust prices, reevaluate your current promotional policy, or borrow additional capital. Making any of these decisions without information would be unwise. In short, whatever retail decisions need to be made can be made better with information.

THE AMOUNT OF INFORMATION

All decision making in retailing can be improved with more information. Unfortunately, however, retail executives cannot usually obtain complete information. Complete or perfect information is extremely expensive or often impossible to obtain, for example, the sales of a competitor. The expense would not only be in terms of direct dollar outlay for the information but also in the time needed to gather and analyze it. This extended period can represent another cost, that of postponing a decision. For example, if you own and operate a Mexican restaurant and you want to open

Exhibit 17.1

XYZ Retailer
Long Island Metro New York Weekly Sales Summary—November 20

	1 Week Ended			4 Weeks Ended			8 Weeks Ended			34 Weeks Ended		
	1989	1988	% Incr	1989	1988	% Incr	1989	1988	% Incr	1989	1988	% Incr
Americana	39.4	45.4	−13.2	152.7	166.5	−8.3	290.1	310.3	−6.5	1364.3	1326.6	2.8
Bayside (7/15/89)	11.8			48.3			87.4			206.8		
Brooklyn Heights	18.8	21.5	−12.6	70.7	79.2	−10.7	127.7	162.9	−21.6	535.0	514.9	−23.0
Cedarhurst	9.9	8.0	23.8	39.2	31.9	22.9	71.9	61.3	17.3	322.4	287.2	12.3
Centereach	22.8	21.9	4.1	84.7	75.5	12.2	151.8	144.6	5.0	614.2	618.1	−.6
Commack	26.0	23.7	9.7	92.9	82.2	13.0	169.4	160.9	5.3	703.7	702.4	.2
Forest Hills	27.6	18.4	50.0	98.7	75.8	30.2	180.8	152.3	18.7	712.2	670.8	6.2
Green Acres	31.5	26.3	19.8	122.3	101.9	20.0	219.9	202.2	8.8	898.6	862.7	4.2
Hicksville	26.2	33.4	−21.6	92.5	110.0	−15.9	169.9	208.1	−18.4	766.7	928.4	−17.4
Holbrook	23.3	21.0	11.0	95.5	74.8	27.7	169.1	141.8	19.3	693.2	605.1	14.6
Madison	24.2	25.4	−4.7	99.1	95.3	4.0	174.4	188.3	−7.4	727.8	810.5	−10.2
Riverhead	14.3	11.6	23.3	55.3	43.3	27.7	103.5	87.2	18.7	428.1	377.4	13.4
Roosevelt Field	103.6	104.3	−.7	387.0	365.1	6.0	716.4	704.4	1.7	3001.9	3003.7	−.1
Sands (2/26/89)	21.3			80.7			146.5			633.6		
South Shore Mall	49.1	39.8	23.4	177.0	136.2	30.0	323.1	259.3	24.6	1295.8	1102.0	17.6
Walt Whitman	55.6	59.0	−5.8	209.9	190.3	10.3	382.4	356.6	7.2	1615.1	1576.7	2.4
Wheatley	22.4	23.9	−6.3	87.9	87.2	.8	171.3	172.7	−.8	740.6	729.9	1.5
Total	527.8	483.6	9.1	1994.4	1715.2	16.3	3655.6	3312.9	10.3	15260.0	14116.4	8.1
Comparative	494.7	483.6	2.3	1865.4	1715.2	8.8	3421.7	3312.9	3.3	14281.1	14116.4	1.2

Exhibit 17.2
**Retail Planning
and
Management
Model**

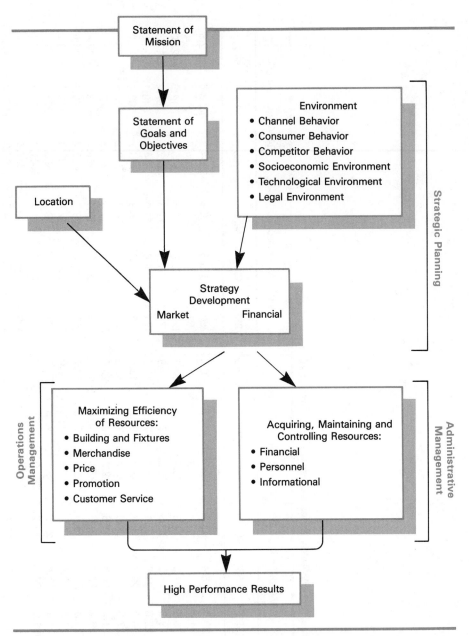

a second restaurant in the same city, you may decide to gather data on the best location. The longer you take to gather the information on the best possible site, the longer you will postpone opening a potentially profitable restaurant. If you wait too long, your competition may open another restaurant or restaurants, which could saturate the proposed market and lower the likelihood that your new restaurant will be profitable.

SOURCES OF RETAIL INFORMATION

The two major sources of retailing information are internal and external. **Internal information** is found within the retailer's records. Retailers generate a wide range of useful information in the normal course of their business (operating or income statements, sales records, credit reports, shipping records, purchasing invoices, inventory records, customer charge account records, personnel records, accounts payable and receivable, and past merchandise budgets). By applying certain statistical and analytical procedures, retailers can generate information on a number of different topics.

One of the newest ways for retailers to make use of internal information is the planogram for use in shelf-space management.[1] Most planograms are produced by the manufacturer for retailers at the manufacturer's expense. Sales information from the store's own scanner data is put into a computer and analyzed until the best design for the retailer's needs emerges. In the ideal situation, retailers benefit because they stock the most lucrative brands and manufacturers benefit because their best-sellers are now rarely out-of-stock. Most planogram programs are sold by one of three firms: Information Resources, which produces Apollo software; Logistics Data Systems which offers the Spaceman system, and Sage Worldwide which offers Accuspace. Exhibit 17.3 is an example of a planogram that a major manufacturer prepared for a supermarket chain. Exhibit 17.3A shows the actual recommendation for shampoo/conditioner area of a supermarket. Exhibit 17.3B is a description of the bottom

Illus. 17.1

Internal information—operating or income statements, sales records, credit reports, shipping records, purchasing invoices, inventory records, customer charge account records, personnel records, accounts payable and receivable and past merchandise budgets—is found within the retailer's records.

Exhibit 17.3A

A Planogram for Shampoo/Conditioners for a Large Supermarket Chain

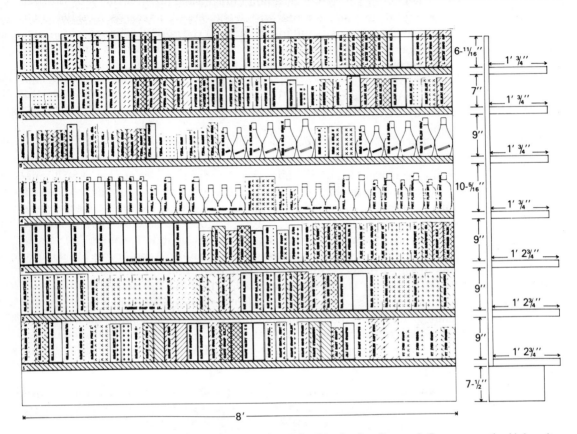

SOURCE: Bert C. McCammon, Jr. and the Distribution Research Program at the University
of Oklahoma, 1988.

shelf's contents. Exhibit 17.3C is the financial recap of the adaptation of such a plan. The final exhibit shows the allocation for shelf space and projected sales by manufacturer.

A retailer serviced by three or four different manufacturers for the same product category may receive three or four different planograms, each slightly different: scanner data is open to interpretation, and manufacturers do favor their own brands. But it really doesn't do a manufacturer any good to mislead retailers on its planogram, since its competition comes from other manufacturers, not retailers. Most major supermakret

Exhibit 17.3B

Bottom Shelf Layout By Items

Bar Code	Name	Manufacturer	# of Facings	# of Units
37824	WELLA BALSAM COND 24.0	Wella	1	4
37826	WELLA BALSAM COND EX BODY 24.0	Wella	1	4
38280	WELLA BALSAM SHAM 24.0	Wella	1	4
38282	WELLA BALSAM CND/SH EX BDY 24.0	Wella	1	4
37813	SUAVE COND REG BALSAM 16.0	Helene Curtis	1	6
37814	SUAVE BLSM PROT XBDY COND 16.0	Helene Curtis	2	12
37815	SUAVE MOIST CON XTRA BODY 16.0	Helene Curtis	2	12
37818	SUAVE X-G COND X-BDY 16.0	Helene Curtis	1	5
38215	SUAVE BLSM PROT SHAMP REG 16.0	Helene Curtis	2	12
38230	SUAVE SHAMP X/BODY BALSAM 16.0	Helene Curtis	2	12
38224	SUAVE DANDRUF SHAM COND 16.0	Helene Curtis	1	6
38225	SUAVE DANDRUF SHAMP REG 16.0	Helene Curtis	1	6
38220	SUAVE SHAM HONEYSUCKLE 16.0	Helene Curtis	1	6
38217	SUAVE SHAMP OILY BALSAM 16.0	Helene Curtis	2	12
38236	SUAVE MOIST SH X BODY 16.0	Helene Curtis	2	12
38228	SUAVE SHAMP FULL BOD NORM 16.0	Helene Curtis	1	6
38227	SUAVE XGNTL XBDY SHAMP 16.0	Helene Curtis	1	6
38234	SUAVE SHAMP GOLDEN 16.0	Helene Curtis	1	6
37816	SUAVE COND STRAWBERRY 16.0	Helene Curtis	1	6
38223	SUAVE STRAWBERRY SHAMP 16.0	Helene Curtis	2	12
33507	J&J BABY SHAMPOO 7.0	J&J	1	18
33508	J&J BABY SHAMPOO 11.0	J&J	1	14
33509	J&J BABY SHAMPOO 15.0	J&J	1	7
33510	CUDDLES BABY SHAM 15.0	P/L	2	14
38205	ST IVES SHAMP ALOE VERA 18.0	St. Ives	1	5
38206	ST IVES HENNA 18.0	St. Ives	1	5
38203	ST IVES SHAMP JOJOBA 18.0	St. Ives	1	5
38208	ST IVES CHAMOMILE 18.0	St. Ives	1	5

and general merchandise chains that can afford to produce their own planograms do so, but they are still interested in seeing the manufacturer-supplied planograms. Exhibit 17.4 is a planogram that Wal-Mart developed itself for irons.

Another source of useful internal information for retailers is shown in Exhibit 17.5. This exhibit shows the actual payroll summary for a 13-week period. A closer look at this exhibit will show that four outlets (Roosevelt, Walt Whitman, S.S.M., and Americana) are all under budget. This could mean that the budget was wrong, or that service at these stores is poor due to a lack of employees. In either case, this is as serious as being over budget.

Exhibit 17.3C
Financial Recap of Recommended Shampoo/Cond. Set

Projected Sales	1141.25	20.379 Per Ft.
Lost Sales	0.00	
Gross Profit	321.96	28.211 % Of Sales
		5.749 Per Ft.
Lost Gross Profit	0.00	
Annual Gross Profit ROII	5.05	0.090 Per Ft.
Direct Product Profit	321.96	28.211 % Of Sales
		5.749 Per Ft.
Annual DPP ROII	5.05	0.090 Per Ft.
Inventory Value	3328.08 Avg.	3954.90 Cap.
Annual Inventory Turns	17.89 "	15.06 "
Days On Hand	20.41 "	24.26 "
Back Room Requirement	0.00 Sq. Ft.	
Items Allocated	194	
Items Unallocated	0	

Exhibit 17.3D
Allocation by Manufacturers for Shelf Space and Projected Sales

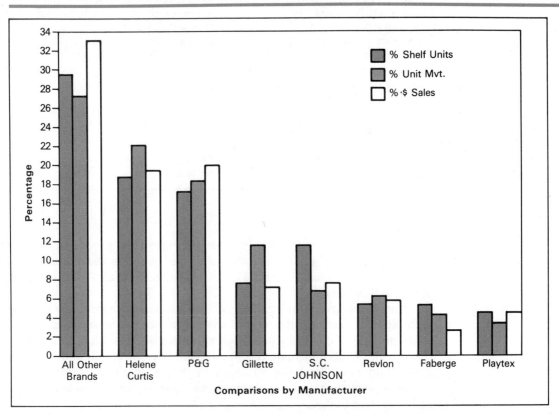

Exhibit 17.4
Planogram

F410AL Black & Decker	＊ 12501 Sunbeam	11411 Sunbeam	F310BD Black & Decker	12256 Sunbeam	11409 Sunbeam

Manufacturer's Display Rack

F363BED Black & Decker	12156 Sunbeam	F392WH Black & Decker	I1400 Proctor Silex	I1309 Proctor Silex	TC502 Rival

Manufacturer's Display Rack

14" Shelf

13"

F410AL Black & Decker Automatic Shut Off Iron	＊ 12501 Sunbeam Monitor Select Steam Iron	11411 Sunbeam Steam/Dry Monitor Iron White	10079 Sunbeam Garment Steamer Gray	WA-111SE Franzus Home/Travel Clothes Steamer

14" Shelf

13"

F310BD Black & Decker Self-Clean II	12156 Sunbeam Spray/Mist/ Shot of Steam Almond	11409 Sunbeam Steam Dry Iron	12256 Sunbeam Comfort Spray Mist Iron	TC502 Rival Travel Iron

14" Shelf

14"

F392WH Black & Decker Light N Easy Spray Steam N Dry Iron	F363BED Black & Decker Light N Easy Steam N Dry Iron	I1400 Proctor Silex Steam N Dry Iron	I1309 Proctor Silex Lightweight Steam Dry Iron (I Facings + I Sideview)

＊ Indicates "Top 300" Item

Exhibit 17.5

XYZ Retailer
Payroll Summary
13 Weeks Ended September 25, 1988

LI/Metro NY

Store	Spvsr	Actual Hours	Budget Hours	Actual Dollars	Budget Dollars	Dollars (Over)/Under Budget	Actual Sales	Act % To Sales	Avg Hrly Rate
Americana	DB	6,120	6,760	31,698	37,047	5,349	547,000	5.79%	5.18
Bayside (6/22/88)	DB	2,605	2,600	13,601	13,601	0	119,400	11.39%	5.22
Brooklyn	DB	4,650	4,810	27,103	28,048	945	191,700	14.14%	5.83
Cedarhurst	DB	2,661	2,340	14,780	13,000	(1,780)	130,700	11.31%	5.55
Centereach	SC	3,496	4,030	18,235	20,501	2,266	237,500	7.68%	5.22
Commack	SC	3,776	4,160	20,750	23,829	3,079	277,800	7.47%	5.50
Forest Hills	DB	4,411	4,160	23,974	22,256	(1,718)	264,600	9.06%	5.44
Green Acres	DB	5,569	5,200	28,498	28,402	(96)	350,200	8.14%	5.12
Hicksville	SC	4,039	5,070	23,205	26,390	3,185	294,600	7.88%	5.75
Holbrook	SC	3,822	3,900	23,041	24,248	1,207	261,900	8.80%	6.03
Madison	DB	4,588	4,680	27,364	28,002	638	266,300	10.28%	5.96
Riverhead	SC	2,669	2,860	14,763	16,192	1,429	173,400	8.51%	5.53
Roosevelt	DB	11,472	14,300	67,280	81,868	14,588	1,168,700	5.76%	5.86
Sands	SC	3,628	3,900	19,761	20,722	961	248,300	7.96%	5.45
S. S. M.	SC	5,455	6,760	27,960	34,710	6,750	516,900	5.41%	5.13
Walt Whitman	SC	6,485	8,190	34,711	43,521	8,810	633,900	5.48%	5.35
Wheatley	DB	4,116	3,965	26,771	26,332	(439)	280,200	9.55%	6.50
Total		79,562	87,685	443,495	488,669	45,174	5,963,100	7.44%	5.57

External information is obtained from sources outside of the firm. This information includes:

1. Published statistics. A vast amount of statistical data is published by a variety of public and private sources. The major public source is the federal government; however, private publishers, such as *Sales and Marketing Management's Survey of Buying Power*, are also included here. Exhibit 17.6 provides a more complete listing of these sources.

2. Standardized retailing information services. Many research agencies compile data on market trends and consumer behavior and sell the data in standardized form to interested retailers. Included here is the *Nielsen Retail Index*, which tracks data on individual brands and their price, market share and promotion. *The Nielsen Retail Index* is based on a sample of 1,600 supermarkets, 750 drugstores, and 150 mass merchandisers.

3. Publicly circulated research reports. These usually appear in business journals or are published by trade associations. Exhibit 17.7 shows a composite income statement for a retailer selling floor covering that is readily available from The American Floor-

Exhibit 17.6

Sources of Retail Information from Publications

Advertising Age	Home Furnishing Daily
American Fabrics and Fashion	Juvenile Merchandising
Auto Merchandising New	Luggage and Leather Goods
Beverage World	Marketing & Media Decisions
Business Week	Mart Magazine
Chain Store Age	Merchandising Week
Clothing and Textiles Research Journal	Modern Jeweler
Clothes	Office Products Dealer
Discount Merchandiser	Office Products News
Distribution	Progressive Grocer
Drug Topics	Retail Advertising Week
Dun's Business Month	Retail Control
DYI Retailing	Retail Technology
Floor Covering Weekly	Sales and Marketing Management
Florist	Sports Merchandiser
Fortune	Stores
Furniture News	Supermarket Business
Hardware Age	Supermarket News
Hardware Merchandiser	Visual Merchandising
Hardware Retailing	Volume Retail Merchandising
Harvard Business Review	Wall Street Journal
	Women's Wear Daily

Exhibit 17.7

Composite Income for Floorcovering Retailers and Various Segments

	All Firms	High Profit Firms	Retail Oriented Firms	Contract Oriented Firms	Sales Volume			
					Under $500,000	$500,000 to $1 Mil	$1 Mil to $2 Mil	Over $2 Mil
Number of Firms Reporting	202	47	137	65	17	53	64	68
Typical Sales Volume ($1,000's)	$1,371.9	$1,129.3	$1,167.7	$2,000.9	$394.2	$741.3	$1,378.3	$3,136.7
Income Statement								
Net Sales	100.0%	100.0%	100.0%	100.0%	100.0%	100.0%	100.0%	100.0%
Cost of Goods Sold	69.8	69.9	68.7	72.0	64.3	68.2	70.3	71.9
Gross Margin	30.2	30.1	31.3	28.0	35.7	31.8	29.7	28.1
Operating Expenses:								
Salaries, Wages & Bonuses	14.0	12.5	13.7	13.1	9.1	12.5	13.4	14.1
Payroll Taxes	1.1	0.9	1.2	1.3	0.7	1.1	1.3	1.0
Employee Benefits	0.7	0.8	0.7	0.7	0.8	0.7	0.8	0.8
Advertising & Sales Promotion	2.1	1.7	2.7	1.2	3.1	2.2	1.8	1.9
Samples	0.5	0.7	0.7	0.4	1.1	0.7	0.6	0.3
Utilities & Telephone	1.0	0.9	1.1	0.8	1.8	1.2	1.1	0.8
Rent or Occupancy Expense	2.7	2.1	3.0	2.2	4.9	3.0	2.4	2.3
Depreciation & Amortization	0.9	0.6	0.9	0.8	1.7	1.3	0.9	0.6
Bad Debt Expense	0.1	0.2	0.1	0.3	0.1	0.2	0.2	0.1
All Other Operating Expenses	4.5	4.1	4.8	4.3	6.5	5.8	4.6	4.0
Total Operating Expenses	27.6	24.5	28.9	25.1	29.8	28.7	27.1	25.9
Operating Profit	2.6	5.6	2.4	2.9	5.9	3.1	2.6	2.2
Other Income	0.4	0.3	0.3	0.4	0.0	0.3	0.5	0.3
Interest Expense	0.5	0.2	0.4	0.6	1.3	0.5	0.3	0.6
Other Expenses	0.0	0.0	0.0	0.0	0.0	0.0	0.0	0.0
Profit Before Taxes	2.5	5.7	2.3	2.7	4.6	2.9	2.8	1.9
Income Taxes	0.5	1.1	0.4	0.5	0.3	0.2	0.6	0.3
Profit After Taxes	2.0%	4.6%	1.9%	2.2%	4.3%	2.7%	2.2%	1.6%
Forecasted Sales Increase ('88 versus '87)	11.6%	11.9%	11.7%	11.1%	26.1%	11.4%	13.2%	10.2%

SOURCE: Reprinted with permission of The American Floorcovering Association.

covering Association. Such information is usually segmented by types of outlets and store size.

THE SCOPE OF A RIS

A retail information system should have a broad scope. Exhibit 17.8 shows a model RIS. You can see that a RIS should have two major subsystems. One subsystem should be reserved for the identification of problems or potential problems confronting the retail enterprise. This subsystem should be designed to continuously compile information on events affecting the retail enterprise. The other subsystem should be dedicated to the solution of recurring or nonrecurring problems that the retailer faces.

An inspection of the RIS in Exhibit 17.8 will show that the **problem identification subsystem** monitors and scans trends in behavioral, environmental, and operating performance areas. In the behavioral area, three patterns are monitored: consumers, channels, and competitors. In the environmental domain, three environments are scanned: legal, socioeconomic, and technological. Finally, in the area of operating performance, asset, revenue, and expense trends are monitored.

The problem solution subsystem can be utilized to obtain information on recurring or nonrecurring problems in strategic planning, administrative management, and operations management. Strategic planning problems relate to mission, goals, and objectives; opportunity analysis; or contingency planning. Administrative management problems involve capital structure and generation, organization structure, human resources, or location analysis. Operations management problems are related to either assets or revenue and expense management.

This chapter will discuss each component of the model RIS, giving you a general understanding of the information requirements of retail decision makers.

THE PROBLEM IDENTIFICATION SUBSYSTEM

The central goal of this problem identification subsystem is to highlight for the retail executive, on a continuing basis, major problems that the retailer is about to encounter or is presently encountering.

BEHAVIORAL TRENDS: MONITORING CONSUMERS

Most retailers scan the behavior of their customers in a casual manner. Small retailers may simply listen to customer complaints or casually converse with regular customers about their needs, wants, and level of satisfaction. This can be quite cost-effective for the small, single-outlet retailer. Other retailers may read magazines such as *Chain Store Age,*

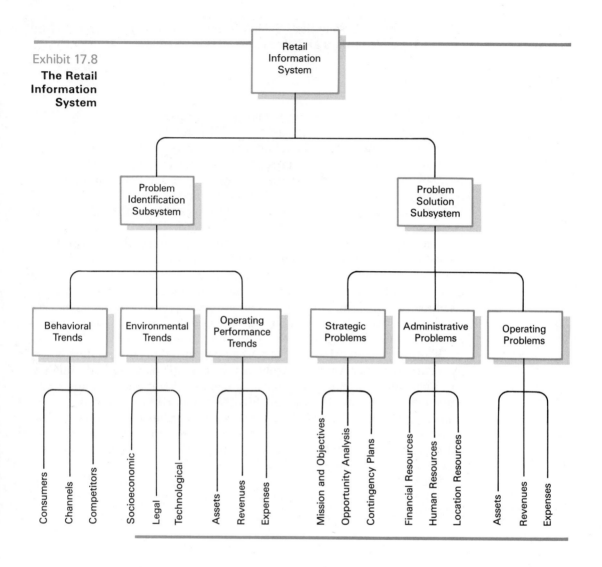

Exhibit 17.8

The Retail Information System

Home Furnishings Daily, Stores, Progressive Grocer, etc., in order to obtain information on future consumer trends. Others might use more formal means to foresee the future. Some of these means include the analysis of purchases, charge account customers, and consumer panels. Many small service retailers merely look at local economic forecasts. It is important for small retailers to realize that while more sophisticated methods may provide a better monitor, they may not be worth the expense involved.

The larger the retail enterprise, the more likely it is to benefit from a formal and continuous monitoring of consumer behavior trends. As the retail enterprise grows, the retail decision-makers become increasingly re-

Illus. 17.2
**Many motels
and restaurants
ask their patrons
to fill out a brief
questionnaire
on how satisfied
they were with
their visit or
meal. Source:
Marriott Hotels
and Resorts.**

moved from regular face-to-face contact with the consumer. Most large-scale retail enterprises would benefit from a continual monitoring of consumer behavior patterns. One top executive of a leading department store stated that by monitoring charge card records, the store noticed a heavy influx of mail orders from customers in Texas and Chicago. This led management to research the feasibility of expansion into these markets. Thus, the decision-maker cannot obtain a casual or subjective appreciation for changes the consumer is experiencing.

If the retailer decides that a continual monitoring of consumer behavior patterns is warranted, regular data collection is needed on three crucial consumer behavior variables: purchase probabilities, attitudes, and consumer satisfaction.

Purchase Probabilities.   Information on **purchase probabilities** (how likely a consumer is to purchase a particular product within the next six months) will allow the retailer to keep apprised of the products it should stock and promote. The Survey Research Center at the University of Michigan reports quarterly on the future plans of American consumers to purchase major durables like automobiles. On the local level, many city newspapers provide continuing consumer surveys of their market areas as a service to advertisers. For example, the *Des Moines Register and Tribune* covers the shopping behavior and purchase intentions of not just Des Moines area consumers, but the entire state. Thus a Des Moines car dealer, armed with knowledge about the target market's purchase probabilities, can develop special promotions and merchandising programs to attract car-purchasing consumers to their dealerships. The same kind of information is used by home builders and real estate firms to determine home purchase probabilities. One retail consultant has even developed a probabilities model to say that if consumers pay X dollars for an item, they will then purchase a companion product costing Y dollars. For example, if a consumer pays between $75 to $120 for a blazer, she will want to purchase a skirt costing $60 to $80 and shoes costing $41 to $61. This model enables the retailer to know what price ranges should be used and what inventory levels must be maintained, given previous purchases.[2]

Consumer Attitudes.   Consumer attitudes toward the retailer's store and operation can be a significant determinant of patronage behavior. Changing attitudes can forewarn the retailer of problems on the horizon. Remember, K mart tried to upgrade consumer's attitudes towards its stores, while Dollar General and Family Dollar were satisfied with how consumers perceived their stores.

Customer Satisfaction.   Information on customer satisfaction with both the merchandise and service will indicate whether the customer's visit to the store was a good experience or a bad experience. If there is dissatisfaction with both the merchandise and service, the customer is less likely to choose that store in the future, thus decreasing sales. Retailers have found that customer dissatisfaction is usually the result of discrepancies between:

1.   What the consumer actually expected and what the retailer thought the consumer wanted in terms of service and merchandise.
2.   What the retailer thought the consumer wanted and what the store actually delivered in terms of service and merchandise.
3.   What the retailer promised in its promotional messages and what was delivered.

In an effort to eliminate, or at least reduce, the first type of discrepancy, retail managers must spend time on the floor, interacting with customers and checking to see if their expectations of what customers want is correct. When placing top management on the floor is impossible, management should at least talk regularly to customer-contact personnel. It is important to have these expectations of customers' wants shaped by the personnel with the hands-on experience.

The second type of discrepancy reflects a lack of commitment to the customer. By making the customer secondary to profits, gross margin, market share, price points, or cost reduction, management tells employees that the expected service or merchandise shouldn't be delivered unless the other objectives are first achieved. Many motels and restaurants ask their patrons to fill out a brief questionnaire on how satisfied they were with their visit or meal. Many auto dealers and furniture retailers send recent customers a letter encouraging them to call a toll-free number if they are dissatisfied with their recent purchase. These retailers obtain information on customer satisfaction at a relatively low cost and take corrective action if dissatisfaction seems to be rising. Retailing in Action 17-1 provides additional insights into the proper use of customer surveys.

The final type of discrepancy occurs when retailers exaggerate the quality of their merchandise or services, resulting in customers expecting more than the retailers provide. This exaggerated promise could come from the retailers' ads, in-store displays, or salesforce. Retail managers can become aware of this type of discrepancy by spending time on the floor or conferring with customer-contact personnel.

RETAILING IN ACTION   17-1

The Proper Use of Consumer Surveys

Customer feedback from surveys helps retailers determine their position against competitors and identifies their weak spots in regard to service and merchandise. The authors are familiar with a restaurant which moved from a mall to a strip center location, a florist which started staying open an hour later on weeknights, and a hotel which reorganized its check-in procedures, all because of feedback from customer surveys.

All retailers recognize the value of consumer surveys, but the real question is, how do you get customers to respond to them? Customers who experienced poor service or a bad meal will generally respond; but what about those who experienced a pleasant meal and service? What will motivate these satisfied customers to respond? Millions of consumer surveys mailed out to consumers each year go unanswered. Some retailers advocate the use of incentives (cash, free products or services) but others claim that incentives only bias the results.

The real issue is whether the nonrespondents represent a particular segment of the market or have a viewpoint that is different from those who respond to the surveys. If incentives are unable to get those market segments who have different observations to respond, they have not made a significant contribution to the results. If incentives enable the retailer to obtain data from all market segments, something that would not be otherwise obtainable, then the retailer should use them.

Another question raised by retailers doing surveys is whether they should require the consumers to use their names. Generally, an answer is more honest if names are not requested.

BEHAVIORAL TRENDS: MONITORING THE MARKETING CHANNEL

The retailer is part of a channel system that few retailers can control. Most retailers must adapt to the behavior of other organizations in the channel. Therefore, the behavior of channel members should be monitored.

In Chapter 3 we discussed some of the intricacies of adapting to the marketing channel. Here, let us focus on obtaining information on alternative merchandise sources, alternative facilitating agencies, financial performance of channel partners, and channel conflicts.

Merchandise Sources.   If retailers become too dependent on a few sources of merchandise, their ability to bargain and negotiate with the suppliers will be hampered. The suppliers may even try to dictate how the retailers should conduct their business. The best way to avoid this is to be continually aware of alternative supply sources. Even if retailers have found that Supplier X always has the best merchandise for the lowest price, they should not become complacent and stop looking for a better deal. This is especially true for retailers who rely heavily on foreign manufacturers. Delivery times and currency fluctuations make it extremely important to keep updating information on these sources of merchandise.

Every retailer should have an ongoing system of information collection to alert the retailer to the best deals. For instance, many supermarkets constantly evaluate their present wholesale sources of supply against alternative sources. This helps them assess the terms of their present suppliers. Also, present suppliers will be more cooperative if they know the retailer is keeping abreast of the terms being offered by their competitors.

Finally, retailers need to be aware of consumer-led boycotts against certain products. In the recent past, boycotts have been carried out against Coors Beer, California grapes, Campbell Soups, and Playboy Magazine.[3] Retailers selling these products need to be aware of these situations, not to prevent picketing outside the store, but also to prepare alternative sources of supply.

Facilitating Agencies.   Most retailers rely on a number of facilitating agencies (banks, ad agencies, brokers, insurance firms, etc.). Just as retailers should monitor alternative merchandise supply sources, they should also monitor the availability, strengths, and weaknesses of alternative facilitating agencies. Are there public warehouses or advertising agencies that can do a better job at a more competitive price? Retailers should have access to any information that can help answer such basic questions.

Financial Performance of Channel Partners.   As much information as possible should be obtained about the financial performance of channel partners. What is happening to their profit margins, inventory turnover, credit policy, cash flow, labor, and productivity sales growth? Whenever any member of a marketing channel begins to have financial problems, it will start to squeeze its channel partners (for instance, cutting credit terms, increasing minimum order size, or raising prices) to increase its performance at the expense of the retailer. By monitoring channel member performance, retailers can have countermoves already developed to minimize any unfair pressure from poorly performing suppliers. Certainly, retailers can help a supplier in need, but they should not allow a supplier to take advantage of them.

Retailers may be able to obtain more information about suppliers than they may realize. Most large suppliers are publicly held corporations, and any stockholder of record can receive annual and quarterly financial statements. Also, any publicly held corporation must file a 10K report with the Securities and Exchange Commission (SEC). The 10K report, which is a matter of public record, is available through the SEC or directly from the reporting company. The 10K has a wealth of financial information that is typically not provided in the standard annual report to stockholders. Retailers do not have to hold stock in a supplier to get this information. Disclosure, Inc., a company based in Dallas, will provide a copy of any corporation's 10K or annual report at a modest cost. Investors Management Service, based in Denver, can provide similar data on computer tape for more than 5,000 publicly held companies in the United States.

Channel Conflict.   The final area of channel behavior that should be monitored is the level of conflict. For every significant channel interface, retailers should identify potential sources of conflict. Specifically, they must regularly ask themselves questions like: To what extent do the channel partners have goals that are not compatible with ours? To what extent does each channel partner try to unduly control aspects of our business? To what extent do channel partners perceive significant events in the economic, social, legal, and technological environments differently than we do? It is better to know of potential conflict than to learn about it after the conflict has become manifest and is more difficult to resolve.

BEHAVIORAL TRENDS: MONITORING COMPETITORS

Almost all retail executives will tell you that they are more interested in what their competitors are doing than in how channel partners or consumers are behaving, but all three behaviors are equally important.

All executives have some means of monitoring competitors' activities. At the simplest level, this may consist of reading or listening to competitors' ads and shopping their stores personally to inspect merchandise, prices, displays, and store decor. More sophisticated monitoring may involve systematic collection and analysis of data on all relevant aspects of competitor market shares and trading areas.

Market Saturation.   The extent to which a particular trading area is populated with retailers in a particular line of trade is called **market satura-tion**. One measure of market saturation is the **index of retail saturation**.[4] The index is found by multiplying the number of households in the market area by the average household retail expenditures per line of trade, then dividing that figure by the square feet of retail selling space for the line of trade. The formal equation is:

$$IRS_1 = (H_1 \times RE_1)/RF_1$$

where

IRS_1 = Index of retail saturation

H_1 = Number of households in the market area

RE_1 = Average retail expenditures per household for line of trade.

RF_1 = Total retail square feet of selling space per line of trade, including the proposed store.

When the IRS is low in comparison with the product line in other market areas, the market is saturated with retail space and competitors compete more aggressively for consumer expenditures. The IRS is a good indication of potential profits in a particular market area. The higher the IRS, the greater the profit potential and vice versa.

Pricing.   The retailer should determine a bundle of goods on which it desires to be most competitive. For example, a grocery store may identify 135 items out of the 4,200 it stocks on which it wants to be visibly price-competitive. Once the bundle has been established, the retailer should compute price indices that show its price for each item compared to the price each of its major competitors is charging. These indices should be constructed regularly, probably weekly or monthly. Trends in these price indices will vividly demonstrate the extent to which the retailer is price competitive.

Merchandise Mixes.   How strong is the retailer's assortment of merchandise in relation to key competitors? Is it deeper, wider, and of a higher quality? How has it changed over time? In short, are the retailer's assortments of merchandise competitive? Only ongoing data collection can provide a meaningful answer to this important question. Retailers should regularly shop competing retailers for the answers.

Promotion.   There are two fundamental questions retailers will want their information system to answer regarding competitor's promotional efforts. First, how much are competitors spending on promotion? Second, what is the quality of competitors' promotional activities?

Neither question is easily or inexpensively answered. A detailed analysis of competitors' advertising, sales promotion activities, publicity efforts, and personal selling would be necessary to answer these questions completely. Because such a task would be a burden, most retailers collect data on a regular basis only on competitor's advertising, and in some cases on their sales promotion activities. For example, many apparel retailers have a file of competitors' newspaper advertising. Competitors' ads are clipped daily and placed in this file and then once a month the intensity and quality of competitors' advertising is analyzed. This simple process allows the retailer to spot any significant deterioration in its advertising in relation to competitors.

Market Share.   What are the respective market shares of the retailer and its competitors, and how are these changing? The best indicator of future profit performance is market share.[5] If retailers observe their market share slipping, that is a warning of future profitability problems.

Retailers that sell a wide range of merchandise should ideally obtain market share data by merchandise line. Rather than only comparing competitors' market shares as a whole, a department store manager may find it most useful to have market share data on particular departments: household furnishings, menswear, women's apparel, children's clothes, sporting goods, jewelry, toys, and lawn and garden equipment. However, the collection of such information is extremely expensive and may not be worth the cost.

Trading Area.   Is the retailer's trading area stable, shrinking, or expanding? A shrinking trading area is a bad omen; an expanding one is good. Market saturation, competitive pricing, competitive merchandise assortments, and competitive promotional strength all affect trading area size. The less competitive the retailer's pricing, merchandise assortment, and promotion, the more its trading area will shrink. The more saturated the market, the more the trading area will shrink.

It is relatively easy to obtain information about the trading area. If the retailers have the addresses of store patrons, the retailer can easily construct a trading area map. One owner-manager of a record store continually held contests in which patrons of the store would fill out entry blanks with their names and addresses to qualify for a weekly drawing of a free album. Each month the color of the entry blanks would change. At the end of each month, the owner could plot on a map where patrons came from, enabling him to notice quickly any change in the size or nature of his trading area.

ENVIRONMENTAL TRENDS: MONITORING THE SOCIOECONOMIC ENVIRONMENT

Events in the socioeconomic environment that should be monitored can be categorized into demographic, psychographic, and economic trends. These trends were discussed in detail in Chapter 4.

Major demographic trends that may be particularly useful to monitor are changing household size, educational levels, age distribution of household members, population growth, and geographic migration. Psychographic trends that may be particularly insightful are changes in leisure time activities, work habits, and religious, family, and cultural values. Economic trends that should be followed are changes in disposable personal income, household expenditure patterns, discretionary income, or the use of credit.

Highly personalized, continuous data on demographic, psychographic, and economic trends is not cheap. National data is readily available, but tells retailers little about the socioeconomic dynamics of their trading area. Data on a particular area may be available from a local newspaper. See Retailing in Action 17-2 for an example of such information. These surveys collect data on a large number of demographic, economic, and in some cases, psychographic variables. If the retailer advertises in the newspaper conducting the survey, much of the data can be obtained free or at modest cost.

The United States Census Bureau can provide a wealth of demographic data on census tracts. However, this data is collected only once every ten years and is quickly dated. Trade associations and publications like *Sales and Marketing Management* publish some of this data on an annual basis. Retailing in Action 17-3 provides an example of the data that is available from a trade association. Occasionally, local governments or universities will conduct special surveys to obtain current demographic data.

RETAILING IN ACTION 17-2

Retailers Should Make Use of Newspaper Research Staffs

Most large-city newspapers provide their advertisers with various types of market research to assist with their advertising strategies. Two such types of research are shown below. The first study shows demographic data for a retail chain's downtown Los Angeles store, as well as the circulation data for the newspaper in reaching this market.

The second study shows the percentage of Los Angeles households that visited various regional shopping centers within the last 30 days and a comparison with an earlier study. The study also shows a comparison of one shopping center's customer profile with the total Los Angeles market.

First Study

Demographic data for: STORE #1—DOWNTOWN

Housing Tenure		*Condominiums*	
Own	23.4%	Percent of total	
Rent (including		dwelling units	1.2%
no cash rent)	76.6		
Total Occupied Units	100.0%	*Household Type*	
		1 person household	27.9%
		2 or more persons: family	66.6
Rent		2 or more persons: non-family	5.5
No cash rent	1.3%		
Less than $200	69.1	Total Occupied Dwelling Units	100.0%
$200–$299	23.2		
$300–$399	4.9	*Presence of Children*	
$400–$499	1.0	Have children under 18	45.1%
$500 or more	.5	No children under 18	54.9
Total Specified Renter		Total Occupied Dwelling Units	100.0%
Occupied Dwelling Units	100.0%		
		Marital Status of Persons	
Median Rent	$143	*Age 15 and Over*	
		Married	42.3%
Number of Units		Single	37.4
at Address		Widowed, divorced,	
1	54.5%	separated	20.3
2–9	21.6		
10 or more	23.7	Total	100.0%
Mobile home	.2		
		Sex of Population	
Total Dwelling Units	100.0%	Male	50.3%
		Female	49.7
		Total	100.0%

First Study

Data for: STORE #1—DOWNTOWN

Los Angeles Times

Current Population	Current Occupied Dwelling Units	Circulation Distribution		Percent Coverage	
		Weekday	Sunday	Weekday	Sunday
777,661	233,136	47,774	37,722	21.15%	16.9%

Age of Population		*Education—Persons*		*Household Income*	
Under 6	12.3%	*Age 25 and Over*		Under $15,000	68.9%
6–13	13.6	Less than 4 years		$15,000–$19,999	12.4
14–17	6.9	high school	61.3%	$20,000–$24,999	7.6
18–24	16.0	4 years high school	20.2	$25,000–$34,999	6.9

Data for: STORE #1—DOWNTOWN

Los Angeles Times

Current Population	Current Occupied Dwelling Units	Circulation Distribution		Percent Coverage	
		Weekday	Sunday	Weekday	Sunday
777,661	233,136	47,774	37,722	21.15%	16.9%

25–34	17.7	1–3 years college	11.0	$35,000–$49,999	3.0
35–44	10.1	4+ years college	7.5	$50,000–$74,999	.8
45–54	7.9			$75,000 and over	.4
55–64	6.7	Total	100.0%		
65 and over	8.8			Total	100.0%
		Median School			
Total	100.0%	Years Completed	9.8	Median Household	
				Income	$10,889
Median Age	25.7	*Employment—Employed*			
		Persons Age 16 and Over		*Home Value*	
Race of Population		Professional specialty	5.1%	Under $50,000	51.1%
White	40.5%	Exec, Administrator, Mgr	4.7	$50,000–$79,999	33.9
Black	19.4	Tech, Sales; Adm support	22.9	$80,000–$99,999	8.2
Asian-Pacific Islander	7.4	Precision prod, Craft/Repair	12.3	$100,000–$149,999	5.1
All Other	32.7	Operators, Laborers	36.2	$150,000–$199,999	1.1
		All Other	18.8	$200,000 and over	.6
Total	100.0%				
		Total	100.0%	Total Specified	
(Spanish/Hispanic				Owner Occupied	
origin)	61.5%			Dwelling Units	100.0%
				Median Home	
				Value	$48,951

SOURCE: Los Angeles Times Marketing Research Department, estimates based on data supplied by various governmental agencies, Southern California Association of Governments. Reprinted with permission of the Los Angeles Times.

Second Study

Percent of Los Angeles Households Shopping Specified Regional Shopping Centers in the Last 30 Days

	Current			Two Years Ago		
	Rank	Percent of Households	Number of Households	Rank	Percent of Households	Number of Households
South Coast Plaza	1	8.8%	311,572	1	7.9%	273,146
Glendale Galleria	2	8.7	308,032	7	5.5	190,165
Del Amo Fashion Center	3	8.2	290,329	2	7.0	242,028

Percent of Los Angeles Households Shopping Specified Regional Shopping Centers in the Last 30 Days

	Current			Two Years Ago		
	Rank	Percent of Households	Number of Households	Rank	Percent of Households	Number of Households
Los Cerritos Center	4	5.9	208,895	4	6.0	207,452
Fox Hills Mall	5	5.5	194,733	8	4.6	159,047
Westminster Mall	5	5.5	194,733	4	6.0	207,452
Beverly Center	7	5.4	191,192	32	2.0	69,151
Lakewood Center Mall	8	5.1	180,570	3	6.3	217,825
Northridge Fashion Center	9	4.8	169,949	6	5.7	197,080
Santa Monica Place	10	4.7	166,408	10	4.4	155,132
Brea Mall	11	4.4	155,786	14	3.6	124,471
Santa Anita Fashion Park	12	4.1	145,164	9	4.5	155,589
Puente Hills Mall	13	3.7	131,002	12	3.9	134,844
Topanga Plaza	14	3.2	113,299	13	3.8	131,386
West Covina Fashion Plaza	15	3.0	106,218	11	4.0	138,302
Buena Park Mall	16	2.8	99,137	17	3.2	110,641
Sherman Oaks Galleria	17	2.7	95,596	15	3.3	114,099
Century City Shopping Center	17	2.7	95,596	23	2.6	89,896
Fashion Island	19	2.5	88,515	21	2.7	93,354
Huntington Center	19	2.5	88,515	17	3.2	110,641
Hawthorne Plaza	19	2.5	88,515	23	2.6	89,896
Eagle Rock Plaza	22	2.2	77,893	*	*	*
Stonewood Shopping Center	23	2.1	74,353	25	2.5	86,438
Laguna Hills Mall	24	2.0	70,812	27	2.4	82,981
Mission Viejo Mall	24	2.0	70,812	29	2.3	79,523

*Less than 2.0%.

Second Study

Del Amo Fashion Center
Percent Distribution of All Los Angeles Households and Los Angeles Households Shopping Del Amo Fashion Center in the Last 30 Days by Selected Demographics

	All Los Angeles Households	Households Shopping Del Amo Fashion Center
Annual Household Income		
$50,000 or more	17.5%*	22.5%**
$35,000–$49,999	18.8	23.2
$25,000–$34,999	18.9	24.5
$20,000–$24,999	12.4	10.4
$15,000–$19,999	10.6	6.9
Under $15,000	21.8	12.5

Del Amo Fashion Center

Total	100.0%	100.0%
(Base)***	(4,956)	(432)
Median income	$27,721	$33,208
Age, Household Head		
Under 30	20.3%	22.1%
30–39	25.5	28.5
40–49	18.6	20.5
50–64	21.8	18.8
65 or over	13.8	10.1
Total	100.0%	100.0%
(Base)***	(5,776)	(474)
Median age	42.3	39.8
Education, Household Head		
College graduate or more	32.7%	39.8%
Some college	28.0	29.7
High school graduate	27.4	25.9
Some high school or less	11.9	4.6
Total	100.0%	100.0%
(Base)***	(5,790)	(475)
Occupation, Household Head		
Professional/technical	19.8%	24.9%
Manager/official/proprietor	20.1	21.1
Clerical/sales	13.6	15.1
Craftsman/foreman/operative	13.7	12.5
Retired	16.7	12.9
All others	16.1	13.5
Total	100.0%	100.0%
(Base)***	(5,674)	(465)

*Example: 17.5% of all Los Angeles households have an annual household income of $50,000 or more.

**Example: 22.5% of the Los Angeles households shopping Del Amo Fashion Center in the last 30 days have an annual income of $50,000 or more.

***Excludes refused/don't know responses.

Reprinted with permission of the Los Angeles Times.

ENVIRONMENTAL TRENDS: MONITORING THE LEGAL ENVIRONMENT

Although it is disquieting to most retailers, the legal environment is always in a state of flux. To avoid costly legal errors, the RIS should be designed to keep the retailer apprised of changes in the legal environment.

RETAILING
IN
ACTION

17-3

Trade Associations Can Provide Data on Consumer Trade

An example of the types of data available from trade associations is provided by the Photo Marketing Association. One of their survey's most interesting findings was that level of income determines where consumers get film developed. Households with incomes under $10,000 a year are most likely to process their film via the mail, because it is less expensive. These low-income households are not likely to take their film to a one-hour minilab or to a parking lot drive-up booth, since this decrease in turnaround time usually doubles the price. Those households with annual incomes of $40,000 or more, were least likely to use mail-order developers and most likely to use the convenience of the drive-up booth or one-hour minilabs.

Of all film processing outlets, one-hour minilabs have the most demographically select clientele. The largest share of minilab patrons have household incomes of $40,000 or more, are under 35, and are college graduates or have post-graduate degrees.

In view of this it is not surprising that many photo developers are locating in shopping centers catering to this up-scale market.

Another interesting finding was the occasions on which pictures are taken. Christmas/Hanukkah continues to be number one with both still and video cameras. Travel/vacations and birthdays are numbers two and three for stills, and birthdays and children/baby are numbers two and three for video movies.

Source: The Photo Marketing Association International, 300 Picture Place, Jackson, MI 49201. Printed with permission.

The larger the retail enterprise, the higher priority this area should receive.

No retail manager or store owner can be expected to monitor all the relevant changes in the legal environment. Fortunately, all the major retail trade associations devote a fair amount of space in their publications to the retail implications of pending legislation at both federal and state levels. Many large retail enterprises even have a legal staff to keep top management aware of changes in the legal environment. Sears, J. C. Penney, and McDonald's all have sizeable legal staffs.

The legal area of most immediate practical concern to the retailer is tax law. Changes in tax laws generally have a significant effect on retail decisions. For example, a favorable change in the investment tax credit can make store remodeling or expansion attractive. Tax laws can influence decisions about inventory valuation methods, executive compensation plans, or recording of credit sales.

Retail corporations that are publicly held should also stay informed of the regulations of the Securities and Exchange Commission (SEC) and the accounting standards established by the Financial Accounting Standards Board (FASB). All publicly held retailers must abide by the SEC guidelines in reporting to stockholders. The FASB develops the generally accepted accounting principles (GAAP). These are not legal requirements, but retailers that want their financial statements to receive an unqualified opinion by a certified external auditor will follow GAAP.

ENVIRONMENTAL TRENDS: MONITORING THE TECHNOLOGICAL ENVIRONMENT

Technology is the application of science to develop new methods of doing things. It is always at work, slowly but continually changing the nature and scope of retailing.

The retailer can monitor the technological environment at the basic science stage or the applied science stage. In either case, the retailer will want to monitor technology as related to four areas of innovation: management techniques, merchandising techniques, equipment and fixtures, and construction and building.

A retailer desiring to monitor any of the four areas at the basic science stage could read academic journals in the fields of management, marketing, engineering, computer science, or architecture. For example, to monitor management and merchandising at the basic science level, the retailer might read such journals as the *Journal of Finance, Journal of Retailing, Journal of Marketing*, or *Administrative Science Quarterly*. Unfortunately, most topics and concepts discussed in academic business journals are a long way from being applied, and many practical problems of implementation need to be worked out. For example, the use of experimental designs to test the effectiveness of promotional displays was proposed in

Illus. 17.3

To monitor technology at the applied level, executives should attend trade shows and read trade-related publications on a regular basis.

the *Journal of Marketing Research* in the 1960s and is just now receiving widespread acceptance by retailers.

Generally, it is more beneficial for the retail executive to monitor technology at the applied level. To do this most effectively, executives should regularly attend trade shows and read trade-related publications. Exhibit 17.6 contains a list of some of the publications that report on innovations that can be or are being applied to retailing.

Rosenbloom and Tripuraneni found that technology was fourth behind competition, consumer behavior, and the economy (and ahead of government regulation) in environmental factors monitored by retailers' strategic planning committees. The authors concluded that "perhaps the very rapid developments in recent years in POS systems, computerized billing, and inventory control, as well as the dramatic changes in consumer electronics products, have made a strong impression on retailers."[6] Considering that nonstore retail sales are expected to pass the $100 billion mark by 1992[7] it is easy to see why interest in technology is increasing. Keeping up with technology can make the difference between achieving or not achieving high-performance results.

OPERATING PERFORMANCE TRENDS: MONITORING ASSETS

The accounting system should be part of the RIS, since it can be an important source of information about operating performance trends.[8]

A RIS should have the capability to monitor the retailer's assets continually. At the most basic level, a retailer may design the RIS to construct a balance sheet at the end of each operating period (typically a month or a quarter) for assessing the magnitude and composition of its assets. By comparing the current balance sheet to prior ones, retailers can assess the growth of their asset base and changes in the composition of their assets. More detailed analysis of period-to-period balance sheets and the general ledgers used to construct them will provide information on the sources and uses of capital. The balance sheet is one of the most useful pieces of information available to retailers.

A RIS can also provide a merchandise management report as shown in Exhibit 17.9. This report shows the total inventory available at retail, at cost, and in units.

One service retailer that does an excellent job of using a RIS to monitor its assets is Avis. Avis employs what it calls a rate-shoppers' guide. The specifics are secret, but, in general, the Wizard system (Avis' Reservation System) allows agents to quote up-to-the-minute prices that change with the availability of the fleet at a particular location. If the cars aren't moving, a lower price will kick in. If the fleet is tight, the price stays up. Avis, the first rental car company to unveil a computerized reservation system in 1972, is now using the power of its RIS much more creatively.[9]

Exhibit 17.9

A Merchandise Management Report

King Stores	** Merchandise Management Report **
Merchandise Group 81–87	Week From
All Stores	02/06/89

Beginning Inventory at Retail	$973,683,744.23
Purchases at Retail	$192,845,605.70
Vendor Returns at Retail	$.00
Net Sales at Retail	$32,700.00
Customer Returns at Retail	$.00
Authorized Point of Sale Markdowns at Retail	$.00
Unauthorized Point of Sale Markdowns at Retail	$1,500.00
General Markdowns at Retail	$560,210.60
Price Adjustments at Retail	$.00
Distributions and Transfers at Retail	$.00
Unit Adjustments at Retail	$329,400.00
Planned Shrinkage at Retail (Memo)	$98.10
Ending Inventory at Retail	$1,166,264,339.33
Beginning Inventory at Cost	$439,874,795.48
Purchases at Cost	$92,584,883.70
Vendor Returns at Cost	$.00
Freight and Duty at Cost	$303,000.00
Net Sales at Cost	$14,534.00
Customer Returns at Cost	$.00
Authorized Point of Sale Markdowns at Cost	$.00
Unauthorized Point of Sale Markdowns at Cost	$666.00
General Markdowns at Cost	$351,243.73
Vendor Discounts and Allowances at Cost	$.00
Price Adjustments at Cost	$58,907.93
Distributions and Transfers at Cost	$.00
Unit Adjustments at Cost	$146,400.00
Planned Shrinkage at Cost (Memo)	$43.60
Ending Inventory at Cost	$532,298,543.38
Beginning Inventory in Units	2,952,012
Purchases in Units	7,557,434
Vendor Returns in Units	0
Net Sales in Units	760
Customer Returns in Units	0
Authorized Pos Markdowns in Units (Memo)	0
Unauthorized Pos Markdowns in Units (Memo)	300
Distributions and Transfers in Units	0
Unit Adjustments in Units	7,320
Planned Shrinkage in Units (Memo)	0
Ending Inventory in Units	516,006

Performance Standards.   Using basic balance sheet data, the retail ana-lyst can compute financial ratios to evaluate the retailer's liquidity. **Li-quidity** represents the firm's ability to meet its current payment obligations.

Liquidity is important to the retailer because it protects the company from economic downturns and potential insolvency, and provides the needed flexibility to capitalize on unexpected merchandising opportunities.

Financial analysts generally use three financial ratios to evaluate li-quidity: the current ratio, the quick ratio, and the liquidity ratio. You may want to review Chapter 2 to see how these ratios are calculated.

In any RIS, retailers must first have some target level for each of these three ratios. That is, they must have a desired level of liquidity, probably based on industry norms. Generally, the goal reflects a desired range for the financial ratio; for instance, the target current ratio may be 1.9 to 2.1. Second, retailers must compare actual performance to targeted performance and note any significant deviation from the target. Third, significant deviations from targeted performance should be investigated. This third step takes us into the problem solution subsystem of the RIS.

Exhibit 17.10 gives a control chart for the current ratio for King Bing's Furniture Sales. The dashed lines show that management wants

Exhibit 17.10

Control Chart for Current Ratio for King Bing Furniture Sales

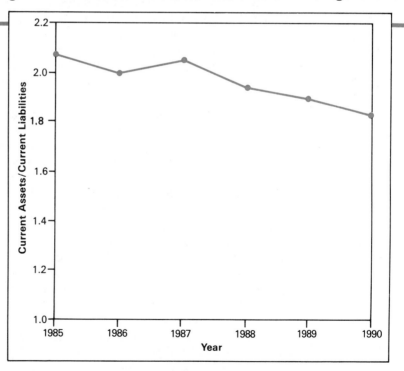

the current ratio to fall between 1.9 and 2.1. Between 1985 and 1989 it fell within this range, but in 1990 it fell below 1.9. Management needs to investigate the cause of this significant drop in liquidity. A careful investigation of the possible causes might reveal that credit customers have significantly slowed their rate of payment on installment sales.

Retailers can also use data from the balance sheet, in conjunction with other data, to measure how well they are utilizing their assets. Some popular measures are:

1. **Sales per dollar invested in inventory** (total dollar sales/average inventory investment.) This is a measure of inventory turnover that shows how productive the retailer's investment in inventory has been. A high rate of turnover is better than a low one if everything else is held constant.

2. **Sales per square feet of selling space** (total dollar sales/square feet of selling space). This is a measure of space productivity. The higher its value, the more productively the retailer is using its selling space.

3. **Sales per dollar invested in assets** (total dollar sales/total dollars invested in assets). This is a basic measure of asset productivity. It shows how much the retailer has generated in sales for each dollar invested. It is a key component of the strategic profit model that was introduced in Chapter 2.

4. **Credit sales per dollar invested in accounts receivable** (total dollar credit sales/average accounts receivable). This measure shows how quickly retailers are collecting from customers who purchase on credit. The larger the measure, the better.

For each of these measures, retailers should develop standards of performance. After these performance measures have been established, one method of control is the **Steering Marketing Control Model (STEMCOM)**.[10] STEMCOM predicts a final outcome and then monitors progress toward that outcome. The model is open-looped, which means that the identification of reasons that cause the process to go out of control and the necessary corrective action is external to the model. STEMCOM alerts managers to deviations from some specified level of performance. Management must then determine the cause of the deviation and whether or not corrective action is necessary.

In one application of STEMCOM, management specified 12 indicators of performance for departments within a department store. These indicators, which are commonly furnished by trade associations, are listed in Exhibit 17.11 along with the mean scores for departments that were successful, mediumly successful, or unsuccessful in performance. For example, for successful departments, the stock turnover rate was 4.2; for medium performance departments the rate was 3.2; and for unsuccessful departments the rate was 2.7.

Exhibit 17.11

Mean Performance Indicators for Successful, Medium, and Unsuccessful Indicators in a Retail Department Store

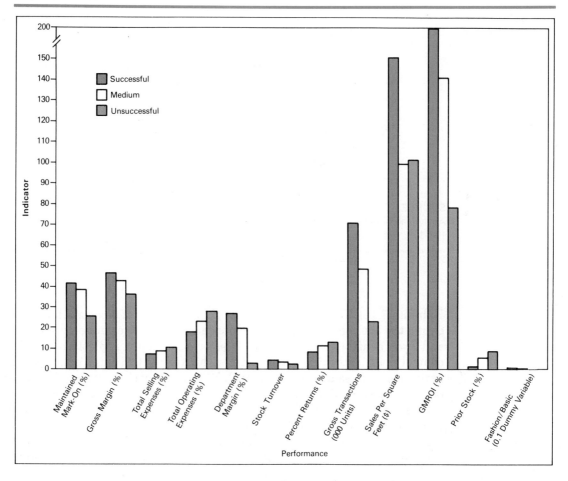

SOURCE: Subhash Sharma and Dale D. Achabal, "STEMCO: An Analytical Model for Marketing Control," *Journal of Marketing,* (Spring 1982), pp.104-113. (Reprinted with AMA permission.)

These indicators were combined into a composite performance index. For successful departments, the composite index value ranged from 1 to 2. Management could monitor the performance of a given department, and if the performance index dropped below 1, managers would examine why the deviation occurred and what, if any, corrective action was necessary.

The major objective of STEMCOM is to indicate to management whether actual performance has deviated from target performance. A control chart similar to those used in quality control can be developed (see

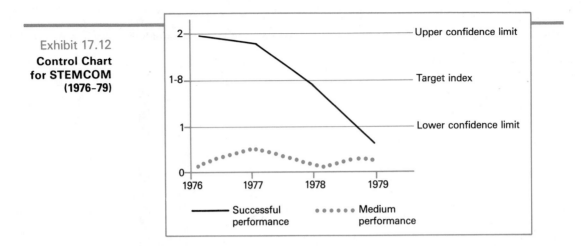

Exhibit 17.12

Control Chart for STEMCOM (1976-79)

SOURCE: Subhash Sharma and Dale D. Achabal, "STEMCO: An Analytical Model for Marketing Control," *Journal of Marketing*, (Spring 1982), pp. 104-113. (Reprinted with AMA permission.)

Exhibit 17.12). The standard control chart consists of a central line indicating the average or target performance and other lines indicating upper and lower control limits. An actual performance index is plotted onto the control chart. If the performance lies within the control limits established, performance is said to be in control. Where the performance index falls outside the control limits, management has been alerted that corrective action may be needed. The control chart can also be used to observe trends in the actual performance index. A downward trend would indicate a deterioration in performance over time, and management may decide to take corrective action before performance falls below an acceptable level.

Auditing Assets.   Imagine yourself as a retail executive making decisions based on accounting information. You would want to be sure that you have valid information. This would be especially true if you were a top executive for a large chain, since you would not be able to visit each store regularly. You would have to rely totally on accounting data to keep you informed of what was happening at each store. If the balance sheet tells you that there is $4 million in inventory on hand, how do you know that this is true? Unless you count the inventory yourself, you probably don't know.

For these reasons, the retailer should regularly have an independent audit of its accounting records and system to ensure their validity. In fact, the SEC requires an independent audit of the annual financial statements to stockholders of publicly held corporations.

Retailers would also be well advised to implement an ongoing internal audit, to ensure continual protection of its assets. The internal audit department would regularly want to answer questions such as:

- Are merchandise shipments made only on the basis of approved instructions?
- Are stringent physical controls and paperwork procedures exercised over in-store transfers?
- Are departmental inventory records maintained in total and on an individual store basis?
- Are merchandise units that show erratic or unusually high shrinkage policed on an interim basis?
- Are customer refunds properly approved and controlled?
- Are sales drawers locked while a cashier is on break?
- Does electronic surveillance equipment receive a daily check?
- Are physical inventories of stores' fixtures and equipment taken periodically with discrepancies reported to management?[11]

Retail managers should also be concerned with some non-merchandising questions. For example, what is the market value of the property purchased in 1948 for our downtown store? Is it the $140,500 carried on the books or is it worth millions today? Can it be used to finance other retail operations via some type of lease-back sales agreement? What can the accounts receivables be sold for? Naturally, these are only a few of the questions that the internal audit department should be regularly answering. In short, the internal audit department's job is to protect the retailer's assets and ensure that the accounting records and information derived from them reflect reality.

OPERATING PERFORMANCE TRENDS: MONITORING REVENUES AND EXPENSES

By monitoring revenues and expenses, retailers are able to readily identify any significant gaps in planned profit levels and develop appropriate remedial actions.

Income Statement.   All of the revenue and expense data that the retailer needs to be kept informed about can be presented in a detailed income statement, which was discussed in Chapter 9. Thus, at the most fundamental level of analysis, retailers will want to design their RIS to regularly generate a detailed income statement.

Since the dollars on a retailer's income statement can change from period to period, it is best to have the income statement constructed in both dollars and percentiles (in which sales are equated to 100 percent). The percentile income statement facilitates the comparison of operating periods over time. Thus, a retail executive can quickly tell if advertising, utilities, wages, or any expense is behaving differently in relation to sales than it has historically.

The percentile income statement allows a retailer to apply standards of performance. A standard income statement can be developed in which each expense is programmed to be a standard percentage of sales. Percentages on the actual income statement can then be compared to the standard in order to gauge performance and identify problem areas. Many retail trade associations conduct annual studies of operating results, which show the average operating performance of the retailers that belong to the trade association. These studies can help the retailer develop standards.

It is important that retailers give careful consideration to the frequency with which their RIS generates income statement data. The income statement should be prepared often enough to allow management to take corrective action if an expense is out of control or if revenues are below standard. An annual income statement will not suffice; monthly or bimonthly statements are better. If you were a retail manager, you would not want to find out about a problem months after it occurred; at that point it may be too late.

Segmental Reporting.   In most cases, it is advantageous for retailers to develop individual income statements for separate segments of the enterprise. For example, if a retailer's enterprise consists of a chain of 48 drugstores, it would be beneficial to prepare a separate income statement for each drugstore and a composite income statement for all 48. This allows performance problems to be pinpointed more easily. Another method of segmental reporting is to look at which divisions of a large retail corporation accounted for what percentage of sales, operating profits, assets utilized, and capital expenditures. Exhibit 17.13 shows the performance of various segments of the Dayton Hudson Corporation for a recent year.

Segmental reporting can also be implemented by merchandise line. A chain of home improvement centers may wish to analyze separately the profit performance of its lumber products, lawn and garden products, small tools and appliances, and home decorating and fixtures. It may construct an income statement for each category, assigning expenses to each.

In 1981, Sears, for the first time in its 94-year history, developed precise sales, expense, and profit goals for every sales level right down to each individual store.[12] Many other large chain retailers are also beginning to employ segmental reporting and planning as part of their RIS.

THE PROBLEM SOLUTION SUBSYSTEM

Once the RIS problem identification subsystem has been used to spotlight problems, the problems must be solved. Frequently, this problem solving requires additional information, and it is the role of the problem solution subsystem to gather that information. There are three broad categories of problems, which parallel the three aspects of retail management

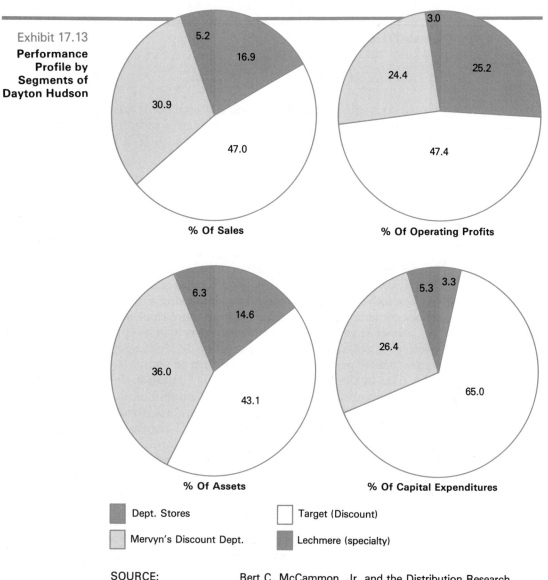

Exhibit 17.13

Performance Profile by Segments of Dayton Hudson

% Of Sales

5.2
16.9
30.9
47.0

% Of Operating Profits

3.0
24.4
25.2
47.4

% Of Assets

6.3
14.6
36.0
43.1

% Of Capital Expenditures

5.3   3.3
26.4
65.0

Dept. Stores

Target (Discount)

Mervyn's Discount Dept.

Lechmere (specialty)

SOURCE: Bert C. McCammon, Jr. and the Distribution Research Program at the University of Oklahoma, 1988.

in Exhibit 17.2: strategic planning, administrative management, and operations management. Let us look at some of the major problems that can occur in each of these areas and briefly discuss the types of information needed to solve them.

STRATEGIC PLANNING PROBLEMS

Three strategic planning problems that can occur are (1) obsolescence of mission or objectives, (2) faltering strategy, and (3) inadequate contingency plans. The retailer can use its RIS to help solve each type of problem.

Mission and Objectives.   A retailer may have serious problems if its mission and objectives are obsolete. This will usually occur when the retailer's environment and competition change significantly. For example, most drugstores between 1910 and 1950 could have had a mission of providing their immediate neighborhood (a 10- to 12-block radius) with its medicinal needs. But such a mission today would be questionable given the advent of the combo drug and food stores with more than 60,000 square feet of space, capable of merchandising a wide variety of nondrug products and drawing consumers from more than a three-mile radius.

Alternatively, a retailer's mission may still be appropriate but its objectives may be out of touch with reality. In 1980, with an inflation rate of more than 15 percent, a 20 percent return on equity objective was reasonable. But in the late 1980s, with rates of inflation below 4 percent, this goal was unobtainable except for the most skillful retailer.

Retailers may occasionally need to conduct research on the appropriateness of their mission and objectives. A change in the retailer's mission and objectives should not be based only on intuition. The entire planning process hinges on the statement of mission and objectives; if they are not appropriate, the entire planning process will suffer. It is in a retailer's best interest to spend money and time to collect relevant information before restating its mission and objectives.

Faltering Strategy.   Retailers may be comfortable with their mission and objectives but uncomfortable with the ability of their present strategy to fulfill them. Therefore, a detailed search for new strategic opportunities may be warranted.

Using data on significant behavioral and environmental trends obtained from the RIS, retailers may be able to readily identify several significant opportunities. Once opportunities have been identified, retailers will need to collect additional information on each and thoroughly analyze and evaluate it. Finally, the best opportunities will be selected for strategic development and implementation. Consider the case of Dayton Hudson Corporation, which is serving the full-service department store mar-

Illus. 17.4
Dayton-Hudson Corp. serves several markets due to strategy developed after thoroughly reviewing market opportunity. Target serves only the discount department store market.

ket (stores are Hudson's and Dayton's), the limited-service department store market (Mervyn's), the discount department store market (Target), and the specialty merchandise market (Lechmere). Each of these operations is the result of a strategy that was developed after thoroughly reviewing market opportunities.

Inadequate Contingency Plans.   Perhaps a retailer is satisfied with its mission and objectives and its current strategy. However, upon analysis of data from the problem identification subsystem of its RIS, the retailer notices considerable turbulence in the social, economic, and legal environments. It begins to question how well it is positioned against negative developments in these environments. In short, a retailer may see that although it is currently very successful, it does not have any contingency plans. The retailer must conduct special research to help formulate contingency plans before it is too late. A good example is the case of a retailer in the Southwest who, realizing that 30 percent of its business came from Mexican citizens, had contingency plans for almost any government interference in currency valuation or trade agreements. When the peso dropped by 30 percent overnight and a limit was imposed on currency exchanges, the retailer was ready with Plans A & B. Plan A was to use a Mexican supplier as an alternative source for some merchandise. The retailer could accept the Mexican peso from its customers, instead of the restricted dollar, and then use the peso to pay the Mexican supplier for merchandise. Plan B involved the use of another American business firm operating in Mexico. This other business used Mexican laborers for certain operations in Mexican communities. The retailer had made arrangements to sell his business pesos at a slight reduction from the official exchange rate, in return for dollars. As a result of this planning, the retailer survived what would have been an economic nightmare.

ADMINISTRATIVE MANAGEMENT PROBLEMS

Administrative management problems are related to the acquisition and management of the resources the retailer needs to carry out its strategy. Three types of resources are especially prone to problems: financial, human, and locational.

Financial Resources.   The problem identification subsystem of the RIS can identify financial resource problems that the problem solution subsystem of the RIS can help solve. For example, monitoring of economic trends using the problem identification subsystem may alert a retailer to the fact that interest rates are rising rapidly and are expected to remain high for at least a year. Or monitoring of the balance sheet may alert the retailer that a $10 million bond issue is maturing in six months. This pair of events should trigger problem recognition. The problem, which must be solved with the help of the problem solution subsystem, is how to generate $10 million in capital to retire the bond issue and subsequently restructure the balance sheet. Obviously, additional information will need to be collected to solve this complicated problem.

Other examples of capital-related problems that require a special research effort are evaluation of how to finance the construction of a new warehouse, analysis of the economics of factoring accounts receivable, exploration of new technology for increasing the productivity of capital invested in inventory, and evaluation of a new cash management system.

Human Resources.   The problem solution subsystem can also be used to help solve the retailer's human resource problems. Once again, the problem identification subsystem may have been instrumental in calling to the retail executive's attention the presence of a human resource problem—such as deteriorating sales per employee. But it is the problem solution subsystem that must obtain the necessary information to solve the problem.

Human resource problems can include morale problems, motivation problems, productivity problems, turnover problems, conflict problems, and organizational design problems. Often, these problems can best be solved by using the talents of external consulting organizations, which provide an independent analysis and opinion of the cause. People in the retail organization are often too close to the human element of the problem to be objective researchers. Using outside consultants to conduct the research falls within the domain of the RIS. The retail manager needs to recognize that information is needed, but that it can obtain the most valid information by contracting with an independent consulting agency to conduct the research and analyze the results.

Location Resources.   A retailer's location is one of the most valuable resources in its arsenal. But this resource can change in value as the retailer's trading area changes. A retailer may discover that its once-valuable location is no longer optimal.

To solve a location problem, retailers need information to help them evaluate alternatives. Reasonable alternatives may be to close the store, modify its merchandise mix, modify the store image, or keep the store operating as is but seek a new location.

OPERATIONS MANAGEMENT PROBLEMS

Operations management problems are those which are related to day-to-day management activities, as illustrated in Exhibit 17.2. Most can be quickly and effectively solved by an experienced and talented retail manager. However, for the occasional unique problem, special information is needed. Most operations problems are related to assets, revenues, or expenses. Let us briefly examine these problem areas.

Assets.   Operations problems may be related to any of the individual assets the retailer must manage on a day-to-day basis. Consider the following problems:

- Inventory is disappearing from the stockroom daily.
- There has been a significant slowdown in customers paying their bills.
- The roof of the store has developed a leak.
- The air conditioning system repeatedly breaks down.

To solve these problems properly, the manager may require information that is not readily available; he or she will thus turn to the RIS.

Let us illustrate a typical problem in more detail. Assume you are a store manager and the air conditioner regularly breaks down. Would you conclude that the old air conditioner needs to be replaced with a new unit?

We hope not. Careful analysis of the technological environment will reveal that there is a wealth of new air conditioning technology, which can have a significant effect on operating costs. At the same time, these lower operating costs must be compared to the higher initial cost of a technologically superior air conditioning system. Also, there may be less tangible costs and benefits. What will be the effect of a new air conditioning system on employee morale and customer loyalty? Even an apparently simple problem, like whether to replace an air conditioner, cannot be properly solved in the absence of substantial information.

Revenues and Expenses.   Other operating problems that arise can be related to various revenue and expense items. The ability to solve these problems may require more information than the manager has at his or her disposal. What might be some of these problems? Consider the following:

- Sales of a previously popular merchandise line drop 8 percent.
- Employee overtime hours increase by 14 percent in a single month.
- Gross margin declines by 3 percent.

Retail managers would probably only have hunches about the causes of these problems unless the preceding situations had been closely studied. Additional information is required to determine which hunch is correct. In one fast-food restaurant chain, sales of new products accounted for a decline in the previously popular items. In addition, overtime was caused by employees inexperienced with handling the new lines. Management, when presented with all the information, developed new operations procedures so that the new products, although reducing the sales of the previously popular items, drew additional customers, resulting in a profit increase of more than 10 percent the following year.

When we discussed the problem identification subsystem, we explained a framework for comparing standard with actual performance. This framework can be a good source for identifying significant revenue and expense problems. The problem solution subsystem can then be used, if needed, to gather additional information to solve these problems.

ORGANIZING THE RIS

How should the RIS be organized in a retail enterprise? The answer depends on the scope of the RIS. If the RIS is nothing more than a beefed-up accounting system, then the company controller is probably the best person to manage it. However, if the RIS is a comprehensive system consisting of both problem identification and problem solution subsystems, a RIS manager may be needed.

A RIS manager would manage both RIS subsystems. This manager would need inputs from the controller, the legal counsel, the store or department managers, the buyers, and anyone else in the enterprise who is either a potential user or a potential provider of information to the RIS. The RIS manager has to be a very talented individual. In order to interact with a wide range of people on a broad array of topics over which he or she had little authority, the manager would have to be persuasive and diplomatic; also, he or she would need to be knowledgeable in all aspects of the retail enterprise. The RIS manager must be equally comfortable conversing with a store manager, a warehouse manager, a buyer, or a corporate lawyer.

A RIS manager is not a necessity. The RIS manager's contribution to the organization must justify the cost. If the RIS manager—or even the RIS itself—won't help decision-makers make more profitable decisions, then the position is an unnecessary luxury.

Obviously, the retailer with only a few employees cannot justify a comprehensive RIS, much less a RIS manager. But small retailers should be cognizant of changes in consumer, competitor, and channel behavior; of changes in the socioeconomic, legal, and technological environments; and of changes in asset, revenue, and expense performance. Further, when significant problems occur, even small retailers should try to get the best data available within their established cost constraints to solve the problem.

SUMMARY

In this chapter we delineated the nature and scope of a retail information system (RIS). A RIS was defined as a blueprint for the continual and periodic systematic collection, analysis, and reporting of relevant data about past, present, or future developments that could influence or have influenced the retailer's performance.

A RIS should have two major operating subsystems. The problem identification subsystem should provide constant feedback on behavioral, environmental, and operating performance trends in order to identify current or potential problems. Behavioral monitoring should involve scanning the behavior of consumers, competitors, and channel members. Environmental monitoring should involve scanning the socioeconomic, legal, and technological environments. Monitoring operating performance should involve regular analysis of the retailer's assets, revenues, and expenses.

The problem solution subsystem should be designed to generate information to help solve special management problems in strategic planning, administrative management, and operations management. For each, special research may be necessary for effective problem solving.

The types of strategic planning problems for which the problem solution subsystem may need to generate information are related to reformulation of the retailer's mission and objectives, identification and analysis of strategic opportunities, and development of contingency plans. Administrative management problems that may involve special data collection may be categorized as capital, human resources, and location problems. Finally, operations management problems can be asset, revenue, or expense related.

1. Well-known French philosopher Paul Valery has stated, "Once, destiny was an honest game of cards which followed certain conventions with a limited number of cards and values. Now the player realizes in amazement that the hand of his future contains cards never seen before and the rules of the game are modified by each play." Comment on the relevance of this statement in regard to the need for and design of retail information systems.
2. How is the problem identification subsystem different from the problem solution subsystem?
3. How much information should retail decision-makers have at hand when making decisions? Does your answer vary depending on the type of decision being made?
4. Who should manage the retail information system?
5. Is it more crucial to monitor the consumer or the marketing channel?
6. If you were the owner-manager of a local furniture store, how would you obtain information about your competitors?
7. Explain how operating performance standards can be used to help identify key management problems in retailing.
8. What are the various external information sources available to all retailers?
9. Assume you are the owner-manager of a local hardware store in a city of 140,000 people. You wish to design a basic, low-cost retail information system. What should be the major subcomponents of this system? Prioritize your information needs (that is, what is the most important information you desire, the second most important, and so on).
10. Get copies of the local newspaper for the last two weeks. Clip all the supermarkets ads. Analyze the ads for content and write a 500-word statement on the competitive behavior of several of the supermarkets in your city.

11. Obtain copies of the last 12 issues of *Chain Store Age Executive* and *Stores*. What information can you obtain on technology, legal developments, and the socioeconomic environment as related to retailing?
12. Visit a small independent merchandise retailer, a small independent service retailer and a large chain retailer and discuss their use of RIS. What suggestions could you offer any of these retailers?

SUGGESTED READINGS

Bolfing, Claire P., and Sandra L. Schmidt. "Utilizing Expert Database Services." *Industrial Marketing Management* (1988): 141–151.

Dodge, H. Robert, and E. Terry Deiderick. "Retail Metamorphosis: A Fundamental Change In Strategic Orientation." Proceedings of the AMS and ACRA Special Conference, 1988, 12–16.

Lodish, Leonard. "A Marketing Decision Support System for Retailers." *Marketing Science* (Winter 1982): 31–56.

McIntyre, Shelby H., and Sherry D. F. G. Bender. "The Purchase Intercept Technique (PIT) in Comparison to the Telephone and Mail Surveys." *Journal of Retailing* (Winter 1986): 364–383.

Walters, D., and C. A. Rands. "Computers in Retailing." *International Journal of Physical Distribution and Materials Management* (Winter 1983): 3–12.

ENDNOTES

1. The material in this section is based on "Planograms: Friend Or Foe?" *Marketing & Media Decisions* (May 1988): 48–54.

2. "Information System Helps Retailers to Mine Overlooked 'Acres of Diamonds,'" *Marketing News* (May 11, 1984): 4.

3. Dennis E. Garrett, "The Effectiveness of Marketing Policy Boycotts: Environmental Opposition to Marketing," *Journal of Marketing* (April 1987): 46–57.

4. Bernard LaLonde, "The Logistics of Retail Locations," Proceedings of the AMA Educations Conference, 1961, p. 572.

5. Sidney Schoeffler, "Nine Basic Findings on Business Strategy," *PIMS Letter*, No. 2, 1977.

6. Bert Rosenbloom and Ravi V. Tripuraneni, "Strategic Planning In The One Hundred Million Club," Proceedings of Retail Workshop on Research and Teaching in Retailing, 1984, p. 20.

7. "Electronic Shopping," *Chain Store Age Executive* (July 1988): 15.

8. Robert Stevens, "Using Accounting Data to Make Decisions," *Journal of Retailing* (Fall 1975): 23–28.

9. "Vittoria in the Driver's Seat," *American Way* (August 1988): 44–52.

10. Subhash Sharma and Dale D. Achabal, "STEMCOM: An Analytical Model for Marketing Control," *Journal of Marketing* (Spring 1982): 104–13.

11. These questions are only a few of hundreds of questions suggested in *A Retailer's Guide to Accounting Controls* (New York: Price Waterhouse).

12. "New Sears Retail Plan Sets Precise Goals for Sales, Costs, Profits at Every Store," *Wall Street Journal*, 3 December 1980, 25.

aisle

VI Part
The Future of Retailing

18 Chapter

Retailing in the Year 2001

OVERVIEW

In this chapter we will speculate about retailing in the twenty-first century. To properly do this we will provide a brief description and explanation of the discipline of futures research. We will give special attention to some of the methods for conducting futures research and relate these to understanding the future of retailing. An analysis of what we believe the socioeconomic and technological environment of retailing will be like in the year 2001 will be offered. We will provide a portrait of the typical consumer, the typical marketing channel, and the typical competitor in 2001. In the final analysis we construct an image of what a shopping center might be like in the future. This prototype for the future is referred to as Town Center USA.

II. Socioeconomic Environment: 2001
   A. More Needs and Wants, But Less Time
   B. More Parents Than Children
   C. Higher Incomes, But Less Flexibility
   D. More Decisions, But Less Power
   E. More Work, But Less Family Harmony
   F. Segmented Market Growth
      1. Children's Market
      2. Hispanic Market
      3. Seniors Market
      4. Men Under 35
      5. Career/Professional Women
III. Technological Environment: 2001
   A. Integrated Information Management Systems
   B. Expert and AI Systems
   C. Performance and Technology
IV. Consumer 2001: A Portrait
   A. Time as a Cost
   B. Transportation as a Cost
   C. Maintenance as a Cost
   D. Compromise Costs
   E. Risk as a Cost
   F. Price as a Cost
V. Channel 2001: A Portrait
VI. Competitor 2001: A Portrait
   A. Convenience
   B. Merchandise
   C. Customer Service
   D. Price
VII. Town Center USA: Prototype for 2001
   A. Infrastructure Components
   B. Services Retailing
   C. Merchandise Retailing

What will retailing be like in 2001? Can we predict the future of retailing in the United States one decade from now? Is it necessary for the student of retailing and the retail manager to be concerned about the future of retailing in the year 2001? These are questions that will be addressed in this final chapter of *Retail Management*.

As observers of the retail marketplace, it is easy for us to recognize that retailing does change and that change is no stranger to retail executives.[1] It is fair to say, though, that although change is no stranger to retail managers, retailers have not been good students of change, often lagging in appropriate responses to a changing environment.

Retailing today is different than it was just 15 years ago. In 1975 retailing in the United States did not include television cable shopping, computer stores, hypermarkets, telephone stores, or ten-minute lube shops. Predictably, in the year 2001 retailing will again be different—perhaps in ways we have not yet envisioned. Because changes will continue to occur we must try to understand the forces that help to bring about these changes. These forces are not hidden; one can identify current trends and then anticipate the consequences of these trends for retailing.

UNDERSTANDING THE FUTURE TODAY

Understanding external environments is the key to understanding the future today. Retailing operates in an open environment. This open environment consists of the socioeconomic, technological, and legal environments and the behavior of competitors, channel members, and consumers. If one understands these elements of the environment, one has a basis for understanding the future. Changes in the environment today are lead indicators for retail developments in the future. Socioeconomic, technological, or legal environment changes change behavior by competitors, channel members, or consumers, and this stimulates strategic redirections in retailing. The process is illustrated in Exhibit 18.1.

Consider the following illustration. The typical household has less discretionary time and inflation beats down any modest income gains, thus decreasing discretionary income. The result is that many gasoline service stations convert to self-service because they can sell at lower prices; in fact, convenience stores such as Circle K and 7-Eleven begin to sell gas just like they sell milk and bread—on a self-service basis. Consequently, the opportunity arises for ten-minute lube stores to enter the market be-

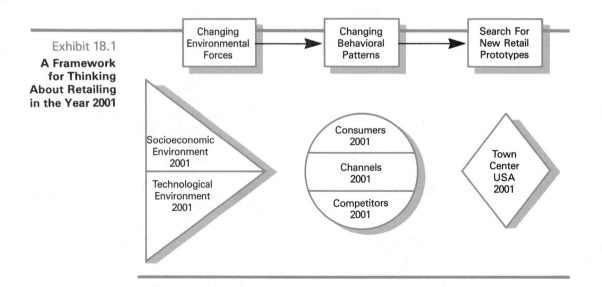

Exhibit 18.1

A Framework for Thinking About Retailing in the Year 2001

Changing Environmental Forces → Changing Behavioral Patterns → Search For New Retail Prototypes

Socioeconomic Environment 2001

Technological Environment 2001

Consumers 2001

Channels 2001

Competitors 2001

Town Center USA 2001

cause they can perform services that historically were performed at service stations.

Remember, the fundamental process never changes: (a) a change in the socioeconomic, technological, or legal environment occurs, which (b) changes consumer, competitor, or channel behavior and (c) encourages strategic redirection in retailing. If you keep this three step process in mind you should not have any trouble thinking about the future.

THINKING

The most important thing you can do to prepare for the future is to think about the future. Thinking is hard work; try to sit in a quiet room for 30 minutes and do nothing but day-dream about the future. Question your dreams. Why can your dream come to reality or why can it not come to reality? If you can do this for 30 uninterrupted minutes, you deserve to be complimented.

The seasoned retail manager is constantly thinking about the future—about how societal values are changing, how the economy is behaving, how competitor strategies are changing, and so on. Thinking takes time. Many retail managers fall into the trap of being crisis managers, and crisis managers do not have time to think. Managers with no time to think about the future will find the future has no time for them. Managers must escape from daily pressures to contemplate the future.

Contemplation cannot occur unless the manager is well-read and informed. The retail executive must be constantly reading about the future. At minimum, the retail executive should regularly read the Sunday edition of *The New York Times*; *American Demographics*, a publication on changing demographics in the United States and marketing implications; and *The Futurist*, a publication on futures research and major trends in the technological, economic, and social environments. These publications will provide information to help the executive think about the future.

THE ROLE OF FUTURES RESEARCH

Futures research can increase the retailer's ability to assess future retail environments. This can occur only if retail executives understand and feel comfortable using the tools and techniques of futures research. First, however, it is important to recognize that futures research cannot predict the future. The future is too complex to be predicted accurately. Instead, futures research can be used to achieve the following, more modest, objectives:

1. To make explicit the assumptions that the retail manager holds about future retail environments.
2. To anticipate alternative futures.

3. To trace possible consequences of important current and past developments.

4. To shape and guide current strategies that might affect the future.

A **futurist**—a person who works in futures research—holds the view that the future is partially controllable if it can be anticipated.

In order to conduct futures research, futurists use three basic types of research methods. These methods have been borrowed from economics, mathematics, statistics, and management, and help the futurist gather perceptions systematically and formulate projections about the future. The basic methods as depicted in Exhibit 18.2 are authority methods, conjecture methods, and mathematical modeling.

Authority Methods.   Perhaps the oldest way to obtain an outlook for the future is to consult an authority. Ancient and modern history are replete with examples of persons being consulted because of the sense they possessed about the future. The Greeks had oracles, rulers in the Middle Ages conferred with wizards, and various American and African tribes utilized medicine men. Even today, many people rely on astrologers.

Just as the ancients and primitives consulted those with the second sight, retailers sometimes solicit the views of an expert, a sole-source au-

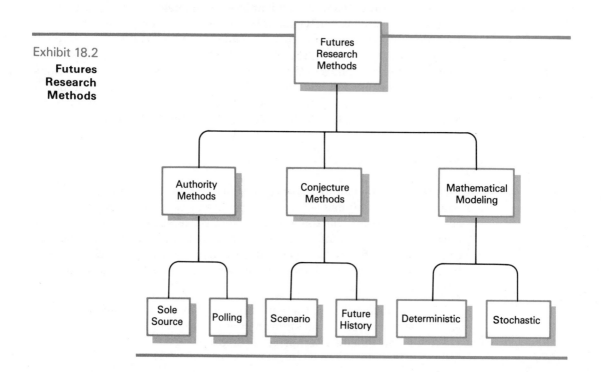

Exhibit 18.2

Futures Research Methods

thority. For instance, a supermarket chain might call on a leading retail academician to draft a report on the future of food retailing. The educator then uses her expertise and existing information to project developments in the macro environment that the supermarket firm will probably face.

In Retailing in Action 18-1, we learn how some retail experts see the future of retailing. All of the individuals quoted are respected authorities in the field of retailing.

RETAILING IN ACTION

18-1

Retail Experts Discuss the Challenges of Today and the Future

- It seems that in every aspect of industry, the rate of change continues to accelerate: the shorter life cycles of products we offer, the fads and tastes of our customers, and the compression of time available for shopping.
- The old marketing methodology of consumer demographics will give way to psychographics, which will enable retailers to serve very narrow and profitable segments, or more likely micro-segments.

    William R. Howell (Chairman, J. C. Penney Company, Inc.), "Tomorrow's Critical Issues," *Retail Control* (June/July 1987): 13–19.

- . . . in the future, proportionally fewer message dollars will be spent getting the customer to the store. But more dollars will be spent inside the store acquainting the customer with your total offering and the value you provide.
- Merchandise will have to be presented more cost effectively in terms of content, fixturing, and floor space.

    Bernard M. Fauber (Chairman of the Board, K mart Corporation), "Critical Issues In Preparing For Tomorrow," *Retail Control* (April/May 1987): 2–6.

- By and large, the majority of households will continue to be short on time. We've been seeing the reaction to that in the preference people have for one-stop shopping.

    Martha Farnsworth Riche (Senior Editor, American Demographics, Inc.), "Vital Trends In Consumer Demographics (I)," *Retail Control* (March 1987): 20–36.

- Retailers have to finally embrace technology, become high-tech oriented, and manage the information explosion.
- . . . The power base of the future will be with those who can amass and utilize information . . .

    Bruce Donald Johnson (National Director, Retail Consulting, Ernst & Whinney), "Retail Trends And Challenges," *Retail Control* (February 1987): 44–64.

- Time-efficient retailing is becoming increasingly important as a large and growing number of consumers become 'time-buyers.' Whereas consumers may be able to make more money, they cannot make more time.

Leonard L. Berry (Professor, Texas A& M University), "Retail Positioning Strategies for the 1980s," *Business Horizons* (November–December 1982): 45–50.

• Stores most likely will be of two strains: Super large stores. . . . and super-specialized 'niche' stores.

Muriel J. Adams, "Robots in the Future?" *Stores* (April 1988).

• Private labels will grow. National brands will dominate.

Walter J. Salmon (Professor, Harvard Business School) and Karen A. Cmar (Associate, McKinsey & Company), "Private Labels Are Back in Fashion," *Harvard Business Review* (May–June 1987): 99–106.

• Competition in the marketplace is driving retailers toward the same kinds of efficiencies that manufacturers are obtaining with Just-in-Time inventory plans and Distribution Resource Planning.

Jules Abend, "UPC + QR = JIT Inventory Replenishment," *Stores* (May 1987).

The polling method, an extension of the sole-source authority method, uses a group of experts instead of only one. Using more than one person to assess the future provides the following advantages:

1. A group of experts can generate and analyze more alternative futures.
2. A broader set of facts can be relied on, more opinions can be expressed, and more estimates of the future can be developed.
3. Specialists as well as generalists can be utilized in areas of high importance to help synthesize facts, refine opinions, and secure estimates.

One method for polling experts that has received considerable attention in many disciplines is the Delphi technique, which was developed at the Rand Institute.[2] Essentially, the **Delphi technique** is used to attain a consensus from a group of experts without having the experts confront each other, but still allowing them to know the opinions of the other experts involved. In futures research, this usually involves having a group of experts independently estimate the likelihood of some future events. The results are then tabulated, and the participants are asked if they desire to revise their estimates in light of the initial estimates given by the other experts. This procedure can be repeated through several rounds. Experiments have shown that, over repeated trials, the range of responses will decrease and that the group response, or median, will move in the direction of the most likely answer.[3]

The Delphi technique can be used in retailing to help the firm assess future retail environments. Of extreme importance to the retail firm are the socioeconomic, technological, and legal environments. Experts from each of these areas, coupled with a few generalists, could enable a retailer to use the Delphi technique to assess likely future environments.

Conjecture Methods.   **Conjecture methods** are reasoned and systematic efforts to identify and describe alternative futures. Conjecture methods employ authorities to develop ideas about the future, but the participants develop whole pictures, whereas in authority methods they produce speculated facts. Two commonly used conjecture methods are scenario construction and future histories.

A **scenario** is a background narrative that describes an alternative future. The scenario can be thought of as a description of some point in the future, a prehistory, so to speak. A scenario for technology in retailing in 2001 might posit a period of fantastic new developments that will alleviate many of the current retail productivity problems. An alternative scenario might describe 2001 as a period when an antitechnology backlash by society grew to fruition and reduced the amount of technological innovation in retailing to a level below its current level.

Familiarity with many alternative scenarios can prevent retail managers from experiencing future shock. The retailer who is aware of possible future scenarios will be able to react to the future in a more positive way.

Another advantage of scenario construction is that it provides an excellent vehicle for retail managers to plan for the future unselfishly. Typically, retail managers try to protect their individual departments in the planning process, because each manager is likely to continue to manage the same department for the next year or two. However, if the managers are asked to construct a scenario for a decade from today, they will do so very open-mindedly, because they do not plan to be in the same administrative position ten years from now and will not try to protect their domain. Ten-year scenarios can then be translated into shorter-range plans formulated to achieve or avoid the contemplated scenarios.

A **future history**, like a scenario, is a conjecture based on facts and assumptions. In contrast to a scenario, however, the future history traces the course of developments and events over time to explain how a particular scenario developed. Thus, whereas a scenario might portray department store retailing in 2001, a future history might begin with totally computerized banking in 1994, leading to a mass system of cashless financial transactions by 1998, and finally to an automated, cash-free department store in 2001. Three key elements in the formulation of a future history are the enumeration of heavy trends, the development of coupling events, and the analysis of branch points.

Heavy trends are those which will have a large effect on the future. For example, if the trend of less and less discretionary time continues, it will drastically alter the fabric of retailing. Consumers will be less willing to search for their ideal bundle of goods and services and will expect

Illus. 18.1

**A two-profes-
sional-
career family—
with little time
left for leisure
and shopping—
will be even
more evident
in the future.**

stores to be conveniently located within minutes of home. McDonald's, for example, now defines its trading area as three to five minutes. Their goal is to have the average household within 3 to 5 minutes of a McDonald's. An excellent source of information about potential heavy trends is the *Trend Analysis Program* published by the Institute of Life Insurance. Exhibit 18.3 profiles some recent TAP reports.

Another important element in the formulation of future histories is the coupling of events. **Coupling of events** refers to the manner in which the occurrence or nonoccurrence of one event affects the likelihood of a subsequent event. For instance, a retailer might ask, "What will be the effect of continual declines in real household purchasing power over a five-year period (the antecedent event) on the average length of time that households keep a durable good such as a TV, car, sofa, etc. (the consequent event)?"

In coupling of events, one is forced to identify **branch points**. These are events whose occurrence or nonoccurrence will affect the retailer's future significantly. For example, a major branch point for food retailers might be the successful development of a pill that provides 100 percent of a person's total nutritional requirements.

Mathematical Modeling.   The third futures research method is mathematical modeling. A model is an abstraction of reality. Therefore, **mathematical modeling** is the construction of mathematical relationships to portray relationships in the real world of retailing. These models can be used to help understand, as well as forecast, the events with which they

Exhibit 18.3
Typical Trend Analysis Reports

Forces in Motion: Identifying Potential Crises (Summer 1983)
Called to our attention are five major crises that could dramatically affect the world. These are the greenhouse effect, the water shortage, decay of the physical infrastructure, collapse of the global financial superstructure, and nuclear armageddon.

The Changing Work Place: Perceptions Reality (March 1984)
This report examines the changing nature of work and gives special attention to high technology skills, better educated and more affluent workers, new technological imperatives, and labor management cooperation. Also the report addresses several central problem areas which must be confronted and these are economic growth, displaced workers and declining areas, underclass and feminization of poverty, and working longer.

Debt Problems, Trade Offensives, and Protectionism (February 1985)
Examined in this report is the trend toward the U.S. becoming an international debtor. The report examines how OPEC's decade of wealth during the 1970s set the stage for the stagnant 1980s. In addition an international system is discussed which is infected by debt and protectionism and the role of the Reagan revolution. The role and implication of the United States as a capital importer is discussed.

New Immigrants New Minorities (July 1986)
The large increase in Hispanics and Asians in the U.S. is discussed. Historical trends are reviewed and projections made through 2030. Special attention is given to the impact on societal sectors of the new immigrants/ new minorities.

Information Technologies (October 1988)
This report examines the critical importance of information technologies to business survival in the future. Some interesting new information technologies are discussed and their impact on the life insurance industry examined.

SOURCE: All Trend Analysis Reports are written and published under the direction of the American Council of Life Insurance.

deal. In futures research, models are more concerned with understanding a system than with forecasting. In retailing, models can be constructed for relatively small sectors of activity (e.g., a single retailer's sales) or for large sectors of retail activity (e.g., total monthly or quarterly retail sales in the United States).

Mathematical models can be classified as static or dynamic. **Static models** ignore time as a variable, whereas **dynamic models** consider time as an independent variable. Because retailers are concerned with the future, they tend to deal more with dynamic models. Dynamic models can be of two basic types—deterministic or stochastic. **Deterministic models** operate under conditions of certainty (i.e., the retail model builder assumes he knows the parameters of the model). With deterministic models, the futurist is able to arrive at a specific forecast of the future.

Consider a local department store retailer attempting to forecast sales for 2001. It has sales in 1990 of $20 million. The retail model builder might develop a model that links retail sales to such factors as trading area population, number of competitors, average household discretionary income, and cost of personal transportation. In addition, interactions between these factors might need to be modeled. A deterministic model would state a very rigid relationship between retail sales and these factors; it might state that on average the projections of these factors will result in sales increasing 5.8 percent annually through the year 2001. The important point here is that 5.8 percent is assumed with certainty. The model thus will be able to forecast $37.2 million in retail sales in 2001. This estimate will probably be wrong, because the assumption of certainty, in regard to the mathematical relationship between retail sales and the four causal factors, is unrealistic.

The fact that deterministic models assume certainty about an uncertain future is their major weakness. However, deterministic models have the strong advantage of being easier and less expensive to construct than stochastic models. When deterministic models are used by retail analysts, the results are usually adjusted in consideration of the uncertainty inherent in future environments.

Stochastic models operate under conditions of risk and, therefore, the parameters of the model take on a series of possible values rather than only one value. As a consequence, the forecast of the future takes on a series of values. Consider the example that, as previously outlined, a department store has sales of $20 million in 1990 and that it projects that sales will increase by 5.8 percent per year through 2001. However, the forecaster believes that the rate of annual growth could possibly be as low as 3.1 percent or as high as 7.9 percent. In essence, the forecaster is saying that the rate of growth is stochastic and can take on a series of values between 3.1 percent and 7.9 percent with an expected growth of 5.8 percent. Exhibit 18.4 shows the possible range of sales that the department store may have in 2001. By considering all possible variables, the retail researcher is able to generate a series of projections for retail sales in 2001 ranging from $28 million, if sales grow at 3.1 percent annually, to $46.2 million if sales grow at 7.9 percent annually. The most likely forecast is sales of $37.2 million based on a growth in sales of 5.8 percent annually. These projections are illustrated in Exhibit 18.4. A stochastic mathematical model gives the retail manager not only a level of sales to expect in 2001, but also the level of uncertainty that surrounds that projection. Obviously, this type of forecast is more useful and realistic; in addition, it is less likely to be misleading.

Mathematical models are not as simple as the preceding illustrations indicate. Usually, they consist of multiple equations instead of a single equation.

Our discussion will now turn to projections we have developed about the socioeconomic and technological environments in 2001. We will not develop any projections about the legal environment, because we believe our projections would be too speculative. We believe that our projections of the socioeconomic and technological environment are reasoned and log-

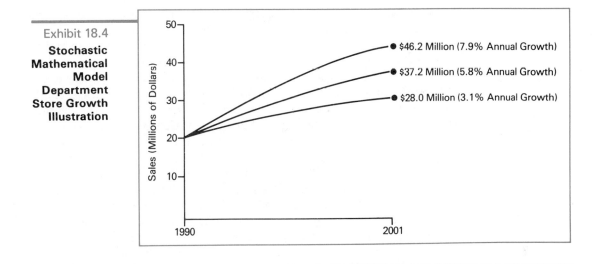

Exhibit 18.4

**Stochastic
Mathematical
Model
Department
Store Growth
Illustration**

ical. Obviously, the future of retailing is more complex than we make it out to be in this chapter.

SOCIOECONOMIC ENVIRONMENT: 2001

We believe that the socioeconomic environment in 2001 will be characterized by six major developments that are beginning to occur today and will accelerate throughout the 1990s. These trends are:

- More needs and wants, but less time
- More parents than children
- More income, but less flexibility
- More decisions, but less power
- More work, but less family harmony
- Segmented market growth

Each of these trends will briefly be reviewed with regard to how they might change retailing in the twenty-first century.

MORE NEEDS AND WANTS, BUT LESS TIME

In the year 2001, the majority of the population will have been born after the year 1960. After World War II our society entered an era of marketing and high consumption; marketing and consumption accelerated even more in the 1960s. During this time Ralph Nader gained popularity in his struggle to protect the consumer from the marketplace. By the 1970s marketers were selling, not just toothpaste, but political candidates, legal advice, health care, social causes, and careers in the United States Army. During the 1980s, the tools of marketing became even more pervasive. The last thirty years have witnessed levels of marketing and consumption that were never before thought possible. We have become a society of durable goods junkies and fast-food addicts, who vote for political candidates on the basis of image, not substance. In the year 2001, the average 40-year-old will have grown up watching television several hours a day, experimenting with computers and possibly drugs in the 1970s, being a yuppie in the 1980s, and wanting more and more of the good life in the 1990s. This individual will want, want, want, and have needs that seem to grow geometrically with time. The 40-year-old in 2001 was "born to shop" in 1961 and will "live to consume." The ability to shop and consume will be halted, not so much by income constraints, but by time constraints. In the year 2001 the average 40-year-old will be working 50 hours a week. A white-collar, salaried job will be the norm. Most couples will have two professional careers. With time at work, commuting to work and other necessary encroachments on time such as sleep, personal care, and child care, this household will be starved for time.

How will people cope? They will cocoon themselves in their own personally controlled habitat. They will be exhausted by the work environment and other interaction with the external world, and thus will equip the home for satisfying experiences and for privacy. The kitchen will be less of a nourishment center, than a place for the mind. This kitchen will have an electronic information center, where goods and services can be purchased electronically and where entire libraries can be accessed. The bathroom will be a health activity center, where the body can be maintained via exercise, relaxation, meditation, and self-diagnosis (facilitated by expert medical systems the individual can use). The family room will be a place to socialize with family members and visitors. Big-screen televisions and wall-to-wall stereo will be commonplace. In brief, houses will allow people to create their own special environment, meeting their needs and protecting them from the external world. Such a home will offer the ultimate in time and place convenience and utility.

MORE PARENTS THAN CHILDREN

The average number of children per family will approach 1.5 to 1.7, so parents will outnumber children. Because of this, and because the large number of divorces will continue, children will receive special attention—not in terms of time, but in terms of materialistic favors.

Children will increasingly become the key influencers on household purchases, because they will have the time to gather information and shop. Children will also have more power over their parents, since parents will spend less time with them and will have to allow children to decide more things for themselves. Children will become addicts to materialism at an early age, and will obtain part-time jobs to support their consumption habits. This income from part-time work, plus sizable weekly allowances, will result in children becoming a large market segment which retailers must recognize. Regardless of social class, children will have money to spend; if they don't receive it in allowance, they will work to obtain spending money.

HIGHER INCOMES, BUT LESS FLEXIBILITY

Household incomes will increase throughout the 1990s, primarily because of productivity gains in the economy and the continued trend of two-income households. However the typical household will have less discretionary income because of two forces. First, taxes will continue to increase. The huge federal deficit will not be able to be controlled with only spending cuts and taxes will have to increase. Second, households will go further into debt. More income will be used to service debt payments, which will leave less discretionary income for current expenditures. Education and day-care expenses will also become increasingly expensive and these will take their toll on discretionary income. Because they are so time-constrained, people will believe that eating out is a necessity. By 2001, two out of three meals will be eaten out of the home.

In brief, more and more of income will go for what people view as necessities and people will have less flexibility on how to spend their income. As a result, people will feel powerless.

Illus. 18.2
By the year 2001, two out of three meals will be eaten out of the home. Source: Jeff Greenberg.

MORE DECISIONS, BUT LESS POWER

2001 will be a time of increased complexity. Products will be technologically complex and the typical consumer will not understand the functioning of most products. This is already true of autos and electronic equipment. Consumers will increasingly understand only the service or satisfaction delivered by the product. Managing a household or life during this period of complexity will be difficult. Consumers will feel that they lack the knowledge about such basic things as the best car, the most nutritional cereal, or the most energy-efficient air conditioner to purchase. The responsibility for making these decisions will be reluctantly shifted to the retailer.

Because consumers will not understand the complexity of products, they will increasingly feel that they do not have the power to make intelligent purchase decisions. In other cases the consumer will feel powerless because large institutions control the alternatives available in the marketplace. All sectors of economic activity will be increasingly controlled by national organizations. This has been a trend for many decades in retailing but will spread to banking, health care, child care, and most other sectors of economic activity which were historically controlled at a local level. This trend will reinforce the feeling of powerlessness on the part of households.

Individuals are also experiencing increasing powerlessness because of the complexity of society. We feel that our small voice doesn't count and that the choices we have are all unattractive. Thus, even if we exercise free choice, it is over options we find unacceptable. These feelings of powerlessness were especially evident during the 1988 presidential election—many people were not satisfied with either candidiate.

MORE WORK, BUT LESS FAMILY HARMONY

A typical household with children will consist of a loosely joined set of individuals who spend very little time together. Husband and wife will be working and children will be at school, day care, or participating in extracurricular activities. A household of four (parents and two children) will seldom be together except for Sundays, holidays, and vacations, and then they may be only together for a few hours or days. In fact, it is likely that on Sundays, holidays, and vacations, each household member will go their own way. Attendance at different churches, separate vacations, and dividing holidays between natural parents and stepparents will be common. Because of the need for both marriage partners to work, the time for family togetherness will all but evaporate and thus family harmony will be the exception instead of the norm.

Another factor causing family disharmony will be care of the elderly parent(s). Children planned for and born when the parents are in their mid-thirties will need to be concerned about caring for their aging parents shortly after graduating from college. Households will feel sandwiched between raising their own children and caring for their aged parents.

SEGMENTED MARKET GROWTH

Markets in general will not see spectacular growth in the 1990s. Often short-run fluctuations in the economy mask underlying realities. The reality is that the United States is a mature, slow-growth economy. Despite this, selected market segments will experience explosive growth. Retailers that respond to these market growth opportunities will be able to experience above-average growth during the early part of the twenty-first century. The market segments that are expected to grow in the next few decades are depicted in Exhibit 18.5 and discussed in the following pages.

Children's Market.   In the year 2001 there will be more than 16 million children under five and more than 48 million children between 5 and 17. This market will have more than $350 billion in annual purchasing power. Parents will spend more money on fewer children; grandparents will overindulge their grandchildren, especially those from divorced families; children will be responsible for more shopping chores; children will receive larger allowances and earn their own spending money; children will increasingly influence their parents' purchase decisions.

Retailers must recognize that children develop brand and store preferences at a very young age. These children can and do influence household purchasing and grow up to purchase goods and services on their own.

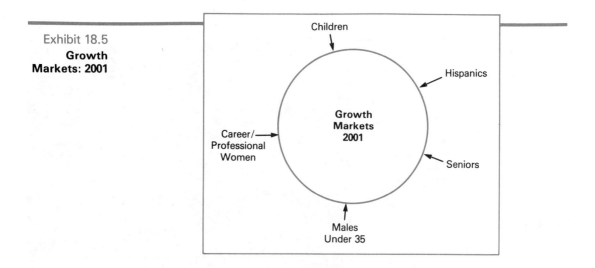

Exhibit 18.5
Growth Markets: 2001

Hispanic Market.   During the 1980s the Hispanic population in the United States grew more than 35 percent to 20 million. By 2001 this market will be more than 25 million strong and spend more than $200 billion. Some analysts predict that by 2015 there will be more Hispanics in the United States than Blacks.[4]

The Hispanic market is concentrated in nine states (California, Texas, New York, Florida, Illinois, Arizona, New Jersey, New Mexico, and Colorado) and two states—California and Texas—have more than half of the Hispanic population. Although by 2001 the Hispanic population will be somewhat more dispersed, these nine states will continue to have more than 75 percent of the Hispanic population. Retailers in these states must begin to develop strategies to get a part of this large market. Hispanics spend heavily on items for the house and are fashion-conscious. One forward-thinking retailer that is responding to this market opportunity is J. C. Penney, which has Patricia Asip as its manager of special segment marketing. J. C. Penney Company has been especially aggressive in Hispanic promotion of its mail-order catalog.

Seniors Market.   In 2001 there will be more than 35 million individuals in the United States over 65 and more than 60 million over 55. Due to increased social security benefits, pension plans, high personal savings, equity in real estate, and few fixed payment obligations, this market represents an enormous market opportunity. By 2001, the average life expectancy will be more than 75 years; thus, people will be spending for many years after age 65. In fact we will only think of old age as being over 85. People in their sixties will be active in outdoor activities, feel healthy, and have the time and money to enjoy themselves. Increasingly these individuals will view retirement as a time to become who and what they always wanted to be. They will spend time with their grandchildren because the

Illus. 18.3
By 2001, the average life span will be more than 75 years. People in their 60s will be active and will have the time and money to enjoy themselves.

parents of the grandchildren will not have the time and/or be divorced. They will also spend heavily on gifts for these grandchildren.

Men Under 35.   Historically, young men have been fashion laggards. They spent proportionately less on apparel and personal care than their female counterparts. By the year 2001 this will have changed dramatically. With the breakdown of sex roles in the 1970s young men learned to experiment with fashion and personal care products. These males will enter the twenty-first century as fashion-conscious consumers. In 2001 there will be 31 million males between 18 and 34. They will have market purchasing power for apparel as great as the female market of similar age.

Career/Professional Women.   Today the career/professional woman is a fact of life. By the year 2001 these women will be entering the ranks of senior executives and their large incomes will accelerate the growth of this market segment. The market itself will become more segmented since young, career-oriented women will have different needs and capabilities in terms of purchasing power than the senior-ranking career women.

Retailers need to recognize that the career-oriented female shopper hates shopping. She hates long lines, insensitive clerks, poorly organized stores with poor signing, uncertainty in terms of merchandise performance, and spending time to shop. The retail store that can help the career-oriented female overcome these hates by catering to her likes will experience spectacular growth.

Retailing in Action 18-2 illustrates the importance of keeping an eye on the future, and shows what happens when the future is ignored.

RETAILING
IN
ACTION
18-2

Pier 1: Keeping an Eye on the Future

The senior management at Pier 1 knows well the importance of keeping an eye on changing demographic and life-style trends and projecting these trends into the future. The firm was founded in 1962 under the name, "Cost Plus", as an outlet for rattan furniture and imported housewares. In 1966, with sixteen stores, the company was sold to new owners and the name changed to Pier 1. In the 1960s the firm was clearly in touch with the long-hair-and-love-beads set. The stores were known as antiestablishment and offered incense, soap, beaded curtains, bedspreads, peacock feathers, and other hallmarks of the hippie cult.

The 1970s, however, were a disappointment for Pier 1, as it stood by and witnessed its sales drop by half from 1971 to 1980. Pier 1 drifted unfocused into the 1970s; it failed to move from the age of Aquarius to the age of disco.

Today, however, the story is different. Pier 1 is revitalized, in tune with today and the future. It now has a strategic plan that will lead it to the year 2000. Sales have skyrocketed from $117 million in 1980 to $327 million in 1988. This has in part occurred because the company now believes in market research and aggressively acts on the results of this research. The research is heavily oriented to the future. Witness the following excerpt from the 1988 *Annual Report to Stockholders of Pier 1 Imports.*

Illus. 18.4

Sales at Pier 1 Imports have skyrocketed, in part because the company now believes in market research and aggressively acts on the results of this research. Source: Pier 1 Imports, Inc.

Pier 1 Imports is a market-driven company. Our primary mission is to identify our customers' needs and wants, and then meet those needs with appropriate products and outstanding service.

The company places great importance on understanding its target customer. Through ongoing consumer research, the company obtains valuable feedback that guides it today and keeps it attuned to the emerging trends of tomorrow.

Pier 1 Imports' research program also analyzes the broader American consumer market to see how trends in this arena affect our customer base. Two factors of particular significance are the aging of the baby boom generation and the massive introduction of women into the work force.

. . . Over the next ten years, baby boom households will be forming in record numbers. Analysts have called this trend the "middle-aging of America." This process will create a broadening interest in the home and home furnishings. Thus Pier 1 Imports places special emphasis on understanding the needs of this important age group.

These excerpts tell us that Pier 1 Imports is a forward-looking, market-oriented retail organization that is engineering its merchandising and marketing efforts to reach its target customer and achieve for itself high performance results. Not surprisingly the firm earned an after-tax return on stockholders' equity of more than 20 percent in 1988.

Sources: Bill Crawford, "Bringing It All Back Home," *Texas Monthly* (January 1989): 122–125; and *Pier 1 Imports 1988 Annual Report*.

TECHNOLOGICAL ENVIRONMENT: 2001

The technological environment of the year 2001 will be an extrapolation of current leading-edge technologies in the computer field. The most important developments will be in software, especially in the development of expert systems and artificial intelligence. These developments will improve financial performance for those retailers that adopt the new technologies. We refer to these new technologies as integrated information management system technologies (IIMS). IIMS is the management information system (MIS) of the future.

INTEGRATED INFORMATION MANAGEMENT SYSTEMS

The components of IIMS are available today.[5] Over the next decade they will be integrated with sophisticated software which will eliminate the need for many middle managers in retailing enterprises. Let us examine the building blocks.

Point of Sale (POS) scanning systems and computerized registers are already very common in retailing.[6] These systems allow the retailer to continuously collect sales data by item. To use scanning technology, items must be marked with a product code symbol. The most dominant coding technology is the Universal Product Code (UPC).[7] In the future, not only products, but customers will have codes. This will be voluntary, so not all customers will participate; however, those that do will be given some sort of incentive such as discount coupons, free prizes, etc. By being able to capture both product data and customer data at the point of sale the retailer will be constructing a database of awesome potential. For instance, a supermarket will be able to determine which customers prefer a particular brand and when they are most likely to purchase the brand, based on past purchase patterns. This information would allow the retailer to more effectively and profitably manage inventory investments.

A second piece of IIMS is **electronic data interchange (EDI)**.[8] EDI allows the retailer's computer to talk directly to the supplier's computer to transmit intercompany transactions. Currently, only 10 percent of retail-

Exhibit 18.6
**Critical
Components:
Integrated
Information
Management
Systems**

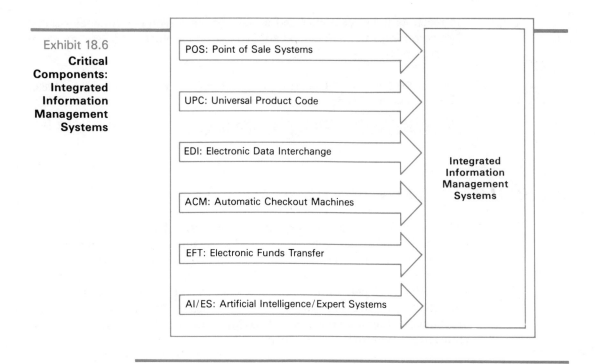

ers are using EDI,[9] but by 2001 90 percent of all retailers will be participating. The primary advantage of EDI is the increased speed of doing
business with suppliers—replenishment orders can be transmitted instan-
taneously. If replenishment is based on monitoring sales via POS systems, the speed is increased even more. The most important factor in determining the growth of EDI will be cooperation between retailers and
suppliers. If retailers and suppliers are going to have access to each other's computers, trust and cooperation will be important.

The customer will become a part of IIMS either through in-home
shopping or traditional shopping at a store. In a store, customers will
have the opportunity to check themselves out of the store via **ACM (automatic checkout machines)**. This phenomenon has already occurred in
banking with ATMs (automatic teller machines). With ACMs the customers will scan their own purchases with the POS system, enter their
customer identification card (similar to an ATM card), and receive clearance to exit the store. This data could then be transmitted to suppliers
with EDI technology.

The entire IIMS technology will rely heavily on **electronic funds
transfer (EFT)**.[10] EFT, which has been with us since the late 1970s, allows
banks to be electronically linked with their customers in order to make
and receive payments. EFT will allow customers to check themselves out

of the store and pay for their merchandise by having their purchases automatically debited from their bank accounts.

EXPERT AND AI SYSTEMS

Two important software developments in retailing will enable IIMS to become dominant by 2001—**artificial intelligence** and **expert systems**. These systems will be able to make important recurring retail decisions without human interference. The expert systems will be modeled on the decision rules of retail experts. We believe that these software developments will occur within the next decade.[11] Specifically, we predict that:

1. **Space Manager (SM).** The space manager will be an expert system which automatically analyzes customer demand and matches this with product availability to constantly realign space in the store to maximize financial returns. In brief, the store will be planogrammed with artificial intelligence. The space manager software will have the ability to conduct its own experiments and statistically analyze the results. For instance, it could decide to reduce the space assigned to 7-Up and increase the space assigned to Kellogg's Rice Krispies, and then assess the results to determine the effectiveness. Based on the results of this experiment, store personnel would be directed by the computer to alter space configurations on a more permanent basis.

2. **Replenishment Manager (RM).** This piece of AI-based software will automatically reorder merchandise and handle all billing, payment, receipt, and stocking of merchandise. The replenishment manager software will manage delivery dates and assign personnel to receive, mark, and stock the merchandise. Primitive forms of this system have appeared already. More sophisticated software will enable the replenishment manager to communicate with new suppliers to assess purchasing opportunities for frequently stocked items.

3. **Demand Manager (DM).** The demand manager software will analyze sales patterns and decide when to mark down merchandise and how long to maintain the markdown. In addition the demand manager will select the items to advertise, prepare the advertisements, and schedule the advertisements. The demand manager will also have a customer database to keep track of customer purchases by item, price, and time of purchase.[12] This component will allow the demand manager to make better pricing and promotion decisions. The demand manager will interface with the replenishment manager and space manager.

4. **Human Resource Manager (HRM).** All retail personnel will be assigned tasks by the human resource manager software. The time taken to complete these tasks will be monitored. The HRM will

report to senior management and recommend corrective actions when value judgements are required. For routine personnel matters, the HRM will act on its own; for example, hiring of more part-time help for a holiday season or compiling weekly schedules.

5. **Working Capital Manager (WCM).** The working capital manager software will manage the current section of the balance sheet for individual stores or an entire chain of stores. It will interface with the replenishment manager in determining when to pay suppliers and with the customer manager in determining when to offer credit to customers. The investment of cash in short-term income-earning financial instruments will also be managed by the WCM.

PERFORMANCE AND TECHNOLOGY

We predict that the high-performance retailers in 2001 will be those that embrace the information technologies we have just reviewed. Already some of these new information technologies have shown to be keys to increased profitability.[13] Collectively these technologies will offer the following benefits:

- Fewer stockouts and better customer service, leading to higher sales
- Less speculative inventory and fewer markdowns, which will lead to higher profit margins
- More rapid replenishment of stocks, which will improve inventory turnover
- Better management of credit, which will result in reduced bad-debts expense
- More scientific pricing, which will result in fewer markdowns and consequently higher profit margins
- Fewer middle managers and reduced payroll costs
- More efficient use of employees and reduced payroll costs

CONSUMER 2001: A PORTRAIT

If we were to paint a portrait of the United States consumer in 2001, what would the portrait look like? America is a society of heterogeneity, and not homogeneity; it is less of a melting pot than a salad bowl. With some risk of oversimplification, we will paint a portrait of the customer of the twenty-first century.

We will refer to this consumer of the twenty-first century as the "Smart Shopper". The **Smart Shopper** will believe that shopping wisely can be a source of improved living standards. Smart shoppers will have a new value orientation. The old value orientation was driven by price and quality: get the most units of quality for the least cost. The new value orientation will be driven by minimizing the total costs of shopping and consumption. This is a radical departure from the past, but it is already beginning to shape the future of retailing in the United States. What are the costs the smart shopper will be concerned with minimizing? Let's take a look.

TIME AS A COST

A construction worker drives up to a Circle K or 7-Eleven convenience store and purchases a sandwich, soft drink, and small packet of cookies. The cost is $4.59. The sandwich is not very tasty and the soft drink and cookies are much more expensive than at the supermarket 500 feet away; in addition the cashier was not polite. Nevertheless, the construction worker feels this was a good deal. Why? Because the entire transaction (from entering the store until exiting) took 2.5 minutes; in brief, the shopping experience was efficient.[14] The twenty-first century consumer will consider time in all purchase decisions. The smart shopper will recognize that a good deal results when time is released for other activities. Retailers that recognize this will gain market share; those that ignore this will lose market share.[15]

TRANSPORTATION AS A COST

In 2001 the typical new car will cost $25,000 and the cost per mile to operate the auto will be $.60. Traveling to the regional shopping mall a mere 13 miles away will cost $15.60 in roundtrip transportation. Congestion will be a serious problem. As a result, the smart shopper will not travel a long distance for a low price, because the reduction in price will be negated by the added transportation and time costs. It will not be uncommon for convenience stores to define their trading area as 90 seconds in travel time. Because transportation will be viewed as a cost, the smart shopper will search less by traveling from store to store and search more from the home electronically. When the smart shopper sets out to purchase an item, she will know exactly where to find it. Also the smart shopper will recognize that mail order retailing is often a good deal because time and transportation costs will be saved.

MAINTENANCE AS A COST

All products have a cost beyond initial price. Maintenance and repair costs are a function of product quality and the costs of side effects from use of the product. For instance, the cost of cigarettes is the current price plus the long-term cost of deterioration in personal well-being and the associated cost of repairing the body. Certainly insurance companies recognize this when they establish insurance premiums on smokers vs. non-smokers; on drivers of Corvettes vs. station wagons; on homes with security and fire protection systems vs. those without. The smart shopper will consider these costs in purchase decisions. The smart shopper will recognize that a low-priced product may be a bad deal when a higher priced product has lower maintenance costs.

COMPROMISE COSTS

The smart shopper will recognize that an ideal product consists of a set of objective and subjective attributes. When a product is purchased that deviates from this ideal, the smart shopper will view this as the cost of compromise. A customer will select a higher priced product if it is closer to the ideal product because the cost of compromise will be less. A piece of clothing that does not fit perfectly is a good illustration of this point. If the dress fits precisely as one would desire, a higher price will be paid than if it does not fit well. A very low dollar price is paid for a dress that does not fit well, but the compromise costs are high. Retailers that recognize that matching products to precise customer needs will decrease compromise costs for the customer can charge higher prices and at the same time be viewed as offering a good deal.

RISK AS A COST

The smart shopper will be concerned about taking risks and will view risk taking as a cost. When the smart shopper purchases a product and is uncertain about how it will perform, function, or provide anticipated benefits, these uncertainties will be viewed as a psychological cost. If a product is found that performs and functions well, the cost of switching to a new product will be viewed as great. The same logic applies to selection of a retail store; the consumer will select stores that minimize risk and will be loyal to such stores.

Warranties and guarantees that reduce uncertainty will be worth a lot to the smart shopper. Nordstroms is very successful because it stands behind everything it sells. At Nordstrom's if you don't like the product, your money or a substitute is returned, regardless of whether the product had a manufacturer's warranty. Clearly Nordstrom's has recognized that uncertainty is a cost. Customers willingly pay a higher merchandise price because their uncertainty costs are reduced. This will increasingly be true of consumers in 2001.

PRICE AS A COST

The purchase price will continue to be viewed as a cost, but the smart shopper will consider financing costs as part of the purchase price. The smart shopper will not look at the monthly cost of a new car but the deferred payment price. Because other costs (interest rates, time, transportation, maintenance, risk, compromise) will be considered, the smart shopper will begin to view the purchase price as often less than 50 percent of the total cost. Retailers must begin to promote on the basis of these other costs. Retailers that can reduce the time, transportation, maintenance, compromise, and risk costs of the merchandise they sell will be at a distinct advantage in the mind of the smart shopper.

CHANNEL 2001: A PORTRAIT

What will the typical marketing channel be like in 2001? The most successful marketing channels will be those that are marketing support systems and these systems will be characterized by cooperation. *Cooperation* is the single word that helps us to paint the portrait of the channel in 2001.

Too often today, marketing channels are characterized by conflict. This occurs because most chief executive officers, presidents, and marketing vice presidents are myopic when it comes to their firm's resources. Although they recognize the usefulness of middlemen, they do not acknowledge that they are off-balance sheet resources. **Off-balance sheet resources** are resources that can be drawn on for support and assistance but which are not recorded on the retailer's balance sheet. When retailers do not realize the marketing channel is an off-balance sheet resource, the tactics for using middlemen and the channel will not be strategically based and channel conflict will arise.

In 2001, marketing channels will be characterized as **marketing support systems.**[16] A marketing support system is a marketing channel where all channel members work together to support the marketing efforts of each other. The underlying premise of marketing support systems is that the function of institutions in the marketing channel is to support the marketing effort of those involved in the channel. Those channel institutions that serve one another are key off-balance sheet resources for the channel partners, and integrated strategies for interorganizational marketing enhance the effectiveness of the channel process.

Retailers in 2001 will recognize that they are very powerful in the marketing channel because they control both information and access to consumers. High-performance retailers will not abuse this power but use it to assist the marketing support system. In brief these retailers will recognize that:

1. They are in business to support the marketing effort of manufacturers or suppliers, and they will dedicate their resources to that end.
2. They are more than just another company to process goods through the marketing channel; they are a marketing support system.
3. They are an off-balance sheet marketing resource for manufactur-

ers and suppliers, and manufacturers and suppliers are off-balance sheet resources for them.

Manufacturers and suppliers who participate in the marketing support system will have a spirit of cooperation toward retailers. These suppliers will be in existence:

1. To discover opportunities. Suppliers will help retailers discover and exploit opportunities to improve customer service and profits. These suppliers will ask retailers to tell them about their marketing plans so they can be meshed with the suppliers' plans.
2. To discover problems. Suppliers will help retailers discover potential customer-service problems before they erode profits. These suppliers will ask retailers about their customer-service objectives and will use their resources to help retailers attain their objectives.
3. To solve problems. Suppliers will help retailers solve existing customer-service problems that are harming profits. These suppliers will ask retailers about their marketing processes and design their operations around these marketing processes.
4. For strategic reasons. Suppliers will offer help in designing and implementing the retailer's strategy for getting goods to the target market. Suppliers will help retailers exploit marketing opportunities.
5. For operational reasons. Suppliers will offer assistance in designing and implementing tactics for getting goods to the target market. Suppliers will want to know about retailers' operational problems and work on them as if they were their own—because they are.
6. To improve retailers' profit. Suppliers will be available to help retailers manage the costs associated with getting goods to the target market. Suppliers will ask retailers to tell them about their operating processes and offer to help manage costs based on an understanding of these operating processes.

In brief, the marketing support system will be a cooperative system in which all channel partners view themselves as resources for each other. They will work as extensions of each others' operations with the common goal of satisfying the customer.

COMPETITOR 2001: A PORTRAIT

In general, competitors in 2001 will be more sophisticated in the ways they compete. Retailers have learned that price competition has a destructive impact on profits. In 2001 the retailer will compete on four dimensions: convenience, merchandise, customer service, and price. As retailers push nonprice competition, price will become less important as a competitive weapon.

CONVENIENCE

Because customers are time-constrained, retailers will increasingly define their trading areas not in terms of miles, but in terms of minutes. As we previously mentioned, McDonald's already defines its trading area as three to five minutes. Retailers that have a distinct convenience advantage will make it easier for customers to patronize their stores. Time savings will be recognized not only in terms of travel to the store, but also in time spent shopping the store and checking out. One-stop shopping will add to convenience. Well designed and signed stores where merchandise can be found quickly, where check-out and payment for merchandise is quick, and where store personnel are courteous, will result in a significant competitive advantage in 2001.

The director of the Center for Retailing Studies at Texas A & M University has said, "Stores that steal the consumer's time—stores that are difficult to get to or through—will generally need a more compelling offer to compete than will stores that are more convenient to use. To survive, time-inefficient stores need to offer outstanding bargains, service, atmosphere, or entertainment. To waste the consumer's time, and to be mediocre in other respects, is to commit competitive suicide in today's retailing environment."[17]

MERCHANDISE

Merchandise assortments will also be used as a competitive weapon. For this weapon to be effective, assortments must be planned in relation to competitive differential advantage. To have this competitive differential advantage, retailers will need four types of assortments.

1. **Dominant Assortments.** These will be merchandise assortments the retailer can dominate with breadth and depth in a particular category. These will be the assortments for which the retailer will be known and will be the assortments for which customers shop the retailer.
2. **Intercept Assortments.** These will be assortments in which breadth and depth are not dominant but the mere presence of which will allow the retailer to take customers away from the traditional retailer for this type of merchandise.
3. **Competitive Assortments.** These will be assortments which will be a subset of the dominant assortments. The retailer will offer these assortments at very attractive prices in order to attract customers to the store and build traffic. These assortments do not

necessarily directly generate profits, but they indirectly help to
sell other goods.

4. **Opportunistic Assortments**. These will be assortments which the
retailer is able to obtain from suppliers on very special terms. The
retailer will become the liquidator of this merchandise and attract
new customers to the store and/or reward existing customers with
a very special deal.

CUSTOMER SERVICE

The primary reason customer service will be important as a competitive
tool is because it will allow the retailer to develop relationships with customers[18] and because retailers have ignored service over the last 30
years.[19] Superior customer service will allow the retailer to bond to its customers and beat competitors. Once this is accomplished, a competitor will
have extreme difficulty in diverting customers to its stores.

A competitive strategy based on customer service will be based on
three factors. First, retailers must guarantee the customer that what they
purchase will be what they receive. If the suit is promised for delivery the
next day, it must be delivered the next day; if the tire is promised to provide 40,000 miles, it must deliver 40,000 miles; if the perfume is promised
to make the person feel beautiful, it must. If it does not, the retailer must
ask no questions and return the customer's money. In brief, customer service must reduce the risk of purchasing to zero. The retailer must be the
bearer of risk. Second, retailers must assist the customer in and out of the
store in the most courteous and friendly manner possible. The retail clerk
must become a professional to whom the customer looks for advice, guidance, and friendship. Third, customer service must provide extras which
augment the product being purchased. That means allowing the customer
to take the merchandise home to see if their spouse likes it before a final
purchase is made; offering product installation and educational services
to show the customer how to use the product; providing special delivery
so the customer can receive the product immediately if needed. In brief, a
competitive strategy based on customer service attempts to sell and compete on the *intangible* aspects of the product.

PRICE

Retailers in 2001 will compete on price—it's unavoidable. However, price
will not be the key element of competition as it was during the 1980s and
early 1990s. When retailers use price as a weapon, it will be on competitive and opportunistic assortments and not dominant or intercept
assortments.

TOWN CENTER USA: PROTOTYPE FOR 2001

It would be possible to develop prototypes for several different retail stores of the future. Instead, however, we will develop a prototype of the shopping center of the future. This allows us to discuss the fabric of retailing in a much richer sense. In this approach we assume that most shopping will continue to take place outside the home vs. at-home via computers, the television, or the mail.[20]

Since 2001 is just a decade away, it is unlikely that this prototype will dominate retailing by 2001. Remember, the role of futures research is not to predict the future but to help us understand what the future might be. The Town Center USA prototype we are about to develop is an exercise in making explicit our assumptions about the future and in tracing the consequences of current developments. We certainly believe that the prototype is feasible and that, in principle, such a prototpye could be built today. It is a prototype which could shape the environment of the community in which it is located, since it is as much an engineering feat as it is a marketing innovation.[21]

Town Center USA is much more than a *shopping center* as we currently use that term. Town Center USA is a community center built to serve a population greater than 100,000. It succeeds because it offers local citizens a community place. This is critical to its success because the community orientation and philosophy has been decaying in America; Town Center USA returns to a community orientation. To bring back a sense of community, people need a place to gather and discuss, learn, and become enriched. Since people are time constrained, the shopping center is an ideal place of community. The shopping center of the future will be a new town center, serving community needs for togetherness and individual needs for shopping and materialistic consumption. The three major advantages of bringing the community and shopping center together are: (1) the customer will be able to be a smart shopper more easily, (2) entertainment and shopping can be combined, and (3) people will feel they have more of a sense of control over their community. Notice how these advantages relate to the socioeconomic environment and consumer portrait we developed for 2001.

INFRASTRUCTURE COMPONENTS

Town Center USA will need to begin with the planning of a large infrastructure to support community activities. The focal point of the infrastucture will be *Main-Street USA*, a cobble-paved street which will bisect Town Center USA and serve as the major focal point of the center. Main Street will be used for holiday parades, street festivals, athletic events, organized protests, and street peddlers. It will be a place for social interaction and relaxation. Clusters of benches will be set along Main Street where people can sit and read or wait for the Town Trolley.

Town Trolley USA will be an electric trolley which will transport individuals throughout Town Center USA. The Town Trolley will be entertaining to ride. Trolley operators will be friendly and conversant with the passengers, and dressed in an attire that reflects the history of the community. Both outside and inside the trolley, important advertising for nonprofit organizations and public service messages will be displayed. The Town Trolley will not only go up and down Main Street, but up and down Broadway Street, the other major traffic artery in Town Center USA. *Broadway Street* will focus on services retailing, Main Street will focus on merchandise retailing.

Riverfront USA will flow from a small 10 to 15 acre man-made lake stocked with ducks and fish. The riverfront will have a tranquil and soothing effect on the visitors to Town Center USA. It will be a place for picnics, festivals, athletic events, and relaxation. *River Boat USA* will ferry people between restaurants that are positioned along the riverfront. Several of the restaurants will have outside eating areas that overlook the river. At the point where the lake flows into the river will be a farmers' market where fresh flowers, vegetables, and other items can be purchased. On occasion this open market will be used for the merchandising of arts and crafts or for major-event retailing such as July Fourth, Labor Day or Octoberfest.

At the intersection of Main and Broadway Streets will be *Town Hall USA*, which will be used for civic meetings, social clubs, and charitable organizations. Information about all town or community events will be available. The *Town Learning Center* will also be located at the intersection of Main and Broadway and will have a public library, current periodicals reading room, classrooms for do-it-yourself educational, remedial, and personal enrichment courses. Religious events can also be scheduled for the Town Learning Center.

SERVICES RETAILING

Town Center USA will house service retailers, located primarily on Broadway Street, who will offer the following services.

- Financial services, including banking, real estate, insurance and tax planning.
- Health care services, including general physicians, dentists, optometrists, chiropractors, wellness clinics, diet centers, and day care services for the senior citizens.
- Personal care services, including beauty and hair care services, ex-

ercise services, color consultants, personal shopping services, child-care services, etc.
- Legal services.
- Entertainment services, including travel agencies and movie theatres.
- Instructional services in dance, music, self defense, computer operation, home repair, etc.
- Food services, including a complete catering service.
- Repair services, including shoe repair, appliance repair, clothes alteration, auto repair, etc.

MERCHANDISE RETAILING

Town Center USA will have a host of general merchandise and specialty retailers to allow the smart shopper of 2001 to get the best possible deals on a total cost perspective. Included will be:

1. *Category Killers.* These will be stores that have merchandise dominance in a particular category[22] such as Toys-'R'-Us has today in the toy category or Home Depot has in the hardware category.
2. *Conventional Department Stores.* An upscale conventional department store such as Nordstrom's will offer merchandise of high quality and high customer service.
3. *Discount Department Store.* A discount operation such as Wal Mart or K mart will offer competitive prices and self-service selection on general merchandise categories.
4. *Highly Focused Specialty Stores.* These will be relatively small (less than 5,000 square feet) and serve special market niches with unique product assortments. A current example would be The Limited or Hickory Farms.
5. *Food Retailers.* There will be at least one large supermarket and several specialty food stores such as bakeries, butchers, or health food stores. The large-scale supermarket will compete on time convenience, customer service, merchandise and price; it should not be a discount-oriented supermarket.

SUMMARY

In this last chapter of *Retail Management* we shared some thoughts on the future of retailing. The chapter began by highlighting the need for retail managers to think about the future if they are to play a part in shaping it. The tools of futures research should be familiar to the retail manager, especially the authority methods, conjecture methods, and mathematical modeling methods.

The socioeconomic and technological environments will shape the behavior of consumers, channels and competitors over the next decade. Environments influence behavior, and behavior influences the need for new retail prototypes.

Six major trends will characterize the socioeconomic environment over the last decade of the twentieth century. These are (1) more needs and wants among households, but less time, (2) more parents than children, (3) higher incomes, but less flexibility, (4) more decisions, but less power, (5) more work, but less family harmony, and (6) segmented market growth. The United States is experiencing very slow growth overall, but spectacular growth in five important market segments. These are the children's, Hispanic, seniors, men under 35, and career/professional women markets.

The technological environment during the last decade of the twentieth century will be an extrapolation of current trends in the information technology arena. Especially important will be further developments in electronic funds transfer, electronic data interchange, point of sale equipment, and universal product coding. Very shortly, all of this technology will be integrated to provide a completely integrated information management system (IIMS). This system will be based on expert and artificial intelligence systems and will largely eliminate the need for middle managers in retailing. Space, merchandise, promotion, pricing, personnel, and working capital will be managed by sophisticated software systems.

The typical consumer in 2001 will have a new shopping orientation. Shopping will be driven by the search for the lowest total cost. In addition to price, costs will include time, transportation, maintenance, compromise, and risk. In brief, the customer of the year 2001 will be a smart shopper.

Channels in 2001 will be characterized by cooperation. In fact, they will be referred to as marketing support systems. They will view their job as supporting the marketing efforts of all institutions in the channel in pleasing the final consumer.

Competition in 2001 will be more sophisticated and will move away from the aggressive price competition retailers experienced during the 1980s and early 1990s. Retailers will compete on convenience, merchandise assortments, customer services, and price. Especially important will be customer services, since these services are the best means for a retailer to develop a lasting relationship with customers and thus develop store loyalty.

Undoubtedly, many new retail institutions will be introduced by 2001. We closed this chapter by offering a prototype for the shopping center in 2001—Town Center USA. This center is both a community and shopping place and includes a trolley, river, lake, town hall, restaurants, a complete array of services, and breadth and depth of merchandise assortments. Town Center USA is a place for recreation, learning, socializing, and shopping. It is a place of community and will help to replace the loss of community America has suffered.

1. What is futures research and what are its primary purposes?
2. If a retail chain was attempting to design a prototype for ten years in the future, what futures research tools might be most useful? Explain your answer.
3. Develop a scenario for hardware or home improvement center retailing in the year 2001.
4. Of the six major trends identified in the socioeconomic environment, which do you believe will have the most dramatic impact on food retailing?
5. What are some major branch points which could affect the growth and attractiveness of the seniors market?
6. A noted retail futurist has predicted that within 20 years there will be no middle managers in retailing—they will all be replaced by artificial intelligence or expert systems. Do you agree or disagree? Explain your response.
7. Do you see any reasons why the smart shopper may not emerge as predicted or become dominant by 2001?
8. Do you anticipate any trends that would result in marketing channels in 2001 not becoming marketing support systems?
9. Develop a scenario in which price competition would be the dominant form of retail competition in 2001.
10. Town Center USA does not include any predictions about specific lines of retail trade in 2001. What do you see happening to the following lines of retail trade over the next decade?
    a. department store retailing
    b. menswear retailing
    c. grocery stores
    d. auto dealerships

Bellah, Robert N. et al. *Habits of the Heart.* (New York: Harper & Row Publishers, 1985).

Blinder, Alan S. *Hard Heads Soft Hearts.* (Reading, MA: Addison-Wesley Publishing Company, Inc. 1987).

Kidder, Rushworth M. *An Agenda for the Twenty-first Century.* (Cambridge, MA: The MIT Press, 1988).

Howell, William R. "Tomorrow's Critical Issues." *Retail Control* (June/July 1987): 13–19.

Fauber, Bernard M. "Critical Issues In Preparing For Tomorrow." *Retail Control* (April/May 1987): 2–6.

Johnson, Bruce Donald. "Retail Trends and Challenges." *Retail Control* (February 1987): 44–64.

ENDNOTES

1. J. Alan Ofner, "How To Manage Change And Growth," *Retail Control* (March 1988): 9–16; William R. Howell, "Tomorrow's Critical Issues," *Retail Control* (June–July 1987): 13–19; Bernard M. Fauber, "Critical Issues In Preparing For Tomorrow," *Retail Control* (April–May 1987): 2–6.

2. Norman Dalkey and Olaf Helmer, "An Experimental Application of the Delphi Method to the Use of Experts," *Management Science* 9, (April 1963): 458–67.

3. Olaf Helmer, *Social Technology* (New York: Basic Books, 1966).

4. "If You Want A Big, New Market. . . ," *Fortune* (November 21, 1988): 181–188.

5. "Computerization: The Future Is Now," *Progressive Grocer* (January 1987): 40–44; "Shaw's Integrates Store Functions," *Progressive Grocer* (September 1987): 43–45.

6. "NRMA's New POS Study," *Stores* (April 1987): 67–73.

7. "Update On The UPC," *Stores* (March 1987): 48–57.

8. "EDI: Another Competitive Edge for Retailers," *Discount Merchandiser* (October 1987): 78–79; "UCS: The Bandwagon Begins to Roll," *Progressive Grocer* (May 1988): 166–172.

9. "Retail MIS Field Reflects Technology Trends," *Chain Store Age Executive* (March 1988): 100+.

10. "What's New in EFT," *Progressive Grocer* (August 1985): 59–66.

11. Harris Gordon, "Trends in Retailing—A Look At The Future," *Retail Control* (June–July 1986): 16–26.

12. "A New Dimension In Marketing," *Progressive Grocer* (May 1987): 133–136.

13. "Direct Product Profitability—A Worthwhile Investment?" *Discount Merchandiser* (August 1987): 116–118; "MIS Helps Speed Turns For Warehouse Club," *Discount Merchandiser* (January 1987): 84–86.

14. "The Convenience Factor," *Progressive Grocer* (December 1987): 44–51.

15. Jeremy Schlosberg, "The Demographics Of Convenience," *American Demographics* (October 1986): 36–42.

16. James A. Constantin and Robert F. Lusch, "Discover the Resources in Your Marketing Channel," *Business* (July–September 1986): 19–26.

17. Leonard Berry, *Arthur Andersen & Co Retailing Issues Letter* (November 1987): 4.

18. Leonard L. Berry and Larry G. Gresham, "Relationship Retailing: Transforming Customers into Clients," *Business Horizons* (November–December 1986): 43–47.

19. "Service: Retail's No.1 Problem," *Chain Store Age, General Merchandise Trends* (January 1987): 19–20.

20. George P. Moschis, Jac L. Goldstucker, and Thomas J. Stanley, "At-Home Shopping: Will Consumers Let Their Computers Do the Walking?" *Busi-*

ness Horizons (March–April 1985): 22–29; John A. Quelch and Hirotaka Takeuchi, "Nonstore Marketing: Fast Track or Slow?" *Harvard Business Review* (July–August 1981): 75–84; Larry J. Rosenberg and Elizabeth C. Hirschman, "Retailing Without Stores," *Harvard Business Review* (July–August 1980): 103–112.

21. The authors' conception of Town Center USA has been greatly influenced by discussions with Wayne Copeland.

22. "Bang, Bang, You're Dead," *Chain Store Age, General Merchandise Trends* (December 1987): 12–15.

Acknowledgments

The authors would like to acknowledge and thank the following persons who have written cases for this book:

Donald J. Bowersox, Michigan State University
James W. Camerious, Northern Michigan University
M. Bixby Cooper, Michigan State University
Roger Dickinson, University of Texas at Arlington
Jack Gifford, Miami University, Oxford, Ohio
Pat Gifford, Elder-Beerman Stores
John I. Coppett, University of Houston at Clear Lake
David C. Karp, Loyola Law School, Los Angeles
Douglas M. Lambert, Michigan State University
Michael W. Little, Virginia Commonwealth University
Virginia Newell Lusch
William A. Staples, University of Houston at Clear Lake
Robert A. Swerdlow, Lamar University
Donald A. Taylor, Michigan State University
Heiko de B. Wijnholds, Virginia Commonwealth University

Myron Gable
Patrick M. Dunne
Robert F. Lusch

Cases

Jack Gifford
Miami University
Oxford, Ohio
Pat Gifford
Elder-Beerman Stores

CASE 1

TOM BORCH TRADITIONAL CLOTHIER

The Carltons were at a turning point in the late fall of 1986. Sales volume at their store, Tom Borch Traditional Clothier, was erratic. Cash flow was poor and profits for the second quarter were not looking good. However, plans had been made for better merchandise and financial controls for 1987, and new promotions were envisioned. Would this be enough to warrant continued efforts to maintain the business, possibly with additional bank loans and/or injections from Mr. & Mrs. Carlton's personal resources? Mr. Carlton was particularly concerned that they were falling behind planned sales. If sales were not strong through the fall, Mrs. Carlton was afraid they would have to consider closing the store.

HISTORY OF THE BUSINESS

Tom Borch Traditional Clothier was located in Bowling Green, Ohio, a small college community in the north-central part of the state. Steve Carlton, the owner, opened his business August 15, 1984. His parents had just died leaving him two farms in south-central Ohio. He was not interested in farming, having spent several years in retailing following his graduation from Kent State University in 1975. He was able to lease the farms and wanted to use the proceeds to finance the opening of his own business. After two years of investigating various areas, Mr. Carlton settled on Bowling Green as a location.

Owing to his expertise in the field, Carlton wanted to open a traditional menswear store. He had spent six years buying menswear for L. L. Bean and two years managing a menswear store in Maine. Bowling Green had only three men's specialty clothing stores at the time. A fourth, successful men's traditional store had recently closed because the building in which it was located had to be razed.

Mr. Carlton leased a freestanding building on Dover Street, one block off Main Street, the main thoroughfare of Bowling Green. At the time this was the best location and building he could find, although he had heard that businesses off Main Street often suffered from lack of visibility and low student pedestrian traffic. Tom Borch's custom fixturing and furnishings were in the country gentry style. Clothing and accessories were traditional and of very good quality. As an afterthought, Mr. Carlton added some women's clothing to his stock which he was able to get through his menswear suppliers. Upon opening, about 85 percent of the merchandise was for men and 15 percent for women.

Business was slow and most of the traffic was female. Within a short time Mr. Carlton knew that he needed to find a place on Main Street and change his merchandise split to favor women. By August of 1985, Mr. Carlton was able to negotiate an agreement to get out of his lease and secure a spot on Main Street. He moved into the lower level of a newly constructed brick building between a new restaurant and a camera/art/card store. The building had three levels; all were open to the street with outside stairways connecting them. The interiors were long and narrow, about 18 feet × 55 feet. There was a gift store on the second level and a quick print shop on the third level. A three-year lease at $750 a month was negotiated for this space. Fifty percent of his stock was devoted to women's apparel. Sales began to improve dramatically.

Mr. Carlton was married in the Spring of 1986. His wife, Dawn, was a former buyer at Symphony, an exclusive Toledo women's specialty store, and also had experience in computer hardware and software sales. Her expertise proved to be a great asset for Mr. Carlton and the business. She became full-time manager of Tom Borch's in August of 1986.

During the spring of 1986 Mr. and Mrs. Carlton made the decision to go entirely into women's wear beginning with the fall, 1986 season. They would be able to offer a better selection to the women, who continued to make up the vast majority of their business. The fall season sales got off to a slow start in August and continued to be soft in September and October, producing a sales volume decline from the same months in the previous year.

MERCHANDISING STRATEGY

Bowling Green is located 35 miles south of Toledo, Ohio. Its permanent residents number 9,226, while the student population of Bowling Green State University's residential campus is 15,100. Bowling Green merchants traditionally have targeted their merchandise offerings primarily to the student population, with permanent Bowling Green residents as a secondary market. There has been some success in drawing summer visitor traffic from the nearby Maumee State Park, but June, July, and early August are usually slow selling periods.

A September, 1986 survey of Bowling Green residents' buying habits conducted by Bowling Green University marketing students revealed that of the 570 students surveyed, 11.7% made their last purchase of women's clothing in Bowling Green, and 6.2% made their last purchase of men's clothing in Bowling Green. Of the 559 permanent residents surveyed, 17.8% made their last purchase of women's clothing in Bowling Green, while 12.3% made their last purchase of men's clothing in Bowling Green. A large proportion of the students bought their clothing at home before they came to school, and a majority of the Bowling Green permanent residents shopped in Toledo or Maumee shopping malls.

The Carltons had identified their target market over time through conversations with other local merchants and observations of customers in their store.

MARKET CENTERS

There were two major shopping areas in Bowling Green, the uptown area and Southgate Mall. The uptown area was adjacent to the main entrance of Bowling Green University. It was six blocks long with the vast majority of businesses facing Main Street, the main east-west thoroughfare, or on the side streets, extending one block north or south of Main Street. The primary north-south thoroughfare, Phillip Street, was three blocks from campus and tended to be an invisible barrier for student pedestrian traffic. Bowling Green merchants who expected to primarily cater to student pedestrian traffic felt that it was necessary to locate within the three blocks of Main Street closest to campus. Businesses in the uptown area included fast-food restaurants; restaurant/bars; book stores; stationery and art supply stores; drug stores; florists; movie theaters; gift shops; copying services; ice cream shops; services such as banks, insurance, travel agencies; and two gas stations. In terms of apparel, Lee's Bookstore carried some junior women's and men's clothing. Hudson's College Shop, (a division of Minneapolis-based Dayton Hudson's Department stores) retailed junior and women's fashions and accessories; The Nutmeg was a chain that carried traditional women's apparel; David Brood's Shoes sold men's and women's shoes; and finally there was Tom Borch Traditional Clothier.

Southgate Mall was generally service oriented. A new Kroger's superstore had replaced a smaller Kroger's at that location in the summer of 1986. There were also a Super-X drugstore, K mart, Penney's catalogue store, card store, beauty shops, a fabric store, two dentists' offices, a Radio Shack, and miscellaneous small convenience stores. The Mall was a mile and a quarter from the main business district and two miles from the center of campus.

SALES VOLUME

The fiscal year for Tom Borch accounting records ran from August 15, 1984 to June 30, 1985, and July 1, 1985 to June 30, 1986. Although these periods are not exactly the same in length, they were used for purposes of comparison. The beginning of the second fiscal year coincided roughly with the opening of the second location, thus the two sets of fiscal data prove valuable in comparing the success of the two locations, especially in terms of sales volume. Sales for Tom Borch rose dramatically from 1985 to 1986 (Exhibit 1). Higher traffic and a year's experience in the Bowling Green market enabled the Carltons to better assess the needs of their customers and make the necessary adjustments to inventory. Mr. and Mrs. Carlton also started to cultivate customers from Toledo and other surrounding areas, which may have contributed a small amount to the increased volume. Sales volume was closely tied to the academic year and holidays.

Exhibit 1

Tom Borch Traditional Clothier
Monthly Credit and Cash Sales

	1984	1985	% Change 1984–1985	1986	% Change 1985–1986
January					
Credit		$ 593.00	N/A	$ 120.00	−79.76
Cash		10,295.00	N/A	21,790.00	111.66
Total		$ 10,888.00	N/A	$21,910.00	101.23
February					
Credit		$ 1,449.00	N/A	$ 440.00	−69.63
Cash		15,878.00	N/A	15,113.00	−4.82
Total		$ 17,327.00	N/A	$15,553.00	−10.24
March					
Credit		$ 134.00	N/A	$ 476.00	225.22
Cash		5,836.00	N/A	8,506.00	45.75
Total		$ 5,870.00	N/A	$ 8,982.00	50.45
April					
Credit		$ 1,168.00	N/A	$ 455.00	−61.04
Cash		12,374.00	N/A	16,033.00	29.57
Total		$ 13,542.00	N/A	$16,488.00	21.75
May					
Credit		$ 1,684.00	N/A	$ 457.00	−72.86
Cash		8,816.00	N/A	10,633.00	20.61
Total		$ 10,500.00	N/A	$11,090.00	5.62
June					
Credit		$ 486.00	N/A	$ 278.00	−42.80
Cash		2,991.00	N/A	6,636.00	121.87
Total		$ 3,477.00	N/A	$ 6,914.00	98.85
July					
Credit		$ 586.00	N/A	$ 364.00	−37.88
Cash		6,882.00	N/A	10,127.00	47.15
Total		$ 7,468.00	N/A	$10,491.00	40.48
August					
Credit	$ 455.00	$ 881.00	93.63	$ 734.00	−16.69
Cash	1,972.00	17,424.00	783.57	14,968.00	−14.10
Total	$ 2,427.00	$ 18,305.00	654.22	$15,702.00	−14.22

Continued

Exhibit 1—*Continued*

	1984	1985	% Change 1984–1985	1986	% Change 1985–1986
September					
Credit	$ 299.00	$ 581.00	94.31	$ 1,226.00	111.02
Cash	6,538.00	18,840.00	118.16	9,490.00	−49.63
Total	$ 6,837.00	$ 19,421.00	184.06	$10,716.00	−44.82
October					
Credit	$ 315.00	$ 1,469.00	366.35		N/A
Cash	12,018.00	21,653.00	80.17		N/A
Total	$12,333.00	$ 23,122.00	87.48		N/A
November					
Credit	$ 834.00	$ 900.00	7.91		N/A
Cash	8,460.00	20,304.00	140.00		N/A
Total	$ 9,294.00	$ 21,204.00	128.15		N/A
December					
Credit	$ 1,418.00	$ 2,121.00	49.58		N/A
Cash	16,004.00	21,333.00	33.30		N/A
Total	$17,422.00	$ 23,454.00	34.62		N/A
Overall Total	$48,313.00	$174,678.00	261.55		N/A

COST STRUCTURES

Mr. Carlton conceded that he was the type of person who worked on hunches and gut feelings concerning the store, and believed that he had been lucky with the business to this point. He was, however, beginning to see the need for closer control over the financial and merchandising aspects of the business. The financial accounting procedures were performed by an accountant on retainer by the corporation. Mr. Carlton relied on him for advice and assistance, but communication was difficult as both were very busy. No specific goals were set in terms of the cost structures. The accountant was simply to suggest cost saving measures and keep taxes at a minimum. Exhibit 2 provides income statements for fiscal 1985 and 1986.

The Carltons hoped to increase their profits for 1987. They also wanted to draw $20,000 in salaries from the business ($10,000 more than last year), which would add to current expenses. The projected income statement is included in Exhibit 2.

FINANCING

Tom Borch was owned by Mr. Carlton as a corporation under Subchapter S. The corporation had limited liability, limited stockholders, and shareholders were taxed as individuals. Mr. Carlton sustained a loss during his

Exhibit 2

Tom Borch Traditional Clothier
Income Statements for June 30, 1985 & 1986

	Fiscal 1985	Fiscal 1986	Projected 1987
Income			
Sales	$ 87,641.22	$195,780.70	$240,000.00
Alterations	542.57	3.00	0.00
Miscellaneous	260.09	4,391.69	9,000.00
Returns & Allowances	(1,965.15)	(2,414.74)	(3,000.00)
Total Income	$ 86,478.73	$197,760.65	$246,000.00
Less Cost of Goods Sold	$ 64,726.58	$132,652.88	$155,000.00
Gross Profit	$ 21,752.15	$ 65,107.77	$ 91,000.00
Selling & Admin. Expenses			
Officer's Salaries	$ 1,473.49	$ 10,000.00	$ 20,000.00
Office Salaries	7,436.13	11,055.40	12,000.00
Cleaning and Sanitation	53.40	125.00	125.00
Telephone	1,174.40	1,701.30	1,800.00
Utilities	1,568.77	1,450.07	1,500.00
Insurance	1,527.75	1,838.61	2,000.00
Travel & Entertainment	0.00	0.00	0.00
Office Supplies & Postage	368.72	521.55	650.00
Selling and Admin. Expenses			
Legal & Accounting	607.50	1,371.55	900.00
Advertising	3,263.12	1,118.06	1,500.00
Dues & Subscriptions	910.31	733.00	750.00
Bad Debts	0.00	0.00	0.00
Auto & Travel Expenses	163.50	63.38	100.00
Depreciation	777.42	2,888.02	3,500.00
License Fees	10.00	0.00	0.00
Employee Welfare	0.00	0.00	0.00
Interest	0.00	0.00	330.00
Miscellaneous	875.00	1,557.84	1,975.00
Employment Insurance	183.77	539.87	540.00
Workman's Compensation	0.00	0.00	0.00
Payroll Taxes	2,473.95	2,259.29	2,300.00
Personal Property Taxes	0.00	410.86	450.00
City Income Taxes	0.00	0.00	0.00
Real Estate Taxes	0.00	0.00	0.00
Supplies	895.65	670.08	700.00
Freight	382.20	195.99	200.00
Rent	7,675.00	11,952.74	9,000.00
Bank Charges	9.35	0.00	0.00
Repairs	89.50	0.00	0.00
Refunds	224.18	499.38	650.00
Discounts Allowed	22.05	120.23	150.00
Contract Labor	2,137.13	6,082.72	800.00
Total S & A Expenses	$ 34,302.29	$57,154.94	$ 61,920.00
Net Profit or Loss	$(12,550.14)	$ 7,952.83	$ 29,080.00

first year of business and has not had to pay taxes on the corporation since its inception, due to the loss carryforward provisions of the IRS (see Exhibit 2).

Investment requirements for Tom Borch include cash, accounts receivable-trade, inventory, pre-paid expenses (the first year only), furniture, leasehold improvements, and a car (see Exhibit 3). Tom Borch had no formal store charge accounts under most circumstances. A few preferred customers deferred half of the purchase price for two weeks and then paid the remainder bi-weekly. These instances were few and did not show up on accounts receivable on the balance sheets from either year. Stockholders equity, which included common stock, retained earnings, and profit (loss), was not sufficient to cover the investment requirements. Mr. Carlton had to contribute to the business from his personal funds in the form of an officer's loan.

The Carltons had made it a practice to pay for all merchandise purchases within the discount period (usually 10 days from the receipt of invoice) in order to get a reduction in the cost of merchandise. This reduction was usually 8 percent. The ability to gain these discounts had required adequate cash flow. When current sales did not adequately cover the business needs, Mr. Carlton dipped into his personal assets to pay the bills. In mid-September of 1986, Mr. Carlton was in a temporary cash bind for the business and personally decided to borrow money from the bank in order to pay his business bills within the discount period and take care of a personal financial need. His track record was such that he had no difficulty getting the two-year loan which totaled $11,200, $8,000 of which was for the business. Interest on the loan was "prime" (which was 13 percent) plus 2 percent variable at the first of each month.

MERCHANDISE

Mr. Carlton conceived Tom Borch as a fine, traditional apparel store, targeted toward college students and townspeople who had discriminating taste in quality clothing at a reasonable price. The interior of the store was designed to create a casual but tasteful atmosphere, an appropriate backdrop for the merchandise. The original women's line included slacks, shirts, sweaters, a few suits and outerwear jackets. Resources were Thomson, David Brooks, Robert Scott, Aston, and Sero. Belts and canvas bags rounded out the store. Later some dresses and nightgowns by Lanz were added to the women's line.

As the first months of operation passed and Mr. Carlton found that he had more female customers than he had anticipated, he began to increase the proportion of women's clothing and tried a few dresses and more sweaters and pants. He found that the market for traditional men's clothing was not as great as he had earlier thought. He guessed that male students were only interested in jeans and t-shirts and that the taste level and price of his merchandise wasn't matched to the needs of the majority of professors on moderate budgets with a need for practical clothing.

Exhibit 3

Tom Borch Traditional Clothier
Balance Sheets, Yr. End
FPR 1985 and 1986

	Balance Sheet as of 1985	Balance Sheet as of 1986
Assets		
Current Assets		
Cash in bank	$ 3,616.19	$ 2,136.59
Accounts Receivable—Trade	1,501.13	1,688.21
Inventory	47,089.62	48,077.75
Prepaid Expenses	2,110.00	0.00
Total Current Assets	$54,316.94	$51,902.55
Noncurrent Assets		
Furniture & Fixtures	$ 851.00	$ 9,656.96
Less: Accum. Depn.	(85.10)	(1,005.80)
Leasehold Improvements	3,173.25	3,173.25
Less: Accum. Depn.	(317.32)	(634.64)
Auto	8,531.36	8,531.36
Less: Accum. Depn.	(375.00)	(2,025.00)
Total Noncurrent Assets	$11,778.19	$17,696.13
Total Assets	$66,095.13	$69,598.68
Liabilities		
Current Liabilities		
Accounts Payable—Trade	$ 1,026.17	$ 0.00
Accrued Payroll Taxes	313.86	505.12
Accrued Sales Tax	817.44	294.12
Notes Payable—Bank	8,887.80	3,132.26
Estimated Federal Income Taxes	0.00	0.00
Total Current Liabilities	$11,045.27	$ 3,931.50
Noncurrent Liabilities		
Notes Payable—Officers	$62,600.00	$65,264.49
Total Noncurrent Liabilities	62,600.00	65,264.49
Total Liabilities	$73,645.27	$69,195.99
Stockholders Equity		
Common Stock	$ 5,000.00	$ 5,000.00
Retained Earnings	0.00	(12,550.14)
Current Profit or Loss	(12,550.14)	7,952.83
Total Stockholders Equity	$ (7,550.14)	$ 402.69
Total Liabilities & Stockholders Equity	$66,095.13	$69,598.68

Most of the brands carried by Tom Borch during the first year and a half were available at better department stores—often at lower prices than Mr. Carlton could afford to sell his merchandise. After the 1985 fall season, Mr. Carlton took a hard look at the store and its directions for the future. By this time he had moved to the new location, sales had picked up, and business seemed to be better, but there were still things that needed to change.

He was by now doing quite well selling women's wear, with 60 to 65 percent of his stock in female apparel. But the men's business was doing poorly. He had direct competition on much of his women's wear from The Nutmeg Shop, located down the street. That store carried many of the same brands of sweaters, pants, and skirts as Tom Borch, had a broader selection, and sometimes lower prices. The Bowling Green Nutmeg was part of a 15-store chain and had buying power that Tom Borch did not have as a single unit. Mr. Carlton joined a resident buying office in New York in March, 1986 and was hoping to reap the benefit of experts in the market.

During the first few months of 1986, the Carltons made their decision to go entirely into women's wear, to drop many of the suppliers they shared with nearby stores, and to try to forge a few, more unique merchandise line for Tom Borch. The new strategy was initiated with the fall 1986 line. Mrs. Carlton, the store manager since late summer of 1986, and then buyer for the store, planned to develop this more unique, sophisticated merchandise look for the spring and beyond. She found that the college students bought their everyday sweaters and corduroys at other stores, but were coming to Tom Borch for "special" clothes, and that Bowling Green women were beginning to look at Tom Borch for "something different." Many parents who visited their children at college were delighted to find Tom Borch and frequently bought for themselves as well as their daughters. Merchandise available in the fall included the categories previously carried with the addition of raincoats, a few more one- and two-piece dresses, and more accessories—ties, belts, purses, briefcases, umbrellas, and a limited line of jewelry. Generally there was a broader range of all merchandise. New resources were Boston Trader, Jason Younger, Needleworks, Scotland Yard, Numa, British Khaki, and several two- or three-of-a-kind sweaters and sweater dresses. For spring 1987, Mrs. Carlton again sought the unusual and ordered many interesting fabrications in styles with a new twist.

MERCHANDISE CONTROL

During the first two years of operation, Mr. Carlton did all the buying for the store. He visited the New York apparel market twice a year, once for his fall line and once for his spring line. He also ordered some merchandise from sales representatives who visited the store and by phone through the buying office. Mr. Carlton did not use a formal buying plan when he went to market. He normally had some idea of what he wanted, worked the market to see what was offered, and ordered what he concluded to be the appropriate merchandise. He did not attempt to control for the cost or the specific units of merchandise purchased.

Mrs. Carlton, from her previous experience in retail buying, was aware of the need for greater controls and was in the process of setting up procedures for inventory control in the store. She also attempted a more organized method of planning her spring purchases during her market trip for spring 1987. The Carltons have never taken a physical inventory. Mr. Carlton did not know why his accountant never asked for one for tax purposes, and assumed that he has used the book inventory to derive data for income statements and balance sheets.

PRICING

Mr. and Mrs. Carlton generally priced merchandise with a 50 percent markup, assuming that this would cover expenses and provide some profit. Virtually all the merchandise in the store was priced at what is considered the upper end of "moderate" or the low end of "better." Mr. Carlton estimated that his annual reductions were 27 percent of net sales.

PROMOTION

The Carltons changed their promotional emphasis over the two years of operations and drastically reduced their advertising costs from 1985 to 1986. They reduced expensive newspaper advertising in local university and community newspapers, which was not effective. They decided to focus on such things as gift certificates for new sorority pledges; sponsorship of various Greek activities, including style shows; ads in selected playbills and game programs; and only occasional newspaper advertising. Tom Borch did not advertise on the radio. Mrs. Carlton did some direct mailing for special store events. In addition, she tried to reach customers outside the immediate Bowling Green area, by hosting Sunday brunches in the store. She was considering fashion shows, direct mailing, and perhaps special events directed at women in Bowling Green and nearby towns.

The Carltons took great pride in their store and the Bowling Green community. They were members of the Chamber of Commerce and the Bowling Green Retail Merchants Association. They made special efforts to generate goodwill in their store, with other businesses, and the community in general.

This teaching case has been prepared as a basis for class discussion. All names—persons, location, university, stores—have been changed to ensure the confidentiality of the retailer.

1. How well have the Carltons integrated the merchandise assortment, pricing, promotion, financial, and control elements of their business? Are there specific problems or inconsistencies?
2. What methods of data collection and control are needed and feasible for this small retailer in order to improve performance?
3. What methods for determining merchandise preferences of target customers are available to the small retailer?
4. Given 1987 financial projections, what is the breakeven point for the store? Have any expenses been omitted? Are the projections realistic? What are the odds of the Carltons successfully competing in Bowling Green in 1987? What specific recommendations would you make to Mr. and Mrs. Carlton?

CASE 2

William A. Staples
University of Houston
Robert A. Swerdlow
Lamar University

BURNSIDE FURNITURE AND APPLIANCE CENTERS, INC.

In June of 1976, Thomas and James Burnside were confronted with a major operating decision that would affect the future development of their furniture and appliance business. The decision centered on whether or not to add a fourth store in the southern section of Des Moines, Iowa. Thomas, as president and financial officer, was reluctant to open a new store, although James, serving as vice president with responsibility for marketing operations, thought the time had come for an additional Burnside Furniture and Appliance Center.

BACKGROUND

In September 1948, Alexander Burnside opened a retail furniture store in Des Moines. Alexander had previously been employed as a furniture salesperson by a large department store. The store on the east side of Des Moines initially carried furniture only. Although the first few years were very difficult, by 1953 Alexander had achieved financial stability. In 1959, due to the growth of Des Moines and the success of the original east side store, Alexander opened a second store on the north side of Des Moines. It was at this time that Alexander decided to add appliances to the product mix of both of his stores.

During the 1960s, the two Burnside Furniture and Appliance Centers were very successful. Between 1962 and 1965, Alexander Burnside brought his two sons, Thomas and James, into the daily operation and management of his retail stores. Thomas and James were both college graduates and had received degrees in business administration from the University of Iowa and Drake University, respectively. Thomas had majored in finance; James was a marketing major.

Due to the large number of people employed in insurance, publishing, and state government, Des Moines continued to grow during the 1960s. The major growth of Des Moines was occurring in the western section of the city. Thomas and James Burnside concurred with their father that a third furniture and appliance center should be opened on the west side of town. In 1969, this idea became a reality.

During the early 1970s, all three stores continued to prosper, although the sales of the first outlet had stabilized and the major sales growth was occurring in the newest (west side) store, followed by the outlet in north Des Moines. In 1973, Alexander Burnside retired from the day-to-day operation of the business, although he retained his position as chairman of the board of the corporation. Thomas Burnside was appointed president of the company with James serving as vice president.

CURRENT SITUATION

In 1976, Thomas and James Burnside were faced with a decision of whether or not to establish their fourth furniture and appliance center, on the south side of Des Moines. While the population of Des Moines had grown between 1970 and 1975, the growth rate was not as high as for the 1950s and 1960s. While the total population had not grown dramatically, there was a major growth area. Due to new real estate developments, the southern section of Des Moines had attracted a large number of young families with children. The new residents of the south side also were above average with respect to years of education, income levels, and percentage of heads of households with white-collar occupations. James Burnside believed that this group should be a prime target for their business and suggested that a new store should be opened on the south side. Thomas Burnside was skeptical of the idea due to the slowed overall growth rate of Des Moines. He believed that major attention should be directed at furthering the development of the three existing stores, where sales were beginning to level off.

James and Thomas Burnside decided that an informal market analysis of the south side was in order. Due to his marketing background,

James took a leadership role in assembling some secondary information for further study. Exhibit 1 shows the boundaries of the south side area. The boundary on the north was the C&M Railroad, while the east side was marked by the Des Moines River. The western and southern borders were marked by Interstate 80 and State Highway 28, respectively. By consulting the Des Moines Chamber of Commerce's Research Division, James was able to determine the estimated 1975 median household incomes for the southside census tracts. Census records revealed that all of the census tracts on the south side were either in the upper- or middle-income tracts for the entire city. An analysis of city building permits revealed that the major building areas during the early 1970s had been in the south, west, and northwest sections of Des Moines. In addition, the Des Moines Planning and Zoning Commission was able to supply James with their estimate of the population growth for Des Moines for 1970 to 1990.

James Burnside, after assembling the data, reanalyzed the past location decisions with respect to the stores on the north and west sides of Des Moines. He determined that there were special levels of household incomes, building permit growth, and population changes that must be considered. The critical values were $13,400 in household incomes, 3 percent in average annual building permit growth, and 10 percent population growth rate of 1970 to 1990.

James realized that in order to make a complete assessment of the situation, an analysis of the competition and available store sites was in order. Exhibit 2 presents an analysis of the south side with respect to

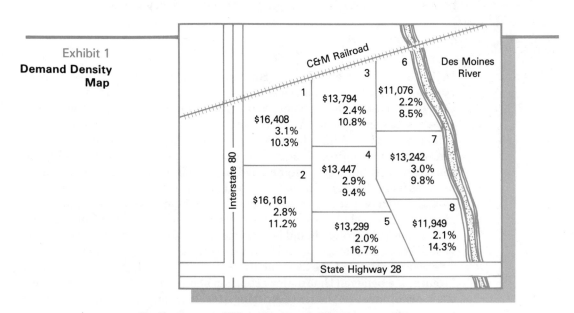

Exhibit 1
Demand Density Map

Top Number = 1975 median household income
Middle Number = Average annual growth in building permits over last five years (1970–75)
Bottom Number = Projected population growth rate (1970–90)

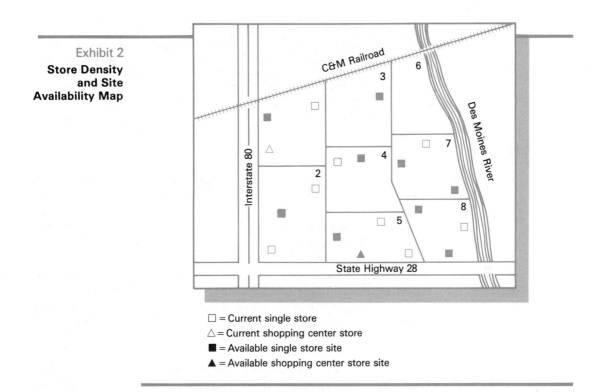

Exhibit 2

**Store Density
and Site
Availability Map**

☐ = Current single store
△ = Current shopping center store
■ = Available single store site
▲ = Available shopping center store site

store density and site availability. The competition on the south side was diverse in that there were appliance stores, furniture stores, plus combination furniture and appliance outlets. In addition, a large department store chain, Adler's, which carried furniture and appliances, had a store in the shopping center off Interstate 80. Another major competitor would be Odom Appliances, which had two stores on the south side. James Burnside knew of at least nine furniture or appliance outlets that could provide strong competition for a new store in the area under consideration.

QUESTIONS

1. How would the demographic characteristics of the population on the south side affect the demand for furniture and appliances?
2. Evaluate the census tracts in Exhibit 1 with respect to the criteria outlined by James Burnside. Which tracts appear to be appropriate for further consideration?
3. What effects would the boundaries of the southern section of Des Moines, Iowa, have on a retail business?
4. What store sites in Exhibit 2 appear to be most promising?
5. If the next step was to select a specific site for a fourth store, what additional factors should Thomas and James Burnside consider?

Michael W. Little
Virginia Commonwealth University
Heiko de B. Wijnholds
Virginia Commonwealth University

CASE 3

CITY DRUGSTORES, INC.

BACKGROUND

Michael James is vice president of City Drugstores, a privately-owned pharmacy chain headquartered in Fairfax, Virginia. Recently, Michael commissioned a feasibility study for a new site location. He has mixed feelings about the location, however, believing there are better opportunities elsewhere. There is some difference of opinion between Michael and his father, Morton James, who is president.

Until now, little market research has been used for store locations. In the past, Michael's father would locate a store near a major supermarket chain or in a university town. Michael strongly believes market analysis must replace this outdated type of location analysis. Michael and his father have agreed that before a decision is made on the proposed site, research will be done.

Over the years, City Drugstores has grown from a single store in Fairfax to a profitable corporation with 62 stores located in central cities throughout Virginia. This expansion was due to a combination of acquisitions, mergers, and new store construction.

City Drugstores enjoys a good reputation because of its convenient locations, competitive prices, and carrying branded product lines. Like many drugstore chains, City Drugstores has four core departments. The most profitable is prescription drugs, followed by over-the counter drugs (OTC), and cosmetics and toiletries. Orders for prescription drugs must be presented to a registered pharmacist with a doctor's written order, whereas OTC drugs, such as pain relievers and vitamins, can be sold without such restrictions. Cosmetics and toiletries are referred to as health and beauty aids and add to a drugstore's product mix. A medium-size store must register approximately $750,000 in sales annually to break even. A profitable store will produce $150 in annual sales per square foot of selling space, with prescription drugs the product line most instrumental in generating volume.

THE PROPOSED LOCATION

Michael's father has asked him to consider a site near the local university, a state-supported institution with 15,000 students located in Fairfax. Morton James graduated from the Pharmacy School there in 1949. Recently, a fellow graduate, who is owner of Paramount Pharmacy and wishes to retire, offered to sell James his drugstore.

Paramount Pharmacy is within one block of the university's three student residence halls and is located on the corner of a busy one-way street heading to the downtown business district. If this site was purchased, Paramount Pharmacy would be razed and a modern City Drug unit built in its place. Estimated construction costs are $950,000 and other capital needs (assets) would amount to $475,000. Annual fixed costs for operating a new drugstore are $160,000, with cost of goods expected to be 67 percent of sales and other variable costs estimated at 5 percent of sales.

Paramount Drugstore attracts a small but loyal group of low- to middle-income customers and some university students and faculty. The Paramount Pharmacy, however, has not been very profitable nor competitive in recent years despite being the only drugstore within the immediate area. For example, Paramount has not taken advantage of university health service contracts for prescription drugs, which are based on bidding. Often these contracts include prescriptions for several hundred students during the academic year.

Upon Michael James' urging, marketing faculty at the university were contacted for the study. It was agreed that a telephone survey of a representative sample of 200 residents living within census tracts surrounding the present Paramount Drugstore and university fringe would be questioned. In addition, a survey was mailed to 250 college students living in the nearby dorms.

An estimate was to be made of the traffic flow past the planned store and the proportion of customers it could attract from this traffic. A guesstimate was also to be provided on walk-in traffic from other students, faculty, and staff. With this information, annual sales potential for the proposed site could be estimated.

The Jameses must decide within 30 days whether or not to buy Paramount Drugs and build one of their own drugstores. Michael has reviewed the data that the researchers collected and needs to make a recommendation to his father.

RESEARCH FINDINGS

A summary of responses to some key questions in the resident survey are presented in Exhibit 1.

Exhibit 1

Do You Buy Prescription Drugs? (N=201)

	N	%
Yes	134	67
No	67	33

Where Do You Buy Prescription Drugs? (N=134)

	N	%
People's Drugs	46	34
City Drug	37	28
Paramount	19	14
Revco	19	14
Other	53	40

(Scores do not add up to 100% due to multiple responses).

Buying Frequency and Expenditures on Drugstore Items
N=179

Frequency	Expenditures				
	Under $3	$3–$5	$5–$15	>$15*	Total
Daily	2	1	1	2	6
Twice per week	3	3	2	3	11
Once per week	9	8	19	2	38
Twice per month	7	10	14	9	40
Once per month	12	9	17	19	57
Other**	5	11	6	5	27
Total	38	42	59	40	179

*Assume none over $25
**Assume once per six months on the average

Would You Shop at Modern Drugstores?

	N	%
Yes	107	55
No	52	27
Don't Know	37	18

Would You Shop at City Drugstores?

	N	%
Yes	166	84
No	15	8
Don't Know	15	8

Why Would You Shop at City Drugstores?

	N	%
Close and Convenient	142	71
Cheaper Prices	52	26
Products	21	11
Already Loyal to City Drug	28	14
Loyal to Paramount	8	4
Other	20	10

(Scores do not add up to 100% due to multiple responses.)

The data above are responses from households represented by randomly selected adults (18 years and older). The expenditure data tabulated represents individual purchases and has to be converted to household expenditure by multiplying it by the average number of adult spenders, i.e., 1.18. Average overall household size amounts to 2.27. [Hint for estimating expenditures; try to substitute average dollar amounts for the tabulated ranges.]

According to the latest United States Census data, the number of people living in the target area numbers 2,949. Unfortunately, this data is four years old. The City's Planning Department has estimated that this mostly low-income population has been declining at an approximate rate of one percent per annum. According to the survey, the average household makes approximately 65 percent of all its drugstore purchases at one store (average purchase ratio).

In the student survey, on-campus dormitory students, as a whole, appear to have little store preference when buying prescription drugs. Approximately 28 percent of the respondents didn't purchase prescription drugs. When buying health and beauty aids, however, a significant number of respondents shop near campus.

More than half the students surveyed buy something at a drugstore at least twice a week. More than one-third buy at least once a month. This indicates a sizable number of students who are frequent purchasers of drugstore products. In fact, on their last visit to a drugstore, these students spent approximately $5 on the average.

When asked if they would shop at a modern drugstore at the Paramount site, half the dormitory student respondents were not sure, implying price, product offerings, and distance as factors to their decision to shop. If the drugstore were City Drug, almost two-thirds would shop there, with about one-third undecided.

Based on the survey data, the dormitory students' total monthly per capita expenditure in drugstores is estimated at $21.80 during the regular academic year. (Academic year is 7.5 months due to Christmas and other holidays.) Average purchase ratio was found to be 60 percent while 62 percent of the students indicated they would shop at the new drugstore.

According to university records, the fall and spring dormitory population is 2,232 (all singles). During the three summer months, approximately 20 percent of this number attends school and stays in these dorms. Summer students spend approximately the same (per capita) monthly amount in drugstores. Some decline in student population, including dormitories, is expected during the next ten years.

Traffic flow past the new store is estimated at 5,000 per day for approximately 300 days per year (allowing for Sundays, holidays, and bad weather). This figure includes an estimated 20 percent duplication of the student population above. It is estimated that 5 percent of this traffic results in actual store visits and purchases averaging $5 per trip.

Based on a very limited survey and some rough estimates, walk-ins, representing faculty, staff, and other students, are expected to spend roughly $30,000 per annum at drugstores in the vicinity of the intended new store.

QUESTIONS

1. Estimate the market potential for all drugstore sales in the area and, using this figure as a base, estimate the sales potential for the new City Drugstore.
2. Determine the expected profitability of the proposed store.
3. What are the main arguments for and against locating a City Drug unit on the intended site?
4. Based on your answers to the questions above, what should Michael James do? Why?

Robert Staples
University of Houston
John I. Coppett
University of Houston

CASE 4

COMPETITECH LEARNS TO USE TELEMARKETING

Brenda Johnson, vice president of Marketing, was confronted with a major problem. Her company, Competitech, a retailer of computer supplies, had recently started to feature a toll-free 800 number in all of its advertisements, direct mail pieces, and catalogs. The public was responding very well to this easy-to-use, economical method of ordering products. Response rate reports indicated that sales should have been up by 12 to 15 percent. Actual sales, however, were just about the same as before Competitech started using telemarketing. As Johnson studied the report, she saw that her three telemarketing service representatives had received approximately 4,000 calls during the last 20 working days. Johnson was pleased to note that about 50 percent of the callers had never previously purchased anything from Competitech. The fact that the telephone was ringing but the cash register wasn't was cause for deep concern.

Later that day Johnson called a meeting of the managers of the telemarketing operation, the shipping and inventory management group, the mail order department, and customer service department. The meeting focused on determining where and how business was being lost. The managers spent most of the time discussing the steps of order processing as depicted in Exhibit 1.

The telemarketing personnel, when they received a call for a computer part or a software package, recorded the customer's name, address, product identification information, credit card information, and then they asked the caller where he/she saw a Competitech advertisement or other promotional information. This last bit of information was considered vital by Johnson to learn which media were stimulating the most responses. At the end of the workday, the telemarketers forwarded all orders to the mail order department where that day's orders were totalled. The orders were then passed on to the shipping and inventory management department. Shipping and inventory verified credit worthiness if necessary and then order-pickers filled each request and prepared the products for shipment.

If the requested merchandise was out of stock, a written notice of the shortage and the customer's name and address were forwarded to customer service. Customer service sent a letter apologizing for the tempo-

Exhibit 1

Order-Processing Operations

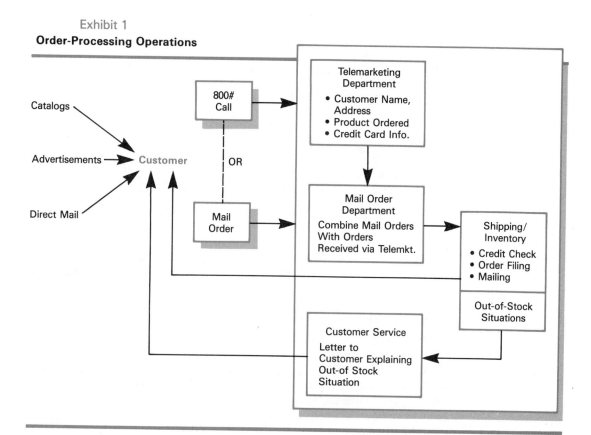

rary delay in completing the order and indicated when Competitech anticipated the back-ordered product could be shipped.

The telemarketing group was beginning to receive calls from customers stating that they did not want to wait for back-orders and wished
to cancel their order. Some customers angrily said that if they had known
about this delay they would have never done business with Competitech.

Johnson realized that Competitech was not only losing an opportunity to capitalize on the new business but, even worse, was alienating
some customers. She wondered if telemarketing might hold the solution
to some of the problems.

QUESTIONS

1. What could the telemarketers do if they had on-line computer access
   to inventory status information?
2. How could telemarketing be used to more efficiently support the customer service function?
3. What information does Ms. Johnson need to determine where the
   problem(s) are in Competitech?
4. Assuming the telemarketing representatives knew what the inventory status was of every product Competitech sold, how could Ms.
   Johnson motivate the telemarketing personnel to sell more?

CASE 5

Roger Dickinson
University of Texas at Arlington

ELEGANT, INC.

The three discount stores run by Elegant, Inc. have been in business for
12 years. Dollar sales have gone from $3 million in 1976 to $60 million in
1987. While profits have been erratic, the stores have been profitable
every year and in 1987 netted $300,000 after taxes. Harry Spalding was
the founder of the firm and is presently its major stockholder.

The Elegant stores handle many types of merchandise. They have
small appliance, television, and major appliance departments, as well as
home building departments with a substantial commitment in plumbing
supplies. Their automotive sections also do well. The stores carry many
other types of goods, including sporting goods, toys, cameras, and fashion merchandise.

Presently there are ten buyers divided along what Spalding feels are reasonable lines. Nevertheless, he believes that the decision-makers in the firm are not getting enough of the information they need. For the past 12 years the store has been on the cost system. Thus, the buyers do not get rapid information on data such as margins, stock positions, and open-to-buy. They do, however, get rapid feedback on the sales of items (SKUs) and the dollar sales of the merchandise areas that are their responsibility. While the store has done reasonably well with this system and the buyers are used to it, Spalding is considering a change to the retail method.

Spalding sees many advantages in the retail method. His buyers and other executives would get reports on the initial markup and stock figures for their decision areas every two weeks. Therefore, they should be able to quickly spot incorrect prices on merchandise. In addition, they could spot trends in stocks and in initial and maintained markup by classification. Furthermore, Spalding and his assistant will be able to see a variety of figures by merchandise area. This will enable them to offer advice and spot trouble before it happens. For example, inventory and markup figures will be available either every two weeks or every month, depending on the decision area. Another advantage of the retail method, Spalding thinks, is that with it he will get a picture of the differences between the book inventory value and the actual physical inventory; and thus get some idea of how much merchandise is missing. With the drastically increasing theft rate, this factor is very important to him.

Elegant, Inc. would have introduced the retail method several years ago had it not been for the opposition of Kevin Wilson, the financial officer of the firm. Wilson maintained that the system was not worth the additional $60,000 that he felt it would cost. In his opinion, most of the benefits that were envisioned with the retail method would not be realized. It was nice to have additional information, but most of the information generated by the retail method was unnecessary. While it was true that one got information such as initial markup, maintained markup, gross margins, and profit statements, this information ended up as a composite of many other decisions. If one priced optimally, took markdowns intelligently, created assortments imaginatively and analytically, and utilized effective inventory techniques, the retail method could do little to improve decision making. It gave management potentially more control, but with the right buyers, this would not be important. In any case, more control could be as negative an influence in the firm as a positive one. The major advantage of the retail method, according to Wilson, was that it would provide figures on how much was being stolen by employees and customers in each store. But he wasn't really sure that he would trust the figures anyway. He personally knew the controller of two stores in which the buyers "fudged" the books so badly that the stores showed overages. And there were many bookkeeping errors.

Kevin Wilson concluded that the disadvantages of the retail method outweighed the advantages. He felt that in addition to the $60,000 it would take to maintain the system, there would probably be other costs: (a) The increased information would take up the buyer's time and would require two merchandise managers to control it. Presently the buyers reported directly to Harry Spalding. With additional information, buyers would need more supervision. (b) The figures generated by the retail method would not be accurate, particularly in the beginning years. Thus, profits would probably be overstated unless sufficient reserves were set up to compensate for the inaccuracies. (c) The firm had been built on an aggressive price image. He feared that the store would lose some of this. In his experience, stores under the retail method tended to charge indirect costs to the decision area on the basis of sales and thus charged higher prices.

QUESTIONS

1. Is there validity to Kevin Wilson's objections?
2. Can other arguments be made in favor of the retail method?
3. Should Harry Spalding introduce the retail method into his firm? Why?

CASE 6

Roger Dickinson
University of Texas at Arlington

EVANS DEPARTMENT STORE

John Evans received a MBA in marketing from a leading graduate school of business. Upon completing his degree, he had gone to work in Evans Department Store, a growing, profitable organization with three stores and a volume of $160 million. The organization had been built up over the years by Louis Evans, John's father.

After starting in the stockroom and progressing to a sales associate, John became an assistant buyer, a buyer, and a merchandise manager. He worked pretty much within the established patterns of the store systems as they had been developed over the years. If the operating results of the areas to which John was assigned were accepted as a guide, John had done well.

In February 1987, Louis Evans died. According to the wishes indicated in his will, John was installed as president and chief executive officer of Evans Department Store.

One of the first of John's concerns was the business's lack of sophistication. Louis Evans had run the firm by what professors would call seat-of-the-pants decision-making. However, Louis had been first in his graduating class at Yale and would spend days deliberating over the pros and cons of the key decisions that he had to make. While John was sure that his business school professors were correct and that this seat-of-the-pants decision-making was wrong, he had not seen many ways during his years at the store in which the method of making these decisions could be improved. The growth of the operation's sales and profits was reasonable.

John, therefore, decided to address the area of the consumer. What could be more important to the future of the store than consumers? After all, he did have a MBA in marketing, which had a heavy consumer orientation. He reviewed what his father had done in this area. Louis Evans had the controller examine the credit records every two years by random sampling techniques. Credit customers in the three stores were analyzed with respect to where they lived, their incomes, family position, occupation, and so forth. In addition, Louis had once paid a consultant to run a similar survey of cash customers. There did not seem to be any managerially significant differences between cash and credit customers, so Louis decided he would assume that the two types of customer were approximately the same. Furthermore, 60 percent of the Evans Stores' business was conducted on credit, so that the credit customers represented a significant portion of the overall business.

Louis Evans had also utilized a very short, simple questionnaire that was filled out by customers at each of the three stores every two years. Initially, he had hired a statistician to insure that the survey results would be representative of all the customers. However, a check of the statistician's sample against a nonrandom sample designed by a store executive indicated that there was little difference in the results. Therefore, because the nonrandom design had cost one-fifth of what the randomized one had cost, nonrandom sampling was used in all subsequent surveys.

John Evans decided to follow the same inexpensive sampling procedure. His father had designed a questionnaire to ascertain how the store was rated on seven attributes. In addition, respondents were asked to identify any special strengths and weaknesses of the store. See Exhibit 1 for a copy of this questionnaire. The results of the questionnaire were distributed to the key executives, and action was taken where deemed appropriate.

The above "research" cost almost nothing, and indeed, the information was only supplemental to the information generated by the firm's more sophisticated systems for determining what the customer was buying in the three stores. John knew that all retail operations emphasize what has been sold, and Evans Department Store was no exception.

John's problem was that he was not sure what to do to learn more

Exhibit 1

Consumer Questionnaire

Q. Please rank the Evans Department Stores along each of the following dimensions, considered separately (put an X under the number that comes closest to your impression):

	7	6	5	4	3	2	1	
Helpful Salespeople	•	•	•	•	•	•	•	Unhelpful Salespeople
Pleasant Salespeople	•	•	•	•	•	•	•	Unpleasant Salespeople
A Large Selection of Merchandise	•	•	•	•	•	•	•	A Small Selection of Merchandise
Very High Prices	•	•	•	•	•	•	•	Low Prices
Poor Displays	•	•	•	•	•	•	•	Very Exciting Displays
Credit Easy to Obtain	•	•	•	•	•	•	•	Credit Difficult to Obtain
Attractive Advertising	•	•	•	•	•	•	•	Unattractive Advertising

Q. In addition, would you please mention:

Any Special Strengths of Evans _____

Any Special Weaknesses of Evans _____

about the customers. His education had made him familiar with many advanced research techniques. He also knew that many other industries were using sophisticated approaches to consumer behavior, but that retailing executives were not enthusiastic about their potential. He decided to seek the advice of two people, Morton Kondyke, the general merchandise manager, and George Rachander, his old professor.

Morton Kondyke was a man of some stature; as a retailer, he had an outstanding reputation. Kondyke asserted flatly that the reason advanced consumer techniques did not permeate retailing was that they were of no value. While it was true that advanced consumer research techniques could yield new information, they simply did not yield enough to justify their incremental cost. Furthermore, the minds of retail executives had always been trained to analyze what items had been sold. Most retail executives were not even very good at that. Indeed, in certain key areas, merchandise executives were not sure whether they should be concerned with unit sales of an item or the unit sales in relation to stock on hand. Morton Kondyke concluded that retailers in general and Evans in particular should spend their incremental research dollars on perfecting the analysis of what has been sold. In his opinion, a creative analysis or systems analysis of what had been sold would provide all the information generated by sophisticated consumer models, and at a much lower cost. In defense of his position, he argued that many very sophisticated economists did not ask customers about the economy. Rather, they used what had happened to the economy as a basis for their projections. However, Morton Kondyke was for continuing the consumer research started by Louis Evans because this aided the store greatly in spotting problems and in opening new stores. He suggested that the store might consider analyzing these data by merchandise classification.

Professor Rachander suggested that times had changed. All leading retail firms interviewed consumers. Each was trying to gain an advantage over the others. Competition was more severe than it was 30 years ago. Firms could no longer assume loyalty of their customer. Retailers had to constantly monitor the changing values of customers—find out what was important to their customer targets. And each retailer had to position itself on those patronage values that were most important to their targets. Professor Rachander went on to suggest that the demise of many leading retailers could be traced to their inability to position themselves effectively with customers.

QUESTIONS

1. If you were John, how would you make use of your marketing education to find out about consumers?
2. Whose advice would you take? Why?

CASE 7

Myron Gable
Shippensburg University

THE FISH MART

Tom Mosher owns and operates a small fish market, The Fish Mart, in Baltimore, Maryland. Mosher buys fish and seafood six days a week from the Chesapeake Bay fishermen. He also has fresh fish and seafood flown in from other sections of the United States (e.g., Maine). These shipments always arrive on Tuesdays and Fridays.

The Fish Mart is unique because it carries a wide variety of fish and seafood all year long. If the fish or seafood is out of season in the area, Mosher has it shipped in from another part of the United States. Therefore, people can rely on The Fish Mart to have what a person wants. Mosher will also stock special requests. For example, one of his regular customers likes a pound of Louisiana crawfish once a month, and Mosher makes sure that he has it. The Fish Mart also has such a good reputation for a variety of fresh fish and seafood that it even supplies a few of the neighborhood restaurants.

Mosher's father was a fisherman on the Chesapeake Bay, and Mosher often helped him. He learned a great deal from his father about fish and fishing. Living along the bay also enabled Mosher to enjoy all kinds of fish and seafood. When Mosher graduated from high school, he traveled all over the United States for a year, eating all kinds of foods and tasting many types of fish and seafood. Mosher then came home and went to a local college in Baltimore. While attending college, Mosher helped his aunt with her small fish market. During Mosher's sophomore year his aunt died, leaving him the market. He eventually decided to quit school and manage the fish market. He expanded the product line by adding fish and seafood he had enjoyed while touring the United States. Mosher's basic fish stock includes bass, trout, flounder, blowfish, monkfish, catfish, cod, herring, bluefish, tuna, albacore, and swordfish. In seafood, The Fish Mart carries whole Maryland crabs (in season), Alaskan crabs and crablegs, crabmeat, shrimp, mussels, oysters, prawns, and Main lobster and lobster tails. The Fish Mart also carries shark, squid, snails, and caviar. Mosher also uses his aunt's recipes and sells freshly made crabcakes and stuffed flounder to be cooked at home. He also sells his father's special seasoning which can be used for fish or seafood.

Mosher manages The Fish Mart very well, but he does have a problem with promotion. Mosher would like to increase business and attract more customers, but he is not sure how to do so. Most of Mosher's advertising is by word of mouth. His current customers tell their friends about The Fish Mart. Mosher has never advertised. When he has specials, he sets up posters in the store a week in advance advertising the special, and has fliers distributed within a one-mile radius of The Fish Mart. In addition to customers purchasing fish for use in their homes, Mosher would like to supply more restaurants with fish and seafood. Most of the restaurants that Mosher currently supplies are small, but they require a constant supply of fish and seafood. Therefore, restaurants are a very important segment for The Fish Mart, but Mosher does not know how to attract the restaurant business outside of The Fish Mart's general vicinity.

QUESTIONS

1. Should Tom attempt to attract the restaurant market?
2. Develop a comprehensive promotional plan for The Fish Mart.

Myron Gable
Shippensburg University

CASE 8

FLOWERS, ETC.

Susan Long owns a small florist shop, Flowers Etc., in a growing area one hour outside of Philadelphia, Pennsylvania. Until recently, Flowers Etc. and a smaller flower shop located three miles away were able to easily satisfy the demand for flowers and floral arrangements in the area. Susan believes there is room for another store because of the increasing number of people moving from Philadelphia to this suburb.

Long sells more than just flowers, which gives her a competitive advantage over other flower shops. She also sells novelty items such as figurines, candles, potpourri, and house plants. These other items make up 25 percent of Susan's gross sales.

The shop has been very busy and sales are growing rapidly. The store is often very crowded between 4:30 p.m. and 6:30 p.m., and Long is contemplating expanding her business or opening another location. She does not have the financial capability to do both. The expansion would be less expensive, but another location may attract more customers. Current customer information is available in Exhibit 1.

Flowers Etc. is currently located at the edge of town on one of the main traffic arteries (Route 30). Long is considering two possible locations: One is in the middle of town, two miles away from the current location (A); the other location is on another main road leading out of town (B). Exhibit 2 indicates the two possible locations, the current location, and the competitor's location.

Location A is very centrally located, and Susan feels that this location would attract many people who shop at the restored downtown shopping area. Location B, on the other hand, is conveniently located along the main road in a small shopping complex. Susan feels that a new store would be best, but she cannot decide on which location to choose, or whether she should renovate and expand the existing store. She can choose only one alternative.

Exhibit 1

Approximate current population	163,000
Current sales	$982,000
Sales growth rate (annual, past three years)	25%
Percent of customers living within 3 miles	43%
Percent of customers living within 3 to 6 miles	30%
Percent of customers living more than 6 miles	27%
Average income of those living within 3 miles	$ 27,000
Average income of those living within 3 to 6 miles	$ 35,000
Average income of those living more than 6 miles	$ 42,000

Exhibit 2

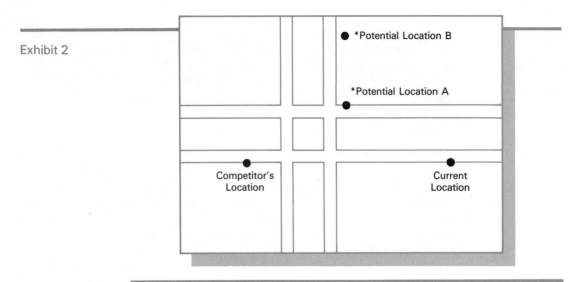

QUESTIONS

1. Evaluate the data in Exhibit 1.
2. Evaluate the extent of trading area overlap between the current location and the two potential locations.
3. Should Susan open another shop or should she expand at her current location?
4. Assuming you recommended an additional store, which location would you choose? Is there any additional information you would like to have to make a better decision?

CASE 9

Robert F. Lusch
University of Oklahoma

FREY'S FLOORCOVERING

Over the last 11 years, Stephen Frey has catapulted Frey's Floorcovering from a small one-person operation to a business with more than $1 million in annual sales and a staff of ten employees (including Stephen). Stephen, now approaching his thirty-fifth birthday, is having visions of transforming Frey's into a chain of floorcovering stores.

BACKGROUND

Stephen is the sole owner of Frey's and proud of it. He single-handedly started the firm, in a midwestern town of 81,000 people, in February, 1976, immediately after completing a two-year program at a local junior college. Before college, Stephen spent four years in the Air Force and during those four years managed to save $4,000. After completing college, Stephen had close to $5,000 and with that and a $2,500 loan from a local bank he started Frey's Floorcovering. One month later he married Sally Tiedeman.

Originally Frey's was located in a 50-year-old 1,500 square foot building near a warehousing district. The rent was cheap but retail customers were few and far between. In those early years, Stephen would often leave Sally to tend the store and he would go out to search for customers. He built quite a business calling on local builders, and by year end 1976 was selling 40 percent of the carpet installed in new houses in the area. Selling to builders resulted in more slender margins, but they were adequate to cover out-of-pocket expenses.

Frey's ended 1977 with sales of $130,000. In addition, by year end 1977 Stephen had repaid the $2,500 bank loan. All of this was accomplished with one part-time employee and Sally's help.

The following year, sales approached $200,000. During this year Stephen added another employee and made a significant effort to capture a portion of the retail market. Several thousand dollars were put into radio and newspaper advertising and the retail market responded favorably.

In late 1978 Stephen spotted an old building on the outskirts of town that was for sale. The building was on the major highway leading to town. The price was reasonable, but the building was in poor condition. Sally was strongly against purchasing the building. She argued with Stephen: "You're crazy to try to buy that building. The roof leaks and it is five times the size of our present building. We simply don't need that much space to sell a couple hundred thousand dollars worth of carpet." Stephen replied, "I don't care. We must own our own building. How can we ever get ahead by paying rent to someone else? Anyway, who cares if it costs $85,000 as long as we can borrow most of the money?" Sally interrupted, "We've paid rent on our house since we've been married. If you don't want to pay rent, and if you want to own something, then let's buy a house. With the baby due in six months we need a house of our own more than that old run-down building!" Stephen didn't reply. The conversation was over. Sally hoped that she had made her point.

Two days later when Stephen came home from work, he informed Sally that he had put a $6,000 down payment on the building. For a few years it was rough. At first, the building *was* too large. It was not until 1983, when sales surpassed the $500,000 mark, that space was beginning to be efficiently utilized. In 1986, when sales exceeded $1 million, the building decision finally seemed right.

CURRENT SITUATION

By 1986 Stephen and Sally had their own home and two children. Things looked splendid. Frey's Floorcovering made more than $12,000 in profit for 1986, after Stephen drew a $30,000 salary for himself. Sales were in excess of $1 million, with 42 percent coming from the building contract market and 58 percent from residential retail sales.

Stephen had worked hard to get his business to the $1 million sales level. His next goal was to start a chain of floorcovering stores. He had determined that there were 20 towns with populations between 30,000 and 60,000—within a 100-mile radius of his base operation—none of which had their own floorcovering store.

The plan was simple. Stephen would convert his existing outlet into a warehouse that would supply all stores. With one truck and driver, he felt that supplying up to twenty stores within a 100-mile radius would be no problem. Since his existing outlet would be converted to a warehouse, Stephen planned to build a new retail outlet for his existing business or possibly try to rent a vacant building temporarily.

The first additional outlet—besides the warehouse and Stephen's own new outlet—would be opened in a town 30 miles southeast. The population of this town is 41,000 and Stephen's brother-in-law, Scott Stern, would be the manager. Scott recently married Stephen's younger sister. Scott is a high-school graduate and has been managing the produce department in a local supermarket for the last two years.

Stephen feels he could open at least one new outlet per year over the next ten years. By the time he reaches age forty-five, Stephen would like to have ten or more outlets, with total sales surpassing $5 million.

Stephen doesn't want any partners. He wants to be the owner and ultimate decision-maker. Scott recently suggested, "Why don't we form a partnership on the store you want me to manage? I've been able to save $7,500, which I was planning to use as a down payment on a house, but that can wait." Stephen immediately rejected this suggestion: "I need

Exhibit 1

Sales Growth Profile (1976–1986)

Year	Sales
1976	$ 82,000
1977	130,000
1978	197,000
1979	231,000
1980	260,000
1981	257,000
1982	408,000
1983	548,000
1984	711,000
1985	903,000
1986	1,114,000

people, not capital. I can get all the money I need from the bank. I've never been late on a payment, even though sometimes it's been extremely close.'' Stephen has a good credit standing with the largest bank in the county. He has a revolving line of credit of $75,000 at two points over the prime rate—presently at about 12 percent. In addition he has a long-term note with an outstanding balance of approximately $86,000. This note has an interest rate of 10 percent.

In January of 1987 Stephen set up an appointment with his banker. At the meeting he presented Jack Black, vice president of commercial loans, with his idea of transforming Frey's Floorcovering into a full-fledged chain store enterprise. Stephen talked of ten stores in ten years as a reasonable goal. Jack Black appeared to be taken by surprise. He seemed to hesitate; no reassurance was forthcoming. Stephen spoke again: ''Don't you see how we can both make money on this deal?'' Jack firmly responded, ''Stephen, you're a valuable customer, but your balance sheet and income statement will simply not justify expansion at this time. To open even one additional outlet you would need at least $30,000, and that is if you can find a store to rent rather than purchase.'' Stephen stood up, ''Mr. Black, I've built Frey's to more than $1 million in sales without defaulting on any loans and you say my balance sheet and income statement are too weak!'' Jack responded in a soft and reassuring voice, ''Don't get irrational, Stephen. We can work something out, but first sit down and let me tell you something.'' Stephen reluctantly sat down, although still uneasy. ''With sales of $1 million you should be walking home with a lot more than $42,000 per year. You may have built sales, but your profit performance is dismal. Take my advice, Stephen, try to squeeze more profit out of your current operation; then let's sit down together in another year or two and discuss your expansion plans more seriously.''

Stephen went home that evening disgusted and had trouble sleeping that night. He was going to show Jack Black that now was the time to expand, not in another year or two. The next day at the office he ran across a copy of the *1986 Operating Results Study of Floorcovering Retailers* prepared by a major trade association. While reading the report, Stephen saw a section of the report entitled ''High Performance Retailing.'' In this portion of the report a typical high-profit floorcovering retailer in the $2 million range was profiled in terms of operating performance. Relevant data from this profile are presented in Exhibits 2 to 4 with comparable data on Frey's Floorcovering.

When Stephen was driving home that evening he was pondering how he could use this data to show Jack Black how his performance was respectable or, alternatively, how he could use data in this report to better program Frey's for high-performance results. When he got home, Scott Stern was there. Sally had told Scott about the turndown by the bank. Scott blurted, ''Stephen, I want you to know that I still have the $7,500 if you want to form a partnership on that new outlet.''

Exhibit 2

Operating Statements for Frey's and a High Performance Floorcovering Retailer

Item	Frey's	High Performance Floorcovering Retailer
Net sales	100.00%	100.00%
Cost of sales	70.58	70.28
Gross margin	29.42%	29.72%
Operating expenses		
Payroll	12.82%	15.90%
Advertising	2.99	2.81
Samples	.33	—
Utilities and telephone	1.71	.65
Rent or occupancy	3.98	1.44
Depreciation (trucks, fixtures, and equipment)	.44	.41
Bad debt losses	—	.30
Interest paid	1.64	.66
All other	3.53	2.62
Total operating expenses	27.44%	24.79%
Operating profits	1.98%	4.93%
Net other income	(.33)	(.52)
Net profits (before taxes)	1.65%	4.41%
Net profits (after taxes)	1.10%	2.95%

Balance Sheets for Frey's and a High Performance Floorcovering Retailer

Item	Frey's	High Performance Floorcovering Retailer
Assets		
Current assets		
Cash (including marketable securities)	10.39%	10.30%
Accounts receivable	30.00	39.38
Inventory	45.42	40.47
All other	1.29	—
Total	87.10%	90.15%
Fixed assets	12.90	9.85
Total assets	100.00%	100.00%

Liabilities and net worth

Current liabilities

Accounts payable	23.80%	23.33%
Notes payable	13.43	7.78
Customer deposits	4.87	—
All other	5.93	4.34
Total	48.03%	35.45%
Long-term liabilities	21.05	—
Net worth	30.92	64.55
Total liabilities and net worth	100.00%	100.00%

Exhibit 4

Productivity Ratios for Frey's and a High Performance Floorcovering Retailer

Item	Frey's	High Performance Floorcovering Retailer
Net sales per dollar invested in inventory	$ 5.94	$ 10.55
Net sales per square foot	128.99	168.32
Net sales per full-time salesperson*	222,806.00	364,695.00
Net sales per full-time employee*	111,403.00	136,761.00
Net sales per dollar invested in assets	2.70	4.30

*Two part time employees equal one full-time employee.

QUESTIONS

1. Is Frey's financially able to grow and become a multiple-outlet operation?
2. Using the data from the Operating Results Study, identify Frey's major operating problems.
3. Should a partnership with Scott Stern be formed?
4. Can you develop a strategy that would allow Frey's to generate enough capital internally to finance new outlets?
5. Would you say that Frey's problems are in most part strategic, administrative, or operating?

C A S E 10

Roger Dickinson
University of Texas at Arlington

GENERAL DEPARTMENT STORES

Michael Farnsworth is president of General Department Stores. He recently read a book of quotations and came across a statement attributed to John Wanamaker. In essence, the quotation was that Wanamaker was sure half his advertising was a waste and that he spent a great deal of time trying to determine which half. Farnsworth had also come across a quotation, attributed to Wrigley, to the effect that once a plane got off the ground, one did not test various elements to find out what made it work. One might find out all right, but by then it might be too late.

General Stores had grown over the years. However, there had never been a complete review of the firm's advertising expenditures. An advertising committee created by the president had maintained a budget of about 3 percent of sales. In some years the budget was not used up because of the difficulty in getting adequate newspaper space around Christmas. In other years a little more was spent to meet particular competitive activities of other stores. The initial budget was not held to religiously but adapted to the competitive environment as it evolved. The president kept a close eye on the store's volume figures; and if an area looked in need of additional advertising, he gave it more money. As merchandise areas developed individual hot items, additional advertising revenues were allocated.

The quotations bothered Farnsworth. He decided to call a meeting of his key executives to get their feelings on how much money the stores should spend on advertising and how these funds should be allocated among merchandise areas on the one hand and advertising media on the other.

All the executives agreed that the store had to spend at least 1 percent of sales on advertising or go out of business. The customers had to be convinced that General was still in business and had representative merchandise offerings. No one could say why the minimum was 1 percent rather than 2 or 3; it just seemed like a reasonable figure. The question was, "How much above this figure should General go?"

Farnsworth asked the opinion of Henry Jones, his tough-minded controller. Jones suggested that the answer was easy: each advertisement had to pay for itself. After all, General's advertising over the years had been merchandise advertising. Each department should be held to a contribution to overhead. If the decision-maker were held to this goal, he should be allowed to make his own advertising decisions. If the decisions were that bad, he should be fired and replaced by someone who could make effective decisions. It was the merchandise area heads, Jones continued, who should add up the requests of the individual merchandise areas. The advertising budget would then be more or less a summation of these requests. The decision makers would not be acting blindly, since they would be instructed in marginal analysis. Each buyer would ask himself: "Does the advertising for my area of concern pay or not?" If the summation of the various areas was less than 1 percent, then some method of allocating advertising up to 1 percent would be devised. But he felt that the requests of the areas would in fact add up to about 3 percent of sales.

Adrian Keller, formerly president of the company and now consultant, basically agreed with the controller; except that he argued that, in his experience, few advertisements paid for themselves completely. After all, there were substantial benefits of advertising other than short-run and immediate returns to the department. There were sales generated in the other parts of the store as a result of the customers coming in; some customers were even introduced to the store for the first time. The increasing number of mobile customers made advertising to new customers of continuing importance. In addition, there were image dimensions to the advertising. Keller suggested that each department receive a credit of 25 percent of its space charges for the benefit that this advertising was to the total store. Beyond that he was willing to accept the merchandise areas' requests for space and time. If allocation were necessary, the areas that could prove their claim to the largest incremental margin return from the dollars spent should get the money.

Paul Campbell, advertising vice-president, had a different perspective. He suggested that what had made General work over the years was the effective image it had built up with its customers, and that advertising had not really done its share. In his experience as vice president of an advertising agency on Madison Avenue, most of the really important advertising campaigns had been image-changing campaigns. The key role for advertising at General should be to favorably influence the attitudes of its customers. Historically, advertising at General had been only merchandise advertising. Campbell suggested that this was wrong. The company should first decide what image it wanted, and then go out and develop this image. To the extent that merchandise advertising was needed in this context, it should be used. But if merchandise advertising was not necessary, it should not be used. The merchandise advertising was just an element in image creation; it should not be the whole thing.

Irving Everett, vice president in charge of hard goods, did not buy the "image forever" approach. Everett felt that of course the firm's image was important, and of course he wanted to improve it. But the image was a constraint, not the purpose, of the advertising. It was merchandising that made the store exciting and merchandise that was the key differentiating feature of the store. Let the merchandise areas create the advertising and be charged 100 or some other percent for it, but let them make sure at the same time that the advertisements conformed to an image-enhancing format. And each merchandise manager should make sure that the merchandise being promoted conformed to the desired store image.

Louis Small, vice president in charge of soft goods, believed neither in a firm budget nor in the firm allocation of that budget to merchandise areas. Small thought that the key to all budgets was the reaction to circumstances, mainly to competition. True, one needed a budget. And one might as well start with last year's dollar figure or with some percentage of sales as with any other figure. One should, however, carefully monitor the sales results and the competition's advertising. Sales should be watched to see if any areas were in trouble. Troubled areas should be examined to see what was wrong. To the extent that advertising could correct the trouble, it should be utilized. Hot items should be promoted when appropriate. Customers and potential customers should be interviewed every six months to see if and how the image of the store had been altered. Again, since image was important, appropriate action should be taken where relevant.

Margaret Cohen, the general merchandise manager, held a slightly different view. She suggested that, basically, buyers and merchandise managers were responsible not just for net profits or contribution to overhead but for the growth of the store and its image. The store tended to use the volume of the merchandise areas as an indication of how the future growth criteria of the department were being met. And the initial and maintained markup were carefully monitored as separate entities to make sure that the volume was not obtained at the cost of the store's image. The promotion of goods at low markups was thought to damage this image, particularly if the merchandise promoted was not a famous brand. Therefore, one could not develop a budget or allocate that budget according to just one criterion—a criterion that few observers would accept at that—namely, short-term contribution or profits. While everyone would like to make the advertising budget scientific and relate this to one goal, perpetual hankering after this ideal was mental masturbation. Three goals—sales growth, high markup, and short-term profit—had to be kept in mind all the time. One simply had to do the best that one could; advertising was an art, not a science.

Cohen concluded that last year's budget should be used as a base, adjusted, if necessary, for exceptional performance the year before. The managers of each area should use the money the best way they know how, recognizing that these three goals apply to most of the areas.

Michael Farnsworth was more confused than ever after the meeting. He had expected more agreement among people who had been in merchandising so long.

QUESTIONS

1. How would you suggest that Michael Farnsworth set the firm's advertising budget?
2. How should he allocate that budget among the various merchandise areas?

CASE 11

Roger Dickinson
University of Texas at Arlington

GILES FURNITURE STORE

Giles Furniture Store is the leading furniture store in a city of 500,000 in the Southeast. Giles guarantees all of the products sold in the furniture department for one year from the date of delivery.

The Cranford family bought a sofa for $450.00 at Giles. After 15 months, the fabric started to pull away from the frame. Mrs. Cranford was quite disturbed by the occurrence. She did not feel that this was reasonable wear for a sofa at that price. She went back to the salesperson who had sold her the merchandise. She was promptly but courteously turned down. The salesperson was very sympathetic. He related that just two years ago, his automobile transmission had gone bad after just 13 months. He had to pay $400.00 to get it fixed. Mrs. Cranford was not satisfied with the answer. She decided to pursue the problem with the complaint manager of the store.

QUESTIONS

1. Was the salesperson correct in turning down Mrs. Cranford?
2. Do you want additional information? If so, what additional information do you want?

CASE 12

Donald J. Bowersox
M. Bixby Cooper
Douglas M. Lambert
Donald A. Taylor
Michigan State University

W. T. GRANT COMPANY

On February 6, 1976, the committee of secured creditors, composed of six bankers and five merchandise suppliers, voted 7–4 for liquidations of W. T. Grant. Thus, the doors were closed on the nation's seventeenth largest retailer. The collapse of W. T. Grant Company represented the biggest retailing failure in the history of the United States, and the closing of

Grant's 1,073 retail stores meant that 80,000 employees lost their jobs. The demise of the giant retailer, whose 1973 sales were $1.8 billion, is a classic example of mismanagement. Facing changing channels of distribution at the retail level, Grant countered with vigorous expansion in the absence of management information systems, controls, well-conceived performance measures, or a management team trained in basic merchandising principles.

BACKGROUND

The first W. T. Grant Store was opened in Lynn, Massachusetts, in 1906 by William T. Grant, who invested his entire savings of $1,000. Grant, age 30, had more than a decade of retailing experience and believed that there was a market for a retailer offering prices above those of the five-and-ten-cent stores such as Woolworth's and Kresge's, but below those of the expensive department stores. The concept was a success and first-year sales of $99,000 were achieved.

Between 1907 and 1917, 29 stores were added and sales reached $4,511,000. The chain grew to 157 stores by 1927 with sales of $43,744,000. In 1924, the founder gave up active management for the position of chairman of the board, which he held until 1966. Grant became a successful retail giant on the sales of basic, staple merchandise such as infants' wear, children's wear, white goods, and curtains and draperies, which had provided the basis for growth.

The year 1966 represented W. T. Grant Company's sixtieth year and the chain boasted 1,104 "Friendly Family Stores in 46 States" and sales of $920 million. In 1968, sales passed the $1 billion mark and the company made the following statements in the annual report:[1]

> Credit service is available at all stores, with approximately 25 percent of all sales being sold on credit.
>
> Over half of the present company stores have been opened during the last ten years. There has been a rapid increase in the size of the average store opened. These newer stores, freestanding and in shopping centers, are complete promotional department stores offering broad merchandising assortments and services.
>
> Over half the stores have restaurants.
>
> More than one-third offer major appliances and have outside garden shops.
>
> There are over 60 auto service centers.
>
> 17 appliance service centers inspect, deliver, install, and service our "Bradford" brand of appliances.

---

[1]W. T. Grant Company *1986 Annual Report.*

Five major distribution centers warehouse and deliver merchandise to the stores.

Net earnings for the year were almost $38 million and management made the following projection.[2]

Having reached this significant milestone of $1 billion in sales, the company will continue to build a bigger and stronger company for the benefit of Grant customers, stockholders, vendors, and employees.

A CRITICAL CHANGE IN TOP MANAGEMENT

On June 27, 1966, on the occasion of his ninetieth birthday, William T. Grant resigned as a director and chairman of the board. He was replaced by his brother-in-law, Edward Staley, formerly vice-chairman of the board. Staley, a long-time Grant employee, was president of the company from 1952 to 1959. Louis C. Lustenberger remained as president, a position he had held since 1959. However, a number of organizational changes took place that would shape the future destiny of the firm. For example, in October 1966, Harry E. Pierson, former president of Pacific Coast Properties, Incorporated, and, prior to 1960, a Grant real estate attorney and negotiator, was elected vice president of store expansion. Also, effective February 1, 1967, James G. Kendrick, formerly sales and store expansion vice-president, again became president of Zeller's Limited, Grant's Canadian subsidiary. Kendrick had previously been president of Zeller's Limited from 1958 until 1964. Richard W. Mayer, financial vice president and treasurer, who had set up the company's credit operation and had held the positions of national credit manager and treasurer, became sales vice president. John G. Curtin, formerly president of Zeller's Limited from 1965 to 1967, was elected financial vice-president and treasurer.

Effective February 1, 1968, Louis C. Lustenberger, president of the company since August 25, 1959, retired under the terms of the employee retirement plan. Under his direction, W. T. Grant's sales had more than doubled and earnings had increased from $9,850,000 to more than $32,000,000. In addition, new Grant stores had tripled in size, and total selling area had more than doubled. In the 1967 fiscal year, W. T. Grant Company set all-time records in both sales and earnings.

Lustenberger's choice for his successor was James G. Kendrick, then president of Zeller's Limited. Kendrick had joined Grant's store management program in 1935 after completing his education at the University of Minnesota. However, Lustenberger and Staley, the chairman of the board, had long been rivals on whether Grant was competing for the same market as K mart or if its target market was the same as Ward's and Penney's. Kendrick had openly disagreed with Staley over the direction of

[2]1968 Annual Report.

the company's expansion program. He believed that store interiors should be upgraded to match the change in merchandise mix. By changing store interiors, Kendrick felt they would create a consumer image that would be consistent with the objective of selling better merchandise. Staley, on the other hand, wanted to keep opening costs per store to the barest minimum and was against upgrading the interiors.[3] Also, Staley was not about to let Lustenberger's retirement slip by without strengthening his own position. Consequently, "a Staley man," Richard W. Mayer, was elected as Grant's ninth president on August 27, 1968.

THE STALEY-MAYER EXPANSION YEARS

Under the direction of the Staley-Mayer management team, Grant began an ambitious expansion program that "placed a great strain on the physical and human capability of the company to cope with the program. These were all large stores we were opening—6 million to 7 million square feet per year—and the expansion of our management organization just did not match the expansion of our stores."[4]

During the six years from 1968 to 1973 inclusive, Grant opened 410 new stores, enlarged an additional 36, and in the process spent $117,284,000 (Exhibit 1 contains a summary of Grant's store growth from 1964 through 1973). The new stores ranged in size from 60,000 square feet to Grant City "superstores" of 180,000 square feet. The smaller stores were built in neighborhood and convenience shopping centers and the big stores were either freestanding or in medium-sized malls, with Sears, Ward's, or a discounter as co-anchor.

The merchandise mix in the larger stores emphasized major appliances, televisions, stereo equipment, automobile accessories, furniture, sporting goods, and camera equipment. Major appliances and televisions were sold under Grant's private label, called Bradford. While this was similar to the Sears position with its Kenmore line, it was in contrast to K mart's strategy of marketing a line of major appliances under the Whirlpool brand name.

By the early 1970s the average store stocked more than 21,000 items, 71 percent of which were private label goods. Family fashions, which had once contributed about half of Grant's annual sales volume, represented less than 25 percent of sales in the early 1970s. In an effort to stimulate sales of big-ticket items, credit sales were emphasized. One former finance executive said: "We gave credit to every deadbeat who breathed."[5] Credit sales continued to account for as much as 25 percent of Grant's sales volume.

[3]Based on information obtained from James G. Kendrick during a telephone conversation on December 19, 1977.
[4]James G. Kendrick in "How W. T. Grant Lost $175 Million Last Year," Business Week (February 24, 1975), p. 75.
[5]"Investigating the Collapse of W. T. Grant," Business Week (July 19, 1976), p. 61.

Exhibit 1
Store Growth Program, 1964–73

Year	Number of Stores Opened	Number of Stores Enlarged	Capital Expenditures	Store Closings	Net Number of Stores at Year End
1973	77	4	$23,537,000	96	1,189
1972	92	5	26,983,000	52	1,208
1971	83	5	26,476,000	31	1,168
1970	65	8	15,995,000	44	1,116
1969	52	3	13,668,000	49	1,095
1968	41	11	10,625,000	35	1,092
1967	24	13	7,792,000	42	1,086
1966	51	11	14,856,000	35	1,104
1965	27	13	7,846,000	31	1,088
1964	31	12	5,262,000	20	1,092

SOURCE: W. T. Grant Company Annual Reports.

THE BEGINNING OF THE END

The year 1969 was a significant turning point for Grant. It marked both the eighth consecutive year of improved sales and profit and the last year that such a claim could be made. A summary of selected financial data covering the years 1969 through 1973 is contained in Exhibit 2. Although sales increased by almost 53 percent from 1969 to 1973, accounts receivable rose 62 percent, merchandise inventories more than doubled, short-term and long-term debt combined more than tripled, and earnings per share fell from $2.99 to $0.59. Even more significant, income before taxes from retail operations fell from $.0649 per dollar to $.008 per dollar of sales.

As early as 1971, significant dangers were evident. Sales per square foot reached an abysmal $30.74, less than half the rate achieved by Grant's major competitors. Return on net worth was 10.8 percent, down from 14.4 percent, and inventory and credit accounts receivable were increasing as a percent of sales. Also, short-term and long-term debt increased 68 percent on sales increases of 13.5 percent over 1969 levels. Alarmed by the direction in which the company was moving, former president Lustenberger and Raymond H. Fogler, also a past president and a Grant director, tried unsuccessfully to mobilize the outside directors. A former board member said: "The outside directors had to become more

Exhibit 2

W. T. Grant Company: Selected Financial Data, 1969-73

	1973	1972	1971	1970	1969
Sales	$1,849,802,346	$1,644,747,319	$1,374,812,791	$1,254,131,857	$1,210,918,068
Cost of merchandise sold, buying and occupancy costs	1,282,944,615	1,125,261,115	931,237,312	843,191,987	817,671,347
Interest expense	51,047,481	21,127,084	16,452,635	18,874,134	14,919,228
Net earnings	8,429,473	37,787,066	35,212,082	39,577,087	41,809,300
Per common share	.59	2.70	2.51	2.87	2.99
Dividends paid per preferred share	3.75	3.75	3.75	3.75	3.75
Dividends paid per common share	1.50	1.50	1.50	1.50	1.40
Employee compensation and benefits	434,368,156	397,133,721	336,311,735	295,882,263	271,650,884
Cents per sales dollar	23.5	24.1	24.5	23.6	22.4
Accounts receivable, net	598,798,552	542,751,365	477,324,069	419,731,126	368,267,131
Merchandise inventories	450,636,556	399,532,793	298,676,170	260,492,329	222,127,620
Store properties, fixtures and improvements	100,983,800	91,419,748	77,173,498	61,832,352	55,310,732
Short-term commercial notes and bank loans	453,096,715	390,033,500	237,740,700	246,420,216	182,132,200
Accounts payable for merchandise	58,191,731	60,973,283	Unavailable	80,681,456	70,853,108
Long-term debt	220,336,000	126,672,000	128,432,000	32,301,000	35,402,000
Net worth	323,738,431	334,338,566	325,745,094	302,036,424	290,688,499
Income from retail operations before taxes[a]	1,502,000	59,901,000	59,059,000	69,806,000	78,598,000
Cents per sales dollar	.08	3.64	4.30	5.57	6.49
Percent earned on net worth	2.6%	11.3%	10.8%	13.1%	14.4%
Inventory as a percent of sales	24.4%	24.3%	21.7%	20.8%	18.3%
Cost of goods sold as a percent of sales	69.36%	68.42%	67.74%	67.23%	67.52%
Accounts receivable as a percent of sales	32.37%	33.00%	34.72%	33.47%	30.41%
Square feet of store space at year end	56,224,000	50,618,000	44,718,000	38,157,000	33,855,000
Sales per square foot	32.90	32.49	30.74	32.87	35.77
Dividends paid—common	20,828,989	20,806,653	20,793,621	20,426,251	19,279,815
Dividends paid—preferred	293,054	344,709	345,813	395,031	456,858

[a]1973 Annual Report, Comparative Statement of Operations, p. 27.

active if they were going to fulfill their responsibilities as company directors."[6]

THE 1973 ANNUAL REPORT

On October 1, 1973, Edward Staley retired as chairman of the board of directors and became chairman of the executive committee. Mayer became chairman of the board and chief executive officer, and Harry Pierson was elected president and chief operating officer, effective February 1, 1974. These changes were no doubt related to the 1973 performance of the firm.

Sales for 1973 increased to $1,849,802,346, but profits fell 78 percent to $8,429,473, the lowest profit since 1961 when sales were $574,502,000. Short-term commercial notes and bank loans and long-term debt reached $673,432,715, more than twice the net worth. It is interesting that with profits of less than $8.5 million, the company continued to pay dividends in excess of $21 million.

In the 1973 annual report, Mayer and Pierson addressed the issue of the company's lack of image at the consumer level.[7]

During the last six years your Company opened 410 large stores of over 50,000 square feet, enlarged 36 successful stores, and closed 307 smaller units. In view of the decline in earnings in 1973, you might well ask . . . WHY?

Retailing is synonymous with change. Selling methods, size and types of stores, and lines or departments of merchandise change as the demands of the American Consumer dictate. The Management of your Company recognized this inevitable shift from smaller, limited stores to larger "full line" stores and committed itself to the complete restructuring of the Company.

As this proceeded, a frequent question asked was "We do not understand or recognize your image." Ten years ago, the Company had been "understood and recognized" as a large chain of Variety Stores. Our image was clear. We sold limited price items in smallwares, wearing apparel and soft goods for the home. Times changed and retailing changed . . . to the one-stop, complete store of over 50,000 square feet which we call Grant City and that is the direction your Company followed.

To convert a chain of approximately 1,000 successful limited variety stores to a Company with approximately half of its units composed of Grant City or "full-line" stores, while at the same time adding all of the necessary back-up services, merchandise distribution centers,

[6]"How W. T. Grant Lost $175 Million Last Year," Business Week (February 24, 1975), p. 74.
[7]W. T. Grant Company 1973 Annual Report, p. 2.

data processing, and major appliance warehousing, home delivery and service in a relatively short span of time was not easily accomplished. Our image may have become blurred. We do have both small and large stores. This has to be. Ten years ago, from Maine to California, Grant operated small stores with limited merchandise assortments. Today, in hundreds of communities, the Grant City store is recognized as a store with complete assortments of merchandise for the home and family. Our Grant City stores may not yet have the general acceptance of some of our major competitors, but we firmly believe our quality is good, our pricing and values excellent, and that our reputation and acceptance as a Grant City full line store improves each year. We are still relatively new to the full-line store field, but we intend to stay—and to improve each year.

In this letter to Stockholders we will cover more fully the factors influencing operations in 1973 and our prospects for the future.

In addition, Mayer used the opportunity to attempt to justify the ill-fated credit system which he had expanded, promoted, and directed for a number of years.[8]

In 1946, the Company first introduced a credit service to aid its customers to purchase wanted merchandise and pay on an installment plan. The stores were small and stocked with merchandise limited in lines and price. The credit coupon book was selected as the most practical method as these coupons could be used as cash and the customer did not have to wait for individual sales slips on each item purchased. It gave us a method of granting credit without incurring the expense of a sophisticated credit system to keep customer credit limits under control. For smaller stores, this type was not only popular with customers—but it was tailor-made for the simplified operation of this small unit. However, as the Company developed new full-line Grant City stores, customers indicated a preference for the revolving credit charge plan. In addition, governmental regulations have made it increasingly difficult and expensive to administer the coupon-type credit plan. Primarily, in recognition of the customer preference for revolving credit charge accounts, this plan was promoted in 1973, and this emphasis will continue in the future. This change from the credit coupon book plan produces less service charge revenue and is more expensive to operate. During 1973, although credit sales were $45,000,000 higher, service charge revenues were down by over $7,000,000. On the other hand, our experience in the past year indicates that Grant City customers prefer the revolving credit charge and will purchase more merchandise with this plan.

[8] *1973 Annual Report,* pp. 2–3.

In spite of the looming financial disaster, Grant continued with its expansion plans for 1974 and its diversification into catalog showroom stores.[9]

In 1973 the Company opened 77 new stores and enlarged 4 existing units, for an additional 5,606,000 square feet of new store space. In addition, construction of the new 475,000 square foot Distribution Center in Windsor Locks, Connecticut, was completed in late fall 1973.

In 1974, we will open approximately 45 new stores and enlarge 1 unit for approximately 3,000,000 square feet. The reduction, both in number of stores and square footage from 1973 levels, is due to developers encountering difficulty in securing necessary materials to complete centers on schedule, inability to start some projects because of the high cost of interim financing, and the increased time required to be spent before beginning a project in satisfying environmental control requirements. It is our estimate at this time that the 1975 program will be of the same magnitude as 1974, or smaller, and management feels that this is a more workable program in view of present conditions. This will, of course, reduce pre-opening costs and the additional funds required for investment in capital expenditures, inventories, and to carry customer receivables, from the peaks of the last few years.

The program of closing older Grant stores, typically of a smaller size, was accelerated in 1973 with 96 closings. All expenses pertaining to this program were charged to the year of closing. Since the closing of unprofitable stores not only reduces investment in inventory but eliminates the burden of operating costs, this program will be continued in 1974.

In 1973, GranJewel, the company's joint venture participation in catalog showroom retailing with Jewelcor, opened 11 stores and purchased Edison Jewelers and Distributors Co. of Forth Worth, Texas, which operates 4 units. In 1974, an additional 7 catalog showroom stores are planned.

Mayer and Pierson concluded their messages to the stockholders as follows.[10]

We will continue opening full-line Grant City stores and will continue to expand our revolving credit charge account plan. This year, the economy will be uncertain, but Management will continue to take aggressive steps to strengthen its entire operation, whether in limited or full-line Grant City Stores. We will continue to change the Company

[9]*1973 Annual Report*, p. 4.
[10]*1973 Annual Report*, p. 5.

to meet the demands of customers. In the final analysis, our customers will determine the success of the Company. We feel that Customers are aware of the positive changes that are occurring and that, as a result, the acceptance of the Grant City stores—as full line stores—will continue to increase.

Exhibit 3 contains a list of Grant directors as of the 1973 year-end.

CRISIS MANAGEMENT AT GRANT

The dismal 1973 financial performance was followed by $10 million loss for the first 6 months of 1974. Effective June 30, 1974, Richard Mayer resigned as chairman and chief executive officer of Grant's and Edward Staley resigned as a director. Fogler and Lustenberger also resigned from the board. One former director made the following observation about the reorganization:[11]

> ... it is a pretty safe bet that Staley's resignation would not have been forthcoming if his old foes didn't leave, too.

Exhibit 3

Grant Directors as of 1973 Year-End with Company Affiliations

Richard W. Mayer	Chairman of the Board and Chief Executive Officer
Harry E. Pierson	President and Chief Operating Officer
Edward Staley	Chairman of the Executive Committee
A. Richard Butler	Executive Vice President—Merchandising
Joseph W. Chinn, Jr.	Director and Chairman, Consulting Committee, Wilmington Trust Company
Raymond H. Fogler	Retired, former President of W. T. Grant Company
John D. Gray	Chairman of the Board and Chief Executive Officer, Hart, Schaffner & Marx
John Hinsey	Partner, White & Case
James G. Kendrick	President and Chief Executive Officer of Zeller's Limited
E. Robert Kinney	President and Chief Operating Officer of General Mills, Inc.
John J. LaPlante	Personnel Vice President
Robert A. Luckett	Corporate Service Vice President and Comptroller
Louis C. Lustenberger	Retired, former President of W. T. Grant Company
DeWitt Peterkin, Jr.	Vice Chairman of the Board, Morgan Guaranty Trust Company of New York
Charles F. Phillips	President Emeritus, Bates College
Clarence W. Spangle	Executive Vice President of Honeywell, Inc.
Asa T. Spaulding	Consultant to Boyden International Group, Inc., of Los Angeles

[11]"How W. T. Grant Lost $175 Million Last Year," *Business Week* (February 24, 1975), p. 76.

On September 3, 1974, James G. Kendrick became chairman and president of W. T. Grant after leading Zeller's Limited for a total of approximately 13 years of impressive sales and profit growth. He believed that the most critical problems facing him were: (1) to increase the company's sales per square foot, (2) to revise significantly the merchandise program back to the basic lines that the company had built its reputation on, (3) to reduce the substantial losses associated with the company's credit operation, and (4) to revise and strengthen its financial policies and controls.[12]

One of Kendrick's first accomplishments was refinancing the short-term notes with a $600 million line of credit with 143 banks headed by Morgan Guaranty Trust Company. Three banks put up $300 million, eleven banks doled out about $200 million, and the remaining $100 million came from 129 banks. Grant used its 50.2 percent interest in Zeller's Limited and $600 million in credit accounts receivable as collateral.

Kendrick planned to reduce the company's reliance on private label merchandise and to replace an inventory of slow-selling items with fresh, new, wanted merchandise. With rising credit delinquencies, Grant began accepting Bank Americard and Master Charge sales. In addition, nervous suppliers had to be assured that Grant would continue to pay its bills since the American Credit Indemnity company had canceled its credit insurance policy.[13] In an effort to gain immediate consumer support, $6 million was budgeted for television advertisements in 35 major markets in fall 1974.

In spite of these changes, Grant suffered losses in 1974 of $175 million on sales of $1.7 billion. Contributing to the massive loss were credit losses of more than $90 million, $24 million in store closing expenses, heavy interest charges, and a substantial markdown budget. Also, Grant filed suit against three former real estate employees, including John A. Christensen, former real estate vice president, for taking what Kendrick described as "hundreds of thousands of dollars in bribes in connection with store leases."[14]

THE COLLAPSE

In 1975, Kendrick began a program to close another 126 stores and the maturity date on Grant's agreement with the banks was extended from June 1975 to March 31, 1976. To satisfy the banks, Robert Anderson, former vice president of Sears, was hired as president and chief executive officer in April 1975 for a guaranteed salary and pension totaling $2.5 million. At this point, any anxious supplier could have brought down the company by filing a Chapter X proceeding.

By October 1975 losses were mounting and Grant was having great

[12]Based on a telephone interview with James T. Kendrick on December 19, 1977.
[13]"It's Get-Tough Time at W. T. Grant," Business Week (October 19, 1974), p. 46.
[14]"How W. T. Grant Lost $175 Million Last Year," Business Week (February 24, 1975), p. 74.

difficulty obtaining merchandise from suppliers. As a result, the company filed under Chapter XI. Under Chapter XI, stores west of the Mississippi River were closed and plans were initiated to reduce further the number of stores to 359 in the Northeast. However questionable financial data and an uncertain future resulted in liquidation:[15]

> The final blow came when the consultants cautioned the creditors that it would take six to eight years to determine whether Grant would survive. The bankers favored liquidation and were hungrily eyeing the $320 million in cash accumulated from store closings and liquidations. Trade creditors, by contrast, were uncertain. They were fully secured and doing business with Grant. But on February 6, the committee voted 7–4 for liquidation.

EPILOGUE

In December 1977, former president Kendrick was asked whether he believed in September 1974 when he returned to Grant's from Zeller's that he could save the company. He replied: "I would not have accepted the job if I had not. However, at that point in time I was not aware of just how bad the credit situation was." In addition, Kendrick was asked whether he could have accomplished his objectives if he had been named president seven months earlier (on February 1, 1974, Pierson became president). Keeping in mind the impending legal cases, he observed that, with the benefit of 20/20 hindsight, it might be possible for some people to reach that conclusion.

QUESTIONS

1. What channel decisions do you see in the W. T. Grant Company case?
2. When did it become evident that Grant was headed for financial trouble? What were the danger signs? What measures of financial performance would have provided management with additional useful information?
3. What were the primary causes of the bankruptcy of the W. T. Grant Company?
4. What role in the collapse of the W. T. Grant Company was played by the American Credit Indemnity Company? The decision to private label big-ticket items? Grant's credit department?

[15]"Investigating the Collapse of W. T. Grant," Business Weekly (July 19, 1976), p. 62.

William A. Staples
University of Houston
John I. Coppett
University of Houston

CASE   13

HADE HARDWARE CENTERS

In 1982, Harve Hade opened his first hardware store in the southwestern part of Houston, Texas. The opening of the store fulfilled a life-long dream of Harve Hade to have his own business. The store offered a variety of hardware and do-it-yourself items including tools, paint, wallpaper, and a variety of other products, such as locks, light bulbs, and extension cords.

Due to the booming economy in Texas, and particularly Houston, during the early 1980s, Harve Hade opened an additional hardware store in northwest Houston in 1984. At the time of the second store opening, Hade decided to shift from a "hardware store" to a "hardware center" concept. This shift in emphasis was accompanied by an expanded product mix, including lawn care equipment, lumber, and a limited line of plumbing items. Both the southwestern and northwestern stores were positioned as hardware centers and carried the same product lines.

During the mid-1980s the Houston economy slumped dramatically due to a declining oil and gas industry. As Hade contemplated opening another store in 1988, only one area in the metropolitan Houston area seemed attractive. In the southeastern part of Houston was an area called Clear Lake City, a residential and commercial project of the Friendswood Development Company, a subsidiary of the Exxon Corporation. The project, which was begun in the early 1960s with the establishment of NASA's Johnson Space Center, was, due to the growth of the space program, the one shining economic area in Houston.

The major cities in this area included the communities of Friendswood, League City, and Webster, as shown in Exhibit 1. Hade had received information on traffic flows and patterns for this area from the City of Houston's Department of Traffic and Transportation, the Harris County Engineer's Office, and the Texas State Department of Highways and Public Transportation. Two major highways, Interstate 45 and State Highway 3, were in the area as well as major thoroughfares such as Bay Area Boulevard in Friendswood, NASA Road 1 in Webster, and FM 518 in League City.

In order to determine the feasibility of locating in this area, Hade had hired a marketing research firm to provide him a report of various economic indicators. Harve Hade believed that the demand for products in a hardware center was influenced by a number of factors. Based on his experience with his first two stores, he attached different weights to each factor: 40 percent on an area's population, 30 percent on retail sales, 20 percent on traffic flows, and 10 percent on building activity (See Exhibit 2).

Exhibit 1
Area Map

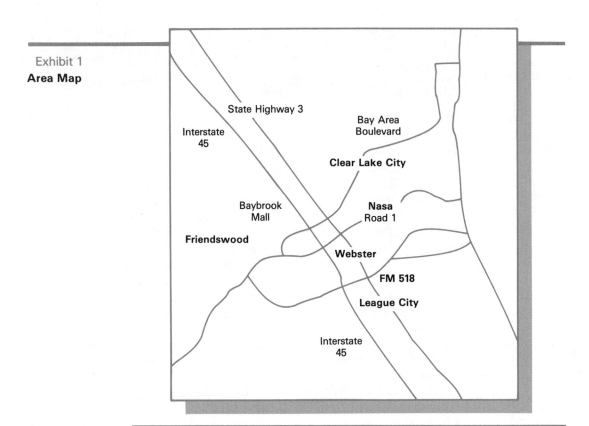

Exhibit 2

Area Economic Indicators

City	Population	Retail Sales (000,000)	Major Traffic Flows*	Building Permits (000,000)
Friendswood	12,472	$ 44.8	42,000	$18.2
League City	16,578	$ 82.9	25,000	$14.6
Webster	8,168	$139.6	29,000	$ 5.6

*Vehicles per 24 hours going both ways on the major street in each city.

He also believed that in order to draw enough customer traffic to a new location that it would be best to be located in a neighborhood shopping center since it would be more accessible and economically feasible than a regional shopping center (See Exhibit 3).

Exhibit 3

Shopping Centers: Space, Vacancy Rates, and Rental Rates

City	Space (Sq. ft.)	Vacancy Rate	Rental Rate
Friendswood	1,870,000	8.4%	$1.00/sq. ft.
League City	582,000	22.7%	$ .77/sq. ft.
Webster	1,689,000	26.2%	$1.07/sq. ft.

Hade realized that adding a third store was a major decision and that success in the first two stores would not guarantee a successful third location. He also knew that a good analysis of the situation could enable him to capitalize on an economic opportunity. The task confronting him was to evaluate each city in terms of the key economic indicators he believed were critical to locating a new hardware center.

QUESTIONS

1. In looking at Exhibit 1, what factors might influence the location decision by Hade for a new hardware center?
2. If you were in Hade's situation, what other information would you want before making this location decision?
3. Based on the information in Exhibits 2 and 3, what city would you select for the new hardware center using Hade's criteria? Why?

CASE 14

Robert F. Lusch
University of Oklahoma

HEALTH-MORE PHARMACIES, INC.

Jane Hoover is the president and principal stockholder of Health-More Pharmacies, Inc. She is in a quandary over how to reorganize the corporation so that it will be able to continue its rapid growth. In six years the firm has grown form a single pharmacy to a group of five pharmacies. Hoover is finding it increasingly difficult to manage and control the five stores.

BACKGROUND

In 1980, Jane Hoover graduated from college with a degree in pharmacy and immediately took a job as a pharmacist for Walgreen Drugs. It didn't take her long to recognize that the day-to-day activities of a pharmacist were not very exciting and challenging. Hoover frequently found herself daydreaming about operating her own drugstore.

In April of 1982, while visiting a friend in a nearby city, Hoover accidentally ran across a small drugstore for sale. The present owner had operated the store for twenty-two years and was nearing retirement. The store was located in a neighborhood shopping center and was easily accessible to many households within eight blocks of the store. Luckily for Hoover, the owner was having difficulty finding a buyer, and she was able to purchase the store (which had a five-year lease remaining) for the book value of the inventory (which was $60,000) and $10,000 for fixtures and equipment. The owner was willing to finance most of the $70,000 purchase price, and Hoover purchased the drugstore with only $7,500 of her own funds. By June 1982 Hoover was in business for herself.

Hoover operated the drugstore with the help of two part-time clerks while she served as the full-time pharmacist. Although the new venture did not free her of her role as a pharmacist, she was enjoying herself since there were many other duties to perform besides filling prescriptions. The accounting records had to be kept, employees supervised, merchandise bought and priced, and sales promotions planned. Not surprisingly, she quickly found herself taking night courses at a local university in accounting and marketing.

By October 1983 Hoover had spotted another small drugstore for sale. It, too, was located in a neighborhood shopping center. The price was $110,000 and the owner would not finance any of the purchase price. Hoover acquired outside capital by incorporating and selling stock to friends and acquaintances who had been impressed with how well she had managed the first store. She was also able to convince the existing owner of the store to take $10,000 of the purchase price in stock of Health-More Pharmacies, Inc.

The first store was turned over to a manager and the new store was managed by Hoover. Also at this point she added a part-time bookkeeper to handle the records for both stores.

In 1985, 1986, and 1987, three more drugstores were acquired—all from individual proprietors desiring to get out of the drugstore business. The two most recently acquired stores were located in a city of 47,000 people 21 miles from the first three stores. Stores acquired in 1985, 1986, and 1987 were financed through retained earnings and issuing stock in Health-More Pharmacies, Inc., to the prior owner. Every time a store was acquired, Hoover would become the manager and turn the store she was presently managing over to a new manager.

CURRENT SITUATION

As 1988 ended, Hoover began to recognize that she did not have the time to keep a close watch over all the stores. At the beginning of 1986, she had hired a full-time assistant to help her with the buying and in late 1986 added a full-time accountant. But still there were too many problems that required her special attention and that were taking her away from managing a store. Hoover also wished she had more time to follow up on other possible drugstore acquisitions. Recently she heard of a small group of four drugstores for sale in a city 54 miles away.

The income statement and balance sheet for Health-More Pharmacies, Inc., are provided in Exhibits 1 and 2. These financial statements reflect the composite performance for all five stores as of the end of 1988. All five stores are located in neighborhood centers and are 4,000 to 5,000 square feet in size. Approximately 40 percent of sales were prescription drugs and the remainder was divided among the following product catego-

Exhibit 1

Health-More Pharmacies, Inc., Income Statement (1988)

Item	Dollars	Percent
Net Sales	$2,420,663	100.0
Cost of goods sold	1,575,852	65.1
Gross margin	844,811	34.9
Operating expenses		
Wages	455,085	18.8
Rent	60,517	2.5
Advertising	29,048	1.2
Utilities and phone	31,469	1.3
Insurance	24,206	1.0
Legal and professional fees	12,103	.5
Delivery	9,683	.4
Repairs	26,627	1.1
Interest	21,786	.9
Bad debts	7,262	.3
Miscellaneous	70,199	2.9
Total expenses	$ 747,985	30.9
Profit (before taxes)	96,826	4.0
Taxes	36,794	1.5
Profit (after taxes)	$ 60,032	2.5

Exhibit 2
Health-More Pharmacies, Inc., Balance Sheet (12/31/88)

Assets		Liabilities and Net Worth	
Current assets		Current liabilities	
Cash	$ 30,103	Accounts payable	$112,041
Accounts receivable	96,827	Notes payable	44,955
Inventory	387,306	Other	35,964
Other	68,163	Total	$192,960
Total	$582,399		
		Long-Term Liabilities	$118,274
Fixed Assets		Net worth	$380,384
Equipment	79,209		
Leasehold improvements	30,010	Total liabilities	
Total	$109,219	and net worth	$691,618
Total assets	$691,618		

ries; health and beauty aids, magazines, books, newspapers, tobacco, candy, greeting cards, and small gifts ($5 to $25). Each store carries 9,500 SKUs. An item is defined as one size of one product. For example, a bottle of vitamin pills containing 200 tablets was considered as one item, even though there may be a dozen bottles of that size and description in stock.

Drugstores are complicated in terms of legal regulations. There are state and federal laws which druggists must comply with since they handle products with dangerous ingredients. Also licenses need to be obtained from the State Board of Pharmacy. In addition, some dangerous drugs need to be ordered by serial number and regularly inventoried and reported to government agencies.

QUESTIONS

1. What are the advantages and disadvantages of a multiple-store organization?
2. How should Health-More Pharmacies, Inc., be reorganized to improve control and give Hoover the time she needs to direct the corporation?
3. Analyze the financial performance of Health-More Pharmacies, Inc.
4. Does Jane Hoover have a strategy for Health-More Pharmacies, Inc.?

CASE   15

Roger Dickinson
University of Texas at Arlington

HENRY'S FRIED CHICKEN

High employee turnover has always plagued the fast-food industry. After being trained, the employee quits for one reason or another. Henry's is taking steps to reduce their turnover rate.

Henry's hires prospective employees at minimum wage for a 28-day period. If the employee remains with the company after the trial period, the employee receives a pay increase of five cents per hour. The training program at the store level includes working for badges that are earned for demonstrated skill in cutting, cooking, and counter service. Employees are given a manual and audiovisual aids to help them learn. A badge and another five-cent-per-hour raise is awarded following the successful completion of both a written and physical test of skills.

When an employee earns three badges, he qualifies as a team leader. Team leaders are eligible to attend one of the five training schools. The training school is a three-week program that combines academic training with the maintenance of management/customer relations.

Since many of Henry's units are located in lower-income areas, the vast majority of the students attending the classes are from the ghettos and not necessarily well-educated. In order to train and motivate the students, they are paired up with students of comparable ability. They work together and test one another on the concepts and skills they learn. The program uses several steps to teach them how to study. The program is self-paced. A student must master the first step before going on to subsequent steps. Each student is awarded points for every accomplishment, and these points are graphed on a daily basis. Discussion groups are held at the end of the day, and students receive feedback for their work and validation for their accomplishments. Problems are also reviewed at this time.

After the successful completion of the training program, the students return to their respective areas as assistant managers. They hold the position for a minimum of two years before becoming store managers. Henry's also provides store managers an opportunity for store ownership.

QUESTIONS

1. How would you improve Henry's program?
2. Why will the employee turnover rate still be high?

3. Henry's has been bitterly criticized for paying low wages. For example, their wages are often well under 50 percent of those paid by supermarkets. Should Henry's pay more than they have to?

James W. Camerius
Northern Michigan University

CASE 16

K MART CORPORATION: CORPORATE STRATEGY AT THE CROSSROADS

K mart, Inc., in 1988, included discount department stores, variety stores, restaurants, financial services, home improvements centers, and specialty shops in the United States and several foreign countries, including Canada, Australia, China, and Puerto Rico. Measured in sales volume it was the second largest retailer and the largest discount department store chain in the United States.

By the mid-1980s, the discount department store industry was perceived to have reached maturity. In 1985, K mart had a retail management strategy that was developed in the late 1950s. The firm was at a crossroads in terms of corporate strategy. The problem was what to do over the next 20 years.

THE EARLY YEARS

K mart was the outgrowth of an organization founded in 1899 in Detroit by Sebastian S. Kresge. The first S. S. Kresge store represented a new type of retailing that featured low-priced merchandise for cash in low-budget, relatively small (4,000 to 6,000 square feet) buildings with sparse furnishings. The adoption of the "5 and 10 cent" or "variety store" concept, pioneered by F. W. Woolworth Company in 1879, led to rapid and profitable development of the S. S. Kresge Company.

Kresge believed it could substantially increase its retail business through centralized buying, control, developing standardized store operating procedures, and expanding with new stores in heavy traffic areas. In 1917, the firm was incorporated. It had 150 stores and, next to Woolworth's, was the largest variety chain in the world. Over the next forty years, the firm experimented with mail order catalogues, full-line department stores, self-service, a variety of price lines, and the opening of stores in planned shopping centers.

By 1957, corporate management became aware that the development of supermarkets and the expansion of drug store chains into general merchandise lines had made inroads into market categories previously dominated by variety stores. It also became clear that a new form of store with a discount merchandising strategy was emerging.

THE CUNNINGHAM CONNECTION

In an effort to regain its competitiveness and possibly save the company, Frank Williams, then president of the S. S. Kresge Company, nominated Harry B. Cunningham as general vice president in 1957. This maneuver was undertaken to free Cunningham, who had worked his way up the ranks in the organization, from operating responsibility. He was being groomed for the presidency and was given the assignment to study existing retailing business and recommend marketing changes.

In his visits to Kresge stores, and those of the competition, Cunningham became interested in discounting—particularly a new operation in Garden City, Long Island. Eugene Ferkauf had recently opened large discount department stores called E. J. Korvette. They had a discount mass-merchandising emphasis that featured low prices and margins, high turnover, large freestanding departmentalized units, ample parking space, and a location typically in the suburbs.

Cunningham was impressed with the discount concept, but he knew he had to first convince the Board of Directors, whose support would be necessary for any new strategy to succeed. He studied the company for two years and presented it with the following recommendation:

> "We can't beat the discounters operating under the physical constraints and the self-imposed merchandise limitations of variety stores. We can join them—and not only join them, but with our people, procedures, and organization, we can become a leader in the discount industry."

In a speech delivered at the University of Michigan, Cunningham made his management approach clear by concluding with an admonition from British author Sir Hugh Walpole: "Don't play for safety, it's the most dangerous game in the world."

The Board of Directors had a difficult job. Change is never easy, especially when the company has a proud heritage. Before the first presentation to the Board could be made, rumors were circulating that one shocked senior executive had said:

> "We have been in the variety business for 60 years—we know everything there is to know about it, and we're not doing very well in that, and you want to get us into a business we don't know anything about."

The Board of Directors accepted H. B. Cunningham's recommendations. When President Frank Williams retired, Cunningham became the new president and chief executive officer and was directed to proceed with his recommendations.

THE BIRTH OF K MART

Management conceived the original K mart as a conveniently located one-stop shopping unit where customers could buy a wide variety of quality merchandise at discount prices. The typical K mart had 75,000 square feet, all on one floor. It generally stood by itself in a high-traffic, suburban area, with plenty of parking space and with a floor plan common to other units in the organization.

The firm made an $80 million commitment in leases and merchandise for 33 stores before the first K mart opened in 1962 in Garden City, Michigan. As part of this strategy, management decided to rely on the strengths and abilities of its own people to make decisions rather than employing outside experts for advice.

The original variety store operation was characterized by low gross margins, high turnover, and concentration on return on investment. The main difference in the K mart strategy would be the offering of a much wider merchandise mix.

The company had the knowledge and ability to merchandise 50 percent of the departments in the planned K mart merchandise mix, and contracted for operation of the remaining departments. In the following years, K mart took over most of those departments originally contracted to licensees. Eventually all departments, except shoes, were operated by K mart.

THE MATURATION OF K MART

By the late 1970s, corporate management at K mart considered the discount department store industry to be at a level of maturity. K mart itself was the largest discount department store organization, with 2,100 stores serving 80 percent of the population. The industry was characterized by a reduced number of store openings, reduced expansion of square feet of floor space, and similar product offerings by competitors. Although maturity was sometimes looked on with disfavor, K mart executives felt that this did not mean a lack of profitability or lack of opportunity to increase sales. The industry was perceived as being "reborn." It was in this context that a series of new marketing programs, designed to upgrade the K mart image, were developed.

By the mid-1980s, the discount department store industry began to undergo a series of fundamental changes. Nearly a dozen firms like E. J. Korvette, W. T. Grant, Arlans, and Atlantic Mills passed into bankruptcy or reorganization. Many regional firms such as Wal-Mart Stores, Target Stores, and ShopKo Stores began carrying more fashionable merchandise in more attractive facilities and shifted their emphasis to more national markets. Specialty discounters such as Toys 'R' Us were making big inroads in toys, sporting goods, paint, and other lines. The so-called "superstores" of drug and food chains were rapidly discounting more and more general merchandise. The discount divisions of other big retailers [e.g., Gold Circle, Caldor, and Venture (May Department Stores)] had emerged as well financed and professionally managed organizations; and some firms like Woolworth (Woolco) had withdrawn from the field entirely after years of disappointment.

Many retailers, such as Target, a division of Dayton-Hudson, who adopted the discount concept, attempted to go after an upscale customer. The upscale customer tended to have a household income of $25,000 to $44,000 annually. Other pockets of population were being served by firms like Zayre, which served consumers in the inner city, and Wal-Mart, which served the needs of the more rural consumer in secondary markets. Senior management at K mart felt that all firms in the industry were facing the same situation. First, they had been very successful 5 or 10 years ago but were not changing and, therefore, were becoming somewhat dated. Management that had a historically successful formula was having difficulty adapting to change, especially at the peak of success. Management would wait too long and then would have to scramble to regain competitiveness.

K mart executives found that discount department stores were being challenged by several new retail formats. Some retailers were assortment-oriented, with a much greater depth of assortment within a given product category. Toys 'R' Us was an example of a firm that operated 20,000 square-foot toy supermarkets. Toys 'R' Us prices were very competitive within an industry that was very competitive. When consumers entered a Toys 'R' Us facility, there was usually no doubt in their minds that if the product wasn't there, no one else had it.

Other retailers were experimenting with the off price apparel concept, where name brands and designer goods were sold at 20 to 70 percent discounts; home improvement centers which were warehouse-styles stores with a wide range of hard-line merchandise for do-it-yourselfers and professionals; and drug supermarkets, which offered a wide variety of high-turnover merchandise in a convenient location.

In these cases, competition was becoming more risk-oriented, putting $3 to $4 million in merchandise at retail value in an 80,000 square-foot facility and offering genuinely low prices. F & M stores in the Detroit market, Drug Emporium in the Midwest, and a series of independents were employing an entirely new concept of the drug supermarket.

Competition was offering something that was new and different in terms of depth of assortment, competitive price image, and format. K mart management perceived this as a threat because they were viable businesses that hindered K mart in its ability to improve and maintain market share in specific merchandise categories.

Corporate research revealed that K mart served 80 percent of the population. One study concluded that one out of every two adults in the United States shopped at a K mart at least once a month. Despite this popular appeal, strategies that had allowed the firm to have something for everybody were no longer felt to be appropriate for the 1990s. K mart found that it had a broad customer base because it operated on a national basis. Its strategies had assumed the firm was serving everyone in a market.

K mart was often perceived as aiming at the low-income consumer. The financial community believed the K mart customer was blue collar, low income and upper lower class. In reality, the market served was more professional and middle class because K mart stores were initially in suburban communities where growth was occurring.

Although K mart has made a major commitment in recent years to secondary or rural markets, these were areas that had previously not been cultivated. The firm, in its initial strategies, perceived the rural consumer as different from the urban or suburban customer. In readdressing the situation, it discovered that its assortments in rural areas were too limited and there were too many preconceived notions regarding what the Nebraska farmer really wanted. The firm discovered that the rural consumer didn't always shop for bib overalls and shovels, but for microwave ovens, just as everyone else did.

The goal was not to attract more customers but to get the customer coming in the door to spend more. Once in the store the customer was thought to demonstrate more divergent tastes. The upper-income consumer would buy more health and beauty aids, cameras, and sporting goods. The lower-income consumer would buy health and beauty aids, toys, and clothing.

In trying to capture a larger share of the market and get people to spend more, the firm began to recognize a market that was more upscale. When consumer research was conducted and management examined the profile of the trading area and the profile of the person who shopped at K mart in the past month, they were found to be identical. K mart was predominately serving the suburban consumer in suburban locations.

In 'life-style' research in markets served, K mart determined there were more two-income families, families were having fewer children, and customers tended to be homeowners. Customers were very careful how they spent their money and wanted quality. This was a distinct contrast to the 1960s and early 1970s, which tended to have a "throw away" orientation. The customer had said, "What we want are products that will last longer. We'll have to pay more for them but we still want them and at the lowest price possible." Customers wanted better quality products but still demanded competitive prices. According to K mart Annual Report, "Consumers today are well educated and informed. They want good value and they know it when they see it. Price remains a key consideration, but the consumer's new definition of value includes quality as well as price."

MARKETING STRATEGIES

Several new marketing programs emerged as the result of an overall reexamination of existing corporate strategies. The area receiving initial attention was improvement in the way products were displayed. Before 1980, the traditional K mart layout was by product category.

Often these locations for departments were holdovers from the firm's variety store past. Many departments would not give up prime locations. As part of the new marketing strategy, the shop concept was introduced. Management recognized that it had a sizable do-it-yourself store. "The hardware department was right smack in the center of the store because it was always there. The paint department was over here and the electrical department was over there." "All we had to do," management contended, "was put them all in one spot and everyone could see that we had a very respectable do-it-yourself department." The concept resulted in a variety of new departments such as "Soft Goods for the Home," "Kitchen Korners," and "Home Electronic Centers." The goal behind each department was to sell an entire life-style concept to consumers, making goods complementary so shoppers would buy several interrelated products rather than just one item.

The programs also involved utilizing and revitalizing the space K mart already had under its control. This took the form of remodeling and updating existing stores. Initial effort was concentrated in key major markets such as Indianapolis, Atlanta, Denver, Chicago, Detroit, and Buffalo. Stores were also identified in smaller markets which had rapid growth and significant new competition. A key to implementing this program was remerchandising assortments, which required changing the firms' preconceived notions about what the customer would or would not buy and under what conditions. The new look featured a broad "poppy"; new racks: round, square, and honeycombed that displayed the full garment; relocating jewelry and women's apparel to areas closer to the entrance, and redesigning counters to make them look more upscale and hold more merchandise.

Name brands were added in soft and hard goods as management recognized that the customer transferred the product quality of branded goods to perceptions of private label merchandise. In the eyes of K mart management, "if you sell Wrangler, there is good quality. Then the private label must be good quality."

Additional programs emphasized the quality image. In a joint venture with *McCall's*, a new magazine called *Betsy McCall*, aimed at girls ages 6 to 12, was launched. Pro golfer Fuzzy Zoeller was engaged to promote golf equipment and other associated products. Mario Andretti who races in the Championship Auto Racing Teams' Indy car series agreed to co-sponsorship of his car with associated promotion. Dusty Lenscap, an animated marketing character, was introduced to promote photo developing equipment. K mart hired Martha Stewart, an upscale Connecticut author of lavish best-sellers on cooking and home entertaining, as its life-style spokesperson and consultant. Martha Stewart was featured as a corporate symbol for housewares and associated products in advertising and in store displays. Management visualized her as a representative of its interest in life-style trends—the next Betty Crocker.

In 1982, K mart initiated its own off-price specialty apparel concept called Designer Depot. A total of 28 Designer Depot stores were opened in 1982, to appeal to customers who wanted quality upscale clothing at a budget price. A variation of this concept, called Garment Rack, was opened to sell apparel that normally would not be sold in Designer Depot. A distribution center was added in 1983, to supplement both of the above ventures. K mart attempted an unsuccessful joint venture with the Hechinger Company of Washington, D.C., a warehouse home center retailer. However, after much deliberation, K mart chose instead to acquire Home Centers of America of San Antonio, Texas. This division was to build 80,000 square-foot warehouse home centers named Builders Square. It would capitalize on K mart's real estate, construction and management expertise and Home Centers of America's merchandising expertise.

Waldenbooks, a chain of 877 book stores, was acquired from Carter, Hawley Hale, Inc. in 1984. It was part of a strategy to capture a greater share of the market with a product category that K mart already had in its stores. K mart had been interested in the book business for some time and took advantage of an opportunity in the marketplace to build on its knowledge base.

The Bruno's Inc., joint venture in 1987, formed a partnership to develop large combination grocery and general merchandise stores or hypermarkets. The giant, one-stop shopping facilities of 225,000 square feet would trade on the grocery expertise of Bruno's and the general merchandise experience of K mart to offer a wide selection of products and services at discount prices.

In 1988, the company acquired a controlling interest in Makro Inc., a Cincinnati-based operator of warehouse club stores. Makro, with annual sales of about $300 million, operated member-only stores stocked with low-priced fresh and frozen groceries, apparel and durable goods in suburbs of Atlanta, Cincinnati, Cleveland, Washington, and Philadelphia.

THE PLANNING FUNCTION

Corporate planning at K mart was the result of executives, primarily the senior executive, recognizing change. The role played by the senior executive was to get others to recognize that nothing is good forever. Good planning was perceived to be the effort of those who recognized that at some point they would have to get involved. Poor planning was done by those who didn't recognize the need for it. When they did, it was too late to survive. Good planning, if done on a regular and timely basis, was assumed to result in improved performance. K mart's director of planning and research contended, "Planning, as we like to stress, is making decisions now to improve performance tomorrow. Everyone looks at what may happen tomorrow, but the planners are the ones who make decisions today. That's where I think too many firms go wrong. They think they are planning because they are writing reports and are aware of changes. They don't say, 'because of this, we must decide today to do this to accomplish this goal in the future.'"

The Director of Planning and Research believed that K mart had been very successful in strategic planning. "When it became necessary to make significant changes in the way we were doing business," he suggested, "that was accomplished on a fairly timely basis." When the organization made the change in the 1960s, it recognized there was a very powerful investment opportunity and capitalized on it—far beyond what anyone else would have done. "We just opened stores," he continued, "at a great, great pace. Management, when confronted with a crisis, would state, 'It's the economy, or it's this, or that, but it's not the essential way we are doing business.'" He continued, "Suddenly management would recognize that the economy may stay like this forever. We need to improve the situation and then do it." Strategic planning was thought to arise out of some difficult times for the organization.

K mart had a reasonably formal planning organization that involved continual evaluation of what was happening in the marketplace, what competition was doing, and what kinds of opportunities were available. Management felt a need to diversify because it would not be a viable company unless it was physically growing. Management felt it was not going to physically grow with the K mart format forever. The Director of Planning and Research felt that, "Given a 'corporate culture' that was accustomed to challenges, management would have to find ways to expand that energy. A corporation that is successful," he argued, "has to continue to be successful. It has to have a basic understanding of corporate needs and be augmented by a much more rigorous effort to be aware of what's going on in the external environment."

A planning group at K mart reports directly to the chairman of the board through its director of planning and research. The group represents a number of functional areas of the organization. Management describes it as an "in-house consulting group" with some independence. It is made up of (1) financial planning, (2) economic and consumer analysis, and (3) operations research. The chief executive officer (CEO) is the primary planner of the organization.

THE CHALLENGE

On April 6, 1987 K mart Corporation announced that it agreed to sell most of its 55 Kresge and Jupiter variety stores in the United States to McCrory Corporation, a unit of the closely held Rapid American Corporation of New York. The move left the firm with approximately 4,000 retail

units including discount department stores, restaurants, home improvement centers, financial and real estate service centers, and specialty shops
in the United States and several countries including Canada, Australia,
China and Puerto Rico. Appendixes A, B and C provide financial information about K mart.

In the light of a corporate climate of asset-disinvestment and asset
redeployment, the firm was at a crossroads in terms of corporate strategy. The question was, what to do now?

QUESTIONS

1. Evaluate the strategies that K mart has introduced as part of its new
   marketing program. How much impact will these strategies have in
   the competitive environment as the firm seeks to maintain its position and grow in the future?
2. How much importance is placed on the planning function at K mart?
3. Why do you think planning is important to an organization like
   K mart?
4. Discuss the importance of changes in the external environment. How
   much impact do they have on strategic plans in retailing firms such as
   K mart?

Appendix A

K mart Corporation
Financial Summary
1987 Annual Report
Consolidated Statements of Income

| | Fiscal Year Ended | | |
(Millions, except per-share data)	January 27, 1988	January 28, 1987	January 29, 1986
Sales	$25,627	$23,812	$22,035
Licensee fees and rental income	237	234	223
Equity in income of affiliated retail companies	92	83	76
Interest income	22	23	23
	25,978	24,152	22,357
Cost of merchandise sold (including buying and occupancy costs)	18,564	17,258	15,987
Selling, general and administrative expenses	5,296	4,936	4,673

Appendix A—*Continued*

(Millions, except per-share data)	Fiscal Year Ended		
	January 27, 1988	January 28, 1987	January 29, 1986
Advertising	617	581	554
Interest expense:			
Debt	156	171	205
Capital lease obligations	174	178	181
	24,807	23,124	21,600
Income from continuing retail operations before income taxes	1,171	1,028	757
Income taxes	479	458	181
Income from continuing retail operations	692	570	472
Discontinued operations	—	28	(251)
Extraordinary item	—	(16)	—
Net income for the year	**$ 692**	**$ 582**	**$ 221**
Earnings per common and common equivalent share:			
Continuing retail operations	$ 3.40	$ 2.84	$ 2.42
Discontinued operations	—	.14	(1.27)
Extraordinary item	—	(.08)	—
Net income	**$ 3.40**	**$ 2.90**	**$ 1.15**
Weighted average shares	203.5	201.5	197.4

Appendix B

K mart Corporation
Financial Summary
1987 Annual Report
Consolidated Balance Sheets

(Millions)	January 27, 1988	January 28, 1987
Assets		
Current Assets:		
Cash (includes temporary investments of $134 and $296, respectively)	$ 449	$ 521
Merchandise inventories	5,571	5,153
Accounts receivable and other current assets	353	390
Total current assets	6,373	6,064
Investments in Affiliated Retail Companies	379	317

Appendix B—*Continued*

(Millions)	January 27, 1988	January 28, 1987
Property and Equipment—net	3,744	3,594
Other Assets and Deferred Charges	610	603
	$11,106	$10,578
Liabilities and Shareholders' Equity		
Current Liabilities:		
Long-term debt due within one year	$ 2	$ 4
Notes payable	—	296
Accounts payable—trade	2,309	2,207
Accrued payrolls and other liabilities	606	639
Taxes other than income taxes	242	223
Income taxes	211	162
Total current liabilities	3,370	3,531
Capital Lease Obligations	1,557	1,600
Long-Term Debt	1,191	1,011
Other Long-Term Liabilities	379	315
Deferred Income Taxes	200	182
Shareholders' equity	4,409	3,939
	$11,106	$10,578

Appendix C

Financial Performance
K mart/S. S. Kresge Company 1960–1986

Year	Sales (000)	Assets (000)	Net Income (000)	Net Worth (000)
1960	418,200	269,343	11,120	205,757
1961	432,838	274,293	8,863	205,791
1962	452,561	281,897	9,014	205,493
1963	510,531	315,265	10,278	209,109
1964	692,499	344,272	17,150	212,700
1965	862,441	394,015	23,470	229,597
1966	1,102,688	442,740	28,609	251,803
1967	1,401,168	525,536	34,915	275,632
1968	1,757,750	657,825	47,611	319,450
1969	2,185,298	797,526	54,089	367,519
1970	2,595,155	926,227	66,994	456,761

Appendix C-*Continued*

Year	Sales (000)	Assets (000)	Net Income (000)	Net Worth (000)
1971	3,139,653	1,095,948	96,116	548,469
1972	3,875,183	1,383,439	114,674	779,726
1973	4,702,504	1,652,773	138,251	924,512
1974	5,612,071	1,896,110	104,772	1,016,600
1975	6,883,613	2,377,541	200,832	1,197,825
1976	8,483,603	2,865,572	266,574	1,441,793
1977	10,064,457	3,428,110	302,919	1,687,817
1978	11,812,810	4,836,260	343,706	1,915,666
1979	12,858,585	5,642,439	357,999	2,185,192
1980	14,204,381	6,102,462	260,527	2,343,172
1981	16,527,012	6,673,004	220,251	2,455,594
1982	16,772,166	7,343,665	261,821	2,601,272
1983	18,597,900	8,183,100	492,300	2,940,100
1984	20,762,000	9,262,000	503,000	3,234,000
1985	22,035,000	9,991,000	472,000	3,273,000
1986	23,812,000	10,578,000	570,000	3,939,000

SOURCE: Fortune Financial Analysis/Annual Reports
*After taxes & Extraordinary Credit or Charges

REFERENCES

"Where K mart Goes Next Now That It's No. 2." *Business Week* (June 2, 1980): 109–110, 114.

Bussey, John. "K mart Is Set To Sell Many Of Its Roots To Rapid-American Corp's McCrory." *Wall Street Journal*, 6 April 1987, p. 24.

Carruth, Eleanore. "K mart Has To Open Some New Doors On The Future." *Fortune* (July, 1977): 143–150, 153–154.

"Why Chains Enter New Areas." *Chain Store Executive* (December, 1976): 22, 24.

"It's Kresge . . . Again." *Chain Store Executive* (November, 1975): 16.

Dewar, Robert E. "The Kresge Company And The Retail Revolution." *University of Michigan Business Review* (July 2, 1975): 2.

Guiles, Melinda G. "Attention, Shoppers: Stop That Browsing And Get Aggressive." *Wall Street Journal*, 16 June 1987, p. 1, 21.

Guiles, Melinda G. "K mart, Bruno's Join To Develop 'Hypermarkets,' " *Wall Street Journal*, 8 September 1987, p. 17.

Ingrassia, Paul. "Attention Non-K mart Shoppers: A Blue-Light Special Just For You." *Wall Street Journal*, 6 October 1987, p. 42.

Key, Janet. "K mart Plan: Diversify, Conquer: Second Largest Retailer Out To Woo Big Spenders." *Chicago Tribune*, 11 November 1984, p. 1-2.

Main, Jerry. "K mart's Plan To Be Born Again." *Fortune* (September 21, 1981): 74–77, 84–85.

Mitchell, Russell. "How They're Knocking The Rust Off Two Old Chains." *Business Week* (September 8, 1986): 44–48.

Schwadel, Francine. "K mart Is Trying to Put Style on the Aisle," *Wall Street Journal,* 9 August 1988, p. 6.

Sternad, Patrica. "K mart's Antonini Moves Far Beyond Retail 'Junk' Image." *Advertising Age* (July 25, 1988): 1, 67.

Wellman, Michael. Interview with Director of Planning and Research, K mart Corporation, August 6, 1984.

CASE 17

Roger Dickinson
University of Texas at Arlington

KELLY'S DISCOUNT STORE

Kelly's Discount Store was having its once-a-year "Believe It or Not" sale. Spectacular values were offered throughout the store. One of the advertised values was a flatware set formerly $38.00, now $18.00. The advertisement was to appear on Sunday for a 10 a.m. Monday opening. Gordon Linquist, housewares buyer, was shocked when he saw that the newspaper had left out the *1*, representing the price as $8.00. Linquist rushed to the store at 8 a.m. on Monday and had the newspaper deliver an apology. The newspaper was extremely sorry about any problems that had been caused. The error was all theirs.

At 10 a.m., 30 customers came running to the department for the $8 set of flatware. Linquist showed the customers the newspaper retraction. He told the customers that the store could and would not sell the item at that price. And it certainly was under no legal obligation to sell any of the sets at $8. Three customers came roaring into the complaint department.

QUESTIONS

1. Was Gordon Linquist's action correct?
2. What action should the complaint department manager take?
3. Would your decision have been different if the store had a slogan, "The customer is always right at Kelly's."? Explain.

CASE 18

Robert F. Lusch
University of Oklahoma

A. B. KING'S

In mid-1987 Vance Womack, menswear buyer at A. B. King's, requested permission from the general merchandise manager to change the present pricing policy on men's suits. Womack felt that a change in pricing was necessary due to increased local competition in this merchandise category.

BACKGROUND

A. B. King's is a locally owned and operated full-line department store in a midwestern city of approximately 250,000 inhabitants. The store was founded by Alfred Bailey King in 1902. The store remains in its original downtown location and is still primarily owned and operated by the King family. Tom King, the grandson of A. B. King, is the current president and chief executive officer. In 1986 annual sales approached $12 million. The company has consistently shown a profit every year since 1902 except 1932, 1933, and 1957.

Since 1974, competition has intensified in King's trading area, which happens to be its entire MSA. Sears remodeled its downtown store and opened another store in a regional shopping mall on the outskirts of the city. In addition, K mart has built three new stores since 1979. Specialty store competition has also intensified, especially in women's apparel and menswear. A. B. King's has always been one of the most fashionable places for upper-middle and upper-class residents to purchase their clothing. Several generations of families have purchased their clothes at King's.

In the area of menswear, one competitor that has grown to be a dominant market leader is Franklin's. Franklin's is a locally owned company founded in 1969. The store sells only menswear and women's apparel in about a 65/35 mix. Franklin's first store was located downtown, directly across the street from A. B. King's. In 1980 their sales were $1.8 million. Today they have a total of five stores, and in 1986 their sales were $5.3 million. Franklin's sells moderate- to good-quality clothing at a relatively low markup. They are very promotion- and price-oriented and concentrate on high inventory turnover. Recently they have introduced a line of high-grade men's suits priced at $249, which most local retailers (including A. B. King's) sell in the $300 to $350 price range. This line has been heavily promoted in the local newspaper.

CURRENT SITUATION

Vance Womack is concerned about the sales performance of the men's suit lines at A. B. King's. In 1982 King's sold 1,445 suits, but in 1984 that number had dropped to 1,208, and in 1986 suit sales were only 940. 1987 results look even less promising.

On July 24, 1987, Vance wrote a memo to John Stern, the general merchandise manager, about this slackening of demand.

Memorandum

TO: John Stern, General Merchandise Manager
FROM: Vance Womack, Buyer, Menswear

It is time we came up with a strategy to combat our declining sales of men's suits. The inroads that Franklin's and other specialty stores are making into our market share is increasingly becoming a problem. We continue to hold on to our loyal patrons but the transient, bargain-seeking shopper is being intercepted by competition. The problem is not one of poor buying. We have as good a selection and assortment of suits as anyone in town. And our sales assistance and alteration department are superior. In short, I believe we are simply not price-competitive. Given the level of competition, our present prices are simply too high.

Stern immediately phoned Womack and told him that he concurred with his observation. He instructed Womack to put together relevant merchandising statistics for men's suits for the first six months of 1987 and also to develop hypothetical merchandising statistics based on his proposed price changes. These statistics are provided in Exhibits 1 and 2.

After Womack had started to compile these statistics, he realized that A. B. King's did not have the selection he initially thought they had, especially in the moderate- to lower-price range. In fact, they currently had no suits priced under $189. As a result, two lower-price lines were added—one at $129 and another at $98, and the $189 line was reduced to $169. Neither of these lines was expected to be a best-seller, but Womack thought they might help to generate more traffic in the menswear department.

Womack also suggested an increased level of advertising. Currently advertising of men's suits had been averaging 1.9 percent of net sales. Womack proposed this be increased to 3.8 percent of net sales. Most of the advertising would be directed at the $298 and $398 lines and the $98 and $129 lines. Some consideration was given to putting the $98 line in a new bargain basement department of the store, but Womack felt this would defeat the purpose of generating more traffic in the upstairs menswear department.

Exhibit 1

Merchandising Statistics for Men's Suits (1/1/87–6/30/87)

Price Line	Cost Range (billed cost)	Average Markup[a]	Average Unit Stock	Unit Sales	Workroom Cost Per Unit	Cash Discounts (as percentage of billed cost)	Retail Reductions (as percentage of original retail)[b]
$419	$200–240	$213	60	50	$21	2%	8.1%
329	160–199	155	90	108	18	2	9.8
259	125–159	118	120	154	13	2	18.1
189	90–124	80	70	47	12	2	19.4

[a]Average markup represents original markup over original billed cost.
[b]Retail reductions include markdowns, employee discounts, and shortages as a percent of original retail.

Exhibit 2

Projected Annual Performance on Men's Suits

Price Line	Cost Range (billed cost)	Average Markup[a]	Planned Unit Stock	Planned Unit Sales	Planned Workroom Cost Per Unit	Cash Discounts (as percentage of billed cost)	Planned Reductions (as percentage of original retail)[b]
$398	$200–240	$192	78	140	$20	2%	3.1%
298	160–199	124	96	312	16	2	6.2
219	125–159	78	128	420	12	2	10.4
169	90–124	60	96	164	11	2	9.8
129	74–89	48	96	140	9	2	6.1
98	54–73	37	78	116	9	2	5.1

[a]Average markup represents original markup over original billed cost.
[b]Retail reductions include markdowns, employee discounts, and shortages as a percent of original retail.

1. Why did A. B. King's wait so long to respond to its declining sales volume in men's suits?
2. Will the price cuts be profitable?
3. How will competition react to the price cuts?
4. What are the pros and cons of advertising both high- and low-priced men's suits?
5. What are the pros and cons of starting a bargain basement department?

CASE 19

Myron Gable
Shippensburg University

LEBO DEPARTMENT STORE

PART A

The buyer for the women's sweater department has purchased wool sweaters for $28, and she wants to sell them at a 43 percent markup on selling price. At what price should this sweater be sold?

PART B

The buyer for men's shirts has a price point of $20 and requires a markup of 38 percent. What would be the highest price he should pay for a shirt to sell at this price point?

PART C

The buyer for housewares hopes to achieve net sales of $1,000,000 for the coming year. Operating expenses are $190,000; retail reductions are $80,000. Management has set a profit goal of $110,000. What should the initial markup percent be?

PART D

The women's dress department wants to produce a 15 percent operating profit on forecasted sales of $550,000. The divisional merchandise manager has made the following estimates:

Alterations Income	$ 700	Operating Expenses	$150,000
Alteration Costs	1800	Markdowns	55,000
Stock Shortages	3000	Cash Discount Earned	400
Employees Discounts	1500		

Based on this information, what initial markup percent will you need?

CASE 20

Myron Gable
Shippensburg University

LINENS UNLIMITED

Linens Unlimited opened for business on February 1, 1988. The store was located in a strip shopping center on a major traffic artery in Norristown, Pennsylvania, a major suburb of Philadelphia. It carried a complete assortment of sheets, pillow cases, towels, tablecloths, napkins, and related merchandise. The merchandise assortment was designed to meet the needs of the middle-class market residing within a five mile radius of the store.

It is now February 10, 1989 and Jane Tabbot, the owner, would like to assess the store's performance during its first fiscal year of operation. All available information is presented in Exhibits 1 through 3. Because markups differ for various items, Linens Unlimited has been advised by its accountant to use the retail inventory method. A major trade journal in the linen industry released figures in its November, 1988 issue indicating the median inventory turnover for stores with sales volumes of less than $1,000,000 was 3.6; for superior stores (the top 10 percent), the turnover figure was 4.1. Based on the information you possess, answer the following questions.

Exhibit 1

Merchandise Available for Sale
February 1, 1988–January 31, 1989

	Cost	Retail
Beginning Inventory (2/1/88)	$120,000	$210,000
Purchases	530,000	800,000
Freight Charges	12,000	
Markdowns		40,000
Sales		790,000
Ending Inventory (Book Value)		180,000
Ending Inventory (Based on physical inventory 1/31/89)		175,000

Exhibit 2

Operating Costs
February 1, 1988–January 31, 1989

Cost	Amount
Rent	$ 44,000
Utilities	4,000
Insurance	2,000
Salaries	160,000
Advertising	38,000
Miscellaneous	5,000

Exhibit 3

Beginning of Month Inventory (at Retail)

Date	Amount
5/1/88	$220,000
8/1/88	200,000
11/1/88	245,000*

*Reflects a build-up in inventory for the Christmas season.

1. Was it a wise decision to use the retail inventory method?
2. Using the retail inventory method, what was the net profit or loss for Linens Unlimited in its first year of operation?
3. Do you think Linens Unlimited performed well during its first year? Would you desire any additional information to answer this question? What would that information be?

C A S E   21

Myron Gable
Shippensburg University

NEYLAND'S

Tina Hoover was recently hired by a large New York-based department store to be department manager for china and gifts. The previous manager left suddenly more than four months ago for another position. Since then, the department has been operating without a manager because there was a temporary hiring freeze for lower management positions. The store's board of directors had fired a number of the top executives, including the president. The board restructured the organization and promoted certain individuals. The new president is 20 years younger than the previous president and has a more open style of management. The chain has seven department stores in suburban New York. They have a prestigious image, but often run excellent sales that attract many customers. The china and gifts department is important because it attracts many customers to the store.

The operations manager of hard goods at the store, which includes china and gifts, had been keeping an eye on the department by visiting it two or three times a week to make sure everything was running smoothly while the department was without a manager. While in the department, she would look at the displays and the overall appearance of the department. She would also look at the sales figures, but she did not take the time to find out what merchandise was selling or to really look at the books. During this period, two of the salesclerks in china and gifts, Laura and Steve, were responsible for maintaining the daily operations of the department. Their responsibilities included scheduling, recording sales and markdowns, authorizing checks and employee discounts, and keeping in contact with buyers about fast-moving merchandise.

Laura is working at the store to pay her way through a local, two-year business college. Steve is attending a nearby junior college, and both will graduate next month. They hope to get into the store's executive training program after graduation. Most of the applicants who have been accepted into the program have had four-year degrees, but the new management is placing more emphasis on experience than education when accepting applicants into the executive training program.

The Operations Manager is very impressed with Laura and Steve and with the work they did in the department while it was without a manager. She has told Hoover what a great job Laura and Steve did and how well they assumed responsibility. If it were up to her, Steve and Laura would have no problem getting into the store's executive training program.

Tina has been at the store for a week, and she feels that Steve and Laura are excellent salespeople and customers enjoy being waited on by them. The department's sales are very good, almost always achieving targeted sales goals. Stock turnover is above average, but Hoover has noticed a high percentage of markdowns recorded on the books during the past few months, which is troubling, since markdowns are usually not as high when sales are good and inventory turnover is at the desired level. In analyzing markdowns still further, Hoover noticed that markdowns were usually not for a line but for a small number of items. Since Laura and Steve had been in charge, they had approved these markdowns. These marked down items were usually in the store less than a month. Hoover talked to the buyers about the merchandise that Laura and Steve had marked down and they told her that they had found it difficult to keep the department stocked with these newer items.

Tina is wondering if she should report her findings to the operations manager of hard goods or just talk to Steve and Laura about the markdowns.

QUESTIONS

1. Why do you think there was this unusual pattern of markdowns?
2. Is there a reason for Tina to talk to the operations manager about Steve and Laura?
3. Do you think Steve and Laura are ready to be admitted into the firm's executive training program?

Robert F. Lusch
University of Oklahoma

C A S E   22

OAKLAND DEPARTMENT STORE

Rodney Hayes is merchandise manager of the shoe department for Oakland Department Store. Oakland Department Store is in a large metropolitan city of more than 750,000 people in the Southwestern United States. Oakland has 250,000 total square feet of floor space and 80 percent is selling space. In 1987 the store had $42 million in sales and 3.8 percent of this total was attributed to the shoe department. The shoe department occupies 6,500 square feet of selling floor space. The 1987 income statement for Oakland Department Store is presented in Exhibit 1.

Currently, Hayes is in the process of preparing a merchandise budget for the fall/winter 1988 selling season. The fall/winter season consists of the months August through January; the spring/summer season consists of February through July. The distribution of sales for the fall/winter season for the last three years is presented in Exhibit 2.

Toni McClain, the store controller, has informed all department managers that overall store sales in 1988 should be 5 to 6 percent above 1987. This forecast is based on an assumption of continued moderate inflation and increased competition. Oakland Department Store has been especially hard hit by a growing number of price- and promotion-oriented retailers such as Mervyn's and factory outlet malls. Also, a growing number of specialty shoe stores, such as Thom McAn, Athlete's Foot, and Open Country have had a detrimental impact on the performance of the shoe department at Oakland. Over the last ten years the shoe department has

Exhibit 1

**Oakland Department Store
1987 Income Statement**

Gross Sales	$43,210,000
Less: Return and Allowances	1,210,000
Net Sales	42,000,000
Less: Cost of Goods Sold	27,510,000
Gross Profit	14,490,000
Less: Operating Expenses	11,760,000
Net Profit (before taxes)	2,730,000

Exhibit 2

Oakland Department Store Shoe Department
Distribution of Annual Sales by Month

Year	Aug.	Sept.	Oct.	Nov.	Dec.	Jan.
1985	10.1%	9.2%	6.3%	8.4%	8.0%	5.9%
1986	10.1	9.1	6.5	8.2	8.1	6.0
1987	9.9	9.4	6.4	8.3	8.2	5.8

generally experienced a rate of annual growth in sales lower than the overall growth in store sales (see Exhibit 3).

Since 1983 the shoe department has used a 55 percent planned initial markup for preparing its seasonal merchandise budget. However Hayes is considering raising this to 60 percent because of the increased level of markdowns over the last several years. The need for higher markdowns is the result of increasing competition. When Hayes mentioned to McClain his desire to raise the initial markup to 60 percent, she suggested that a better solution may be to cut the initial markup to 50 percent. She argued that this should reduce the need for markdowns and may also result in higher sales because of lower everyday prices. Actual reductions from the initial markup for the 1987 fall/winter season are presented in Exhibit 4.

In prior years the seasonal merchandise budget for the shoe department was prepared using the beginning-of-the-month stock/sales ratios as shown in Exhibit 5. This year Hayes was contemplating using the basic

Exhibit 3

Oakland Department Store
Sales Growth (1978–1987)

Year	Total Store	Shoe Department
1978	6.4%	5.2%
1979	11.8	10.3
1980	12.1	11.4
1981	10.3	10.1
1982	4.9	5.0
1983	6.2	5.7
1984	7.9	6.3
1985	11.2	9.8
1986	10.1	6.9
1987	7.3	5.4

Exhibit 4

**Oakland Department Store Shoe Department
Reductions from Initial Markup (1987)**

Reductions	Aug.	Sept.	Oct.	Nov.	Dec.	Jan.
Markdowns	12.1%	12.4%	18.2%	11.5%	11.0%	17.5%
Discounts	5.0	4.0	4.5	5.0	5.0	3.0
Shortages	1.0	.9	1.0	1.0	1.0	.9

Exhibit 5

**Oakland Department Store Shoe Department
BOM Stock/Sales Ratios**

Month	BOM Ratio
Aug.	5.34
Sept.	5.01
Oct.	4.45
Nov.	5.95
Dec.	5.84
Jan.	4.10

stock method to develop the seasonal merchandise plan because this method allowed him to plan for a target stockturn. Hayes was especially concerned about achieving a planned stockturn of 2.5 times per year because this is one of the standards by which senior management will evaluate his performance. They have also established a 40 percent target gross margin for the shoe department. Hayes was told to plan to have beginning-of-the-month retail stock of $400,000 for February 1988.

Hayes is somewhat concerned about his ability to achieve a 40 percent gross margin and retail stockturn of 2.5 since he had no control over advertising expenditures. In 1987 his department was allocated $25,000 for advertising for the fall/winter season. Hayes believes that if he could double his advertising, sales would grow by at least 20 percent.

It was five days before his merchandise budget was due to McClain when Hayes realized that his long run future at Oakland was to be largely determined by his ability to reverse the declining performance of the shoe department. He wanted to develop a no-nonsense merchandise budget to convince McClain that his department required special resources and attention.

QUESTIONS

1. Prepare a seasonal merchandise budget for the Oakland shoe department using both the BOM stock method and basic stock method. Which budget should Hayes submit to McClain?
2. How can Hayes convince McClain of the need to double the advertising budget for the shoe department?
3. What should the planned initial markup be?

CASE 23

Roger Dickinson
University of Texas at Arlington

PAGEANT STORES

Nancy Driscoll has just taken over as handbag buyer for a ten-store chain of women's fashion outlets called Pageant Stores, located in a large eastern metropolitan area. She has been the assistant buyer in the handbag department, and prior to that was department manager of one of the largest of the ten stores.

Driscoll was superbly qualified for her job. She even had an M.B.A. from a leading business school. At school she had been exposed to the Robinson-Patman Act. Her impression at that time was that it was illegal for a buyer to solicit discounts from suppliers unless she was sure that other stores were also being offered the discount.

Since coming to Pageant Stores, Driscoll had not heard much discussion of the Robinson-Patman Act. Irma Schultz, the buyer for whom she had worked, did not discuss it. She knew that Schultz bargained very aggressively; but she did not know how, if at all, her activities were altered by the Robinson-Patman Act. As assistant buyer this did not bother her. Now, however, she was the buyer. According to the way business was conducted at Pageant Stores, Driscoll had all the responsibilities for negotiation.

Driscoll decided that she would find out about the law. A reasonable first step was to read it. She finally located a copy of the law in the back of a book. Section 2(a), she discovered, suggested that price discrimination by the supplier was illegal if, and only if, in addition to other things, the effects of such discrimination were anti-competitive. Since Pageant's ten stores were small by comparison with, say, Sears, there appeared to be little Driscoll could do to be anti-competitive. Furthermore, Section 2(b) of the Act permitted suppliers to meet competition in good faith. Driscoll felt that this would justify almost any action by a domestic supplier, since all other suppliers were doing almost anything imaginable to get the business, particularly with the threat of imports. Driscoll also found that Section 2(f), which was directed toward buyers, applied only to the prohibitions of Section 2(a), which alluded only to price discrimination. Driscoll felt assured that all her activities were probably legal.

Soon after her promotion, Driscoll ran into an attorney friend of hers at a party. During their conversation, he stated that the Courts had basically ignored the anti-competitive provisions of the Act. Furthermore, while the Act had held buyers responsible only for price violations of the Act, the Courts had held that buyers were indeed responsible for other aspects of negotiation such as advertising and services. Lastly, while the need to meet competition was a defense against violations, it was a very difficult defense for a buyer to use, mainly because much of the data on meeting competition was in the supplier's hands.

Driscoll was now confused. What should she do? She did not want to break the law, but what was it? She knew that bargaining was a key element in the handbag industry, and she had tried to find out the practices of other buyers. But there was no way that she could find out what other buyers in her competitive area were paying for anything. As she thought about her problem, there appeared to be three general approaches that she might use.

First, she need not bargain at all. This procedure appeared safe legally, although the Act implied that she could still be held liable because of its suggestion that it is unlawful "knowingly to induce or receive a discrimination in price which is prohibited by this section." One need not induce a discrimination; receiving the discrimination under certain conditions would be enough. There were other ways to be safe within the Robinson-Patman Act. For example, a buyer might deal with suppliers who qualified in the legal sense as dealing only in intra-state traffic. She might also deal only with suppliers who sold exclusively to large stores. Presumably, the problem would not then be as important. Indeed, she might try to become the only account of a few firms, although Pageant was probably too small a chain for this. A clear alternative was to try to develop private brands. While these did not exclude one from the Robinson-Patman Act in and of themselves, goods of not like grade and quality are exempt from the provisions of the Act.

Another alternative that occurred to her was to bargain vigorously but in a manner that was likely to be considered legal. But for this it was necessary to become fairly knowledgeable about the Act. Driscoll would have to find out things like: (a) What did it mean for a supplier to meet competition? (b) Could a supplier meet an illegal price? (c) Where was the burden of proof? In instances where the burden of proof was on the government, it is unlikely that any buyer would be caught. (d) What types of legal defense were permitted for the various kinds of discrimination? For example, cost defense was permissible under several conditions.

A third alternative was to disregard the Act in some intelligent manner. Most buyers did not understand it very well anyway; they lacked either the time, or the legal training, or both. Driscoll thought most buyers bargained aggressively. But few were investigated. A buyer who chose to disregard the Act need not be excessivelys stupid about negotiating. She would conduct herself with discretion.

QUESTIONS

1. Which alternative would you have chosen if you had been in Driscoll's position?
2. Do you think buyers should have legal training? If so, how much?

CASE 24

Myron Gable
Shippensburg University

THE SHOE BOUTIQUE

Diane Wentworth is the owner of a women's shoe store, The Shoe Boutique, located in the New York suburb of White Plains. The basic merchandise assortment consists of high-quality shoes which are also high in price. Her two top lines are Angelique and Kenya, with Angelique shoes being slightly more expensive than the Kenyas. Wentworth has carried the Kenya line for more than five years; the Angelique line has been sold for only the past two years. The Shoe Boutique sells a wide variety of fashionable shoes in current styles. Also maintained are a stock of casual loafers and flats. Most styles of shoes come in an assortment of colors, sizes, and in a variety of textures including leather, snakeskin, and suede. A third major line carried at the store is the Kinley brand which attracts women who cannot afford the Angelique and Kenya brands but still want quality and stylish shoes. This brand offers a variety of styles in fashionable colors and texture such as imitation leather, snakeskin, and suede.

The Shoe Boutique attempts to have interesting and eye-catching window displays. For example, Wentworth recently created a window display showing the step-by-step process of how Angelique shoes are made. Many customers made favorable comments about the display. Eye-catching displays are especially important for the Angelique line because Wentworth's primary competitor also carries this line. While both stores are located in the major shopping area of downtown White Plains, Foot Fantasy, the competitor, is located in the most heavily trafficked area, whereas The Shoe Boutique is located three blocks away in a secondary trading area. The entire business district has deteriorated somewhat, and some residences a block away from the business district are rundown.

Wentworth's primary customers are Black and Puerto Rican businesswomen, secretaries, school teachers, and a few blue-collar workers residing in the neighborhood. In addition, some people working in downtown White Plains shop at the store. Generally, very few individuals residing in surburban White Plains come downtown to shop, and this affects all downtown retailers.

In May, 1988, a representative of Catri Shoes contacted Wentworth about possibly carrying the Catri brand in her store. Catri has a good, high-quality reputation which would add to the prestige of Wentworth's store. Wentworth is somewhat apprehensive about carrying this brand because of the Angelique Company. She has heard that her competitor has been urging Angelique to drop Wentworth as a customer so that Foot Fantasy could be the exclusive retailer of Angelique shoes in downtown White Plains. The line is also being carried by two stores at the regional mall near White Plains. Angelique is a prestigious brand, and many women purchase a pair of shoes because they are Angeliques. The Shoe Boutique also has other nearby competition from two national chains. Fortunately, none of these outlets carries the same brands that The Shoe Boutique stocks.

Wentworth is also hesitating in carrying the Catri line because of the large initial cash outlay required to order the basic stock. The minimum purchase requirement is four different colors or textures of eight different styles. To maintain an adequate stock, twenty pairs of each color must be purchased. An example of the size breakdown is shown in Exhibit 1.

If one style is carried and the cost for a pair is $30, the investment would be $2,400 ($30 × 20 pairs × 4 colors). To stock eight styles, assuming an average cost of $30, would represent an investment of slightly less than $19,200 ($2,400 × 8 styles).

Catri has an excellent co-op advertising policy. Retailers carrying the line are eligible to receive not only a flat allowance of $2,000 annually, but also an accrual based on purchases. Eight percent of purchases will be added to the $2,000 amount. The Shoe Boutique can select any media and need not contribute to an ad. Catri, in addition, provides retailers with a guaranteed sale privilege. All unsold merchandise can be returned to the vendor by the retailer anytime after being in the retail store for 60 days. The refund privilege expires 90 days after purchase. Retailers receive full credit on their return. The only cost to the retailers is the transportation cost to the manufacturer's warehouse. This privilege only holds for styles that both Wentworth and the Catri sales representative feel would sell in White Plains. With this guaranteed sale privilege, Wentworth would not have to worry about having slow-moving merchandise or markdowns.

The retail price range of the Catri line is similar to that of Angelique, but Catri's cost structure is slightly lower than Angelique's, which would allow Wentworth to have a 50 percent markup on retail. For example, a pair of shoes purchased from Angelique for $44 would retail for $80. A pair of shoes purchased from Catri for $40 would also sell for $80. Special orders are also encouraged for the styles that are carried, because of the problem of stockouts. For example, when the store has sold its one pair of $7\frac{1}{2}$ N in a particular style and color, and another customer requires a $7\frac{1}{2}$ N, the order will be air mailed and delivered to The Shoe Boutique within seven business days. Shoe Boutique would pay for the transportation charges.

Wentworth has a tough decision to make. The advantages of stocking the Catri line include:

1. Availability of co-op advertising dollars
2. A 100 percent return privilege
3. An easy and efficient special order arrangement
4. A high quality line with a better-than-average markup

But, Wentworth must also consider the effect the Catri line would have on her business relationship with Angelique, and whether she can move enough stock during the slow season to warrant the large initial investment necessary to stock the Catri line. The Shoe Boutique has available display and stockroom space for the line and would have no problem borrowing the money to acquire the basic stock. She has asked a close friend who is very experienced in the retail shoe business and her salespeople for their opinions. Her friend thinks she should wait until fall, but her salespeople feel that they could sell enough of the shoes before fall to warrant getting the stock now, since many customers have asked if they carry the Catri brand. Wentworth's husband is concerned that the investment in Catri Shoes will have a negative impact on inventory turnover

Exhibit 1

Size

Width	$5\frac{1}{2}$	6	$6\frac{1}{2}$	7	$7\frac{1}{2}$	8	$8\frac{1}{2}$	9	10
N			1	1	1	1	1		
B	1	1	1	2	2	2	2	1	1
C	1	1							

and profits (e.g., interest cost in borrowing from the bank) and does not recommend adding the line. It is now Wednesday and the representative has left some catalogs and pamphlets for Wentworth to look at. The sales representative is returning at the beginning of next week, and Wentworth must have her decision made by then.

QUESTIONS

1. Should Diane Wentworth add the Catri brand to her product line?
2. Would accepting Catri's offer cause Angelique to withdraw its line from The Shoe Boutique?
3. Are the opinions of Wentworth's husband, friend, and salespeople sufficient information on which to make a decision?
4. Why do Wentworth's salespeople want to add the Catri line?

CASE 25

Myron Gable
Shippensburg University

TANNING EXPRESS

Lisa Evans has recently purchased a small tanning salon, Tanning Express, in a small college town in Minnesota. She is originally from Philadelphia and is new to the area. She moved here because her husband recently got a job as a history professor at the college. The town is small (population of 6,000) with the college being its major employer. Most of the people are very friendly, but they are not too stylish or up on trends. Approximately 5,000 undergraduates attend the college, equally distributed between males and females.

Evans paid a very low price for the salon since the previous owner did not do well. In fact, if Evans had started the business from scratch, it would have cost more to buy new beds and fixtures than it did to buy the complete business. Evans feels that she can make the salon a success since she attended tanning salons often while in college. The salon only has two tanning beds, but if things go well, Evans plans to add more. She also plans to sell a line of sun products to be used in the tanning beds in the near future. The salons that Evans visited in Philadelphia also sold beachwear, bathing suits, and beach towels.

Evans has owned Tanning Express for more than a month, but she is not doing as well as she had hoped. If business does not pick up, Evans will have to close the salon within a few months.

Evans's current customers are mostly professors from the college and young women from the area (not college students) who had attended the salon previously. These customers had purchased a number of sessions in advance. Evans had hoped to attract more college students to the salon. A few have come in, but they were usually disappointed with the results and did not return. Most of these women dislike laying out in the sun because it takes too long and they thought a tanning bed would give them an instant tan. They did not know that a tanning bed also takes a while if a person does not have a base tan. One half-hour session is equivalent to approximately four hours in the sun and one or two half-hour sessions a week are a good way to start the tanning process. Once a person has a tan, it can be maintained by using a tanning bed for one half-hour a week.

When people come in for an appointment, Evans directs them to the bed and turns it on for a half hour. Whenever Evans attended tanning salons in Philadelphia, she always had to fill out a card asking for skin type, age, and tanning ability. She always hated filling out these cards, and she does not require her customers to do so.

Evans currently places a small ad in the local newspaper once a week. The ad, which is placed near the classified section, shows the name of the salon, the address, and the phone number. Evans thought the prices for sessions and package plans were too low. She is used to paying $12 per session while the previous owner charged only $5 per session. Therefore, Evans has increased the prices to $8 per session and adjusted the package plans accordingly. A customer can get five sessions for $35, ten sessions for $65, or twenty sessions for $120.

Evans is trying to think of ways to increase business. She thinks that more advertising and special promotions are needed. Evans is still trying to find out how to attract more college students.

QUESTIONS

1. Can Lisa Evans attract more college students to Tanning Express?
2. What can Evans do to improve the business?
3. Do you think this business will succeed?

CASE   26   **Robert F. Lusch**
University of Oklahoma

TAYLOR'S FURNITURE

Taylor's Furniture is located in a city of roughly 200,000 in the South-western United States. The company is owned and operated by Tom Prescott, who acquired the company in 1983 from Benny Taylor. Over the last five years Prescott has experienced good success in owning and operating Taylor's. In 1987 sales were $997,000, which produced a profit (after taxes) of $26,500. The profit was after Prescott paid himself a $36,000 salary for managing the store. Prescott, with the help of seven full-time and three part-time employees, operates all aspects of the firm. Sales volume since has grown at an annual rate of 12.1 percent. Unfortunately, however, first quarter 1988 results were not as encouraging. Sales were off 2.1 percent from the corresponding 1987 quarter, and profits were a mere 0.6 percent of sales.

BACKGROUND

Since Prescott acquired Taylor's in 1983 he has worked at positioning the firm as a promotion-oriented home furnishings retailer with a liberal credit policy and a broad assortment of merchandise. Approximately 7 percent of sales are spent on advertising, which is considerably above the industry average for home furnishing retailers. In addition, 70 percent of all sales are made on credit. The installment credit plan that Prescott designed requires that the customer put at least 10 percent down on an item and that the balance be paid off in six, nine, or twelve equal monthly installments. The interest charge is 1.5 percent per month on the unpaid balance. In every year since 1983, Taylor's has made money on its credit operation. That is, interest income has more than offset the cost of capital, bad debts, and expenses of administering the credit program.

Prescott believes that Taylor's risks in selling on credit are relatively low because of the financial stability of Taylor's target market. Taylor's typical customers are 25 to 44; have at least some college; have a household size of three or four members; own rather than rent; are self-employed, a professional, or a manager; and have an annual income of more than $25,000. The quality of this target market has resulted in bad debt expense typically being only 1.4 percent of sales.

Exhibit 1

Listening Profile of Seven Radio Stations in Metropolitan Area (First Quarter 1988)

Station	Age		Education		Family Size			Residence	Occupation	Income
	25-34	35-44	Some College	College Graduate	2	3	4	Single Family	Professional, Managerial, or Self-Employed	Over $25,000
KEGN-AM	32.2%	17.9%	35.7%	14.3%	14.3%	32.1%	17.9%	78.6%	28.6%	43.1%
KEGN-FM	35.8	14.8	37.5	22.5	34.6	19.8	21.0	71.6	35.8	52.0
KFDE-AM	7.8	22.1	11.8	11.8	35.1	15.6	11.7	76.6	32.9	44.1
KFDE-FM	19.6	21.5	25.5	15.7	27.5	23.5	9.8	78.4	33.4	44.8
KBDI-FM	15.6	18.8	27.0	33.3	34.9	17.5	17.5	88.9	36.5	53.3
KOKE-AM	30.7	21.8	30.7	28.7	31.0	25.0	19.0	87.1	44.5	51.6
KBCT-AM	25.0	3.6	38.1	8.3	31.0	23.8	15.5	68.7	33.5	43.2

Exhibit 2

Anticipated Purchasers in Seven Radio Station Audiences in Metropolitan Area[a]
First Quarter 1988

Item	KEGN-AM	KEGN-FM	KFDE-AM	KFDE-FM	KBDI-FM	KOKE-AM	KBCT-AM
Mattress or box springs	700	700	3,300	500	1,700	1,900	2,100
Major household appliances	1,400	4,000	2,400	2,900	1,400	3,100	5,700
Antiques	1,200	1,400	1,700	1,900	2,100	3,800	3,600
Furniture	1,400	5,700	2,400	2,100	3,100	7,400	6,900
Carpeting	1,700	3,300	2,100	1,900	1,900	3,800	4,800
Draperies or other interior decorating items	1,900	5,500	3,600	3,600	4,000	6,900	6,700
Major home remodeling	500	1,900	1,700	1,900	2,400	3,300	1,700
Television	700	2,600	1,700	1,900	1,900	1,900	3,800
Radio or stereo	3,100	6,700	1,000	2,600	700	5,500	8,600
Buying a house	1,700	4,000	2,100	2,100	1,200	3,800	6,400

[a]Responses in the categories above indicate that one or more persons in the respondent's household is considering purchasing or spending money on an item in the indicated category within the next three months. The numbers reported are projected households in the survey area (rounded to the nearest hundred) anticipating a purchase. All station names are disguised.

CURRENT SITUATION

In early 1988 the economy began to slow down. Most households had overspent for Christmas. Interest rates began to climb. Taylor's itself was facing a 12 percent cost of capital from its local bank just to finance inventory during the slowdown. Prescott believed that if Taylor's could move inventory more rapidly, even if it did so by selling the merchandise on credit, it would be better off.

Prescott felt the time was never better for households to purchase major appliances and home furnishings. Manufacturers and retailers were cutting prices to move inventory, and retail credit in terms of its cost to the consumer could not go beyond its present level of 18 percent annually because of state usury laws. Also consumers could be almost certain that prices of furniture and appliances would be significantly higher in the future.

Prescott believed that consumer resistance could be overcome with a strong 30-day promotional program. He felt that up to $10,000 could be committed to this promotional campaign with the goal of moving $150,000 (at retail) of excess and old inventory. Part of the promotional campaign would consist of direct-mail advertising to all past charge customers over the last 24 months. This would comprise about 1,600 households. The second part of the promotional campaign would consist of heavy radio advertising for 30 consecutive days. Radio was selected because it offered the best potential for communicating with a specific target market. To assist in selecting the best station on which to advertise, Prescott ordered the most recent copy of the Radio Audience Profile (RAP) from the Marketing and Economic Research Corporation in Oklahoma City. Selected data from this RAP report are presented in Exhibits

Exhibit 3

Radio Station Rates for 30-Second Spots

Station	Program Format	30-Second Spot	180/30/30 Buy[a]	240/30/30 Buy	360/30/30 Buy	720/30/30 Buy
KEGN-AM	Contemporary	$ 6	$ 972	$1,152	$1,512	$2,592
KEGN-FM	Contemporary	9	1,539	1,836	2,592	4,860
KFDE-AM	Modern country	9	n/a	1,944	2,592	4,536
KFDE-FM	Progressive country	8	n/a	1,824	2,448	4,320
KBDI-FM	Beautiful music	7	1,197	1,512	2,142	3,780
KOKE-AM	Middle-of-the-road	9	n/a	1,836	2,430	3,888
KBCT-AM	Album-oriented rock	10	n/a	1,920	2,340	3,600

[a]A 180/30/30 buy consists of 180, 30-second spots broadcast over 30 days; other combinations are similar.

Exhibit 4
Taylor's Merchandise Statistics (1987)

Merchandise Line	Net Sales to Total Sales	Inventory Turnover[a]	Gross Margin	Percentage of Purchases on Installment Credit
Living room furniture	32.4%	3.4x	42.8%	83.1%
Dining room furniture	8.7	1.6	40.7	78.0
Bedroom furniture	11.3	2.0	41.3	76.4
Bedding	9.1	3.7	43.4	10.8
Kitchen furniture	3.1	2.5	47.1	70.4
Floor coverings	6.1	2.9	34.6	65.8
Draperies and Curtains	2.5	3.1	39.1	48.1
Radio and stereo	3.0	2.2	37.0	87.2
Television	5.6	2.6	24.2	83.4
Washers, dryers, irons	4.8	2.5	32.0	67.1
Lamps and shades	2.1	1.1	48.1	21.4
Refrigerators	2.9	3.1	29.1	79.4
Stoves and ranges	4.9	3.0	33.7	80.7
All other	3.5	1.8	36.7	58.1

[a]Sales divided by inventory at cost.

1 and 2. All of the radio stations had special package buys. Typically these special buys consisted of from 180 to 360 spots over a 30-day period at a substantial discount over the single-spot price. Relevant data on these special buys is provided in Exhibit 3.

Prescott is not sure which items he should try to promote most heavily. He has even considered not promoting any specific merchandise lines but rather to merely advertise storewide savings. Prescott requested that his controller prepare merchandise statistics for 1988 so that he could better decide which merchandise lines might warrant special attention. These statistics are displayed in Exhibit 4.

QUESTIONS

1. Does it make sense for Taylor's to try to shift some of its inventory investment into accounts receivable?
2. Should Taylor's use radio as the major media vehicle for their special thirty-day promotional campaign?
3. What would be Taylor's best radio buy?
4. What should Taylor's try to communicate through its 30-day promotional program?

David C. Karp
Loyola Law School
Los Angeles

C A S E   27

TOPCO ASSOCIATES, INC.

Following World War II, the food retailing industry in the United States experienced tremendous change as grocers, both independents and chains, switched their retail facilities from the traditional, small, corner store to the large supermarket. This change continued into the 1960s, fueled by the conversion of an increasing number of chains to supermarket-type retail outlets.[1] By 1963, 57 percent of all supermarkets in the United States were chain stores.[2] Large national food chains became the dominant force in the industry and set the competitive pace for all food retailers. In 1967, 85.6 percent of all chain sales were attributable to the 25 largest chains.[3]

COMPETITION IN THE RETAIL FOOD INDUSTRY

THE LARGE CHAIN RETAILERS

During this time, the national and regional chain stores became more powerful, as independent grocers and smaller chains disappeared at an accelerating rate. Exhibit 1 illustrates the nationwide decline in the total number of stores between 1940 and 1963.[4] Due to their size, these large chains were able to obtain several advantages over their smaller competitors. As large purchasers, the chains were able to:

1. demand the best products at favorable prices;
2. purchase products through efficient centralized purchasing departments;
3. institute their own testing laboratories and quality control programs;
4. engage in product and packaging innovations; and
5. purchase or create their own production, warehousing, and food distribution facilities.

These advantages enabled them to control costs and sources of supply, and to receive a profit at all levels of the chain of distribution.[5]

The large chains were also able to obtain certain advantages with respect to marketing, such as:

1. gaining access to the best store locations;
2. building modern and efficient stores;

Exhibit 1
Store Population (1940–1963)

	Number of Stores		
Year	Independent	Chain*	Total
1940	405,000	41,350	446,350
1945	365,000	33,400	398,400
1950	375,000	25,700	400,700
1955	324,000	18,800	342,800
1960	240,000	20,050	260,050
1963	210,000	21,000	231,000

SOURCE: Adapted from the *Progressive Grocer 46th Annual Report of the Grocery Industry*, p. 11.
*Through 1951, firms were labeled chains if they operated four or more stores; after 1951, firms operating eleven or more stores were labeled as chains.

3. expanding into new areas with enough stores to enable use of local warehouses and local sales forces;
4. amortizing retail sales promotion activities;
5. taking advantage of fuller advertising exposure than that available to smaller competitors;
6. using loss leaders and other incentives to increase customer volume;
7. "leveraging" themselves into new areas by operating at a loss in new markets, while making up that loss through profits received from stores in areas where the chain was well-established; and
8. developing and using other sophisticated and highly effective marketing techniques.[6]

THE RISE OF PRIVATE LABEL BRANDS

The three largest chains, A & P, Safeway, and Kroger,[7] along with National Tea, pioneered the use of private label products. These were commonly purchased items sold under a brand name owned by the chain. Due to the chains' large size, they were each able to secure sources of supply, or even manufacture products, which they then sold under private label in their respective stores.[8] Numerous benefits accrued to retailers who could offer private label merchandise in their stores. These products provided consumers with a lower-price alternative to national brands, thereby allowing a store to attract brand-conscious *and* cost-conscious consumers. They also enabled retailers to reduce prices on nationally branded goods whenever the profit margin on private label goods was high enough to offset the lower margin received for the national brand. Private label products also aided the large chains by reducing their dependence on the national brand manufacturers and by creating a broader supply base for their stores.[9] Private labels also benefited the big chains in the following ways:

1. the retailer was vested with exclusive control over specifications, sources of supply, quality control, packaging, physical distribution, pricing, and promotion of its own brands and products;
2. the retailer received higher profit margins at the same time it obtained a low-price image by providing consumers with a lower-price alternative;
3. the retailer was able to exercise greater control over its product mix;
4. the retailer obtained consumer recognition of private label values, thereby easing acceptance of new items introduced under the same label; and
5. the retailer benefited as consumer goodwill was transferred from store to store within the chain.[10]

Just as the chains benefited from the new private label brands, so did consumers. The store labels increased the selection available to a store's customers. The new labels were also less expensive than nationally branded products. On average, advertised prices for national brands were 20 percent higher than private label prices. Finally, consumers benefited as national brand manufacturers responded to this competition by innovating, by lowering prices, and by providing better service.[11]

Each chain, of course, maintained exclusive control over its private labels. No other retailer could use a given retailer's brand. Sales of private label products became increasingly important to these large retailers, as in several product categories more than half of a chain's sales were captured by its private label.[12]

ESTABLISHMENT OF A PRIVATE LABEL PROGRAM

A retailer's size was crucial in determining if it could institute a private label program. Such a program required high sales volume in each product category to make its adoption feasible. A competitive private label line would require annual sales of at least $250,000,000, and an optimally efficient line probably required annual sales of nearly $500,000,000. Additionally, it was necessary for a store to offer a private label selection of hundreds of items, and it was often necessary to offer a given item in several quality lines. A & P, Safeway, and Kroger each offered more than one thousand items under their respective private labels.

Although they required a large investment and the promise of high sales volume to be effective, the private label items gave the big chains a unique competitive advantage: products which emphasized lower cost, guaranteed quality, and lower consumer prices that could not be precisely duplicated by the competition.[13]

TOPCO AND ASSOCIATES

THE NEED

It was obvious that small chains could not hope to offer a selection of private label brands to compete with those of the big retailers. The cost of instituting a private label program was much too high for any one small retailer to undertake. Therefore, a number of these small, local grocery chains formed Food Cooperative, Inc., (later to be known as Topco Associates, Inc.). Their purpose was to secure, for the members, a low-cost, competitive private label program that would enable them to better compete with the national and regional chains.[14]

TOPCO'S MEMBERS

Topco was a Wisconsin corporation wholly owned and operated by 25 small independent grocery chains in 33 states. Each member was a separate entity, distinctly owned and operated by independent management. The members were each shareholders in the corporation. Members were licensed to sell, and did sell, Topco branded products in their retail stores. Each member bore the cost of promoting Topco brands in its own territory. In 1967, Topco members' overall sales varied widely, from $1.6 million to $182.8 million. Eighteen of its members had sales well under $100,000,000. In that same year, Topco's members' total retail sales were greater than $2.3 billion, an increase over the 1964 figure of $2 billion. Only A & P, Safeway, and Kroger experienced greater sales.[15] Exhibit 2 illustrates the 1966 market share of each Topco member in its respective geographic market.

Topco members could be found across the United States. They were located in distinct geographic markets and each competed with at least one of the national or regional chains, as well as with other local chains and independents.[16] Membership was not frozen. Older members could leave, and the corporation's bylaws provided that new members were able to join the organization.[17]

TOPCO OPERATIONS

Topco acted as a cooperative buying organization for its members. It bought and distributed more than a thousand different products under brand names owned by Topco. Some of these brand names were Babysoft,

Exhibit 2
Market Share of Topco Members (1966)

Topco Member	Market Share Percentages
Allied Supermarkets, Inc.	8.6%
American Community Stores Corp.	9.5
Big Bear Stores Company	8.0
A.J. Bayless Markets, Inc.	15.3
Brockton Public Markets	1.5
A.W. Cullum & Co., Inc.	8.9
Delchamps, Inc.	7.5
Eagle Food Centers, Inc.	4.7
Furr's, Inc.	9.1
Giant-Eagle Markets, Inc.	5.5
Giant Food, Inc.	8.6
Hill's Korvette Supermarkets, Inc.	2.8
Holyoke Food Marts, Inc.	3.6
The Liberal Market, Inc.	8.2
McCarty-Holman Co., Inc.	14.6
Meijer's Supermarkets, Inc.	7.7
Fred Meyer, Inc.	4.6
Milgram Food Stores, Inc.	9.5
Supreme Markets, Inc.	1.4
Penn Fruit Company	3.8
Pick-N-Pay Supermarkets	16.3
Schultz-Sav-O-Stores, Inc.	4.4
Star Markets (Cambridge)	5.5
Star Supermarkets, Inc. (Rochester)	14.1
J. Weingarten, Inc.	9.1
Average Market Share Percentage	5.87%

SOURCE: *United States v. Topco and Associates, Inc.,* 319 F.Supp. at 1033 (N.D.Ill. 1970).

Bo Peep, Top Fresh, Mel-O-Sweet, Topco, and Valiant. Topco also purchased nonbranded items and non-Topco branded items for its members, but did not purchase national brands.

In addition, Topco set product specifications and standards, tested products, developed new product ideas, engaged in quality control, and designed labels. In connection with these activities, Topco arranged for the manufacture of labels and packaging, negotiated with suppliers, and distributed its products. During fiscal 1968, Topco obtained and sold to its members items amounting to 10 percent of their total sales ($236,871,000). Of this total, 60 percent ($133,871,000) was attributable to Topco brands.[18]

DIVISION OF MARKETS

Topco's bylaws set forth three categories of territorial licenses that could be granted to members of the association:

1. exclusive territorial licenses allowed the members to sell all Topco-labeled products specified in the license, and denied any other retailer in the territory the ability to purchase and sell these products;
2. nonexclusive territorial licenses allowed a member to sell all Topco-labeled products specified in the license, but not to the exclusion of any other members who were licensed to sell those products in the same territory; and
3. co-exclusive territorial licenses allowed two or more members to sell Topco-labeled products specified in the license, and denied any other retailer in the territory the ability to purchase and sell these products.[19]

An applicant for membership in Topco was required to note the type of license it preferred. An applicant would be accepted for membership if it was approved by Topco's Board of Directors and 75 percent of Topco's members. A further provision enabled the member whose operations were closest to those of the applicant, or any member with operations located within 100 miles of the applicant, to trigger a stricter standard for admission, merely by voting against the applicant. In such cases, an 85 percent vote of the existing membership was required to join the association.

In practice, a "no" vote by a member acted as a veto over the applicant's admission because existing Topco members normally accommodated the wishes of their dissenting associate. Further, in most cases, an exclusive license was granted, and those few nonexclusive and co-exclusive territories that were granted actually operated as if they were exclusive.[20]

It was not necessary for a member to operate in the entire territory granted by the association. Exclusive territories were available to members who indicated a desire to expand sometime in the future.[21] As a result, a territory allocated to one member might never actually be served by Topco-branded products.

Thus, exclusive licenses, combined with an existing member's effective veto power over new membership, enabled members to prevent the sale of Topco products by their competitors. Further, the association's bylaws also prevented competition between members. If a member violated its license by selling Topco products in an area outside its territory, it could be terminated.[22]

Topco licenses also restricted sales of Topco products, labeled or unlabeled, at wholesale. To sell at wholesale, a member had to obtain permission from the association. Before permission could be granted, other licensees would be consulted. If the member was allowed to sell at wholesale, sales were restricted to a certain geographic area, and restrictions on sales were often imposed. In practice, applications to sell at wholesale were often denied.[23]

THE LAWSUIT

The Antitrust Division of the United States Department of Justice brought suit against the association in the United States District Court for the Northern District of Illinois, the district where Topco's headquarters was located. The government sought an injunction which would prevent Topco from limiting or restricting the territories in which members could sell Topco brands, or from limiting or restricting memberships on a territorial basis. The Antitrust Division's complaint asserted that the system set up in the bylaws was a *per se* violation of Section 1 of the Sherman Antitrust Act.[24]

Topco answered, claiming that its system was pro-competitive, and that any restriction on its members, as well as on attaining membership, was far outweighed by the enhanced ability of its members to compete with the large national and regional chains.

On November 16, 1970, the district court judge, having heard the evidence and argument noted above, issued his decision in the case.

QUESTIONS

1. Why did the Antitrust Division bring suit against Topco?
2. Based on what you have learned about the Sherman Act, what type of violation do you think was alleged by the government?
3. Place yourself in the position of the district court judge. Apply the law to the facts and render your own decision. What are the legal and factual bases for your decision?
4. Assume that Topco won the lawsuit. What recourse would be available to other small retailers situated similarly to Topco members, but unable to obtain Topco products?
5. Assume Topco's practices violated the Sherman Act. What alternative system of distribution could Topco's members create which would decrease the likelihood of an alleged or actual antitrust violation?

ENDNOTES

1. Louis P. Bucklin, *Competition and Evolution in the Distributive Trades* (Englewood Cliffs, N.J.: Prentice-Hall, 1972), 85–87.
2. Bucklin, 104.

3. *United States v. Topco Associates, Inc.*, 319 F.Supp. 1031, 1034 (N.D.Ill. 1970), *reversed*, 405 U.S. 596 (1972).

4. Other evidence indicated a similar decline (only with different numbers) from 386,897 total grocery stores in 1939 to 244,833 in 1963. *Topco Associates, Inc.*, 319 F.Supp. at 1034.

5. *Topco Associates, Inc.*, 319 F.Supp. at 1034.

6. *Topco Associates, Inc.*, 319 F.Supp. at 1034.

7. *United States v. Topco Associates, Inc.*, 405 U.S. 596, 600 (1972).

8. *Topco Associates, Inc.*, 319 F.Supp. at 1035.

9. *Topco Associates, Inc.*, 405 U.S. at 599.

10. *Topco Associates, Inc.*, 319 F.Supp. at 1035.

11. *Topco Associates, Inc.*, 319 F.Supp. at 1035.

12. *Topco Associates, Inc.*, 319 F.Supp. at 1035–36.

13. *Topco Associates, Inc.*, 319 F.Supp. at 1036.

14. *Topco Associates, Inc.*, 319 F.Supp. at 1033.

15. *Topco Associates, Inc.*, 319 F.Supp. at 1032–33.

16. *Topco Associates, Inc.*, 319 F.Supp. at 1033.

17. *Topco Associates, Inc.*, 319 F.Supp. at 1038.

18. *Topco Associates, Inc.*, 319 F.Supp. at 1033.

19. *Topco Associates, Inc.*, 405 U.S. at 601–02.

20. *Topco Associates, Inc.*, 405 U.S. at 602.

21. *Topco Associates, Inc.*, 405 U.S. at 602.

22. *Topco Associates, Inc.*, 405 U.S. at 602.

23. *Topco Associates, Inc.*, 405 U.S. at 604–04.

24. 15 U.S.C. §1.

CASE 28

Myron Gable
Shippensburg University

THE WEST MALL

During the early spring of 1987, Gladys Miller, the executive director of West Mall, was concerned about how the Mall was perceived by shoppers. The Mall is located in the mid-eastern United States, adjacent to a city of approximately 75,000 people. The Mall has 125 stores, including two nationally known department stores, three major chain operations, and a substantial number of chains in specific merchandise lines. In addition, there are approximately 75 independent retailers. With the exception of a supermarket, all types of retail stores are represented at the Mall.

In the late spring of 1987, under the direction of Dr. Mervin Legab, a professor of marketing at a nearby state college, a survey was conducted at the West Mall. The major findings of this study are found in Exhibits 1

Exhibit 1

Driving Time to the West Mall (in minutes)

Driving Time	All Shoppers #	All Shoppers %	Frequent Shoppers #	Frequent Shoppers %	Infrequent Shoppers #	Infrequent Shoppers %
Less than 10	111	14.7	85	25.2	26	6.2
10–14	179	23.7	97	28.8	82	19.6
15–19	176	23.2	84	24.9	92	22.0
20–29	137	18.2	48	14.3	89	21.2
30–59	88	11.6	19	5.6	69	16.4
60 or more	65	8.6	4	1.2	61	14.6
Total	756	100.0	337	100.0	419	100.0

through 4. Frequent shoppers were defined as those shopping at the Mall four or more times monthly. Of the total of 756 female shoppers, 337 were classified as frequent; the balance being infrequent shoppers.

Approximately 80 percent of all shoppers traveled less than 30 minutes driving time to the shopping center; 93 percent of frequent shoppers traveled 30 minutes or less. Exhibit 1 indicates that infrequent shoppers

Exhibit 2

Shoppers Opinions Toward Attitudinal Statements

Statement	Mean Score All Shoppers	Mean Score Frequent Shoppers	Mean Score Infrequent Shoppers
1. Compared to other malls, West Mall is one of the nicer places to shop.	4.20	4.27	4.14
2. The stores at the Mall keep me informed by their advertisements and shopping flyers.	3.53	3.73	3.37
3. I can always find whatever product I am seeking at the Mall.	3.37	3.46	3.30
4. I like to read ads or receive shopping flyers before going to shop.	3.81	3.88	3.77
5. When going shopping, I basically look for sale items.	3.59	3.51	3.65

*A mean score close to 5 indicates strong agreement, while a score close to 1 indicates strong disagreement.

Exhibit 3

Age of Shoppers

Age	All Shoppers		Frequent Shoppers		Infrequent Shoppers	
	#	%	#	%	#	%
20 and under	120	15.9	59	17.5	61	14.6
21 to 30	230	30.4	98	29.1	132	31.5
31 to 40	120	15.9	44	13.1	76	18.1
41 to 50	112	14.8	45	13.3	67	16.0
over 50	131	17.3	67	19.9	64	15.3
No Response	43	5.7	24	7.1	19	4.5
Total	756	100.0	337	100.0	419	100.0

Exhibit 4

Annual Family Income of Shoppers (In $'s)

Income Level	All Shoppers		Frequent Shoppers		Infrequent Shoppers	
	#	%	#	%	#	%
Under $20,000	132	17.5	63	18.7	69	16.5
From $20,000–$30,000	372	49.3	170	50.4	202	48.3
Over $30,000	159	21.0	70	20.8	89	21.2
No Response	93	12.2	34	10.1	59	14.0
Total	756	100.0	337	100.0	419	100.0

spend a greater time traveling. In fact, 31 percent travel 30 minutes or longer. The trading area of the Mall was, therefore, quite large. With regard to Statement 1 in Exhibit 2, frequent and infrequent shoppers agree that the West Mall is a nice place to shop, with the frequent shoppers ranking it a little higher. The results indicate the stores at the Mall keep shoppers reasonably well informed; frequent shoppers feeling they are better informed. Shoppers are reasonably pleased with product assortment, but the results indicate improvement is needed. Shoppers like to read ads or receive flyers before going to shop. Statement 5 in Exhibit 2 indicates that, overall, shoppers do look for sale items—infrequent shoppers seeking them out to a greater degree than frequent shoppers. According to Exhibit 3, approximately 46 percent of all shoppers are under the age of 30, with 62 percent being under 40. According to Exhibit 4, the average family income of infrequent shoppers was slightly higher than that of frequent shoppers. A survey at a similar sized mall in another part of the state indicated 33 percent in the $30,000 and over category.

In early 1988 Miller again contacted Dr. Legab. She wanted him to conduct another study focusing on shoppers' attitudes toward the stores at the Mall and ascertain whether a different type of shopper was coming to the Mall. She was interested in the following types of information:

1. How long did it take the shopper to drive to the Mall?
2. Did the shoppers have a price or quality orientation toward merchandise?
3. How many shopping trips does the shopper make each week?
4. Does the shopper rely on advertising media? If so, which media?
5. What is the age and income of shoppers coming to the Mall?
6. What type of image do shoppers have of the West Mall?

Dr. Legab, in deciding on the type of questionnaire to use, thought of the semantic differential rating scale. See Exhibit 5 for a partial listing of these scales and their dimensions.

Exhibit 5
A Partial Listing of the Scales and Their Dimensions[1]

			Dimension
Good		Bad	Evaluative
Fast		Slow	Activity
Large		Small	Potency
Strong		Weak	Potency
Clean		Dirty	Evaluative
Sharp		Dull	Activity
Beautiful		Ugly	Evaluative
Active		Passive	Activity
Heavy		Light	Potency

[1]C. Osgood, G. Suci, and P. Tannenbaum, *The Measurement of Meaning* (Urbana, Illinois: University of Illinois Press, 1957) 37.

QUESTIONS

1. Do you think that the semantic differential would provide a good way to ascertain shoppers' opinions? Defend your answer.
2. What are the elements of the image of a shopping mall? Explain why you selected these elements.

3. What is the consumer profile of frequent shoppers and infrequent shoppers at the West Mall? Describe.
4. Formulate a research recommendation to Gladys Miller.

CASE   29

Myron Gable
Shippensburg University

WHAT'S IN

Frank and Anna Carlton own a small store located near a very large state university in the northeastern United States. More than 35,000 students (undergraduate and graduate) are currently enrolled. The store, What's In, handles a variety of merchandise, such as clothes, posters, recorded music, and miscellaneous items that are popular with college students, such as stuffed animals, pins, and bumper stickers. A breakdown of the percentage of total sales that each area had last year is shown in Exhibit 1. Sales for 1988 were $520,000.

The Carltons are in the process of forecasting next fiscal year's sales. They keep thorough records of every item sold. Computerized registers enable the Carltons to code the merchandise tickets so the number can be entered in the register and the computer will translate the number into the exact item which will be printed on the dated sales receipt with the price. Depending on the item, the color, size, and style can also be printed on the receipt. This helps to keep track of clothes, records, and tapes and permits easy reordering of goods.

These receipts are then compared to actual inventory and entered into journals to help maintain accurate records of what has been sold. Unusual events such as holidays, sales days, snowstorms, rainy days, and heat waves are also recorded. This year, the Carltons would like to develop a quantitative model to help forecast annual sales.

Exhibit 1

Merchandise Area	Last Year's % Share
Clothing	60
Records	20
Posters	5
Miscellaneous	15

In the past, What's In has often been sold out of popular items and overstocked with slow-moving merchandise at the same time. The Carltons would like to use forecasting methods to help them maintain an optimal inventory. They are going to look at the upcoming university enrollment and they will also consider several economic factors, such as the gross national product, inflation, disposable income rate, rate of savings, consumer buying expectations, and other general economic conditions to help make forecasts as accurate as possible.

The Carltons have an intuitive belief that there is a correlation between sales and the rate of disposable income. They feel that as the level of disposable income increases, discretionary income will also increase, which will leave more money available to spend on merchandise like that carried at What's In. They are going to look at the annual figures for the past five years to see whether this is true. If there is a correlation, the Carltons would like to develop a quantitative model that includes this relationship and use it to predict future sales.

Past sales data can also enable the Carltons to help predict sales. This is a form of time series analysis. The problem with this type of analysis, however, is that it relies on past data to predict future sales, and it is hard to determine how well sales from a year or two ago can help predict future sales. Sales often depend on when college students have money to spend, and whether What's In has the merchandise that will satisfy their tastes. This greatly affects sales.

Also making the forecasting task more difficult is the fact that the Carltons don't know their current competitors' promotion or merchandising plans, so they really can't predict how competitive strategies will affect sales at What's In. These competitors are all located near the university. What's In is conveniently located, less than a block away from campus. However, a new clothing store, Trends, Inc., is expected to open up in a couple of months. It will also be close to campus and only two blocks away from What's In. The new store is part of a large retail chain that locates stores in college towns along the eastern coast. It specializes in trendy clothes that appeal to college students. Many students are familiar with Trends, Inc. and they are excited that a store is opening in town.

The Carltons' success is dependent on stocking merchandise that appeals to college students. They, therefore, must be able to accurately read and detect trends and fads. They encourage their college workers and other students to make comments and suggestions about their merchandise.

QUESTIONS

1. What other factors can help the Carltons forecast sales more accurately?

2. Is sales forecasting needed for a small retail store such as What's In to be successful? Explain your answer.

3. Should the sales forecast be based on a unit or dollar basis? Explain your answer.

CASE | 30

Roger Dickinson
University of Texas at Arlington

WILEY'S DISCOUNT STORE

Wiley's Discount Department Store was founded in the early 1960s. It offers low prices on quality, name-brand merchandise from lawnmowers to perfume. Today they have 400 stores. Most are about 60,000 square feet in size and are located in southern states. Their success apparently stems from offering fashion clothing at a discount price in the ladies', men's, and infants' areas.

John Bolling, a recent college graduate, had just completed his two-month training program at Wiley's. He had been given the position of Department Manager in the Ladies' Fashion Department. The department carries ladies' sportswear, dresses, and lingerie. The ladies' department generates 20 percent of the store's total sales, while only taking 15 percent of the floor space. Bolling supervised twelve employees, including two stock clerks. His primary responsibility was to make sure the right merchandise was in the right location in the department at the appropriate time. Three weeks before a new season began, the regional office sent merchandise layouts to each store suggesting the possible locations of each type of merchandise. The ordering and reordering of merchandise was controlled by the buyers in the two regional offices. The department manager had no control over how many or what kind of merchandise was received at the store level.

Bolling was anxious to succeed. If he did well as a department manager, he would be promoted to store manager, and then, hopefully, to the regional office level. Advancement in the company depended on the profitability of the areas under a manager's control at each level. Bolling felt that the key to success was high turnover in merchandise. Increases in sales would result in higher profits. Bolling approached his position with the idea of substantially increasing sales.

Since Wiley's is a discount store, Bolling felt the customers would be looking for bargains; i.e., they would buy merchandise on sale or marked down significantly. Thus, the front of his department was always filled with sale merchandise. Bolling marked down a piece of merchandise every two weeks until it sold. Bolling kept the regularly priced items toward the rear of the department to make room for the sale merchandise. Bolling directed his staff to keep large quantities of future sale merchandise in the stockroom.

The store manager was very pleased with the weekly sales increases in the ladies' department. However, he was troubled by the appearance of the department. The manager commented to Bolling that the front of his department looked cluttered with sale signs.

After the fiscal year, the profitability reports came out. Bolling's department showed an impressive 25 percent increase in sales over last year, but only a 4.1 percent increase in profit. The reports also indicated a markdown percent of 18, compared to 12.6 percent last year.

Bolling was shocked by the low profitability of the year-end report. He considered the factors he controlled. He had nothing to say about the items being advertised or about the items being purchased for sale. Indeed, he could not even reorder. Further, he did not know how the profit percentage was calculated. He was considering asking the buyers to come to his store and check the merchandise mix of this Wiley's store with that of the competition.

QUESTIONS

1. Should Bolling have been given more freedom with respect to what to order and reorder?
2. Was Bolling's authority equal to his responsibility?
3. What factors probably caused the low profit percentage of sales?
4. Should a discount store place sale merchandise in front or back of a department?

C A S E 31

Virginia Newell Lusch

ZIG ZAG

In May of 1987, two friends who had met in college, Tina Rhodes and Art Ramirez, decided to become partners in a retail venture. The retail enterprise they jointly envisioned would be a specialty store of modest size but, they hoped, sufficient magnitude to provide them with a reasonable income while allowing them both to pursue careers they felt would be fulfilling. Tina had just completed her undergraduate degree in art with an emphasis in fashion design. She believed that the retail venture would be a good vehicle for using her creative talents. Art had just finished a two-year junior college program in business administration. He was eager to try the skills he had acquired in college in the real world and envisioned the retail enterprise in which he and Tina planned to be partners as a way to apply his analytical training.

The store would be located in a coastal city in Texas of approximately 300,000 people. It would cater to the young adult (18 to 26) of moderate income. The merchandise mix would feature unisex clothing (custom T-shirts, Mexican and other imported clothing) and also custom-made beach wear. In addition to the clothing, the store would carry unique accessories for men and women, handmade jewelry, candles, and gift items. The store would be called Zig Zag.

Several months later, on a sultry Friday morning, Zig Zag was opened. But before opening day, Tina and Art had done considerable planning and preparation. After conceptualizing the store, they had to go through all the legal paperwork involved in establishing a partnership: find a location; obtain financing; buy merchandise; develop advertising messages; and much more. They quickly found out that the planning and preparation was more time-consuming and complex than they had anticipated. Nonetheless, the big day finally arrived and they held their Grand Opening on August 1 and 2, 1987.

The building they had chosen was located, according to Art's calculations, in an excellent spot to attract its target customers. The store was in a neighborhood shopping center composed of specialty shops, a nationally affiliated supermarket, and a movie theater. The center was on one of the main highways leading out of the city in the direction of one of the busiest beaches in the metropolitan area. The building was only five years old, in excellent condition, and the right size for Zig Zag (2,400 square feet). It had previously been used by a real estate firm, which had recently moved its office to a more central location. The store was located near the end of the strip of shops, between a shoe store and an exclusive dress shop.

During the planning and preparation stages, Art had handled most of the financial and marketing problems while Tina concentrated on the store decor and layout. Her artwork decorated the walls and storefront. Exhibit 1 shows the storefront Tina designed and Exhibit 2 illustrates the layout she developed for Zig Zag.

CURRENT SITUATION

A month after the opening, Art announced that sales had not been quite as good as they had anticipated (see Exhibit 3). Ironically, however, the number of people who had come into the store had been greater than expected. Art attributed the low sales to the fact that school had recently

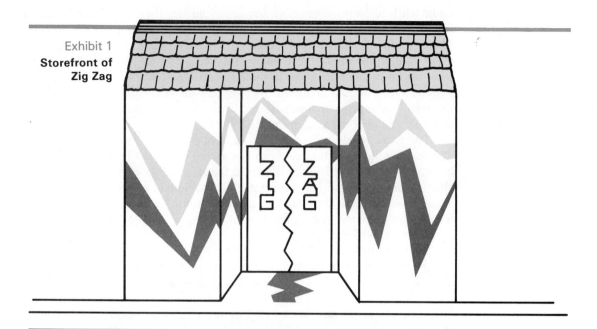

Exhibit 1
Storefront of Zig Zag

started and that a significant proportion of their target group had less discretionary income to spend for a couple of months. "Things will pick up," he assured Tina.

Another month went by, and the traffic began to drop off. Sales were down, but something more astounding was happening. Merchandise was missing. Tina first noticed this one afternoon after four teenage girls left the store after trying on some new embroidered tops. When Tina went back to clear the dressing room for the day, she discovered several empty hangers. Discouraged by this, she went into the storage room to unpack some more of the tops. On entering, she spied an old purse stuffed under some shelves. When she bent to pull it out she knocked several boxes of T-shirts off the shelves. "This really isn't my day!" she muttered. Picking up the boxes she noticed how light in weight they were. Opening them, she found them empty. At this moment the bells on the entrance jangled, indicating a customer. She left the storeroom and reentered the sales area.

Two middle-aged women had just entered and were looking at the gifts. Tina wished that Art would return from the bank so that she could show him what she had discovered in the storeroom but, putting on a happy face, she approached the two women. "May I help you?" she asked, smiling.

One of the women turned to her and answered, "No, I don't think you have anything here that we want. We were at Marcelle's next door and thought your store looked interesting. We have appointments at the Beauty Salon across the street every week, and usually come over here to

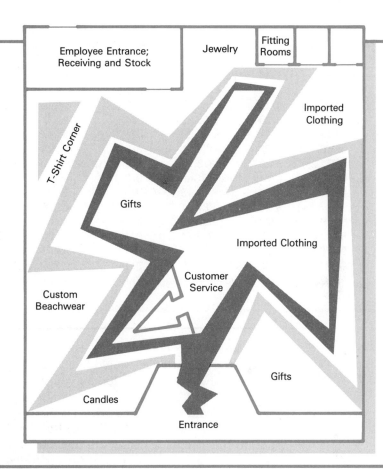

Exhibit 2

Interior Layout of Zig Zag

do a little shopping while waiting for the bus. This is a cute place, but we have to go now. Goodbye."

Several days later, Art was beginning to close for the night when a couple in their late teens entered.

"Hi," said Art, "Can I do something for you?"

"Yes," said the girl. "My boyfriend wants to buy me a custom bikini for my birthday. I heard that you have them here."

"Right over here," Art indicated. "Pick out the style and size from the samples hanging on the rack, then choose the fabric. The prices are on the tags. Let me know if I can help you. The fitting rooms are in the back. Just following the Zig Zag Rainbow carpet. Closing time is in fifteen minutes, but if you need a little extra time it's OK."

Art went back to straightening the imported tops and jeans when he overheard the two young people as they made their way to the fitting rooms.

"Wow!" exclaimed the boy, "I see what Sheila meant when she said that this place was weird. This "follow the Zig Zag Rainbow" routine

Exhibit 3

Zig Zag Daily Sales Volume (first two months of operation)

8/1	$248.16	8/17	Closed (Sunday)	9/1	$ 29.21	9/16	$ 58.41
8/2	311.37	8/18	$ 61.38	9/2	41.73	9/17	71.29
8/3	Closed (Sunday)	8/19	60.41	9/3	48.48	9/18	98.81
8/4	54.18	8/20	88.39	9/4	99.77	9/19	134.47
8/5	84.13	8/21	96.38	9/5	151.47	9/20	149.35
8/6	98.46	8/22	136.31	9/6	147.28	9/21	Closed (Sunday)
8/7	164.72	8/23	178.74	9/7	Closed (Sunday)	9/22	40.55
8/8	168.98	8/24	Closed (Sunday)	9/8	49.43	9/23	51.79
8/9	189.47	8/25	73.18	9/9	57.30	9/24	98.71
8/10	Closed (Sunday)	8/26	84.71	9/10	62.28	9/25	224.49
8/11	59.79	8/27	109.41	9/11	89.99	9/26	288.37
8/12	87.41	8/28	279.34	9/12	119.30	9/27	290.41
8/13	94.70	8/29	271.87	9/13	149.47	9/28	Closed (Sunday)
8/14	161.37	8/30	346.38	9/14	Closed (Sunday)	9/29	58.71
8/15	198.32	8/31	Closed (Sunday)	9/15	41.32	9/30	92.91
8/16	182.44						

sounds like something out of the Wizard of Oz. Who does this turkey think he is anyway? I think I would like you in style D made out of the blue flowered Hawaiian stuff. What do you think?"

The girl replied, "That would be super. It would be the prettiest suit at the beach, but did you see the price?"

"Don't worry about that. Mr. Zig Zag Rainbow must be loaded. All of the people in this shopping center are rich. He doesn't need our money."

"Excuse me, sir," the boy called, "My girlfriend likes one of the suits. Can you help her decide on the fabric?"

Putting the overheard conversation out of his mind, Art replied, "Sure. Let's go back to the beachwear area and I'll show you some samples."

Together they went back to the beachwear area where Art unfolded the five fabric samples she indicated and laid them on the counter. Among them was the blue flowered Hawaiian material they had discussed earlier.

"We like this one," stated the boy, indicating a multicolored stripe cotton, "but don't you have it in any other color combinations?"

"I don't think so," Art replied, "but here's a print that's nice for that suit."

"No, we like the stripes. Is this all of your sample stock?"

"Well, no. Actually, I just received a shipment this afternoon that isn't unpacked yet. If you can come back tomorrow I'll show it to you. I'm certain there are several striped pieces in the order."

"We can't do that! This place is ten miles from her house and I have to work tomorrow. Anyway, today's her birthday, and I'd really like to do it now. Couldn't you check and see if the stripes are there? We can wait."

"OK," said Art, "I'll be right back."

"We'll just look around while you look."

Art went back to the storeroom and opened the box from the fabric mill. He was right. There were several different striped samples. When he returned to the sales area, the couple was looking at the T-shirts.

"Here are the samples," Art called as he went back to the beachwear area.

"We're coming," laughed the girl, "along the Zig Zag Rainbow."

The couple ordered a suit made out of a multishade green fabric and left fifteen minutes past closing time.

Art was tired, but at least, he thought to himself, he had closed a sale for his extra effort. As he refolded the fabrics he had shown them, he noticed that the blue Hawaiian print was missing, and as he found out later, so was the style D, size 9 sample unit, several T-shirts, a hand-hammered copper chain, and a belt. He felt sick. Looking at the order form for the custom suit, he realized that the address given was for the public library.

After only two months of operation, Art and Tina had realized that Zig Zag had a real problem. The location was good, but the store just wasn't drawing the right customers. The middle-aged women who shopped in the other stores or frequented the beauty salon were coming in but rarely purchasing anything. There were also numerous young teens who came in packs from the school nearby. Some of them made purchases, and most seemed really turned on to the store atmosphere.

Art decided something had to be done. He spent that entire weekend taking physical inventory to identify all thefts and preparing a profit and loss statement for the first two months of operation (Exhibit 4) and a bal-

Exhibit 4

Zig Zag Profit and Loss Statement (8/1/87–9/30/87)

Sales		$ 6635
Less: Cost of goods sold		3666
Gross profits		$ 2969
Less: Operating expenses		
Rent	$2400	
Advertising	600	
Wages	2000	
Theft and pilferage	749	
Utilities	343	
Insurance	200	
Phone	96	
Interest	884	
Miscellaneous	371	
Total operating expenses		7643
Profits or (loss)		$(4674)

ance sheet as of September 30, 1987 (Exhibit 5). In addition, he spent considerable time developing some merchandise operating statistics for the seven major merchandise lines Zig Zag handled (Exhibit 6).

After the long weekend with the books and paperwork, Art informed Tina that they were losing almost as much money as they were taking in. Somewhat depressed, he bluntly told Tina they could probably get out of their six-month lease, close the doors, and take their losses. Alternatively, he mentioned, they could try to hold things together for a couple more months while rapidly making some changes to try to improve sales and profits.

Exhibit 5

Zig Zag Balance Sheet (9/30/87)

Assets		Liabilities and Net Worth	
Current assets		Current liabilities	
Cash	$ 483	Accounts payable	$ 3,443
Inventory	22,292	Note payable	30,000
Total	$22,775	Total	$33,443
Fixed assets		Long-term liabilities	0
Equipment and fixtures	$ 9,400	Net worth	$ 1,107
Leasehold improvements	2,375		
Total	$11,775	Total liabilities and net worth	$34,550
Total assets	$34,550		

Exhibit 6

Zig Zag Operating Statistics (first two months of Operation)

Merchandise Line	Square Feet[a]	Dollar Sales	Average Inventory (at Cost)	Gross Margin Percent[b]
Candles	150	876	$1,732	45.3
Custom beach wear	170	375	692	47.1
T-shirts	222	1,291	1,608	31.3
Gifts	388	429	9,240	39.2
Jewelry	137	1,647	4,659	43.7
Accessories	93	1,408	3,043	29.4
Imported clothing	400	609	3,038	34.0

[a]Total square feet was 2,400; that not devoted to merchandise lines was for aisles, checkout, fitting rooms, and the stockroom.
[b]Gross margin percent equals sales minus cost of goods divided by sales.

1. What do you see as the major problems that have afflicted Zig Zag?
2. What steps should Art and Tina take to correct their problems? Should they close the doors and quit?
3. Draw a new layout pattern that would improve efficiency and security while promoting the proper atmosphere.

Glossary

A

above market pricing A pricing method used when retailers want a highly specialized or prestige image and set their price above the market price. Used when little or no competition is at hand.

accounts payable Money owed vendors by retailers for goods and services.

achieved markup Actual selling price minus cost.

acid-test ratio A measure of liquidity, it is cash (and its equivalent) divided by current liabilities.

administered vertical marketing systems Marketing channels in which one of the channel members takes the initiative to lead the channel by applying principles of effective interorganizational management.

administrative management The acquisition, maintenance, and control of resources (financial, personnel, and informational) necessary to carry out a retailer's strategy.

advertising Any paid form of nonpersonal presentation and promotion of ideas, goods, and services by an identified sponsor.

advertising efficiency The extent to which advertising has produced the desired result at the least cost.

affective dimension of attitude That aspect of attitude which is concerned with the feelings of like or dislike toward an object.

allocation The breaking down of homogeneous supplies into a smaller lot size as needed by members of the channel.

anchor store A major store (generally a department store) which is expected to draw customers to the shopping center.

arbitration A form of conflict resolution in which parties voluntarily submit their dispute to a third party whose decision will be considered final and binding.

aspirational group A reference group to which a person does not currently belong but to which one desires to belong.

asset Anything of value that is owned by the retail firm.

asset turnover Annual net sales divided by total assets. This is a basic measure of how productively the retailer is using its assets to generate sales.

assorting The building up of a variety of products for use in association with each other in order to provide a market what it wants.

atmosphere The image a store projects as a result of its layout and fixtures. The main determinants are the type and density of employees, merchandise, fixtures, sound, and odor and visual factors.

atmospherics The conscious designing of a store layout and its various dimensions to evoke certain effects in buyers.

attitude A learned predisposition to respond consistently in a certain manner with respect to a given alternative.

authority method A method of formulating projections about the future which involves consulting an expert (i.e., an authority).

automatic checkout machines (ACM) A system that will allow customers to check themselves out of the store.

G1

award   The result of a settlement that is paid to one party in a conflict when both parties have agreed to accept the verdict of an outside person or agency rather than continue the conflict.

B

bait-and-switch advertising   A deceptive form of promotion in which merchandise is advertised at unusually attractive prices and then, once customers are in the store, they are persuaded that the low-price model is not a good buy because of its poor quality or durability and are directed toward a high-price model.

balance sheet   Accounting statement showing the financial condition of a retailer's business at a particular point in time. It shows the assets, liabilities and net worth of the firm.

basic stock   The smallest number of units deemed necessary to have on hand without losing sales during the slowest part of a merchandise season.

basic stock method   Method of inventory control used by retailers to provide a given level of inventory at all times. It assumes that the retailer will always have a fixed level of inventory regardless of expected sales volume. In addition, a variable level based on projected sales will be added at the beginning of each period.

beginning inventory   The total inventory investment with which a department or store begins a merchandise period (month or season). May be expressed in dollars or units.

behavioral dimension of attitude   The aspect of attitude which refers to the action tendencies toward an object.

behavioral intention   The subjective probability that beliefs and attitudes will be acted on.

beliefs   Information that links a given alternative to a specified evaluative criterion, specifying the extent to which the alternative possesses the desired attribute.

below market pricing   A pricing method used when retailers use price points that are below the competition's.

bona fide occupational qualification (BFOQ)   Criteria that a retailer may use that are exceptions to the federal law that prohibits the retailer from discrimination on the basis of race, color, religion, sex, age, or national origin. A BFOQ should pertain only to qualifications needed to perform the duties expected of the employee.

book inventory   An inventory method which provides a running total of the cost value on hand at a given time. This cost value can then be converted into a retail value if needed.

boutique layout   A form of free-flow layout that creates mini-stores aimed at specific target groups within a larger store. Each mini-store is aimed at a specific market and is often a grouping of merchandise from a single country, company or designer.

brainstorming   A technique of creative thinking in which participants freely toss out ideas, which are recorded but not discussed. The purpose is to gather the greatest number of ideas possible on the chance of obtaining one or more that is innovative.

breadth   The number of merchandise brands in the merchandise line. This is also referred to as assortment.

buyer   The title of a retail employee responsible for a department's or area's buying and selling activities.

buying power index (BPI)   A single-weighted measure combining effective buying income, retail sales, and population size into an overall indicator of a market's potential, based on data published by *Sales and Marketing Management Magazine*.

C

capital allocation   The distribution of the total funds a retailer has decided to commit to a store among the available options.

cash discount   Discounts earned by retailers for payment of the vendor's invoice within an agreed upon period of time. Usually expressed in terms such as 2/10, net 30, where a 2% discount is given for payment within 10 days. If not paid in 10 days, the full amount is due in 30 days. The purpose of these discounts is to encourage prompt payment of invoices.

category killers   Stores that have merchandise dominance in a particular category.

central business district   The geographic point where most cities originated. Also, it is typically the geographic point at which all public transportation systems converge.

central place   A center of commerce composed of a cluster of retail institutions; i.e., a village, town, or city.

central place theory   A location theory developed

by Walter Christaller in 1933 in which central places are established in a geographic space so as to minimize aggregate travel costs for the consumer.

chain store retailers Retailers with 11 or more outlets.

closure The point where evidence conclusively suggests to the consumer that the product or service being offered should be bought.

coercive power Power based on B's belief that A has the capacity to punish or harm B if B doesn't conform to A's desire.

cognitive dimension of attitude That aspect of attitude which refers to the understanding or perception of an object.

community shopping center A shopping center which provides a range of soft lines and hard lines in addition to the day-to-day goods of a neighborhood center. The major anchor is usually a discount store or supermarket.

compensation The direct dollar payments (wages, commissions, and bonuses) and indirect payments (insurance, vacation time, and retirement plans) to the employees.

competitive assortments Assortments which the retailer offers at a very attractive price, not to build profit, but to attract customers to the store.

compromise The result of a situation in which each party to a conflict has different positions but is willing to settle for something less than the ideal rather than continue the conflict.

conflict An inevitable occurrence between retailers and suppliers because of their interdependence. Conflict is any action taken by one party that is inconsistent with the goals of the other.

conjecture method A method of formulating projections about the future as a whole picture, rather than as speculated facts.

consignment sales Sales in which the supplier retains title to the merchandise while the retailer has physical possession and attempts to sell the merchandise. Typically when the merchandise is sold the retailer pays the supplier.

Consumer Price Index (CPI) Figure computed by the Bureau of Labor Statistics to measure the cost of purchasing a "fixed market basket" of goods and services in the current period compared with the same basket in the previous period.

contingency strategy A strategy that the firm has on hand, in case the most likely configuration of environmental factors does not occur and the core strategy becomes obsolete.

contractual vertical marketing systems A type of channel arrangement in which channel leadership is assigned through a legal agreement.

contribution profit percentage Contribution profit divided by net sales.

contribution profit Net sales less cost of goods sold and any expenses that are directly traceable to the goods sold.

conventional marketing channel A type of channel in which each member is loosely aligned with the other members and is relatively autonomous from the others.

core strategy A mainstream strategy that blends with the configuration of external forces that management anticipates.

corporate vertical marketing system A type of channel system in which one firm owns and operates the successive stages of distribution.

cost complement The portion of retail price attributed to cost.

cost method An accounting system which values current inventory at cost plus freight.

cost of goods sold Firm's cost of merchandise sold during a period. Net sales minus cost of goods sold.

coupling of events The manner in which the occurrence or nonoccurrence of one event affects the likelihood of a subsequent event.

coverage The theoretical maximum percentage of a retailer's target market that can be reached by an advertising medium, not the percentage actually reached.

creativity The ability to generate ideas and solutions.

cumulative quantity discounts A price discount that grows larger as an increased volume of goods is purchased over a period of time. The intent is to get retailers to return to a particular supplier again and again.

cumulative reach The actual coverage that is accumulated by an ad or a series of ads over a specified period of time.

current assets Cash and other items which the retailer can convert into cash within a relatively short period of time—usually a year.

current liabilities Short-term indebtedness payable within a year.

current ratio Current assets divided by current liabilities. This is a basic measure of a retailer's solvency. Analysts suggest retailers should have a current ratio of 2.0 times.

customer service   All the activities performed by a retailer which influence the customer's satisfaction with the service or merchandise before, during, or after the transaction.

D

Delphi technique   A method of formulating projections about the future which obtains a consensus from a group of experts without having them confront each other, but still allowing them to know the opinions of the other experts involved.

demand density   The extent to which potential demands for the retailer's goods and services is concentrated in certain census tracts, ZIP Codes, or parts of a community.

demand elasticity of price   The percentage change in quantity demanded divided by the percentage change in price.

demand manager (DM)   Software of the future that will analyze sales patterns and decide when to mark down and how long to maintain the markdown.

demographics   The study and description of individuals and groups of people in terms of such variables as race, sex, age, and marital status. These variables are frequently used by retailers as a basis for market segmentation.

department store   A departmentalized retail outlet, often large, offering a wide variety of products and generally providing a full range of customer services.

depth   The average number of stock keeping units (SKUs) within each brand of the merchandise line.

deterministic models   Mathematical models which operate under assumptions of certainty to arrive at a specific forecast of the future.

direct product profit   The gross margin dollars of an item, plus discounts and allowances, less direct handling, selling, and inventory holding costs.

direct selling establishments   Retailers primarily engaged in the sale of merchandise by telephone or house-to-house canvass.

discount store   A retail outlet that sells merchandise at low prices as a result of cutting back on "services" and "extras" provided to customers.

dissociative groups   A reference group with which the individual does not want to be identified.

dissonance   Post-choice doubt motivated by awareness that unchosen alternatives also have desirable attributes or that chosen merchandise may have undesirable attributes.

diverter   An unauthorized member of a channel who buys and sells excess merchandise from authorized channel members.

divertive competition   When retailers intercept customers from the competition. For example, supermarkets, when they sell auto parts, divert customers from service stations, discount stores and auto supply stores.

divisional merchandise manager (DMM)   Manager responsible for merchandising activities for particular lines of merchandise.

domain dissensus   Disagreement among channel members about who has the power to make decisions.

dominant assortment   Merchandise assortments the retailer can dominate with breadth and depth in a particular category.

dual distribution   Occurs when a manufacturer sells to independent retailers and also through its own outlets.

dynamic models   Mathematical models that consider time as an independent variable.

E

earnings per share   Total earnings available to common stockholders divided by shares of common stock outstanding. It shows the profit that each share of common stock has earned.

electronic data interchange (EDI)   A system that allows the retailer's computer to talk directly to the supplier's computer to transmit intercompany transactions.

end-of-month dating   A method of billing which allows the full payment period to begin on the first day of the following month instead of on the invoice date.

Equal Credit Opportunity Act   A law which seeks to reduce or eliminate credit discrimination by making it unlawful to discriminate against an applicant for credit on the basis of race, color, religion, national origin, sex, marital status or age; or because all or part of an applicant's income is obtained from public assistance; or because the applicant has in good faith exercised any right under the Consumer Credit Protection Act.

expectancy theory   A process theory addressing the relationship between effort, performance, and organizational outcome, assuming the employee understands this relationship and is influenced in one way or another.

expert power   Power based on B's perception that A has some special knowledge in a particular area.

express warranties   Explicit verbal or written agreements between buyer and seller covering from one to all attributes of purchased merchandise.

external information   Information obtained from sources outside the firm (e.g., trade magazines, government, trade associations).

external search   The seeking of information from any source outside the individual (e.g., advertising, store salespeople).

F

facilitating institution   A member of the marketing channel that does not take title to the goods it handles but facilitates the marketing process by specializing in the performance of certain marketing functions.

family life cycle   The changes in family composition that, over time, substantially alter family needs, decision making, and market behavior.

felt conflict   Stress, tension, or conflict resulting from perceiving a conflict.

FIFO (First In, First Out)   Assumes that the oldest merchandise is sold before recently purchased merchandise.

financial leverage ratio   Total assets divided by owners' net worth. This shows the extent to which the retailer is using debt in its total capital structure. A ratio around 2.0 times is generally considered comfortable for a retailer.

financial performance objectives   Those objectives which can be stated in monetary or economic terms.

fixed assets   Assets that cannot be converted into cash in a short period of time (e.g., buildings, fixtures, and equipment).

fixed component compensation plan   A compensation plan comprising some base wage per hour, week, month, or year or an annual, monthly, or weekly salary.

fixed costs   Those costs which do not change over the short run as a result of a change in sales volume.

fixed liabilities   Long-term indebtedness (e.g., bonds).

FOB (free on board)   A delivery term that identifies where the buyer assumes title and is responsi-

ble for all further transportation costs and other risks.

FOB destination   Delivery term under which the seller pays the freight and the buyer takes title on delivery.

FOB shipping point (sometimes called FOB factory) Delivery term in which the buyer assumes title and pays transportation costs from the seller's location.

formal organization structure   The organizational structure representing the way employees should behave in terms of lines of authority and responsibility.

forward buying   Retailers buying in advance of needs in order to take advantage of promotional discounts offered by suppliers.

franchise   A contractual vertical marketing system. A form of licensing by which the owner of a product, service, or method obtains distribution through affiliated dealers.

free-flow layout   Store layout in which the fixtures and merchandise are grouped into patterns or left freestanding, thereby creating an unstructured traffic pattern.

free-lance broker   A facilitating institution with no permanent ties to any manufacturers, which may negotiate sales for a large number of manufacturers.

freestanding retailer   A retailer usually located along a major traffic artery without any adjacent retailers.

frequency   The average number of times each person who is reached by an advertising medium is exposed to a particular advertisement during a given time period.

fringe benefit package   A compensation plan that includes such things as health insurance, disability benefits, life insurance, retirement plans, automobiles, and financial counseling.

functional discount   See trade discount.

futures research   The analysis of future environments.

futurist   A person who works in futures research and who holds the view that the future is partially controllable if it can be anticipated.

G

general merchandise manager (GMM) Executive for a large retail firm responsible for planning, budgeting, and controlling all merchandising activities. Divisional merchandise managers report to the GMM.

goal incompatibility A situation in which the goals of the supplier or retailer, if pursued, would hamper the goal attainment of the other.

goal setting A process theory that shows a way to achieve the firm's objectives, resulting in inducing a person to behave in the desired manner.

gray marketing A situation whereby a supplier's products are sold through unauthorized channels.

grid layout Store layout in which all the counters and fixtures are at right angles to each other, forming a maze.

gross margin Net sales less cost of goods sold.

gross margin percentage Gross margin divided by net sales.

Gross National Product (GNP) The total value of all goods and services produced in a country during one year.

gross sales The total of the retailer's sales whether the sales were later returned or allowances were given.

H

high performance results A retailer achieves high performance results when it achieves financial performance in the upper 25 percent of all retailers selling its merchandise lines in terms of profitability, liquidity, and growth.

highly focused specialty stores Relatively small (less than 5,000 square feet) stores that serve special market niches with unique product assortments (e.g., Foot Locker, Kinney, Payless Shoesource).

horizontal price fixing An illegal arrangement in which a group of competing retailers establish a fixed price at which to sell their merchandise.

human resource audit A careful examination by top management or an outside consultant of the strengths and weaknesses of all employees.

human resource manager (HRM) Software of the future that will assign tasks to retail employees and monitor the time taken to complete these tasks.

hypermarkets A huge retail outlet, usually over 100,000 sq. ft., which is typically discount-oriented that sells a wide variety of goods and performs some functions ordinarily performed by wholesalers.

I

implied warranty of fitness for a particular purpose Warranties that arise when a customer relies on the retailer to assist the customer or to select the right goods to serve a particular purpose.

implied warranty of merchantability The retailer's implied promise that merchandise is fit for the ordinary purpose for which such goods are typically used.

income statement Summary of the sales and expenses for a given time period, usually monthly, quarterly, or annually.

index of retail saturation The ratio of aggregate household demand to aggregate retail supply for a particular location.

informal organizational structure The organizational structure depicting how employees within the retail organization actually behave in terms of lines of authority and responsibility.

initial markup The markup placed on the merchandise when the store receives it; initial markup = initial selling price less cost.

interest rate Price paid for the use of money.

internal information Information found in a retailer's normal records (e.g., customers' charge accounts).

internal search The mental recall or review of what the consumer has learned from prior shopping behavior or prior processing of information.

interorganizational management The management of relationships between organizational entities.

intertype competition Competition between different types of retail outlets selling the same lines of merchandise in the same trade area.

intratype competition The most common type of competition that occurs when two or more retailers of the same type compete with each other for the same households.

J

job enrichment The process of enhancing core job characteristics for the purpose of increasing worker motivation, productivity, and satisfaction.

L

labor productivity Net sales divided by number of full-time equivalent employees.

latent conflict An underlying situation that, if left

unattended, could eventually result in conflicting behavior between channel members.

layout   The arrangement of selling and nonselling departments, aisles, fixtures, displays, and equipment in the proper relationship to each other and to the fixed elements of the building structure.

leadership pricing   Establishing a price on an item at a markup significantly lower than the demand warrants for that item. Used to build traffic and generate sales for related items.

leased department retailer   An independent retailer who owns the merchandise to be sold but who leases floor space from another retailer, usually operating under that retailer's name.

legitimate power   Power based on A's right to influence B, or B's belief that he should accept A's influence (e.g., salesclerk doing what the department manager wants based on superior-subordinate relationship).

liability   Any legitimate claim against the retailer's assets.

lifestyle   The patterns in which people live and spend time and money (activities, interests and opinions).

LIFO (Last In, First Out)   Inventory costing method in which the cost of goods sold is based on the cost of the most recently purchased inventory. Useful in inflationary times as a technique for reducing taxes.

limited item store   Offers the consumer lower prices with less product assortment (e.g., 1,000 or fewer grocery SKUs).

liquidity   A measure of how many of the firm's assets can be readily converted to cash. Reflects the firm's ability to meet its current payment obligations, measured by the acid-test ratio, current ratio, and quick ratio.

M

mail order houses   Establishments primarily engaged in the retail sale of products by catalog and mail order through catalog offerings.

maintained markup   The actual selling price minus the cost.

manifest conflict   The behavioral or action stage of conflict.

manufacturer's agent   A facilitating institution that acts as the salesforce for several manufacturers at the same time within a prescribed market

area. They may take possession of goods but do not take title.

mark   Any word, symbol, design, or combination of these used to identify a product or service.

markdown   Reductions in the price of an item to stimulate sales. Markdowns are necessary because of buying errors, pricing errors or promotion errors.

market performance objectives   Objectives which compare your position in the marketplace to that of the competition.

market segmentation   The process of breaking a heterogeneous group of consumers into smaller more homogeneous groups.

marketing channel   A set of institutions that move goods from point of production to point of consumption.

markup   The difference between the cost of the merchandise and the selling price.

markup on cost   Markup divided by the cost of the merchandise.

markup on retail (or markup on selling price)   Markup divided by the selling price of the goods.

mathematical modeling   The construction of mathematical relationships to portray relationships in the real world of retailing.

maximum demand price   The highest price that a consumer would be willing to pay for one unit of a product.

membership group   A reference group in which a person is a recognized member.

merchandise budget   A formal plan for the merchandising activities of an upcoming season. The budget includes projected sales, planned inventory, planned gross margin, planned purchases and reductions for the period.

merchandise line   A group of products that are closely related because they are intended for the same end use, are sold to the same customer group, or fall within a given price range.

merchandise management   The analysis, planning, acquisition, handling, and control of the merchandise investments of a retail operation.

merchandise productivity   Net sales divided by average dollar investment in inventory.

merchandising   The planning and control involved in the buying and selling of goods and services.

Metropolitan Statistical Areas (MSAs)   Census

Bureau term for metropolitan areas with populations greater than 50,000.

middle-of-month dating   Billing method using middle of the month as starting point for cash discount period.

mission statements   Description of the fundamental nature, rationale, and direction of a firm.

model stock plan   An inventory plan giving precise items and their respective quantities that should be on hand for each merchandise line.

motivation   The drive within a person to excel.

multi-mode organization   Retailers that are organized not around single-mode functions, locations, or merchandise categories, but around several modes.

multiple transaction premium   Gift the consumer will receive or may qualify for after more than one transaction.

N

neighborhood business district   A shopping area that evolves to satisfy the convenience-oriented shopping needs of a neighborhood.

neighborhood shopping center   A shopping center which provides for the sale of convenience goods and personal services for the day-to-day living needs of the immediate neighborhood. Usually the major anchor store is a supermarket.

net sales   Total dollar sales (gross sales) less any returns and merchandise allowances.

net worth   See owner's equity.

noncumulative quantity discount   A price discount determined by the size of the individual order. The larger the order, the bigger the discount on that order. The purpose of this discount is to encourage large order sizes.

nonstore retailing   Retail selling operations that occur outside of a retailer's fixed location.

O

odd prices (sometimes called odd-even prices)   A price that is a few cents less than the nearest round dollar price. The intent is to psychologically "lower" the price of the item.

off-price retailers   Independent retailers that aggressively promote nationally known brands at low prices.

100 percent location   The location with the greatest amount of the kind of traffic desired for a given store. Note: a 100 percent location for one type of retailer may not be one for another type of retailer.

one-way exclusive dealing   Supplier agrees to give the retailer the exclusive right to merchandise the supplier's product in a particular trading area without the retailer agreeing to do anything. This is legal.

open-to-buy (OTB)   The dollar amount currently available to a buyer to spend on merchandise without exceeding planned dollar stocks.

operating expenses   Those expenses the retailer incurs in operation of the business.

operating margin percentage   Operating profit divided by net sales.

operating profit   A measure of performance defined either as a) The difference between gross margin and operating expenses or b) Net sales less the cost of goods sold, direct expenses, and a share of all indirect expenses the retailer incurs.

operations management   The management of the operational (building and fixtures, merchandise, price, promotion, and customer service) aspects of a retail business that seeks to maximize the efficiency of these resources.

optimal merchandise mix   That combination of variety, breadth and depth which maximizes a retailer's returns.

order getter   Salesperson who is primarily responsible for developing business for the retailer.

organizational structure   An arrangement of human resources in terms of lines of authority and responsibility.

overage   A condition that occurs when physical inventory is greater than the book inventory.

overall review   Analysis of the overall performance of the retailer to see if the objectives are reasonable and the strategy is workable.

overbought   A condition whereby the buyer has become committed to purchases in excess of planned purchases. Also occurs when purchases of merchandise are in excess of customer demand.

owner's equity   Part of a balance sheet that reflects the difference between an owner's assets and liabilities.

ownership groups   Retail enterprises that have purchased previously independent retailers or other retail chains. These groups allow individual stores to maintain their image and management and merchandising programs, except for the centralizing of some staff functions.

P

palming-off   A form of deceptive merchandising where a retailer represents goods as being made by a firm other than the true manufacturer; an illegal practice.

patent   The government's granting of a 17-year legal monopoly for the marketing of a process or product.

payroll payable   Money due employees on past labor.

perceived conflict   A cognitive stage at which either the retailer or the supplier becomes aware of latent conflict.

percentage variation method   A method of dollar merchandise planning postulating that the percentage fluctuations in monthly stock from average stock should be half as great as the percentage fluctuations in monthly sales from average sales.

perceptual incongruity   Results when the retailer and supplier have different perceptions of reality.

performance review   The formal, systematic assessment of how well employees are performing their jobs in relation to established standards, and the communication of that assessment to employees.

perpetual inventory system   An inventory control system that provides a running total of the cost value of inventory on hand at a given time. Inventory is not physically counted; rather, invoices and other accounting records are used to keep track of inventory on paper.

personal objectives   Relate to helping people employed in retailing fulfill some of their needs.

personal selling   An oral presentation in a conversation with one or more prospective purchasers for the purpose of making a sale.

planning   The anticipation and organization of what needs to be done to reach an objective.

planogram   An individualized, computer-generated plan for maximum use of shelf space between the various products.

point of indifference   The breaking point at which shoppers are indifferent to shopping at either of two different trading centers.

point of purchase material (POP)   Any promotional communication vehicle within the store, including signs, banners, and elevator cards, used to attract attention to specific products where those products are purchased.

population density   The number of persons or households per square mile.

posttransaction service   Service provided to the customer after the sale has been made, including complaint handling, return policies, merchandise repair, servicing, and delivery.

power   The ability to affect the decision variables of others. The more dependent one member of a channel is on another, the more power that other member has.

predatory pricing   An illegal pricing strategy of pricing merchandise low solely to eliminate competition.

prepaid expenses   Goods and services that the retailer has already paid for but has not yet received.

price discrimination   A situation that occurs when two retailers buy identical merchandise from the same supplier but pay different prices. This is not necessarily illegal.

price lining   A custom or strategy whereby retailers sell merchandise only at given price points.

price point   A specific price within a price zone.

price zone   A range of prices for a particular merchandise line that appeals to customers in a certain demographic group.

primary individual   A household head living alone or with nonrelatives.

primary marketing institution   A member of the marketing channel that takes title to the goods it handles.

problem identification subsystem   That part of a RIS that monitors and scans trends in behavioral, environmental, and operating performance areas.

problem recognition   Stage that occurs when the consumer's ideal state of affairs departs sufficiently from the actual state of affairs to place the consumer in a state of unrest.

process theories   Theories concerned with how to motivate an individual.

profit and loss statement (sometimes called an income statement)   Summary of the sales and expenses for a given time period, usually monthly, quarterly, or annually.

profit margin   The ratio of net profit to net sales, showing how much profit a retailer makes on each dollar of sales after all expenses and taxes are paid.

programmed merchandise agreements A joint venture in which a specific retail account and a supplier develop a comprehensive merchandising plan to market the supplier's product line.

promotional discount Discount received by the retailer for performing an advertising or promotional service for the manufacturer.

prospecting The search for customers who have the ability and willingness to purchase a product.

psychographics (sometimes referred to as life-style analysis) The examination of a person's day-to-day pattern of living (expressed in the activities, interests, and opinions of the individual).

public warehouse Independent warehouse that will store goods for safekeeping in return for a fee.

publicity Any nonpersonal stimulation of demand for a product, service, or business unit by planting commercially significant news about it in a published medium or obtaining favorable presentation of it upon radio or television, that is not paid for by the sponsor.

purchase probabilities How likely a consumer is to purchase a particular product within the next six months.

purchasing agents Members of the marketing channel who operate on a contractual basis for a limited number of customers and receive a commission just as sales agents do.

push money (PM) (spiffs) Money given to retailers by suppliers to pass on to the retailers' salesforce for aggressively selling certain items.

Q

quantity discounts Price reduction offered as an inducement to purchase large quantities of merchandise.

quick ratio The ratio of current assets less inventory to current liabilities. Analysts suggest a quick ratio of 1.0 times for retailers.

R

range The maximum distance a consumer is willing to travel for a good or service.

reach The percentage of a retailer's market that is exposed to an advertisement carried by a given medium.

real income growth Growth in income minus the effect of inflation.

receipt of goods dating (ROG) Billing method in which the starting date for the discount period is the date the goods are received.

reconciliation A situation in which the value systems of the parties to the conflict change so that they now both want the same state of affairs so that conflict is eliminated.

referent power Power based on the identification of B with A. B will go along with A because of a desire to be associated with A.

regional center Shopping center which provides general merchandise, apparel, furniture, and home furnishings in depth and variety. Usually, the anchors are several major department stores.

regression model A series of mathematical equations showing the relationship between sales and a variety of independent variables.

Reilly's Law Two cities attract trade from an intermediate place in direct proportion to the population of the two cities, and in inverse proportion to the square of the distance from the two cities to the intermediate place.

replenishment manager (RM) Artificial intelligence-based software of the future which will automatically reorder merchandise and handle all billing, payment, receipt, and stocking of merchandise.

retail information system (RIS) A blueprint for the continual and periodic systematic collection, analysis, and reporting of data about any past, present, or future developments as relevant to the retailer's performance.

retail inventories Merchandise that the retailer has in the store or in storage and that is available for sale.

retail method of inventory A method of inventory accounting whereby the ending inventory is calculated at retail value and converted to cost by applying the cost complement.

retail price The price at which an item is to be sold; this price includes both cost and markup.

retailer-owned cooperatives A contractual vertical marketing system organized and owned by retailers that offers scale economies and service thus allowing them to compete with larger chain organizations.

retailing All the business activities necessary to sell goods and services to the final consumer. The final stage in the progression of merchandise from producer to consumer.

retractive advertising   Occurs when the FTC orders a retailer who has made false or deceptive claims to run new ads in which the former statements are contradicted and the truth stated.

return on assets   The ratio of net profit to total assets. This shows the return on all assets employed by the retailer regardless of how they were financed.

return on net worth   Same as return on investment. Net profit divided by net worth (owners' or stockholders' equity) which shows the return on capital that the owners or stockholders have invested in the firm.

reward power   Power based on the ability of A to mediate rewards for B.

S

salary plus commission   A compensation plan where the salesperson is paid a fixed salary plus a percentage commission on all sales.

sales agent   A member of the marketing channel who has long-term arrangements with one or very few manufacturers. Sells the entire output for the manufacturer and has no limitation on territory, prices, terms, or conditions of sale.

sales promotions   Any marketing activities other than personal selling, advertising, or publicity that stimulate consumer purchasing and dealer effectiveness, such as displays, shows, exhibitions, and demonstrations.

sales ratio   The amount of stock needed at the beginning of each month to support the forecasted sales for that month.

scrambled merchandising   A strategy of carrying any merchandise line which can be sold profitably, even if the lines are not traditionally associated with each other (e.g., supermarket selling greeting cards).

seasonal discount   Discounts earned by retailers for purchasing goods in the off-season.

secondary business district   A shopping area that is smaller than the central business district and that evolves around at least one department or variety store at a major street intersection.

servicemark   Any word, symbol, design, or combination of same that identifies a service, such as a car wash.

shopping center   A centrally owned or managed shopping district which is planned, has balanced tenancy, and is surrounded by parking facilities.

shortage of inventory   A condition that occurs when physical inventory is less than the book inventory.

sink or swim method   A method of training in which new employees are thrust into the job and have to learn in any way possible or else get fired.

SKU (Stock Keeping Unit)   The lowest level of identification of merchandise. It is usually defined by department, store, vendor, style, color, size, and location.

social class   Relatively permanent and homogeneous divisions in a society in which individuals or families share similar values, life-styles, interests, and behavior.

societal objectives   Those objectives which are phrased in terms of helping society fulfill some of its needs.

sorting out   Breaking down heterogeneous supplies into more homogeneous groups.

space manager (SM)   An expert system which automatically analyzes customer demand and matches it with product availability to constantly realign space in the store to maximize financial returns.

space productivity   Net sales divided by total square feet of retail selling space.

sponsorship method   A method of training a new employee in which the employee is assigned to a senior employee for on-the-job instruction.

Standard Industrial Classification (SIC) codes   Codes used by the U.S. Bureau of the Census to classify groups of firms in similar lines of business.

standard layout   A retail layout consisting of an entrance, a counter, a checkout area, and an exit.

statement of cash flow   A detailed list of the sources and types of all expenditures and revenues for a given period.

static model   Mathematical models which ignore time as a variable.

stochastic models   Mathematical models which operate under conditions of risk. The parameters of the model take on a series of possible values rather than only one value.

stock-to-sales method   Inventory planning method using a ratio of stock to estimated sales to establish desired inventory level for a period of time.

store attributes   The evaluative criteria consumers use to evaluate stores. Attributes can be both objective and subjective. The most frequently used attributes are price, merchandise, layout, physical characteristics, sales promotion, advertising, convenience, service and personnel.

store positioning   A retail strategy of identifying a well defined market segment using demographics or life-style variables and appealing to this segment with a clearly differentiated approach.

store saturation of a market   A condition under which existing store facilities are utilized efficiently and meet customer needs.

straight commission   A compensation plan where income of the salesperson is limited to a percentage commission on sales generated.

straight salary   A compensation program where the retail employee receives a fixed salary per time period (usually per week) regardless of the level of sales generated or orders taken.

strategic planning   Planning which involves adapting the resources of a firm to the opportunities and constraints of the environment.

strategic profit model   A measure of a retailer's profit performance obtained by multiplying the retailer's profit margin by its rate of asset turnover to get return on assets. Return on assets is then multiplied by the retailer's financial leverage to yield its return on net worth.

super-regional center   A shopping center with extensive variety in general merchandising, apparel, furniture, and home furnishings, and a variety of service and recreational facilities.

supply density   The extent to which retailers are concentrated in a particular geographic area.

T

target market   A fairly homogeneous group of customers to whom a retailer's strategy appeals.

task analysis   The process of identifying all tasks the retailer needs to perform, and breaking those tasks into jobs.

territorial restrictions   Attempts by a supplier to limit the geographic area in which a retailer may resell its merchandise.

three-dimensional demand function   The relationship of price, distance, and demand. For retailers, quantity demanded by a household is inversely related to prices charged and distance to store.

threshold   The minimum amount of consumer demand that must exist in an area for a store to be economically viable.

trade discount (sometimes referred to as a functional discount)   A compensation the buyer may receive for performing retailing or wholesaling services for the vendor.

trademark   A registered and legally protected mark (word, symbol, design, or combination of) that identifies a product.

trading area   A geographically delineated region, containing potential customers for whom there exists a probability of their purchasing a product or service from a particular firm or from a particular agglomeration of firms.

transient customer   The customer who does not shop at a store on a regular basis.

two-way exclusive dealing   Supplier offers the retailer the exclusive distribution of a merchandise line or product if, in return, the retailer will agree to do something for the supplier. This is usually not handling competing brands and is potentially illegal.

tying agreements   When a seller with a strong product or service forces a retailer to buy a weak product or service as a condition for buying the strong one; not necessarily illegal.

U

unit stock planning   Planning for the assortment of items that will comprise the merchandise mix.

V

Values and Lifestyles (VALS) program   A systematic classification of American adults into four comprehensive groups divided into nine life-styles, each defined by distinct values, drives, beliefs, needs, dreams, and points of view.

variable costs   Those costs which change in proportion to sales volume.

variety   The number of different lines the retailer stocks in the store.

vertical cooperative advertising   An arrangement in which a retailer and the supplier share the cost of advertising.

vertical price fixing   An illegal arrangement whereby a retailer collaborates with its supplier to resell an item at an agreed-on price. Sometimes referred to as resale price maintenance or fair-trade.

W

warehouse store   A no-frills, low-service, high-tonnage approach to retailing where the showroom facility doubles as a storage place for stock.

week's supply method   A method of dollar stock planning in which stocks are set equal to the demand for a predetermined number of weeks.

wholesaler sponsored voluntary groups   A group of independently owned retailers who rely on the same wholesaler for a coordinated buying program that provides economies of scale.

within-market opportunity analysis   A step in retail location analysis consisting of evaluation of the supply and demand within each market, by census tract or other meaningful geographic area.

working capital manager (WCM)   Software of the future that will manage the current section of the balance sheet for individual stores or entire chains of stores.

Subject Index

Name Index

Company Index